KU-334-857

popular dogs

DOG LOVERS COMPLETE GUIDE

Edited by

DENNIS B. SPRUNG

ARCO PUBLISHING COMPANY, INC.
219 Park Avenue South
New York, New York 10003

Library of Congress Catalog Card Number 75-796
ISBN 0-668-03795-4
Printed in the United States of America

ACKNOWLEDGEMENTS

I wish to express my gratitude to the management and staff of Popular Dogs Magazine for the overwhelming amount of time and effort devoted to this work. In a period of only eleven weeks they produced this invaluable reference work, containing every official breed standard as recognized by the American Kennel Club and over 200 photographs, so that dog fanciers may have a complete up-to-date Guide.

Many of the general breed descriptions and histories were written by Dr. Alvin Novick and were reprinted here through his kind permission for which we are most grateful.

My appreciation to all those photographers whose work appears in the Guide, and a special thanks to the following photographers who contributed a major portion of the photos and without whom we could not have brought this complete reference to the dog loving public . . . again many thanks:

William P. Gilbert
Stephen Klein
Joan Ludwig
Susan Sprung
Richard Wasserman
Missy Yuhl

Dennis B. Sprung
Editor
1975

Dedicated

To The Memory Of

"Fauna"

INTRODUCTION

The First Edition of *Dog Lovers Complete Guide* is a dependable reference book of all recognized American Kennel Club breed standards. The purpose of this work is to acquaint the dog-loving public with the proper appearance of their purebred pet and with its general characteristics.

Included in this book is a book-within-a-book entitled, "The Blue Book of Dog Breeders," which is devoted to the listing of reputable breeders of the purebred dog. This ready reference can be used as a source material for all who are interested in obtaining a purebred dog. Buying a dog from a reputable breeder will prove to be very satisfactory. The purchaser will gain further appreciation of his dog by personal contact with the breeder. The use of "The Blue Book" will help to eliminate the heartbreak which can result from the purchase of a "puppy mill pet." We hope to bring you an even more complete listing in subsequent editions, which addenda may easily be inserted in this edition.

You can keep current in your pursuit of additional information on the care, training, feeding, grooming and general welfare of your dog—pet or show—by subscribing to our monthly publication, *Popular Dogs*. There are articles each month by such well-known authorities as M. Josephine Deubler, VMD, University of Pennsylvania, School of Veterinary Medicine, who answers questions of pertinence to all owners; Elizabeth M. Ent, eminent attorney, each month discusses the ever-changing legal problems of dog ownership; among the many other regular feature columnists are: Nigel Aubrey-Jones, Ruth Tongren, Capt. Arthur Haggerty and Patty Alston who have also contributed articles of special interest which are contained in this edition.

Every effort has been directed to offer the reader the latest most complete accurate guide to the purebred dog.

TABLE OF CONTENTS

ALL ABOUT YOU AND YOUR PUPPY

NIGEL AUBREY-JONES

SHOULD YOU OWN A PUPPY?

Dogs are like people. There are nice people and nasty people. Sometimes I think there are more nasty people than nice ones. I am sure there are more nice dogs than nasty ones.

If you accept that, then you will probably go along with my idea that there are amusing dogs and dull ones; friendly and unfriendly; intelligent and stupid; kind and vicious. Fortunately, not so many of the vicious.

Of this much I am certain: dogs become very much like their owners. Not so much in looks (as used to be said) but in nature. Show me a neurotic dog and I'll show you a neurotic owner.

Not all people should keep a dog. To get the best out of it one requires know-how, time, patience and a special regard for animals. Love is such a misused word. Some who say they love dogs love only themselves. They are just as likely to say they love Frank Sinatra and adore Elizabeth Taylor. Why not, a lot do.

Loving a dog is more than this. Nor is it like loving a wife or a husband, a mistress or a child. A dog belongs to you in a special sense. Whereas people belong to themselves, you have the power of life and death over a dog. A man's best friend is a dog, they used to say. I believe a man or a woman is a dog's best friend, or should be.

If you put nothing into life and take out a lot, you're lucky. You won't get much out of a dog if you don't make an effort. Treat a dog badly and you'll get a poor sort of friend. Treat a nice dog kindly and you'll get a warm response. Understand his needs like proper feeding, exercise, care, attention and affection, particularly affection, and you'll get a happy dog. Most times anyway.

A rich, selfish, unhappy, bad-tempered woman complained to me about one of her dogs. She "hated it," she said. I wasn't surprised. They were so much alike. I believe dogs instinctively know more about people than the other way round.

Don't keep a dog if you don't like animals and don't have a "feel" for them. Don't keep a dog if you haven't the time or the patience. But if you have, and will obey a few simple rules, you will be richly rewarded. Take it from me; I've been rewarded.

IT DEPENDS ON YOU

If I've made it appear that as much depends on you as the dog, that's a good thing. If I've made you *think* before you rush out and buy a pup, that's a good thing too. When people write to me, as a lot do because I write a column about dogs, and say, "I want a pup", I always reply: "Are you sure? Have you thought about it enough? Do you know what it entails?" I say this because those of us who care about dogs (and there are a lot of us) get very angry when we read about dogs being abandoned. Many are, every year, especially after Christmas when it's discovered that you can't throw a dog away like an old toy.

One of the worst things we did was to listen to the pleadings of a sweet child and her indulgent parents and give her an equally sweet pup. They were tired of it in a month. They "discovered" it had to go out at regular intervals and be fed at regular intervals. Fortunately we found a better and more understanding home.

Now if I haven't made it all seem too difficult and you really want a pup, spend a little time studying the subject in general. It's just as important to learn how to keep a pup as it is to learn how to drive a car, and everyone accepts that.

Yet a pup is made of flesh, bone and blood—behaving differently on different days—and you have to put more into it than gasoline, oil and water. Even more regularly. Besides, you can put a car in the garage and forget about it. Not so a pup. It comes into your house. You should be very particular about who comes into your house and how they behave. Pups don't know until you teach them.

This article is not intended for large-scale breeders or those who want to have big kennels, though it may be of some use to them. It is for the many thousands who want to start with a puppy as a companion, bring it up to maturity, possibly breed it, show it maybe (though not in that order), and take an interest generally in canine matters. Equally, it can apply to those who want a pet and a companion and have no intention of either competing or breeding. Many start out like that and find themselves drawn into the sport, or "the dog game," as we call it.

I hope, also, to help those who are not so much concerned about dogs with pedigrees. Mind you, this much is certain: the basic principles are the same for a dog with a pedigree or one without. They both need proper treatment, feeding and exercise. And this also is certain: it takes just as much time and care and money to keep a mongrel as it does to keep a pedigree dog. The initial outlay will be greater, and that's about all.

Take it a step further: if you are concerned about cost (and most of us are) it costs just as much to keep a good dog (in the show sense) as a bad one. And above all, I put temperament. I'd rather have a good-tempered, useful girl around the place than an up-tight beauty queen! Have both rolled in one and you're laughing.

Remember this, too, when you buy a pup with a known pedigree, you can be pretty sure about the sort of dog it will become - its size when fully mature, its coat and color. You will also be able to find out about its temperament and character for its birth will have been planned and the breeders will be able to tell you about its family.

BASIC PRINCIPLES

They used to say, "if you want to know something about the girl you are going to marry, look at her mother." There's something in this with dogs. And I would add: look at father, too.

Pay no heed to those who say mongrel dogs are more intelligent than pedigreed dogs. It is not so. Stupid parents often have stupid children, pedigree or not. Not always. But where there is an honest pedigree (they usually are) the background is known. The mating has been controlled. It is more likely to produce pups with known character, size, color, coat and shape.

I do not say it is impossible to get a good-natured intelligent mongrel. I do say the chances of getting a good-natured, intelligent pure-bred dog is greater. And you know what you are getting, providing the parents have been intelligently bred.

I shall not deal at length with genes and chromosomes —I will not attempt to blind you with science. Instead I will talk in down-to-earth terms and basic principles. Here is an important one; don't be put off by the widely held opinion (many widely-held opinions are wrong) that pedigreed dogs are more nervous and weaker than mongrels, and that closely-bred dogs (meaning of the same family) are stupid and often plain daft. It is the nature and character of the parents, grandparents and others in the background that really matters. The closeness of the breeding (with certain safeguards) does not produce weakness of itself. It must be there first. It intensifies, but does not create, in the same way good characteristics can be intensified and fixed.

I'm glad we've got that out of the way for it bothers many. The basic thing to get hold of is this: if you like the father and mother; if you approve of their character, size, shape, color and coat, you will most probably like their pups.

They may not always become such good show specimens, but they will be so close that you'll have a pretty good idea which the pup will turn out to be. In the words of old dog folk, "like breeds like." It's not absolutely true, or absolutely certain; there are the recessive characteristics that pop up suddenly. But you can risk this; you have to take a chance with most things. Well, haven't you?

So we know a little about basic principles. We're certain we want a pup. We know what sort of pup and the sort of dog it will grow into because we have studied pictures, been to a dog show or two and talked to people with dogs who will certainly confuse the issue. (Dog people are always more difficult to understand than dogs.) However, our minds are made up. How do we go about it? There's a right way and a wrong way, as with most other things in life. Let's continue with the adventure, and don't blame me!

HOW TO CHOOSE A BREED

First check the *Dog Lovers Complete Guide*. Those listed in the *Complete Guide* are members of breed and dog-show-giving clubs whose purpose is to breed better specimens of their breed. This of course includes soundness and temperament in addition to standardization. In this book you will find a great deal of information, some of which you won't understand. Don't worry, we're all baffled occasionally. What you will be interested in are the Breeder Listings, Advertisements and Calendar of coming shows —there are scores held regularly in most parts of the U.S.

I advise you to go and have a look, first trying a local match show or small championship show, leave the big championship events for a bit. Notice I don't say you must go to Westminster in New York City, Chicago International or Beverly Hills which are some of the greatest dog shows in the world. You can, but you will find them big, noisy and crowded. Many of the exhibitors, a lot of them breeders, will be far too busy presenting their dogs and winning prizes to talk to you.

Now that little bit of advice will get me into trouble as some of the best dogs in the world are to be seen there, and they are the breeders' shop window. They are. But I'm trying to save you, the novice, from getting an off-putting rebuff. As someone must have said at some time or another: there's a time and place for everything - if you know what I mean.

Anyway, I bet a dollar to a penny (if there is such a thing) that you will go, get pushed around, get tired and confused. And enjoy it. I always do.

But for a starter, don't ignore the little shows where the breeders are more relaxed and have time to discuss their dogs with you. You will find them a friendly bunch on the whole, much divided in their opinions and inclined to have violent likes and dislikes. Be patient with them if you expect them to be patient with you.

Just let a lot of stuff about rotten judges and who did what to whom go in one ear and out of the other. Most of them are good friends underneath, though you'd hardly guess it. They also have a language of their own, which it takes time to understand.

After a first look round and time spent studying the breeds in which you are interested, and reading about them in several issues of POPULAR DOGS, you will be provided with lots of information about shows, breeders and other matters you will get to know about later-if you live that long.

You must make a big decision. What sort of dog do you want? They come in all shapes and sizes, all colors, and with long coats or short coats. Only you can decide. If you still don't know, there are many books published, and easily obtainable, which will give more help, for they provide not only details of the various breeds, but also pictures in color. Study them.

You will notice that dogs roughly fall into groups: tiny dogs, called the toys, some with short coats and some with long coats; medium-sized ones and big ones. These also are short or long coated. We have proper names for these groups, and they go like this: Sporting, Hound, Working, Terrier, Toy and Non-Sporting. But you don't have to worry at this stage.

Your decision is: big, medium or small; long coat or short coat. I keep mentioning coat because, like a girl with hair down to her waist, you have to work harder on it than a girl with an Eton crop or a shingle, as they used to call it in my young days. Which shows how un-with-it I am.

The point is this: a long coat takes a lot of looking after and it needs time; a short coat needs looking after too, but it's a quicker job. There are all sorts of preparations and brushes and combs that help to make it easier.

There's a further point: it is possible to cut off a longhaired dog's coat if you are not bothered about showing it, but it isn't a once-for-all job. It grows again and you have to clip at regular intervals. You either learn to do this yourself, which takes some skill, or you pay a dog beauty parlour or grooming shop to do it for you, which can be expensive.

Size matters because, believe it or not, a little dog doesn't take up so much room as a big one, and they don't eat as much either. If you want a dog to sit on your lap and sleep on the end of your bed, I would suggest a small one. Not that bigger ones don't enjoy the same treatment, but they are bigger and they take a lot of room.

Don't be put off by those who speak contemptuously of lap dogs, as if they were inferior and spoiled brats. They can be, but to generalize is rubbish. There are hounds (and this was particularly so in years gone by) kept in kennels which rough it and "go out huntin', by gad, Sir." They still do, and good luck to them. It's all very admirable, but I'm more concerned about the thousands of dogs that are constant companions and are part of the family.

Some dog people, bless 'em, have bees in their bonnets about dogs being bred for the job for which they were originally intended, from pulling sleds and carts to fighting bulls. It's a lot of bull. Humans used to live in caves, eat raw meat and pull in women by the hair. They don't do it any more; not much round our way, anyway.

Animals in their wild state are not cared for in anything like the same way as domesticated ones; they are often in poor condition and mostly frightened. I've seen them.

Life has changed, times have changed, and dogs must no longer, in any circumstances, be turned loose except when under proper control in the countryside. Besides this, man has decided what shape and size dogs will be. We make them smaller, sometimes bigger, and the job for which they were originally intended, like mine, no longer exists. Remember this: a dog will mate with any sort of dog of the opposite sex—which is something many breeders hold against them; blackbirds don't mate with robins!

Big dogs are just as wonderful companions as medium or small ones. Many friends have been brought up with Great Danes which are very large but mostly gentle creatures. But take my word for it. they do need room, and this goes for all the big ones. They are also strong, and you need to be pretty bright to control them. I also think you need experience. The big ones with big coats also take a great deal of looking after. There's a lot of coat and a lot of dog.

Are they better guards? They can be, but not always. Little dogs, like little people, are usually quicker and sharper. In many homes it's the small dog which speaks first and the large one which follows up with much greater weight, gruffer voice and authority.

But let me appeal to your reason. All dogs need training and correction at some time. If you don't have much space, it must be easier to deal with something small, even if it does make a fuss, than with something big and as strong as you are.

But don't be misled by anyone who tells you that a medium-sized dog can't live in a small house or flat. A champion Boxer, I know well, lived in a flat with a devoted girl owner. She cared for him like a brother, exercised him morning and night and fed him regularly. He was beautifully behaved, crossed the world with her and lived happily to a ripe old age.

You can keep a dog in any reasonably-sized accommodation anywhere - city or country. But you must not let a dog loose in a built-up area. It can be a menace in traffic and I join with those who object to dogs that mess up the pavements. I blame the people who own them, not the dogs.

So that's decided then, you know what you want (lucky you)! How do you get it?

WHERE TO PICK THE PUPPY

I wouldn't go to a pet shop to buy a pup. And that doesn't mean a thing against pet shops. Some, I'm told, are good. Some have weak unhealthy pups of questionable parentage. I'd go to the breeder. For good reasons. The breeder knows more about the pup and about its parents, probably about its grandparents too, and that's all to the good. If you're considering price (according to quality), then going to the accredited breeder listed in the *Dog Lovers Guide* is like going directly to the factory to buy your clothes, etc. You eliminate the middle man, shop overhead and shipping.

Don't imagine all breeders are lining up to sell you one of their pups. Some are, but not the dedicated ones.

They will want to know something about you and what sort of home the pup is going to. Besides that, it all depends on what sort of pup you want: a pet, a show prospect (which can also be a pet), a dog or a bitch.

A beginner won't know a show prospect from a woolly bear, even experts make mistakes. Many a champion has been sold and pups retained get nowhere in the show ring. That's part of the luck and fascination of the game. But, as a general rule, the beginner will have to take the expert's advice.

Don't be in a hurry. If one breeder can't help, there are others. You may even have to book a puppy before it's born.

I advise you to carefully select your breeder which is why you need the *Dog Lovers Guide*. Take their word. Most of those listed in the *Dog Lovers Guide* are thoroughly reliable and dedicated people, and will help you.

I've read lots of stuff about how to pick a puppy, how to know whether it's fit and well, how to discern its character, and, believe it or not, how to decide whether it will become a champion.

In fact, a good breeder (and I'm insisting that you go to one) won't sell you a sick puppy and most times will try not to sell you a future champion if they know you are only interested in a pet. As for character, it would be easy for me to say, "take the pup that comes to you, the extrovert rather than the shy one." Most writers say that, plus you must see that: the nose is not dry; the skin is loose; there's no sign of stomach upset; the pup is clear in eye, plump and living in proper conditions.

If you go to a bad breeder or an uncaring owner of a pet shop, you might worry about these points, but not where I'm sending you. A good breeder will have the pups as fat as butter balls, bright as sparks and spanking clean.

WHICH PUPPY TO PICK

Now this matter of character. We all like a bouncy pup at eight weeks waddling around and getting into all sorts of trouble, but don't overlook the aloof one that isn't so sure of you. Why should it be on first acquaintance? A very shy pup that hides is not one I'd select, but I wouldn't despair of it providing the mother is not nervous and father is a bold dog—I like bold stallions—but I would be cautious.

All this, of course, depends on whether there is a choice. It could be there is; on the other hand, you may not be so lucky. But you must see his mother, study her, for she is a guide as sure as any guides can be. Listen also to the owner, of whom you should know something from your reading of the *Dog Lovers Guide* and your dog show experience.

I have a preference for well established owners that have themselves successfully shown the breed you are interested in. If they haven't, take care, but do not necessarily discard them. We all had to start.

THE BEST TIME TO PICK A PUPPY

"The best age to pick a pup for the show ring is 11 months and 364 days," is the old dog man's quip. But you'll have to do it long before then because the breeders don't keep pups to that age save for themselves. Besides, the whole point of the exercise is that the pup is going to grow up with you and you are going to have the fun of it. Eight to twelve weeks is about the time, certainly not before eight, especially in winter.

Let's clear up the point about the sex: dog or bitch? For some reason many beginners go for a dog. I believe they are unwise. Bitches, when you take them out, as you must all pups, will spend a penny in one go. There's none of this dodging from one tree to another. Bitches are more faithful when they grow up, for the best dog on earth will forsake you, if he can, when he knows there's some loving to do. And he will know, for not all owners are careful.

True, bitches come into season, about once every six months, but today they can be put on the pill like all the girls—but get your vet's advice. And if you don't want to do this, there are preparations available which, when applied, will deceive the males who go by smell not by looks. They're not the slightest bit interested in the shape of the "Miss Canine World."

Another thing - and you can absolutely rely on this: you'll only be able to breed a litter yourself one day if you have a bitch!

If you do buy a dog, and don't let me stop you, don't think that when he's grown up he must have a girl friend just once and then he won't be frustrated! Never start him on this lark unless he's a stud dog—another matter altogether—for once is like blood to a tiger, and they say tigers care about blood! Pet male dogs should not be introduced to either the joys or frustrations of womanizing. It is not for them. If it happens by accident, that's too bad. He won't forget it.

It is possible, too, by surgical operation to render a dog or bitch unfit for breeding. But this again is a matter for you and your vet. Personally, I don't care about it. You won't be able to show the animal.

Lots of advice has been given on how to send for a pup and what to do when it arrives by train or plane. The answer is this: if you can't bother to fetch a pup, don't have one. I speak generally and not about special cases like guide dogs for the blind, and others. Then a friend is needed. Sometimes the breeder will oblige, which also gives them an opportunity to see the new home.

About breeding terms. The buyer may not be able to afford a pup outright and the breeder may not wish to part with a bitch outright. An arrangement can be made whereby some money is paid, and it is agreed that when the pup grows up and is mated a certain number of pups go back to the original breeder. There are many variations of this arrangement. It must be in writing and neither side must be greedy. Be clear who is going to be the one registered breeder, and who pays the stud fee, and how many pups go back and from how many litters. Unless this is put down in black and white, disputes are more than likely to arise. I can't tell you exactly how the arrangements should be worked out, because different ideas are held by different breeders. The principle is that both sides are happy about it; that the breeder doesn't take all and that the buyer appreciates that in return for the help given there must be concessions. That is generous. Oddly, established breeders are sometimes more generous than comparative newcomers.

I'm not going to tell you how to feed your pup. How can I? I don't know which of the infinite varieties you are going to feed. The breeder of the pup will give you a diet sheet with the pup's pedigree. The breeder will know best, especially the experienced sort I've discussed. Do what they say. You don't know better, even if you think you do. It's very simple. Breeders will have their own ideas, based on experience of rearing many pups. There are many variations of diet.

I have reared scores of pups, and they have not been treated all the same by any means: some are greedy; some are more difficult; some have to be encouraged; others have to be checked. In broad, very broad, terms treat your pup like a baby. And if you haven't had a baby, use your imagination. And you can always ring up the breeder, of the pup I mean.

So, you're off home with your pup. You have his pedigree (which will mean little to you, but you will learn), his diet sheet, and the documentation which the breeder will tell you about and which you can check with the American Kennel Club.

Keep the little beggar warm as you travel, be sweet to him (or is it her?), talk to him. He's leaving his mum and he won't be happy. You've got to make him happy and if you do the response will be quick and warm. I hope you have made preparations at home; you've got his food in; his bed ready. Now you've got to learn how to bring up a pup. That's the next lesson.

BRINGING UP PUPPY

Rearing a puppy is a matter of common sense—uncommon sense if you like. A lot of people are short of it. You must feed the pup right (you have a diet sheet for that) and you must treat it like a baby. Babies don't go to the lavatory by themselves; you have to train them. Unhappily you can't put a nappy on a puppy and a grown dog doesn't go to the lavatory and pull the chain either! I wish they did. If you haven't got a garden into which you can send your pup, or if you have a garden and don't like it used by the dog, or if you live on a street, you must take your pup out regularly. That's all there is to it. Puppies, like children, need to go more often than grown ups.

Simple and true. It's up to you. When there's a mistake it's your fault. And if you hit a pup or rub its nose in it for a mistake for which you are to blame, then you're a fool, besides being unkind. I'm not going to insult your intelligence by telling you how many times a pup must go, or shall I?

My latest pup never made a mistake and she was taken out first thing in the morning, after every meal and last thing at night. It became a matter of habit, and dogs who live with the family are creatures of habit. You have to work out a routine for yourself. One that suits you and the pup. We have one rule: never let a pup roam about by itself. Unlike a child it can't tell you of its need. If you are an aware person you will know when a dog wants to go out.

Of course there are exceptions to these rules. Work them out for yourself. Dogs that live in kennels are treated very differently. You clean up after them. Grown male dogs pee around to let the bitches know they're about, but not in the house, if you have brought them up properly. So do some bitches when they are in the mood.

When a friend came to see me she brought a pet bitch. It peed in the sitting room three times. I was furious. By the way, when this does happen squirt soda water on the spot immediately and then mop up, or your carpets will suffer. Then use a nice-smelling spray so that other dogs don't get the wrong idea.

Some dog writers gloss over this side of nature. I don't because it is most important, unless you don't mind a smelly house which is horrid. My dogs sit on chairs. Some people don't care about it and it's possible to train them to stay on the floor. I don't mind them on chairs. If you brush your pup regularly there isn't all that much dead hair left around. With some breeds none at all, others lose their coats regularly.

I had a friend who was very particular about his clothes. He was not a dog man, and all our dogs knew it. They would insist on rubbing against him, gazing at him intently with dark brown eyes and breathing heavily. He doesn't seem to visit us much nowadays.

GOOD GROOMING—GOOD MANNERS

Brushing and cutting nails must be done regularly. Just like a child again. There's no need to make a meal of it. Ten minutes brushing a day for the short-coated breeds and somewhat longer for the longhaired ones. Some Poodle owners, for example, never seem to stop and if it's a show Poodle it's quite a performance. Other breeds come into the same category and for the details and the best way of doing these jobs you'd best get one of the books about your own breed. Buy a Breed Book written by an experienced breeder, not one of those books that tells a little about your breed and the rest of the material is generalizations to be found in half a dozen or more books on other breeds by the same author.

Life is made much easier nowadays by preparations specially made for dogs' coats. They are easily applied. Excellent brushes and combs are also available.

Pups pick up simple words of command very quickly, providing you use the same words firmly and few of them. Come, sit, down, are three I use. But you must be patient and you must reward for prompt and good behavior—not always with a tidbit, that helps, but with a pat and a kind word. Good girl brings a tail-wag. It's the tone of voice that matters.

Many dogs can be trained to a high degree for work of all kinds and they are very happy about it. If you are interested go to see obedience rings at dog shows. Classes are held all over the country. Obedience schools and trainers are available. There are also working and field trials. These are subjects for which you will need further information which is readily available.

When a child has good manners it's a joy. So with a pup, but you must be the teacher. I recommend patience and kindness. Rough people are not attractive either in speech or manner and I loathe seeing a dog roughly treated. Firmness is sometimes needed, but spare the rod and improve the child.

Certainly we are soft with our dogs, and they are not the best behaved in the world, but they are devoted to us and we love them, we hope in the best way. Dull people are boring, so are dull dogs.

Keep your pup warm. We've often put a stone hot water bottle, well covered, into a pup's bed and also a loud ticking clock to keep the pup company. Pups like toys.

I like a regular bed, so does a pup. They can put up with going to a strange one occasionally. So can I. But always warm and never a draft.

NUTRITION AND CARE

Good food, vitamins and minerals are good for children, so they are for pups. And you can get all the necessary vitamins, including calcium (very important) quite easily these days. Many firms package these things very neatly and give clear instructions. You can rely on them. With their help, and if the pup was healthy to start with, you'll be pretty certain of getting a healthy, happy dog.

Do I have to tell you that if the pup needs more than home help you phone the doctor? They call him a Vet, and he'll be in the phone book.

Some folks love diseases and are always talking about them. Some dog books list so many ailments that you would imagine that a dog is sick most of its time. If you care for the dog it isn't. Caring for it means proper food, sufficient exercise (which means very little for a young pup and more for a grown up dog), regular brushing and care of ears and nails.

There's little else. Except this: make certain the pup has the right injections ("shots" if you like) for protection against Distemper. The good breeder will have seen to this before you collect your pup, and if anything else is required, will tell you. For this you need the Vet. Make no mistake about this point. Check on it, do the right thing and forget about it. The modern shots are very good and are absolutely reliable. It was different in the old days.

A pup can't tell you when it's sick, except by its behavior. You must bring yourself to look at its stools and see they are firm. There are simple remedies to put this right, and you must consider whether the diet is correct for your particular pup. Some breeds are more prone to upset turns than others. Observe how the pup meets you first thing in the morning. Bert Lloyd, one of Britain's great dog men, said to me, "When I call the pups in the mornings, I always watch. If one is lingering it always puts me on my guard." Good advice.

Ears need to be cleaned gently with cotton once a week, more often if you like. Treat the pup's ears as if they were your own. The pup can't do it for himself. Cut nails and file once a week, for long nails are ugly and can become uncomfortable, and notice whether the eyes are clear and bright. One of my pups needed her eyes to be wiped and mucous gently removed daily. I regularly squirted in, very gently, a little ointment suggested by the Vet and this cleared it up. There are ear remedies and others for fleas.

Some people don't wash or bathe their dogs. We do, in warm water and then shampoo them. It's a good thing; why not? You take a bath don't you? That old stuff about destroying the natural oils is rubbish. But you must dry thoroughly and don't let the dog rush out if it's cold. Just use your head and a proper dog shampoo.

Many dogs get a bit of skin trouble occasionally despite all precautions. There are some excellent ointments that get to the root of the trouble. Inquire about an injection the Vet can give if it persists.

If you read the Veterinary Column, "Ask Your Doctor", printed monthly in POPULAR DOGS - also your Breed Column - I am sure you will receive many helpful hints toward understanding, as well as prevention of health problems.

TRAINING & EXHIBITING YOUR PUPPY

Your pup is growing up. The diet will have changed to more food but less often. Don't be too rigid about it. Like us, dogs are individualists. For example, a fully grown dog, "they" say, needs one meal a day. Mine prefer two, or one, if you like divided into two, except on show days when the routine is varied. It doesn't hurt them to wait occasionally, and some breeders give no food at all on one day each week. I suspect the fast is for their own convenience.

There are others, cranks, who maintain that, in the natural state, dogs eat only when they can get food (and may have to wait some time for the next lot), therefore it's all right for them to gorge themselves one day and then starve. That's rubbish! Having changed the lives of dogs and having "made" the various breeds ourselves, they are no longer in their natural state.

If you want to show that pup of yours (and why not?) look at the announcements in the Dog Show Calendar, send for a premium list and post your entry. What to do is made clear. I advise the beginner to try a little show first, possibly a match show, and leave the championship ones till later. By then you will have your own ideas. In any event, you must get some training in first. All this means is to get your pup to stand still, look its best and move briskly up and down when called on to do so. Notice I've said that's all you have to do. In fact it is an art to do it well, and a dog's chances in the show ring can be made or ruined by clever handling. Many clubs run ringcraft classes. They are worth looking at and there are also classes for children. In the end it depends on you and the dog.

Some people will never be able to handle well; some pick it up quickly. If you feel unsure, discuss it with a professional handler. It requires a lot of know-how and and understanding between dog and handler. I would watch the experienced experts before having a go. It's possible to write a book on this one aspect, but that's not our purpose. Watch and learn, and remember it's the dog, not you, that's being judged. Some forget that.

You need time to do the job properly. It astonished me that some quite experienced owners will take a pup into the ring without training at home. Never do this. Most exhibitors will start "setting up" their pups at eight weeks and continue each day before showing them, perhaps at ten months.

Between dog and handler there grows a great sympathy and understanding. There should be quick response—and it is done on a loose lead. None of this life-and-death struggle one so often sees. So, go to a show, see what is required, and return home and practice, practice, practice.

Some quick but important points. In puppy classes dogs and bitches are eligible between six and twelve months. So if you enter at six months you can be giving away a lot unless, which is the case at some shows, the puppy classes are divided 6-9 months and 9-12 months. In some breeds this is more important than others. And some pups mature much quicker than others. Only experience will help here.

Your pup must be shown in the best condition possible and there are many aids that will provide for this. If yours is a long-coated breed you must particularly find out about presentation. There is so much to be said about this, and again I advise you to get a book written solely about your breed. Study the color photographs and don't be dismayed by all the beautiful animals you will see. Their owners had to start like you, though some came from homes where dogs have been bred and shown for many years. This is an advantage, but you can catch up.

Short-coated dogs also need preparation, and if the breeder you bought your pup from is knowledgeable (as I sincerely hope), he should help you. If this is impossible then there is nothing to do but to watch and read, or invest in a professional.

DO YOU HAVE A CHANCE?

You are likely to have some successes and many disappointments. Remember above all, that a judge is only giving an opinion. It's not like horse racing where the first past the post is winner. This is a matter of judgment, and some are much better at it than others. Say to yourself on those occasions when you don't get a prize: there will be another day and another judge. Besides, when coat, condition and fitness come into it, dogs look better some days than others, and the competitors are not always the same. One thing is certain: you can't win if you don't have a go, and you won't always win, or lose either.

Don't get involved in dog "politics". (Oh, yes, they do exist as in most sports.) But you will, of course! And take with a pinch of salt the stories you will hear about judges being bribed. I've been connected with this sport and others for many years, and I believe the dog game is as clean as any.

I've skated over the ground, but the idea is to give you the taste. Millions of people who own dogs never go near a show ring—like families who own a pony—and they're perfectly happy. So will you be.

A dog can mean much, or little, to you. They can be a great comfort. When I worked in a highly competitive world I could pretty well tell how I was doing by the way some people greeted me. It made no difference to my dogs, up or down, without a dime in my pocket. They neither knew nor cared. True friends are like that.

You will find all types in the dog show game: some are rich and have nothing else to do; some are lonely; some have lived colorless lives and seek recognition they can't find elsewhere; some are in it for the money; some are true dog lovers and enjoy the competition. There's only one good reason to join: because you like it. I think you will.

From your puppy classes you will progress and find other classes restricted by age (the pup's not yours), the number of wins obtained, and finally those classes open to all. At these championship shows you can win the points which are needed to make up (as we call it) a champion. That's a long way ahead for you and you will have to compete against professional handlers and toughened knowledgeable exhibitors from famous kennels.

Do you have a chance? Of course. But a greater chance when you also have experience. A really good dog will win eventually no matter who owns it providing it's given the opportunity. You can't keep a good man down, or a good dog either. But it stands to reason, the experienced exhibitors with many dogs are better placed than the novice with one dog to start with. But you can do it, and many have. This is a game in which knowledge and luck play a part. Above all you've got to have a good dog.

YOUR FIRST LITTER

That's a brief glance at the show ring, now what about your first litter. Remember, once again, that I write in general terms. The only thing certain in dogs is the uncertainty. Bitches come into season about once every six months, if nature is allowed to take its course. But I do not believe in mating them, apart from show ring considerations, until they are at least 12 months for the smaller ones and 18 months for the larger—mature, or nearly so, but still young and slim. Breeds vary considerably.

As at all times, the bitch must be in sparkling health, built up with good food and vitamins. You will need to have her mated around the 12th day of her season, but, goodness me, that varies too. We've had success much earlier and later. It's experience you need to gauge the right moment, so why not inquire from the breeder who sold you your pup. He will know. And I've been told about a new scientific method of telling the right moment. Ask your Vet. If he doesn't know (and it's possible), ask him to find out.

You have, of course, decided on the stud dog. Even in these modern days the male is still necessary for this little job. Which dog will you use? You can be blinded by science about it. Thousands of words have been written about in-breeding, line-breeding and out-cross breeding. Broadly this means mating close relations, near relations and no relation at all. We've tried it all ways and I've done my bit towards confusing the innocents by rabbling off the jargon about genes recessive and otherwise. I'm not going to bother you. If you want to find out get a book on the subject. Two or three if you like, and I doubt if you'll be much wiser and more successful at the end of it.

Such heresy will drive some of my friends mad. I don't mind a bit; we've bred champions by line-breeding and by out-crossing. So what does that prove? Nothing.

Here is my advice. Study your breed, find out which stud dog is having, or has had, success in the show ring, and has already sired winners. It's not always possible to do this, but aim for it. Then go and see him, make up your own mind, paying regard to his color and many other characteristics. Study photographs, remembering that these do not always give a completely true picture. That breeder who sold you your pup can help, but it's time you were making up your own mind. Study pedigrees, but they might not tell you very much, because you probably won't know what the dogs looked like. Pedigrees don't tell you that. That knowledge will come. You must also have made up your mind in what way your bitch can be improved.

So, if you follow me (amid howls of protest), you will work on the principle that it's best to mate good looking girls to good looking boys, if you want good looking children. You'll have time to experiment when you have had a dozen litters (that is your bitches have). Avoid putting fault to fault. By that I mean that a long-backed bitch mated to a long-backed dog, for example, is more likely to get long-backed pups than short-backed ones. This applies to other parts of the animals. Light eyes to light eyes, short necks to short necks and so on.

But it's not nearly so easy as that. Stud dogs will probably have some characteristics you like and not others. And to crown it all, the expectation that long backs will make long backs may not be realized at all. Mother Nature (if there is such a thing) is most provoking and quite unpredictable. I've known two well bred champions, and close bred at that, produce nothing outstanding and I've known an "accident" to produce a beauty.

That's the luck of the game, and this is where a big kennel may beat you at first, because they have taken more tickets in the lottery, for that's what it is. Almost anyway. And above all, pay regard to temperament, call it character if you like. Personality can be passed on as well as make and shape. And that by no means indicates that a bright pair will produce sparkling children. But I think you stand a better chance.

So I've made it simple for you, or have I? Need I say you must ring up the owner of the stud dog and make your own arrangements and you take, not send, your bitch to be mated. The stud dog owner will almost certainly be experienced, though God knows I've dealt with some who still think the whole thing is done under a gooseberry bush. If they are not experienced, have no part of it.

Pay the stud fee on the male if you can, for if the owner of the male agrees to pick of litter instead of a fee, he will certainly take the best pup if he can. And justifiably so. You should also come to an understanding that if no pups result the bitch will be mated free next time. Stud fees to champions in this country range from about $100.00 to $250.00. A few less, some more.

Don't be above taking advice from the stud dog owner on this your first time round, for remember they usually know a lot more than you and are just as particular. They like taking fees most of them (rightly so), but they like good bitches to come to them too, for a stud dog gains his reputation by the quality of his children. To coin that well worn phrase: handsome surely is as handsome does. And don't be so naive to believe that if all doesn't go well and you don't get a beautiful litter, it's all the stud dog's fault. This really is a matter of cooperation.

Some more don'ts. If you want to breed good pups don't use the dog next door. It's worth traveling a long way if necessary. Don't in any circumstances let your bitch out either during her season or sometime after unless she's on a lead. That is pretty unnecessary advice you may think. Don't believe it. I wonder how many experienced breeders can look you in the eye and say they've never had a mistake. I well remember the day when a neighbor's small son came in and announced, "Rex is marrying Trixie on the lawn." Actually the mating turned out very well, but that's hardly the point.

In normal circumstances your bitch will not take her pregnancy as a great burden until near her time in nine weeks. Give her lots of good meat, milk, eggs and building vitamins. But don't get her fat. Fat bitches don't get pregnant as easily as slim bitches and fat bitches don't have puppies as easily as slim bitches. And I'll be dogmatic about that one. After a month we didn't let our bitches race around by themselves. We counselled them: take care my dear, we are expecting great things of you.

So you await your first litter; it's an interesting time. You are now completely immersed in "the dog game", it's a sport the whole family can play at and enjoy.

HAS THE BREEDER LOST HIS SHOWCASE

BY

RUTH H. TONGREN

"Can you tell me where I can find the Welsh Terriers, Pugs, Poodles, Afghans or whatever?"

"Everyone breeds to the top winner."

"I went reserve but didn't wait to see who got Best of Breed."

"I don't know anyone in my breed anymore."

"All the fun has gone out of dog shows."

Though no surface relationship is evident in these familiar quotations, they are in truth all related to the passing of benched shows.

The eager searchers for a specific breed can be a family who have gone to a dog show hoping to talk to breeders and see a selection of their chosen breed.

Their dreams are dashed by the chilling expediency of the unbenched show. The breed was judged at 10 o'clock and all have left. However, if they choose to wait until Group time, they can see the top winner. One who, being of this stature, is scarcely the cuddly puppy our family is looking for to love and maybe, "show at the local matches." We can all identify with this—who among us bought our first dog dreaming of the dedication to follow?

So . . . where to go?

Few potential buyers are sufficiently aware of procedure to call the AKC. Most don't know about dog magazines. Classified ads involve expensive phone calls and fruitless trips to learn, "The last one is sold," or it's the wrong age, sex, color or any of the many detriments to confuse the uninitiated.

The warm professional welcome of the ubiquitous Pet Shop offers infinite variety with no waiting or tiresome Sunday driving. As an added fillip, there's a ten year guarantee!

Ironically, anyone reading this is aware of the Pet Shop Pitfalls, so how is the breeder to reach the trusting souls who at this moment are awaiting the call, "Your puppy is in, you can pick him up today"?

Benched shows made us available to the buying public . . .

"EVERYONE BREEDS TO THE TOP WINNER!" Often people wanting to breed will go to shows to formulate their opinion of type. The only breeder available is the owner of the top winner who is staying for the group. There is no poll of ideas to be assessed; no one to advise on pedigrees or bloodlines; no one to talk to.

They were there at benched shows . . .

"WE WENT RESERVE BUT DIDN'T WAIT FOR THE BREED!" An attitude greatly responsible for the vast turnover in show enthusiasts. No real breeder was ever created by a frenetic spin around a ring and home again. The true dog person is one who feels the flavor of shows, who knows each worthy competitor in his breed, then in his Group, and ultimately every important regular in the Best in Show ring. Who, by constant exposure, feels at home when he arrives on the show grounds. Who understands that no judge is infallible; that competition, condition and expertise can make or break a show dog. The only road to this awareness is time spent becoming part of it. It can't be learned from a book or from inept speculations of other neophytes. It is an intangible we can call absorption . . . .

Benched shows made people wait and absorb.

"I DON'T KNOW ANYONE IN MY BREED ANYMORE!" Of course not, only during the actual judging is there a community of exhibitors. A time when tension is too high for introductions, tempers are frayed, the winners exultantly seeking close ones to rejoice. It is human for the defeated to resent the victors. Animosities are created among some who in a more relaxed hour could find mutual interests and a splendid relationship.

As the last ribbon is handed out, dog and handler flee to their corner of the far flung acreage of today's enormous sites and then home. There is no geographical center for each breed where V.I.P. is benched next to the novice, who finds that the face seen in magazines or the Group ring is in reality a human being and not a distant demi-god. Where time permits amenities and an exchange of ideas. Where preconceived misconceptions based on an ill chosen word or superficial gesture are shattered because there is no time for communication. When sometimes an apparent hauteur is a veil for timidity cloaking an anxious hope for acceptance.

Benched shows forced communication . . .

"ALL THE FUN HAS GONE OUT OF DOG SHOWS!" At the risk of sounding like a "good old days" reactionary, I admit this is where my heart is. Could a party really swing if each guest stood in a separate room? The comparison may sound strange but it is valid. There was a party flavor about weekly benched shows. Lunches and well-stocked bars were shared and exchanged. Precious bits of gossip were savored for special ears. Arriving in the morning there was time to relax and moan about yesterday's judging. It was a meeting place for friends. "I'll be at the Afghan bench," was destination pinpoint. It was fun sitting on the bench and boasting to Mr. and Mrs. John Q. as they filed by. There was solace in the blue ribbon tacked up even if your neighbor knew the awful truth.

Deep rooted animosities were rare. Who could harbor a grudge against someone with whom you shared four feet of space? The same principle as a double bed. You can't stay mad at someone you can't avoid.

There was a safe place for coats and bags and best of all a comfortable secure spot for your dog, alleviating the necessity of dragging crates into the overcrowded handlers' area. There was always someone to keep an eye on your dog and it was reciprocal.

It was a showcase where prospective buyers could see dogs and talk to breeders. Many puppies were sold and friendships made from these encounters

"Let's all stop for dinner," was the norm once the day's business was dispatched. Restaurant owners would be taxed beyond endurance when 15 or more bedraggled, jabbering dog show folk would descend, demanding one big table. It was fun; the griping, crowing, rehashing and rejudging while we ate, drank, laughed and fought often until too late at night. Many a wary novice has become an old timer because he tagged along to these post-show dinners and was made welcome.

Only at benched shows would proximity have demanded an invitation!

Don't shake a finger and spout statistics at me. I recognize the inevitablility of unbenched shows. I know all about cramped space and mushrooming costs and I bow to the validity of reason. I can't help one small reservation though. Why is it that Westminster, Philadelphia, Eastern, Hartford, International, Heart of America and some of the other wonderful shows seem to be doing business at the same old stand with the excitement and prestige of old still intact?

As one whose many years of discomfort, bankruptcy and mental torture have proven my loyalty inviolate, benched or unbenched, I love it. So, permit me my last wistful glance backwards and forgive my rueful smile when I hear "Great, we can leave as soon as we are judged."

You don't know what you missed!

The handlers have profitted, but the breeder has lost his showcase.

Only a benched show can provide that . . . .

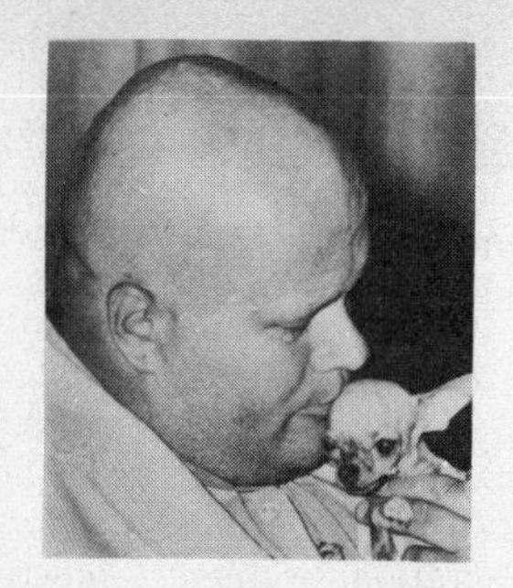

EUROPEAN TRAVEL WITH YOUR DOG

BY CAPTAIN ARTHUR J. HAGGERTY

Liz and Richard Burton had a simple solution to travel with their dogs. Before the famous couple broke up they trotted all over Europe. England with its ridiculous six month quarantine would have separated the Burtons from their assortment of dogs and other pets. Simple solution: hire a yacht to anchor in the Thames on which the animals were kept . . . the dogs never entered England, hence, no quarantine! The cost of many thousands of dollars daily did not bother the Burtons. Unless you are able to afford a yacht on the Thames, you would be best advised not to take your dog to the British Isles. What will you do with your house dog on your trip to Europe?

A friend of mine went to California and left his Maltese with a cousin. The little dog was getting underfoot so the well-meaning cousin put him in the den. At this point the Maltese started to bark. This was ignored by the relatives, because a Maltese just does not make that much noise. Later on when they went in to see the dog they found him choking on the rug that he was chewing. They did not want the rug ruined so they gave the little dog run of the entire house. They forgot that the door was open and the white ball of fluff scooted out the door. The owner was frantic. A reward of $1,000 enabled them to recover their dog. Their solution to this true story is that they are not going unless they can take their dog along with them.

If the dog was put in a good boarding kennel, he would not have been permitted to bark incessantly. Someone would have investigated what was troubling the dog and made sure that the dog did not go home with a hoarse throat. If the kennel had rugs, the kennel help would have seen the dog chewing on the rug and removed it. Granted, the dog may not have a rug to lie on but he would not choke to death. On the third and most important matter, any kennel worth its salt would have at least two doors the dog would have to go through in order to get out and they would be closed. Nonetheless, these people are going to take the Maltese with them from now on. Let's see what we have to do to get around Europe.

Getting there is half the fun. How do you like your pleasure . . . sea or air? Luxury sea travel is more relaxing and the food and entertainment found aboard ship is well worth the extra time and money. Quality ship travel assures your dog of the best conditions throughout the voyage. This will include special menus and a kennel master to tend to your dog's needs. If you are the adventuresome type that prefers being one of the few passengers on a freighter (either to save money or get away from it all), you will find that freighters do not have facilities for your dog. If your dog is accepted, you probably will not be charged for your dog as they do on deluxe steamship lines. The dog will be your full responsibility and, until you meet a sympathetic cook, you'll have to feed him from your "doggy bag."

A cruise, where the ship is your hotel, eliminates the problem of clearing your dog through customs. Keep your dog on shipboard and he won't enter the country. You can, unencumbered by "Rover", enjoy the local sights.

The cost of transporting your dog by ship can be less expensive than by air. As a matter of fact, airlines charge you more for your dog than they do for you. It is not just the weight that costs! Put a dog in a crate and it takes up a lot of space. The airlines take advantage of this situation and they have a cute little trick here. They charge you for cubic displacement. A seventy pound dog in a thirty pound crate weighs one hundred pounds. If the crate measures 30" high by 24" wide by 37" long, you have 138 pounds of cubic displacement and pay the higher rate. The cost from New York to Frankfurt is $1.78 per pound for a grand total of $245.64 ONE WAY. On actual weight the cost would only be $178.00. You can be assured that your dog will be on the flight with you if you ship him excess baggage. Excess baggage charges are $2.55 per pound which would cost $351.90 for the same dog to the same destination. It might be cheaper to bring your wife along—or somebody else's wife—that way there would be someone at home to watch the dogs . . . in both households.

A smaller dog can simplify the problem. If you have a real tiny Toy, you can smuggle it into the aircraft cabin. Airlines continually change their policy as to dogs in the cabin. With a well disguised carrier you will get on board with the dog. Once you are airborne no one is going to turn a 747 around to discharge a Papillon. The people who give you a thorough search before you board your plane are security personnel, not airline personnel. They are not required to enforce a particular airline's regulation and are probably not even aware of them. They want to be sure that you are not carrying guns and will not concern themselves with Yorkies.

A trip to Europe can include a quick side trip to North Africa. This interesting side of the world is not as strict as some European countries regarding entry documentation.

People are often confused between the terms "Embassy" and "Consulate." The Embassy is the main office of a foreign country located in the national capitol of a country with which they have diplomatic relations. It is where the Ambassador generally hangs out. The Consulates are the "branch offices" in large metropolitan areas. The larger the country, the more Consulates it has. Lichtenstein *does not* have a Consulate in Fargo, North Dakota. If you need further information to change your travel plans to another country, remember that the countries must have diplomatic ties. You may be forced to put your dog in a foreign boarding kennel in order to change your travel plans rapidly. European boarding rates, once considerably lower than ours, are comparable to Stateside rates today with the weakening of the dollar.

Travel by ship or plane will be simplified if you bring a crate along. One of the folding wire varieties can be recommended. If you rent a car, you will be able to fold and pack the crate along. A couple of firms manufacture a solid aluminum folding crate which is a good idea. The weight of the crate is important from *your* point of view, not the airlines. Years ago that aluminum crate made a difference on airline freight charges. As pointed out earlier, you will be paying for cubic displacement. When you get off the plane you will have to "schlepp" the crate around. Dollies are handy for dog shows as well as international travel. Skycaps are like taxi drivers and policemen—you can never find one when you need him. The wealthy European working man now finds it demeaning to do this type of work and the foreign airports often have no one to help you.

Europe lacks the American sophistication in shipping, crating and containing dogs. The American show fancier has developed this to a fine art. Do not think that you will be able to pick up American type of equipment in Europe. Even if you could, you would not save any money. The dollar lacks the strength that it once had.

Convenience type dog food is not readily available in Europe. Many

Europeans refuse to feed the inexpensive dry commercial dog food that is now available to them. They feel that dogs should be fed meat and the principle diet of European dogs, even in kennels, is meat. While the dry food is catching on, it is not as easily found as in the States. The canned food is also scarce. Frozen food is not popular in Europe and the meat that the dogs eat may consist of unrefrigerated tripe fresh from the slaughter house. Most kennels will get a week's supply at a time. At the end of the week the tripe is ripe! Freezer and refrigerator space is limited in Europe. Homes do not have refrigerators and if they do have one, it is like our itty-bitty bar refrigerators. Our big combination freezer-refrigerators would astound the average European.

"There is no such thing as dog food in Russia," warns Pam Cole of Dornwald German Shepherds. "You'll have to line up at meat markets to get regular cuts of meat," she continued in an interview. Ms. Cole strongly advises against bringing dogs into the Soviet Union. Tourists are put on a tight schedule by their intourist guides and they do not have time to queue up for meat.

BATTLING THE BUREAUCRATS

The attached information will give you ammunition with which to bombard the bastion of bureaucratic bungling that you will meet at the borders. Make sure that you have the proper documentation. If not, you may find yourself closed out of a country. Different countries have different types of people at the border. You can tell a country's political leanings by its border check points. These regulations are subject to change at any time so use the chart as a guide and not the final word. A few years ago the rigid British quarantine system slipped and rabies were found in the British Isles. The English extended their quarantine period from six to nine months and then to one year. Dogs that had entered quarantine for a six-month stay had their time extended. In fairness to the British government, it must be said that they paid the added expenses while the dog was in quarantine. Normally all quarantine expenses are paid by the owner. The one year quarantine was in effect for such a short period of time that no dog actually did spend one year in quarantine. These laws can and do change, so be prepared. Problem areas to watch out for on your trip are Poland and Czechoslovakia that require health certificates be issued no more than four and two days respectively, before entry.

Most countries require that forms be issued by "official" veterinarians. The nearest equivalent that we have to this is our licensed veterinarians. Have your veterinarian use rubber stamps and embossing machines on any documentation required. Make it look as official as possible. In Europe, your hotel bills will look more officious than a Harvard diploma. Have your veterinarian use Latin terms wherever possible. As the official language of medicine, it will reduce confusion.

The average border guard is not familiar with the regulations on importing pets. In western Europe be as sure of yourself as possible. This will eliminate the need for the customs' personnel to check with a superior, or the regulations, in order to pass you on. If you are queried about your certificates, explain to them that it is in order and exactly what their government requires. Customs' people, who are unsure of themselves, will delay you. Do not become overbearing or they will become uncooperative. The ultimate bureaucrats, the Germans, will insist that everything is in order. The Communist block countries also have a highly developed bureaucracy which will also make the entry of a dog a matter of precise record. You will not be able to talk your way around these people. They are afraid to make decisions themselves and will check with their superiors, meaning delays. The Communists are more interested in what *leaves* their country than what comes in. The free world is interested in what comes *in* rather than what goes *out*. North African countries have a tendency to be slipshod in their handling of paperwork which will make it easier for you.

Germany and Austria are the greatest dog-loving countries in Europe. Dogs are welcome everywhere, restaurants, street cars (a muzzle is required), and assorted stores and shops. Prohibitions are starting to rear their heads in bakeries. In most places a well behaved dog is not only welcome but fawned over.

Iceland, technically a Nordic and therefore European country, is noted for one thing to travelers. Their national airline is the cheapest one with scheduled flights to Europe. One trip on their planes will tell you the reason why this is true. The next logical thought is that you can fly your dog cheaper with Icelandic Airlines.

Not true! The airline does not even carry dogs. Dogs are "persona non grata" in Iceland. The fact that this country has such prohibitive laws against dogs is reason enough for me not to fly Icelandic Airlines.

The Swiss have an interesting approach to dogs whose owners want to enter a food store. The store has chains with snaps outside just like the old hitching post.

Before your trip make sure your dog is in the best of health. The trip, changes in climate, changes in food and water will put a strain on your dog. Cut his nails before the trip. You may not have too much of a chance to do this on your journey. Bring along at least one dish to feed and water your dog.

Remember to keep your dog on a leash. Your dog's I.D. tag should have "USA" after the address. It is a good idea to add, "or the American Embassy," after the address.

While most Europeans like dogs, they do not like unruly dogs. Your pet should be well mannered, trained and not destructive. You are responsible for your dog's actions. Respect other people's property and watch where your dog relieves himself. We have heard about the "Ugly American." Let's not hear about the "Ugly American's Dog."

With documentation problems, inoculations, health checks, unavailability of dog food, a declining dollar, etc., you may want to leave your dog at home. Aunt Nell doesn't know the symptoms of bloat, how to handle the over-heated dog or loose bowels. Do not leave the dog with her! Leave your dog with an experienced boarding kennel that knows how to handle these problems. If you do take your dog along, lots of luck and "Bon Voyage!"

IMPORT REQUIREMENTS FOR DOGS

Compiled by Capt. Arthur J. Haggerty

Austria: No requirements, no restrictions.

Belgium: Rabies. Live virus w/2 yr. protection or inactive w/1 yr. protection, either one administered at least 30 days before arrival.

Bulgaria: Health certificate and statement that country is epidemic free.

Czechoslovakia: Health certificate no more than 2 days before arrival w/statement the area within 40 kilometers (25 miles) is rabies free.

Denmark: Dogs over 4 mos. must have rabies inoc. 4 wks. to 12 mos. before arrival. Dog can be inoc. & examined at border for nominal fee. Save your papers. They can be used for re-entry.

Finland: Rabies. Inactive. Distemper. Inoculations 21 days before arrival. Dog must be worm free. Health certificate. Permission from government to bring dog in. 4 mos. ouarantine and 2 mos. house quarantine.

France: Rabies good for 1 yr. administered 30 days before arrival.

Germany [Communist East]: Health certificate from home town saying the dog is free of diseases communicable to dog and man.

Germany [West]: Health certificate stating free of contagious disease and no rabies within 20 Km (12 miles) of place of origin in last 3 mos. Must be in German.

Greece: Rabies good for 1 yr.

Great Britain: 6 mos. quarantine followed by inoculations. Government permission.

Hungary: Health certificate.

Ireland [Free State]: 6 mos. quarantine.

Israel: Rabies 14 days before arrival. Health certificate notarized at Israel Consulate.

Italy: Rabies innoc. at least 30 days before trip w/11 mo. immunity. Health certificate good for 30 days.

Lebanon: Rabies inoculation and health certificate.

Luxemburg: Rabies inoculation and health certificate.

Morocco: Rabies inoculation and health certificate.

Netherlands: Rabies. Live virus w/2 yr. protection or inactive w/1 yr. protection. Either one administered at least 30 days before arrival.

Norway: Government Approval. 4 mos. quarantine and 2 mos. house quarantine.

Poland: Rabies w/12 mos. protection. Health certificate no more than 4 days old.

Portugal: Rabies w/1 yr. protection. Health certificate and must remain under veterinarian observation after arrival as long as there is any suspicion of disease.

Romania: Rabies innoculation and health certificate.

Russia: Health certificate.

Spain: Rabies inoculation with 1 yr. protection. Health certificate that certifies dog is from epidemic free area. Certified at Spanish Consulate.

Sweden: Government approval. 4 mos. quarantine and 2 mos. house quarantine.

Switzerland: Rabies inoculation at least 30 days before arrival. Health certificate. Plane and train through flights require no documentation.

Tunisia: Rabies inoculation no more than 3 mos. prior to arrival. Health certificate.

Turkey: Rabies inoculation. Duplicate rabies and health certificate. Obtain forms and certificate from Turkish consulate. Both must be translated into Turkish.

Yugoslavia: 6 mos. Rabies protection at least 15 days before arrival. Health certificate.

U.S.A.: If you want to get back into the States, you need a rabies certificate stating the dog has been inoculated more than a month before return but not more than 36 mos. w/chick embryo vaccine or 12 mos. w/a nervous tissue vaccine. If you are bringing in a pup less than 3 mos. old, you don't need a certificate, if you certify the puppy will be kept confined until 3 mos. of age and then inoculated. If you are returning with your own dog, bring some documentation to prove that this is the case. If not, you may have to pay 3.5% duty on the declared value. For some strange reason there is a law on the books that requires breeds of dogs that are used for sheep herding to be accompanied by an affidavit sworn to by the owner. The affidavit has to say that the dog will not be used for sheep herding. Fortunately most of the customs officials either are not familiar with this law or look the other way.

N.B.: The above information on different countries has not gone into requirements for bringing in puppies. Some of the above countries have special rulings on pups.

More than 600 championship-level dogs paraded with their owners around the football field setting of the Japan Kennel Club's Asia Championship All-Breed Dog Show held at Yokota Air Base, Japan.

JUNIOR SHOWMANSHIP

BY PATTY ALSTON

Let's start out by getting to know each other. Name: Patty Alston....Address: c/o POPULAR DOGS will do just fine....Old enough to be a mother, young enough (I hope) to try to bridge the gap...Profession: Mother, proprietor of a grooming establishment, and professional handler. This is probably the place to add that I'm a very "ex" Jr. Handler, having been active in the Junior classes from 1950-56. When those dates are actually down on paper, there's no denying that many years have passed since then, and many changes have taken place in the physical make-up of Junior classes in the last twenty (gasp) years. Let's see how my "Garden" stacks up against yours.

We were, of course, in the old Madison Square Garden. Exhibitors complained about the facilities just as much as they do today regarding the new Garden. Possibly even more so as the grooming and benching areas were downstairs, while judging rings were upstairs. Dogs were required to be benched both days of the show instead of only on the day of judging. Junior Handling dogs had to be entered in the breed classes as well as for handling. All groups were judged on Tuesday night, not split up as they are now. These requirements all combined to make Westminster a very trying and tiring show for dogs and exhibitors alike. On the plus side, Monday evening offered an interesting and varied program which is now missing. We were treated to demonstrations by award winning obedience teams, and the famous Macy's Canine Guard Dogs. For me, the most exciting exhibition was that given by well-known field handlers and their wonderfully trained gun dogs. How those dogs could work so eagerly and flawlessly under such fake field conditions never ceased to amaze. The Statler was then, as well as now, the gathering spot for dog people, but remember, it was three cold and windy city blocks to and from the show grounds. By the time an exhibitor was lucky enough to squeeze into an elevator going up, he was not only mumbling and grumbling, but downright complaining about how "This will be the last time I'll ever come here." With or without him, Westminster has survived and I, for one, will continue to show up year after year with hopes of winning at what many still consider to be the prestige show of the year.

Junior Showmanship, although very different physically, was much the same emotionally. We gathered in the corridor with, believe it or not, the ever popular Paul Nigro in charge. We did not have to pre-enter so our eligibility cards were checked right then before entering the ring. If you could wander back in time, you would see many familiar faces in that corridor, but their place in the action would be slightly different. You might catch a glimpse of Tommy Glassford (not quite skinny but definitely slim); George Alston (without that harried look); Barbara Worcester Keenan, Lydia Coleman Hutchinson, Sari Brewster and Marsha Hall Browne (all on the business end of the lead); Susan Heckman Fisher (without Bob); and me without a batch of kids. All of these and many others have continued beyond Junior Handling and made a place for themselves in the world of dog shows. We all waited to enter the ring, half the size of the entire Garden, just like yours. Our adjacent ring was occupied by group judging in process; you will share the spotlight with another ring full of Juniors. Our feelings are all the same as we wait. Pride at having made it this far, discomfort with some article of our clothing, and fear that we'd mess up the job at hand. Most of all, we're conscious of that weird feeling that starts somewhere around the bottom of the stomach and kind of vibrates all the way up, reaching the lump in our throats. The want and need to win, so badly that it almost hurts, is present in all of us. We enter the ring and miraculously, the anxiety disappears. There is only a child, a judge, and a dog. The others don't really count, only in relationship to ourselves. The feeling is not how did they do, but did they do better than I? Selfish? Yes, very. But that's what makes a winner. That terrible need to be better than the others.

As the judge examines the entrants carefully, you watch to get the feel of his judging procedure. We rehearse in our minds how we'll handle a given situation when and if it arises....the moment is at hand. Our dog is approached. The hind end is slipping on those blankity-blank unmentionable mats. (The Garden mats will be slippery forever.) Our hands tremble just the slightest bit, as this is the moment we've been working toward all year. Head, bite, front, shoulders, topline, rear, and a final overall look. It's over except for moving. Courtesy turn, speed just right, watch for that slight ridge in the mat, correct corners, pay attention, stop and bait beautifully....Thank you....it's done, for better or for worse. The remaining entrants are judged and then it's mind-blowing time as the judge cuts the class down in size. Six or eight kids have been selected for another look. If the judge is a mover, it's easy. You have a reason to keep busy. If he's a looker, it becomes more difficult; how hard can you push before you start over-handling? How many times can that slipping foot be replaced before the dog must be re-stacked? And finally, it really is over. For us, four placings were made. The ring filled with officials and trophy presenters. Fathers took snapshots. Kids surrounded us from all corners of the ring, giving and accepting congratulations, many times through a mist of tears....of success..of defeat..no matter really. Those kids are your friends, suddenly they all matter again. The aloneness is gone and once again we are able to feel their emotions as we feel our own. Grace, poise, sportsmanship; all are necessities now. Your success, you will find, is difficult to handle and how you handle it will make you or break you in the eyes of your peers. I know, you see, I've been there. For us, it was over at that elating moment. For you, only two will be chosen from each class, to return for the finals. For you, the whole thing must be repeated. The let-down after the preliminaries has to be tremendous as you realize in your moment of triumph that you haven't really won, you've just moved up one more step toward success. You must now compete with the finest. Will you succeed? I hope so, for it is an unforgettable experience; one that I will always cherish and have tried to share with you here. Those who do not succeed in the ring have not lost, they can only gain by sharing such a wonderful moment with this year's Westminster winner.

Even though we were judged by professional handlers and you are judged by breed judges, we competed in classes for boys or for girls and you compete according to your age and skill, and our classes were, of course, much smaller than yours. Junior Handling has not really changed much in twenty years. You are doing the same things we did and for exactly the same reasons. I might say that I think you do it with a little more grace and polish than we did but your generation is lucky enough to have our generation as teachers.

JUNIORS IN ACTION

GLOSSARY

AKC: American Kennel Club. Registration body for purebred dogs.
ALMOND EYES: Tissue surrounding the eye is almond shaped.
ANGULATION: The angle formed by the junction of the bones of the shoulder, upper arm; stifle and hock.
ANUS: Posterior opening of the alimentary canal.
APPLE HEAD: Topskull round and humped rather than flat.
APRON: Long hair on chest. Frill.
BALANCED: The dog is proportioned symmetrically, each part to another and overall, all parts to the whole.
BARREL: Rounded rib section.
BAT EAR: Ear is erect, broad across the base and rounding at the top. The orifice directly to the front.
BEARD: Thick, long hair growth on the underjaw.
BENCH SHOW: A dog show at which dogs are "benched" or leashed on benches.
BEST IN SHOW: Award to the only undefeated dog in the show.
BITCH: A female dog.
BITE: The relationship of the upper and lower teeth to each other when the mouth is closed.
BLAZE: White or light colored strip on the face or the center of the head between the eyes.
BLOCKY: Head square in shape.
BLOOM: Appearance of coat in top condition.
BLUE MERLE: Black coat which is mixed with blue and gray.
BOBTAIL: Docked tail or a tail cut very short. A dog which is naturally tailless.
BRACE: Two dogs working together.
BREED: Dog strains produced and maintained by man which are purebred and alike in size and characteristics.
BRINDLE: Mixture of black hairs with lighter color ones.
BRISKET: Forepart of body below the chest, between the forelegs.
BROKEN COLOR: Mono-color or self color is broken by white or any other color.
BROKEN UP FACE: Stop deep, nose receding, wrinkle and undershot jaw.
BROOD BITCH: A female used for breeding purposes.
BRUSH: A bushy tail. Also a utensil for grooming.
BURR: The inner part of the ear, usually irregular in shape and visible.
BUTTERFLY NOSE: A nose which is parti-colored (dark spotted with light).
BUTTOCKS: Rump.
BUTTON EAR: Flap folds forward with the tip lying close to the skull, covering the orifice and pointing toward the eye.
CANINES: Fang-type pointed teeth just behind the incisors. Two in the upper and two in the lower jaws.
CAT FOOT: The foot is compact, round and short with short third digits.
CHARACTER: Expression, temperament, general behavior and intelligence.
CHEEKY: Cheeks prominently rounded; thick, protruding.
CHINA EYE: Clear blue eye.
CHISELED: Clean cut in head, particularly beneath the eyes.
CHOPS: Jowls or pendulous flesh of the lips and jaws.
CLIP: The distinctive trim of the coat of some dogs.
CLODDY: Low, thick set, comparatively heavy.
CLOSE COUPLED: Short bodied from withers to hipbones.
COBBY: Short bodied, compact.
COLLAR: The marking around the neck, usually white.
CONFORMATION: Adherence in structure, size, shape and arrangement of body parts to the standard of the breed.
CORKY: Active, fiery, lively, alert.
COUPLING: Body part which joins hindquarters to front parts of body, the loin, flank.
COURSING: The sport of chasing the hare by dogs.
COW HOCKED: Hock turned inward, toward each other.
CRANK TAIL: A crooked, crank like shaped tail.
CREST: Arched upper position of neck.
CROPPING: Ear leather is trimmed to force the ears to stand erect.
CROUP: Part of back above hind legs and over tail set.
CROWN: Highest part of the head.
CRYPTORCHID: Undescended testicles in the adult dog.
CULOTTE: Longer hair on back of the thighs.
CUSHION: Fullness of the upper lip.
CYNOLOGY: The study of canines.
DAM: The female parent.
DAPPLED: Mottled marking of different colors, no one color predominating.
DEWCLAW: An extra claw on the inside of the leg.
DEWLAP: Loose, pendulous skin under the throat.
DISH FACED: Nasal bone formed in such a way that the nose is higher at the tip than the stop.
DOCK: To shorten the tail by means of cutting.
DOG: A male dog.
DOMED: Evenly rounded top skull.
DOUBLE COAT: Dual coat; under coat and outer coat.
DOWN-FACED: Muzzle inclines downward.

DOWN IN PASTERN: Weak or faulty pastern causing pronounced angulation at the pastern.
DROP EAR: The end of the ears fold or droop forward.
DRY NECK: Skin on the neck is taut, neither loose nor wrinkled.
DUAL CHAMPION: Dog that is a bench show and field trial champion of record.
DUDLEY NOSE: Flesh colored nose.
ELBOW: The joint between the upper arm and the forearm.
ELBOWS OUT: Turning out from the body, not held close.
EWE NECK: Concave outline at top of neck.
FEATHERINGS: Long hair fringe on body, tail legs, or ears.
FETLOCK: Joint between the pastern and the lower arm.
FIDDLE FRONT: Forelegs out at elbows, pasterns close, and feet turned out.
FIELD TRIAL: Competition in which breeds are judged on ability in finding and/or retrieving game.
FLANK: Side of body between last rib and hip.
FLARE: A blaze that widens as it approaches the topskull.
FLAT BONE: Leg bones elliptical rather than round.
FLEWS: Lips pendulous, particularly at inner corners.
FLYING EARS: Ears carried so that they appear to stand or fly.
FOREARM: Foreleg between elbow and pastern.
FOREFACE: Front part of head lying between eyes. The muzzle.
FROGFACE: Extended nose accompanied by a receding jaw, (usually overshot).
FRONT: Forepart of the body; forelegs, chest, brisket, shoulders.
FURROW: A median line down the center of the skull to the stop.
GAIT: The way in which a dog runs, trots, or walks.
GAY TAIL: When the tail is carried up.
GAZEHOUND: A sight hunting hound.
GOOSE RUMP: Too steep or sloping a croup.
GRIZZLE: Bluish-gray color.
GUARD HAIRS: The hair which grows through the undercoat and helps conceal it.
GUN DOGS: A dog used to find and retrieve game.
HACKNEY ACTION: High lifting of the front feet, as in the Hackney horse.
HANDLER: Person who handles a dog in the show or at a field trial.
HAREFOOT: An elongated foot.
HARLEQUIN: Patches or pied color, usually black and white.
HAW: A third eyelid on the eyes inside corner.
HEAT: Female seasonal period.
HEIGHT: Measurement of dog from the ground to the withers.
HOCK: Joint between the metatarsal and the second thigh.
HOUND MARKED: White, tan and black markings.
HUCKLEBONES: Top of the hipbones.
INCISORS: Upper and lower front teeth between canines.
JOWLS: Flesh of lips and jaws.
KINK TAIL: A sharply bent tail.
KNUCKLING OVER: Wrist bends forward.
LAYBACK: Angle of the shoulder blade.
LEATHER: Flap of the ear.
LEVEL BITE: Front teeth of upper and lower jaws meet edge to edge (Pincer Bite).
LIPPY: Lips that do not fit tightly.
LITTER: Puppies or puppy of one whelping.
LOADED SHOULDERS: Shoulder blades are shoved out from the body by overdevelopment of the muscles.
LOIN: Region of the body on either side of the vertebral column between the last rib and the hindquarters.
LOWER THIGHS: Area from stifle to hock. Also known as second thigh.
MANE: Long hair growth on top and sides of the neck.
MANTLE: Darker-shaded part of the shoulder, back and side coat.
MASK: Dark shadowing on the foreface.
MATCH SHOW: Informal show where no title points are given.
MATE: Breeding of a dog or bitch.
MERLE: Mixture of blue-black-gray hair.
MUZZLE: Area of face in front of eyes.
MUZZLE BAND: White markings around the muzzle.
OCCIPUT: Upper back part of the skull.
OUT AT ELBOWS: Elbows turn out from the body.
OUT AT SHOULDER: Shoulder blades are so that joints are too wide.
OVERSHOT: Front teeth of the upper jaw overlap the front teeth of the lower jaw.
PADS: Soles of the dog's feet.
PAPER FOOT: A thin padded foot.
PARTI-COLOR: Variegated in patches of two or more colors.
PASTERN: Foreleg between fetlock and foot.
PEDIGREE: Written record of a dog's descents.
PENCILING: The black lines dividing the tan on the toes.
POINTS: Color on face, ears, legs and tail; usually white, tan, or black.

POMPOM: Rounded tuft of hair left on the end of the tail when the coat is clipped.
PREMIUM LIST: Advance notice containing details of upcoming dog shows.
PRICK EAR: Carried erect and usually pointed at tip.
PROFESSIONAL HANDLER: AKC licensed person who shows dogs for a fee.
PUPPY: Dog under 12 months old.
QUARTERS: Both hindlegs.
RACY: Tall, comparatively slight build.
RAT TAIL: Root thick and covered with soft curls, tip devoid of hair.
REGISTER: To record a dog's papers with the American Kennel Club.
RETRIEVE: To bring back game to the handler.
RING TAIL: Carried up and almost in a circle.
ROACH BACK: An arched or a convex spine, going towards the loin.
ROAN: Mixture of colored hair with white hairs.
ROMAN NOSE: Convex curved top line of the muzzle.
ROSE EAR: Small ear that folds over and back to reveal burr.
RUFF: Thick, long hair around the neck.
SABER TAIL: Tail carried in a semi-circle.
SABLE: Intertwining of black hairs over a lighter ground color.
SADDLE: Darker coat markings over back.
SCREW TAIL: A naturally twisted short tail.
SECOND THIGH: Hindquarters from the stifle to the hock.
SELF COLOR: One color or whole color except for lighter shades of same.
SEMI PRICK EAR: Ear carried erect with the tips leaning in a forward position.
SEPTUM: The line between the nostrils extending vertically.
SHOULDER HEIGHT: Dogs height measured from ground to withers.
SICKLE TAIL: Carriage of tail out and up in a semi-circle.
SIRE: Male parent of a litter.
SLAB SIDES: Sides lacking enough spring of rib.
SLOPING SHOULDER: Shoulder blade that is laid back or set obliquely.
SNIPY: A muzzle too sharply pointed, narrow, weak.
SOUNDNESS: State of good mental and physical health.
SPAY: Removal of a bitch's ovaries.
SPLAYFOOT: Flat foot with spread toes.
SPRING OF RIBS: Amount of roundness to ribs.
SQUIRREL TAIL: Carriage of tail up and curving forward.
STANCE: Way in which a dog stands.
STERN: Tail of a hound or sporting dog.
STERNUM: Breastbone.
STIFLE: Joint above the hock, corresponds to man's knee.
STRAIGHT-HOCKED: Hocks lacking bend or angulation.
STRAIGHT SHOULDERS: Shoulder formation with blades too upright.
STUD BOOK: Written record of breedings.
STUD DOG: Male dog used for breeding.
SUBSTANCE: Amount and strength of bone.
SWAYBACK: Sagging spine, concave from withers to pelvis.
TESTICLE: Genital glands of the male.
THIGH: The hindquarters from hip to stifle.
THROATINESS: Superfluous amount of skin under the throat.
TOPKNOT: Tuft of hair on top of the head.
TRACE: Dark strip running down the back of the Pug.
TRIANGULAR EYE: Eye set in tissue of triangular shape.
TRI-COLOR: Three color. White, tan, black.
TUCK-UP: Shallow body depth at the loin.
TULIP EAR: Ears with slight forward curvature.
TURN UP: An uptilted foreface (jaw).
TYPE: Characteristic qualities of a breed.
UNDERSHOT: Lower incisor teeth project beyond the upper ones.
UPPER ARM: Bone of the foreleg between shoulder blade and forearm.
WALLEYE: Blue eye, fish eye, pearl eye.
WEEDY: Dog lacking sufficient bone.
WHEATEN: Pale yellow or fawn color.
WEAVING: Crossing of the front legs one over the other.
WHEEL BACK: Back line arched over loin.
WHIP TAIL: Carriage of tail that is stiff, straight, pointed.
WHISKER: Long hair on muzzle and underjaw.
WIREHAIR: Coat that is hard, wiry, crisp in texture.
WITHERS: Part between the shoulder bones at neck base.
WRINKLE: Loose folding skin on foreface and/or forehead.
WRY MOUTH: Lower jaw not lining up with upper jaw.

GROUP 1

SPORTING DOGS

POINTER STANDARD

GENERAL APPEARANCE—The Pointer is bred primarily for sport afield; he should unmistakably look and act the part. The ideal specimen gives the immediate impression of compact power and agile grace; the head noble, proudly carried; the expression intelligent and alert; the muscular body bespeaking both staying power and dash. Here is an animal whose every movement shows him to be a wide-awake, hard-driving hunting dog possessing stamina, courage, and the desire to go. And in his expression are the loyalty and devotion of a true friend of man.

TEMPERAMENT—The Pointer's even temperament and alert good sense make him a congenial companion both in the field and in the home. He should be dignified and should never show timidity toward man or dog.

HEAD—The skull of medium width approximately as wide as the length of the muzzle, resulting in an impression of length rather than width. Slifth furrow between the eyes, cheeks cleanly chiseled. There should be a pronounced stop. From this point forward the muzzle is of good length with the nasal bone so formed that the nose is slightly higher at the tip than the muzzle at the stop. Parallel planes of the skull and muzzle are equally acceptable. The muzzle should be deep without pendulous flews. Jaws ending square and level, should bite evenly or as scissors. Nostrils well developed and wide open. *Ears*—Set on at eye level. When hanging naturally, they should reach just below the lower jaw, close to the head, with little or no folding. They should be somewhat pointed at the tip—never round—and soft and thin in leather. *Eyes*—Of ample size, rounded and intense. The eye color should be dark in contrast with the color of the markings, the darker the better.

NECK—Long, dry, muscular and slightly arched, springing cleanly from the shoulders. *Shoulders*—Long, thin, and sloping. The top of blades close together.

FRONT—Elbows well let down, directly under the withers and truly parallel so as to work just clear of the body. Forelegs straight and with oval bone. Knee joint never to buckle over. Pasterns of moderate length, perceptibly finer in bone than the leg, and slightly slanting. Chest, deep and rather wide, must not hinder free action of forelegs. The breastbone bold, without being unduly prominent. The ribs well sprung, descending as low as the elbow-point. *Back*—Strong and solid with only a slight rise from croup to top of shoulders. Loin of moderate length, powerful and slightly arched. Croup falling only slightly to base of tail. Tuck-up should be apparent, but not exaggerated.

TAIL—Heavier at the root, tapering to a fine point. Length no greater than to hock. A tail longer than this or docked must be penalized. Carried without curl, and not more than 20 degrees above the line of the back; never carried between the legs.

HINDQUARTERS—Muscular and powerful with great propelling leverage. Thighs long and well developed. Stifles well bent. The hocks clean; the legs straight as viewed from behind. Decided angulation is the mark of power and endurance. *Feet*—Oval, with long, closely-set, arched toes, well padded, and deep. Cat-foot is a fault. Dweclaws on the forelegs may be removed.

COAT—Short, dense, smooth with a sheen. *Color*—Liver, lemon, black, orange; either in combination with white or solid-colored. A good Pointer cannot be a bad color. In the darker colors, the nose should be black or brown; in the lighter shades it may be lighter or flesh-colored.

GAIT—Smooth, frictionless, with a powerful hindquarters' drive. The head should be carried high, the nostrils wide, the tail moving from side to side rhythmically with the pace, giving the impression of a well-balanced, strongly-built hunting dog capable of top speed combined with great stamina. Hackney gait must be faulted.

BALANCE AND SIZE—Balance and overall symmetry are more important in the Pointer than size. A smooth, balance dog is to be more desired than a dog with strongly contrasting good points and faults. Hound or terrier characteristics are most undesirable. Because a sporting dog must have both endurance and power, great variations in size are undesirable the desirable height and weight being within the following limits:

Dogs:	Height	—25-28 inches
	Weight	—55-75 pounds
Bitches:	Height	—23-26 inches
	Weight	—45-65 pounds

Approved November 12, 1968

BODY: Picture of compact power, dash, grace; great stamina; muscular co-ordination

EYES of ample size; rounded; the darker the better

EARS set at eye level; should reach just below jaw; close to head; little or no folding; somewhat pointed at tip, never round; leather soft, thin

NECK long, dry, muscular; slightly arched; springing cleanly from shoulders

SHOULDERS long, thin, sloping; top of blades close together

BACK strong, solid; slight rise from croup to top of shoulders; loin of moderate length, powerful, slightly arched; croup falling slightly to base of tail

TAIL heavier at root; tapering to fine point; length no greater than to hock carried without curl and not more than 20 degrees above the line of the back

HINDQUARTERS muscular, powerful great propelling leverage; thighs long, well-developed

STIFLES well-bent

SIZE: Balance more important than size; desirable height and weight:
dogs: height 25-28 inches
weight 55-75 pounds
bitches: height 23-26 inches
weight 46-65 pounds

TUCK-UP apparent; not exaggerated

RIBS well-sprung; as low as elbow point

HOCKS clean, legs straight as viewed from behind, decided angulation a mark of power and endurance

PASTERNS of moderate length; finer in bone than leg; slightly slanting

COAT short, dense, smooth, with sheen

HEAD proudly carried; slight furrow between eyes; cheeks cleanly chiseled

SKULL medium width, approximately as wide as the length of the muzzle

STOP pronounced

NOSE black or brown with dark colored coats; lighter shades of coat, nose may be lighter or fleshcolored; nostrils well developed and wide open

JAWS ending level, square; scissors or even bite

CHEST deep rather than wide; must not hinder leg action; breastbone bold but not too prominent

ELBOWS well-down; directly under withers; truly parallel, to work just clear of body

FORELEGS straight; bone oval; knee joint never should knuckle over

FEET oval; well-padded, deep; toes long, arched, closely set

COLORS: Liver, lemon, black, orange; either in combination with white or solid-colored; good Pointed cannot be bad color

CH. ST. ALDWYN'S RADIANCE

RAE WAS IMPORTED BY HER OWNERS AT SEVEN MONTHS OF AGE AND COMPLETED HER CHAMPIONSHIP UNDEFEATED IN THE CLASSES AT JUST EIGHT MONTHS OF AGE. HER RECORD AS OF 11/24/74 IS AS FOLLOWS:

RAE IS #1 POINTER—ALL SYSTEMS

2 BESTS IN SHOW
1 BEST IN SPECIALTY
27 GROUP 1'S
69 GROUP PLACEMENTS
96 BESTS OF BREED

HANDLER: JEFFREY LYNN BRUCKER

OWNER:
SONNIE & ALAN NOVICK
"RUSTIC WOODS"
10 CHELMSFORD DRIVE
MUTTONTOWN,
GLEN HEAD, NEW YORK 11545

The Pointer was a well established type in England as early as 1650. First used for locating and pointing hares, for at least 250 years they have been used as gun-dogs for pointing birds. The breed derives in part from foxhounds, greyhounds, bloodhounds, and setters. The modern Pointer is graceful, agile, powerful, sturdy, and swift. It is a hard-driving dog with staying power, even-tempered, good-natured, responsive and congenial as a companion. A pointer, when hunting, runs with its head held high, testing the air for the scent of gamebirds. When it catches the scent, it freezes to a "point" to indicate where the birds are hiding, the head up, nose pointing, foreleg lifted, and tail out straight behind. The form of the head is very important in this breed and quite distinctive. Liver, orange, lemon, or black either with white or solid, are the most commonly seen colorings. While widely admired, Pointer registration today in the United States is some 600 annually.

STANDARD

THE GERMAN WIREHAIRED POINTER is a dog that is essentially Pointer in type, of sturdy build, lively manner, and an intelligent, determined expression. In disposition the dog has been described as energetic, rather aloof but not unfriendly.

HEAD — The head is moderately long, the skull broad, the occipital bone not too prominent. The stop is medium, the muzzle fairly long with nasal bone straight and broad, the lips a trifle pendulous but close and bearded. The nose is dark brown with nostrils wide open, and the teeth are strong with scissors bite. The ears, rounded but not too broad, hang close to the sides of the head. Eyes are brown, medium in size, oval in contour, bright and clear and overhung with bushy eyebrows. Yellow eyes are not desirable. The neck is of medium length, slightly arched and devoid of dewlap, in fact, the skin throughout is notably tight to the body.

BODY AND TAIL — The body is a little longer than it is high, as ten is to nine, with the back short, straight and strong, the entire back line showing a perceptible slope down from withers to croup. The chest is deep and capacious, the ribs well sprung, loins taut and slender, the tuck-up apparent. Hips are broad, with croup nicely rounded and the tail docked, approximately two-fifths of original length.

LEGS AND FEET — Forelegs are straight, with shoulders obliquely set and elbows close. The thighs are strong and muscular. The hind legs are moderately angulated at stifle and hock and as viewed from behind, parallel to each other. Round in outline, the feet are webbed, high arched with toes close, their pads thick and hard, and their nails strong and quite heavy. Leg bones are flat rather than round, and strong, but not so heavy or coarse as to militate against the dog's natural agility.

COAT — The coat is weather resisting and to some extent water repellent. The undercoat is dense enough in winter to insulate against the cold but so thin in summer as to be almost invisible. The distinctive outer coat is straight, harsh, wiry and rather flat-lying, from one and one-half to two inches in length, it is long enough to protect against the punishment of rough cover but not so long as to hide the outline. On the lower legs it is shorter and between the toes of softer texture. On the skull it is naturally short and close fitting, while over the shoulders and around the tail it is very dense and heavy. The tail is nicely coated particularly on the underside, but devoid of feather. These dogs have bushy eyebrows of strong, straight hair and beards and whiskers of medium length.

A short smooth coat, a soft woolly coat, or an excessively long coat is to be severely penalized.

COLOR — The coat is liver and white, usually either liver and white spotted, liver roan, liver and white spotted with ticking and roaning or sometimes solid liver. The nose is dark brown. The head is brown, sometimes with a white blaze, the ears brown. Any black in the coat is to be severely penalized. Spotted and flesh-colored noses are undesirable and are to be penalized.

SIZE — Height of males should be from 24 to 26 inches at the withers, bitches smaller but not under 22 inches.

Approved February 7, 1959

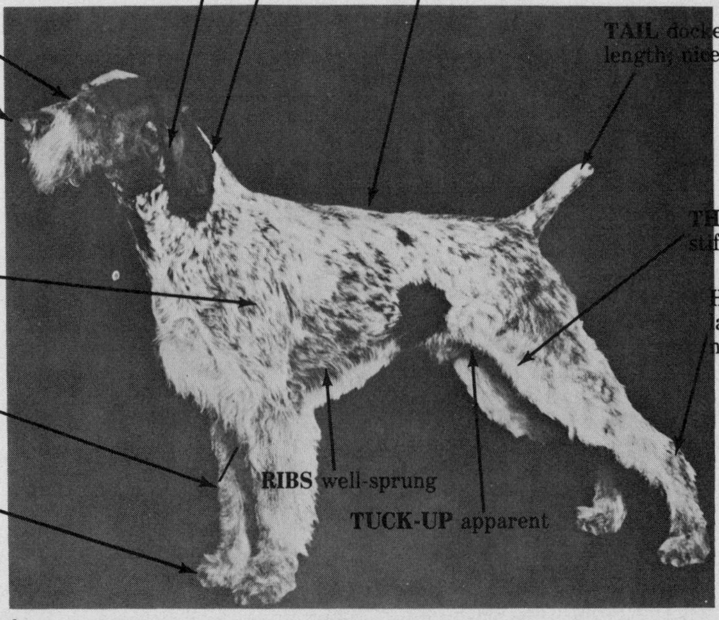

HEAD moderately long; occipital bone not too prominent; skull broad

APPEARANCE: Sturdy build; not too heavy; agile, lively; Pointer type

EYES brown; size medium; oval, bright, clear; overhung with bushy eyebrows; yellow UNDESIRABLE

EARS rounded; not too broad; hanging close to head; brown

NECK length medium; slightly arched; (skin tight to body); no dewlap

BACK short, straight, strong; slope down from withers to nicely-rounded croup. Loins taut, slender. Hips broad

STOP medium

NOSE dark brown; nostrils wide open

TAIL docked approx. 2/5ths orig. length; nicely coated; no feathering

MUZZLE fairly long; nasal bone straight, broad; lips trifle pendulous, close, bearded; teeth strong, scissors bite

THIGHS strong, muscular; stifle moderately angulated

SHOULDERS obliquely set; elbows close

CHEST deep, capacious

HOCK moderately angulated; turning neither in nor out viewed from rear

FORELEGS straight; bone flat rather than round; strong (but not heavy or coarse)

FEET webbed, round; toes close, highly arched; pads thick, hard; nails strong, quite heavy

RIBS well-sprung

TUCK-UP apparent

SIZE: Height, males 24" to 26" at withers; females smaller but not under 22"; length to height, 10 to 9 ratio

COAT weather-resisting, somewhat water-repellent; undercoat dense in winter, thin in summer; outercoat distinctive, straight, harsh, wiry, rather flat-lying, length 1½ to 2"; hair shorter on lower legs, softer between toes; short, close on skull; dense, heavy on shoulder, around tail; underside of tail well-coated but devoid of feathering; a short, smooth, soft, woolly or excessively long coat, severely penalized

COLOR: Liver and white; liver and white spotted; liver roan; liver and white with ticking and roaning; or solid liver; head brown, sometimes with white blaze; black penalized

AM. & MEX. CH. MUELLER MILL'S

CH. MUELLER MILL'S VALENTINO II FINISHED AT 8-MONTHS OF AGE AND WAS RETIRED IN NOVEMBER '74 AT 7-YEARS-OLD. HE COMPILED A RECORD OF OVER 250 BOB'S; 30 GROUP FIRSTS; BOB'S AT BOTH WESTMINSTER AND CHICAGO INTERNATIONAL; BIS, ALL BREED, MEXICO CITY '72, AND BOB '73; '74 WIS. TRI-BREED SPEC.

MORE IMPORTANT HE IS PRODUCING SOUND DUAL PURPOSE OFFSPRING, WITH GOOD COAT AND TEMPERAMENT, WHO WILL CONTINUE TO WIN MORE ENTHUSIASTS FOR THE BREED, THAT HE AND HIS FAMOUS SIRE RUDY, WITH THEIR SHOWMANSHIP, DRIVING GAIT, AND BEAUTIFUL BALANCE, MADE A TOP CONTENDER FOR PLACEMENT IN SPORTING GROUPS FROM COAST TO COAST.

HANDLER: JUDY MURRAY

OWNER:
HELEN B. CASE
DESERT KENNEL
ROUTE 1, BOX 48A
BLUEMONT, VA. 22012
(703) 554-8386

Early Wirehaired Pointers were mostly a combination of breedings of the German Shorthair, Stichelhaar, Griffon, and the Pudelpointer. As a result, many of the fine hunting skills possessed by these ancestors were incorporated into the development of the Wirehaired Pointer. His wire coat enables him to work in various climates, whether in the cold, the water or the underbrush. The true German Wirehaired Pointer should be intelligent, energetic, soundly built and basically Pointer in type.

RETRIEVER [CHESAPEAKE BAY]
STANDARD

HEAD—Skull broad and round with medium stop, nose medium short-muzzle, pointed but not sharp. Lips thin, not pendulous. Ears small, set well up on head, hanging loosely and of medium leather. Eyes medium large, very clear, of yellowish color and wide apart.

NECK—Of medium length with a strong muscular appearance, tapering to shoulders.

SHOULDERS, CHEST AND BODY — Shoulders, sloping and should have full liberty of action with plenty of power without any restrictions of movement. Chest strong, deep and wide. Barrel round and deep. Body of medium length, neither cobby nor roached, but rather approaching hollowness, flanks well tucked up. *Back Quarters and Stifles*—Back quarters should be as high or a trifle higher than the shoulders. They should show fully as much power as the forequarters. There should be no tendency to weakness in either fore or hindquarters. Hindquarters should be especially powerful to supply the driving power for swimming. Back should be short, well-coupled and powerful. Good hindquarters are essential.

LEGS, ELBOWS, HOCKS AND FEET—Legs should be medium length and straight, showing good bone and muscle, with well-webbed hare feet of good size. The toes well rounded and close, pasterns slightly bent and both pasterns and hocks medium length—the straighter the legs the better. Dewclaws, if any, must be removed from the hindlegs. Dewclaws on the forelegs may be removed. A dog with dewclaws on the hindlegs must be disqualified.

STERN—Tail should be medium length—varying from: males, 12 inches to 15 inches, and females from 11 inches to 14 inches; medium heavy at base, moderate feathering on stern and tail permissible.

COAT AND TEXTURE—Coat should be thick and short, nowhere over 1½ inches long, with a dense fine woolly undercoat. Hair on face and legs should be very short and straight with tendency to wave on the shoulders, neck, back and loins only. The curly coat or coat with a tendency to curl not permissible. *Color*—Any color varying from a dark brown to a faded tan or deadgrass. Deadgrass takes in any shade of deadgrass, varying from a tan to a dull straw color. White spot on breast and toes permissible, but the smaller the spot the better, solid color being preferred.

WEIGHT—Males, 65 to 75 pounds; females 55 to 65 pounds. *Height*—Males, 23 inches to 26 inches; females, 21 inches to 24 inches.

SYMMETRY AND QUALITY—The Chesapeake dog should show a bright and happy disposition and an intelligent expression, with general outlines impressive and denoting a good worker. The dog should be well proportioned, a dog with a good coat and well balanced in other points being preferable to the dog excelling in some but weak in others.

The texture of the dog's coat is very important, as the dog is used for hunting under all sorts of adverse weather conditions, often working in ice and snow. The oil in the harsh outer coat and woolly undercoat is of extreme value in preventing the cold water from reaching the dog's skin and aids in quick drying. A Chesapeake's coat should resist the water in the same way that a duck's feathers do. When he leaves the water and shakes himself, his coat should not hold the water at all, being merely moist. Color and coat are extremely important, as the dog is used for duck hunting. The color must be as nearly that of his surroundings as possible and with the fact that dogs are exposed to all kinds of adverse weather conditions, often working in ice and snow, the color of coat and its texture must be given every consideration when judging on the bench or in the ring.

Courage, willingness to work, alertness, nose, intelligence, love of water, general quality, and, most of all, disposition should be given primary consideration in the selection and breeding of the Chesapeake Bay dog.

POSITIVE SCALE OF POINTS

Head, inc. lips, ears & eyes	16
Neck	4
Shdrs. and body	12
Back quarters and stifles	12
Elbows, legs and feet	12
Color	4
Stern and tail	10
Coat and texture	18
General conformation	12
Total	100

APPEARANCE: Well-proportioned, well-balanced; general outline impressive; body length medium; not cobby, not roached

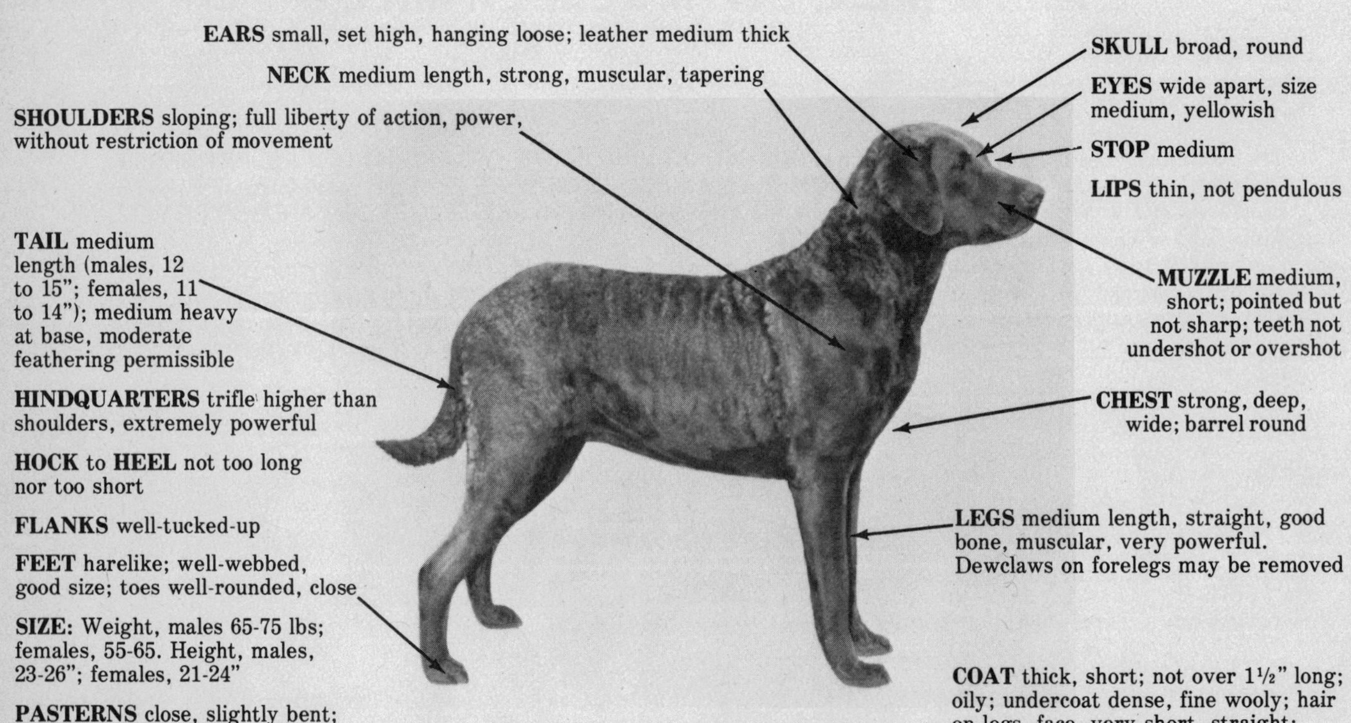

DISQUALIFICATIONS: Black or liver-colored. Dewclaws on hind legs. White on any part of body, except breast, belly or spots on feet. Feathering on tail or legs over 1¾" long. Undershot, overshot, or any deformity. Coat curly or tendency to curl all over body. Specimens unworthy or lacking breed characteristics

COLOR: Dark brown to deadgrass; solid color preferred; white spot on breast and toes permissible, the smaller the better

CAN. & AM. CH. QUEEN COCOA

FINISHED CANADIAN CHAMPIONSHIP — JULY 1974 WITH BEST IN SHOW AT ST. JOHNS, NEWFOUNDLAND. FINISHED AMERICAN CHAMPIONSHIP — SEPT. 1974 OVER SPECIALS AT RICHMOND, VIRGINIA. HAS THREE AMERICAN GROUP PLACEMENTS.

HANDLER: JEFFREY L. BRUCKER

ALBURTA M. DAUGETTE
2312 PINE STREET
GADSDEN, ALABAMA 35901

Note:—The question of coat and general type of balance takes precedence over any scoring table which could be drawn up.

APPROXIMATE MEASUREMENTS

	Inches
Length head, nose to occiput	9½ to 10
Girth at ears	20 to 21
Muzzle below eyes	10 to 10½
Length of ears	4½ to 5
Width between eyes	2½ to 2¾
Girth neck close to shoulder	20 to 22
Girth of chest to elbows	35 to 36
Girth at flank	24 to 25
Length from occiput to tail base	34 to 35
Girth forearms at shoulders	10 to 10½
Girth upper thigh	19 to 20
From root to root of ear, over skull	5 to 6
Occiput to top shoulder blades	9 to 9½
From elbow to elbow over the shoulders	25 to 26

DISQUALIFICATIONS

Black or liver colored. Dewclaws on hind legs, white on any part of body, except breast, belly or spots on feet. Feathering on tail or legs over 1¾ inches long. Undershot, overshot or any deformity. Coat curly or tendency to curl all over body. Specimens unworthy or lacking in breed characteristics.

Approved July 9, 1963

GENERAL APPEARANCE — The general appearance of the Labrador should be that of a strongly built, short-coupled, very active dog. He should be fairly wide over the loins, and strong and muscular in the hindquarters. The coat should be close, short, dense and free from feather.

HEAD — The skull should be wide, giving brain room; there should be a slight stop, *i.e.*, the brow should be slightly pronounced, so that the skull is not absolutely in a straight line with the nose. The head should be clean-cut and free from fleshy cheeks. The jaws should be long and powerful and free from snipiness; the nose should be wide and the nostrils well developed. Teeth should be strong and regular, with a level mouth. The ears should hang moderately close to the head, rather far back, should be set somewhat low and not be large and heavy. The eyes should be of a medium size, expressing great intelligence and good temper, and can be brown, yellow or black, but brown or black is preferred.

NECK AND CHEST — The neck should be medium length, powerful and not throaty. The shoulders should be long and sloping. The chest must be of good width and depth, the ribs well sprung and the loins wide and strong, stifles well turned, and the hindquarters well developed and of great power.

LEGS AND FEET — The legs must be straight from the shoulder to ground, and the feet compact with toes well arched, and pads well developed; the hocks should be well bent, and the dog must neither be cowhocked nor be too wide behind; in fact, he must stand and move true all round on legs and feet. Legs should be of medium length, showing good bone and muscle, but not so short as to be out of balance with rest of body. In fact, a dog well balanced in all points is preferable to one with outstanding good qualities and defects.

TAIL — The tail is a distinctive feature of the breed; it should be very thick towards the base, gradually tapering towards the tip, of medium length, should be free from any feathering, and should be clothed thickly all round with the Labrador's short, thick, dense coat, thus giving that peculiar "rounded" appearance which has been described as the "otter" tail. The tail may be carried gaily but should not curl over the back.

COAT — The coat is another very distinctive feature; it should be short, very dense and without wave, and should give a fairly hard feeling to the hand.

COLOR — The colors are black, yellow, or chocolate and are evaluated as follows:

(a) *Blacks:* All black, with a small white spot on chest permissible. Eyes to be of medium size, expressing intelligence and good temper, preferably brown or hazel, although black or yellow is permissible.

(b) *Yellows:* Yellows may vary in color from fox-red to light cream with variations in the shading of the coat on ears, the underparts of the dog, or beneath the tail. A small white spot on chest is permissible. Eye coloring and expression should be the same as that of the blacks, with black or dark brown eye rims. The nose should also be black or dark brown, although "fading" to pink in winter weather is not serious. A "Dudley" nose (pink without pigmentation) should be penalized.

(c) *Chocolates:* Shades ranging from light sedge to chocolate. A small white spot on chest is permissible. Eyes to be light brown to clear yellow. Nose and eye-rim pigmentation dark brown or liver colored. "Fading" to pink in winter weather not serious. "Dudley" nose should be penalized.

MOVEMENT — Movement should be free and effortless. The forelegs should be strong, straight and true, and correctly placed. Watching a dog move towards one, there should be no signs of elbows being out in front, but neatly held to the body with legs not too close together, but moving straight forward without pacing or weaving. Upon viewing the dog from the rear, one should get the impression that the hind legs, which should be well muscled and not cowhocked, move as nearly parallel as possible, with hocks doing their full share of work and flexing well, thus giving the appearance of power and strength.

APPROXIMATE WEIGHTS OF DOGS AND BITCHES IN WORKING CONDITIONS — Dogs — 60 to 75 pounds; bitches — 55 to 70 pounds. *Height at Shoulders* — Dogs — 22½ inches to 24½ inches; bitches — 21½ inches to 23½ inches.

Approved August, 1963

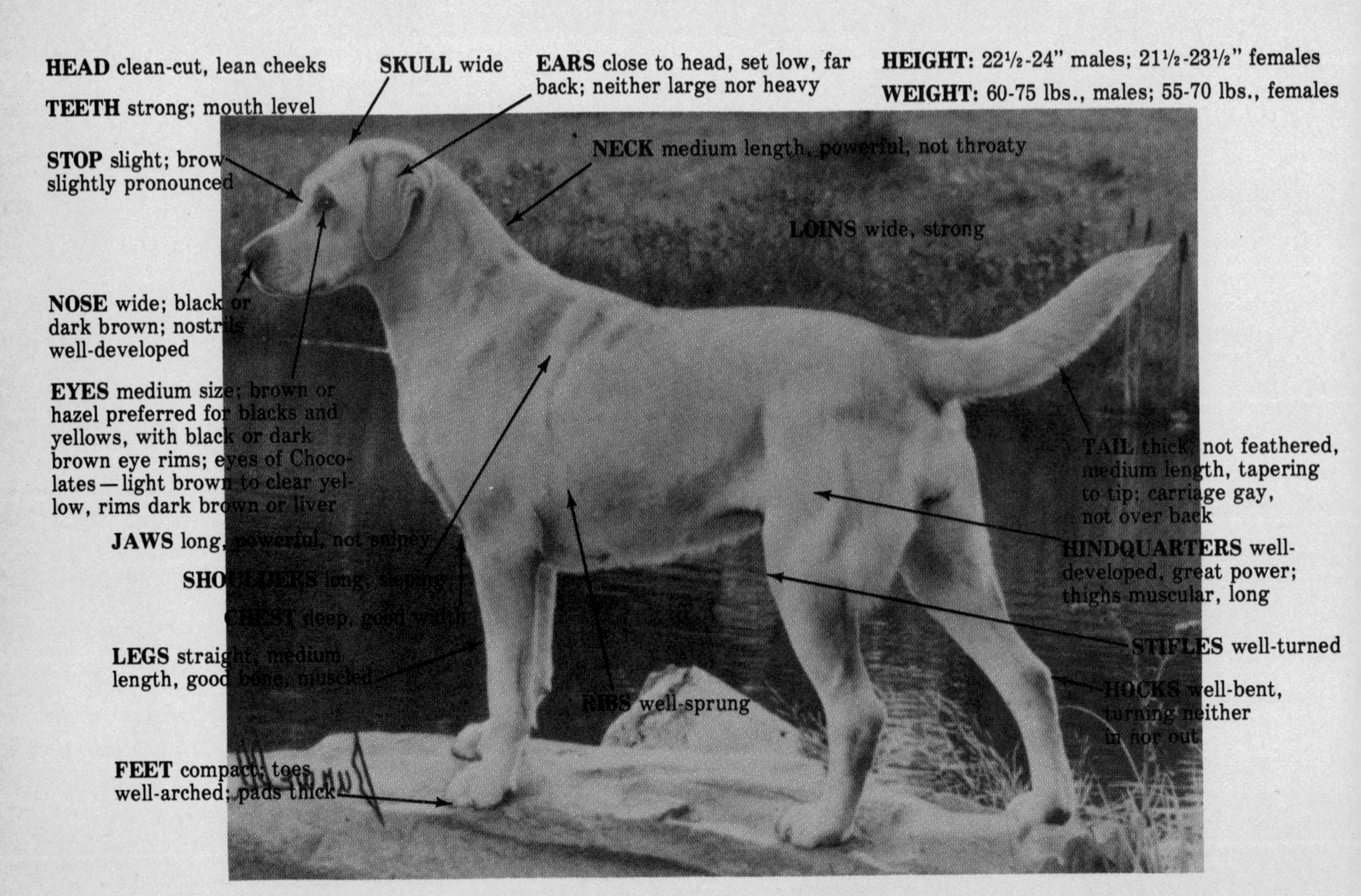

ENG. and AM. CH. KIMVALLEY PICKLEWITCH

OUR PERSONIFICATION OF BREED AND TYPE. BEST OF BREED AT THE 1974 LABRADOR RETRIEVER CLUB OF AMERICA SPECIALTY. SHE IS AN EXAMPLE OF THE TYPE OF LABRADOR SPRINGFIELD KENNELS' BREEDING IS TRYING TO ACHIEVE.
HANDLER: CONSTANCE BARTON

MRS. ROBERT V. CLARK, JR.
SPRINGFIELD FARMS
MIDDLEBURG, VIRGINIA
MANAGER/HANDLER
CONSTANCE BARTON
(703) 687-6424

Labrador Retrievers originated in Newfoundland as assistants to fishermen in the early 19th century. Their jobs are said to have included pulling the ends of the nets to shore, retrieving overboard objects, and even retrieving fish. When the fishing boats called at English ports to sell their catch, the fishermen also sold some of their retrievers. By the 1870's, the breed was apparently established in England but, paradoxically, soon became rare in the New World. Later Labrador Retrievers were reintroduced to the United States, rivaling Irish Setters for first place among sporting dogs. The breed currently ranks 9th among all breeds with some 34,000 registered in 1973. In England, the breed has ranked as number two among all breeds. Labrador Retrievers today are excellent gundogs for upland or water retrieving. They are bred for speed and stamina and love to swim. Their popularity as companions derives from their unusual reliability, docility with children, stability, obedience, and good-humor. The most obvious characteristics of the breed are the short, hard coat, free of feather, which sheds water and ice easily, the dense undercoat, the broad head, and the broad, rounded tail, known as an otter tail, which acts as a rudder and counter weight to a laden mouth in the water. The coat may be solid black, yellow (including a wide range from cream to red), or chocolate. Labrador Retrievers do not appear in the show ring in proportion to their current registrations. The breed ranks only 6th in the Sporting Group in numbers in competition.

HEAD — Long and lean, with a well-defined stop. The skull oval from ear to ear, of medium width, giving brain room but with no suggestion of coarseness, with but little difference between the width at base of skull and at brows and with a moderately defined occipital protuberance. Brows should be at a sharp angle from the muzzle. Muzzle should be long and square, without any fullness under the eyes and straight from eyes to tip of the nose. A dish face or Roman nose objectionable. The lips square and fairly pendant. Nose should be black or dark liver in color, except in white, lemon and white, orange and white, or liver and white dogs, when it may be of lighter color. Nostrils should be wide apart and large in the openings. Jaws should be of equal length. Overshot or undershot jaw objectionable. Ears should be carried close to the head, well back and set low, of moderate length, slightly rounded at the ends, and covered with silky hair. Eye should be bright, mild, intelligent and dark brown in color.

NECK — The neck should be long and lean, arched at the crest, and not too throaty.

SHOULDERS — Shoulders should be formed to permit perfect freedom of action to the forelegs. Shoulder blades should be long, wide, sloping moderately well back and standing fairly close together at the top.

CHEST — Chest between shoulder blades should be of good depth but not of excessive width.

RIBS — Ribs, back of the shoulders, should spring gradually to the middle of the body and then taper to the back ribs, which should be of good depth.

BACK — Back should be strong at its junction with the loin and should be straight or sloping upward very slightly to the top of the shoulder, the whole forming a graceful outline of medium length, without sway or drop. Loins should be strong, moderate in length, slightly arched, but not to the extent of being roached or wheel-backed. Hipbones should be wide apart without too sudden drop to the root of the tail.

FORELEGS — The arms should be flat and muscular, with bone fully developed and muscles hard and devoid of flabbiness; of good length from the point of the shoulder to the elbow, and set at such an angle as will bring the legs fairly under the dog. Elbows should have no tendency to turn either in or out. The pastern should be short, strong and nearly round with the slope from the pastern joint to the foot deviating very slightly forward from the perpendicular.

HIND LEGS — The hind legs should have wide, muscular thighs with well developed lower thighs. Stifles should be well bent and strong. Hocks should be wide and flat. The hind pastern or metatarsus should be short, strong and nearly round.

FEET — Feet should be closely set and strong, pads well developed and tough, toes well arched and protected with short, thick hair.

TAIL — Tail should be straight and taper to a fine point, with only sufficient length to reach the hocks, or less. The feather must be straight and silky, falling loosely in a fringe and tapering to the point when the tail is raised. There must be no bushiness. The tail should not curl sideways or above the level of the back.

COAT — Coat should be flat and of good length, without curl; not soft or woolly. The feather on the legs should be moderately thin and regular.

HEIGHT — Dogs about 25 inches; bitches about 24 inches.

COLORS — Black, white and tan; black and white; blue belton; lemon and white; lemon belton; orange and white; orange belton; liver and white; liver belton; and solid white. *Markings* — Dogs without heavy patches of color on the body, but flecked all over preferred.

SYMMETRY — The harmony of all parts to be considered. Symmetrical dogs will have level backs or be very slightly higher at the shoulders than at the hips. Balance, harmony of proportion, and an appearance of breeding and quality to be looked for, and coarseness avoided.

MOVEMENT AND CARRIAGE — An easy, free and graceful movement, suggesting rapidity and endurance. A lively tail and a high carriage of head. Stiltiness, clumsiness or a lumbering gait are objectionable.

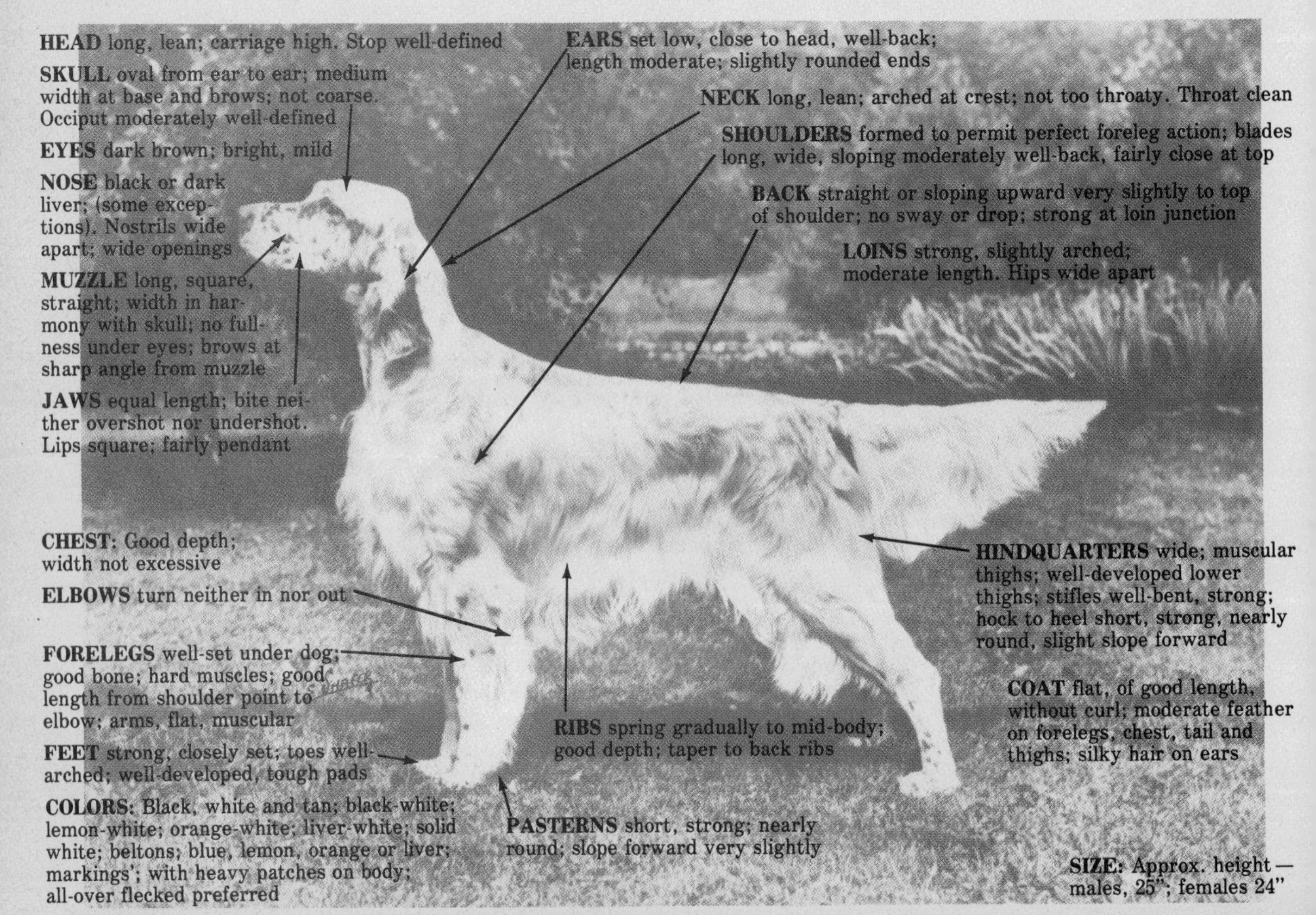

SCALE OF POINTS

Head		
Skull	5	
Ears	5	
Eyes	5	
Muzzle	5	20
Body		
Neck	5	
Chest and shoulders	12	
Back, loin and ribs	10	27
Running Gear		
Forelegs	5	
Hips, thighs and hind legs	12	
Feet	6	23
Coat		
Length and texture	5	
Color and marking	3	8
Tail		
Length and carriage	5	5
General Appearance and Action		
Symmetry, style and movement	12	
Size	5	17
Total		100

Approved May 8, 1951

SETTER [GORDON] STANDARD

GENERAL IMPRESSION — The Gordon Setter is a good-sized, sturdily built, black and tan dog, well muscled, with plenty of bone and substance, but active, upstanding, and stylish, appearing capable of doing a full day's work in the field. He has a strong, rather short back, with well-sprung ribs and a short tail. The head is fairly heavy and finely chiseled. His bearing is intelligent, noble, and dignified, showing no signs of shyness or viciousness. Clear colors and straight or slightly waved coat are correct. He suggests strength and stamina rather than extreme speed. Symmetry and quality are most essential. A dog well-balanced in all points is preferable to one with outstanding good qualities and defects. A smooth, free movement, with high head carriage, is typical.

SIZE — Shoulder height for males, 24 to 27 inches. For females, 23 to 26 inches. *Weight* — Males, 55 to 80 pounds; females, 45 to 70 pounds. Animals that appear to be over or under the prescribed weight limits are to be judged on the basis of conformation and condition. Extremely thin or fat dogs should be discouraged on the basis that under- or overweight hampers the true working ability of the Gordon Setter. The weight-to-height ratio makes him heavier than other setters.

HEAD — The head is deep, rather than broad, with plenty of brain room; a nicely rounded, good-sized skull, broadest between the ears. The head should have a clearly indicated stop. Below and above the eyes should be lean, and the cheek as narrow as the leanness of the head allows. The muzzle is fairly long and not pointed, either as seen from above or from the side. The flews should not be pendulous. The nose should be broad, with open nostrils and black in color. The muzzle is the same length as the skull from occiput to stop, and the top of the muzzle is parallel to the line of the skull extended. The lip line from the nose to the flews shows a sharp, well-defined, square contour. *Eyes* — Of fair size, neither too deep-set, nor too bulging, dark brown, bright, and wise. The shape is oval rather than round. The lids should be tight. *Ears* — Set low on the head approximately on line with the eye, fairly large and thin, well folded and carried close to the head. *Teeth* — The teeth should be strong and white, and preferably should meet in front in a scissors bite, with the upper incisors slightly forward of the lower incisors. A level bite is not to be considered a fault. Pitted teeth from distemper or allied infections should not be penalized.

NECK — Long, lean, arched to the head, and without throatiness.

SHOULDERS — Should be fine at the points, and lying well back, giving a moderately sloping topline. The tops of the shoulder blades should be close together. When viewed from behind, the neck appears to fit into the shoulders in smooth, flat lines that gradually widen from neck to shoulder.

CHEST — Deep and not too broad in front; the ribs well sprung, leaving plenty of lung room. The chest should reach to the elbows. A pronounced forechest should be in evidence.

BODY — The body should be short from shoulder to hips, and the distance from the forechest to the back of the thigh should approximately equal the height from the ground to the withers. The loins should be short and broad and not arched. The croup is nearly flat, with only a slight slope to the tailhead. *Forequarters* — The legs should be big-boned, straight, and not bowed, with elbows free and not turned in or out. The angle formed by the shoulder blade and upper arm bone should be approximately 90° when the dog is standing so that the foreleg is perpendicular to the ground. The pasterns should be straight. *Hindquarters* — The hind legs from hip to hock should be long, flat, and muscular; from hock to heel, short and strong. The stifle and hock joints are well bent and not turned either in or out. When the dog is standing with the hock perpendicular to the ground the thigh bone should hang downward parallel to an imaginary line drawn upward from the hock. *Feet* — The feet should be formed by close-knit, well-arched toes with plenty of hair between; with full toe pads and deep heel cushions. Feet should not be turned in or out. Feet should be cat-like in shape.

TAIL — Short and should not reach below the hocks, carried horizontal or nearly so; thick at the root and finishing in a fine point. The feather which starts near the root of the tail should be slightly waved or straight, having triangular appearance, growing shorter uniformly toward the end. The placement of the tail is important for correct carriage. If the croup is nearly flat, the tail must emerge nearly on the same plane as the croup to allow for horizontal carriage. When the angle of the tail bends too sharply at the first coccygeal bone, the tail will be carried

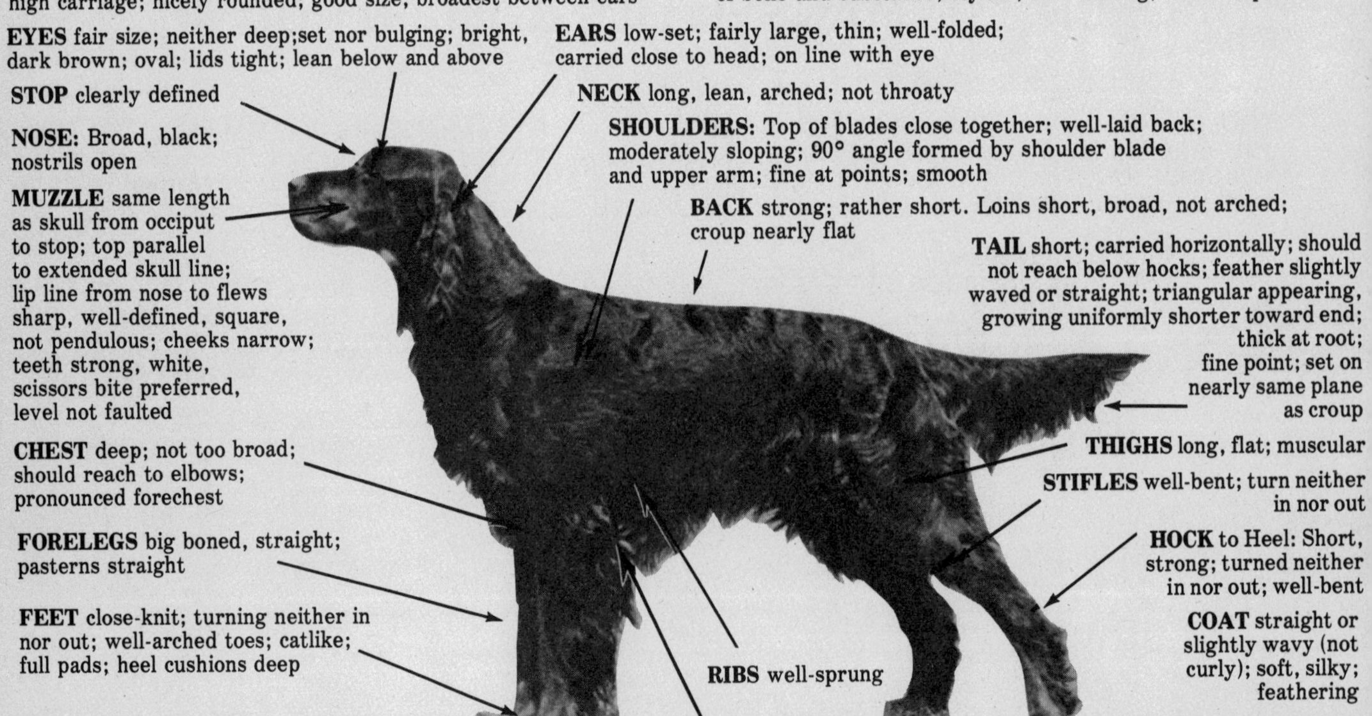

CH. AFTERNOD YANK OF ROCKAPLENTY

YANKEE IS WELL KNOWN FOR HIS ENTHUSIASTIC SHOWMANSHIP. HIS CAREER TO DATE INCLUDES 4 BEST IN SHOWS, 12 GROUP 1 AND 35 OTHER GROUP PLACINGS. YANKEE HAS WON 4 SPECIALTY SHOWS—ALSO BOB AT WESTMINSTER IN 1972 & 1974. HE HAS SIRED SEVERAL CHAMPIONS INCLUDING HIS SPECIALTY WINNING SON. CH. ROCKAPLENTY'S HANG 'EM HIGH. TOP GORDON SETTER 1972 AND 1974.

HANDLER: GEORGE G. ALSTON

MRS. W. W. CLARK
STAR ROUTE, BOX S-78
MAURERTOWN, VA. 22644

too gaily or will droop. The tail placement should be judged in its relationship to the structure of the croup.

TEMPERAMENT — The Gordon Setter should be alert, gay, interested, and aggressive. He should be fearless and willing, intelligent and capable. He should be loyal and affectionate, and strong-minded enough to stand the rigors of training.

GAIT — The action of the Gordon Setter is a bold, strong, driving, free-swinging gait. The head is carried up and the tail "flags" constantly while the dog is in motion. When viewed from the front the forefeet move up and down in straight lines so that the shoulder, elbow, and pastern joints are approximately in line with each other: When viewed from the rear, the hock, stifle, and hip joints are approximately in line. Thus the dog moves in a straight pattern forward without throwing the feet in or out. When viewed from the side the forefeet are seen to lift up and reach forward to compensate for the driving hindquarters. The hindquarters reach well forward and stretch far back, enabling the stride to be long and the drive powerful. The over-all appearance of the moving dog is one of smooth-flowing, well-balanced rhythm, in which the action is pleasing to the eye, effortless, economical and harmonious.

COAT — Should be soft and shining, straight or slightly waved, but not curly, with long hair on ears, under stomach and on chest, on back of the fore- and hind legs, and on the tail. *Color and Markings* — Black with tan markings, either of rich chestnut or mahogany color. Black penciling is allowed on the toes. The borderline between black and tan colors should be clearly defined. There should not be any tan hairs mixed in the black. The tan markings should be located as follows: (1) Two clear spots over the eyes and not over three quarters of an inch in diameter; (2) On the sides of the muzzle. The tan should not reach to the top of the muzzle, but resembles a stripe around the end of the muzzle from one side to the other; (3) On the throat; (4) Two large clear spots

[*continued on page 63*]

GENERAL APPEARANCE — The Irish Setter is an active, aristocratic bird-dog, rich red in color, substantial yet elegant in build. Standing over two feet tall at the shoulder, the dog has a straight, fine, glossy coat, longer on ears, chest, tail, and back of legs. Afield he is a swift-moving hunter; at home, a sweet-natured, trainable companion. His is a rollicking personality.

HEAD—Long and lean, its length at least double the width between the ears. The brow is raised, showing a distinct stop midway between the tip of nose and the well-defined occiput (rear point of skull). Thus the nearly level line from occiput to brow is set a little above, and parallel to, the straight and equal line from eye to nose. The skull is oval when viewed from above or front; very slightly domed when viewed in profile. Beauty of head is emphasized by delicate chiseling along the muzzle, around and below the eyes, and along the cheeks. Muzzle moderately deep, nostrils wide, jaws of nearly equal length. Upper lips fairly square but not pendulous, the underline of the jaws being almost parallel with the top line of the muzzle. The teeth meet in a scissors bite in which the upper incisors fit closely over the lower, or they may meet evenly. *Nose* — Black or chocolate.

EYES — Somewhat almond-shaped, of medium size, placed rather well apart; neither deep-set nor bulging. Color, dark to medium brown. Expression soft yet alert. *Ears*—Set well back and low, not above level of eye. Leather thin, hanging in a neat fold close to the head, and nearly long enough to reach the nose.

NECK — Moderately long, strong but not thick, and slightly arched; free from throatiness, and fitting smoothly into the shoulders.

BODY — Sufficiently long to permit a straight and free stride. Shoulder blades long, wide, sloping well back, fairly close together at the top, and joined in front to long upper arms angled to bring the elbows slightly rearward along the brisket. Chest deep, reaching approximately to the elbows; rather narrow in front. Ribs well sprung. Loins of moderate length, muscular and slightly arched. Top line of body from withers to tail slopes slightly downward without sharp drop at the croup. Hindquarters should be wide and powerful with broad, well-developed thighs. *Legs and Feet*—All legs sturdy, with plenty of bone, and strong, nearly straight pastern. Feet rather small, very firm, toes arched and close. Forelegs straight and sinewy, the elbows moving freely. Hind legs long and muscular from hip to hock, short and nearly perpendicular from hock to ground; well angulated at stifle and hock joints, which, like the elbows, incline neither in nor out. *Tail*—Strong at root, tapering to fine point, about long enough to reach the hock. Carriage straight or curving slightly upward, nearly level with the back.

COAT — Short and fine on head, forelegs, and tips of ears; on all other parts, of moderate length and flat. Feathering long and silky on ears; on back of forelegs and thighs long and fine, with a pleasing fringe of hair on belly and brisket extending onto the chest. Feet well feathered between the toes. Fringe on tail moderately long and tapering. All coat and feathering as straight and free as possible from curl or wave.

COLOR — Mahogany or rich chestnut red, with no trace of black. A small amount of white on chest, throat, or toes, or a narrow centered streak on skull, is not to be penalized.

SIZE — There is no disqualification as to size. The make and fit of all parts and their overall balance in the animal are rated more important. Twenty-seven inches at the withers and a show weight of about 70 pounds is considered ideal for a dog; the bitch 25 inches, 60 pounds. Variance beyond an inch up or down to be discouraged.

GAIT—At the trot the gait is big, very lively, graceful, and efficient. The head is held high. The hindquarters drive smoothly and with great power. The forelegs reach well ahead as if to pull in the ground, without giving the appearance of a hackney gait. The dog runs as he stands: straight. Seen from the front or rear, the forelegs, as well as the hind legs below the hock joint, move perpendicularly to the ground, with some tendency toward a single track as speed increases. But a crossing or weaving of the legs, front or back is objectionable.

BALANCE—At his best the lines of the Irish Setter so satisfy in over-all balance that artists have termed him the most beautiful of all dogs. The correct specimen always exhibits balance whether standing or in motion. Each part of the dog flows and fits smoothly into its neighboring parts without calling attention to itself.

Approved June 14, 1960

HEAD long, lean; length at least double width between ears; oval viewed from above; domed viewed in profile. Brow raised; well-defined occiput. Level line from occiput to brow set above and parallel to straight and equal line from eye to nose

EYES somewhat almond-shaped, medium size; placed rather well apart; expression soft but alert; dark to medium brown

STOP distinct

NOSE black or chocolate; nostrils wide

MUZZLE moderately deep; chiseling delicate around and below eyes, along cheeks; jaws of nearly equal length; upper lips fairly square but not pendulous; scissors bite, or teeth may meet evenly

SHOULDER BLADES long, wide, sloping well back, fairly close together at top; upper arms long, angled so elbows are slightly rearward along brisket

CHEST deep, rather narrow in front; reaching to elbows

FORELEGS strong, sinewy; elbows moving freely; good bone; nearly straight pasterns

FEET rather small, firm; toes arched, close

COAT short, fine on head, front of legs, tips of ears; otherwise flat, glossy; length moderate; feathering long, silky on ears, back of forelegs, thighs, belly, chest, between toes, tail. Entire coat straight as possible

COLOR: Mahogany or rich chestnut red (no black); small white markings on chest, throat, toes, not penalized

BODY sufficiently long for free gait; no disqualification on size; over-all balance

EARS set well back; low, not above eye level; leather thin, hanging close to head in neat fold; nearly reaches nose

NECK moderately long, strong; not thick, slightly arched without throatiness; fitting smoothly into shoulders

TOPLINE: Slight slope downward from withers to tail-set without sharp drop at croup; loins of moderate length, muscular, slightly arched

TAIL strong at root; tapering to fine point; length reaching to hock; carriage straight or curving slightly upward; nearly level with back

HINDQUARTERS wide, powerful; thighs broad, well-developed

HIND LEGS long, muscular from hip to hock; short, nearly perpendicular from hock to ground; stifle and hock joints well angulated, inclining neither in nor out

SIZE: Ideal male, 27" at withers, 70 lbs. Ideal female, 25", 60 lbs. No disqualification as to size. Over-all balance more important

RIBS well-sprung

APPEARANCE: Active, aristocratic; substantial yet elegant; rollicking personality

CH. TIRVELDA DISTANT DRUMMER

DRUMMER IS THE 90TH CHAMPION BRED BY THIS KENNEL. FROM HIS FIRST POINT TO HIS TITLE IN THREE WEEKENDS AT 2½ YEARS OLD. LADIES KENNEL CLUB — BEST OF WINNERS — LUCY JANE MYERS. FRAMINGHAM DISTRICT KENNEL CLUB — BEST OF BREED — MRS. JOHN BRADY. STATEN ISLAND KENNEL CLUB — BEST OF WINNERS — MRS. CLARK THOMPSON. WESTERN NEW YORK SPECIALTY — BEST OF BREED — PETER KNOUP. GENESSEE VALLEY KENNEL CLUB — BEST OF WINNERS — MRS. FRANCES PHILLIPS.

HANDLER: GEORGE ALSTON

TIRVELDA KENNELS
MR. AND MRS. E. IRVING ELDREDGE
MIDDLEBURG, VIRGINIA 22117

By the 18th Century, typy red and white setters had become established in Ireland. Little is known specifically of their ancestry. Later solid, dark red dogs came to be favored. Today only mahogany or rich chestnut red are allowed, with occasional minimal white streaks. The breed had become so outstandingly beautiful by the mid-19th Century as to lead to an explosion of popularity, especially in the United States. This popularity persists and is actually increasing today. Irish Setters lead all other sporting breeds in registrations. Far more are kept as companions today than are used for hunting. Some 54,000 are registered annually with the AKC; the breed having moved into 3rd place last year. The breed also ranks 5th in numbers in show competition and leads the Sporting Group in group wins.

SPANIEL [AMERICAN WATER] STANDARD

GENERAL APPEARANCE — Medium in size, of sturdy typical Spaniel character, curly coat, an active muscular dog, with emphasis placed on proper size and conformation, correct head properties, texture of coat and color. Of amicable disposition; demeanor indicates intelligence, strength and endurance.

HEAD — Moderate in length, skull rather broad and full, stop moderately defined, but not too pronounced. Forehead covered with short smooth hair and without tuft or topknot. Muzzle of medium length, square and with no inclination to snipiness, jaws strong and of good length, and neither undershot nor overshot, teeth straight and well shaped. Nose sufficiently wide and with well developed nostrils to insure good scenting power. *Faults:* Very flat skull, narrow across the top, long, slender or snipy muzzle. *Eyes* — Hazel, brown or of dark tone to harmonize with coat; set well apart. Expression alert, attractive, intelligent. *Fault:* Yellow eyes to disqualify. *Ears* — Lobular, long and wide, not set too high on head, but slilghtly above the eyeline. Leather extending to end of nose and well covered with close curls. *Neck* — Round and of medium length, strong and muscular, free of throatiness, set to carry head with dignity, but arch not accentuated.

BODY STRUCTURE — Well developed, sturdily constructed but not too compactly coupled. General outline is a symmetrical relationship of parts. Shoulders sloping, clean and muscular. Strong loins, lightly arched, and well furnished, deep brisket but not excessively broad. Well-sprung ribs. Legs of medium length and well boned, but not so short as to handicap for field work. *Legs and Feet* — Forelegs powerful and reasonably straight. Hind legs firm with suitably bent stifles and strong hocks well let down. Feet to harmonize with size of dog. Toes closely grouped and well padded. *Fault:* Cowhocks. *Tail* — Moderate in length, curved in a slightly rocker shape, carried slightly below level of back; tapered and covered with hair to tip, action lively. *Faults:* Rat or shaved tail.

COAT — The coat should be closely curled or have marcel effect and should be of sufficient density to be of protection against weather, water or punishing cover, yet not coarse. Legs should have medium short, curly feather. *Faults:* Coat too straight, soft, fine or tightly kinked. *Color* — Solid liver or dark chocolate, a little white on toes or chest permissible.

HEIGHT — 15 to 18 inches at the shoulder. *Weight* — Males, 28 to 45 pounds; females, 25 to 40 pounds.

DISQUALIFICATION

Yellow eyes.

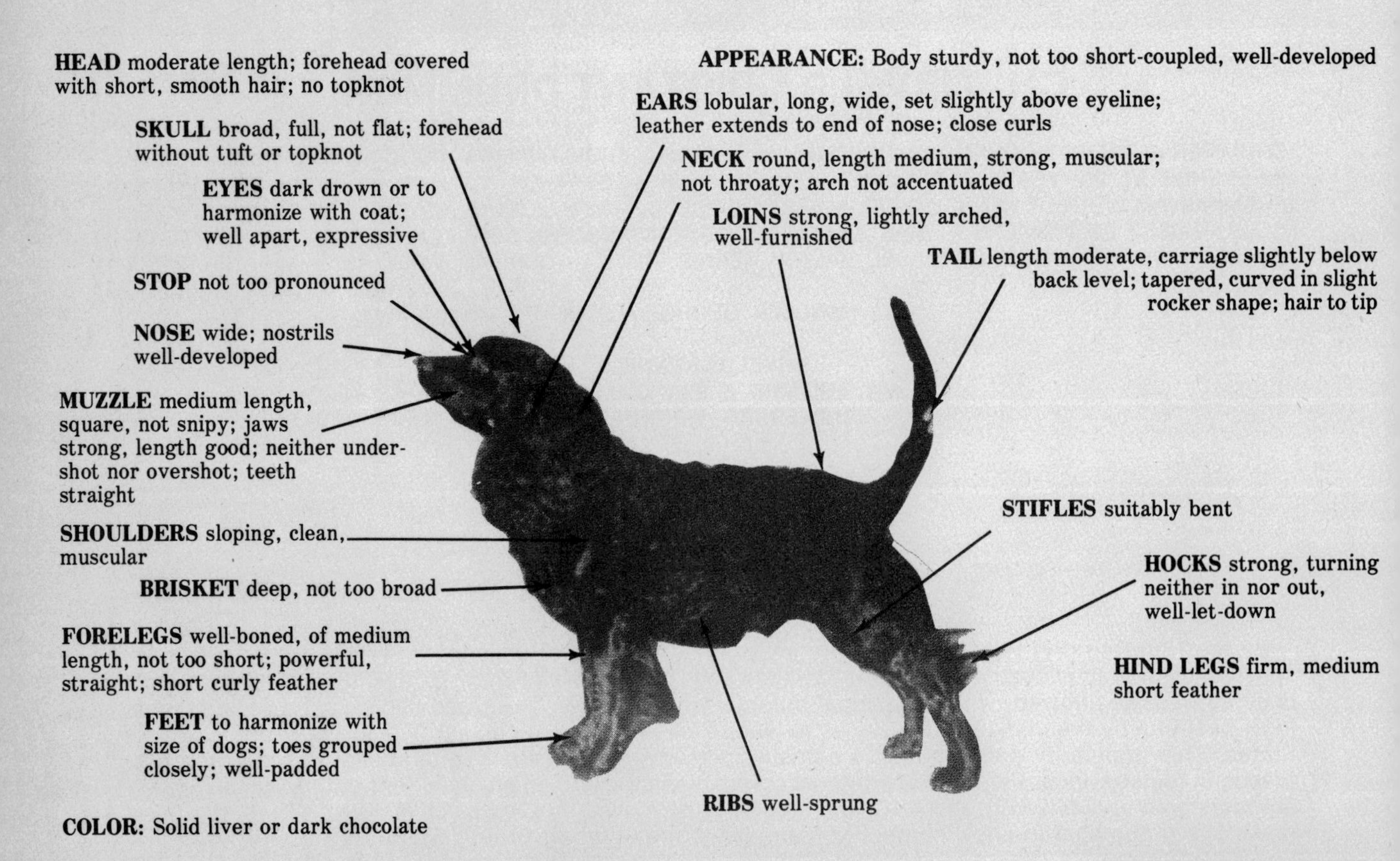

CH. COUNTRYSIDES HAPPY HIRAM

"BEAR" IS SHOWN GOING BOB AT THE 1974 WESTMINISTER SHOW AT 18 MONTHS OF AGE UNDER MRS. TOM STEVENSON. BEAR IS A FINE EXAMPLE OF GREAT TYPE, MOVEMENT, AND SHOWMANSHIP. THESE QUALITIES ARE NOW BEING EXHIBITED BY HIS MANY POINTED GET AND HIS CHAMPION SON, COUNTRYSIDES BIG MAC, WHO FINISHED AT 7 MONTHS OF AGE. BEAR STANDS AT STUD WITH HIS OWNER.

BARBARA SPISAK
3347 STATE ROUTE 42
SPRING VALLEY, OHIO 45370

The American Water Spaniel was used in the United States as a gun dog before it was granted recognition by the American Kennel Club in 1940. He is considered an much desired retrieving dog due to his excellent swimming skill. He can work in the water, woods, rough ground or thicket. His appearance reminds one of a Irish Water Spaniel or a Curly-Coated Retriever; however, he is smaller than both and can certainly hold his own.

GENERAL DESCRIPTION — A compact, closely knit dog of medium size, a leggy spaniel having the appearance as well as the agility of a great ground coverer. Strong, vigorous, energetic and quick of movement. Not too light in bone, yet never heavy-boned and cumbersome. Ruggedness, without clumsiness, is a characteristic of the breed. So leggy is he that his height at the withers is the same as the length of his body. He has no tail, or at most, not more than 4 inches.

WEIGHT — Should weight between 30 and 40 pounds. *Height* — 17½ to 20½ inches — measured from the ground at the highest point of the shoulders. *Disqualifications;* — Any Brittany Spaniel measuring under 17½ inches or over 20½ inches shall be disqualified from bench show competition. Any black in the coat or a nose so dark in color as to appear black shall disqualify. A tail substantially more than 4 inches in length shall disqualify.

COAT — Hair dense, flat or wavy, never curly. Not as fine as in other spaniel breeds, and never silky. Furnishings not profuse. The ears should carry little fringe. Neither the front nor hind legs should carry heavy featherings. *Note:* Long, curly, or silky hair is a fault. Any tendency toward excessive feathering should be severely penalized, as undesirable in a sporting dog which must face burrs and heavy cover. *Skin* — Fine and fairly loose. (A loose skin rolls with briar and sticks, thus diminishing punctures or tearing. But a skin so loose as to form pouches is undesirable.)

COLOR — Dark orange and white, or liver and white. Some ticking is desirable, but not so much as to produce belton patterns. Roan patterns or factors of orange or liver shade are permissible. The orange or liver are found in standard parti-color, or piebald patterns. Washed out or faded colors are not desirable. Tri-colors (liver and white with some orange markings) are to be severely faulted. Black is a disqualification.

SKULL — Medium length (approximately 4¾ inches). Rounded, very slightly wedge-shaped, but evenly made. Width, not quite as wide as the length (about 4-3/8 inches) and never so broad as to appear coarse, or so narrow as to appear racy. Well defined, but gently sloping stop effect. Median line rather indistinct. The occipital crest only apparent to the touch. Lateral walls well rounded. The Brittany should never be "apple-headed" and he should never have an indented stop. (All measurements of skull are for a 19½-inch dog.) *Muzzle* — Medium length, about two-thirds the length of the skull, measuring the muzzle from the tip to the stop, and the skull from the occipital crest to the stop between the eyes. Muzzle should taper gradually in both horizontal and vertical dimensions as it approaches the nostrils. Neither a Roman nose nor a concave curve (dish-face) is desirable. Never broad, heavy, or snipy. *Nose* — Nostrils well open to permit deep breathing of air and adequate scenting while at top speed. Tight nostrils should be penalized. Never shiny. Color, fawn, tan, light shades of brown or deep pink. A black nose is a disqualification. A two-tone or butterfly nose should be severely penalized.

EYES — Well set in head. Well protected from briars by a heavy, expressive eyebrow. A prominent, full or pop eye should be heavily penalized. It is a serious fault in a hunting dog that must face briars. Skull well chiseled under the eyes, so that the lower lid is not pulled back to form a pocket or haw for catching seeds, dirt and weed dust. Judges should check by forcing head down to see if lid falls away from the eye. Preference should be for darker-colored eyes, though lighter shades of amber should not be penalized. Light and mean-looking eyes to be heavily penalized. *Ears* — Set high, above the level of the eyes. Short and leafy, rather than pendulous, reaching about half the length of the muzzle. Should lie flat and close to the head, with the tip rounded very slightly. Ears well covered with dense, but relatively short hair, and with little fringe. *Lips* — Tight to the muzzle, with the upper lip overlapping the lower jaw only sufficiently to cover under lip. Lips dry so that feathers do not stick. Drooling to receive a heavy penalty. Flews to be penalized. *Teeth* — Well joined incisors. Posterior edge of upper incisors in contact with anterior edge of lower incisors, thus giving a true scissors bite. Overshot or undershot jaw to be penalized heavily.

NECK — Medium length. Not quite permitting the dog to place his nose on the ground without bending his legs. Free from throatiness, though not a serious fault unless accompanied by dewlaps. Strong, without giving the impression of being overmuscled. Well set into sloping shoulders. Never concave nor ewe-necked.

BODY LENGTH — Approximately the same as the height when measured at the withers. Body length is measured from the point of the forechest to the rear of the haunches. A long body should be heavily penalized. *Withers* — Shoulder blades should not protrude much. Not too widely set apart with perhaps two thumbs' width or less between

SKULL medium length (approx. 4-3/4"), width less (approx. 4-3/8"); rounded, evenly-made; very slightly wedge;shaped, lateral walls well-rounded; never coarse, "apple-headed" or racy; occiput crest only apparent to touch; indistinct median line

EYES well-set; dark colors preferred; expressive; eyebrows heavy

STOP well-defined; gentle sloping; never indented

NOSE fawn, tan, light brown shades, deep pink; nostrils well-open; neither Roman nor concave curve (dish-face) desirable; (butterfly two-tone) severely penalized)

LIPS tight; dry. Upper lip overlapping lower jaw only to cover under lip. Flews penalized

TEETH well-joined; scissors bite; neither under- nor overshot

MUZZLE medium — 2/3 length of skull (measuring muzzle from tip to stop, skull from occipital crest to stop); tapering gradually toward nostrils; never broad, heavy, snipy; well-chiseled under eyes

CHEST deep; reaching elbow level; neither too wide nor too rounded

FORELEGS perpendicular; not too wide apart; bones clean, graceful, not too fine; supple. Pasterns slightly bent

FEET strong; proportionately smaller than other spaniels; close-fitting, well-arched toes; thick pads

COLORS: Dark orange and white; liver and white; some ticking desirable (not enough for belton pattern). Roan patterns or factors of orange or liver (found in std. parti-color or pied) permissible; washed out or faded colors not desirable; tri-colors (liver, white with some orange markings) severely faulted

APPEARANCE: Compact; closely-knit, strong; rugged without clumsiness; energetic, vigorous, agile; leggy

EARS short, leafy; set high above eye level; reach half-length muzzle; flat, close to head; very slightly rounded tips; dense relatively short hair, little fringe

NECK medium length; strong; well-set into shoulders; not throaty

SHOULDERS sloping; muscular; blade forming nearly 90-degree angle with upper arm; perhaps 2-thumb-widths between blades

BACK short, straight; slight slope from withers to tail-set; short (3-4 finger widths) from last rib to upper thigh; slight drop from hips to tail root

TAIL high-set; tailless, natural or docked, not over 4"

HINDQUARTERS broad, strong, muscular; powerful thighs; rounded, fairly full flanks; hips well-set into short, strong loins; well-bent stifles; hocks firm, turning neither in nor out; hock to heel fairly short

COAT dense, flat, wavy; not too fine; never curly or silky; feathering moderate (excessive severely penalized). Skin fine; fairly loose

RIBS well sprung

SIZE: Height, 17½"-20½", measured from ground at highest point of shoulders; weight, 30-40 lbs. Body length (point of forechest to rear of haunches): approx. same as height

ELBOWS turning neither in nor out; height to elbows approx. equal distance elbows to withers

DISQUALIFICATIONS: Measuring under 17½" or over 20½"; black in coat; nose so dark as to appear black; tail substantially more than 4"

AM. & CAN. CH. FFYNANT'S HAPPY TIME

A BRITTANY SPANIEL, IN 1974 FROM JANUARY 1 UNTIL NOVEMBER 24, HAPPY TIME'S U.S. RECORD IS 74 BOB, 2 BIS, 1 SPECIALTY, 15 GROUP I, 17 GROUP II, 8 GROUP III, 6 GROUP IV. HIS CANADIAN RECORD IS 1 BIS, 8 BOB, 2 GROUP I, 3 GROUP II, 1 GROUP III, AND 1 GROUP IV. AT STUD WITH HANDLER.
HANDLER: TONY GWINNER

the blades. At the withers, the Brittany is slightly higher than at the rump. *Shoulders* — Sloping and muscular. Blade and upper arm should form nearly a 90-degree angle when measured from the posterior point of the blade at the withers to the junction of the blade and upper arm, and thence to the point of the elbow nearest the ribs. Straight shoulders do not permit sufficient reach.

BACK — Short and straight. Slight slope from highest point of withers to the root of the tail. Never hollow, saddle, sway or roach-backed. Slight drop from hips to root of tail. Distance from last rib to upper thigh short, about three to four finger widths. *Chest* — Deep, reaching the level of the elbow. Neither so wide nor so rounded as to disturb the placement of the shoulder bones and elbows, which causes a paddling movement, and often causes soreness from elbow striking ribs. Ribs well sprung, but adequate heart room provided by depth as well as width. Narrow or slab-sided chests are a fault.

FLANKS — Rounded. Fairly full. Not extremely tucked up, nor yet flabby and falling. Loins short and strong. Narrow and weak loins are a fault. In motion the loin should not sway sideways, giving a zigzag motion to the back, wasting energy. *Hindquarters* — Broad, strong and muscular, with powerful thighs and well-bent stifles, giving a hip set well into the loin and the marked angulation necessary for a powerful drive when in motion. Fat and falling hindquarters are a fault.

TAIL — Naturally tailless, or not over four inches long. Natural or docked. Set on high, actually an extension of the spine at about the same level.

FRONT LEGS — Viewed from the front, perpendicular, but not set too wide as in the case of a dog loaded in shoulder. Elbows and feet turning neither in nor out. Viewed from the side, practically perpendicular to the pastern. Pastern slightly bent to give cushion to stride. Not so straight as in terriers.

[*continued on page 63*]

SPANIEL [ENGLISH COCKER] STANDARD

GENERAL APPEARANCE — The English Cocker Spaniel is an attractive, active, merry sporting dog; with short body and strong limbs, standing well up at the withers. His movements are alive with energy; his gait powerful and frictionless. He is alert at all times, and the carriage of head and incessant action of his tail while at work give the impression that here is a dog that is not only bred for hunting but really enjoys it. He is well balanced, strongly built, full of quality and is capable of top speed combined with great stamina. His head imparts an individual stamp peculiar to him alone and has that brainy appearance expressive of the highest intelligence; and is in perfect proportion to his body. His muzzle is a most distinctive feature, being of correct conformation and in proportion to his skull.

CHARACTER — The character of the English Cocker is of extreme importance. His love and faithfulness to his master and household, his alertness and courage are characteristic. He is noted for his intelligence and merry disposition; not quarrelsome; and is a responsive and willing worker both in the field and as a companion.

HEAD — The skull and forehead should be well developed with no suggestion of coarseness, arched and slightly flattened on top when viewed both from the stop to the end of the skull as well as from ear to ear, and cleanly chiseled under the eyes. The proportion of the head desirable is approximately one-half for the muzzle and one-half for the skull. The muzzle should be square with a definite stop where it blends into the skull and in proportion with the width of the skull. As the English Cocker is primarily a sporting dog, the muzzle and jaws must be of sufficient strength and size to carry game; and the length of the muzzle should provide room for the development of the olfactory nerve to insure good scenting qualities, which require that the nose be wide and well developed. Nostrils black in color except in reds, livers, parti-colors and roans of the lighter shades, where brown is permissible, but black preferred. Lips should be square, full and free from flews. Teeth should be even and set squarely. *Faults:* Muzzle too short or snipy. Jaw overshot or undershot. Lips snipy or pendulous. Skull too flat or too rounded, cheeky or coarse. Stop insufficient or exaggerated.

EYES — The eyes should be of medium size, full and slightly oval shaped; set squarely in skull and wide apart. Eyes must be dark brown except in livers and light parti-colors where hazel is permissible, but the darker the better. The general expression should be intelligent, alert, bright and merry. *Faults:* Light, round or protruding eyes. Conspicious haw.

EARS — Lobular; set low and close to the head; leather fine and extending at least to the nose, well covered with long, silky, straight or slightly wavy hair. *Faults:* Set or carried too high; too wide at the top; insufficient feathering; positive curls or ringlets.

NECK — Long, clean and muscular; arched towards the head; set cleanly into sloping shoulders. *Faults:* Short; thick; with dewlap or excessive throatiness.

BODY — Close coupled, compact and firmly knit, giving the impression of great strength without heaviness. Depth of brisket should reach to the elbow, sloping gradually upward to the loin. Ribs should spring gradually to middle of body, tapering to back ribs which should be of good depth and extend well back. *Faults:* Too long and lacking depth; insufficient spring of rib; barrel rib. *Shoulders and Chest* — Shoulders sloping and fine; chest deep and well developed but not too wide and round to interfere with the free action of the forelegs. *Faults:* Straight or loaded shoulders.

BACK AND LOIN — Back short and strong. Length of back from withers to tail-set should approximate height from ground to withers. Height of the dog at the withers should be greater than the height at the hip joint, providing a gradual slope between these points. Loin short and powerful, slightly arched. *Faults:* Too low at withers; long, sway-back or roach back; flat or narrow loin; exaggerated tuck-up.

FORELEGS — Straight and strong with bone nearly equal in size from elbow to heel; elbows set close to the body with free action from shoulders; pasterns short, straight, and strong. *Faults:* Shoulders loose; elbows turned in or out; legs bowed or set too close or too wide apart; knees knuckled over; light bone.

FEET — Size in proportion to the legs; firm, round and catlike with thick pads and strong toes. *Faults:* Too large, too small; spreading or splayed. *Hindquarters* — The hips should be rounded; thighs broad; well developed and muscular, giving abundance of propelling power. Stifles strong and well bent. Hock to pad moderately short, strong and well let down. *Faults:* Excessive angulation; lightness of bone; stifle too short; hocks too long or turned in or out. *Tail* — Set on to conform with the topline of the back. Merry in action. *Faults:* Set too low; habitually carried too high; too short or too long.

HEAD: Skull and forehead well-developed, arched, slightly flattened on top; cleanly chiseled under eyes; no coarseness. Proportion: one-half muzzle, one-half skull

APPEARANCE: Body close-coupled, compact, firmly knit; impression of strength without heaviness

EARS lobular, set low, close to head; leather fine, should extend to nose; well-covered with straight or slightly wavy hair

EYES of medium size, slightly oval shaped; set squarely; wide apart; dark brown except in livers and light parti-colors where hazel is permitted

NECK long, clean, muscular; arched toward head; set cleanly on sloping shoulders

SHOULDERS sloping, fine

BACK short, strong; length from withers to tail-set approx. same as height from withers to ground; height at withers greater than height at hip joints (gradual slope of topline)

NOSE wide, well-developed; nostrils black, brown permitted (black preferred) for reds, livers, parti-colors and lighter roans

LOINS short, powerful, slightly arched

MUZZLE square, free from flews; in proportion with width of skull; definite stop; jaws of sufficient size and strength to carry game; teeth even, set squarely; neither over- nor undershot; lips square, full

TAIL set to conform with topline of back

HIPS well-rounded

THIGHS well-developed, broad, muscular, powerful

CHEST deep, well-developed; not too wide so as to interfere with action

STIFLES strong, well-bent

BRISKET should reach to elbow; sloping upward to loin

HOCK to HEEL moderately short, strong, well-let-down

ELBOWS set close to body

FORELEGS straight, strong; bone size nearly same from elbow to heel

COAT short, fine on head; silky, flat or slightly wavy on body; well-feathered but not so profusely as to hide body lines or interfere with work; undercoat length medium

FEET firm, round, catlike; size in pro portion to legs; pads thick; toes strong

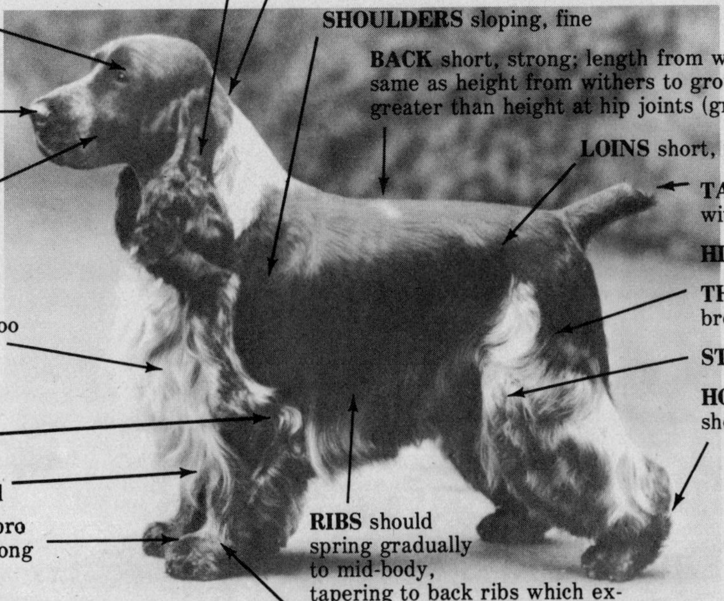

RIBS should spring gradually to mid-body, tapering to back ribs which extend well back; of good depth

SIZE: Height: ideal at withers, males, 16 to 17"; females, 15 to 16"; deviations penalized. Weight: Most desirable, males 28 to 34 lbs; females, 26 to 32 lbs. Conformation and balance more important than weight alone

PASTERNS short, straight, strong

COLORS: Various. White shirt frill undesirable in solid colors. Parti-colors — colors broken, evenly distributed; no large portions of any one color; white on saddle (solid color with white feet and chest not a parti-color). Roans — white hair evenly distributed over body (blue, liver, red, orange, lemon roans). Black and Tans — with tan markings

CH. DUNELM GALAXY

WINNER OF 4 BIS, 26 GROUP FIRSTS, 3 TIMES BOB AT WESTMINSTER. TWICE BOB E.C.S.C.A. SPECIALTY, TWICE BOB AMERICAN SPANIEL CLUB, ONCE FROM THE VETERANS CLASS. HIS GREATNESS LIES IN HIS SIRING ABILITY — HE IS THE TOP SIRE IN THE BREED: SIRE OF 3 BIS DOGS, SIRE OF 8 TOP PRODUCERS, SIRE OF 65 CHAMPIONS.

HANDLER: RICHARD L. BAUER

MRS. RUTH L. COOPER
2327 SWAINWOOD DRIVE
GLENVIEW, ILL. 60025

COLOR — Various. In self colors a white shirt frill is undesirable. In parti-colors, the coloring must be broken on the body and be evenly distributed. No large portion of any one color should exist. White should be shown on the saddle. A dog of any solid color with white feet and chest is not a parti-color. In roans it is desirable that the white hair should be distributed over the body, the more evenly the better. Roans come in various colors: blue, liver, red, orange and lemon. In black and tans the coat should be black; tan spots over the eyes, tan on the sides of the muzzle, on the throat and chest, on forelegs from the knees to the toes and on the hind legs on the inside of the legs, also on the stifle and extending from the hock to the toes. *Faults:* White feet are undesirable in any specimen of self color.

COAT — On head short and fine; on body flat or slightly wavy and silky in texture. Should be of medium length with enough undercoating to give protection. The English Cocker should be well feathered but not so profusely as to hide the true lines or interfere with his field work. *Faults:* Lack of coat; too soft, curly or wiry. Excessive trimming to change the natural appearance and coat should be discouraged.

HEIGHT — Ideal heights at withers: Males, 16 to 17 inches; females, 15 to 16 inches. Deviations to be severely penalized but not disqualified. *Weight* — The most desirable weights: Males, 28 pounds to 34 pounds; Females, 26 pounds to 32 pounds. Proper physical conformation and balance should be considered more important than weight alone.

Approved September 13, 1955

SPANIEL [ENGLISH SPRINGER] STANDARD

GENERAL APPEARANCE AND TYPE — The English Springer Spaniel is a medium-size sporting dog with a neat, compact body, and a docked tail. His coat is moderately long, glossy, usually liver and white or black and white, with feathering on his legs, ears, chest and brisket. His pendulous ears, soft gentle expression, sturdy build and friendly wagging tail proclaim him unmistakably a member of the ancient family of spaniels. He is above all a well proportioned dog, free from exaggeration, nicely balanced in every part. His carriage is proud and upstanding, body deep, legs strong and muscular with enough length to carry him with ease. His short level back, well developed thighs, good shoulders, excellent feet, suggest power, endurance, agility. Taken as a whole he looks the part of a dog that can go and keep going under difficult hunting conditions, and moreover he enjoys what he is doing. At his best he is endowed with style, symmetry, balance, enthusiasm and is every inch a sporting dog of distinct spaniel character, combining beauty and utility. To be penalized: Those lacking true English Springer type in conformation, expression, or behavior.

TEMPERAMENT — The typical Springer is friendly, eager to please, quick to learn, willing to obey. In the show ring he should exhibit poise, attentiveness, tractability, and should permit himself to be examined by the judge without resentment or cringing. To be penalized: Excessive timidity, with due allowance for puppies and novice exhibits. But no dog to receive a ribbon if he behaves in vicious manner toward handler or judge. Aggressiveness toward other dogs in the ring *not* to be construed as viciousness.

SIZE AND PROPORTION — The Springer is built to cover rough ground with agility and reasonable speed. He should be kept to medium size — neither too small nor too large and heavy to do the work for which he is intended. The ideal shoulder height for dogs is 20 inches; for bitches, 19 inches. Length of topline (the distance from top of the shoulders to the root of the tail) should be approximately equal to the dog's shoulder height — never longer than his height — not appreciably less. The dog too long in body, especially when long in loin, tires easily and lacks the compact outline characteristic of the breed. Equally undesirable is the dog too short in body for the length of his legs, a condition that destroys his balance and restricts the gait.

Weight is dependent on the dog's other dimensions: a 20-inch dog, well proportioned, in good condition should weigh about 49-55 pounds. The resulting appearance is a well-knit, sturdy dog with good but not too heavy bone, in no way coarse or ponderous. To be penalized: Over-heavy specimens, cloddy in build. Leggy individuals, too tall for their length and substance. Over-size or undersize specimens (those more than one inch under or over the breed ideal).

COLOR AND COAT — Color may be liver or black with white markings; liver and white (or black and white) with tan markings; blue or liver roan; or predominantly white with tan, black or liver markings. On ears, chest, legs and belly the Springer is nicely furnished with a fringe of feathering (of moderate heaviness). On his head, front or forelegs, and below hocks on front of hindlegs the hair is short and fine. The body coat is flat or wavy, of medium length, sufficiently dense to be waterproof, weatherproof and thorn-proof. The texture fine and the hair should have the clean, glossy, live appearance indicative of good health. It is legitimate to trim about head, feet, ears; to remove dead hair; to thin and shorten excess feathering particularly from the hocks to the feet and elsewhere as required to give a smart, clean appearance. To be penalized: Rough, curly coat. Over-trimming especially of the body coat. Any chopped, barbered or artificial effect. Excessive feathering that destroys the clean outline desirable in a sporting dog. Off colors such as lemon, red or orange not to place.

HEAD — The head is impressive without being heavy. Its beauty lies in a combination of strength and refinement. It is important that the size and proportion be in balance with the rest of the dog. Viewed in profile the head should appear approximately the same length as the neck and should blend with the body in substance. The skull (upper head) to be of medium length, fairly broad, flat on top, slightly rounded at the sides and back. The occiput bone inconspicuous, rounded rather than peaked or angular. The foreface (head in front of the eyes) approximately the same length as the skull, and in harmony as to width and general character. Looking down on the head the muzzle to appear to be about one-half the width of the skull. As the skull rises from the foreface it makes a brow or "stop," divided by a groove or fluting between the eyes. This groove continues upward and gradually disappears as it reaches the middle of the forehead. The amount of "stop" can best be described as moderate. It must not be a pro-

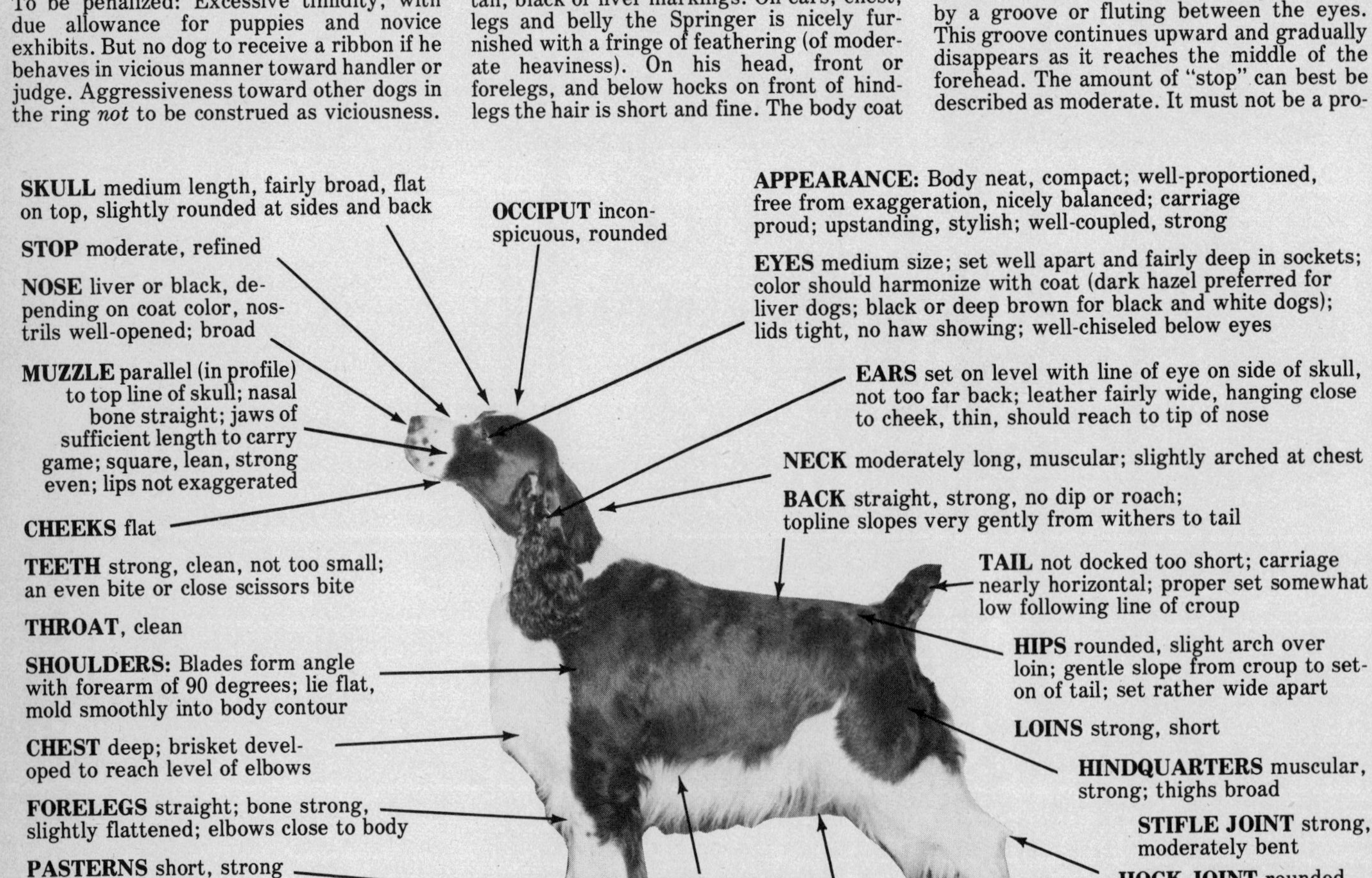

CH. SALILYN'S ARISTOCRAT

CAMPAIGNED FOR 18 MONTHS, HE FINISHED HIS CHAMPIONSHIP WHEN ONLY 9 MONTHS OLD BY GOING BEST OF BREED AND GROUP FIRST FROM THE PUPPY CLASS. HIS SHOW RECORD IS 66 BIS, 108 GROUP FIRSTS, 5 SPECIALTY SHOWS (2 NATIONAL SPECIALTIES). HIS GET NUMBER 120 CHAMPIONS; THESE INCLUDE THE TOP WINNING MALE IN 1969-70-71-72, AND TOP WINNING BITCH IN 1970-71-72. HIS SON CH. CHINOE'S ADAMENT JAMES BROKE ARISTOCRAT'S RECORD FOR GREATEST NUMBER OF BEST IN SHOWS IN ONE YEAR (48 BIS).

SALILYN KENNELS
MRS. F. H. GASOW
4031 COLLIDGE
TROY, MICHIGAN 48084

nounced feature as in the Clumber Spaniel. Rather it is a subtle rise where the muzzle blends into the upper head, further emphasized by the groove and by the position and shape of the eyebrows which should be well-developed. The stop, eyebrow and the chiseling of the bony structure around the eye sockets contribute to the Springer's beautiful and characteristic expression.

Viewed in profile the topline of the skull and the muzzle lie in two approximately parallel planes. The nasal bone should be straight, with no inclination downward toward the tip of the nose which gives a down-faced look so undesirable in this breed. Neither should the nasal bone be concave resulting in a "dish-faced" profile, nor convex giving the dog a Roman nose. The jaws to be of sufficient length to allow the dog to carry game easily; fairly square, lean, strong, and even (neither undershot nor overshot). The upper lip to come down full and rather square to cover the line of the lower jaw, but lips not to be pendulous nor exaggerated. The nostrils, well opened and broad, liver color or black depending on the color of the coat. Flesh-colored ("Dudley noses") or spotted ("butterfly noses") are undesirable. The cheeks to be flat (not rounded, full or thick), with nice chiseling under the eyes. To be penalized: Oval, pointed or heavy skull. Cheeks prominently rounded, thick and protruding. Too much or too little stop. Over heavy muzzle. Muzzle too short, too thin, too narrow. Pendulous slobbery lips. Under- or overshot jaws — a very serious fault, to be heavily penalized. *Teeth* — The teeth should be strong, clean, not too small; and when the mouth is closed the teeth should meet in an even bite or a close scissors bite (the lower incisors touching the inside of the upper incisors). To be penalized: Any deviation from above description. One or two teeth slightly out of line not to be considered a serious fault, but irregularities due to faulty jaw formation to be severely penalized.

EYES — More than any other feature the eyes contribute to the Springer's appeal. Color, placement, size influence expression and attractiveness. The eyes to be of medium size, neither small, round, full and

[contined on page 63]

HEAD — Skull rather large and high in dome with prominent occiput; muzzle square and rather long with deep mouth opening and lips fine in texture. Teeth strong and level. The nose should be large with open nostrils, and liver in color. The head should be cleanly chiseled, not cheeky, and should not present a short wedge-shaped appearance. Hair on face should be short and smooth. *Topknot* — Topknot, a characteristic of the true breed, should consist of long loose curls growing down into a well-defined peak between the eyes and should not be in the form of a wig; *i.e.*, growing straight across.

EYES — Medium in size and set almost flush, without eyebrows. Color of eyes hazel, preferably of dark shade. Expression of the eyes should be keenly alert, intelligent, direct and quizzical. *Ears* — Long, lobular, set low with leathers reaching to about the end of the nose when extended forward. The ears should be abundantly covered with curls becoming longer toward the tips and extending two or more inches below the ends of the leathers.

NECK — The neck should be long, arching, strong and muscular, smoothly set into sloping shoulders. *Shoulders and Chest* — Shoulders should be sloping and clean; chest deep but not too wide between the legs. The entire front should give the impression of strength without heaviness.

BODY, RIBS AND LOINS — Body should be of medium length, with ribs well sprung, pear-shaped at the brisket, and rounder toward the hindquarters. Ribs should be carried well back. Loins should be short, wide and muscular. The body should not present a tucked-up appearance. *Hindquarters* — The hindquarters should be as high as or a trifle higher than the shoulders and should be very powerful and muscular with well-developed upper and second thighs. Hips should be wide; stifles should not be too straight; and hocks low-set and moderately bent. Tail should be set on low enough to give a rather rounded appearance to the hindquarters and should be carried nearly level with the back. Sound hindquarters are of great importance to provide swimming power and drive. *Forelegs and Feet* — Forelegs medium in length, well boned, straight and muscular with elbows close set. Both fore and hind feet should be large, thick and somewhat spreading, well clothed with hair both over and between the toes, but free from superfluous feather.

TAIL — The so-called "rat tail" is a striking characteristic of the breed. At the root it is thick and covered for 2 or 3 inches with short curls. It tapers to a fine point at the end, and from the root-curls is covered with short, smooth hair so as to look as if the tail had been clipped. The tail should not be long enough to reach the hock joint.

COAT — Proper coat is of vital importance. The neck, back and sides should be densely covered with tight crisp ringlets entirely free from wooliness. Underneath the ribs the hair should be longer. The hair on lower throat should be short. The forelegs should be covered all around with abundant hair falling in curls or waves, but shorter in front than behind. The hind legs should also be abundantly covered by hair falling in curls or waves, but the hair should be short on the front of the legs below the hocks. *Color* — Solid liver; white on chest objectionable.

HEIGHT AND WEIGHT — Dogs, 22 to 24 inches; bitches, 21 to 23 inches. Dogs, 55 to 65 pounds; bitches, 45 to 58 pounds.

GENERAL APPEARANCE — That of a smart, upstanding, strongly built but not leggy dog, combining great intelligence and the rugged endurance with a bold, dashing eagerness of temperament. *Gait* — Should be dquare, true, precise and not slurring.

SCALE OF POINTS

HEAD		
Skull and topknot	6	
Ears	4	
Eyes	4	
Muzzle and nose	6	20
BODY		
Neck	5	
Chest, shoulders, back, loin and ribs	12	17
DRIVING GEAR		
Feet, hips, thighs, stifles and continuity of hindquarter muscles	14	
Feet, legs, elbows and muscles of forequarters	9	23
COAT		
Tightness, denseness of curl and general texture	16	
Color	4	20
TAIL		
General appearance and "set on," length and carriage	5	5
GENERAL CONFORMATION AND ACTION		
Symmetry, style, gait, weight and size	15	15
		100

Approved June 11, 1940

CH. MALLYREE MR. MULDOON

MULDOON HAD HIS FIRST BOB AT EASTERN DOG CLUB AT 8 MONTHS, HIS FIRST GROUP PLACEMENT AT SANTA BARBARA AT 15 MONTHS. AT 2 YEARS HE GAINED HIS CHAMPIONSHIP AND HAD GROUP PLACEMENTS AT RAVENNA AND LAKES REGION K.C. HE WAS #1 IRISH WATER SPANIEL IN 1972 AND 1973. AS WINNER OF THE 1974 IWSCA NATIONAL SPECIALTY, MULDOON IS A THIRD GENERATION SPECIALTY WINNER.

MARION L. HOPKINS
MALLYREE KENNELS
CENTER RD.
BRADFORD, N.H. 03221
(603) 938-2164

Water Spaniels are among the oldest documented types of dogs and it is presumably from such ancestry that the Irish Water Spaniels descended. Their resemblance to standard Poodles is striking and is believed to indicate a close relationship. Large and non-spaniel-like in appearance, these dogs are eager and spaniel-like in the field. They quarter and retrieve and are particularly effective with water-fowl. The coat, which is always dark liver, falls into tight curls except on the face, tail, and parts of the legs. There is a dense undercoat as well. Never highly popular in the United States or England, registrations today number only about 100 a year. The breed ranks 105th. Relatively few Irish Water Spaniels appear in show competition.

THE "WELSH SPANIEL" or "SPRINGER" is also known and referred to in Wales as a "Starter." He is of very ancient and pure origin, and is a distinct variety which has been bred and preserved purely for working purposes.

HEAD — *Skull* — Proportionate, of moderate length, slightly domed, clearly defined stop, well chiseled below the eyes. *Muzzle* — Medium length, straight, fairly square; the nostrils well developed and flesh-colored or dark. *Jaw* — Strong, neither undershot nor overshot. *Eyes* — Hazel or dark, medium size, not prominent, nor sunken, nor showing haw. *Ears* — Set moderately low and hanging close to the cheeks, comparatively small and gradually narrowing towards the tip, covered with nice setterlike feathering. A short chubby head is objectionable.

NECK AND SHOULDERS — *Neck* — Long and muscular, clean in throat, neatly set into long and sloping shoulders. *Forelegs* — Medium length, straight, well boned, moderately feathered.

BODY — Not long; strong and muscular with deep brisket, well sprung ribs; length of body should be proportionate to length of leg, and very well balanced; with muscular loin slightly arched and well coupled up. *Quarters* — Strong and muscular, wide and fully developed with deep second thighs. *Hind Legs* — Hocks well let down; stifles moderately bent (neither twisted in nor out), moderately feathered. *Feet* — Round with thick pads. *Stern* — Well set on and low, never carried above the level of the back; lightly feathered and with lively action.

COAT — Straight or flat and thick, of a nice silky texture, never wiry nor wavy. A curly coat is most objectionable. *Color* — Dark rich red and white.

GENERAL APPEARANCE — A symmetrical, compact, strong, merry, very active dog; not stilty, obviously built for endurance and activity.

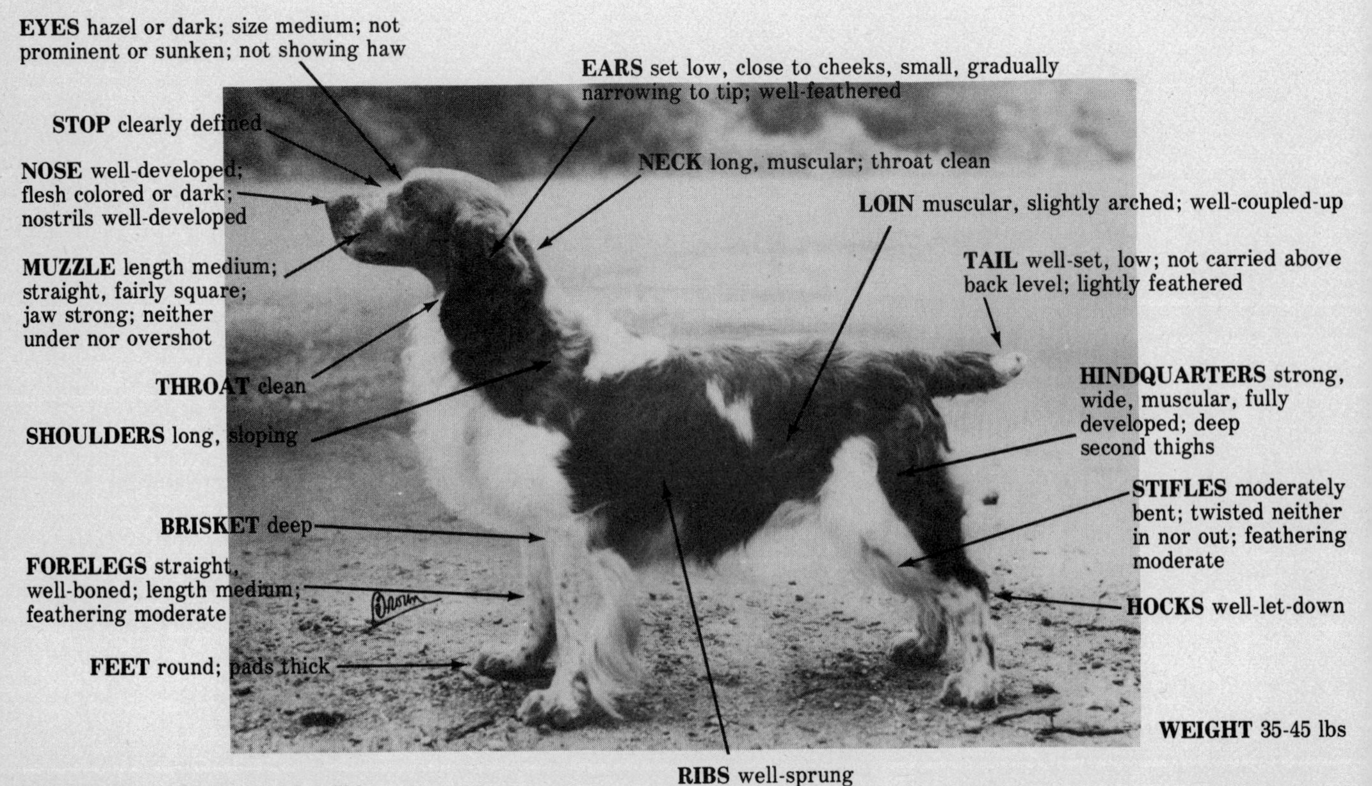

CH. PICKWICK'S BRYCHAN

TOP WINNING WELSH SPRINGER FOR 1973 (IN U.S.).

FIRST WELSH SPRINGER TO BECOME CHAMPION ON

THE WEST COAST. 48 BOB AND 1 GROUP IV.

HANDLER: JOHN DAVIDSON

RICHARD L. PRESTON
185 SHELLEY AVE.
CAMPBELL, CA. 95008

The Welsh Springer Spaniel has long been known in Wales. Its closest ally appears to be the Brittany Spaniel. Excellent gun-dogs though they are, Welsh Springer Spaniels have never enjoyed much popularity in other lands. The Welsh Springer Spaniel is compact, powerfully built, and active. It is built for endurance and falls between the Cocker Spaniel and the English Springer Spaniel. Coat color is rich, dark red and white. Only a few dozen Welsh Springer Spaniels are registered annually in the United States, the breed ranking 112th. They are rarely seen in show competition.

GENERAL APPEARANCE — That of a medium-sized hunting dog of quite distinguished appearance. Robust but rather lightly built, his short coat is an attractive rusty-gold, and his tail is docked. He is a dog of power and drive in the field, and a tractable and affectionate companion in the home.

HEAD — Lean but muscular. The skull is moderately wide between the ears, with a median line down the forehead. Stop moderate. The muzzle is a trifle longer than the skull and although tapering, is well squared at its end. Jaws strong, with well-developed white teeth meeting in a scissors bite. The lips cover the jaws completely but they are neither loose nor pendulous. Nostrils slightly open, the nose brown. A black or slate-gray nose is objectionable.

EARS — Thin, silky, and proportionately long, with rounded-leather ends; set fairly low and hanging close to the cheeks. *Eyes* — Medium in size and depth of setting, their surrounding tissue covering the whites, and the iris or color portion harmonizing with the shade of the coat. A yellow eye is objectionable.

NECK — Strong, smooth, and muscular; moderately long, arched, and devoid of dewlap. It broadens nicely into shoulders which are well laid back.

BODY — Strong and well proportioned. The back is short, the withers high, and the topline slightly rounded over the loin to the set-on of the tail. Chest moderately broad and deep, and reaching down to the elbows. Ribs well sprung, and underline exhibiting a slight tuck-up beneath the loin.

LEGS AND FEET — Forelegs straight, strong, and muscular, with elbows close. The hind legs have well-developed thighs, with moderate angulation at stifles and hocks. Too much angulation at the hocks is as faulty as too little. The hocks, which are well let down, are equidistant from each other from the hock joint to the ground. Cowhocks are faulty. Feet are cat-like, round and compact, with toes close. Nails are brown and short; pads thick and tough. Dewclaws, if any, to be removed. Hare feet are objectionable. *Tail* — Set just below the level of the back, thicker at the root, and docked one-third off.

COAT — Short, smooth, dense, and close-lying, without woolly undercoat.

COLOR — Solid. Rusty gold or rather dark sandy yellow in different shades, with darker shades preferred. Dark brown and pale yellow are undesirable. Small white spots on chest or feet are not faulted.

TEMPERAMENT — That of the natural hunter endowed with a good nose and above-average ability to take training. Lively, gentle-mannered, and demonstratively affectionate. Fearless, and with well-developed protective instinct.

GAIT — Far-reaching, light-footed, graceful, smooth.

SIZE — Males, 22 to 24 inches; females, 21 to 23 inches at the highest point of the shoulders. Any dog measuring over or under these limits shall be considered faulty, the seriousness of the fault depending on the extent of the deviation. Any dog that measures more than 2 inches over or under these limits shall be disqualified.

DISQUALIFICATION

Deviation in height of more than 2 inches from standard either way.

Approved December 10, 1963

CH. TAUNEE'S LOKI SANTANA
"BEAR"

BEAR IS NUMBER ONE VISZLA IN AMERICA. HIS RECORD IS:
6 ALL BREED BEST IN SHOWS
22 GROUP ONES

HANDLER: BOBBY BARLOW

MR. & MRS. JAMES BUTT & LINDA GREENFIELD
R.D. 1, BOX 606
HONEY BROOK, PA. 19344

The Vizsla is a Hungarian gun-dog, good at pointing and retrieving both upland game and waterfowl. Its origins are not known. The Vizsla is medium-sized (22-24 inches at the shoulder), robust but rather lightly built, and rusty-gold in color. He is powerful and driving in the field as well as a biddable and affectionate companion. Some 2,200 are now registered annually in the United States; the breed ranking 48th.

WEIMARANER STANDARD

GENERAL APPEARANCE — A medium sized gray dog, with fine aristocratic features. He should present a picture of grace, speed, stamina, alertness and balance. Above all, the dog's conformation must indicate the ability to work with great speed and endurance in the field.

HEIGHT — Height at the withers: dogs 25 inches to 27 inches; bitches 23 inches to 25 inches. One inch over or under the specified height of each sex is allowable but should be penalized. Dogs measuring less than 24 inches or more than 28 inches and bitches measuring less than 22 inches or more than 26 inches shall be disqualified.

HEAD — Moderately long and aristocratic, with moderate stop and slight median line extending back over the forehead. Rather prominent occipital bone and trumpets well set back, beginning at the back of the eye-sockets. Measurement from tip of nose to stop equal that from stop to occipital bone. The flews should be straight, delicate at the nostrils. Skin drawn tightly, neck clean-cut and moderately long. Expression kind, keen and intelligent. *Ears* — Long and lobular, slightly folded and set high. The ear when drawn snugly alongside the jaw should end approximately two inches from the point of the nose. *Eyes* — In shades of light amber, gray or blue-gray set well enough apart to indicate good disposition and intelligence. When dilated under excitement the eyes may appear almost black. *Teeth* — Well set, strong and even; well-developed and proportionate to jaw with correct scissors bite, the upper teeth protruding slightly over the lower teeth but not more than 1/16 of an inch. Complete dentition is greatly to be desired. *Nose* — Gray. *Lips and Gums* — Pinkish flesh shades.

BODY — The back should be moderate in length set in a straight line, strong and should slope slightly from the withers. The chest should be well developed and deep with shoulders well laid back. Ribs well sprung and long. Abdomen firmly held; moderately tucked up flank. The brisket should extend to the elbow.

COAT AND COLOR — Short, smooth and sleek, solid color. In shades of mouse-gray to silver gray, usually blending to lighter shades on the head and ears. A small white marking on the chest is permitted, but should be penalized on any other portion of the body. White spots resulting from an injury should not be penalized. *Disqualification:* A distinctly long coat.

FORELEGS — Straight and strong, with the measurement from the elbow to the ground approximately equaling the distance from the elbow to the top of withers.

HINDQUARTERS — Well angulated stifles and straight hocks. Musculation well developed.

FEET — Firm and compact, webbed, toes well arched, pads closed and thick, nails short and gray or amber in color. *Dewclaws* — Should be removed.

TAIL — Docked. At maturity it should measure approximately six inches with a tendency to be light rather than heavy and should be carried in a manner expressing confidence and sound temperament. A non-docked tail shall be penalized.

GAIT — The gait should be effortless and should indicate smooth co-ordination. When seen from the rear, the hind feet should be parallel to the front feet. When viewed from the side, the top line should remain strong and level.

TEMPERAMENT — The temperament should be friendly, fearless, alert and obedient.

MINOR FAULTS — Tail too short or too long. Pink nose.

MAJOR FAULTS — Doggy bitches. Bitchy dogs. Improper muscular condition. Badly affected teeth. More than four teeth missing. Back too long or too short. Faulty coat. Neck too short, thick or throaty. Low set tail. Elbows in or out. Feet east and west. Poor gait. Poor feet. Cowhocks. Faulty backs, either roached or sway. Badly overshot, or undershot bite. Snipey muzzle. Short ears.

VERY SERIOUS FAULTS — White, other than a spot on the chest. Eyes, other than gray, blue-gray or light amber. Black mottled mouth. Non-docked tail. Dogs exhibiting strong fear, shyness and extreme nervousness. A color darker than mouse-gray.

DISQUALIFICATIONS

Deviation in height of more than one inch from standard either way. A distinctly long coat.

Approved June 8, 1965

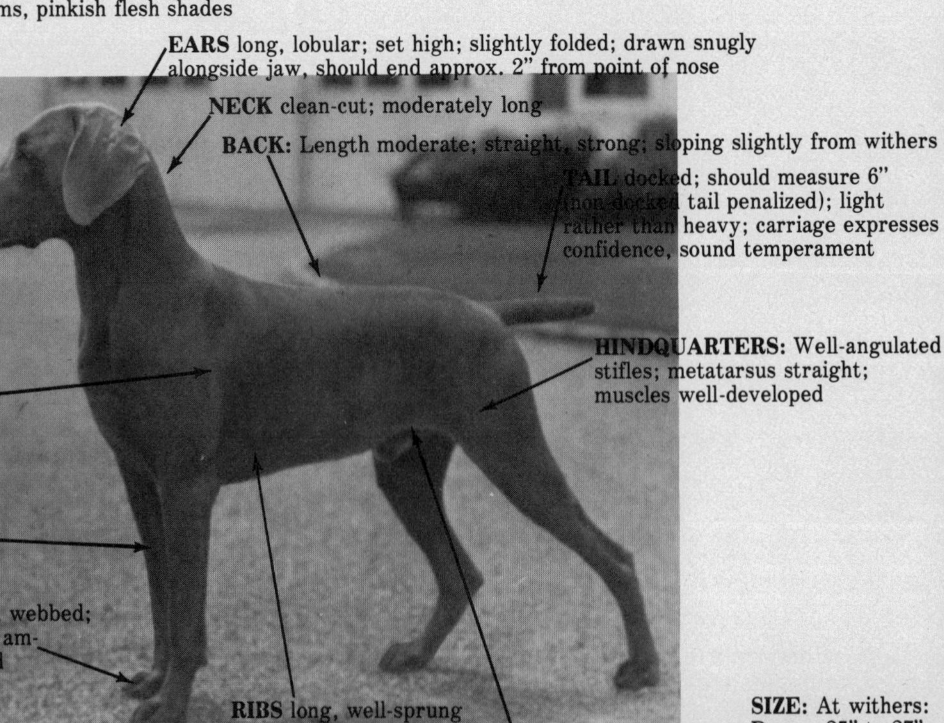

CH. SPRINGDALE RHEA V.D. REITERALM

NUMBER 1 WEIMARANER — BOTH SEXES — 1974. "ONE OF A KIND." RHEA IS THE ONLY BEST IN SHOW BITCH IN THE HISTORY OF THE BREED. SHE BEGAN HER STUNNING CAREER AS THE BEST BITCH IN THE WESTERN BENCH FUTURITY. ALWAYS A STANDOUT AS A SPECIAL, RHEA CONTINUES TO WIN STRONG GROUPS AND PLACEMENTS AGAINST STIFF COMPETITION. HER CAREER AS A BROOD BITCH HAS JUST BEGUN WITH 3 OUT OF 5 PUPPIES ALREADY CHAMPIONS — ONE IS IN THE TOP TEN — AND ANOTHER A GROUP PLACER. OFA-WE 669.

STANLEY FLOWERS — HANDLER

SUSAN ORTH
520 GIUFFRIDA AVENUE
SAN JOSE, CALIFORNIA 95123

The Weimaraner was developed in Germany as a bird dog. Its ancestry is not known. Breeding of Weimaraners was very strictly controlled in Germany and this model was later followed in the United States. The dog's impressive success in the field and in field trials as well as its distinctive appearance and or unusually strong public relations campaign have won it a strong place in the United States. The Weimaraner is graceful, swift, enduring, alert, and balanced. Dogs stand 25 to 27 inches at the withers. The coat is smooth and sleek. The color is a distinctive solid mouse-grey or silver-grey. A blue or black is disqualifying. Some 7,000 Weimaraners are currently registered annually with the AKC. They are less well established in England.

GENERAL APPEARANCE — The over-all picture which is created in the observer's eye should be that of an aristocratic, well-balanced, symmetrical animal with conformation indicating power, endurance and agility and a look of intelligence and animation. The dog should be neither unduly small nor conspicuously large. It should rather give the impression of medium size, but be like the proper hunter, "with a short back, but standing over plenty of ground." Tall, leggy individuals seldom possess endurance or sound movement.

Dogs which are ponderous or unbalanced because of excess substance should be definitely rejected. The first impression should be that of a keenness which denotes full enthusiasm for work without indication of nervous or flighty character. Movement should be alertly co-ordinated without waste motion. Grace of outline, clean-cut head, sloping shoulders, deep breast, powerful back, strong quarters, good bone composition, adequate muscle, well-carried tail and taut coat, all of which should combine to produce a look of nobility and an indication of anatomical structure essential to correct gait which must indicate a heritage of purposefully conducted breeding.

HEAD — Clean-cut, neither too light nor too heavy, in proper proportion to the body. Skull should be reasonably broad, arched on side and slightly round on top. Scissura (median line between the eyes at the forehead) not too deep, occipital bone not as conspicuous as in the case of the Pointer. The foreface should rise gradually from nose to forehead—not resembling the Roman nose. This is more strongly pronounced in the dog than in the bitch, as befitting his sex. The chops should fall away from the somewhat projecting nose. Lips should be full and deep, never flewy. The chops should not fall over too much, but form a proper fold in the angle. The jaw should be powerful and the muscles well developed. The line to the forehead should rise gradually and should never possess a definite stop as in the case of the Pointer, but rather a stop-effect when viewed from the side, due to the position of the eyebrows. The muzzle should be sufficiently long to enable the dog to seize properly and to facilitate his carrying game a long time. A pointed muzzle is not desirable. The entire head should never give the impression of tapering to a point. The depth should be in the right proportion to the length, both in the muzzle and in the skull proper.

EARS — Ears should be broad and set fairly high, lie flat and never hang away from the head. Placement should be above eye level. The ears, when laid in front without being pulled, should about meet the lip angle. In the case of heavier dogs, they should be correspondingly longer. *Eyes* — The eyes should be of medium size, full of intelligence and expressive, good-humored, and yet radiating energy, neither protruding nor sunk. The eyelids should close well. The best color is a dark shade of brown. Light yellow, china or wall (bird of prey) eyes are not desirable. *Nose* — Brown, the larger the better; nostrils well opened and broad. Flesh-colored and spotted noses are not desirable. *Teeth* — The teeth should be strong and healthy. The molars should intermesh properly. Incisors should fit close in a true scissor bite. Jaws should be neither overshot nor undershot.

NECK — Of adequate length to permit the jaws reaching game to be retrieved, sloping downwards on beautifully curving lines. The nape should be rather muscular, becoming gradually larger towards the shoulders. Moderate hound-like throatiness permitted.

BREAST AND THORAX — The breast in general should give the impression of depth rather than breadth; for all that, it should be in correct proportion to the other parts of the body with fair depth of chest. The ribs forming the thorax should be well-curved and not flat; they should not be absolutely round or barrel-shaped. Ribs that are entirely round prevent the necessary expansion of the chest when taking breath. The back ribs should reach well down. The circumference of the breast immediately behind the elbows should be smaller than that of the breast about a hands-breadth behind elbows, so that the upper arm has room for movement.

BACK AND LOINS — Back should be short, strong and straight with slight rise from root of tail to withers. Excessively long or hog-backed should be penalized. Loin strong, of moderate length and slightly arched. Tuck-up should be apparent.

ASSEMBLY OF BACK MEMBERS — The hips should be broad with hip sockets wide apart and fall slightly toward the tail in a graceful curve. Thighs strong and well muscled. Stifles well bent. Hock joints should be well angulated with strong, straight bone structure from hock to pad. Angulation of both stifle and hock joints should be such as to combine maximum combination of both drive and traction. Hocks should turn neither in nor out. *Assembly of Front Members* — The shoulders should be sloping, movable, well covered with muscle. The shoulder blades should lie flat. The upper arm (also called the cross bar, *i.e.*, the bones between the shoulder and elbow joints) should be as

[*continued on page 63*]

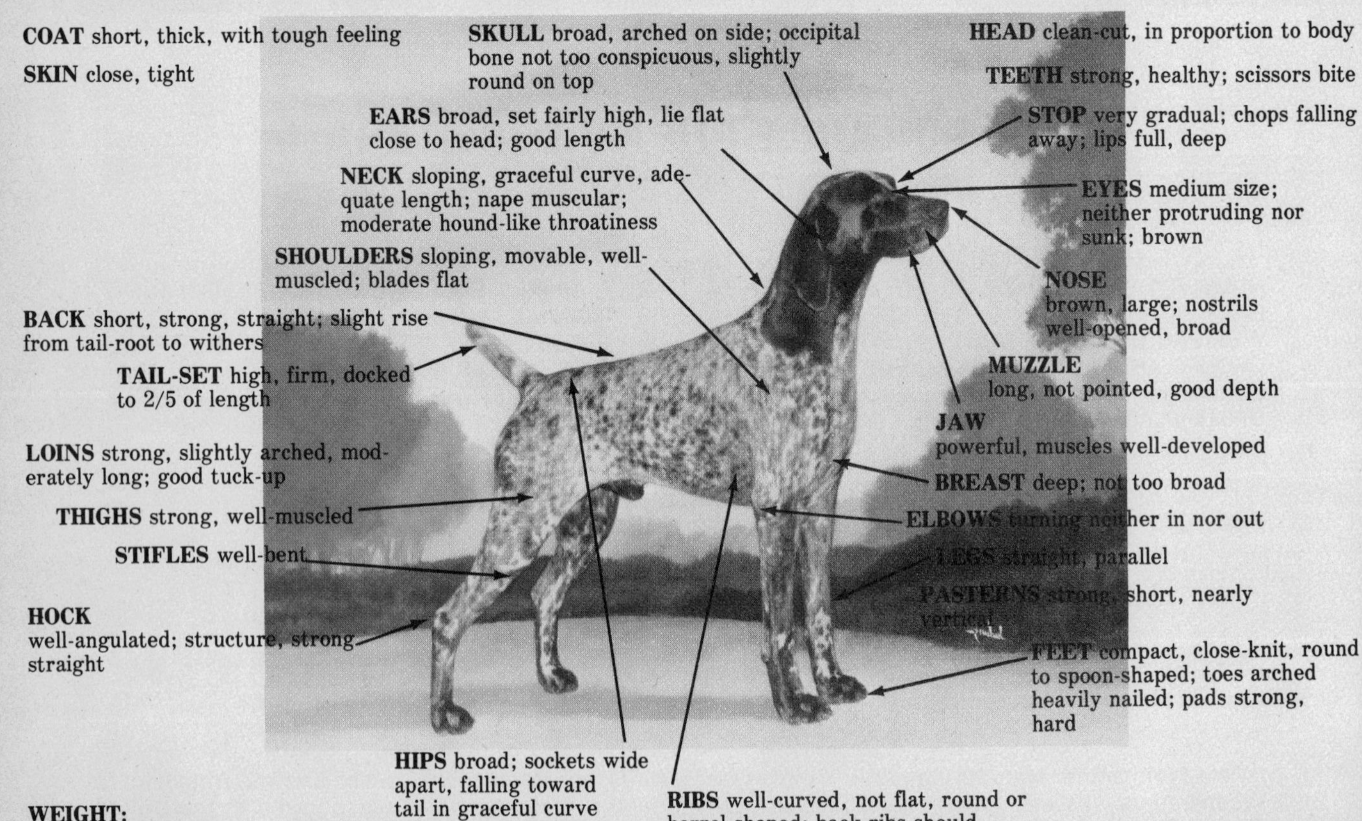

WEIGHT:
55-70 lbs. males;
45-60 lbs. females

HEIGHT:
23-25" males;
21-23" females

COLOR: Solid liver; liver and white spotted; liver and white ticked; liver and white spotted and ticked; liver roan

HEAD—Long and well proportioned, skull not too flat, jaws long and strong but not inclined to snipiness, nose black, in the black coated variety, with wide nostrils. Teeth strong and level. *Eyes*—Black or brown, but not yellow, rather large but not too prominent. *Ears*—Rather small, set on low, lying close to the head, and covered with short curls.

COAT—Should be one mass of crisp curls all over. A slightly more open coat not to be severely penalized, but a saddle back or patch of uncurled hair behind the shoulder should be penalized, and a prominent white patch on breast is undesirable, but a few white hairs allowed in an otherwise good dog. Color, black or liver.

SHOULDERS, CHEST, BODY AND LOINS—Shoulders should be very deep, muscular and obliquely placed. Chest, not too wide, but decidedly deep. Body, rather short, muscular and well ribbed up. Loin, powerful, deep and firm to the grasp.

LEGS AND FEET—Legs should be of moderate length, forelegs straight and set well under the body. Quarters strong and muscular, hocks low to the ground with moderate bend to stifle and hock. Feet round and compact with well-arched toes.

TAIL—Should be moderately short, carried fairly straight and covered with curls, slightly tapering towards the point.

GENERAL APPEARANCE — A strong smart upstanding dog, showing activity, endurance and intelligence.

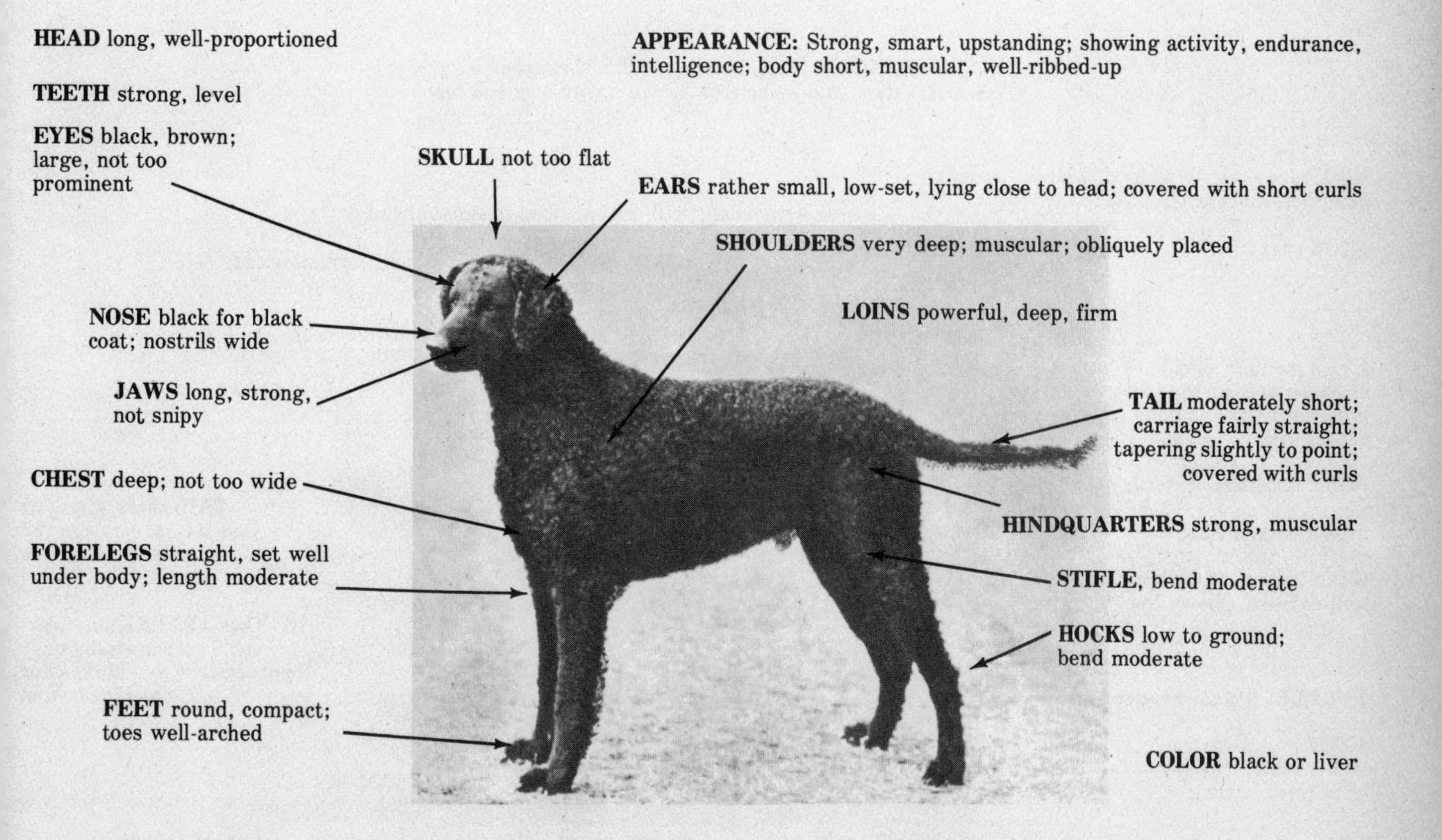
HEAD long, well-proportioned
TEETH strong, level
EYES black, brown; large, not too prominent
SKULL not too flat
EARS rather small, low-set, lying close to head; covered with short curls
APPEARANCE: Strong, smart, upstanding; showing activity, endurance, intelligence; body short, muscular, well-ribbed-up
SHOULDERS very deep; muscular; obliquely placed
LOINS powerful, deep, firm
NOSE black for black coat; nostrils wide
JAWS long, strong, not snipy
TAIL moderately short; carriage fairly straight; tapering slightly to point; covered with curls
CHEST deep; not too wide
HINDQUARTERS strong, muscular
FORELEGS straight, set well under body; length moderate
STIFLE, bend moderate
HOCKS low to ground; bend moderate
FEET round, compact; toes well-arched
COLOR black or liver
COAT: Mass of crisp curls; slightly open coat not severely penalized; but saddle-back or patch of uncurled hair behind shoulders should be penalized; prominent white patch on breast undesirable

GENERAL APPEARANCE—A bright, active dog of medium size (weighing from 60 pounds to 70 pounds) with an intelligent expression, showing power without lumber and raciness without weediness.

HEAD—This should be long and nicely molded. The skull flat and moderately broad. There should be a depression or stop between the eyes, slight and in no way accentuated, so as to avoid giving either a down or a dish-faced appearance. The nose of good size with open nostrils. The eyes, of medium size, should be dark brown or hazel, with a very intelligent expression (a round prominent eye is a disfigurement), and they should not be obliquely placed. The jaws should be long and strong, with a capacity of carrying a hare or pheasant. The ears small and well set on close to the side of the head.

NECK, SHOULDERS AND CHEST — The head should be well set in the neck, which latter should be long and free from throatiness, symmetrically set and obliquely placed in shoulders running well into the back to allow of easily seeking for the trail. The chest should be deep and fairly broad, with a well-defined brisket, on which the elbows should work cleanly and evenly. The fore ribs should be fairly flat showing a gradual spring and well arched in the center of the body but rather lighter towards the quarters. Open couplings are to be ruthlessly condemned.

BACK AND QUARTERS—The back should be short, square and well ribbed up, with muscular quarters. The stern short, straight and well set on, carried gaily but never much above the level of the back. *Legs and Feet*—These are of the greatest importance. The forelegs should be perfectly straight, with bone of good quality carried right down to the feet which should be round and strong. The stifle should not be too straight or too bent and the dog must neither be cowhocked nor move too wide behind, in fact, he must stand and move true all round on legs and feet, with toes close and well arched, the soles being thick and strong, and when the dog is in full coat the limbs should be well feathered.

COAT—Should be dense, of fine quality and texture, flat as possible. Color: black or liver.

APPEARANCE: Bright, active; medium size; showing power, raciness; stand and move true all around on legs and feet

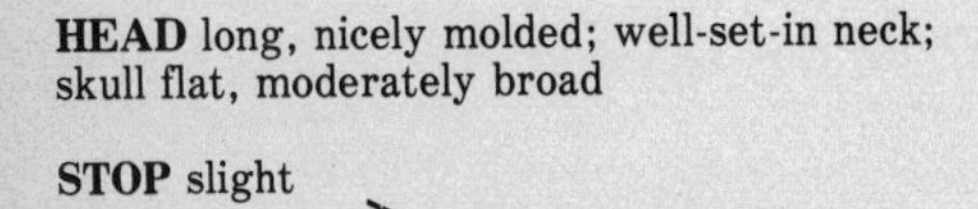

HEAD long, nicely molded; well-set-in neck; skull flat, moderately broad

STOP slight

EARS small, well-set-on; close to side of head

NECK long, free from throatiness; symmetrically set; obliquely placed in shoulders

BACK short, square; well-ribbed-up

EYES medium size; dark brown or hazel; neither round nor prominent nor obliquely placed; expressive, intelligent

NOSE good size; nostrils open

JAWS long, strong

TAIL short, straight; well-set-on; carriage gay but never much above back level

CHEST deep, fairly broad; brisket well-defined; elbows free

HINDQUARTERS muscular; stifle not too straight nor too bent; neither cow-hocked nor too wide behind

FORELEGS straight, good bone

FEET round, strong; toes close; well-arched; pads thick, strong

SIZE: 60-70 lbs.

RIBS (fore) fairly flat with gradual spring; well-arched in center of body; lighter toward quarters; open couplings condemned

COAT dense; fine in quality and texture; flat as possible; limbs well-feathered

COLOR: Black or liver

STANDARD

A SYMMETRICAL, powerful, active dog, sound and well put together, not clumsy or long in the leg, displaying a kindly expression and possessing a personality that is eager, alert and self-confident. Primarily a hunting dog, he should be shown in hard working condition. Over-all appearance, balance, gait and purpose to be given more emphasis than any of his component parts.

SIZE — Males 23-24 inches in height at withers; females 21½-22½. Length from breastbone to buttocks slightly greater than height at withers in ratio of 12-11. *Weight* for dogs 65-75 pounds; bitches 60-70 pounds.

HEAD — Broad in skull, slightly arched laterally and longitudinally without prominence of frontal or occipital bones. Good stop. Foreface deep and wide, nearly as long as skull. Muzzle, when viewed in profile, slightly deeper at stop than at tip; when viewed from above, slightly wider at stop than at tip. No heaviness in flews. Removal of whiskers for show purposes optional. *Eyes* — Friendly and intelligent, medium large with dark rims, set well apart and reasonably deep in sockets. Color preferably dark brown, never lighter than color of coat. No white or haw visible when looking straight ahead. *Teeth* — Scissors bite with lower incisors touching inside of upper incisors. *Nose* — Black or dark brown, though lighter shade in cold weather not serious. Dudley nose (pink without pigmentation) to be faulted. *Ears* — Rather short, hanging flat against head with rounded tips slightly below jaw. Forward edge attached well behind and just above eye with rear edge slightly below eye. Low, houndlike ear-set to be faulted.

NECK — Medium long, sloping well back into shoulders, giving sturdy muscular appearance with untrimmed natural ruff. No throatiness.

BODY — Well balanced, short-coupled, deep through the heart. Chest at least as wide as a man's hand, including thumb. Brisket extends to elbows. Ribs long and well sprung but not barrel shaped, extending well to rear of body. Loin short, muscular, wide and deep, with very little tuck-up. Top line level from withers to croup, whether standing or moving. Croup slopes gently. Slabsidedness, narrow chest, lack of depth in brisket, excessive tuckup, roach or sway back to be faulted.

FOREQUARTERS — Forequarters well coordinated with hindquarters and capable of free movement. Shoulder blades wide, long and muscular, showing angulation with upper arm of approximately 90 degrees. Legs straight with good bone. Pastern short and strong, sloping slightly forward with no suggestion of weakness. *Hindquarters* — Well-bent stifles (angulation between femur and pelvis approximately 90 degrees) with hocks well let down. Legs straight when viewed from rear. Cowhocks and sickle hocks to be faulted.

FEET — Medium size, round and compact with thick pads. Excess hair may be trimmed to show natural size and contour. Open or splayed feet to be faulted. *Tail* — Well set on, neither too high nor too low, following natural line of croup. Length extends to hock. Carried with merry action with some upward curve but never curled over back nor between legs.

COAT AND COLOR — Dense and water repellent with good undercoat. Texture not as hard as that of a shorthaired dog nor silky as that of a setter. Lies flat against body and may be straight or wavy. Moderate feathering on back of forelegs and heavier feathering on front of neck, back of thighs and underside of tail. Feathering may be lighter than rest of coat. Color lustrous golden of various shades. A few white hairs on chest permissible but not desirable. Further white markings to be faulted.

GAIT — When trotting, gait is free, smooth, powerful and well coordinated. Viewed from front or rear, legs turn neither in nor out, nor do feet cross or interfere with each other. Increased speed causes tendency of feet to converge toward center line of gravity.

DISQUALIFICATIONS

Deviation in height of more than one inch from standard either way. Undershot or overshot bite. This condition not to be confused with misalignment of teeth. Trichiasis (abnormal position or direction of the eyelashes).

Approved September 10, 1963

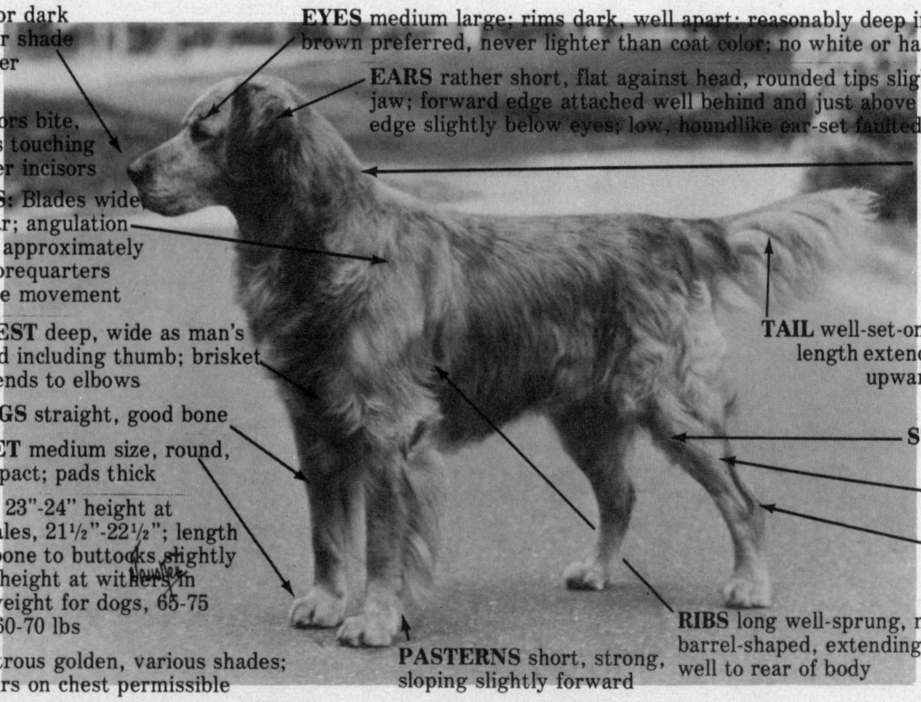

HEAD skull broad; frontal, occipital bones not prominent; good stop; foreface deep, wide, nearly skull length. Muzzle slightly deeper at stop than tip in profile; viewed above, slightly wider at stop than tip. No heaviness in flews

APPEARANCE: Symmetrical, powerful, active, sound; well-put-together; body short-coupled; loin short, muscular, wide, deep, little tuck-up; topline level from withers to croup; croup slopes gently

NOSE black or dark brown (lighter shade in cold weather not serious)

EYES medium large; rims dark, well apart; reasonably deep in sockets; dark brown preferred, never lighter than coat color; no white or haw visible looking ahead

EARS rather short, flat against head, rounded tips slightly below jaw; forward edge attached well behind and just above eyes; rear edge slightly below eyes; low, houndlike ear-set faulted

TEETH scissors bite, lower incisors touching inside of upper incisors

NECK medium long, sloping well back into shoulders; muscular appearance, untrimmed, natural rough; no throatiness

SHOULDERS: Blades wide, long, muscular; angulation with forearm approximately 90 degrees; forequarters capable of free movement

CHEST deep, wide as man's hand including thumb; brisket extends to elbows

TAIL well-set-on; follows natural line of croup; length extends to hock; merry action; some upward curve but never curled over back or between legs

FORELEGS straight, good bone

FEET medium size, round, compact; pads thick

STIFLES well-bent (angulation approx. 90 degrees)

HIND LEGS straight viewed from rear

HOCKS well-let-down

SIZE: Males, 23"-24" height at withers; females, 21½"-22½"; length from breast bone to buttocks slightly greater than height at withers in ratio 12-11; weight for dogs, 65-75 lbs; bitches, 60-70 lbs

RIBS long well-sprung, not barrel-shaped, extending well to rear of body

PASTERNS short, strong, sloping slightly forward

COLOR: Lustrous golden, various shades; few white hairs on chest permissible

COAT dense, water-repellent, good undercoat; texture not as hard as short-coated dog nor as silky as setter; lies flat, straight or wavy; moderate feathering back of forelegs, heavier feathering front of neck, back of thighs and underside of tail, may be lighter than rest of coat

DISQUALIFICATIONS: Deviation in height of more than one inch from standard either way. Undershot or overshot bite (this condition not to be confused with misalignment of teeth). Trichiasis (abnormal position or direction of eyelashes)

GAIT when trotting, free, smooth, powerful, well-coordinated; viewed from front or rear, legs turn neither in nor out, nor do feet cross or interfere with each other; increased speed causes feet to converge toward center line of gravity

STANDARD

GENERAL APPEARANCE AND SIZE — General appearance, a long, low, heavy-looking dog, of a very thoughtful expression, betokening great intelligence. Should have the appearance of great power. Sedate in all movements, but not clumsy. Weight of dogs averaging between 55 and 65 pounds; bitches from 35 to 50 pounds.

HEAD—Head large and massive in all its dimensions; round above eyes, flat on top, with a furrow running from between the eyes upon the center. A marked stop and large occipital protuberance. Jaw long, broad and deep. Lips of upper jaw overhung. Muzzle not square, but at the same time powerful-looking. Nostrils large, open and flesh-colored, sometimes cherry-colored. *Eyes*—Eyes large, soft, deep-set and showing haw. Hazel in color, not too pale, with dignified and intelligent expression. *Ears*—Ears long and broad at the top, turned over on the front edge; vine-shaped: close to the head; set on low and feathered only on the front edge, and there but slightly. Hair short and silky, without the slightest approach to wave or curl.

NECK AND SHOULDERS — Neck long, thick and powerful, free from dewlap, with a large ruff. Shoulders immensely strong and muscular, giving a heavy appearance in front.

BODY—Long, low and well ribbed up. The chest is wide and deep, the back long, broad, and level, with very slight arch over the loin. *Legs and Feet*—Forelegs short, straight, and very heavy in bone; elbows close. Hind legs only slightly less heavily boned than the forelegs. They are moderately angulated, with hocks well let down. Quarters well developed and muscular. No feather above the hocks, but thick hair on the back of the legs just above the feet. Feet large, compact, and well filled with hair between the toes.

COAT AND FEATHERS — Coat silky and straight, not too long, extremely dense; feather long and abundant. *Color and Markings*—Color, lemon and white, and orange and white. Fewer markings on body the better. Perfection of markings, solid lemon or orange ears, evenly marked head and eyes, muzzle and legs ticked. *Stern*—Stern set on a level and carried low.

SCALE OF POINTS

General appearance and size	10	Body and quarters	20
Head	15	Legs and feet	10
Eyes	5	Coat and feather	10
Ears	10	Color and marking	5
Neck and shoulders	15	Total	100

Approved February 6, 1960

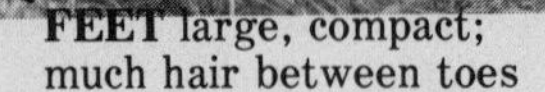
HEAD large, massive, round above eyes; flat on top; furrow between eyes
EARS long, front edge turned over; broad at top; vine-shaped; close to head; set low; slightly feathered
BODY long, low, well-ribbed-up; long in coupling
EYES large, soft, deep-set, showing haw; hazel; expressive
NECK long, thick, powerful; ruff large; no dewlap
SHOULDERS strong, muscular, giving front heavy appearance
STOP marked; occipital protuberance large
BACK long, broad, straight; no droop or bow
NOSTRILS large, open, flesh-colored (or cherry)
LOIN powerful, not too arched
JAW long, broad, deep
TAIL-SET on level, carried low
LIPS full, upper overhung
MUZZLE powerful, not square
QUARTERS shapely, muscular; neither drooping nor stilty
CHEST deep, large
FORELEGS short, straight, heavy bone; in at elbows
HINDLEGS heavy in bone but not as great as forelegs; no feather above hocks; hair thick above foot on back of leg
FEET large, compact; much hair between toes

LENGTH 2½ times height at shoulder

WEIGHT 55-65 lbs. males; 35-50 lbs. females

COLORS: Lemon and white; orange and white; fewer markings the better; solid lemon or orange ears; evenly marked head, eyes; muzzle, legs ticked

COAT silky, straight, not too long, dense; feather long, abundant

SPANIEL [COCKER] BLACK STANDARD

SPANIEL [COCKER] ASCOB STANDARD

SPANIEL [COCKER] PARTI-COLOR STANDARD

GENERAL APPEARANCE — The Cocker Spaniel is the smallest member of the Sporting Group. He has a sturdy, compact body and a cleanly chiseled and refined head, with the over-all dog in complete balance and of ideal size. He stands well up at the shoulder on straight forelegs with a topline sloping slightly toward strong, muscular quarters. He is a dog capable of considerable speed, combined with great endurance. Above all he must be free and merry, sound, well balanced throughout, and in action show a keen inclination to work; equable in temperament with no suggestion of timidity.

HEAD — To attain a well-proportioned head, which must be in balance with the rest of the dog, it embodies the following:

Skull — Rounded but not exaggerated with no tendency toward flatness; the eyebrows are clearly defined with a pronounced stop. The bony structure beneath the eyes is well chiseled with no prominence in the cheeks.

Muzzle — Broad and deep, with square, even jaws. The upper lip is full and of sufficient depth to cover the lower jaw. To be in correct balance, the distance from the stop to the tip of the nose is one half the distance from the stop up over the crown to the base of the skull.

Teeth — Strong and sound, not too small, and meet in a scissors bite.

Nose — Of sufficient size to balance the muzzle and foreface, with well-developed nostrils typical of a sporting dog. It is black in color in the blacks and black and tans. In other colors it may be brown, liver or black, the darker the better. The color of the nose harmonizes with the color of the eye rim.

Eyes — Eyeballs are round and full and look directly forward. The shape of the eye rims gives a slightly almond-shaped appearance; the eye is not weak or goggled. The color of the iris is dark brown and in general the darker the better. The expression is intelligent, alert, soft and appealing.

Ears — Lobular, long, of fine leather, well feathered, and placed no higher than a line to the lower part of the eye.

NECK AND SHOULDERS — The neck is sufficiently long to allow the nose to reach the ground easily, muscular and free from pendulous "throatiness." It rises strongly from the shoulders and arches slightly as it tapers to join the head. The shoulders are well laid back forming an angle with the upper arm of approximately 90 degrees which permits the dog to move his forelegs in an easy manner with considerable forward reach. Shoulders are clean-cut and sloping without protrusion and so set that the upper points of the withers are at an angle which permits a wide spring of rib.

BODY — The body is short, compact and firmly knit together, giving an impression of strength. The distance from the highest point of the shoulder blades to the ground is fifteen (15%) per cent or approximately two inches more than the length from this point to the set-on of the tail. Back is strong and sloping evenly and slightly downward from the shoulders to the set-on of the docked tail. Hips are wide and quarters well rounded and muscular. The chest is deep, its lowest point no higher than the elbows, its front sufficiently wide for adequate heart and lung space, yet not so wide as to interfere with the straightforward movement of the forelegs. Ribs are deep and well sprung. The Cocker Spaniel never appears long and low.

TAIL — The docked tail is set on and carried on a line with the topline of the back, or slightly higher; never straight up like a terrier and never so low as to indicate timidity. When the dog is in motion the tail action is merry.

LEGS AND FEET — Forelegs are parallel, straight, strongly boned and muscular and set close to the body well under the scapulae. When viewed from the side with the forelegs vertical, the elbow is directly below the highest point of the shoulder blade. The pasterns are short and strong. The hind legs are strongly boned and muscled with good angulation at the stifle and powerful, clearly defined thighs. The stifle joint is strong and there is no slippage of it in motion or when standing. The hocks are strong, well let down, and when viewed from behind, the hind legs are parallel when in motion and at rest.

Feet — Compact, large, round and firm with horny pads; they turn neither in nor out. Dewclaws on hind legs and forelegs may be removed.

COAT — On the head, short and fine; on the body, medium length, with enough undercoating to give protection. The ears, chest, abdomen and legs are well feathered, but not so excessively as to hide the Cocker Spaniel's true lines and movement or affect his appearance and function as a sporting dog. The *texture* is most important. The coat is silky, flat or slightly wavy, and of a texture which permits easy care. Excessive or curly or cottony textured coat is to be penalized.

COLOR AND MARKINGS — *Black Variety* is jet black; shadings of brown or liver in the sheen of the coat is not desirable. A small

[continued on page 64]

Example of a Black Cocker Spaniel

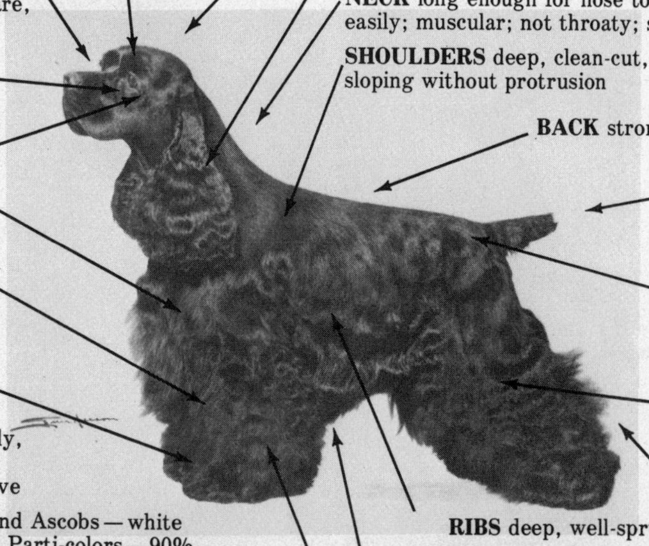

EYES round, full, almond-shaped appearance. Color of iris is dark brown, in general the darker the better

STOP, eyebrows clearly defined; pronounced stop

BODY short, compact; short in coupling and flank; depth at flank less than at last rib

NOSE size to balance muzzle, foreface; black for Blacks, B/Ts; black, brown, liver for other varieties, dark color preferred; well-developed nostrils

TEETH sound, scissors bite

SKULL well-developed, somewhat rounded; no tendency toward flatness; forehead smooth; bone surrounding eye socket well-chiseled

EARS lobular, set on line no higher than lower part of eye; leather fine

MUZZLE broad, deep; jaws square, even; distance from tip of nose to stop approx. one-half from stop to base of skull; upper lip should cover lower jaw

NECK long enough for nose to reach ground easily; muscular; not throaty; slight arch

SHOULDERS deep, clean-cut, sloping without protrusion

CHEEKS smooth, clean-cut; no fullness under eyes

BACK strong, sloping evenly from withers

CHEST deep, lowest point no higher than elbows; not so wide as to interfere with movement

TAIL set on line with topline

FORELEGS straight, muscular, strongly boned; set close to body under shoulder blades

HIPS wide; quarters well-rounded, muscular

FEET compact, turning neither in nor out, round, firm; pads horny

HIND LEGS strongly boned; muscular; stifles well-turned; powerful clearly defined thighs

COAT short, fine on head; on body, flat, slightly wavy, silky, medium length; feathering not too excessive

RIBS deep, well-sprung

ELBOWS well-let-down; turning neither in nor out

HOCKS strong, well-let-down, turning neither in nor out

PASTERNS short, strong

DISQUALIFICATIONS: Blacks and Ascobs — white markings except on chest, throat. Parti-colors — 90% or more of primary color; secondary color or colors limited solely to one location; B/Ts — tan markings in excess of 10%; absence of tan markings in any of the specified locations; white markings except on chest, throat. The markings not readily visible in the ring. Height — males over 15½"; females over 14½

SPANIEL [FIELD] STANDARD

HEAD — Should be quite characteristic of this grand sporting dog, as that of the Bulldog, or the Bloodhound; its very stamp and countenance should at once convey the conviction of high breeding, character and nobility; skull well developed, with a distinctly elevated occipital tuberosity, which, above all, gives the character alluded to; not too wide across the muzzle, long and lean, never snipy or squarely cut, and in profile curving gradually from nose to throat; lean beneath the eyes — a thickness here gives coarseness to the whole head. The great length of muzzle gives surface for the free development of the olfactory nerve, and thus secures the highest possible scenting powers. *Eyes* — Not too full, but not small, receding or overhung, color dark hazel or brown, or nearly black, according to the color of the dog. Grave in expression and showing no haw. *Ears* — Moderately long and wide, sufficiently clad with nice Setter-like feather and set low. They should fall in graceful folds, the lower parts curling inwards and backwards. *Neck* — Long, strong and muscular, so as to enable the dog to retrieve his game without undue fatigue.

BODY — Should be of moderate length, well ribbed up to a good strong loin, straight or slightly arched, never slack. *Nose* — Well developed, with good open nostrils. *Shoulders and Chest* — Former long, sloping and well set back, thus giving great activity and speed; latter deep and well developed, but not too round and wide.

BACK AND LOIN — Very strong and muscular. *Hindquarters* — Strong and muscular. The stifles should be moderately bent, and not twisted either in or out. *Stern* — Well set on and carried low, if possible below the level of the back, in a straight line or with a slight downward inclination, never elevated above the back, and in action always kept low, nicely fringed with wavy feather of silky texture. *Forelegs* — Should be of fairly good length, with straight, clean, flat bone, and nicely feathered. Immense bone is no longer desirable. *Feet* — Not too small; round, with short soft hair between the toes; good, strong pads.

COAT — Flat or slightly waved, and never curled. Sufficiently dense to resist the weather, and not too short. Silky in texture, glossy and refined in nature, with neither duffleness on the one hand, nor curl or wiriness on the other. On the chest, under belly and behind the legs, there should be abundant feather, but never too much, especially below the hocks, and that of the right sort, *viz.*, setterlike. The hindquarters should be similarly adorned.

COLOR — Black, liver, golden liver, mahogany red, or roan; or any one of these colors with tan over the eyes and on the cheeks, feet, and pasterns. Other colors, such as black and white, liver and white, red or orange and white, while not disqualifying, will be considered less desirable since the Field Spaniel should be clearly distinguished from the Springer Spaniel.

HEIGHT — About 18 inches to shoulder. *Weight* — From about 35 pounds to 50 pounds.

GENERAL APPEARANCE — That of a well-balanced, noble, upstanding sporting dog; built for activity and endurance. A grand combination of beauty and utility, and bespeaking of unusual docility and instinct.

SCALE OF POINTS

Head and jaw	15	Feet	10
Eyes	5	Stern	10
Ears	5	Coat and feather	10
Neck	5	General appearance	10
Body	10		
Forelegs	10		
Hind legs	10	Total	100

Approved July 14, 1959

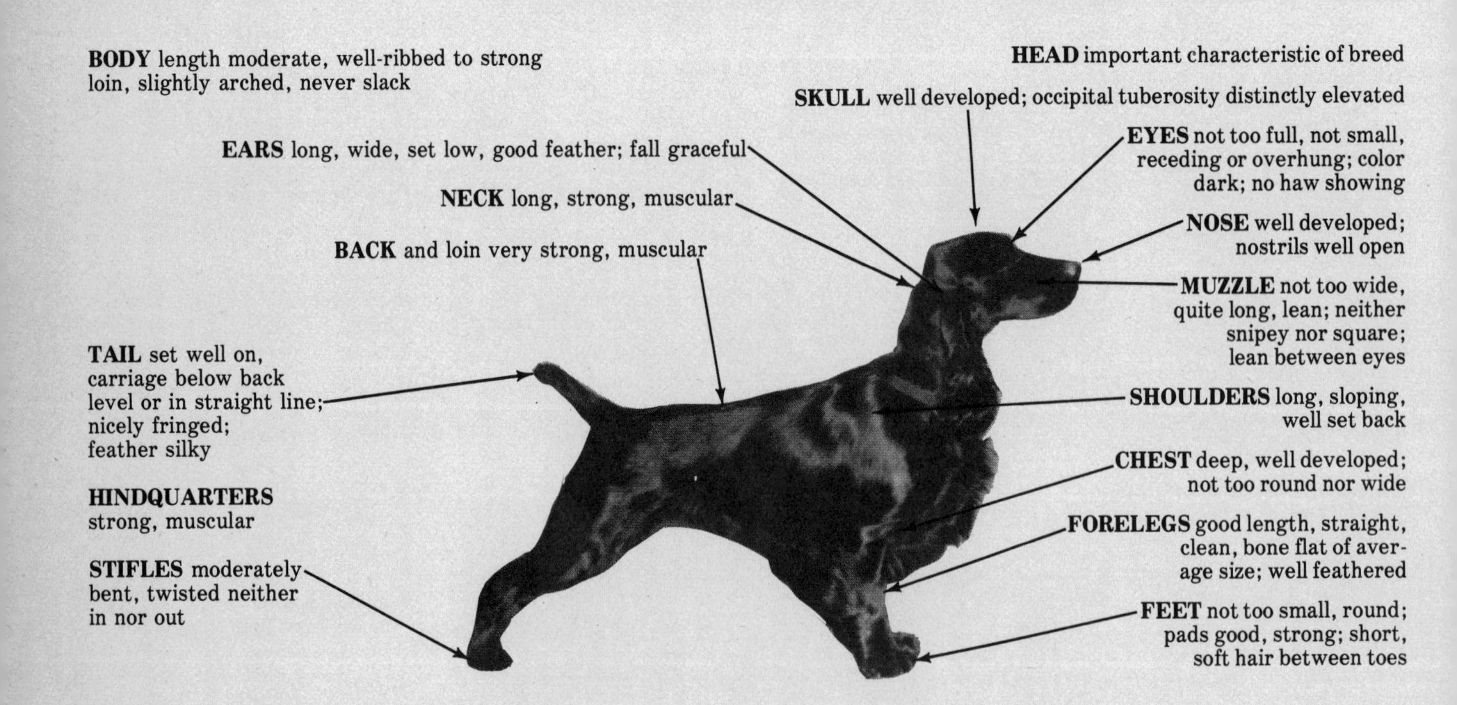

BODY length moderate, well-ribbed to strong loin, slightly arched, never slack
HEAD important characteristic of breed
SKULL well developed; occipital tuberosity distinctly elevated
EARS long, wide, set low, good feather; fall graceful
EYES not too full, not small, receding or overhung; color dark; no haw showing
NECK long, strong, muscular
NOSE well developed; nostrils well open
BACK and loin very strong, muscular
MUZZLE not too wide, quite long, lean; neither snipey nor square; lean between eyes
TAIL set well on, carriage below back level or in straight line; nicely fringed; feather silky
SHOULDERS long, sloping, well set back
HINDQUARTERS strong, muscular
CHEST deep, well developed; not too round nor wide
FORELEGS good length, straight, clean, bone flat of average size; well feathered
STIFLES moderately bent, twisted neither in nor out
FEET not too small, round; pads good, strong; short, soft hair between toes

COLOR: Black or recessive from black (liver, golden liver, mahogany, black and tan, roan, etc.) more desirable than Partis

HEIGHT 18" at shoulder

WEIGHT 35-50 lbs.

COAT flat or slightly curled, dense, not too short, silky, refined; profuse feathering on chest, belly, behind legs; not too much below hocks (Setter-like)

HEAD — The skull should be moderately long and also wide, with an indentation in the middle and a full stop, brows fairly heavy; occiput full, but not pointed, the whole giving an appearance of heaviness without dullness. *Eyes* — Hazel color, fairly large, soft and languishing, not showing the haw overmuch. *Nose* — The muzzle should be about three inches long, square, and the lips somewhat pendulous. The nostrils well developed and liver color. *Ears:* Thick, fairly large and lobe shaped; set moderately low, but relatively not so low as in the black Field Spaniel; carried close to the head and furnished with soft, wavy hair.

NECK — Is rather short, strong and slightly arched, but not carrying the head much above the level of the back. There should not be much throatiness about the skin, but well-marked frill in the coat. *Chest and Shoulders* — The chest is round, especially behind the shoulders, deep and wide giving a good girth. The shoulders should be oblique.

BACK AND BACK RIB — The back and loin is long and should be very muscular, both in width and depth; for this development the back ribs must be deep. The whole body is characterized as low, long and level. *Legs and Feet* — The arms and thighs must be bony as well as muscular, knees and hocks large and strong; pasterns very short and bony, feet large and round, and with short hair between the toes. The legs should be very short and strong, with great bone, and may show a slight bend in the forearm, and be moderately well feathered. The hind legs should not appear to be shorter than the forelegs, nor be too much bent at the hocks. They should be well feathered above the hocks but should not have much hair below that point. The hind legs are short from the hock to the ground, and wide apart. *Tail* — Should be docked from 5 to 7 inches, set low, and not carried above the level of the back, thickly covered with moderately long feather.

COAT — Body coat abundant, flat or slightly waved, with no tendency to curl, moderately well feathered on legs and stern, but clean below the hocks.

COLOR — Rich golden liver; this is a certain sign of the purity of the breed, dark liver or puce denoting unmistakably a recent cross with the black or other variety of Field Spaniel.

GENERAL APPEARANCE — Rather massive and muscular, but with free movements and nice tail action, denoting a cheerful and tractable disposition. Weight from 35 pounds to 45 pounds.

POSITIVE POINTS

Head	10	Legs and feet	10
Eyes	5	Tail	5
Nose	5	Coat	5
Ears	10	Color	15
Neck	5	General appearance	15
Chest and shoulders	5		
Back and back ribs	10	Total	100

NEGATIVE POINTS

Light eyes	5
Narrow head	10
Weak muzzle	10
Curled ears or set on high	5
Curled coat	15
Carriage of stern	5
Topknot	10
White on chest	5
Color, too light or too dark	15
Legginess or light of bone	5
Shortness of body or flat sided	5
General appearance—sour or crouching	10
Total	100

Approved July 14, 1959

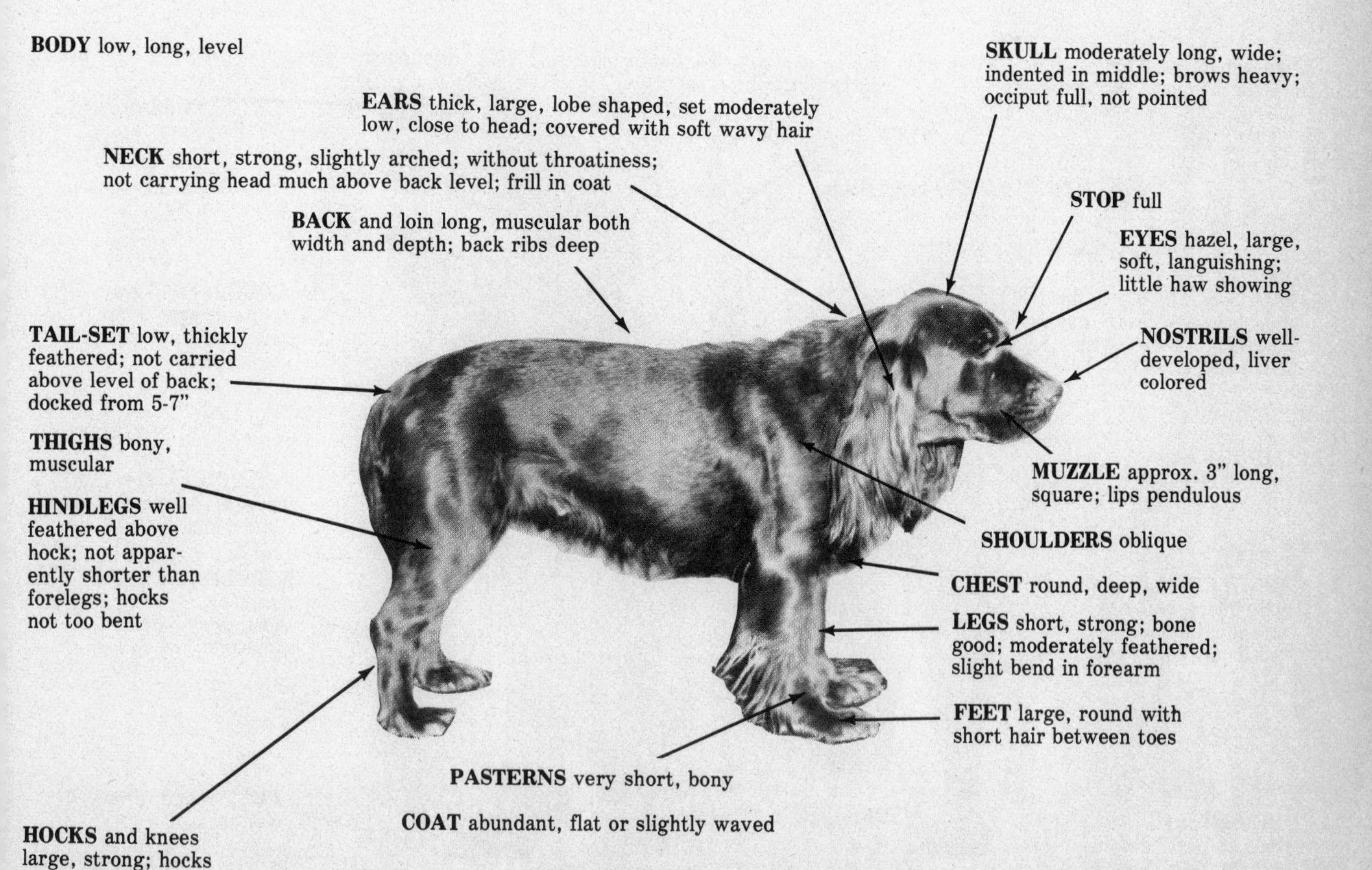
BODY low, long, level
SKULL moderately long, wide; indented in middle; brows heavy; occiput full, not pointed
EARS thick, large, lobe shaped, set moderately low, close to head; covered with soft wavy hair
NECK short, strong, slightly arched; without throatiness; not carrying head much above back level; frill in coat
STOP full
BACK and loin long, muscular both width and depth; back ribs deep
EYES hazel, large, soft, languishing; little haw showing
TAIL-SET low, thickly feathered; not carried above level of back; docked from 5-7"
NOSTRILS well-developed, liver colored
THIGHS bony, muscular
MUZZLE approx. 3" long, square; lips pendulous
HINDLEGS well feathered above hock; not apparently shorter than forelegs; hocks not too bent
SHOULDERS oblique
CHEST round, deep, wide
LEGS short, strong; bone good; moderately feathered; slight bend in forearm
FEET large, round with short hair between toes
PASTERNS very short, bony
COAT abundant, flat or slightly waved
HOCKS and knees large, strong; hocks wide apart; below hocks no feather
WEIGHT: 35-45 lbs.
COLOR: Rich golden liver

WIREHAIRED POINTING GRIFFON STANDARD

THE WIREHAIRED GRIFFON is a dog of medium size, fairly short-backed, rather a little low on his legs. He is strongly limbed, everything about him indicating strength and vigor. His coat is harsh like the bristles of a wild boar and his appearance, notwithstanding his short coat, is as unkempt as that of the long-haired Griffon, but on the other hand he has a very intelligent air.

HEAD — Long, furnished with a harsh coat, forming a mustache and eyebrows, skull long and narrow, muzzle square. *Eyes* — Large, open, full of expression, iris yellow or light brown. *Ears* — Of medium size, flat or sometimes slightly curled, set rather high, very lightly furnished with hair. *Nose* — Always brown.

NECK — Rather long, no dewlap. *Shoulders* — Long, sloping. *Ribs* — Slightly rounded.

FORELEGS — Very straight, muscular, furnished with rather short wire hair.

HIND LEGS — Furnished with rather short stiff hair, the thighs long and well developed. *Feet* — Round, firm and well formed. *Tail* — Carried straight or gaily, furnished with a hard coat without plume, generally cut to a third of its length.

COAT — Hard, dry, stiff, never curly, the undercoat downy. *Color* — Steel gray with chestnut splashes, grey white with chestnut splashes, chestnut, dirty white mixed with chestnut, never black.

HEIGHT — 21½ to 23½ inches for males, and 19½ to 21½ inches for females.

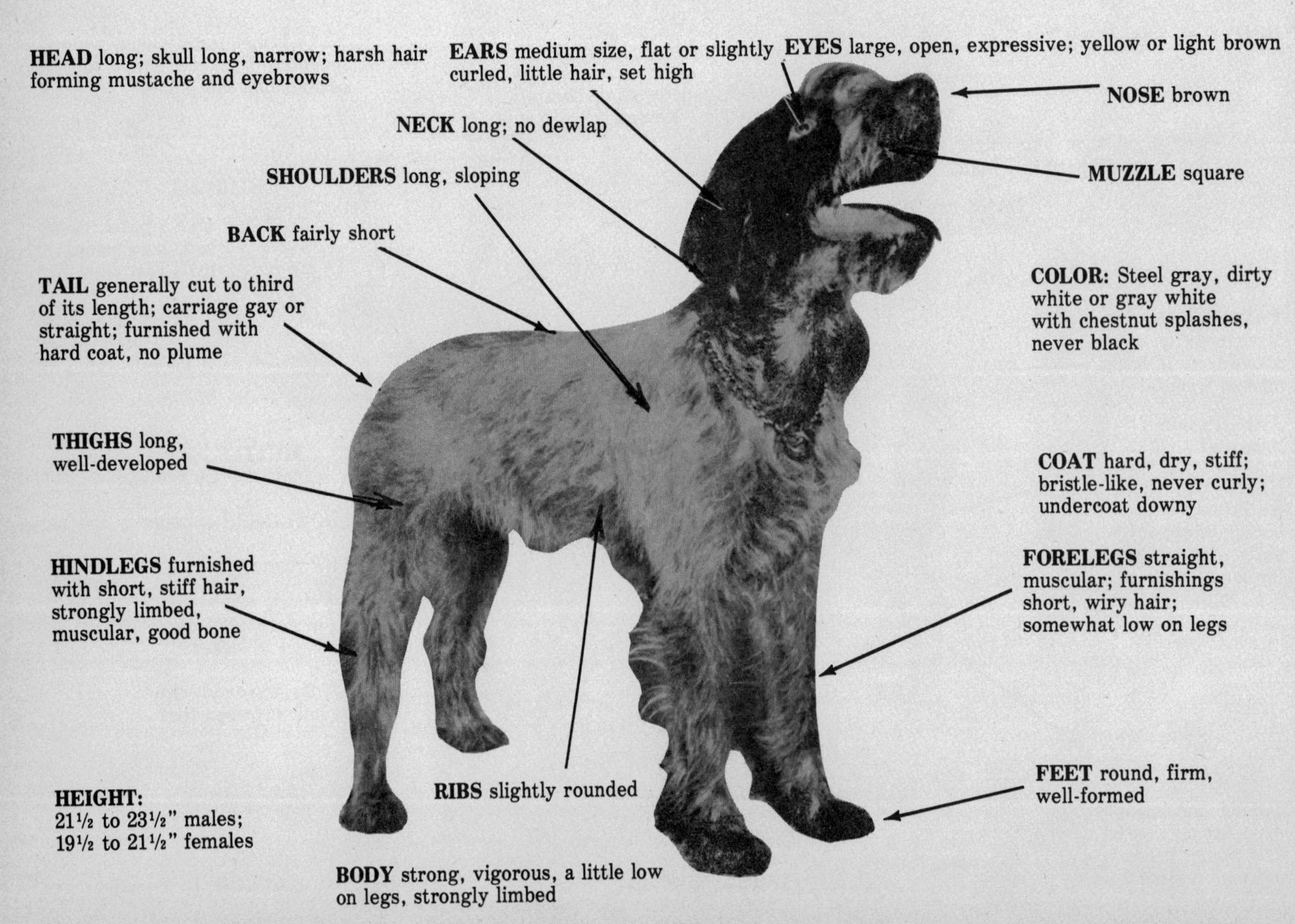
HEAD long; skull long, narrow; harsh hair forming mustache and eyebrows
EARS medium size, flat or slightly curled, little hair, set high
EYES large, open, expressive; yellow or light brown
NOSE brown
NECK long; no dewlap
MUZZLE square
SHOULDERS long, sloping
BACK fairly short
TAIL generally cut to third of its length; carriage gay or straight; furnished with hard coat, no plume
COLOR: Steel gray, dirty white or gray white with chestnut splashes, never black
THIGHS long, well-developed
COAT hard, dry, stiff; bristle-like, never curly; undercoat downy
HINDLEGS furnished with short, stiff hair, strongly limbed, muscular, good bone
FORELEGS straight, muscular; furnishings short, wiry hair; somewhat low on legs
FEET round, firm, well-formed
HEIGHT: 21½ to 23½" males; 19½ to 21½" females
RIBS slightly rounded
BODY strong, vigorous, a little low on legs, strongly limbed

[*Britany Spaniel cont'd. from p. 41*]

Falling pasterns, however, are a serious fault. Leg bones clean, graceful, but not too fine. An extremely heavy bone is as much a fault as spindly legs. One must look for substance and suppleness. Height to the elbows should approximately equal distance from elbow to withers.

HIND LEGS — Stifles well bent. The stifle generally is the term used for knee joint. If the angle made by the upper and lower leg bones is too straight, the dog quite generally lacks drive, since his hind legs cannot drive as far forward at each stride as is desirable. However, the stifle should not be bent as to throw the hock joint far out behind the dog. Since factors not easily seen by the eye may give the dog his proper drive, a Brittany should not be condemned for straight stifle until the judge has checked the dog in motion from the side. When at a trot, the Brittany's hind foot should step into or beyond the print left by the front foot. The stifle joint should not turn out making a cowhock. (The cowhock moves the foot out to the side, thus driving out of line, and losing reach at each stride.) Thighs well feathered, but not profusely, halfway to the hock. Hocks, that is, the back pasterns, should be moderately short, pointing neither in nor out; perpendicular when viewed from the side. They should be firm when shaken by the judge. *Feet*—Should be strong, proportionately smaller than other spaniels, with close-fitting, well-arched toes and thick pads. The Brittany is not "up on his toes." Toes not heavily feathered. Flat feet, splayed feet, paper feet, etc., are to be heavily penalized. An ideal foot is half way between the hare- and cat-foot.

A GUIDE TO THE JUDGE — The points below indicate only relative values. To be also taken into consideration are type, gait, soundness, spirit, optimum height, body length and general proportion.

SCALE OF POINTS

Head	25
Body	35
Running gear	40
Total	100

DISQUALIFICATIONS

Any Brittany Spaniel measuring under 17½ inches or over 20½ inches. Any black in the coat or a nose so dark in color as to appear black. A tail substantially more than 4 inches in length.

Approved September 13, 1966

[*Gordon Setter cont'd. from p. 35*]

on the chest; (5) On the inside of the hind legs showing down the front of the stifle and broadening out to the outside of the hind legs from the hock to the toes. It must not completely eliminate the black on the back of the hind legs; (6) On the forelegs from the carpus, or a little above, downward to the toes; (7) Around the vent; (8) A white spot on the chest is allowed, but the smaller the better. Predominantly tan, red or buff dogs which do not have the typical pattern of markings of a Gordon Setter are ineligible for showing and undesirable for breeding.

SCALE OF POINTS

While not a part of the official breed standard, may be helpful in placing proper emphasis upon qualities desired in the physical makeup of the breed.

Head and neck [incl. ears and eyes]	10	**Color and markings**	5
Body	15	**Temperament**	10
Shoulders, forelegs, forefeet	10	**Size, general appearance**	15
Hind legs and feet	10	**Gait**	12
Tail	5	**Total**	100
Coat	8		

DISQUALIFICATION

Predominantly tan, red, or buff dogs which do not have the typical pattern of markings of a Gordon Setter.

Approved November 13, 1962

[*German Shorthair cont'd. from p. 54*]

long as possible, standing away somewhat from the trunk so that the straight and closely muscled legs, when viewed from in front, should appear to be parallel. Elbows which stand away from the body or are pressed right into same indicate toes turning inwards or outwards, which should be regarded as faults. Pasterns should be strong, short and nearly vertical. *Feet* — Should be compact, close-knit and round to spoon-shaped. The toes sufficiently arched and heavily nailed. The pad should be strong and hard.

COAT AND SKIN — The skin should look close and tight. The hair should be short and thick and feel tough and hard to the hand; it is somewhat longer on the underside of the tail and the back edge of the haunches. It is softer, thinner and shorter on the ears and the head.

TAIL — Is set high and firm, and must be docked, leaving approximately two-fifths of length. The tail hangs down when the dog is quiet, is held horizontally when he is walking, never turned over the back or considerably bent but violently wagged when he is on the search.

BONES — Thin and fine bones are by no means desirable in a dog which should be able to work over any and every country and should possess strength. The main importance accordingly is laid not so much on the size as being in proper proportion to the body. Dogs with coarse bones are handicapped in agility of movement and speed.

DESIRABLE WEIGHT AND HEIGHT — Dogs—55 to 70 pounds. Bitches—45 to 60 pounds. Dogs—23 to 25 inches. Bitches—21 to 23 inches at the shoulders.

COLOR — Solid liver, liver and white spotted, liver and white spotted and ticked, liver and white ticked, liver roan. Any colors other than liver and white (gray white) are not not permitted.

SYMMETRY AND FIELD QUALITY are most essential. A dog well balanced in all points is preferable to one with outstanding good qualities and defects. A smooth, lithe gait is most desirable.

FAULTS — Bone structure too clumsy or too light, head too large, too many wrinkles in forehead, dish-faced, snipy muzzle, ears too long, pointy or fleshy, flesh-colored nose, eyes too light, too round or too closely set together, excessive throatiness, cowhocks, feet or elbows turned inward or outward, down on pasterns, loose shoulders, sway-back, black coat or tri-colored, any colors except liver or some combination of liver and white.

Approved May 7, 1946

[*English Springer cont'd. from p. 45*]

prominent, nor bold and hard in expression. Set rather well apart and fairly deep in their sockets. The color of the iris to harmonize with the color of the coat, preferably a good dark hazel in the liver dogs and black or deep brown in the black and white specimens. The expression to be alert, kindly, trusting. The lids, tight with little or no haw showing. To be penalized: Eyes yellow or brassy in color or noticeably lighter than the coat. Sharp expression indicating unfriendly or suspicious nature. Loose droopy lids. Prominent haw (the third eyelid or membrane in the inside corner of the eye).

EARS — The correct ear set is on a level with the line of the eye; on the side of the skull and not too far back. The flaps to be long and fairly wide, hanging close to the cheeks, with no tendency to stand up or out. The leather, thin, approximately long enough to reach the tip of the nose. To be penalized: Short round ears. Ears set too high or too low or too far back on the head.

NECK — The neck to be moderately long, muscular, slightly arched at the crest gradually blending into sloping shoulders. Not noticeably upright nor coming into the body at an abrupt angle. To be penalized: Short neck, often the sequence to steep shoulders. Concave neck, sometimes called ewe neck or upside down neck (the opposite of arched). Excessive throatiness.

BODY — The body to be well coupled, strong, compact; the chest deep but not so wide or round as to interfere with the action of the front legs; the brisket sufficiently developed to reach to the level of the elbows. The ribs fairly long, springing gradually to the middle of the body then tapering as they approach the end of the ribbed section. The back (section between the withers and loin) to be straight and strong, with no tendency to dip or roach. The loins to be strong, short; a slight arch over loins and hip bones. Hips nicely rounded, blending smoothly into hind legs.

The resulting topline slopes *very gently* from withers to tail — the line from withers to back descending without a sharp drop; the back practically level; arch over hips somewhat lower than the withers; croup sloping gently to base of tail; tail carried to follow the natural line of the body. The bottom line, starting on a level with the elbows, to continue backward with almost no up-curve until reaching the end of the ribbed section, then a more noticeable up-curve to the flank, but not enough to make the dog appear small-waisted or "tucked up." To be penalized: Body too shallow, indicating lack of brisket. Ribs too flat sometimes due to immaturity. Ribs too round (barrel-shaped), hampering the gait. Sway-back (dip in back), indicating weakness or lack of muscular development, particularly to be seen when dog is in action and viewed from the side. Roach back (too much arch over loin and extending forward into middle section). Croup falling away too sharply; or croup too high — unsightly faults, detrimental to outline and good movement. Topline sloping sharply, indicating steep withers (straight shoulder placement) and a too low tail-set.

TAIL — The Springer's tail is an index both to his temperament and his conformation. Merry tail action is characteristic. The proper set is somewhat low following the natural line of the croup. The carriage should be nearly horizontal, slightly elevated when dog is excited. Carried straight up is untypical of the breed. The tail should not be docked too short and should be well fringed with wavy feather. It is legitimate to shape and shorten the feathering but enough should be left to blend with the dog's other furnishings. To be penalized: Tail habitually upright. Tail set too high or too low. Clamped down tail (indicating timidity or undependable temperament, even less to be desired than the tail carried too gaily).

FOREQUARTERS — Efficient movement in front calls for proper shoulders. The blades sloping back to form an angle with the forearm of approximately 90 degrees which permits the dog to swing his forelegs forward in an easy manner. Shoulders (fairly close together at the tips) to lie flat and mold smoothly into the contour of the body. The forelegs to be straight with the same degree of size to the foot. The bone, strong, slightly flattened, not too heavy or round. The knee, straight, almost flat; the pasterns short, strong; elbows close to the body with free action from the shoulders. To be penalized: Shoulders set at a steep angle limiting the stride. Loaded shoulders (the blades standing out from the body by overdevelopment of the muscles). Loose elbows, crooked legs. Bone too light or too coarse and heavy. Weak pasterns that let down the feet at a pronounced angle. *Hindquarters* — The Springer should be shown in hard muscular condition, well developed in hips and thighs and the whole rear assembly should suggest strength and driving power. The hip joints to be set rather wide apart and the hips nicely rounded. The thighs broad and muscular; the stifle joint strong and moderately bent. The hock joint somewhat rounded, not small and sharp in contour, and moderately angulated. Leg from hock joint to foot pad, short and strong with good bone structure. When viewed from the rear the hocks to be parallel whether the dog is standing or in motion. To be penalized: Too little or too much angulation. Narrow, undeveloped thighs. Hocks too short or too long (a proportion of 1/3 the distance from hip joint to foot is ideal). Flabby muscles. Weakness of joints. *Feet* — The feet to be round, or slightly oval, compact, well arched, medium size with thick pads, well feathered between the toes. Excess hair to be removed to show the natural shape and size of the foot. To be penalized: Thin, open or splayed feet (flat with spreading toes). Hare foot (long, rather narrow foot).

MOVEMENT — In judging the Springer there should be emphasis on proper movement which is the final test of a dog's conformation and soundness. Prerequisite to good movement is balance of the front and rear assemblies. The two must match in angulation and muscular development if the gait is to be smooth and effortless. Good shoulders laid back at an angle that permits a long stride are just as essential as the excellent rear quarters that provide the driving power. When viewed from the front the dog's legs should appear to swing forward in a free and easy manner, with no tendency for the feet to cross over or interfere with each other. Viewed from the rear the hocks should drive well under the body following on a line with the forelegs, the rear legs parallel, neither too widely nor too closely spaced. Seen from the side the Springer should exhibit a good, long forward stride, without high-stepping or wasted motion. To be penalized: Short choppy stride, mincing steps with up and down movement, hopping. Moving with forefeet wide, giving roll or swing to body. Weaving or crossing of fore or hind feet. Cowhocks — hocks turning in toward each other.

In judging the English Springer Spaniel the over-all picture is a primary consideration. It is urged that the judge look for type which includes general appearance, outline and temperament and also for soundness especially as seen when the dog is in motion. Inasmuch as the dog with a smooth easy gait must be reasonably sound and well-balanced he is to be highly regarded in the showring, however, not to the extent of forgiving him for not looking like an English Springer Spaniel. A quite untypical dog, leggy, foreign in head and expression, may move well. But he should not be placed over a good all-round specimen that has a minor fault in movement. It should be remembered that the English Springer Spaniel is first and foremost a sporting dog of the spaniel family and he must look and behave and move in character.

Approved June 12, 1956

[Cocker Spaniel cont'd. from p. 59]

amount of white on the chest and throat is to be penalized, and white in any other location shall disqualify.

Any Solid Color Other than Black shall be a uniform shade. Lighter coloring of the feathering is permissible. A small amount of white on the chest and throat is to be penalized, and white in any other location shall disqualify.

Black and Tans, shown under the Variety of Any Solid Color Other than Black, have definite tan markings on a jet black body. The tan markings are distinct and plainly visible and the color of the tan may be from the lightest cream to the darkest red color. The amount of tan markings is restricted to ten (10%) per cent or less of the color of the specimen; tan markings in excess of ten (10%) per cent shall disqualify. Tan markings which are not readily visible in the ring or the absence of tan markings in any of the specified locations shall disqualify. The markings shall be located as follows:

(1) A clear spot over each eye. (2) On the sides of the muzzle and on the cheeks. (3) On the undersides of the ears. (4) On all feet and legs. (5) Under the tail. (6) On the chest, optional, presence or absence not penalized.

Tan on the muzzle which extends upward, over and joins, shall be penalized. A small amount of white on the chest and throat is to be penalized, and white in any other location shall disqualify.

Parti-Color Variety — Two or more definite colors appearing in clearly defined markings, distinctly distributed over the body, are essential. Primary color which is ninety (90%) per cent or more shall disqualify; secondary color or colors which are limited solely to one location shall disqualify. Roans are classified as Parti-colors and may be of any of the usual roaning patterns. Tricolors are any of the above colors combined with tan markings. It is preferable that the tan markings be located in the same pattern as for Black and Tans.

MOVEMENT — The Cocker Spaniel, though the smallest of the sporting dogs, possesses a typical sporting dog gait. Prerequisite to good movement is balance between the front and rear assemblies. He drives with his strong, powerful rear quarters and is properly constructed in the shoulders and forelegs so that he can reach forward without constriction in a full stride to counterbalance the driving force from the rear. Above all, his gait is coordinated, smooth and effortless. The dog must cover ground with his action and excessive animation should never be mistaken for proper gait.

HEIGHT — The ideal height at the withers for an adult dog is 15 inches and for an adult bitch 14 inches. Height may vary one-half inch above or below this ideal. A dog whose height exceeds 15½ inches or a bitch whose height exceeds 14½ inches shall be disqualified. An adult dog whose height is less than 14½ inches or an adult bitch whose height is less than 13½ inches shall be penalized.

Note: Height is determined by a line perpendicular to the ground from the top of the shoulder blades, the dog standing naturally with its forelegs and the lower hind legs parallel to the line of measurement.

DISQUALIFICATIONS

Color and Markings — *Blacks — White markings except on chest and throat.*

Solid Colors Other Than Black — White markings except on chest and throat.

Black and Tans — Tan markings in excess of ten (10%) per cent; tan markings not readily visible in the ring, or the absence of tan markings in any of the specified locations; white markings except on chest and throat.

Parti-Colors — Ninety (90%) per cent or more of primary color; secondary color or colors limited solely to one location.

Height — *Males over 15½ inches; females over 14½ inches.*

GROUP 2

HOUNDS

AFGHAN HOUND STANDARD

GENERAL APPEARANCE — The Afghan Hound is an aristocrat, his whole appearance one of dignity and aloofness with no trace of plainness or coarseness. He has a straight front, proudly carried head, eyes gazing into the distance as if in memory of ages past. The striking characteristics of the breed — exotic, or "eastern," expression, long silky topknot, peculiar coat pattern, very prominent hip bones, large feet, and the impression of a somewhat exaggerated bend in the stifle due to profuse trouserings — stand out clearly, giving the Afghan Hound the appearance of what he is, a king of dogs, that has held true to tradition throughout the ages.

HEAD — The head is of good length, showing much refinement, the skull evenly balanced with the foreface. There is a slight prominence of the nasal bone structure causing a slightly Roman appearance, the center line running up over the foreface with little or no stop, falling away in front of the eyes so there is an absolutely clear outlook with no interference; the underjaw showing great strength, the jaws long and punishing; the mouth level, meaning that the teeth from the upper jaw and lower jaw match evenly, neither overshot nor undershot. This is a difficult mouth to breed. A scissors bite is even more punishing and can be more easily bred into a dog than a level mouth, and a dog having a scissors bite, where the lower teeth slip inside and rest against the teeth of the upper jaw, should not be penalized. The occipital bone is very prominent. The head is surmounted by a topknot of long silky hair.

EARS — The ears are long, set approximately on level with outer corners of the eyes, the leather of the ear reaching nearly to the end of the dog's nose, and covered with long silky hair. *Eyes* — The eyes are almond-shaped (almost triangular), never full or bulgy, and are dark in color. *Nose* — Nose is of good size, black in color. *Faults:* Coarseness; snipiness; overshot or undershot; eyes round or bulgy or light in color; exaggerated Roman nose; head not surmounted with topknot.

NECK — The neck is of good length, strong and arched, running in a curve to the shoulders which are long and sloping and well laid back. *Faults:* Neck too short or too thick; a ewe neck; a goose neck; a neck lacking in substance.

BODY — The black line appearing practically level from the shoulders to the loin. Strong and powerful loin and slightly arched, falling away toward the stern, with the hipbones very pronounced; well ribbed and tucked up in flanks. The height at the shoulders equals the distance from the chest to the buttocks; the brisket well let down, and of medium width. *Faults:* Roach back, sway-back, goose rump, slack loin; lack of prominence of hipbones; too much width of brisket causing interference with elbows. *Tail* — Tail set not too high on the body, having a ring, or a curve on the end; should never be curled over, or rest on the back, or be carried sideways; and should never be bushy.

LEGS — Forelegs are straight and strong with great length between elbow and pastern; elbows well held in; forefeet large in both length and width; toes well arched; feet covered with long thick hair; fine in texture; pasterns long and straight; pads of feet unusually large and well down on the ground. Shoulders have plenty of angulation so that the legs are well set underneath the dog. Too much straightness of shoulder causes the dog to break down in the pasterns, and this is a serious fault. All four feet of the Afghan Hound are in line with the body, turning neither in nor out. The hind feet are broad and of good length; the toes arched, and covered with long thick hair; hindquarters powerful and well muscled with great length between hip and hock; hocks are well let down; good angulation of both stifle and hock; slightly bowed from hock to crotch. *Faults:* Front or back feet thrown outward or inward; pads of feet not thick enough; or feet too small; or any other evidence of weakness in feet; weak or broken down pasterns; too straight in stifle; too long in hock.

COAT — Hindquarters, flanks, ribs, forequarters, and legs well covered with thick, silky hair, very fine in texture; ears and all four feet well feathered; from in front of the shoulders, and also backwards from the shoulders along the saddle from the flanks

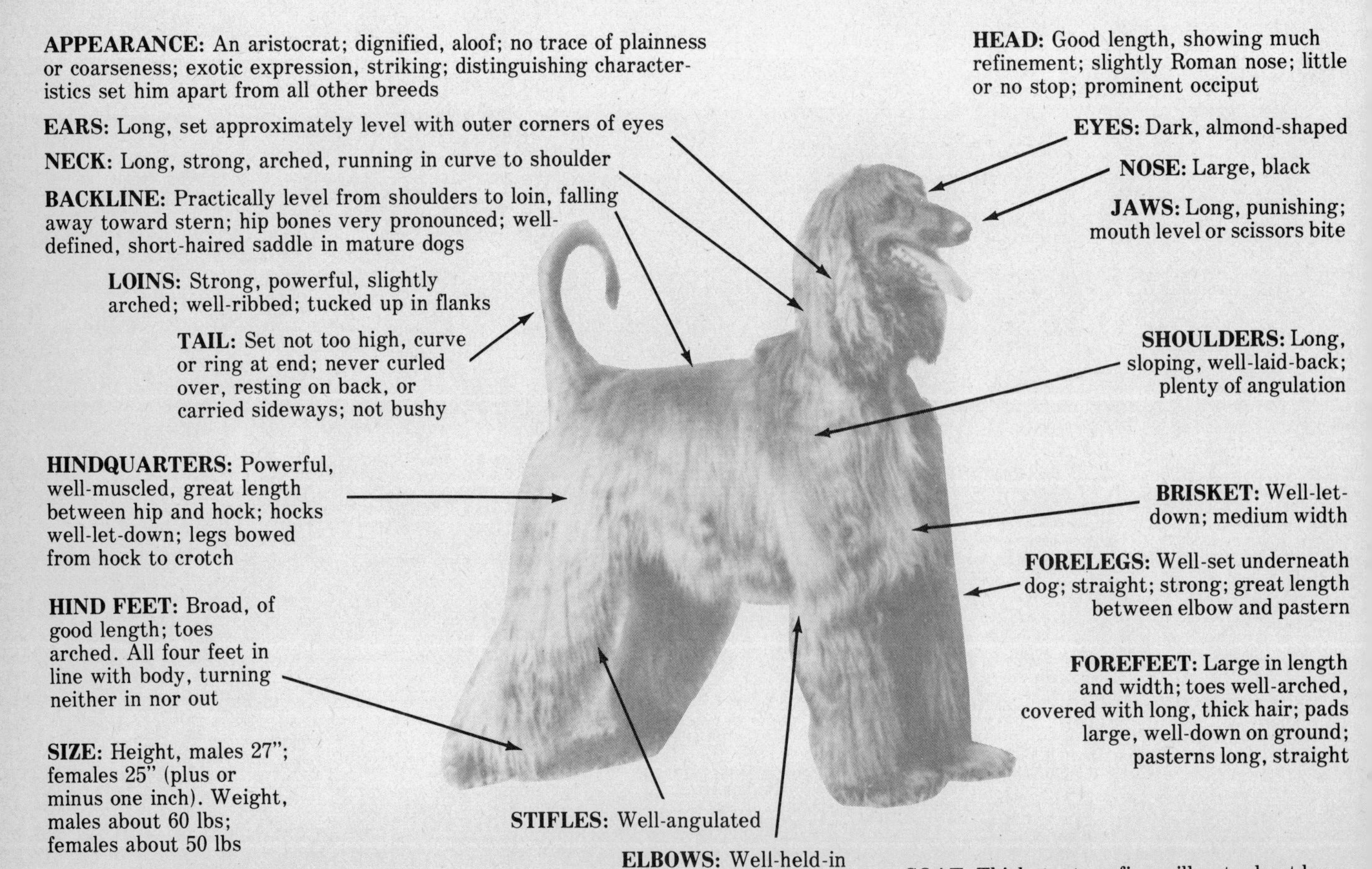

APPEARANCE: An aristocrat; dignified, aloof; no trace of plainness or coarseness; exotic expression, striking; distinguishing characteristics set him apart from all other breeds
EARS: Long, set approximately level with outer corners of eyes
NECK: Long, strong, arched, running in curve to shoulder
BACKLINE: Practically level from shoulders to loin, falling away toward stern; hip bones very pronounced; well-defined, short-haired saddle in mature dogs
LOINS: Strong, powerful, slightly arched; well-ribbed; tucked up in flanks
TAIL: Set not too high, curve or ring at end; never curled over, resting on back, or carried sideways; not bushy
HINDQUARTERS: Powerful, well-muscled, great length between hip and hock; hocks well-let-down; legs bowed from hock to crotch
HIND FEET: Broad, of good length; toes arched. All four feet in line with body, turning neither in nor out
SIZE: Height, males 27"; females 25" (plus or minus one inch). Weight, males about 60 lbs; females about 50 lbs
COLORS: All colors permissible, solid or in combinations
STIFLES: Well-angulated
ELBOWS: Well-held-in
HEAD: Good length, showing much refinement; slightly Roman nose; little or no stop; prominent occiput
EYES: Dark, almond-shaped
NOSE: Large, black
JAWS: Long, punishing; mouth level or scissors bite
SHOULDERS: Long, sloping, well-laid-back; plenty of angulation
BRISKET: Well-let-down; medium width
FORELEGS: Well-set underneath dog; straight; strong; great length between elbow and pastern
FOREFEET: Large in length and width; toes well-arched, covered with long, thick hair; pads large, well-down on ground; pasterns long, straight
COAT: Thick, texture fine, silky; topknot long; ears and feet well-feathered; back smooth, hair short, close; never clipped or trimmed

and the ribs upwards, the hair is short and close, forming a smooth back in mature dogs — this is a traditional characteristic of the Afghan Hound. The Afghan Hound should be shown in its natural state; the coat is not clipped or trimmed; the head is surmounted (in the full sense of the word) with a topknot of long, silky hair — that is also an outstanding characteristic of the Afghan Hound. Showing of short hair on cuffs on either front or back legs is permissible. *Fault:* Lack of shorthaired saddle in mature dogs.

HEIGHT — Dogs, 27 inches, plus or minus one inch; bitches, 25 inches, plus or minus one inch. *Weight* — Dogs, about 60 pounds; bitches, about 50 pounds.

COLOR — All colors are permissible, but color or color combinations are pleasing; white markings, especially on the head, are undesirable.

GAIT — When running free, the Afghan Hound moves at a gallop, showing great elasticity and spring in his smooth, powerful stride. When on a loose lead, the Afghan can trot at a fast pace; stepping along, he has the appearance of placing the hind feet directly in the foot prints of the front feet, both thrown straight ahead. Moving with head and tail high, the whole appearance of the Afghan Hound is one of great style and beauty.

TEMPERAMENT — Aloof and dignified, yet gay. *Faults:* Sharpness or shyness.

Approved September 14, 1948

BASENJI STANDARD

CHARACTERISTICS — The Basenji should not bark, but is not mute. The wrinkled forehead and the swift, tireless gait (resembling a racehorse trotting full out) are typical of the breed.

GENERAL APPEARANCE — The Basenji is a small, lightly built, short backed dog, giving the impression of being high on the leg compared to its length. The wrinkled head must be proudly carried, and the whole demeanor should be one of poise and alertness.

HEAD AND SKULL — The skull is flat, well chiseled and of medium width, tapering towards the eyes. The foreface should taper from eye to muzzle and should be shorter than the skull. Muzzle, neither coarse, nor snipy but with rounded cushions. Wrinkles should appear upon the forehead, and be fine and profuse. Side wrinkles are desirable, but should never be exaggerated into dewlap. *Nose* — Black greatly desired. A pinkish tinge should not penalize an otherwise first class specimen, but it should be discouraged in breeding. *Eyes* — Dark hazel, almond shaped, obliquely set and far seeing.

EARS — Small, pointed and erect, of fine texture, set well forward on top of head.

MOUTH — Teeth must be level with scissors bite.

NECK — Of good length, well crested and slightly full at base of throat. It should be well set into flat, laid back shoulders. *Forequarters* — The chest should be deep and of medium width. The legs straight with clean fine bone, long forearm and well defined sinews. Pasterns should be of good length, straight and flexible.

BODY — The body should be short and the back level. The ribs well sprung, with plenty of heart room, deep brisket, short coupled, and ending in a definite waist. *Hindquarters* — Should be strong and muscular, with hocks well let down, turned neither in nor out, with long second thighs. *Feet* — Small, narrow and compact, with well arched toes. *Tail* — Should be set on top and curled tightly over to either side.

COAT — Short and silky. Skin very pliant. *Color* — Chestnut red (the deeper the better) or pure black, or black and tan, all with white feet, chest and tail tip. White legs, white blaze and white collar optional.

WEIGHT — Bitches 22 pounds approximately. Dogs 24 pounds approximately.

SIZE — Bitches 16 inches and dogs 17 inches from the ground to the top of the shoulder. Bitches 16 inches and dog 17 inches from the front of the chest to the farthest point of the hindquarters. *Faults:* Coarse skull or muzzle. Domed or peaked skull. Dewlap. Round eyes. Low set ears. Overshot or undershot mouths. Wide chest. Wide behind. Heavy bone. Creams, shaded or off colors, other than those defined above, should be heavily penalized.

Approved June 8, 1954

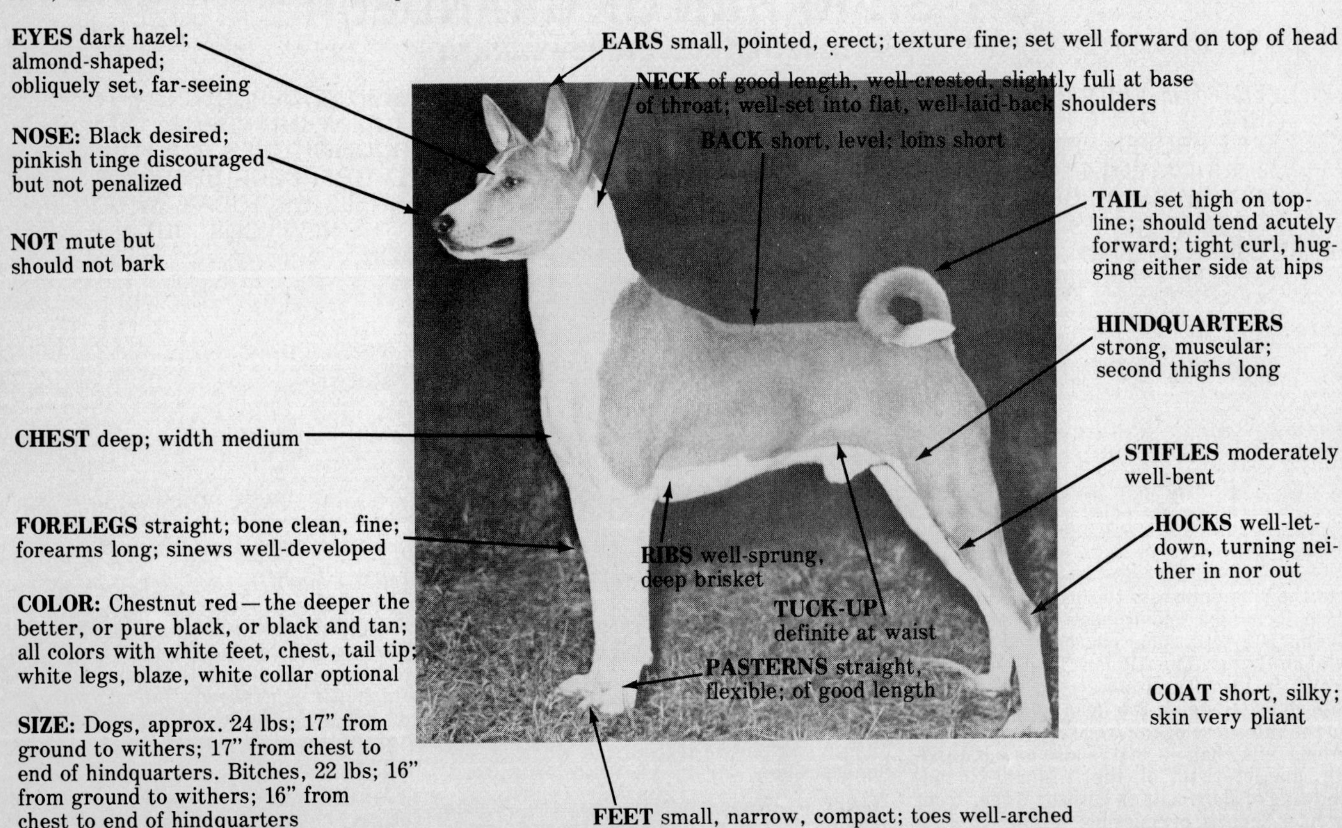
HEAD: Carried proudly; skull flat, well-chiseled; width medium, tapering toward eyes; foreface tapers from eye to muzzle, shorter than skull; muzzle neither coarse nor snipy; cushions rounded; wrinkles on forehead fine, profuse; side wrinkles desirable; no dewlap; teeth level, with scissors bite
APPEARANCE: Body short, small, short-coupled; lightly built; high on leg compared to length; gait swift; tireless
EYES dark hazel; almond-shaped; obliquely set, far-seeing
EARS small, pointed, erect; texture fine; set well forward on top of head
NECK of good length, well-crested, slightly full at base of throat; well-set into flat, well-laid-back shoulders
BACK short, level; loins short
NOSE: Black desired; pinkish tinge discouraged but not penalized
NOT mute but should not bark
TAIL set high on topline; should tend acutely forward; tight curl, hugging either side at hips
HINDQUARTERS strong, muscular; second thighs long
CHEST deep; width medium
STIFLES moderately well-bent
FORELEGS straight; bone clean, fine; forearms long; sinews well-developed
RIBS well-sprung, deep brisket
HOCKS well-let-down, turning neither in nor out
TUCK-UP definite at waist
COLOR: Chestnut red — the deeper the better, or pure black, or black and tan; all colors with white feet, chest, tail tip; white legs, blaze, white collar optional
PASTERNS straight, flexible; of good length
COAT short, silky; skin very pliant
SIZE: Dogs, approx. 24 lbs; 17" from ground to withers; 17" from chest to end of hindquarters. Bitches, 22 lbs; 16" from ground to withers; 16" from chest to end of hindquarters
FEET small, narrow, compact; toes well-arched

CH. REVEILLE BE SIRIUS

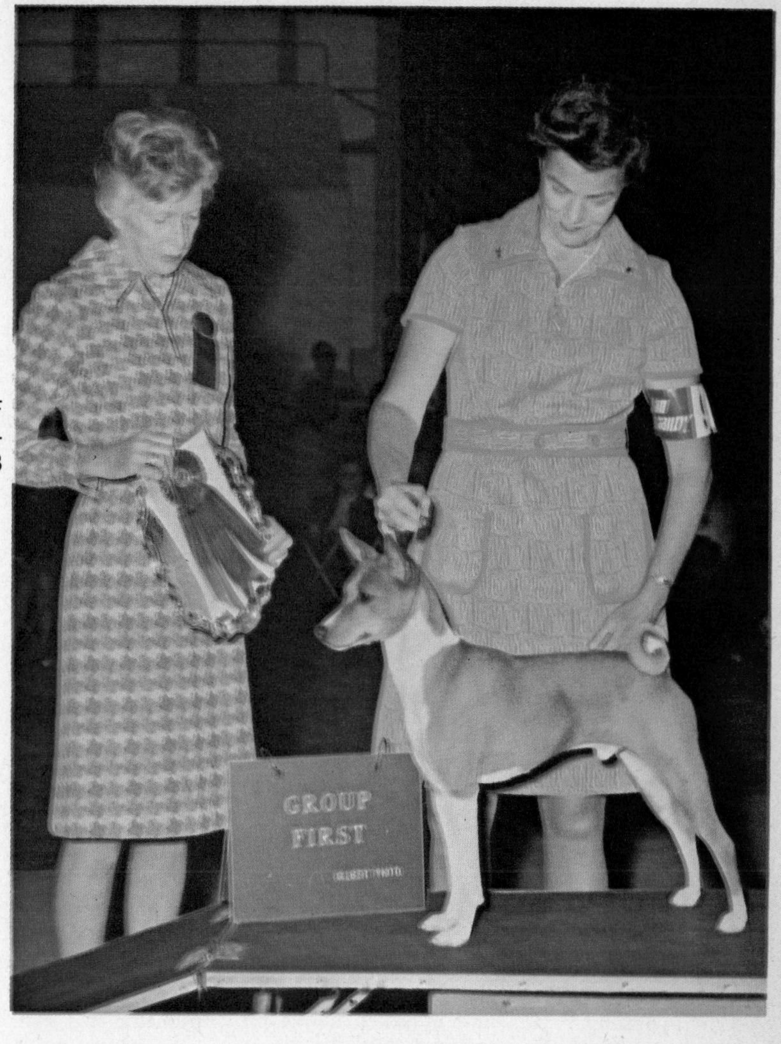

40 GROUP FIRSTS. 5 BESTS IN SHOW. BEST OF BREED — BASENJI CLUB OF AMERICA, EASTERN SPECIALTY. 1974 — TOP TEN HOUNDS. 1973 & '74 — TOP WINNING BASENJI.

OWNER
MRS. JAMES H. SYMINGTON
RT 4, BOX 4
LEESBURG, VA. 22075

HANDLER
DAMARA BOLTE
RT 4, BOX 130
LEESBURG, VA. 22075

Dogs resembling Basenjis, not only in appearance but in favored postures, were depicted by the ancient Egyptians. Their presumed descendants persisted, to this day, in East Africa where they are said to have been used to assist in hunting. Since the late 1800's examples have been brought to Britain and more recently to the U.S., particularly from the areas now known as Sudan and Zaire, but until the 1930's none survived to breed. They were apparently highly susceptible to European dog diseases, especially distemper. The breed is now well established in both Britain and the U.S., where they are favored as pets and companions but are rarely used for hunting. Straightforward in appearance, Basenjis have several unique characteristics. They cannot bark but instead yodel. They wash themselves much in the fashion of a cat and they posture in charming ways when playing or seeking to play. The coat is short and silky, the skin pliant. Deep chestnut red, black, or black and tan, all with white feet, chest, and tail tip are the desired colors. Some 2,400 are registered annually in the U.S., the breed ranking 46th. Though Basenjis rank 18th in number in show competition and 2nd in the Hound Group, they do not do their share of winning. They tied for 9th place in 1972 for Hound Groups wins.

BASSET HOUND STANDARD

GENERAL APPEARANCE — The Basset Hound possesses in marked degree those characteristics which equip it admirably to follow a trail over and through difficult terrain. It is a short-legged dog, heavier in bone, size considered, than any other breed of dog, and while its movement is deliberate, it is in no sense clumsy. In temperament it is mild, never sharp or timid. It is capable of great endurance in the field and is extreme in its devotion.

HEAD — The head is large and well proportioned. Its length from occiput to muzzle is greater than the width at the brow. In overall appearance the head is of medium width. *The skull* is well domed, showing a pronounced occipital protuberance. A broad flat skull is a fault. The length from nose to stop is approximately the length from stop to occiput. The sides are flat and free from cheek bumps. Viewed in profile the top lines of the muzzle and skull are straight and lie in parallel planes, with a moderately defined stop. The skin over the whole of the head is loose, falling in distinct wrinkles over the brow when the head is lowered. A dry head and tight skin are faults. *The muzzle* is deep, heavy, and free from snipiness. *The nose* is darkly pigmented, preferably black, with large wide-open nostrils. A deep liver-colored nose conforming to the coloring of the head is permissible but not desirable. *The teeth* are large, sound, and regular, meeting in either a scissors or an even bite. A bite either overshot or undershot is a serious fault. *The lips* are darkly pigmented and are pendulous, falling squarely in front and, toward the back, in loose hanging flews. *The dewlap* is very pronounced. *The neck* is powerful, of good length, and well arched. *The eyes* are soft, sad and slightly sunken, showing a prominent haw, and in color are brown, dark brown preferred. A somewhat lighter-colored eye conforming to the general coloring of the dog is acceptable but not desirable. Very light or protruding eyes are faults. *The ears* are extremely long, low set, and when drawn forward, fold well over the end of the nose. They are velvety in texture, hanging in loose folds with the ends curling slightly inward. They are set far back on the head at the base of the skull and, in repose, appear to be set on the neck. A high set or flat ear is a serious fault.

FOREQUARTERS — *The chest* is deep and full with prominent sternum showing clearly in front of the legs. *The shoulders* and elbows are set close against the sides of the chest. The distance from the deepest point of the chest to the ground, while it must be adequate to allow free movement when working in the field, is not to be more than one-third the total height at the withers of an adult Basset. The shoulders are well laid back and powerful. Steepness in shoulder, fiddle fronts, and elbows that are out, are serious faults. *The forelegs* are short, powerful, heavy in bone, with wrinkled skin. Knuckling over of the front legs is a disqualification. *The paw* is massive, very heavy with tough heavy pads, well rounded and with both feet inclined equally a trifle outward, balancing the width of the shoulders. Feet down at the pastern are a serious fault. *The toes* are neither pinched together nor splayed, with the weight of the forepart of the body borne evenly on each. The dewclaws may be removed.

BODY — The rib structure is long, smooth, and extends well back. The ribs are well sprung, allowing adequate room for heart and lungs. Flat-sidedness and flanged ribs are faults. The topline is straight, level, and free from any tendency to sag or roach, which are faults.

HINDQUARTERS The hindquarters are very full and well rounded, and are approximately equal to the shoulders in width. They must not appear slack or light in relation to the over-all depth of the body. The dog stands firmly on its hind legs showing a well-let-down stifle with no tendency toward a crouching stance. Viewed from behind, the hind legs are parallel, with the hocks turning neither in nor out. Cowhocks or bowed legs are serious faults. The hind feet point straight ahead. Steep, poorly angulated hindquarters are a serious fault. The dewclaws, if any, may be removed.

TAIL — The tail is not to be docked, and is set in continuation of the spine with but slight curvature, and carried gaily in hound fashion. The hair on the underside of the tail is coarse.

SIZE — The height should not exceed 14 inches. Height over 15 inches at the highest point of the shoulder blades is a disqualification.

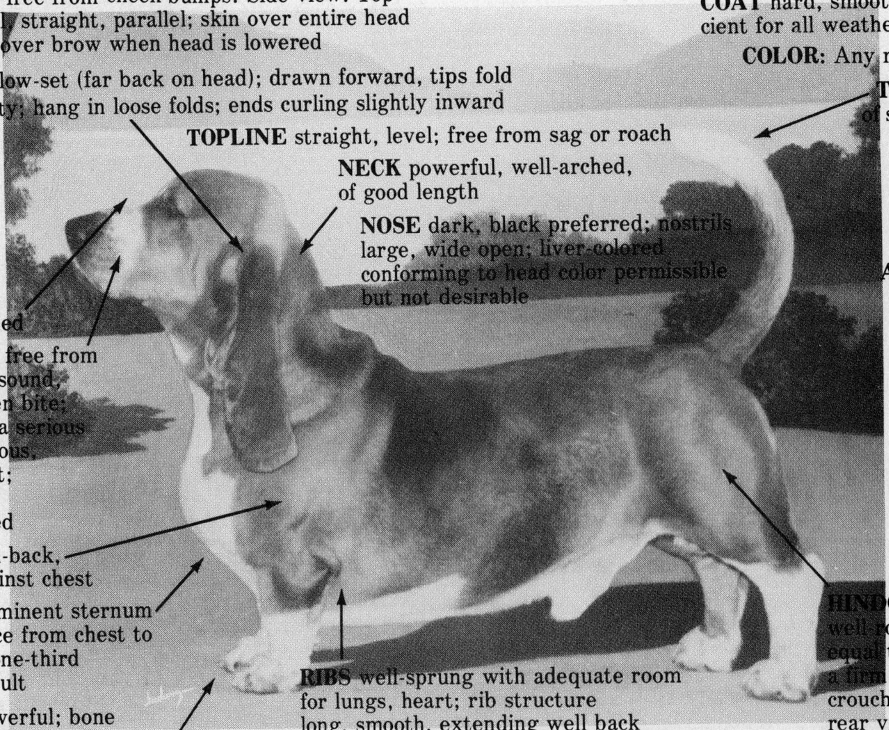

GAIT — The Basset Hound moves in a smooth, powerful, and effortless manner. Being a scenting dog with short legs, it holds its nose low to the ground. Its gait is absolutely true with perfect coordination between the front and hind legs, and it moves in a straight line with hind feet following in line with the front feet, the hocks well bent with no stiffness of action. The front legs do not paddle, weave, or overlap, and the

HEAD: Medium width, large, well-proportioned; length from occiput to muzzle greater than width at brow; skull well-domed; pronounced occipital protuberance; length of nose to stop approx. from stop to occiput; skull sides flat, free from cheek bumps. Side view: Top lines of muzzle and skull, straight, parallel; skin over entire head loose, distinct wrinkles over brow when head is lowered
EARS extremely long, low-set (far back on head); drawn forward, tips fold over end of nose; velvety; hang in loose folds; ends curling slightly inward
EYES slightly sunken, haw prominent; dark brown preferred (lighter, according to coat acceptable); light or protruding eyes, faults
STOP moderately defined
MUZZLE deep, heavy, free from snipiness; teeth large, sound, regular, scissors or even bite; overshot or undershot a serious fault; lips dark, pendulous, falling squarely in front; loose, hanging flews; dewlap very pronounced
SHOULDERS well-laid-back, powerful; set close against chest
CHEST deep, full; prominent sternum in front of legs; distance from chest to ground not to exceed one-third height at withers of adult
FORELEGS short, powerful; bone heavy; skin wrinkled; elbows set close against sides of chest
PAWS massive, very heavy; pads tough, heavy, well-rounded; feet inclinded trifle outward; (down on pasterns, a serious fault); toes, neither pinched nor splayed; dewclaws may be removed
RIBS well-sprung with adequate room for lungs, heart; rib structure long, smooth, extending well back
TOPLINE straight, level; free from sag or roach
NECK powerful, well-arched, of good length
NOSE dark, black preferred; nostrils large, wide open; liver-colored conforming to head color permissible but not desirable
DISQUALIFICATIONS: Height of more than 15" at highest point of shoulder blades; knuckled-over front legs; distinctly long coat
COAT hard, smooth, short; density sufficient for all weather; skin loose, elastic
COLOR: Any recognized hound color
TAIL set in continuation of spine; not to be docked; carriage slight curvature, gay; hair on underside coarse
APPEARANCE: Short-legged, very heavy-boned; movement deliberate but not clumsy; of great endurance; temperament mild, devoted
SIZE: Desired height not to exceed 14"
HINDQUARTERS very full, well-rounded; approx. equal to shoulder width; a firm stance, no crouching; high legs straight; rear view, parallel; stifle, well-let-down; hocks turning neither in nor out; hind feet point straight ahead; dewclaws may be removed

elbows must lie close to the body. Going away, the hind legs are parallel.

COAT — The coat is hard, smooth, and short, with sufficient density to be of use in all weather. The skin is loose and elastic. A distinctly long coat is a disqualification.

COLOR — Any recognized hound color is acceptable and the distribution of color and markings is of no importance.

DISQUALIFICATIONS

Height of more than 15 inches at the highest point of the shoulder blades. Knuckled over front legs. Distinctly long coat.

Approved January 14, 1964

HEAD — The skull should be fairly long, slightly domed at occiput, with cranium broad and full. *Ears* — Ears set on moderately low, long, reaching when drawn out nearly, if not quite, to the end of the nose; fine in texture, fairly broad — with almost entire absence of erectile power — setting close to the head, with the forward edge slightly inturning to the cheek — rounded at tip. *Eyes* — Eyes large, set well apart — soft and houndlike — expression gentle and pleading; of a brown or hazel color. *Muzzle* — Muzzle of medium length — straight and square-cut — the stop moderately defined. *Jaws* — Level. Lips free from flews; nostrils large and open. *Defects:* A very flat skull, narrow across the top; excess of dome, eyes small, sharp and terrierlike, or prominent and protruding; muzzle long, snipy or cut away decidedly below the eyes, or very short. Roman-nosed, or upturned, giving a dish-face expression. Ears short, set on high or with a tendency to rise above the point of origin.

BODY — *Neck and Throat* — Neck rising free and light from the shoulders strong in substance yet not loaded, of medium length. The throat clean and free from folds of skin; a slight wrinkle below the angle of the jaw, however, may be allowable. *Defects:* A thick, short, cloddy neck carried on a line with the top of the shoulders. Throat showing dewlap and folds of skin to a degree termed "throatiness." *Shoulders and Chest* — Shoulders sloping — clean, muscular, not heavy or loaded — conveying the idea of freedom of action with activity and strength. Chest deep and broad, but not broad enough to interfere with the free play of the shoulders. *Defects:* — Straight, upright shoulders. Chest disproportionately wide or with lack of depth. *Back, Loin and Ribs* — Back short, muscular and strong. Loin broad and slightly arched, and the ribs well sprung, giving abundance of lung room. *Defects:* Very long or swayed or roached back. Flat, narrow loin. Flat ribs.

FORELEGS AND FEET — *Forelegs* — Straight, with plenty of bone in proportion to size of the hound. Pasterns short and straight. *Feet* — Close, round and firm. Pad full and hard. *Defects:* Out at elbows. Knees knuckled over forward, or bent backward. Forelegs crooked or Dachshundlike. Feet long, open or spreading.

HIPS, THIGHS, HIND LEGS AND FEET — Hips and thighs strong and well muscled, giving abundance of propelling power. Stifles strong and well let down. Hocks firm, symmetrical and moderately bent. Feet close and firm. *Defects:* Cowhocks, or straight hocks. Lack of muscle and propelling power. Open feet.

TAIL — Set moderately high; carried gaily, but not turned forward over the back; with slight curve; short as compared with size of the hound; with brush. *Defects:* A long tail. Teapot curve or inclined forward from the root. Rat tail with absence of brush.

COAT — A close, hard, hound coat of medium length. *Color* — Any true hound color. *Defects:* A short, thin coat, or a soft quality.

GENERAL APPEARANCE — A miniature Foxhound, solid and big for his inches, with the wear-and-tear look of the hound that can last in the chase and follow his quarry to the death.

SCALE OF POINTS

Head		
Skull	5	
Ears	10	
Eyes	5	
Muzzle	5	25
Body		
Neck	5	
Chest and shoulders	15	
Back, loin and ribs	15	35
Running Gear		
Forelegs	10	
Hips, thighs and hind legs	10	
Feet	10	30
Coat	5	
Stern	5	10
Total		100

VARIETIES — There shall be two varieties. Thirteen Inch — which shall be for hounds not exceeding 13 inches in height. Fifteen Inch — which shall be for hounds over 13 but not exceeding 15 inches in height.

DISQUALIFICATION

Any hound measuring more than 15 inches shall be disqualified.

PACKS OF BEAGLES

Score of Points for Judging

Hounds	
General levelness of pack	40%
Individual merit of hounds	30%
	70%
Manners	20%
Appointments	10%
Total	100%

LEVELNESS OF PACK — The first thing in a pack to be considered is that they present a unified appearance. The hounds

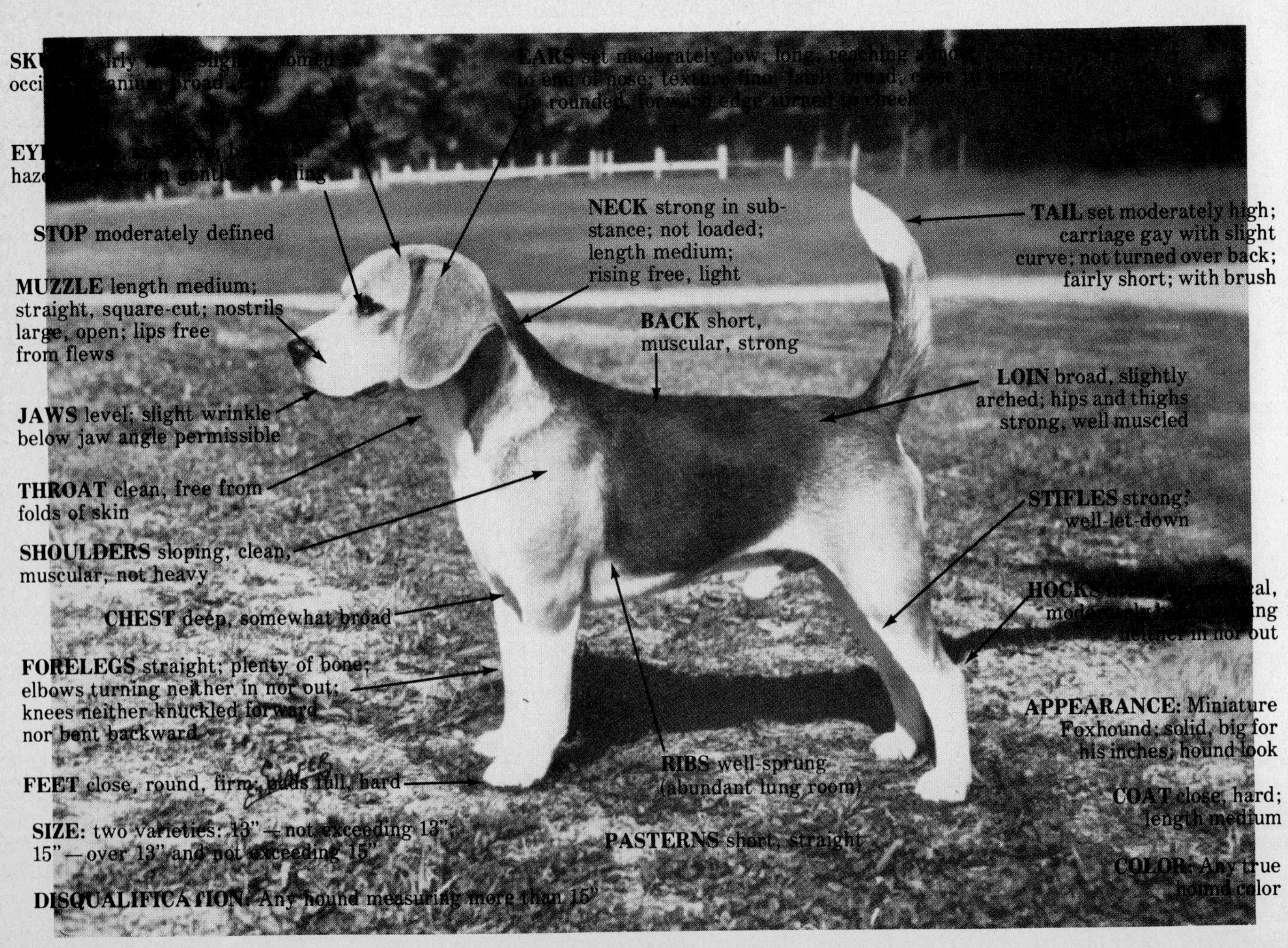

EARS set moderately low; long; reaching almost to end of nose; texture fine; fairly broad; close to head; tip rounded; forward edge turned to cheek

FORELEGS straight; plenty of bone; elbows turning neither in nor out; knees neither knuckled forward nor bent backward

FEET close, round, firm; pads full, hard

SIZE: two varieties: 13" — not exceeding 13"; 15" — over 13" and not exceeding 15"

NECK strong in substance; not loaded; length medium; rising free, light

HOCKS firm, symmetrical, moderately bent; turning neither in nor out

APPEARANCE: Miniature Foxhound; solid, big for his inches; hound look

COAT close, hard; length medium

must be as near to the same height, weight, conformation and color as possible.

INDIVIDUAL MERIT OF THE HOUNDS — Is the individual bench-show quality of the hounds. A very level and sporty pack can be gotten together and not a single hound be a good Beagle. This is to be avoided.

MANNERS — The hounds must all work gaily and cheerfully, with flags up — obeying all commands cheerfully. They should be broken to heel up, kennel up, follow promptly and stand. Cringing, sulking, lying down to be avoided. Also, a pack must not work as though in terror of master and whips. In Beagle packs it is recommended that the whip be used as little as possible.

APPOINTMENTS — Master and whips should be dressed alike, the master or huntsman to carry horn — the whips and master to carry light thong whips. One whip should carry extra couplings on shoulder strap.

RECOMMENDATIONS FOR SHOW LIVERY — Black velvet cap, white stock, green coat, white breeches or knickerbockers, green or black stockings, white spats, black or dark brown shoes. Vest and gloves optional. Ladies should turn out exactly the same except for a white skirt instead of white breeches.

Approved September 10, 1957

BLACK AND TAN COONHOUND STANDARD

THE BLACK AND TAN COONHOUND is first and fundamentally a working dog, capable of withstanding the rigors of winter, the heat of summer, and the difficult terrain over which he is called upon to work. Judges are asked by the club sponsoring the breed to place great emphasis upon these facts when evaluating the merits of the dog. The general impression should be that of power, agility, and alertness. His expression should be alert, friendly, eager, and agressive. He should immediately impress one with his ability to cover the ground with powerful rhythmic strides.

HEAD—The head should be cleanly modeled with medium stop occurring midway between occiput bone and nose. The head should measure from 9 to 10 inches in males and from 8 to 9 inches in females. Viewed from the profile the line of the skull is on a practically parallel plane to the foreface or muzzle. The skin should be devoid of folds or excess dewlap. The flews should be well developed with typical hound appearance. Nostrils well open and always black. Skull should tend toward oval outline. Eyes should be from hazel to dark brown in color, almost round and not deeply set. The ears should be low set and well back. They should hang in graceful folds giving the dog a majestic appearance. In length they should extend well beyond the tip of the nose. Teeth should fit evenly with slightly scissors bite.

BODY — *Neck, Shoulders, and Chest* — The neck should be muscular, sloping, medium length, extending into powerfully constructed shoulders and deep chest. The dog should possess full, round, well-sprung ribs, avoiding flatsidedness. *Back and Tail*—The back should be level, powerful and strong, with a visible slope from withers to rump. Tail should be strong, with base slightly below level of back line, carried free, and when in action at approximately right angle to back.

LEGS AND FEET—The forelegs should be straight, with elbows well let down, turning neither in nor out; pasterns strong and erect. Feet should be catlike with compact, well-arched toes and thick strong pads. *Hindquarters*—Quarters should be well boned and muscled. From hip to hock long and sinewy, hock to pad short and strong. Stifles and hock well bent and not inclining either in or out. When standing on a level surface the hind feet should set back from under the body, and leg from pad to hock be at right angles to the ground when viewed both from profile and the rear. The stride of the Black and Tan Coonhound should be easy and graceful with plenty of reach in front and drive behind.

COAT AND COLOR—The coat should be short but dense to withstand rough going. As the name implies, the color should be coal black, with rich tan markings above eyes, on sides of muzzle, chest, legs and breeching with black pencil markings on toes.

SIZE—Measured at the shoulder: males, 25 to 27 inches; females, 23 to 25 inches. Height should be in proportion to general conformation so that dog appears neither leggy nor close to the ground. Dogs oversized should not be penalized when general soundness and proportion are in favor.

Judges should penalize the following defects: Undersize, elbows out at shoulder, lack of angulation in hindquarters, splay feet, sway or roach-back, flatsidedness, lack of depth in chest, yellow or light eyes, shyness and nervousness. *Fault*—Dewclaws; white on chest or other parts of body is highly undesirable and if it exceeds 1½ inches in diameter should be disqualified.

DISQUALIFICATION

White on chest or other parts of the body if it exceeds 1½ inches in diameter.

Approved July 10, 1945

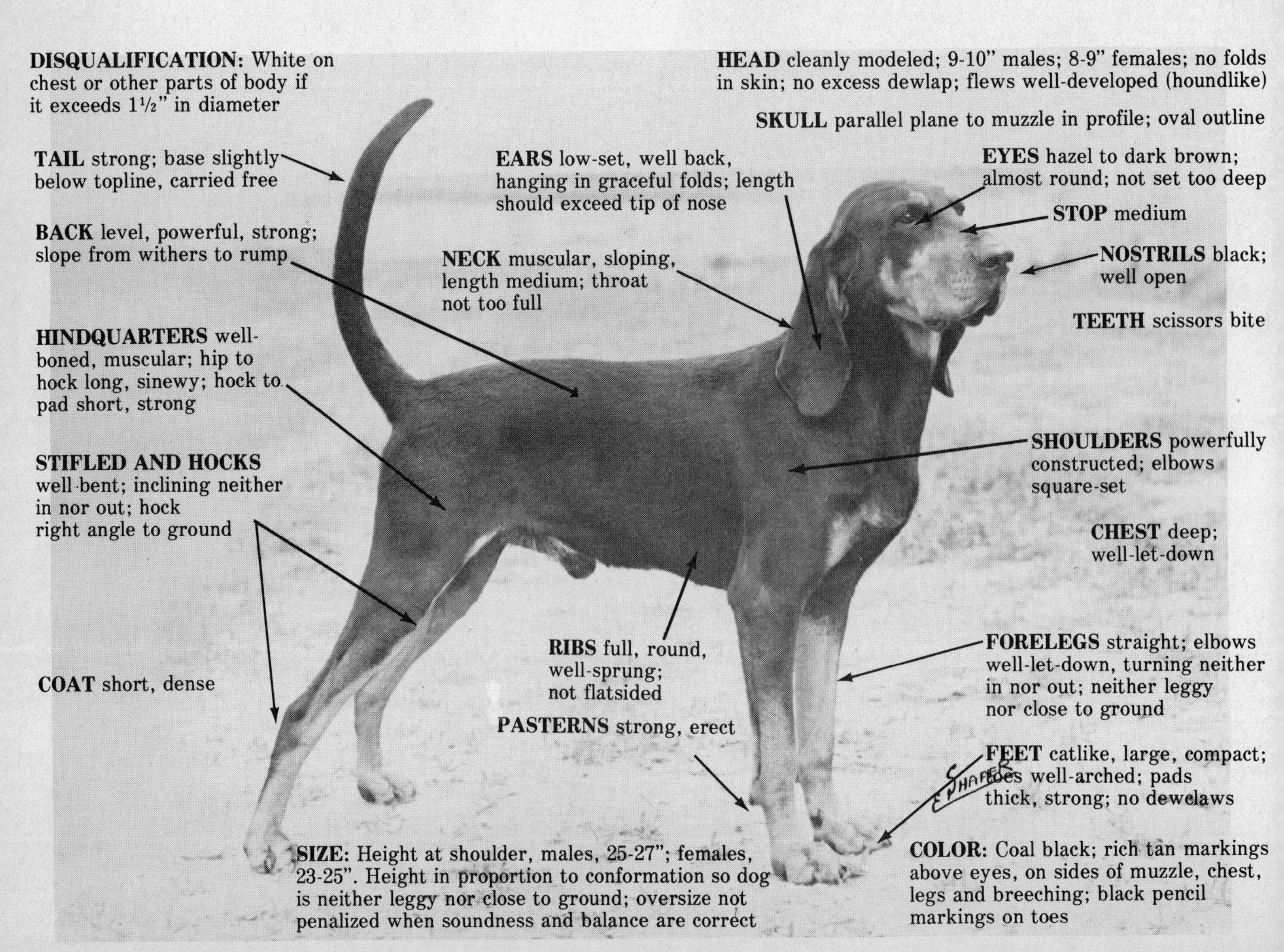
DISQUALIFICATION: White on chest or other parts of body if it exceeds 1½" in diameter
TAIL strong; base slightly below topline, carried free
BACK level, powerful, strong; slope from withers to rump
HINDQUARTERS well-boned, muscular; hip to hock long, sinewy; hock to pad short, strong
STIFLED AND HOCKS well bent; inclining neither in nor out; hock right angle to ground
COAT short, dense
EARS low-set, well back, hanging in graceful folds; length should exceed tip of nose
NECK muscular, sloping, length medium; throat not too full
RIBS full, round, well-sprung; not flatsided
PASTERNS strong, erect
SIZE: Height at shoulder, males, 25-27"; females, 23-25". Height in proportion to conformation so dog is neither leggy nor close to ground; oversize not penalized when soundness and balance are correct
HEAD cleanly modeled; 9-10" males; 8-9" females; no folds in skin; no excess dewlap; flews well-developed (houndlike)
SKULL parallel plane to muzzle in profile; oval outline
EYES hazel to dark brown; almost round; not set too deep
STOP medium
NOSTRILS black; well open
TEETH scissors bite
SHOULDERS powerfully constructed; elbows square-set
CHEST deep; well-let-down
FORELEGS straight; elbows well-let-down, turning neither in nor out; neither leggy nor close to ground
FEET catlike, large, compact; toes well-arched; pads thick, strong; no dewelaws
COLOR: Coal black; rich tan markings above eyes, on sides of muzzle, chest, legs and breeching; black pencil markings on toes
E. SHAFER

CH. MERHABA BANJO (EZRA)

SIRE: CH. MERHABA MAGIQUE MONTEREY (HAWK). DAM: CH. MERHABA MAGIQUE MISSOURI (SNOOPY). WHELPED JUNE 27, 1972. BREEDER: SONIA ALLEN, FULLERTON, CA. EZRA FOLLOWS HIS DAM SNOOPY WHO WAS THE TOP WINNING BLACK AND TAN COONHOUND FOR 1972-1973. AT SCOTTSDALE DOG FANCIERS ASSOCIATION NOV. 16, 1974. BOB, JUDGE MR. TACKER. GROUP FIRST, JUDGE DR. WASKOW.

ARTHUR L. CARTER PHA
1110 MOUNTAIN VIEW ROAD
EL CAJON, CA 92021
(714) 442-1735

The black and tan coonhound, although not one of our popular breeds, has been with us for a long time. He is a descendant from the Talbot Hound which was a popular breed in England under the reign of William I. Through breedings with our own Foxhound (American) and the Bloodhound, the Black and Tan Coonhound developed. The coonhound has a great skill for trailing raccoon and opposum. He trails totally by scent, much like the Bloodhound. In 1945 he was accepted for registration by the American Kennel Club.

GENERAL CHARACTER — The Bloodhound possesses, in a most marked degree, every point and characteristic of those dogs which hunt together by scent (Sagaces). He is very powerful, and stands over more ground than is usual with hounds of other breeds. The skin is thin to the touch and extremely loose, this being more especially noticeable about the head and neck, where it hangs in deep folds.

HEIGHT — The mean average height of adult dogs is 26 inches, and of adult bitches 24 inches. Dogs usually vary from 25 inches to 27 inches, and bitches from 23 inches to 25 inches; but, in either case, the greater height is to be preferred, provided that character and quality are also combined. *Weight* — The mean average weight of adult dogs, in fair condition, is 90 pounds, and of adult bitches 80 pounds. Dogs attain the weight of 110 pounds, bitches 100 pounds. The greater weights are to be preferred, provided (as in the case of height) that qualilty and proportion are also combined.

EXPRESSION — The expression is noble and dignified, and characterized by solemnity, wisdom, and power. *Temperament* — In temperament he is extremely affectionate, neither quarrelsome with companions nor with other dogs. His nature is somewhat shy, and equally sensitive to kindness or correction by his master.

HEAD — The head is narrow in proportion to its length, and long in proportion to the body, tapering but slightly from the temples to the end of the muzzle, thus (when viewed from above and in front) having the appearance of being flattened at the sides and of being nearly equal in width throughout its entire length. In profile the upper outline of the skull is nearly in the same plane as that of the foreface. The length from end of nose to stop (midway between the eyes) should be not less than that from stop to back of occipital protuberance (peak). The entire length of head from the posterior part of the occipital protuberance to the end of the muzzle should be 12 inches, or more, in dogs, and 11 inches, or more, in bitches. *Skull* — The skull is long and narrow, with the occipital peak very pronounced. The brows are not prominent, although, owing to the deep-set eyes, they may have that appearance. *Foreface* — The foreface is long, deep, and of even width throughout, with square outline when seen in profile. *Eyes* — The eyes are deeply sunk in the orbits, the lids assuming a lozenge or diamond shape, in consequence of the lower lids being dragged down and everted by the heavy flews. The eyes correspond with the general tone of color of the animal, varying from deep hazel to yellow. The hazel color is, however, to be preferred, although very seldom seen in red-and-tan hounds. *Ears* — The ears are thin and soft to the touch, extremely long, set very low, and fall in graceful folds, the lower parts curling inwards and backwards.

WRINKLE — The head is furnished with an amount of loose skin, which in nearly every position appears superabundant, but more particularly so when the head is carried low; the skin then falls into loose, pendulous ridges and folds, especially over the forehead and sides of the face. *Nostrils* — The nostrils are large and open. *Lips, Flews, and Dewlap* — In front the lips fall squarely, making a right angle with the upper line of the foreface; whilst behind they form deep, hanging flews, and, being continued into the pendant folds of loose skin about the neck, constitute the dewlap, which is very pronounced. These characters are found, though in a less degree, in the bitch.

NECK, SHOULDERS, AND CHEST — The neck is long, the shoulders muscular and well sloped backwards; the ribs are well sprung; and the chest well let down between the forelegs, forming a deep keel. *Legs and Feet* — The forelegs are straight and large in bone, with elbows squarely set; the feet strong and well knuckled up; the thighs and second thighs (gaskins) are very muscular; the hocks well bent and let down and squarely set.

BACK AND LOIN — The back and loins are strong, the latter deep and slightly arched. *Stern* — The stern is long and tapering, and set on rather high, with a moderate amount of hair underneath.

GAIT — The gait is elastic, swinging and free, the stern being carried high, but not too much curled over the back.

COLOR — The colors are black and tan, red and tan, and tawny; the darker colors being sometimes interspersed with lighter or badger-colored hair, and sometimes flecked with white. A small amount of white is permissible on chest, feet, and tip of stern.

HEAD narrow in proportion to length; long in proportion to body; tapering slightly from temples to end of muzzle; length from end of nose to stop no less than from stop to back of occiput. Entire length from occiput to end of muzzle 12" or more, males; 11" or more, females. Superabundant loose skin falls into loose, pendulous folds

APPEARANCE: Powerful; stands over more ground than other hound breeds. Expression noble, dignified; temperament, affectionate, friendly, sensitive. Skin extremely loose; especially noticeable around head and neck where it hangs in deep folds

EARS low set; extremely long; soft to touch; falling in graceful folds; lower parts curling in and back

SKULL long, narrow; occiput very pronounced

EYES deeply sunk; deep hazel to yellow; lids diamond-shaped; brows not prominent

NOSE: Nostrils large, open

FOREFACE long, deep; even width; square in profile

LIPS fall squarely in front, make right angle with foreface upper line; form deep heavy flews behind; very pronounced dewlap from deep folds of loose skin about neck

CHEST well-let-down between forelegs, forming deep keel

FORELEGS straight; large bone; elbows set squarely

FEET strong; well-knuckled-up

RIBS well-sprung

STERN long, tapering; set-on rather high; moderate amount of hair underneath; carriage high; not too much curled over back

THIGHS (and 2nd thighs) very muscular. Loins strong; deep; slightly arched

HOCKS well-bent; well-let-down; squarely set

SIZE: Height, males, 25"-27" (av. 26"); females, 23"-25" (av. 24"). Weight, males, 110 lbs (av. 90 lbs.), females, 100 lbs (av. 80 lbs.). Greater heights and weights preferred, provided character and quality also combined

COLORS: Black and tan; red and tan; tawny. Darker colors sometimes interspersed with lighter or badger-colored hair, or white flecked. Small amount of white permissible on chest, feet, tip of stern

CH. CRAGSMOOR'S BACCHUS OF MAREVE

BACCHUS, A HOME-BRED CHAMPION, REFLECTS THE CO-BREEDERS, MATTHEW STANDER AND MARION PRUITT'S INTENSE CONCERN TO BREED "TYPEY" BLOODHOUNDS. TAKE NOTE OF BACCHUS' LENGTH OF LEG, HIS PRONOUNCED OCCIPUT REFLECTIVE OF BREED HEAD STANDARD AND HIS MASSIVE BUT ELEGANTLY BALANCED BODY. THIS DOG COULD AND DOES TRAIL.HEWAS THE TOP BLOODHOUND OF 1974!

ALL OF OUR BLOODHOUNDS ARE HAPPILY HANDLED BY TOM GLASSFORD.

MATTHEW STANDER
CRAGSMOOR, NEW YORK 12420

Bloodhounds or hounds very like them in appearance and function have been known from the Ardennes region of France for hundreds of years. Specialists in covering ground and tracking by scent, Bloodhounds have become legendary in America. These dogs are large, 80 to 90 lbs. or more and standing 24 or 25 inches at the shoulder. Powerful, moving with an elastic gait, and tail carried scimitar fashion, Bloodhounds are known for the great loose wrinkles of the skin on their head and neck and their beautiful, pendulous ears. The coat is black and tan, red and tan or tawny, sometimes flecked with white. Gentle in temperament but largely one-man dogs, Bloodhounds are adapted best for open country and field work. About 1,200 are registered annually with AKC, the breed ranking 58th.

BORZOI STANDARD

HEAD — *Skull* slightly domed, long and narrow, with scarcely any perceptible stop, rather inclined to be Roman-nosed; jaws long, powerful and deep; teeth strong, clean and even, neither pig-jawed nor undershot; nose large and black. *Ears* — Small and fine in quality, lying back on the neck when in repose with the tips when thrown back almost touching behind occiput; raised when at attention. *Eyes* — Set somewhat obliquely, dark in color, intelligent, but rather soft in expression, never full nor staring, nor light in color, eyelids dark.

NECK — Clean, free from throatiness, somewhat shorter than in the Greyhound, slightly arched, very powerful and well set on. *Shoulders* — Sloping, should be fine at the withers and free from coarseness or lumber. *Chest* — Rather narrow, with great depth of brisket.

RIBS — Only slightly sprung, but very deep, giving room for heart and lung play. *Back* — Rising a little at the loins in a graceful curve.

LOINS — Extremely muscular, but rather tucked up, owing to the great depth of chest and comparative shortness of back and ribs.

FORELEGS — Bone flat, straight, giving free play for the elbows, which should be neither turned in nor out; pasterns strong. *Feet* — Hare-shaped, with well-arched knuckles, toes close and well padded. *Hindquarters* — Long, very muscular and powerful, with well bent stifles and strong second thighs, hocks broad, clean and well let down. *Tail* — Long, set on and carried low in a graceful curve.

COAT — Long, silky (not woolly), either flat, wavy or rather curly. On the head, ears and front of legs it should be short and smooth; on the neck the frill should be profuse and rather curly. Feather on hindquarters and tail, long and profuse, less so on the chest and back of forelegs. *Color* — Any color, white usually predominating, more or less marked with lemon, tan, brindle, gray or black. Whole-colored specimens of these tints occasionally appear.

GENERAL APPEARANCE — Should be that of an elegant, graceful aristocrat among dogs, possessing courage and combining muscular power with extreme speed.

SIZE — Dogs, average height at shoulder from 28 to 31 inches; average weight from 75 to 105 pounds. Larger dogs are often seen, extra size being no disadvantage when it is not acquired at the expense of symmetry, speed and staying quality. Bitches are invariably smaller than dogs, and two inches less in height, and from 15 to 20 pounds less in weight is a fair average.

SCALE OF POINTS

Head	12	Hindquarters, stifles and hocks	12
Eyes	5	Legs and feet	10
Ears	3	Coat and feather	10
Neck	5	Tail	3
Shldrs and brisket	10	Conformation and gait	15
Ribs, back and loins	15	Total	100

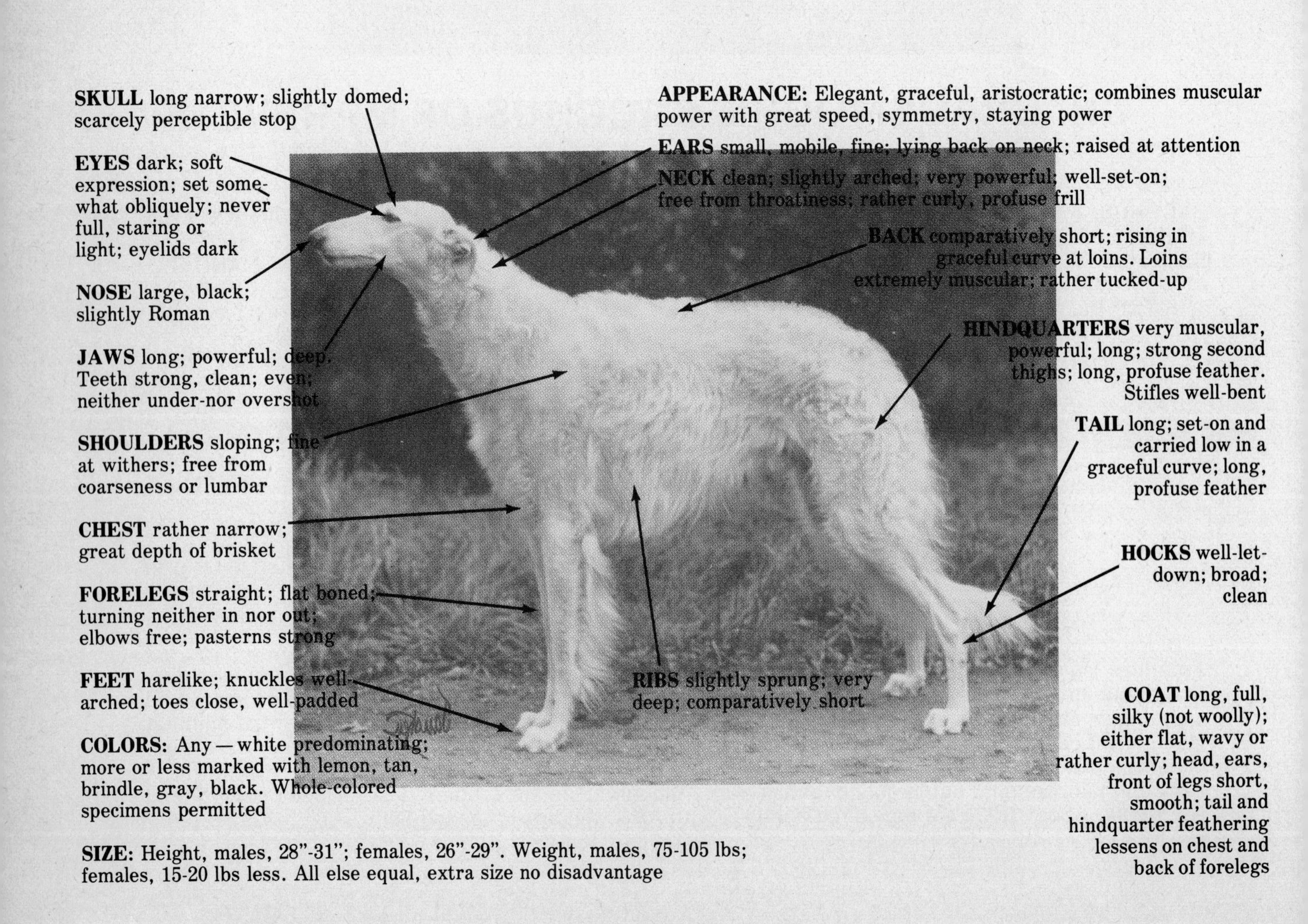

SKULL long narrow; slightly domed; scarcely perceptible stop
EYES dark; soft expression; set somewhat obliquely; never full, staring or light; eyelids dark
NOSE large, black; slightly Roman
JAWS long; powerful; deep. Teeth strong, clean; even; neither under-nor overshot
SHOULDERS sloping; fine at withers; free from coarseness or lumbar
CHEST rather narrow; great depth of brisket
FORELEGS straight; flat boned; turning neither in nor out; elbows free; pasterns strong
FEET harelike; knuckles well-arched; toes close, well-padded
COLORS: Any — white predominating; more or less marked with lemon, tan, brindle, gray, black. Whole-colored specimens permitted
APPEARANCE: Elegant, graceful, aristocratic; combines muscular power with great speed, symmetry, staying power
EARS small, mobile, fine; lying back on neck; raised at attention
NECK clean; slightly arched; very powerful; well-set-on; free from throatiness; rather curly, profuse frill
BACK comparatively short; rising in graceful curve at loins. Loins extremely muscular; rather tucked-up
HINDQUARTERS very muscular, powerful; long; strong second thighs; long, profuse feather. Stifles well-bent
TAIL long; set-on and carried low in a graceful curve; long, profuse feather
HOCKS well-let-down; broad; clean
RIBS slightly sprung; very deep; comparatively short
COAT long, full, silky (not woolly); either flat, wavy or rather curly; head, ears, front of legs short, smooth; tail and hindquarter feathering lessens on chest and back of forelegs
SIZE: Height, males, 28"-31"; females, 26"-29". Weight, males, 75-105 lbs; females, 15-20 lbs less. All else equal, extra size no disadvantage

AM. & CAN. CH. SIRHAN PORASCHAI

ALL TIME TOP PRODUCER IN THE HISTORY OF THE BREED. TOP WINNING BORZOI FOR 1971 & 1972. OVER 100 BEST OF BREEDS, 6 BEST IN SHOWS ONE FROM THE OPEN DOG CLASS AT 11 MONTHS OF AGE, ALSO RECORD HOLDER FOR WINNING 9 SPECIALTIES IN A ROW. 1973 BREED WINNER AT THE GARDEN. ALWAYS OWNER HANDLED. WHELPED APRIL 29, 1968.

(ARISTOFF) ED ABBLETT & GEORGE ROOT
P.O. BOX 102
GLEN ELLEN, CALIF. 95442

The Borzoi has also been called the Russian Wolfhound. Bred, probably for centuries, by the Russian nobility, these coursing, sight-hounds are related to the stock which produced the Saluki, the Afghan, and the Greyhound. In Imperial Russia, after a wolf had been beaten out of cover by peasants on foot, in a highly ritualized hunt which was really a social event, a horseman would unleash a brace of matched Borzoi. The dogs would pursue and throw the wolf, holding it until the huntsman arrived, dismounted, and dispatched it. These hounds must be large, swift, powerful, symmetrical, and elegant. Style is the key word. Special emphasis must be given to sound running gear, a strong neck and jaws, courage, and agility. The long silky coat may be flat, wavy or curly, with profuse feathering on the hindquarters and tail. Any color or combination of colors is acceptable. Mature males should stand at least 28 inches at the withers and weigh from 75-105 lbs. Long scarcely obtainable because of its close association with the nobility, first in Russian and then in England as well, the Borzoi is now popular in the show ring and gaining wide acceptance as a companion. Some 1,700 are registered annually in the U.S., the breed ranking 52nd. The Borzoi is 31st in numbers in show competition and even stronger in Group wins.

GENERAL APPEARANCE — Short-legged, long-bodied, low-to-ground; sturdy, well muscled, neither clumsy nor slim, with audacious carriage and intelligent expression; conformation pre-eminently fitted for following game into burrows.

HEAD — Long, uniformly tapered, clean-cut; teeth well fitted, with scissors bite; eyes medium oval; ears broad, long, rounded, set on high and well back; neck long, muscular.

FOREQUARTERS — Muscular, compact. Chest deep, long, full and oval; breastbone prominent. Broad, long shoulder, and oblique humerus forming right angle; heavy, set close; forearm short, inclined slightly in foreleg straight and vertical in profile, covering deepest point of chest. Feet broad, firm, compact, turned slightly out.

HINDQUARTERS — Well-muscled and rounded. Pelvis, femur and tibia oblique, forming right angles; tarsus inclined forward. Hip should be level with shoulder, back strong, neither sagged nor more than very slightly arched. Tail strong, tapered, well-covered with hair, not carried gaily.

VARIETIES — Three coat types: *Smooth* or Shorthaired, short and dense, shining, glossy. *Wirehaired*, like German Wirehaired Pointer, hard, with good undercoat. *Longhaired*, like Irish Setter.

Note — In each coat variety there are divisions of open classes restricted to Miniatures, under 9 pounds, minimum age 12 months.

COLOR — Solid red (tan) of various shades, and black with tan points, should have black noses and nails, and narrow black line edging lips and eyelids; chocolate with tan points permits brown nose. Eyes of all, lustrous, the darker the better.

FAULTS — Overshot or undershot, knuckling over, loose shoulders; high on legs, clumsy gait, long, splayed or twisted feet, sagged or roached back, high croup, small, narrow or short chest, faulty angulation of fore or hindquarters, weak loins, narrow hindquarters, bowed legs, cowhocks; weak or dish-faced muzzle, dewlaps, uneven or scanty coat.

General Features

GENERAL APPEARANCE — Low to ground, short-legged, long-bodied, but with compact figure and robust muscular development; with bold and confident carriage of the head and intelligent facial expression. In spite of his shortness of leg, in comparison with his length of trunk, he should appear neither crippled, awkward, cramped in his capacity for movement, nor slim and weasel-like. *Qualities* — He should be clever, lively, and courageous to the point of rashness, persevering in his work both above and below ground; with all the senses well developed. His build and disposition qualify him especially for hunting game below ground. Added to this, his hunting spirit, good nose, loud tongue, and small size, render him especially suited for beating the bush. His figure and his fine nose give him an especial advantage over most other breeds of sporting dogs for trailing.

Conformation of Body

HEAD — Viewed from above or from the side, it should taper uniformly to the tip of the nose, and should be clean-cut. The skull is only slightly arched, and should slope gradually without stop (the less stop the more typical) into the finely-formed slightly-arched muzzle (ram's nose). The bridge bones over the eyes should be strongly prominent. The nasal cartilage and tip of the nose are long and narrow; lips tightly stretched, well covering the lower jaw, but neither deep nor pointed; corner of the mouth not very marked. Nostrils well open. Jaws opening wide and hinged well back of the eyes, with strongly developed bones and teeth.

(a) *Teeth* — Powerful canine teeth should fit closely together, and the outer side of the lower incisors should tightly touch the inner side of the upper (scissors bite). (b) *Eyes* — Medium size, oval, situated at the sides, with a clean, energetic, though pleasant expression; not piercing. Color, lustrous dark reddish-brown to brownish-black for all coats and colors. Wall eyes in the case of dapple dogs are not a very bad fault, but are also not desirable. (c) *Ears* — Should be set near the top of the head, and not too far forward, but not too long, beautifully rounded, not narrow, pointed or folded. Their carriage should be animated, and the forward edge should just touch the cheek. (d) *Neck* — Fairly long, muscular, cleancut, not showing any dewlap on the throat, slightly arched in the nape, extending in a graceful line into the shoulders, carried proudly but not stiffly.

FRONT — To endure the arduous exertion underground, the front must be correspondingly muscular, compact, deep, long and broad. Forequarters in detail: (a) *Shoulder Blade* — Long, broad, obliquely and firmly placed upon the fully developed thorax, furnished with hard and plastic muscles. (b) *Upper Arm:* — Of the same length as the shoulder blade, and at right angles to the latter, strong of bone and hard of muscle, lying close to the ribs, capable of free movement. (c) *Forearm* — This is short in comparison to other breeds, slightly turned inwards; supplied with hard but plastic

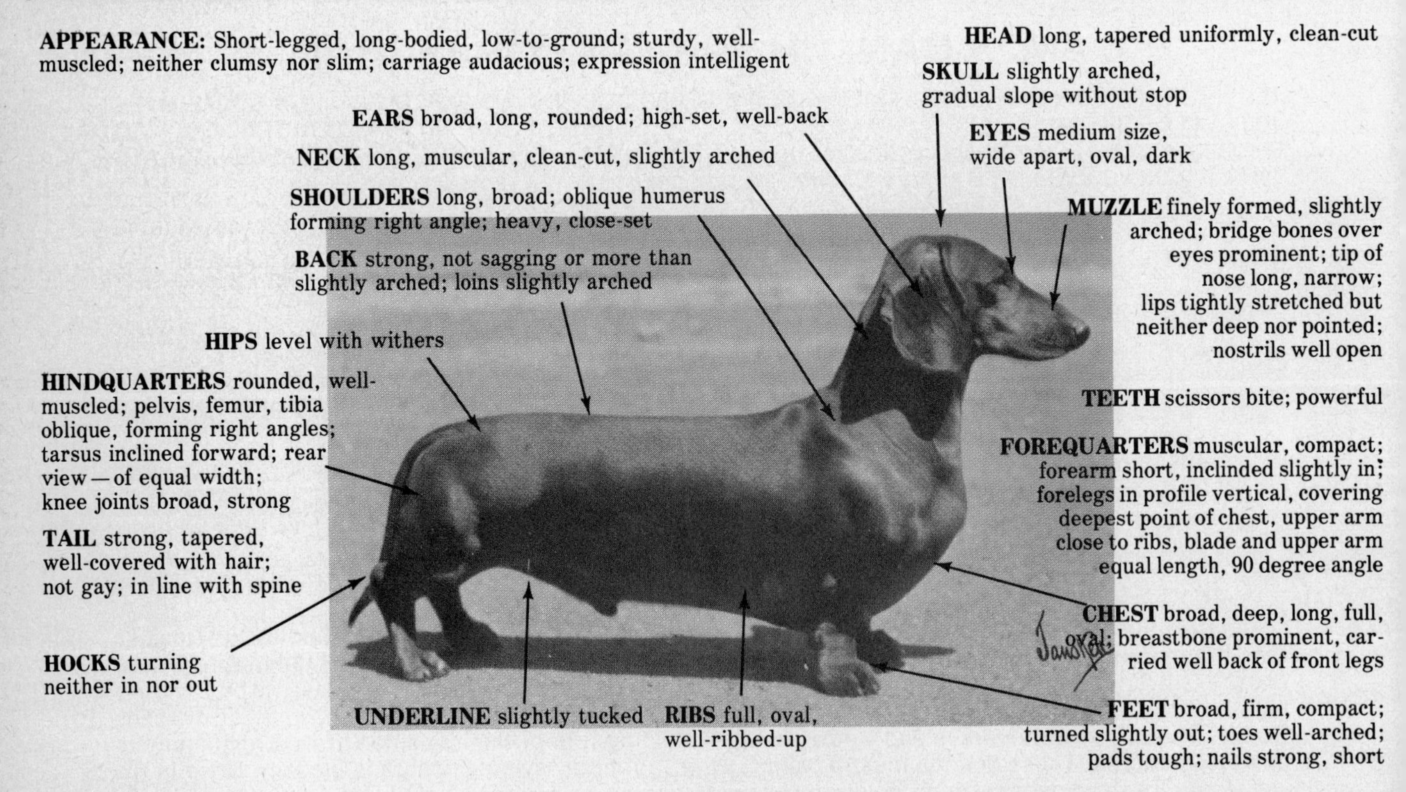
APPEARANCE: Short-legged, long-bodied, low-to-ground; sturdy, well-muscled; neither clumsy nor slim; carriage audacious; expression intelligent
EARS broad, long, rounded; high-set, well-back
NECK long, muscular, clean-cut, slightly arched
SHOULDERS long, broad; oblique humerus forming right angle; heavy, close-set
BACK strong, not sagging or more than slightly arched; loins slightly arched
HIPS level with withers
HINDQUARTERS rounded, well-muscled; pelvis, femur, tibia oblique, forming right angles; tarsus inclined forward; rear view—of equal width; knee joints broad, strong
TAIL strong, tapered, well-covered with hair; not gay; in line with spine
HOCKS turning neither in nor out
UNDERLINE slightly tucked
RIBS full, oval, well-ribbed-up
HEAD long, tapered uniformly, clean-cut
SKULL slightly arched, gradual slope without stop
EYES medium size, wide apart, oval, dark
MUZZLE finely formed, slightly arched; bridge bones over eyes prominent; tip of nose long, narrow; lips tightly stretched but neither deep nor pointed; nostrils well open
TEETH scissors bite; powerful
FOREQUARTERS muscular, compact; forearm short, inclinded slightly in; forelegs in profile vertical, covering deepest point of chest, upper arm close to ribs, blade and upper arm equal length, 90 degree angle
CHEST broad, deep, long, full, oval; breastbone prominent, carried well back of front legs
FEET broad, firm, compact; turned slightly out; toes well-arched; pads tough; nails strong, short

MINIATURE DACHSHUNDS bred in 3 varieties.

COLORS Solid red (tan) of various shades; black with tan points (black noses, nails black line edging lips, eyeligs); chocolate with tan points permits brown nose

VARIETIES three: Shorthaired (smooth); hair short, thick, smooth; red, B/T, dappled, brindle. Wirehaired: hair rough, hard with undercoat; beard, bushy eyebrows. Longhaired: hair long, silky, soft, sleek; feather pronounced; not curly

muscles on the front and outside, with tightly stretched tendons on the inside and at the back. (d) *Joint between forearm and foot* (wrists) — These are closer together than the shoulder joints, so that the front does not appear absolutely straight. (e) *Paws* — Full, broad in front, and a trifle inclined outwards; compact, with well-arched toes and tough pads. (f) *Toes* — There are five of these, though only four are in use. Dewclaws may be removed. They should be close together, with a pronounced arch; provided on top with strong nails, and underneath with tough toepads.

TRUNK — The whole trunk should in general be long and fully muscled. The back, with sloping shoulders, and short, rigid pelvis, should lie in the straightest possible line between the withers and the very slightly arched loins, these latter being short, rigid, and broad. (a) *Chest* — The breastbone should be strong, and so prominent in front that on either side a depression (dimple) appears. When viewed from the front, the thorax should appear oval, and should extend downward to the mid-point of the forearm. The enclosing structure of ribs should appear full and oval, and when viewed from above or from the side, full-volumed, so as to allow by its ample capacity, complete development of heart and lungs. Well ribbed up, and gradually merging into the line of the abdomen. If the length is correct, and also the anatomy of the shoulder and upper arm, the front leg when viewed in profile should cover the lowest point of the breast line. (b) *Abdomen* — Slightly drawn up.

HINDQUARTERS — The hindquarters viewed from behind should be of completely equal width. (a) *Croup* — Long, round, full, robustly muscled, but plastic, only slightly sinking toward the tail. (b) *Pelvic Bones* — Not too short, rather strongly developed, and moderately sloping. (c) *Thigh Bone* — Robust and of good length, set at right angles to the pelvic bones. (d) *Hind Legs* — Robust and well-muscled, with well-rounded buttocks. (e) *Knee Joint* — Broad and strong. (f) *Calf Bone* —In comparison with

[*continued on page 102*]

HEAD — *Skull* — Should be fairly long, slightly domed at occiput, with cranium broad and full. *Ears* — Ears set on moderately low, long, reaching when drawn out nearly, if not quite, to the tip of the nose; fine in texture, fairly broad, with almost entire absence of erectible power — setting close to the head with the forward edge slightly inturning to the cheek — round at tip. *Eyes* — Eyes large, set well apart; soft and houndlike; expression gentle and pleading; of a brown or hazel color. *Muzzle* — Muzzle of fair length — straight and square-cut — the top moderately defined. *Defects:* A very flat skull, narrow across the top; excess of dome; eyes small, sharp and terrier-like, or prominent and protruding; muzzle long and snipy, cut away decidedly below the eyes, or very short. Roman-nosed, or upturned, giving a dish-face expression. Ears short, set on high, or with a tendency to rise above the point of origin.

BODY — *Neck and Throat* — Neck rising free and light from the shoulders, strong in substance yet not loaded, of medium length. The throat clean and free from folds of skin, a slight wrinkle below the angle of the jaw, however, is allowable. *Defects:* A thick, short, cloddy neck carried on a line with the top of the shoulders. Throat showing dewlap and folds of skin to a degree termed "throatiness." *Shoulders, Chest and Ribs* — Shoulders sloping — clean, muscular, not heavy or loaded — conveying the idea of freedom of action with activity and strength. Chest should be deep for lung space, narrower in proportion to depth than the English hound — 28 inches (*girth*) in a 23-inch hound being good. Well-sprung ribs — back ribs should extend well back — a three-inch flank allowing springiness. *Back and Loins* — Back moderately long, muscular and strong. Loins broad and slightly arched. *Defects:* Very long or swayed or roached back. Flat, narrow loins.

FORELEGS AND FEET — *Forelegs* — Straight, with fair amount of bone. Pasterns short and straight. *Feet* — Foxlike. Pad full and hard. Well-arched toes. Strong nails. *Defects:* Straight, upright shoulders, chest disproportionately wide or with lack of depth. Flat ribs. Out at elbow. Knees knuckled over forward, or bent backward. Forelegs crooked. Feet long, open or spreading.

HIPS, THIGHS, HIND LEGS AND FEET — Hips and thighs, strong and muscled, giving abundance of propelling power. Stifles strong and well let down. Hocks firm, symmetrical and moderately bent. Feet close and firm. *Defects:* Cowhocks, or straight hocks. Lack of muscle and propelling power. Open feet.

TAIL — Set moderately high; carried gaily, but not turned forward over the back; with slight curve; with very slight brush. *Defects:* A long tail. Teapot curve or inclined forward from the root. Rat tail, entire absence of brush.

COAT — A close, hard, hound coat of medium length. *Defects:* A short thin coat, or of a soft quality.

HEIGHT — Dogs should not be under 22 or over 25 inches. Bitches should not be under 21 or over 24 inches measured across the back at the point of the withers, the hound standing in a natural position with his feet well under him. *Color* — Any color.

SCALE OF POINTS

Head		
Skull	5	
Ears	5	
Eyes	5	
Muzzle	5	20
Body		
Neck	5	
Chest and shoulders	15	
Back, loins and ribs	15	35
Running Gear		
Forelegs	10	
Hips, thighs and hind legs	10	
Feet	15	35
Coat and Tail		
Coat	5	
Tail	5	10
Total		100

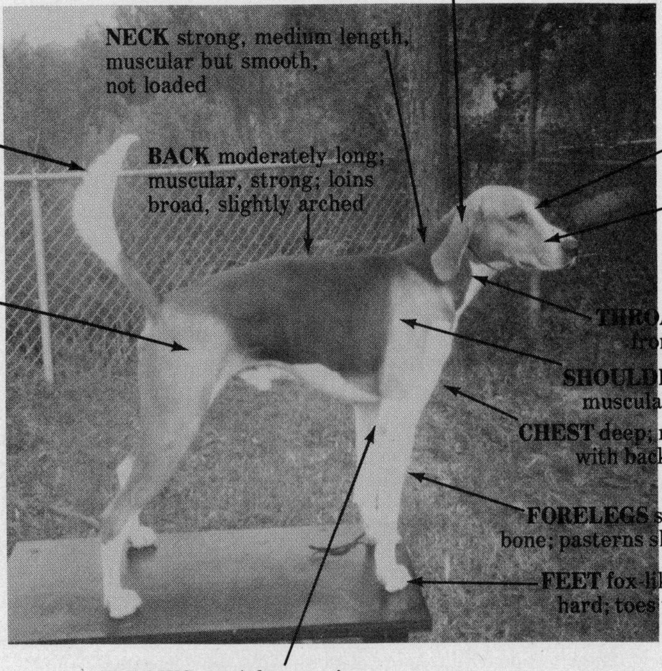

HEAD fairly long; skull domed, broad and full

EARS set on moderately low, close to head, long; texture fine, round at tip, fairly broad

EXPRESSION gentle, pleading

NECK strong, medium length, muscular but smooth, not loaded

TAIL set moderately high; gay carriage with slight curve; slight brush, moderate length

STOP moderately defined

BACK moderately long; muscular, strong; loins broad, slightly arched

EYES large, wide apart, brown or hazel

MUZZLE fair length, straight, square cut

HINDQUARTERS strong, well muscled; stifles strong, well let down; hocks firm, moderately bent; feet close, firm

THROAT clean, free from folds of skin

SHOULDERS sloping, muscular but smooth

CHEST deep; ribs well-sprung with back ribs well-back, not too wide

FORELEGS straight, good bone; pasterns short, straight

COAT close, hard, medium length

FEET fox-like; pads full, hard; toes well-arched; nails strong

ELBOWS straight, turning neither in nor out

HEIGHT at withers, dogs 22-25 inches, females 21-24 inches

CH. DELMAS KENTUCKY LAKE BRAXTON

FINISHED HIS CHAMPIONSHIP FROM THE PUPPY CLASSES AT THE AGE OF 11 MONTHS. TO DATE HE HAS NUMEROUS GROUP PLACEMENTS AND IS SHOWN HERE WINNING THE HOUND GROUP UNDER JUDGE PAT HASTINGS AT THE MANATEE K.C. SHOW, BRADENTON, FLA. HIS SIRE IS CH. KENTUCKY LAKE FLASHER, ONE OF THE GREAT SIRES IN THIS BREED. HIS DAM IS A FLASHER DAUGHTER, KENTUCKY LAKE JEZEBEL II.
HANDLER: PETE DAWKINS

PATRICIA C. KAPPLOW
9820 NOROAD
JACKSONVILLE, FLORIDA 32221

The breeding of hounds for fox hunting in America dates from the 17th century. The Black and Tan Coonhound as well as the American Foxhound descend from this early stock. In the case of the latter, French and Irish hounds were bred into the line after the 1730's, when fox hunting style changed in response to the introduction of the European red fox into the Southern American colonies, especially Virginia. Used in packs or individually, these dogs are swift, cover ground well, have great stamina, and loud, musical voices. They are leggier and lighter bodied than the English Foxhounds of today. They are masters at following a faint scent at a gallop and then, when and if the fox evades them or goes to ground, they can find their way back over long distances, guided by the faint scent trail. Type is very variable. All colors are acceptable. Widely used in the field, the American Foxhound is rarely seen in the ring and almost as rarely kept as a pet. Only a few dozen are registered annually with the AKC, the breed ranking 110th. On the average less than one American Foxhound competes per show in the U.S.

The points of the modern Harrier are very similar to those of the English Foxhound. The Harrier, however, is smaller than the English Foxhound and the most popular size is 19 to 21 inches. They should be active, well balanced and full of strength and quality, with shoulders sloping into the muscles of the back, clean and not loaded on the withers or point.

The back level and muscular, and not dipping behind the withers or arching over the loin. The elbow's point set well away from the ribs, running parallel with the body and not turning outwards. Deep, well-sprung ribs, running well back, with plenty of heart room, and a deep chest.

Good straight legs with plenty of bone running well down to the toes, but not overburdened, inclined to knuckle over very slightly but not exaggerated in the slightest degree. Round catlike feet, and close toes turning inwards. Hind legs and hocks stand square, with a good sweep and muscular thigh to take the weight off the body.

The head should be of a medium size with good bold forehead, and plenty of expression; head must be well set up on a neck of ample length, and not heavy; stern should be set well up, long and well controlled.

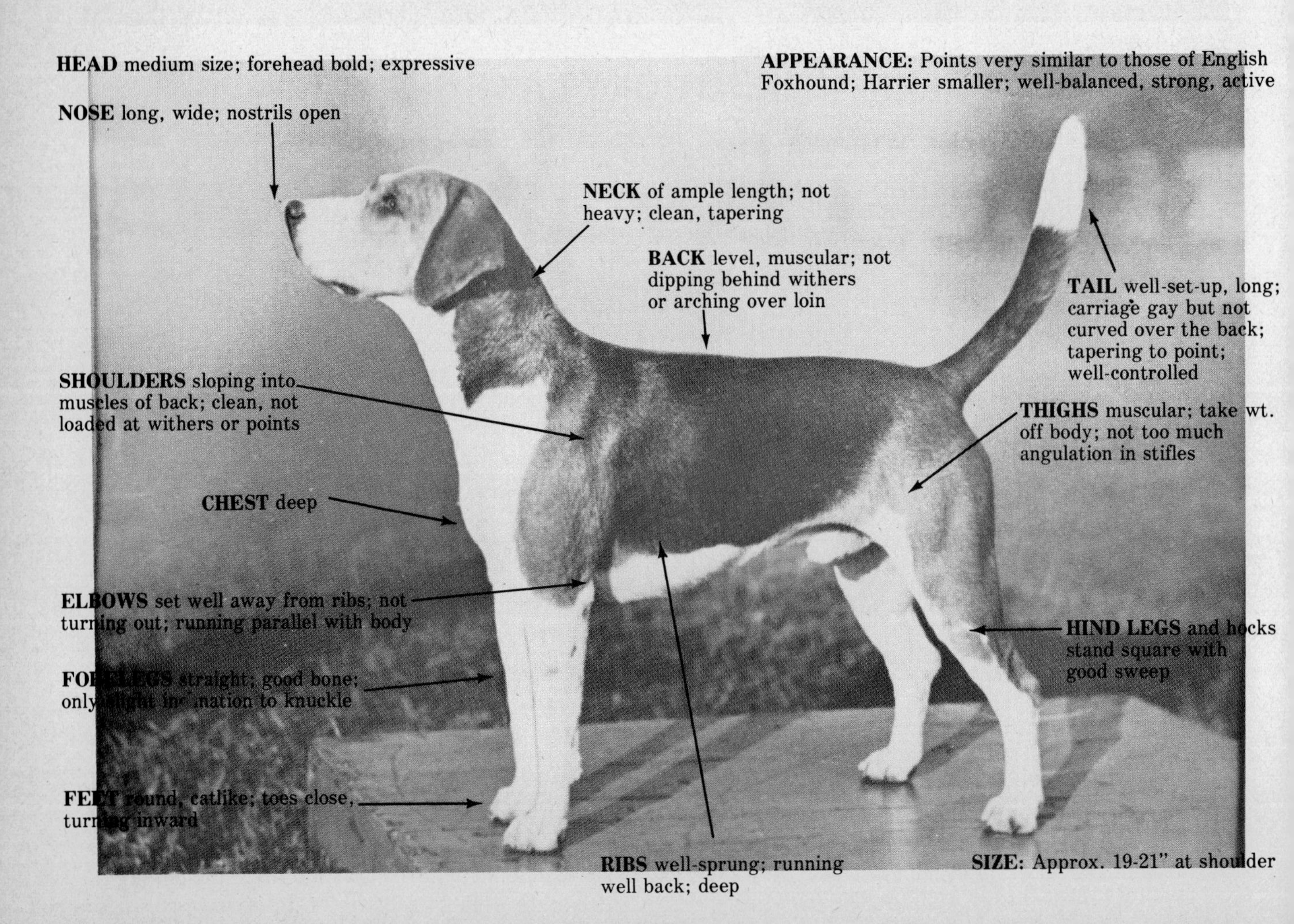
HEAD medium size; forehead bold; expressive
NOSE long, wide; nostrils open
APPEARANCE: Points very similar to those of English Foxhound; Harrier smaller; well-balanced, strong, active
NECK of ample length; not heavy; clean, tapering
BACK level, muscular; not dipping behind withers or arching over loin
TAIL well-set-up, long; carriage gay but not curved over the back; tapering to point; well-controlled
SHOULDERS sloping into muscles of back; clean, not loaded at withers or points
THIGHS muscular; take wt. off body; not too much angulation in stifles
CHEST deep
ELBOWS set well away from ribs; not turning out; running parallel with body
HIND LEGS and hocks stand square with good sweep
FORELEGS straight; good bone; only slight inclination to knuckle
FEET round, catlike; toes close, turning inward
RIBS well-sprung; running well back; deep
SIZE: Approx. 19-21" at shoulder

CH. SPRINGS LANCASHIRE RAF

THE CLOWN PRINCE OF SPRINGS HOUNDS. ELEGANT, SOUND AND TYPEY HE IS A FINE EXAMPLE OF THIS LOVING INTELLIGENT BREED.

SPRINGS HOUNDS
7565 MAVERICK ROAD
COLORADO SPRINGS, CO. 80908
(303) 495-4209

The Harrier of today is very much a smaller edition of the Foxhound, having been bred down to his present size. In the United States they are one, if not the oldest, of the hunting hounds having been used in Colonial times. They have long been used in packs in England, the first one having been started in 1260 by Sir Elias de Midhope. A reason for their popularity as pack dogs is that they travel slowly and can be followed on foot.

IRISH WOLFHOUND STANDARD

GENERAL APPEARANCE — Of great size and commanding appearance, the Irish Wolfhound is remarkable in combining power and swiftness with keen sight. The largest and tallest of the galloping hounds, in general type he is a rough-coated, Greyhoundlike breed; very muscular, strong though gracefully built; movements easy and active; head and neck carried high, the tail carried with an upward sweep with a slight curve towards the extremity. The minimum height and weight of dogs should be 32 inches and 120 pounds; of bitches, 30 inches and 105 pounds; these to apply only to hounds over 18 months of age. Anything below this should be debarred from competition. Great size, including height at shoulder and proportionate length of body, is the desideratum to be aimed at, and it is desired to firmly establish a race that shall average from 32 to 34 inches in dogs, showing the requisite power, activity, courage and symmetry.

HEAD — Long, the frontal bones of the forehead very slightly raised and very little indentation between the eyes. Skull, not too broad. Muzzle, long and moderately pointed. Ears, small and Greyhoundlike in carriage.

NECK — Rather long, very strong and muscular, well arched, without dewlap or loose skin about the throat.

CHEST — Very deep. Breast, wide. *Back* — Rather long than short. Loins arched. *Tail* — Long and slightly curved, of moderate thickness, and well covered with hair. *Belly* — Well drawn up.

FOREQUARTERS — Shoulders, muscular, giving breadth of chest, set sloping. Elbows well under, neither turned inwards nor outwards. *Leg* — Forearm muscular, and the whole leg strong and quite straight.

HINDQUARTERS — Muscular thighs and second thigh long and strong as in the Greyhound, and hocks well let down and turning neither in nor out.

FEET — Moderately large and round, neither turned inwards nor outwards. Toes, well arched and closed. Nails, very strong and curved.

HAIR — Rough and hard on body, legs and head; especially wiry and long over eyes and under jaw.

COLOR AND MARKINGS — The recognized colors are gray, brindle, red, black, pure white, fawn, or any other color that appears in the Deerhound.

FAULTS — Too light or heavy a head, too highly arched frontal bone; large ears and hanging flat to the face; short neck; full dewlap; too narrow or too broad a chest; sunken or hollow or quite straight back; bent forelegs; overbent fetlocks; twisted feet; spreading toes, too curly a tail; weak hindquarters and a general want of muscle too short in body. Lips or nose liver-colored or lacking pigmentation.

LIST OF POINTS IN ORDER OF MERIT

1. *Typical.* The Irish Wolfhound is a rough-coated Greyhoundlike breed, the tallest of the coursing hounds and remarkable in combining power and swiftness. 2. *Great size* and commanding appearance. 3. Movements easy and active. 4. Head, long and level, carried high. 5. Forelegs, heavily boned, quite straight; elbows well set under. 6. Thighs long and muscular; second thighs, well muscled, stifles nicely bent. 7. Coat, rough and hard, specially wiry and long over eyes and under jaw. 8. Body, long, well ribbed up, with ribs well sprung, and great breadth across hips. 9. Loins arched, belly well drawn up. 10. Ears, small, with Greyhoundlike carriage. 11. Feet, moderately large and round; toes, close, well arched. 12. Neck, long, well arched and very strong. 13. Chest, very deep, moderately broad, 14. Shoulders, muscular, set sloping. 15. Tail, long and slightly curved. 16. Eyes, dark.

Note — The above in no way alters the "Standard of Excellence," which must in all cases be rigidly adhered to; they simply give the various points in order of merit. If in any case they appear at variance with Standard of Excellence, it is the latter which is correct.

Approved September 12, 1950

APPEARANCE: Body long; well-ribbed-up; great size, commanding; good height at shoulders; rough-coated; muscular, powerful. Tallest and largest of galloping hounds; gracefully built

HEAD carriage high; level, long; frontal bones of forehead slightly raised; little indentation between eyes

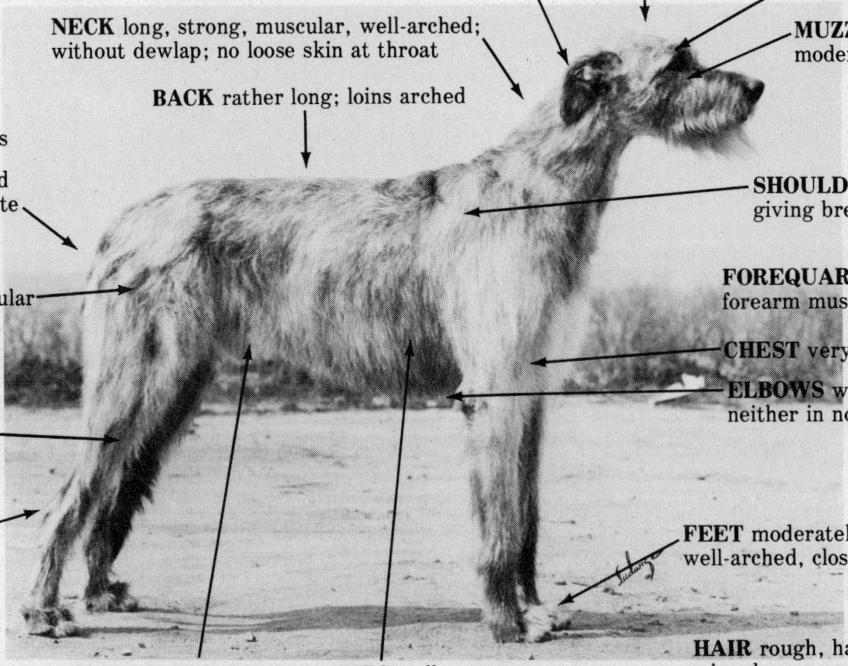

SKULL not too broad

EARS small, carriage Greyhoundlike

EYES dark; keen

MUZZLE long, moderately pointed

NECK long, strong, muscular, well-arched; without dewlap; no loose skin at throat

BACK rather long; loins arched

HIPS great breadth across

TAIL long, slightly curved in upward sweep; moderate thickness; well-covered with hair

SHOULDERS muscular, sloping, giving breadth of chest

FOREQUARTERS straight, strong; forearm muscular; heavily boned

HINDQUARTERS: Muscular thighs; second thigh long, strong

CHEST very deep, breast wide

ELBOWS well-under; turning neither in nor out

STIFLES nicely bent

HOCKS well-let-down, turning neither in nor out

FEET moderately large, round; toes well-arched, closed; nails strong, curved

HAIR rough, hard on body, legs, head; wiry, long over eyes and under jaw

BELLY well-drawn-up

RIBS well-sprung

COLOR: Gray, brindle, red, black, pure white, fawn (or any Deerhound color)

DISQUALIFICATION: Hounds under minimum height and weight

SIZE: Medium height at shoulder, males, 32"; weight 120 lbs. Females, 30" and 105 lbs. This applies to hounds over 18 months of age.

CH. IMPERIAL THE COUNSELOR

FINISHED WITH 4 MAJORS AT 15 MONTHS OLD. STARTING IN APRIL, 1974 COUNSELOR IS NO. 1 IRISH WOLFHOUND WITH 4 BEST IN SHOWS (ALL BREED), 10 GROUP 1'S, AND 24 OTHER GROUP PLACEMENTS (45 BREEDS).

HANDLER: DICK COOPER

LEOPOLD P. & AUDRE W. BORRELLO
63 BENTON RD.
SAGINAW, MICHIGAN 48602
(517) 793-1728

The Irish Wolfhound seems to have been well established as a type in the days of Ancient Greece and Rome. During the ensuing centuries, there are many references to these gigantic dogs bred to hunt wolves, stags, and boars. By the 1840's, the breed was very reduced in numbers and may actually have been extinct. Reduced or extinct, the breed was revived or recreated by the use of what pure or cross-bred stock remained and outcrosses to Scottish Deerhounds and Great Danes. The distinctive size and type were retained. The Irish Wolfhound is a gentle, affectionate beast, dogs standing at least 32 inches at the withers and weighing at least 120 lbs. Being a coursing, sight hound, the Irish Wolfhound must be powerful, swift, and enduring. Soundness of limb, obviously, is particularly important in a breed of such size which is expected to cover ground swiftly. The coat is rough and hard. Recognized colors include grey, brindle, red, black, white, fawn, or any other color appearing in the Scottish Deerhound. Though no longer used substantially in hunting, the Wolfhound has found great favor as a striking companion. Some 1,300 are registered annually with the AKC and their popularity seems to be sharply on the rise. The breed currently ranks 57th. Though Irish Wolfhounds rank only 10th in the Hound Group in numbers in competition, they claimed third place in Group wins in 1972.

NORWEGIAN ELKHOUND STANDARD

GENERAL DESCRIPTION — The Norwegian Elkhound is a hardy gray hunting dog. In appearance, a typical northern dog of medium size and substance, square in profile, close coupled and balanced in proportions. The head is broad with prick ears, and the tail is tightly curled and carried over the back. The distinctive gray coat is dense and smooth-lying. In temperament, the Norwegian Elkhound is boid and energetic, an effective guardian yet normally friendly, with great dignity and independence of character. As a hunter, the Norwegian Elkhound has the courage, agility and stamina to hold moose and other big game at bay by barking and dodging attack, and the endurance to track for long hours in all weather over rough and varied terrain.

In the show ring, presentation in a natural, unaltered condition is essential.

HEAD — Broad at the ears, wedge-shaped, strong, and dry (without loose skin). Viewed from the side, the forehead and back of the skull are only slightly arched; the stop not large, yet clearly defined. The bridge of the nose is straight, parallel to and about the same length as the skull. The muzzle is thickest at the base and, seen from above or from the side, tapers evenly without being pointed. Lips are tightly closed and teeth meet in a scissors bite.

EARS — Set high, firm and erect yet very mobile. Comparatively small; slightly taller than their width at the base with pointed (not rounded) tips. When the dog is alert, the orifices turn forward and the outer edges are vertical.

EYES — Very dark brown, medium in size, oval, not protruding.

NECK — Of medium length, muscular, well set up with a slight arch and with no loose skin on the throat.

BODY — Square in profile and close coupled. Distance from brisket to ground appears to be half the height at the withers. Distance from forechest to rump equals the height at the withers. Chest deep and moderately broad; brisket level with points of elbows; and ribs well sprung. Loin short and wide with very little tuck-up. The back is straight and strong from its high point at the withers to the root of the tail.

FOREQUARTERS — Shoulders sloping with elbows closely set on. Legs well under body and medium in length; substantial, but not coarse, in bone. Seen from the front, the legs appear straight and parallel. Single dewclaws are normally present.

HINDQUARTERS — Moderate angulation at stifle and hock. Thighs are broad and well-muscled. Seen from behind, legs are straight, strong and without dewclaws.

FEET — Paws comparatively small, slightly oval with tightly closed toes and thick pads. Pasterns are strong and only slightly bent. Feet turn neither in nor out.

TAIL — Set high, tightly curled, and carried over the centerline of the back. It is thickly and closely haired, without brush, natural and untrimmed.

COAT — Thick, hard, weather-resisting and smooth-lying; made up of soft, dense, woolly undercoat and coarse, straight covering hairs. Short and even on head, ears, and front of legs; longest on back of neck, buttocks and underside of tail. The coat is not altered by trimming, clipping or artificial treatment. Trimming of whiskers is optional.

COLOR — Gray, medium preferred, variations in shade determined by the length of black tips and quantity of guard hairs. Undercoat is clear light silver as are legs, stomach, buttocks, and underside of tail. The gray body color is darkest on the saddle, lighter on the chest, mane and distinctive harness mark (a band of longer guard hairs from shoulder to elbow). The muzzle, ears, and tail tip are black. The black of the muzzle shades to lighter gray over the forehead and skull. Yellow or brown shading, white patches, indistinct or irregular markings, "sooty" coloring on the lower legs and light circles around the eyes are undesirable. Any overall color other than gray as described above, such as red, brown, solid black, white or other solid color, disqualifies.

GAIT — Normal for an active dog constructed for agility and endurance. At a trot the stride is even and effortless; the back remains level. As the speed of the trot increases, front and rear legs converge equally in straight lines toward a center line beneath the body so that the pads appear to follow in the same tracks (single track). Front and rear quarters are well balanced in angulation and muscular development.

SIZE — The height at the withers for dogs is 20½ inches; for bitches 19½. Weight for dogs about 55 pounds; for bitches about 48 pounds.

DISQUALIFICATIONS

Any overall color other than gray as described above, such as red, brown, solid black, white or other solid color.

HEAD dry (without loose skin); broad at ears, forehead and back of head slightly arched

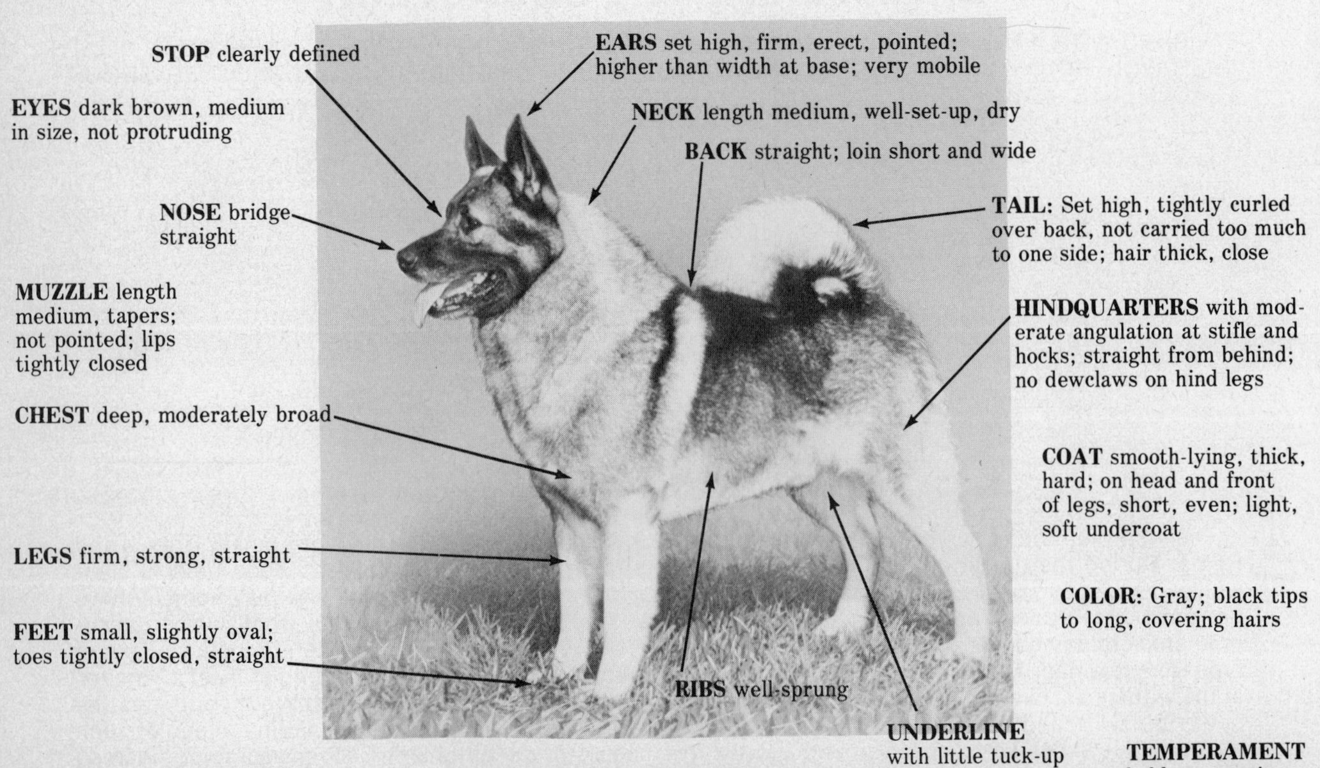
STOP clearly defined
EARS set high, firm, erect, pointed; higher than width at base; very mobile
EYES dark brown, medium in size, not protruding
NECK length medium, well-set-up, dry
BACK straight; loin short and wide
NOSE bridge straight
TAIL: Set high, tightly curled over back, not carried too much to one side; hair thick, close
MUZZLE length medium, tapers; not pointed; lips tightly closed
HINDQUARTERS with moderate angulation at stifle and hocks; straight from behind; no dewclaws on hind legs
CHEST deep, moderately broad
COAT smooth-lying, thick, hard; on head and front of legs, short, even; light, soft undercoat
LEGS firm, strong, straight
COLOR: Gray; black tips to long, covering hairs
FEET small, slightly oval; toes tightly closed, straight
RIBS well-sprung
UNDERLINE with little tuck-up
TEMPERAMENT bold, energetic

SIZE: Height at shoulder—The ideal height for dogs, 20½", for bitches, 19¼"

DISQUALIFICATIONS: Any overall color other than gray as described above, such as red, brown, solid black, white or other solid color

WEIGHT: Dogs, about 55 pounds; bitches, about 48 pounds

VIN-MELCA'S NORTHERN LIGHTS

PICTURED WINNING THE HOUND GROUP FROM THE CLASSES AT THE TENDER AGE OF 16 MONTHS UNDER THE RESPECTED JUDGE MR. RAYMOND BEALE AT THE TUCSON KENNEL CLUB SHOW IN LATE 1974. ALTHOUGH STILL A MERE YOUNGSTER, NORTHERN LIGHTS WAS SELECTED BY HIS BREEDERS FOR THE STANDARD BECAUSE OF HIS MANY FINE QUALITIES SO REMINISCENT OF HIS FAMOUS GRANDSIRE CH. VIN-MELCA'S VAGABOND. A VERY HIGH—STATIONED, HUNTING TYPE HOUND WITH THE TRUE ELKHOUND EYE AND EXPRESSION, NORTHERN LIGHTS IS SIRED BY CH. ARCTIC STORM OF POMFRET X, THE GROUP-PLACING VAGABOND DAUGHTER CH. VIN-MELCA'S NIGHTCAP. HIS OWNERS LOOK FORWARD TO HIS SPECIALS DEBUT.

OWNED BY
LANCE E. MCAFEE
24326 MACFIE DR.
ROMOLAND, CA. 92380

CO-OWNED/BRED/HANDLED BY
PATRICIA V. CRAIGE
1221 FREMONT STREET
MONTERY, CA. 93940

The Norwegian Elkhound belongs to the Spitz group of Arctic breeds. Long used in Scandinavian countries in hunting elk as well as other large game, these dogs are hard, active, and resourceful. The Spitz or Nordic dogs are characterized by sharp, erect ears, a ruff around the neck, a bushy tail curled over the back, and rather straight hocks. The Elkhound has a dense, soft undercoat covered by long, coarse, dark tipped hairs. The color must be gray. The Elkhound is not only a devoted hunting companion but an excellent, adaptable guard dog and a good house pet. Several authorities make a point of warning against overfeeding and obesity in this breed, lest the typical hard appearance be lost. As one might expect, the Elkhound's versatility and vitality have brought it rapid favor. Some 9,000 are registered annually with the AKC; the breed ranking 31st.

OTTER HOUND STANDARD

GENERAL APPEARANCE — The Otter Hound is a large, rough-coated, squarely symmetrical hound. The length of a dog's body from withers to base of tail is approximately equal to its height at the withers. However, a bitch is not to be faulted if her length of body is slightly greater than her height. The Otter Hound is amiable and boisterous. It has an extremely sensitive nose, and is inquisitive and persevering in investigating scents. The Otter Hound should be shown on a loose lead. The Otter Hound hunts its quarry on land and water and requires a combination of characteristics unique among hounds — most notably a rough, double coat and webbed feet.

HEAD — The head is large, fairly narrow, and well covered with hair. The length from tip of nose to occiput is 11 to 12 inches in a hound 26 inches at the withers. This proportion should be maintained in larger and smaller hounds. The *Skull* (cranium) is long, fairly narrow under the hair, and only slightly domed. The muzzle is long and square in cross-section with powerful jaws and deep flews. The *Stop* is not pronounced. The *Nose* is large, dark, and completely pigmented. The *Ears* are long, pendulous, and folded. They are set low and hang close to the head. They are well covered and fringed with hair. The tips of the ear leather reach at least to the tip of the nose. The *Eyes* are deeply set. The haw shows only slightly. The eyes are dark, but may vary with the color of the hound. The *Jaws* are powerful and capable of a crushing grip. A scissors bite is preferred. *Faults:* Bite grossly undershot or overshot.

NECK AND BODY — The *Neck* looks shorter than it really is because of the abundance of hair on it. The neck blends smoothly into the trunk. The *Chest* is deep; the *Ribs* extend well toward the rear of the trunk. The *Topline* is level. The *Tail* is fairly long, reaching at least to the hock. It is well feathered (covered and fringed with hair). It is carried sickle-fashion (not over the back) when a dog is moving or alert, but may droop when the dog is at rest.

FOREQUARTERS — *Shoulders* clean, powerful, and well-sloped. *Legs* heavy-boned and straight.

HINDQUARTERS — Thighs large and well-muscled. *Legs* moderately angulated. Legs parallel when viewed from the rear. *Feet* large, broad, compact, and well padded, with membranes connecting the toes (web-footed). *Dewclaws*, if any, on the hind legs are generally removed; dewclaws on the forelegs may be removed.

COAT — The rough outer coat is three to six inches long on the back, shorter on the extremities. It must be hard (coarse and crisp). A water-resistant inner coat of short woolly hair is an essential feature of the breed. A naturally stripped coat lacking length and fringes is correct for an Otter Hound that is being worked. A proper hunting coat will show the hard outer coat and woolly undercoat. *Faults:* A soft outer coat is a very serious fault as is a woolly-textured top coat. Lack of undercoat is a serious fault. An outer coat much longer than six inches becomes heavy when wet and is a fault.

COLOR — Any color or combination of colors is acceptable. The nose should be darklly pigmented, black or liver, depending on the color of the hound.

GAIT — The Otter Hound moves freely with forward reach and drive. The gait is smooth and effortless and capable of being maintained for many miles. Otter Hounds single-track at slower speed than light-bodied hounds. Because they do not lift their feet high off the ground, Otter Hounds may shuffle when they walk or move at a slow trot.

SIZE — Males range from 24 to 27 inches at the withers, and weigh from 75 to 115 pounds, depending on the height and condition of the hound. Bitches are 22 to 26 inches at the withers and 65 to 100 pounds. A hound in hard working condition may weigh as much as 15 pounds less than one of the same height that is not being worked. Otter Hounds should not be penalized for being shown in working condition (lean, well-muscled, naturally stripped coat).

Approved October 12, 1971

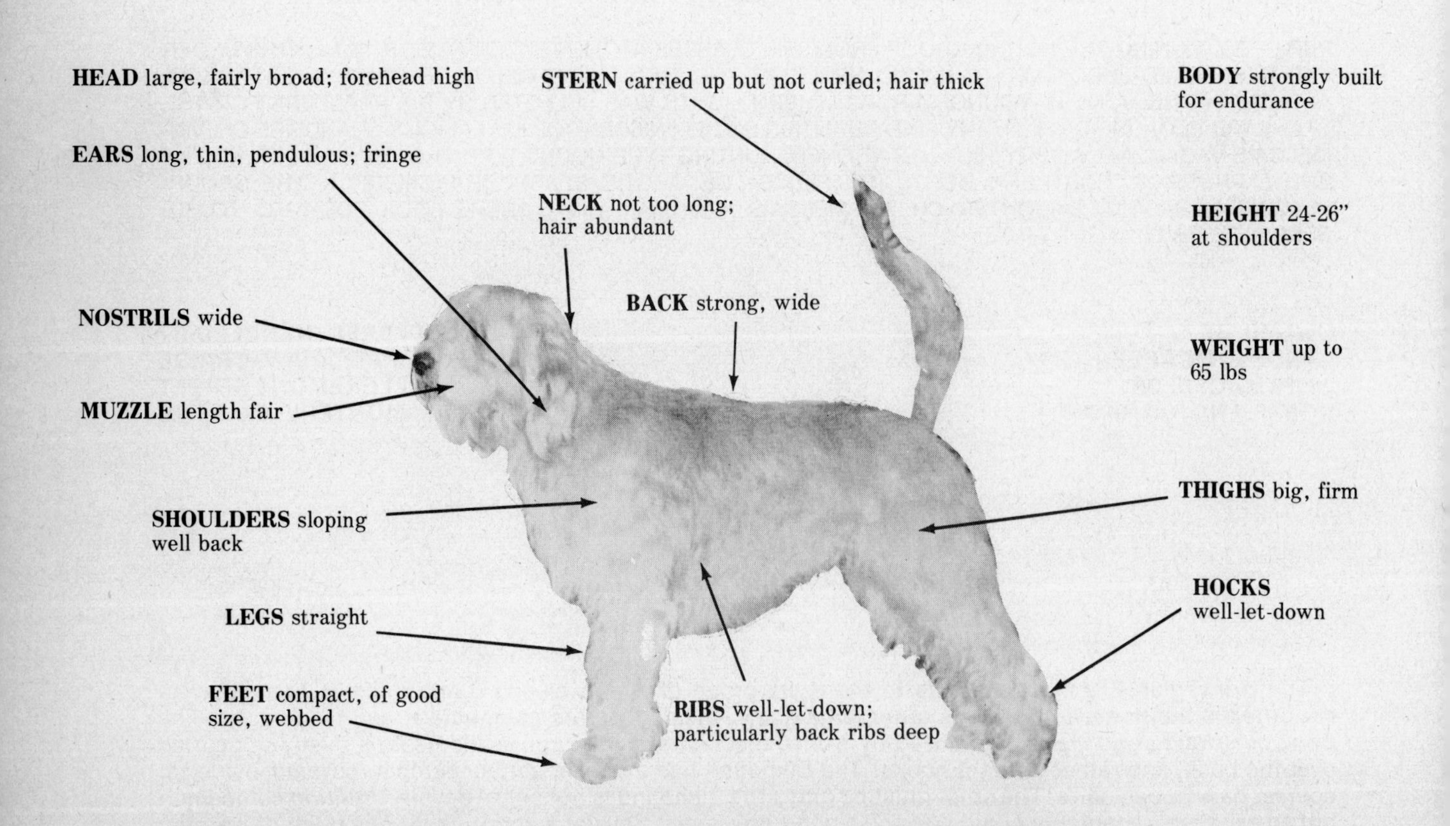

CH. RINJAN'S DANDELION WHINE

A MULTIPLE BEST IN SHOW WINNER "BOO" IS NUMBER 1 OTTER HOUND AND NUMBER 7 HOUND IN AMERICA. "BOO" IS THE TOP ALL TIME WINNING OTTER HOUND IN THE HISTORY OF THE BREED.

HANDLER—BOB STEBBINS

OWNER
ROBERT E. MAYTAG
TAGHOLLOW KENNELS
NEWTON, IOWA 50208

The Otter Hounds hunting skill goes back to the days of Edward II in England. They were used extensively to hunt the Otter so that the fish were left alone to be the fishermans prey. They were most commonly used in packs. His working ability was so renowned that his exhibition at dog shows was somewhat limited. They first appeared at a bench-show in the United States in 1907 at Claremont, Oklahoma. Although they have never been exhibited extensively they have attained a good deal of success in recent years at many shows.

RHODESIAN RIDGEBACK STANDARD

The peculiarity of this breed is the *ridge* on the back, which is formed by the hair growing in the opposite direction to the rest of the coat. The ridge must be regarded as the characteristic feature of the breed. The ridge should be clearly defined, tapering and symmetrical. It should start immediately behind the shoulders and continue to a point between the prominence of the hips, and should contain two identical crowns opposite each other. The lower edges of the crown should not extend further down the ridge than one third of the ridge.

GENERAL APPEARANCE — The Ridgeback should represent a strong muscular and active dog, symmetrical in outline, and capable of great endurance with a fair amount of speed.

HEAD — Should be of a fair length, the skull flat and rather broad between the ears and should be free from wrinkles when in repose. The stop should be reasonably well defined. *Muzzle* — Should be long, deep and powerful, jaws level and strong with well-developed teeth, especially the canines or holders. The lips clean, closely fitting the jaws. *Eyes* — Should be moderately well apart, and should be round, bright and sparkling, with intelligent expression, their color harmonizing with the color of the dog. *Ears* — Should be set rather high, of medium size, rather wide at base, and tapering to a rounded point. They should be carried close to the head. *Nose* — Should be black, or brown, in keeping with the color of the dog. No other colored nose is permissible. A black nose should be accompanied by dark eyes, a brown nose by amber eyes.

NECK AND SHOULDERS — The neck should be fairly strong and free from throatiness. The shoulders should be sloping, clean and muscular, denoting speed.

BODY, BACK, CHEST AND LOINS — The chest should not be too wide, but very deep and capacious; ribs moderately well sprung, never rounded like barrel hoops (which would indicate want of speed), the back powerful, the loins strong, muscular and slightly arched. *Legs and Feet* — The forelegs should be perfectly straight, strong and heavy in bone; elbows close to the body. The feet should be compact, with well-arched toes, round, tough, elastic pads, protected by hair between the toes and pads. In the hind legs the muscles should be clean, well defined, and hocks well down. *Tail* — Should be strong at the insertion, and generally tapering towards the end, free from coarseness. It should not be inserted too high, or too low, and should be carried with a slight curve upwards, never curled.

COAT — Should be short and dense, sleek and glossy in appearance, but neither woolly nor silky. *Color* — Light wheaten to red wheaten. A little white on the chest and toes permissible but excessive white there and any white on the belly or above the toes is undesirable.

SIZE — A mature Ridgeback should be a handsome, upstanding dog; dogs should be of a height of 25 to 27 inches, and bitches 24 to 26 inches. *Weight* — (Desirable) dogs 75 pounds, bitches 65 pounds.

SCALE OF POINTS

Ridge	20	Coat	5
Head	15	Tail	5
Neck and shoulders	10	Size, symmetry, gen. appearance	20
Body, back, chest, loins	10		
Legs and feet	15	Total	100

Approved November, 1955

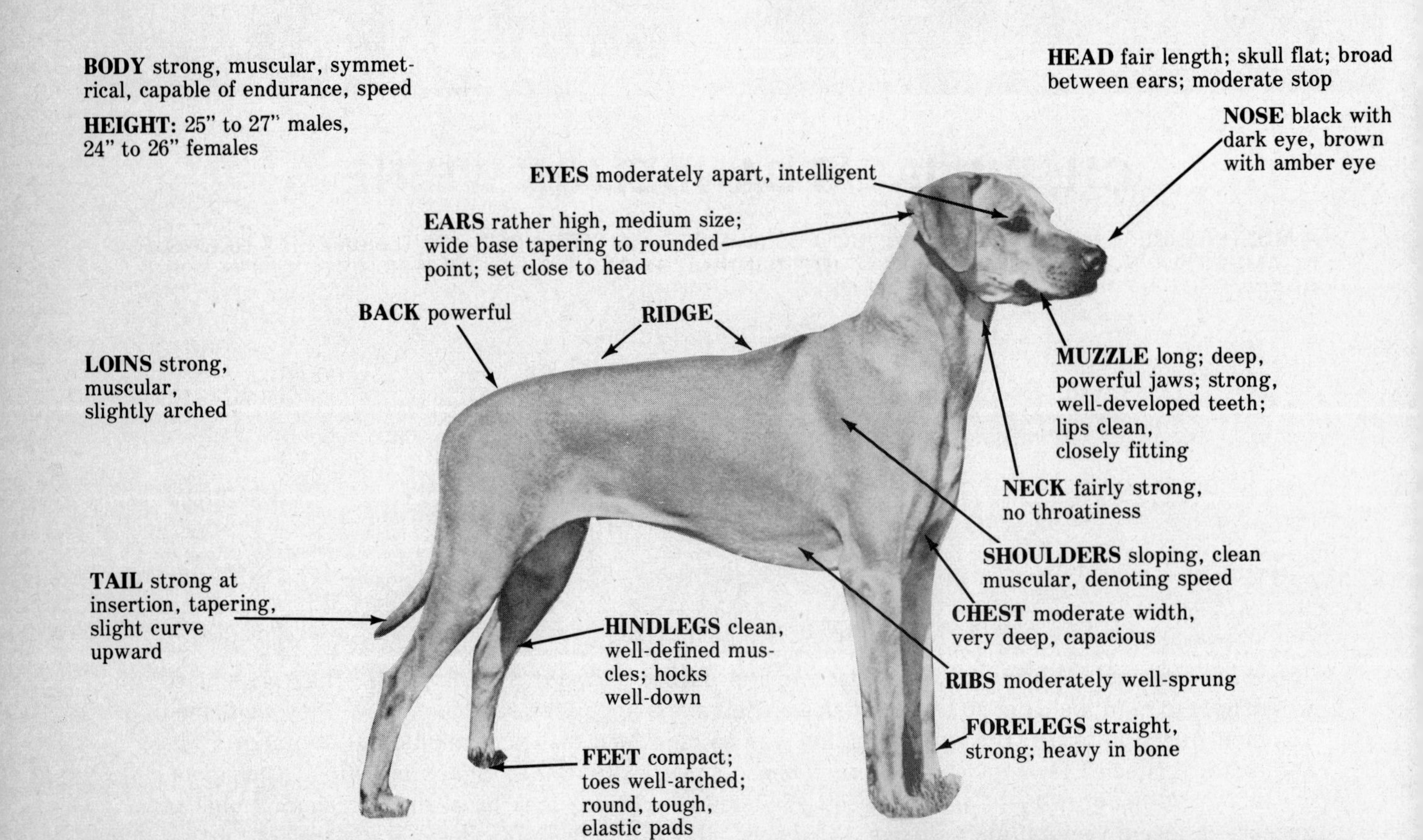

BODY strong, muscular, symmetrical, capable of endurance, speed
HEIGHT: 25" to 27" males, 24" to 26" females
HEAD fair length; skull flat; broad between ears; moderate stop
NOSE black with dark eye, brown with amber eye
EYES moderately apart, intelligent
EARS rather high, medium size; wide base tapering to rounded point; set close to head
BACK powerful
RIDGE
LOINS strong, muscular, slightly arched
MUZZLE long; deep, powerful jaws; strong, well-developed teeth; lips clean, closely fitting
NECK fairly strong, no throatiness
SHOULDERS sloping, clean muscular, denoting speed
TAIL strong at insertion, tapering, slight curve upward
CHEST moderate width, very deep, capacious
HINDLEGS clean, well-defined muscles; hocks well-down
RIBS moderately well-sprung
FORELEGS straight, strong; heavy in bone
FEET compact; toes well-arched; round, tough, elastic pads
COAT short, dense, glossy
COLOR: Light wheaten to red wheaten; little white on chest and toes permissible
RIDGE characteristic of breed; clearly defined, tapering, symmetrical; hair grows opposite direction from immediately behind shoulders to between prominence of hips; two identical crowns opposite each other; crowns not more than 1/3 length of ridge

ROLLING KENNELS RHODESIAN RIDGEBACKS

ROLLING KENNELS WAS FOUNDED IN 1959 AND SINCE THAT TIME HAS BEEN BREEDING CHAMPIONSHIP RHODESIAN RIDGEBACKS. THEY HAVE HAD THE TOP STUD DOG (CH. ROLLINGS TOOWOOMBA) FOR 4 YEARS, AND CH. ROLLINGS LINGA WAS BOB WESTMINSTER 1974.

ROLLING KENNELS
D. JAY HYMAN
ROUTE 109
BARNESVILLE, MD 20703
(301) 652-4223

The Rhodesian Ridgeback took its origin in Southern Africa as the product of many European breeds, possibly crossed with native dogs. By the 20th century, the general type had become well-defined and was used for guard duty, companionship, and hunting. These speedy, durable, and courageous dogs, in fact, became legendary for their daring in lion hunts. The Rhodesian Ridgeback is large, 25 to 27 inches at the shoulder in dogs, muscular, and heavy boned, with no excess flesh whatsoever. The short, dense, glossy coat comes in wheaten shades. A ridge on the back characterizes this breed. The ridge must be clearly defined, symmetrical, and tapering. Anteriorly, immediately behind the shoulders, are two whorled crowns, one on each side. The Rhodesian Ridgeback is highly valued today as a powerful, intelligent guard dog and an excellent and devoted companion. Some 750 are registered annually in the U.S. The breed ranks 70th.

SALUKI STANDARD

HEAD — Long and narrow, skull moderately wide between the ears, not domed, stop not pronounced, the whole showing great quality. Nose black or liver.

EARS — Long and covered with long silky hair hanging close to the skull and mobile.

EYES — Dark to hazel and bright; large and oval, but not prominent.

TEETH — Strong and level.

NECK — Long, supple and well muscled.

CHEST — Deep and moderately narrow.

FOREQUARTERS — Shoulders sloping and set well back, well muscled without being coarse.

FORELEGS — Straight and long from the elbow to the knee.

HINDQUARTERS — Strong, hipbones set well apart and stifle moderately bent, hocks low to the ground, showing galloping and jumping power.

LOIN AND BACK — Back fairly broad, muscles slightly arched over loin.

FEET — Of moderate length, toes long and well arched, not splayed out, but at the same time not cat-footed; the whole being strong and supple and well feathered between the toes.

TAIL — Long, set on low and carried naturally in a curve, well feathered on the underside with long silky hair, not bushy.

COAT — Smooth and of a soft silky texture, slight feather on the legs, feather at the back of the thighs and sometimes with slight woolly feather on the thigh and shoulder. *Colors* — White, cream, fawn, golden, red, grizzle and tan tricolor (white, black and tan), and black and tan.

GENERAL APPEARANCE — The whole appearance of this breed should give an impression of grace and symmetry and of great speed and endurance coupled with strength and activity to enable it to kill gazelle or other quarry over deep sand or rocky mountains. The expression should be dignified and gentle with deep, faithful, far-seeing eyes. Dogs should average in height from 23 to 28 inches and bitches may be considerably smaller, this being very typical of the breed.

THE SMOOTH VARIETY — In this variety the points should be the same with the exception of the coat, which has no feathering.

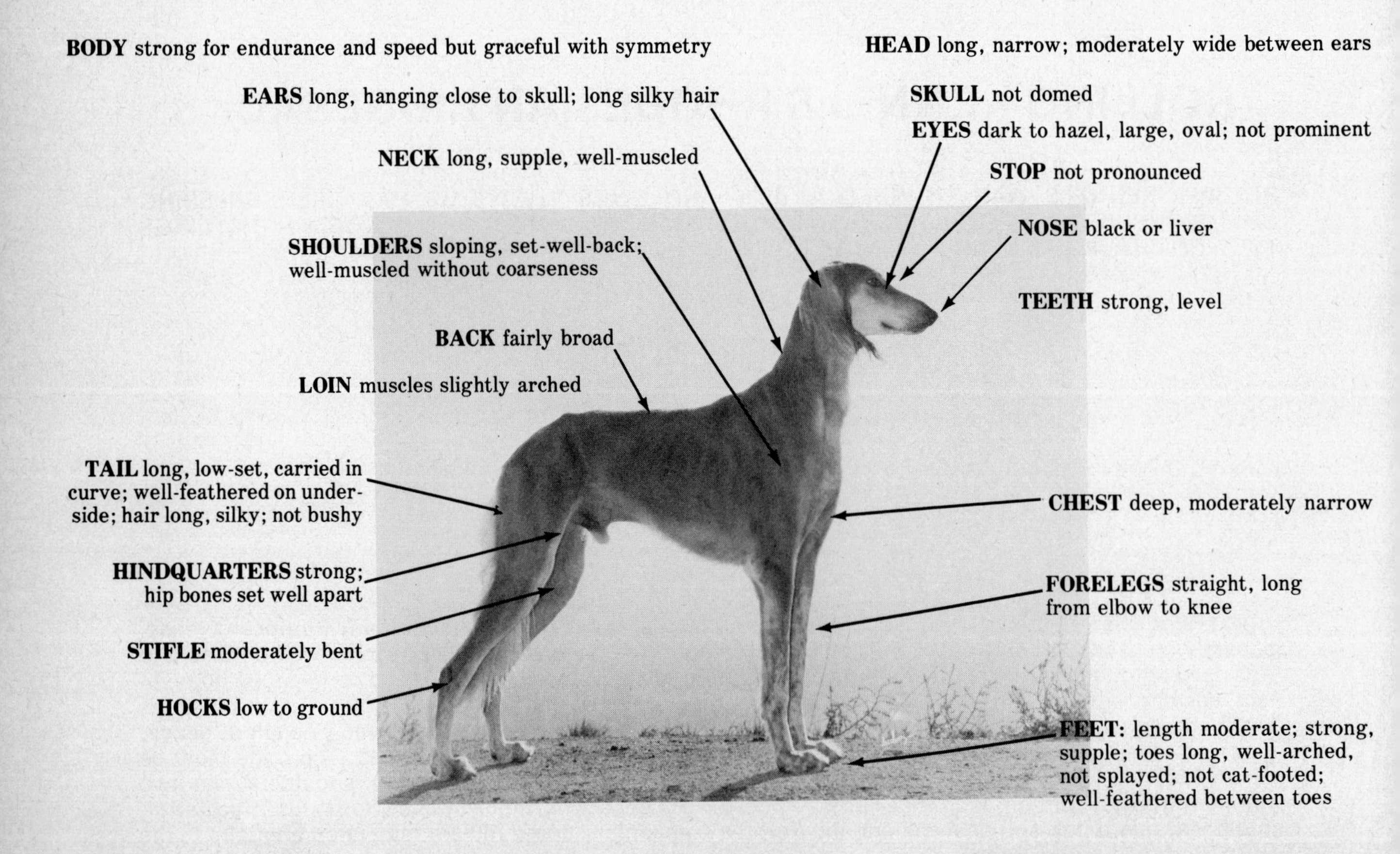

BODY strong for endurance and speed but graceful with symmetry
HEAD long, narrow; moderately wide between ears
EARS long, hanging close to skull; long silky hair
SKULL not domed
EYES dark to hazel, large, oval; not prominent
NECK long, supple, well-muscled
STOP not pronounced
NOSE black or liver
SHOULDERS sloping, set-well-back; well-muscled without coarseness
TEETH strong, level
BACK fairly broad
LOIN muscles slightly arched
TAIL long, low-set, carried in curve; well-feathered on underside; hair long, silky; not bushy
CHEST deep, moderately narrow
HINDQUARTERS strong; hip bones set well apart
FORELEGS straight, long from elbow to knee
STIFLE moderately bent
HOCKS low to ground
FEET: length moderate; strong, supple; toes long, well-arched, not splayed; not cat-footed; well-feathered between toes
HEIGHT: males 23" to 28; females may be considerably smaller
COLOR: White; cream; fawn; golden; red; grizzle; tan; tricolor (white, black, tan); black and tan
COAT smooth; texture soft, silky; slight feather on legs; feather back of thighs; in the smooth variety there is no feathering

Dogs very like today's Salukis were pictured entombed and even embalmed in ancient Egypt. The type, a coursing, gaze hound of the Greyhound group, used for hunting gazelles, has been faithfully preserved in the Near East. The Saluki was permanently introduced into England around the turn of the century and into the U.S. in 1927. The Saluki must give the impression of grace and symmetry, great speed and endurance, strength, and dignity. Type is quite variable, especially in size. Almost all colors are acceptable. In the feathered variety, the smooth silky coat shows slight feathering on the legs, at the back of the thighs, and on the tail. The smooth variety, rarely seen, has no feathering. The Saluki is aloof to strangers but a devoted and warm companion in the home. Some 600 are registered annually in the U.S., the breed ranking 75th. As one might expect of such an elegant breed, the numbers in show competition are large in proportion to the numbers registered and they do very well in Group wins.

SCOTTISH DEERHOUND STANDARD

HEAD — Should be broadest at the ears, narrowing slightly to the eyes, with the muzzle tapering more decidely to the nose. The muzzle should be pointed, but the teeth and lips level. The head should be long, the skull flat rather than round with a very slight rise over the eyes but nothing approaching a stop. The hair on the skull should be moderately long and softer than the rest of the coat. The nose should be black (in some blue fawns—blue) and slightly aquiline. In lighter colored dogs the black muzzle is preferable. There should be a good mustache of rather silky hair and a fair beard. *Ears* — Should be set on high; in repose, folded back like a Greyhound's, though raised above the head in excitement without losing the fold, and even in some cases semierect. A prick ear is bad. Big thick ears hanging flat to the head or heavily coated with long hair are bad faults. The ears should be soft, glossy, like a mouse's coat to the touch and the smaller the better. There should be no long coat or long fringe, but there is sometimes a silky, silvery coat on the body of the ear and the tip. On all Deerhounds, irrespective of color of coat, the ears should be black or dark colored.

NECK AND SHOULDERS — The neck should be long — of a length befitting the Greyhound character of the dog. Extreme length is neither necessary nor desirable. Deerhounds do not stoop to their work like the Greyhounds. The mane, which every good specimen should have, sometimes detracts from the apparent length of the neck. The neck, however, must be strong as is necessary to hold a stag. The nape of the neck should be very prominent where the head is set on, and the throat clean-cut at the angle and prominent. Shoulders should be well sloped; blades well back and not too much width between them. Loaded and straight shoulders are very bad faults.

TAIL — Should be tolerably long, tapering and reaching to within 1½ inches off the ground and about 1½ inches below the hocks. Dropped perfectly down or curved when the Deerhound is still, when in motion or excited, curved, but in no instance lifted out of line of the back. It should be well covered with hair, on the inside, thick and wiry, underside longer and towards the end a slight fringe is not objectionable. A curl or ring tail is undesirable.

EYES — Should be dark — generally dark brown, brown or hazel. A very light eye is not liked. The eye should be moderately full, with a soft look in repose, but a keen, far-away look when the Deerhound is roused. Rims of eyelids should be black.

BODY — General formation is that of a Greyhound of larger size and bone. Chest deep rather than broad but not too narrow or slab-sided. Good girth of chest is indicative of great lung power. The loin well arched and drooping to the tail. A straight back is not desirable, this formation being unsuited for uphill work, and very unsightly. *Legs and Feet* — Legs should be broad and flat, and good broad forearms and elbows are desirable. Forelegs must, of course, be as straight as possible. Feet close and compact, with well-arranged toe. The hindquarters drooping, and as broad and powerful as possible, the hips being set wide apart. A narrow rear denotes lack of power. The stifles should be well bent, with great length from hip to hock, which should be broad and flat. Cowhocks, weak pasterns, straight stifles and splay feet are very bad faults.

COAT — The hair on the body, neck and quarters should be harsh and wiry, about 3 or 4 inches long; that on the head, breast and belly much softer. There should be a slight fringe on the inside of the forelegs and hind legs but nothing approaching the "feather" of a Collie. A woolly coat is bad. Some good strains have a mixture of silky coat with the hard which is preferable to a woolly coat. The climate of the United States tends to produce the mixed coat. The ideal coat is a thick, close-lying ragged coat, harsh or crisp to the touch. *Color* is a matter of fancy, but the dark blue-gray is most preferred. Next come the darker and lighter grays or brindles, the darkest being generally preferred. Yellow and sandy red or red fawn, especially with black ears and muzzles, are equally high in estimation. This was the color of the oldest known strains — the McNeil and Chesthill Menzies. White is condemned by all authorities, but a white chest and white toes, occurring as they do in many of the darkest-colored dogs, are not objected to, although the less the better, for the Deerhound is a self-colored dog. A white blaze on the head, or a white collar, should entirely disqualify. The less white the better but a slight white tip to the stern occurs in some of the best strains.

HEIGHT OF DOGS — From 30 to 32 inches, or even more if there be symmetry without coarseness, which is rare. *Height of Bitches* — From 28 inches upwards. There is no objection to a bitch being large, unless too coarse, as even at her greatest height she does not approach that of the dog, and there-

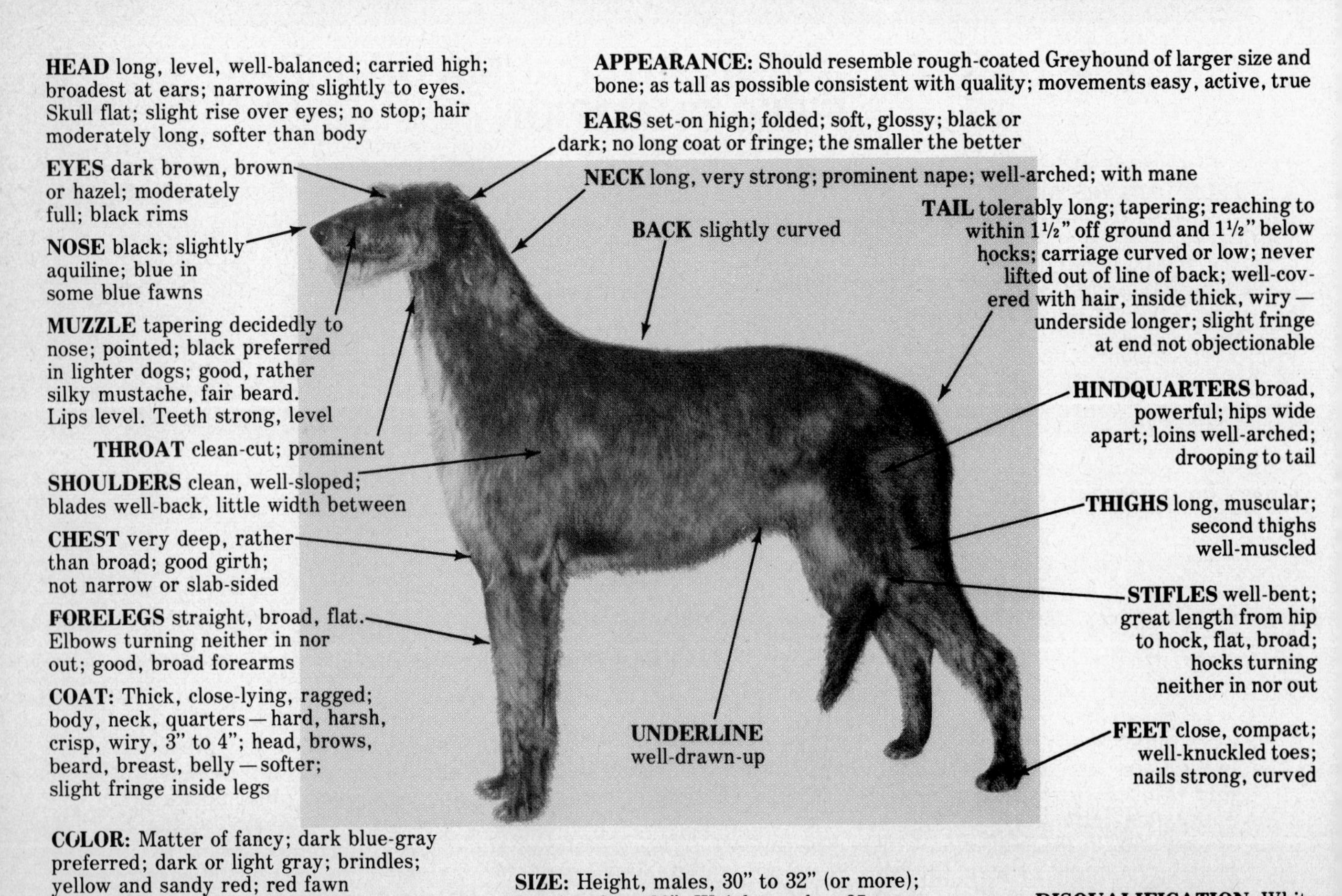
HEAD long, level, well-balanced; carried high; broadest at ears; narrowing slightly to eyes. Skull flat; slight rise over eyes; no stop; hair moderately long, softer than body
APPEARANCE: Should resemble rough-coated Greyhound of larger size and bone; as tall as possible consistent with quality; movements easy, active, true
EARS set-on high; folded; soft, glossy; black or dark; no long coat or fringe; the smaller the better
EYES dark brown, brown or hazel; moderately full; black rims
NECK long, very strong; prominent nape; well-arched; with mane
NOSE black; slightly aquiline; blue in some blue fawns
BACK slightly curved
TAIL tolerably long; tapering; reaching to within 1½" off ground and 1½" below hocks; carriage curved or low; never lifted out of line of back; well-covered with hair, inside thick, wiry — underside longer; slight fringe at end not objectionable
MUZZLE tapering decidedly to nose; pointed; black preferred in lighter dogs; good, rather silky mustache, fair beard. Lips level. Teeth strong, level
HINDQUARTERS broad, powerful; hips wide apart; loins well-arched; drooping to tail
THROAT clean-cut; prominent
SHOULDERS clean, well-sloped; blades well-back, little width between
THIGHS long, muscular; second thighs well-muscled
CHEST very deep, rather than broad; good girth; not narrow or slab-sided
STIFLES well-bent; great length from hip to hock, flat, broad; hocks turning neither in nor out
FORELEGS straight, broad, flat. Elbows turning neither in nor out; good, broad forearms
COAT: Thick, close-lying, ragged; body, neck, quarters—hard, harsh, crisp, wiry, 3" to 4"; head, brows, beard, breast, belly—softer; slight fringe inside legs
UNDERLINE well-drawn-up
FEET close, compact; well-knuckled toes; nails strong, curved

COLOR: Matter of fancy; dark blue-gray preferred; dark or light gray; brindles; yellow and sandy red; red fawn (especially with black ears and muzzles); white chest and toes not objectionable

SIZE: Height, males, 30" to 32" (or more); females, from 28". Weight, males, 85 to 110 lbs; females, 75 to 95 lbs

DISQUALIFICATION: White blaze on head or white collar

CH. GUILLARI ANNIE LAURIE

THIS YOUNG BITCH HAS ALREADY COMPILED A RECORD OF 1 BEST IN SHOW AND NUMEROUS GROUP PLACEMENTS INCLUDING MANY FIRSTS. SHE IS THE NUMBER ONE SCOTTISH DEERHOUND IN THE NATION.

HANDLERS: JANE & ROBERT FORSYTH

DIONNE ELINOR BUTT
R.D. 1, BOX 193
HONEY BROOK, PA. 19344

fore could not be too big for work as overbig dogs are. *Weight* — From 85 to 110 pounds in dogs, and from 75 to 95 pounds in bitches.

Points of the Deerhound
Arranged in Order of Importance

1. *Typical* — A Deerhound should resemble a rough-coated Greyhound of larger size and bone. 2. *Movements* — Easy, active and true. 3. As tall as possible consistent with qualilty. 4. *Head* — Long, level, well balanced, carried high. 5. *Body* — Long, very deep in brisket, well-sprung ribs and great breadth across hips. 6. *Forelegs* — Strong and quite straight, with elbows neither in nor out. 7. *Thighs* — Long and muscular, second thighs well muscled, stifles well bent. 8. *Loins* — Well arched, and belly well drawn up. 9. *Coat* — Rough and hard, with softer beard and brows. 10. *Feet* — Close, compact, with well-knuckled toes. 11. *Ears* — Small (dark) with Greyhoundlike carriage. 12. *Eyes* — Dark, moderately full. 13. *Neck* — Long, well arched, very strong with prominent nape. 14. *Shoulders* — Clean, set sloping. 15. *Chest* — Very deep but not too narrow. 16. *Tail* — Long and curved slightly, carried low. 17. *Teeth* — Strong and level. 18. *Nails* — Strong and curved.

DISQUALIFICATION

White blaze on the head, or a white collar.

Approved March, 1935

GENERAL APPEARANCE — The Whippet should be a dog of moderate size, very alert, that can cover a maximum of distance with a minimum of lost motion, a true sporting hound. Should be put down in hard condition but with no suggestion of being muscle-bound.

HEAD — Long and lean, fairly wide between the ears, scarcely perceptible stop, good length of muzzle which should be powerful without being coarse. Nose entirely black. *Ears* — Small, fine in texture, thrown back and folded. Semipricked when at attention. Gay ears are incorrect and should be severely penalized.

Eyes — Large, intelligent, round in shape and dark hazel in color, must be at least as dark as the coat color. Expression should be keen and alert. Light yellow or oblique eyes should be strictly penalized. A sulky expression and lack of alertness to be considered most undesirable. *Teeth* — White, strong and even. Teeth of upper jaw should fit closely over the lower. *An undershot mouth shall disqualify.*

NECK — Long and muscular, well-arched and with no suggestion of throatiness, widening gradually into the shoulders. Must not have any tendency to a "ewe" neck. *Shoulders* — Long, well-laid back with long, flat muscles. Loaded shoulders are a *very* serious fault.

BRISKET — Very deep and strong, reaching as nearly as possible to the point of the elbow. Ribs well sprung but with no suggestion of barrel shape. Should fill in the space between the forelegs so that there is no appearance of a hollow between them.

FORELEGS — Straight and rather long, held in line with the shoulders and *not* set under the body so as to make a forechest. Elbows should turn neither in nor out and move freely with the point of the shoulder. Fair amount of bone, which should carry right down to the feet. Pasterns strong. *Feet* — Must be well formed with strong, thick pads and well-knuckled-up paws. A thin, flat, open foot is a serious fault. *Hindquarters* — Long and powerful, stifles well bent, hocks well let down and close to the ground. Thighs broad and muscular, the muscles should be long and flat. A steep croup is most undesirable.

BACK — Strong and powerful, rather long with a good, natural arch over the loin creating a definite tuck-up of the underline but covering a lot of ground. *Tail* — Long and tapering, should reach to a hipbone when drawn through between the hind legs. Must not be carried higher than the top of the back when moving.

COAT — Close, smooth and firm in texture.

COLOR — Immaterial.

SIZE — Ideal height for dogs, 19 to 22 inches; for bitches, 18 to 21 inches. These are not intended to be definite limits, only approximate.

GAIT — Low, free moving and smooth, as long as is commensurate with the size of the dog. A short, mincing gait with high knee action should be severely penalized.

DISQUALIFICATION

Undershot mouth.

Approved November 9, 1955

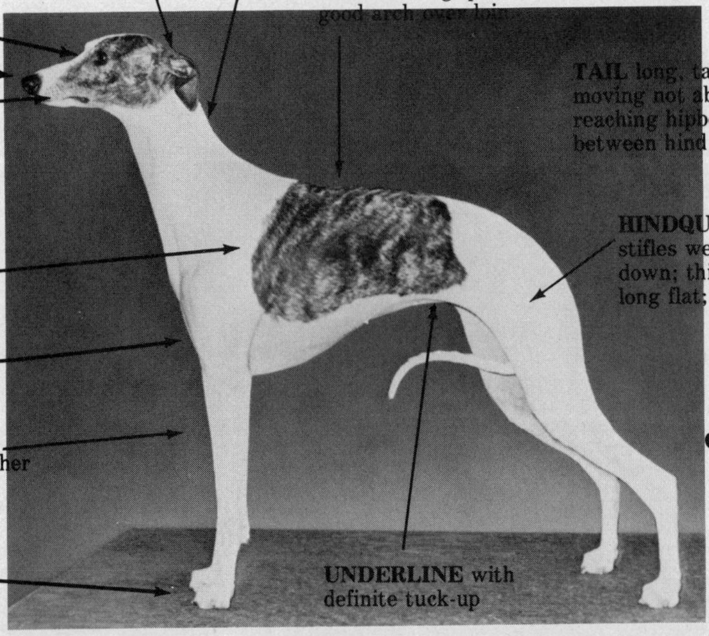

HEAD long, lean; fairly wide between ears; no perceptible stop

EXPRESSION keen, alert

EYES large, round; dark hazel or dark as coat color

NOSE black

MUZZLE good length, powerful but not coarse

TEETH even, strong, white; uppers fit closely over lowers; undershot mouth disqualifies

SHOULDERS long, well-laid-back; muscles flat; long; loaded shoulders serious fault

BRISKET deep, strong; reaching approx. to elbow; ribs well-sprung; no suggestion of barrel shape

FORELEGS straight, rather long; in line with shoulders; elbows turning neither in nor out; good bone; pasterns strong

FEET well-formed; pads thick; toes well-knuckled

SIZE: Height, dogs, 19-22"; females, 18-21" (approx.)

EARS small, fine in texture; thrown back; folded; semi-pricked at attention; gay ears severely penalized

NECK long, muscular, well-arched; no throatiness; widening gradually into shoulders; no "ewe" neck

BACK strong, powerful, rather long; good arch over loin

UNDERLINE with definite tuck-up

BODY: size moderate, alert; condition hard with no suggestion of being muscle-bound

TAIL long, tapering; carriage when moving not above topline; reaching hipbone when drawn through between hind legs

HINDQUARTERS long, powerful; stifles well-bent; hocks well-let-down; thighs broad, muscular, long flat; steep croup undesirable

COAT close, smooth, firm

COLOR: Any color

DISQUALIFICATION: Undershot mouth

CH. RUNNER'S OUR OWN CHARISMA

CHARISMA IS THE #1 WHIPPET AND #7 HOUND IN THE NATION FOR 1974. SHE WON BEST IN SHOW IN JULY, 1974 AT THE VENTURA COUNTY DOG FANCIERS ASSN. SHOW (PICTURED ABOVE) WITH A TOTAL ENTRY OF 4036, UNDER DR. J.D. JONES. CHARISMA STARTED WITH FIRST AKC SHOW BY WINNING BOS SWEEPSTAKE PUPPY AND RESERVE WINNERS BITCH AT THE WESTERN WHIPPET SPECIALTY, ENTRY OF 106, AT 7½ MONTHS OLD. SHE FINISHED HER CHAMPIONSHIP THE FOLLOWING YEAR FROM BBE CLASS, AT THE SPECIALTY. SHOWN AS A SPECIAL IN 1974, HANDLED BY MIKE DOUGHERTY, SHE BECAME THE NUMBER ONE WHIPPET NATIONWIDE WITH ONE BIS, 26 BB, 6 GR I, 2 GR II, 1 GR III, and 3 GR IV. CHARISMA IS EQUALLY AT HOME IN THE SHOW RING OR OPEN FIELD COURSING AND IS ALSO TRAINED FOR RUNNING THE LURE ON THE RACE TRACK. SHE IS TRULY A TOP WINNER WHO CAN STILL FUNCTION IN THE PURPOSE THAT THE WHIPPET WAS BRED TO BE USED FOR. WHELPED DEC. 21, 1971 (BITCH).

HANDLER: MIKE DOUGHERTY

ISABELL STOFFERS
STOFFERS RUNNING RANCH
20827 MESARICA ROAD
COVINA, CALIF. 91724
(213) 332-2190

The Whippet is English in origin but its ancestry is not documented. Apparently the Whippets of the 19th century were a working man's dog, perhaps bred for rough races after hare. The ancestral breeds may well have been the Greyhound and local English Terriers. In any event, the Whippet became a fabulous running machine. Similar in appearance to the Greyhound, the Whippet is smaller, more refined, and gentler. It must be elegant, fit, speedy, powerful, and balanced, with no trace of coarseness. The coat is close, smooth, and firm. Color is immaterial. The gait is low, free-moving, and smooth. A short, mincing gait with high knee action is very faulty. Today the Whippet makes a loving house pet but is also used widely for racing. About 1,000 are registered annually with the AKC, the breed ranking 63rd. Whippets have done very well in Group wins in recent years, placing second only to Afghans among hounds.

FOXHOUND [ENGLISH] STANDARD

HEAD — Should be of full size, but by no means heavy. Brow pronounced, but not high or sharp. There should be a good length and breadth, sufficient to give in a dog hound a girth in front of the ears of fully 16 inches. The nose should be long (4½ inches) and wide, with open nostrils. Ears set on low and lying close to the cheeks. Most English hounds are "rounded" which means that about 1½ inches are taken off the end of the ear. The teeth must meet squarely, either a *pig-mouth* (overshot) or undershot being a disqualification.

NECK — Must be long and clean, without the slightest throatiness, not less than 10 inches from cranium to shoulder. It should taper nicely from shoulders to head, and the upper outline should be slightly convex. The *Shoulders* should be long and well clothed with muscle, without being heavy, especially at the points. They must be well sloped, and the true arm between the front and the elbow must be long and muscular, but free from fat or lumber. *Chest and Back Ribs* — The chest should girth over 31 inches in a 24-inch hound, and the back ribs must be very deep.

BACK AND LOIN — Must both be very muscular, running into each other without any contraction between them. The couples must be wide, even to raggedness, and the topline of the back should be absolutely level, the *Stern* well set on and carried gaily but not in any case curved *over* the back like a squirrel's tail. The end should taper to a point and there should be a fringe of hair below. The *Hindquarters* or propellers are required to be very strong, and as endurance is of even greater consequence than speed, straight stifles are preferred to those much bent as in a Greyhound. *Elbows* set quite straight, and neither turned in nor out are a *sine qua non*. They must be well let down by means of the long true arm above mentioned.

LEGS AND FEET — Every Master of Foxhounds insists on legs as straight as a post, and as strong; size of bone at the ankle being especially regarded as all important. The desire for straightness had a tendency to produce knuckling-over, which at one time was countenanced, but in recent years this defect has been eradicated by careful breeding and intelligent adjudication, and one sees very little of this trouble in the best modern Foxhounds. The bone cannot be too large, and the feet in all cases should be round and catlike, with well-developed knuckles and strong horn, which last is of the greatest importance.

COLOR AND COAT — Not regarded as very important, so long as the former is a good "hound color," and the latter is short, dense, hard, and glossy. Hound colors are black, tan, and white, or any combination of these three, also the various "pies" compounded of white and the color of the hare and badger, or yellow, or tan. The *Symmetry* of the Foxhound is of the greatest importance, and what is known as "quality" is highly regarded by all good judges.

SCALE OF POINTS

Head	5	Elbows	5
Neck	10	Legs and feet	20
Shoulders	10	Color and coat	5
Chest and back ribs	10	Stern	5
Back and loin	15	Symmetry	5
Hindquarters	10	Total	100

DISQUALIFICATION

Pig-mouth (overshot) or undershot.

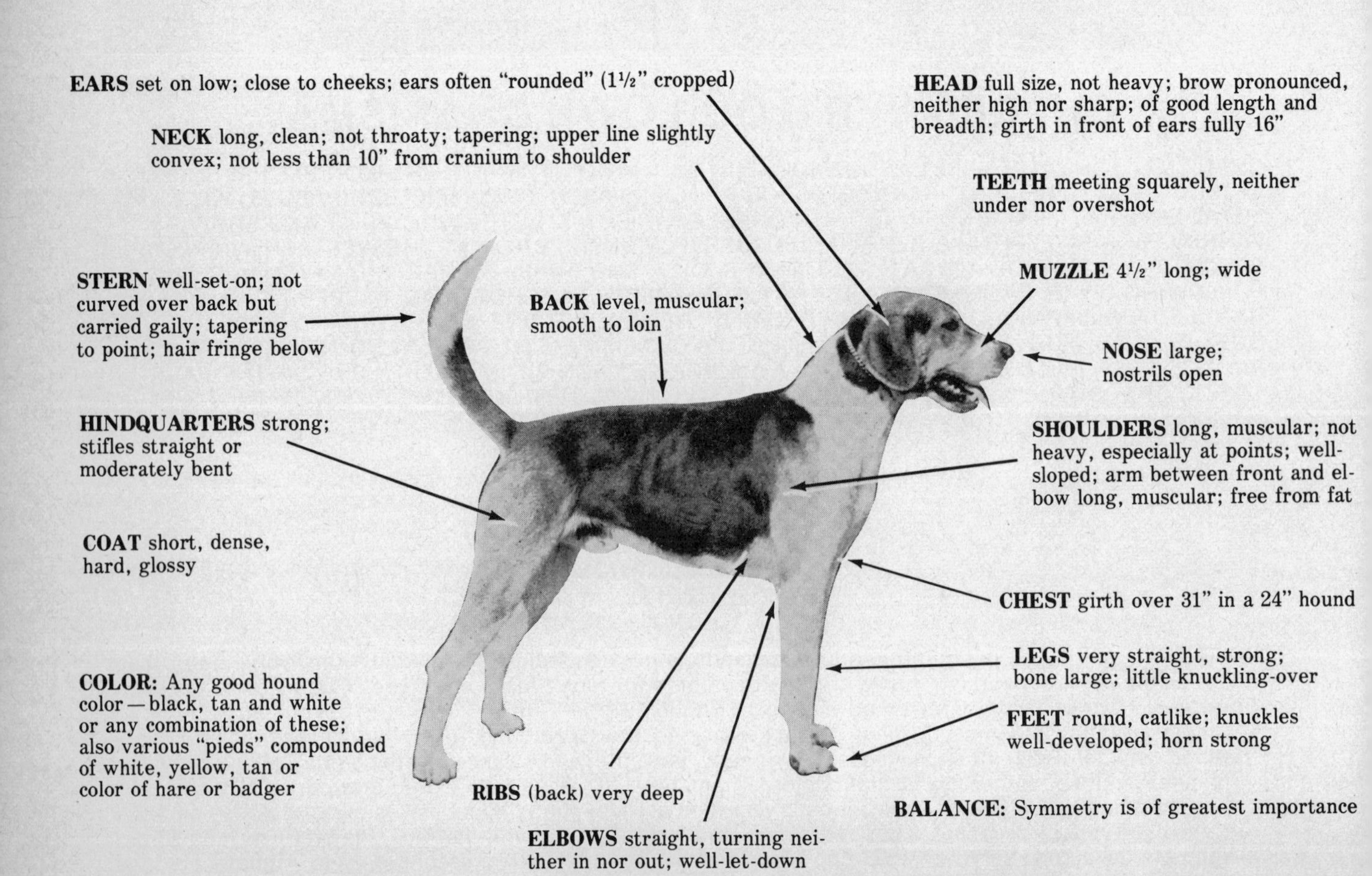

EARS set on low; close to cheeks; ears often "rounded" (1½" cropped)
NECK long, clean; not throaty; tapering; upper line slightly convex; not less than 10" from cranium to shoulder
HEAD full size, not heavy; brow pronounced, neither high nor sharp; of good length and breadth; girth in front of ears fully 16"
TEETH meeting squarely, neither under nor overshot
STERN well-set-on; not curved over back but carried gaily; tapering to point; hair fringe below
BACK level, muscular; smooth to loin
MUZZLE 4½" long; wide
NOSE large; nostrils open
HINDQUARTERS strong; stifles straight or moderately bent
SHOULDERS long, muscular; not heavy, especially at points; well-sloped; arm between front and elbow long, muscular; free from fat
COAT short, dense, hard, glossy
CHEST girth over 31" in a 24" hound
LEGS very straight, strong; bone large; little knuckling-over
COLOR: Any good hound color—black, tan and white or any combination of these; also various "pieds" compounded of white, yellow, tan or color of hare or badger
FEET round, catlike; knuckles well-developed; horn strong
RIBS (back) very deep
BALANCE: Symmetry is of greatest importance
ELBOWS straight, turning neither in nor out; well-let-down
DISQUALIFICATION: Pig-mouth (over-shot) or undershot

GREYHOUND STANDARD

HEAD — Long and narrow, fairly wide between the ears, scarcely perceptible stop, little or no development of nasal sinuses, good length of muzzle, which should be powerful without coarseness. Teeth very strong and even in front.

EARS — Small and fine in texture, thrown back and folded, except when excited, when they are semipricked. *Eyes* — Dark, bright, intelligent, indicating spirit.

NECK — Long, muscular, without throatiness, slightly arched, and widening gradually into the shoulder. *Shoulders* — Placed as obliquely as possible, muscular without being loaded.

FORELEGS — Perfectly straight, set well into the shoulder, neither turned in nor out, pasterns strong. *Chest* — Deep, and as wide as consistent with speed, fairly well-sprung ribs.

BACK — Muscular and broad. *Loins* — Good depth of muscle, well arched, well cut up in the flanks. *Hindquarters* — Long, very muscular and powerful, wide and well let down, well-bent stifles. Hocks well bent and rather close to ground, wide but straight fore and aft. *Feet* — Hard and close, rather more hare than cat-feet, well knuckled up with good strong claws. *Tail* — Long, fine and tapering with a slight upward curve.

COAT — Short, smooth and firm in texture. *Color* — Immaterial. *Weight* — Dogs, 65 to 70 pounds; bitches, 60 to 65 pounds.

SCALE OF POINTS

General symmetry and quality	10
Head and neck	20
Chest and shlds	20
Back	10
Quarters	20
Legs and feet	20
Total	100

HEAD long, narrow; fairly wide between ears; little or no development of nasal sinuses
EYES dark, expressive, indicating spirit
STOP very indistinct
MUZZLE good length; powerful, not coarse
TEETH strong, even in front
SHOULDERS muscular; not loaded; placed obliquely as possible
CHEST deep; wide as consistent with speed
FORELEGS perfectly straight, set well into shoulders; turned neither in nor out
FEET hard, close; more hare-like than catlike; well-knuckled-up; claws good, strong
SIZE: Weight 65;70 lbs, males; 60-65 lbs, females
EARS small, texture fine; thrown back and folded in repose; semi-pricked at attention
NECK long, muscular, slightly arched; widening gradually to shoulder; no throatiness
BACK muscular, broad, well-arched
LOINS good depth of muscle; well-cut-up in flanks
RIBS fairly well-sprung
PASTERNS strong
TAIL long, fine, tapering; slight curve upward
HINDQUARTERS long, very muscular; powerful, wide, well-let-down
STIFLES well-bent
HOCKS well-bent; close to ground, wide, straight fore and aft
COAT short; texture smooth, firm
COLOR: Immaterial

[Dachshund cont'd. from p. 81]

other breeds, short; it should be perpendicular to the thigh bone, and firmly muscled. (g) The bones at the base of the foot (*tarsus*) should present a flat appearance, with a strongly prominent hock and a broad tendon of Achilles. (h) The central foot bones (*metatarsus*) should be long, movable towards the calf bone, slightly bent toward the front, but perpendicular (as viewed from behind). (i) *Hind Paws* — Four compactly closed and beautifully arched toes, as in the case of the front paws. The whole foot should be posed equally on the ball and not merely on the toes; nails short.

TAIL — Set in continuation of the spine, extending without very pronounced curvature, and should not be carried too gaily.

Note: Inasmuch as the Dachshund is a hunting dog, scars from honorable wounds shall not be considered a fault.

Special Characteristics of the Three Coat-Varieties

The Dachshund is bred with three varieties of coat: (1) Shorthaired (or Smooth); (2) Wirehaired; (3) Longhaired. All three varieties should conform to the characteristics already specified. The longhaired and shorthaired are old, well-fixed varieties, but into the wirehaired Dachshund, the blood for otherbreeds has been purposely introduced; nevertheless, in breeding him, the greatest stress must be placed upon conformity to the general Dachshund type. The following specifications are applicable separately to the three coat-varieties, respectively:

Shorthaired (or Smooth) Dachshund

(1) Hair — Short, thick, smooth and shining; no bald patches. Special faults are: Too fine or thin hair, leathery ears, bald patches, too coarse or too thick hair in general. *Tail* — Gradually tapered to a point, well but not too richly haired; long, sleek bristles on the underside are considered a patch of strong-growing hair, not a fault. A brush tail is a fault, as is also a partly or wholly hairless tail.

COLOR OF HAIR, NOSE AND NAILS —

(a) One-colored Dachshund — This group includes red (often called tan), red-yellow, yellow, and brindle, with or without a shading of interspersed black hairs. Nevertheless a clean color is preferable, and red is to be considered more desirable than red-yellow or yellow. Dogs strongly shaded with interspersed black hairs belong to this class, and not to the other color groups. A small white spot is admissible but not desirable. *Nose and Nails* — Black; brown is admissible, but not desirable.

(b) Two-colored Dachshund — These comprise deep black, chocolate, gray (blue), and white; each with tan markings over the eyes, on the sides of the jaw and underlip, on the inner edge of the ear, front, breast, inside and behind the front legs, on the paws and around the anus, and from there to about one-third to one-half of the length of the tail on the under side. The most common two-colored Dachshund is usually called black-and-tan. A small white spot is admissible but not desirable. Absence, undue prominence or extreme lightness of tan markings is undesirable. *Nose and Nails* — In the case of black dogs, black; for chocolate, brown (the darker the better); for gray (blue) or white dogs, gray or even flesh color, but the last named color is not desirable; in the case of white dogs, black nose and nails are to be preferred.

(c) Dappled Dachshund — The color of the dappled Dachshund is a clear brownish or grayish color, or even a white ground, with dark irregular patches of dark-gray, brown, red-yellow or black (large areas of one color not desirable). It is desirable that neither the light nor the dark color should predominate. *Nose and Nails* — As for One- and Two-Colored Dachshund.

Wirehaired Dachshund

(2) The general appearance is the same as that of the shorthaired, but without being long in the legs, it is permissible for the body to be somewhat higher off the ground.

HAIR — With the exception of jaw, eyebrows, and ears, the whole body is covered with a perfectly uniform tight, short, thick, rough, hard coat, but with finer, shorter hairs (undercoat) everywhere distributed between the coarser hairs, resembling the coat of the German Wirehaired Pointer. There should be a beard on the chin. The eyebrows are bushy. On the ears the hair is shorter than on the body; almost smooth, but in any case conforming to the rest of the coat. The general arrangement of the hair should be such that the wirehaired Dachshund, when seen from a distance should resemble the smooth-haired. Any sort of soft hair in the coat is faulty, whether short or long, or wherever found on the body; the same is true of long, curly, or wavy hair, or hair that sticks out irregularly in all directions; a flag tail is also objectionable. *Tail* — Robust, as thickly haired as possible, gradually coming to a point, and without a tuft. *Color of Hair, Nose and Nails* — All colors are admissible. White patches on the chest, though allowable, are not desirable.

Longhaired Dachshund

(3) The distinctive characteristic differentiating this coat from the short-haired, or smooth-haired Dachshund is alone the rather long silky hair. *Hair* — The soft, sleek, glistening, often slightly wavy hair should be longer under the neck, on the underside of the body, and especially on the ears and behind the legs, becoming there a pronounced feather; the hair should attain its greatest length on the underside of the tail. The hair should fall beyond the lower edge of the ear. Short hair on the ear, so-called "leather" ears, is not desirable. Too luxurious a coat causes the longhaired Dachshund to seem coarse, and masks the type. The coat should remind one of the Irish Setter, and should give the dog an elegant appearance. Too thick hair on the paws, so-called "mops," is inelegant, and renders the animal unfit for use. It is faulty for the dog to have equally long hair over all the body, if the coat is too curly, or too scrubby, or if a flag tail or overhanging hair on the ears are lacking; or if there is a very pronounced parting on the back, or a vigorous growth between the toes. *Tail* — Carried gracefully in prolongation of the spine; the hair attains here its greatest length and forms a veritable flag. *Color of Hair, Nose and Nails* — Exactly as for the smooth-haired Dachshund, except that the red-with-black (heavily sabled) color is permissible and is formally classed as a red.

Miniature Dachshunds are bred in all three coats. Within the limits imposed, symmetrical adherence to the general Dachshund conformation, combined with smallness, and mental and physical vitality, should be the outstanding characteristics of Miniature Dachshunds. They have not been given separate classification but are a division of the Open Class for "under 10 pounds, and 12 months old or over."

GENERAL FAULTS

Serious Faults: Over- or under-shot jaws, knuckling over, very loose shoulders.

Secondary Faults: A weak, long-legged, or dragging figure, body hanging between the shoulders; sluggish, clumsy, or waddling gait; toes turned inwards or too obliquely outwards; splayed paws, sunken back, roach (or carp) back; croup higher than withers; short-ribbed or too-weak chest; excessively drawn-up flanks like those of a Greyhound; narrow, poorly-muscled hindquarters; weak loins; bad angulation in front or hindquarters; cow hocks; bowed legs; wall eyes, except for dapple dogs; a bad coat.

Minor Faults: Ears wrongly set, sticking out, narrow or folded; too marked a stop; too pointed or weak a jaw; pincer teeth; too wide or too short a head; goggle eyes, wall eyes in the case of dapple dogs; insufficiently dark eyes in the case of all other coat-colors; dewlaps; short neck; swan neck; too fine or too thin hair; absence of, or too profuse or too light tan markings in the case of two-colored dogs.

Approved January 12, 1971

GROUP 3

WORKING DOGS

ALASKAN MALAMUTE STANDARD

GENERAL APPEARANCE AND CHARACTERISTICS — The Alaskan Malamute is a powerful and substantially built dog with deep chest and strong, compact body, not too short coupled, with a thick, coarse guard coat of sufficient length to protect a dense, woolly undercoat, from 1 to 2 inches in depth when dog is in full coat. Stands well over pads, and this stance gives the appearance of much activity, showing interest and curiosity. The head is broad, ears wedge-shaped and erect when alerted. The muzzle is bulky with only slight diminishing in width and depth from root to nose, not pointed or long, but not stubby. The Malamute moves with a proud carriage, head erect and eyes alert. Face markings are a distinguishing feature. These consist of either cap over head and rest of face solid color, usually grayish white, or face marked with the appearance of a mask. Combinations of cap and mask are not unusual. The tail is plumed and carried over the back, not like a fox brush, or tightly curled, more like a plume waving.

Malamutes are of various colors, but are usually wolfish gray or black and white. Their feet are of the "snowshoe" type, tight and deep, with well-cushioned pads, giving a firm and compact appearance. Front legs are straight with big bone. Hind legs are broad and powerful, moderately bent at stifles, and without cowhocks. The back is straight, gently sloping from shoulders to hips. The loin should not be so short or tight as to interfere with easy, tireless movement. Endurance and intelligence are shown in body and expression. The eyes have a "wolf-like" appearance by their position, but the expression is soft and indicates an affectionate disposition.

TEMPERAMENT — The Alaskan Malamute is an affectionate, friendly dog, not a "one-man" dog. He is a loyal, devoted companion, playful on invitation, but generally impressive by his dignity after maturity.

HEAD — The head should indicate a high degree of intelligence, and is broad and powerful as compared with other "natural" breeds, but should be in proportion to the size of the dog so as not to make the dog appear clumsy or coarse. *Skull* — The skull should be broad between the ears, gradually narrowing to eyes, moderately rounded between ears, flattening on top as it approaches the eyes, rounding off to cheeks, which should be moderately flat. There should be a slight furrow between the eyes, the topline of skull and topline of the muzzle showing but little break downward from a straight line as they join. *Muzzle* — The muzzle should be large and bulky in proportion to size of skull, diminishing but little in width and depth from junction with skull to nose; lips close fitting; nose black; upper and lower jaws broad with large teeth, front teeth meeting with a scissors grip but never overshot or undershot.

EYES — Brown, almond shaped, moderately large for this shape of eye, set obliquely in skull. Dark eyes preferred.

EARS — The ears should be of medium size, but small in proportion to head. The upper halves of the ears are triangular in shape, slightly rounded at tips, set wide apart on outside back edges of the skull with the lower part of the ear joining the skull on a line with the upper corner of the eye, giving the tips of the ears the appearance, when erect, of standing off from the skull. When erect, the ears point slightly forward, but when the dog is at work the ears are sometimes folded against the skull. High-set ears are a fault.

NECK — The neck should be strong and moderately arched.

BODY — The chest should be strong and deep; body should be strong and compactly built but not short coupled. The back should be straight and gently sloping to the hips. The loins should be well muscled and not so short as to interfere with easy, rhythmic movement with powerful drive from the hindquarters. A long loin which weakens the back is also a fault. No excess weight. *Shoulders, Legs and Feet* — Shoulders should be moderately sloping; forelegs heavily boned and muscled, straight to pasterns, which should be short and strong and almost vertical as viewed from the side. The feet should be large and compact, toes tight-fitting and well arched, pads thick and tough, toenails short and strong. There should be a protective growth of hair between toes. Hind legs must be broad and powerfully muscled through thighs; stifles moderately bent, hock joints broad and strong, moderately bent and well let down. As viewed from behind, the hind legs should not appear bowed in bone, but stand and move true in line with movement of the front legs, and not too close or too wide. The legs of the Malamute must indicate unusual strength and tremendous propelling power. Any indication of unsoundness in legs or feet, standing or moving, is to be considered a serious fault. Dewclaws on the hind legs are undesirable and should be removed shortly after pups are whelped.

TAIL — Moderately set and following the line of the spine at the start, well furred and

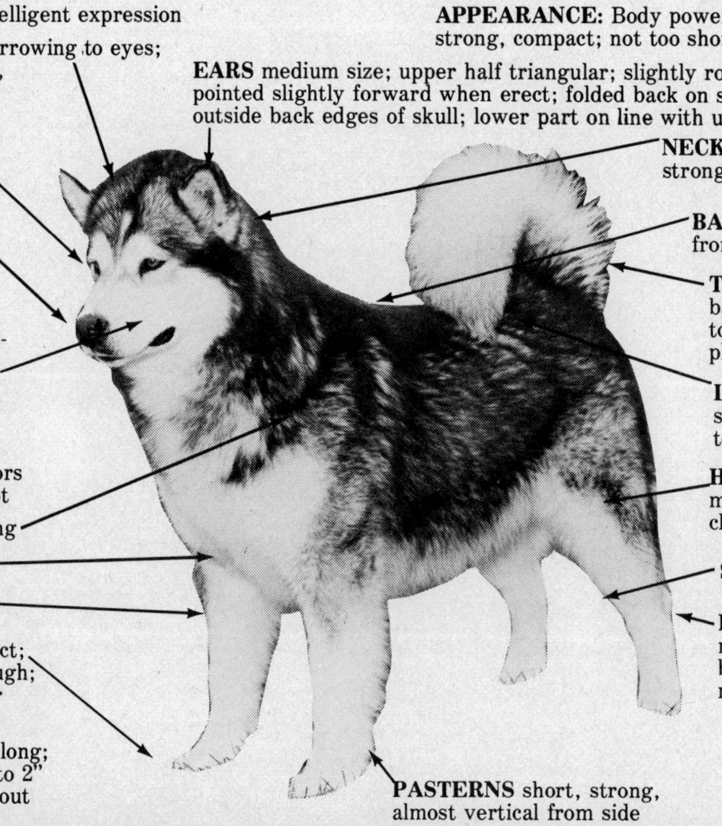

HEAD in proportion to size; intelligent expression

SKULL broad between ears, narrowing to eyes; moderately round between ears, flattening to eyes; rounding off to moderately flat cheeks

EYES almond-shaped, dark, moderately large, set obliquely; slight furrow between

NOSE black

FACE markings cap-like, mask-like; markings distinguishing feature

MUZZLE large, bulky; diminishing little in width or depth from junction with skull to nose; not too long or pointed

LIPS close fitting

JAWS broad; teeth large, scissors bite, neither over- nor undershot

SHOULDERS moderately sloping

CHEST strong, deep

FORELEGS heavily boned, muscular, straight

FEET large, tight, deep, compact; toes well-arched; pads thick, tough; toenails short, strong; thick hair between toes, "snow-shoe" type

COAT thick, dense, coarse; not long; undercoat thick, oily, woolly; 1 to 2" depth; outercoat coarse, stands out

APPEARANCE: Body powerful, substantially built; large, strong, compact; not too short-coupled; carriage proud

EARS medium size; upper half triangular; slightly rounded at tips, set wide apart; pointed slightly forward when erect; folded back on skull when at work; set on outside back edges of skull; lower part on line with upper corner of eye

NECK covered with thick fur; strong, moderately arched

BACK straight, gently sloping from shoulders to hips

TAIL well-furred, carried over back; not too tightly curled to rest on back; "waving plume" appearance

LOINS well-muscled; no surplus weight; neither too short nor too long

HIND LEGS broad, powerfully muscled through thighs; dewclaws on legs undesirable

STIFLES moderately bent

HOCKS well-let-down, moderately bent, joints broad, strong; turning neither in nor out

PASTERNS short, strong, almost vertical from side

COLOR: Wolf-gray, black and white; variations; cap or mask desirable; underbodies always white, also parts of legs, feet, mask; white blaze on forehead desirable; broken color undesirable. Only solid color allowable is all-white

When type, proportion and functional attributes are equal, then the dog or bitch nearest the desired freighting size is to be preferred.

Males: 25" at shoulders, 85 lbs.
Females: 23" at shoulders, 75 lbs.

carried over the back when not working — not tightly curled to rest on back — or short furred and carried like a fox brush, a waving plume appearance instead.

COAT — The Malamute should have a thick, coarse guard coat, not long and soft. The undercoat is dense, from 1 to 2 inches in depth, oily and woolly. The coarse guard coat stands out, and there is thick fur around the neck. The guard coat varies in length, as does the undercoat; however, in general, the coat is moderately short to medium along the sides of the body with the length of the coat increasing somewhat around the shoulders and neck, down the back and over the rump, as well as in the breeching and plume. Malamutes usually have shorter and less dense coats when shed out during the summer months.

COLOR AND MARKINGS — The usual colors range from light gray through the intermediate shadings to black, always with white on underbodies, parts of legs, feet, and part of mask markings. Markings should be either caplike and/or mask-like on face. A white blaze on forehead and/or collar or spot on nape is attractive and acceptable, but broken color extending over the body in spots or uneven splashings is undesirable. One should distinguish between mantled dogs and splash-coated dogs. The only solid color allowable is the all-white.

SIZE — There is a natural range in size in the breed. The desirable freighting sizes are: *Males:* 25 inches at the shoulders, 85 pounds. *Females:* 23 inches at the shoulders, 75 pounds. However, size consideration should not outweigh that of type, proportion, and functional attributes, such as shoulders, chest, legs, feet, and movement. When dogs are judged equal in type, proportion, and functional attributes, the dog nearest the desirable freighting size is to be preferred.

IMPORTANT: In judging Alaskan Malamutes their function as a sledge dog for heavy freighting must be given consideration above all else. The judge must bear in mind that this breed is designed primarily as the working sledge dog of the North for hauling heavy freight, and therefore he should be a heavy-boned, powerfully built, compact dog with sound legs, good feet, deep chest, powerful shoulders, steady, balanced, tireless gait, and the other physical equipment necessary for the efficient performance of his job. He isn't intended as a racing sled dog designed to compete in speed trials with the smaller Northern breeds. The Malamute as a sledge dog for heavy freighting is designed for strength and endurance and any characteristic of the individual specimen, including temperament, which interferes with the accomplishment of this purpose is to be considered the most serious of faults. Faults under this provision would be splayfootedness, any indication of unsoundness or weakness in legs, cowhocks, bad pasterns, straight shoulders, lack of angulation, stilted gait or any gait which isn't balanced, strong, and steady, ranginess, shallowness, ponderousness, lightness of bone, poor over-all proportion, and similar characteristics.

SCALE OF POINTS

General Appearance	20
Head	15
Body	20
Legs and Movement	20
Feet	10
Coat and Color	10
Tail	5
Total	100

Approved April 12, 1960

BELGIAN SHEEPDOG STANDARD

PERSONALITY — The Belgian Sheepdog should reflect the qualities of intelligence, courage, alertness, and devotion to master. To his inherent aptitude as guardian of flocks should be added protectiveness of the person and property of his master. He should be watchful, attentive, and always in motion when not under command. In his relationship with humans he should be observant and vigilant with strangers but not apprehensive. He should not show fear or shyness. He should not show viciousness by unwarranted or unprovoked attack. With those he knows well, he is most affectionate and friendly, zealous of their attention, and very possessive.

GENERAL APPEARANCE — The first impression of the Belgian Sheepdog is that of a well-balanced, square dog, elegant in appearance, with an exceedingly proud carriage of the head and neck. He is a strong, agile, well-muscled animal, alert and full of life. His whole conformation gives the impression of depth and solidity without bulkiness. The male dog is usually somewhat more impressive and grand than his female counterpart. The bitch should have a distinctly feminine look.

SIZE AND SUBSTANCE — Males should be 24-26 inches in height and females 22-24 inches, measured at the withers. The length, measured from point of breast bone to point of rump, should equal the height. Bitches may be slightly longer. Bone structure should be moderately heavy in proportion to his height so that he is well balanced throughout and neither spindly or leggy nor cumbersome and bulky. *Stance* — The Belgian Sheepdog should stand squarely on all fours. Side view: the topline, front legs, and back legs should closely approximate a square. *Expression* — Indicates alertness, attention, readiness for activity. Gaze should be intelligent and questioning.

COAT — The guard hairs of the coat must be long, well-fitting, straight, and abundant. They should not be silky or wiry. The texture should be a medium harshness. The undercoat should be extremely dense, commensurate, however, with climatic conditions. The Belgian Sheepdog is particularly adaptable to extremes of temperature or climate. The hair is shorter on the head, outside of the ears, and lower part of the legs. The opening of the ear is protected by tufts of hair. Ornamentation: especially long and abundant hair, like a collarette, around the neck; fringe of long hair down the back of the forearm; fringe of long hair down the back of the forearm; especially long and abundant hair trimming the hindquarters, the breeches; long, heavy, and abundant hair on the tail.

COLOR — Black. May be completely black or may be black with white, limited as follows: Small to moderate patch or strip on forechest. Between pads of feet. On *tips* of hind toes. On chin and muzzle (frost—may be white or gray). On *tips* of front toes—allowable but a fault.

HEAD — Clean-cut and strong, over-all size should be in proportion to the body. *Skull* — Top flattened rather than rounded. The width approximately the same, but not wider, than the length. *Stop*—Moderate. *Muzzle, Jaws, Lips*—Muzzle moderately pointed, avoiding any tendency to snipiness, and approximately equal in length to that of the topskull. The jaws should be strong and powerful. The lips should be tight and black, with no pink showing on the outside. *Ears* — Triangular in shape, stiff, erect, and in proportion to the head in size. Base of the ear should not come below the center of the eye. *Eyes*—Brown, preferably dark brown. Medium size, slightly almond shaped, not protruding. *Nose*—Black, without spots or discolored areas. *Teeth*—A full complement of strong, white teeth, evenly set. Should not be overshot or undershot. Should have either an even bite or a scissors bite.

TORSO — *Neck* — Round and rather outstretched, tapered from head to body, well muscled, with tight skin. *Topline*—The withers are slightly higher and slope into the back which must be level, straight, and firm from withers to hip joints. The loin section, viewed from above, is relatively short, broad and strong, but blending smoothly into the back. The croup is medium long, sloping gradually. *Tail*—Strong at the base, bone to reach hock. At rest the dog holds it low, the tip bent back level with the hock. When in action he raises it and gives it a curl, which is strongest toward the tip, without forming a hook. *Chest*—Not broad, but deep. The lowest point should reach the elbow, forming a smooth ascendant curve to the abdomen.

ABDOMEN — Moderate development. Neither tucked-up nor paunchy.

FOREQUARTERS — Shoulder — long and oblique, laid flat against the body, forming a sharp angle (approximately 90 degrees) with the upper arm. *Legs*—Straight, strong, and parallel to each other. Bone oval rather than round. Development (length and substance) should be well proportioned to the size of the dog. *Pastern*—medium length, strong, and very slightly sloped.

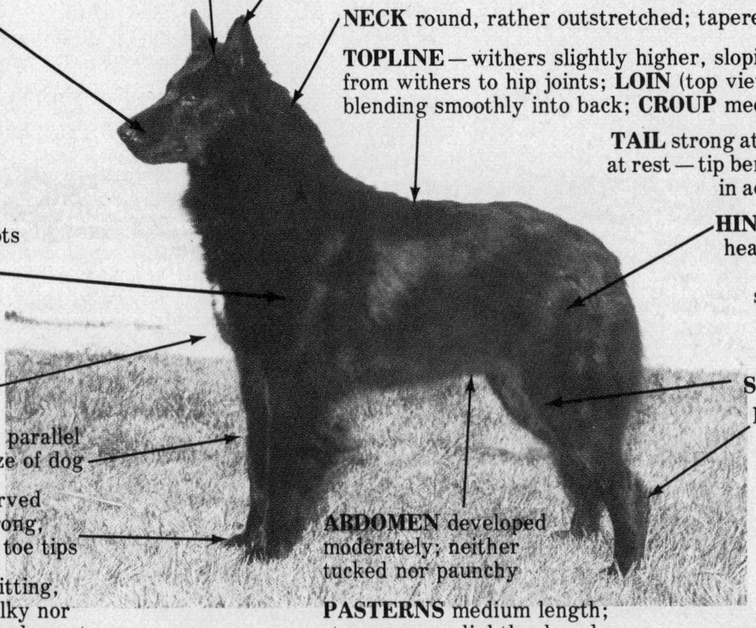

HEAD clean-cut, strong; size in proportion to body; stop moderate

SKULL top-flattened, width approx. same as length, not wider

EYES brown; dark preferred; size medium, slightly almond shaped; not protruding

MUZZLE moderately pointed, not snippy; length approx. that of top skull; **JAWS** strong, powerful; **LIPS** tight, black, no pink on outside; **TEETH** evenly set; neither over- nor undershot; scissors or even bite desirable

NOSE black without spots

SHOULDERS long, oblique, flat against body; approx. 90 degrees with upper arm

CHEST deep, not broad; lowest point reaches elbow

FORELEGS straight, strong, parallel oval bone; in proportion to size of dog

FEET round, catlike; toes curved closely, well-padded; nails strong, black; white nails may match toe tips

COAT guard hair long, well-fitting, straight, abundant, neither silky nor wiry; of medium harshness; undercoat dense (according to climate); hair shorter on head, outside of ears and lower legs; ear opening protected by hair tufts; collarette around neck; hair fringe back of forearm, hindquarters, breeches, tail

EARS triangular, stiff, erect; in proportion to head; base not below center of eye

NECK round, rather outstretched; tapered, well-muscled; skin tight

TOPLINE—withers slightly higher, sloping, level back; straight, firm from withers to hip joints; **LOIN** (top view) short; broad, strong, blending smoothly into back; **CROUP** medium long, sloping gradually

ABDOMEN developed moderately; neither tucked nor paunchy

PASTERNS medium length; strong, very slightly sloped

COLOR: Black; or black with white as follows: white patch or strip on foreches, between pads, on tips of hind toes, on chin and muzzle (frost may be white or gray) and on tips of front toes (latter allowed but faulted)

BODY well-balanced, square, strong, well-muscled; length from breastbone to point of rump equals height; bitches may be slightly longer

TAIL strong at base; bone to reach hock; low at rest—tip bent back level with hock; raised in action with curl strongest at tip

HINDQUARTERS: Thighs broad, heavily muscled; upper and lower thigh bones approx. parallel shoulder blade and upper arm; proportioned to size of dog; bone oval; legs parallel

STIFLE, relatively sharp angle

HOCK, relatively sharp angle; not extreme; metatarsus medium length, strong, slightly sloped; no dewclaws

FEET slightly elongated

HEIGHT: dogs, 24" to 26"; bitches, 22" to 24" measured at withers

DISQUALIFICATIONS: Viciousness. Color—any color other than black (except white spots). Ears hanging. Tail cropped or a stump. Males under 22½" or over 27½". Females under 20½" or over 25½"

AM, CAN. CH. SKIP'S REWARD O'EBON WILL

FEET — Round (cat footed), toes curved close together, well padded. Nails strong and black except that they may be white to match white toe tips.

HINDQUARTERS, THIGHS — Broad and heavily muscled. The upper and lower thigh bones approximately parallel the shoulder blade and upper arm respectively, forming a relatively sharp angle at stifle joint. *Legs* — Length and substance well proportioned to the size of the dog. Bone oval rather than round. Legs are parallel to each other. The angle at the hock is relatively sharp, although the Belgian Sheepdog does not have extreme angulation. Metatarsus medium length, strong, and slightly sloped. Dewclaws, if any, should be removed. *Feet* — Slightly elongated. Toes curved close together, well padded. Nails strong and black except that they may be white to match white toe tips.

GAIT — Motion should be smooth, free and easy, seemingly never tiring, exhibiting facility of movement rather than a hard driving action. He tends to single-track on a fast gait; the legs, both front and rear, converging toward the center line of gravity of the dog. The backline should remain firm and level, parallel to the line of motion with no crabbing. He shows a marked tendency to move in a circle rather than a straight line.

FAULTS — Any deviation from these specifications is a fault. In determining whether a fault is minor, serious, or major, these two factors should be used as a guide: 1. The extent to which it deviates from the Standard. 2. The extent to which such deviation would actually affect the working ability of the dog.

DISQUALIFICATIONS

Viciousness. Color — any color other than black, except for white in specified area. Ears — hanging (as on a hound). Tail — cropped or stump. Males under 22½ or over 27½ inches in height. Females under 20½ or over 25½ inches in height.

Approved June 9, 1959

BELGIAN TERVUREN STANDARD

PERSONALITY — The Belgian Tervuren should reflect the qualities of intelligence, courage, alertness and devotion to master. To his inherent aptitude as guardian of flocks should be added protectiveness of the person and property of his master. He should be watchful, attentive and usually in motion when not under command. In his relationship with humans he should be observant and vigilant with strangers but not apprehensive. He should not show fear or shyness. He should not know viciousness by unwarranted or unprovoked attack. With those he knows well, he is most affectionate and friendly, zealous for their attention and very possessive.

GENERAL APPEARANCE — The first impression of Belgian Tervuren is that of a well-balanced square dog, elegant in appearance, with proud carriage of the head and neck. He is a strong, agile, well-muscled animal, alert and full of life. His whole conformation gives the impression of depth and solidity without bulkiness. The male is usually somewhat more impressive and grand than the female. The female should have a distinctly feminine look. Because of frequent comparisons between the Belgian Tervuren and the German Shepherd Dog, it is to be noted that these two breeds differ considerably in size, substance and structure, the difference being especially noticeable in the formation of the topline and the hindquarters.

SIZE AND SUBSTANCE — Males 24-26 inches in height, and females 22-24 inches, measured at the withers. The length, measured at the withers. The length, measured from point of breastbone to point of rump, should equal the height. Bone structure medium in proportion to height so that he is well balanced throughout and neither spindly or leggy nor cumbersome and bulky. *Stance* — The Belgian Tervuren should stand squarely on all fours. Viewed from the side, the topline, ground level, front legs, and back legs should closely approximate a perfect square.

EXPRESSION — Intelligent and questioning, indicating alertness, attention and readiness for action.

COAT — The guard hairs of the coat must be long, well-fitting, straight and abundant. They should not be silky or wiry. The texture should be a medium harshness. The undercoat should be very dense commensurate, however, with climatic conditions. The Belgian Tervuren is particularly adaptable to extremes of temperature or climate. The hair is shorter on the head, outside the ears and on the lower part of the legs. The opening of the ear is protected by tufts of hair. Ornamentation: especially long and abundant hair, like a collarette, around the neck; fringe of long hair down the back of the forearm; especially long and abundant hair trimming the hindquarters—the breeches; long, heavy and abundant hair on the tail.

COLOR — Rich fawn to russet mahogany with black overlay. The coat is characteristically double pigmented, wherein the tip of each fawn hair is blackened. On mature males, this blackening is especially pronounced on the shoulders, back and rib section. The chest color is a mixture of black and gray. The face has a black mask, and the ears are mostly black. The tail typically has a darker or black tip. The underparts of the body, tail and breeches are light beige. A small white patch is permitted on the chest, not to extend to the neck or breast. The tips of the toes may be white. White or gray hair (frost) on chin or muzzle is normal. Although some allowance is to be made for dogs under 18 months of age, when true color is attained, washed-out color or color too black resembling the Belgian Sheepdog is undesirable.

HEAD — Well chiseled, dry, long without exaggeration. Skull and muzzle, measuring from the stop, should be of equal length. Over-all size should be in proportion to the body. Top of skull flattened rather than rounded, the width approximately the same but not wider than the length. Stop moderate. Muzzle moderately pointed, avoiding any tendency to snipiness. The jaws should be strong and powerful. The lips should be tight and black, with no pink showing on the outside. Ears are equilateral triangles in shape, well cupped, stiff, erect, not too large. Set high, the base of the ear should not come below the center of the eye. Eyes brown, preferably dark brown, medium size, slightly almond shaped, not protruding. Light or yellow eyes are a fault. Nose black, without spots or discolored areas. Nostrils well defined. There should be a full complement of strong white teeth evenly set. Either a scissors or even bite is acceptable. Should not be overshot or undershot. Teeth broken by accident should not be severely penalized, but worn teeth, especially incisors, are often indicative of the lack of proper bite, although some allowance should be made for age. Discolored (distemper) teeth are not to be penalized.

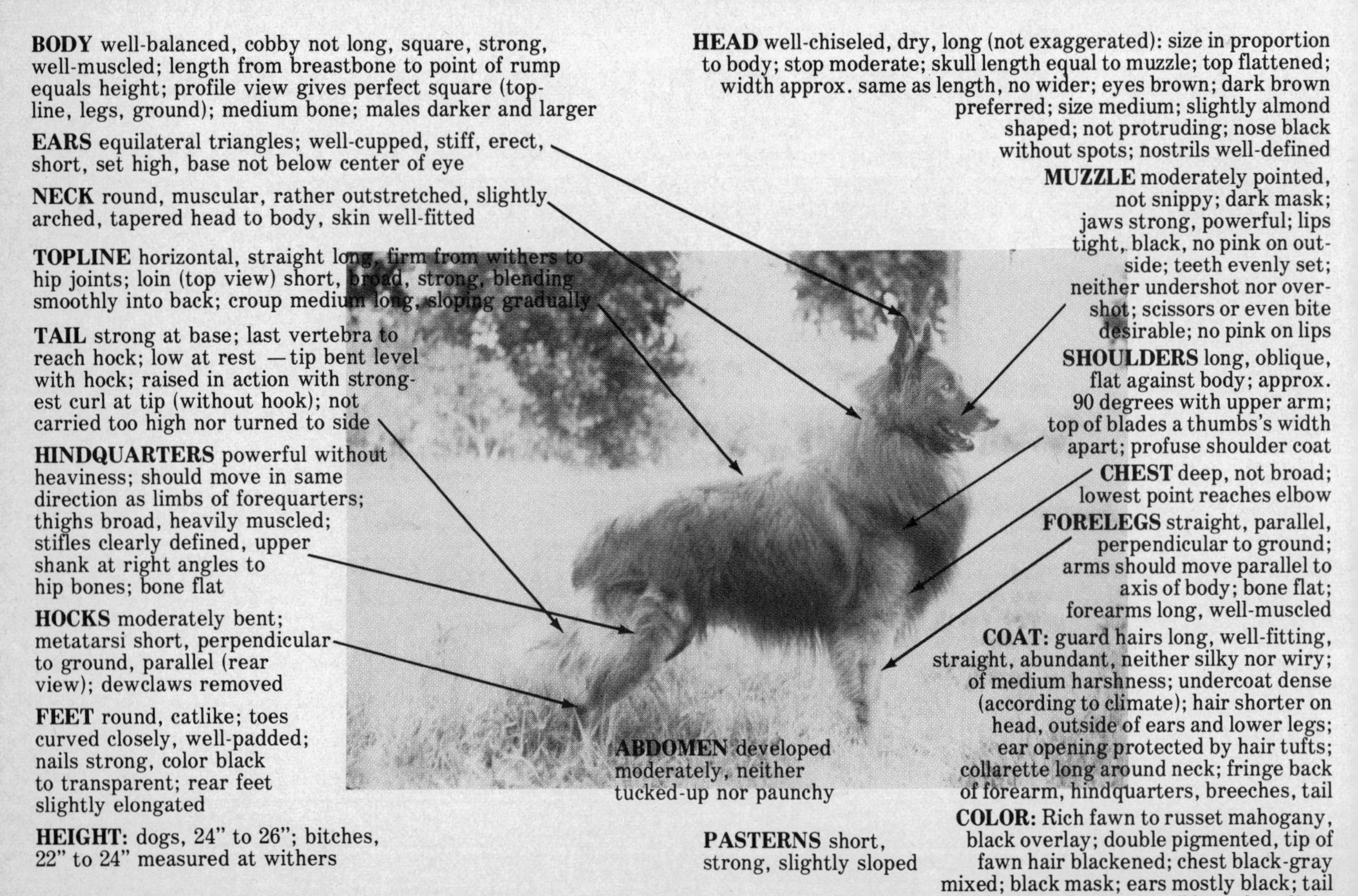
BODY well-balanced, cobby not long, square, strong, well-muscled; length from breastbone to point of rump equals height; profile view gives perfect square (topline, legs, ground); medium bone; males darker and larger
EARS equilateral triangles; well-cupped, stiff, erect, short, set high, base not below center of eye
NECK round, muscular, rather outstretched, slightly arched, tapered head to body, skin well-fitted
TOPLINE horizontal, straight long, firm from withers to hip joints; loin (top view) short, broad, strong, blending smoothly into back; croup medium long, sloping gradually
TAIL strong at base; last vertebra to reach hock; low at rest —tip bent level with hock; raised in action with strongest curl at tip (without hook); not carried too high nor turned to side
HINDQUARTERS powerful without heaviness; should move in same direction as limbs of forequarters; thighs broad, heavily muscled; stifles clearly defined, upper shank at right angles to hip bones; bone flat
HOCKS moderately bent; metatarsi short, perpendicular to ground, parallel (rear view); dewclaws removed
FEET round, catlike; toes curved closely, well-padded; nails strong, color black to transparent; rear feet slightly elongated
HEIGHT: dogs, 24" to 26"; bitches, 22" to 24" measured at withers
ABDOMEN developed moderately, neither tucked-up nor paunchy
PASTERNS short, strong, slightly sloped
HEAD well-chiseled, dry, long (not exaggerated): size in proportion to body; stop moderate; skull length equal to muzzle; top flattened; width approx. same as length, no wider; eyes brown; dark brown preferred; size medium; slightly almond shaped; not protruding; nose black without spots; nostrils well-defined
MUZZLE moderately pointed, not snippy; dark mask; jaws strong, powerful; lips tight, black, no pink on outside; teeth evenly set; neither undershot nor overshot; scissors or even bite desirable; no pink on lips
SHOULDERS long, oblique, flat against body; approx. 90 degrees with upper arm; top of blades a thumbs's width apart; profuse shoulder coat
CHEST deep, not broad; lowest point reaches elbow
FORELEGS straight, parallel, perpendicular to ground; arms should move parallel to axis of body; bone flat; forearms long, well-muscled
COAT: guard hairs long, well-fitting, straight, abundant, neither silky nor wiry; of medium harshness; undercoat dense (according to climate); hair shorter on head, outside of ears and lower legs; ear opening protected by hair tufts; collarette long around neck; fringe back of forearm, hindquarters, breeches, tail
COLOR: Rich fawn to russet mahogany, black overlay; double pigmented, tip of fawn hair blackened; chest black-gray mixed; black mask; ears mostly black; tail darker or black tip; underparts, tail breeches, light beige; white patch permitted only on chest; muzzle may be white or gray frosted; tips of toes may be white
DISQUALIFICATIONS: Ears hanging. Tail cropped or a stump. Color—white anywhere except as specified. Teeth—pronounced undershot. Size—males under 22½" or over 27½"; females under 20½" or over 25½"

CH. RAJAH D'ANTRE DU LOUVE, C.D.

IN ONLY TWO-AND-A-HALF MONTHS OF BEING SHOWN, RAJAH ACCUMULATED 16 BREED WINS, A GROUP IV, 2 GROUP II's, 2 GROUP I's, AND A BEST IN SHOW. THIS IS A TREMENDOUS DOG DESTINED TO HAVE A GREAT IMPACT ON THE BREED.

HANDLER: VINCENT SMITH

SALLYANN COMSTOCK
RT. 2, BOX 133A
HEBRON, INDIANA 46341
(219) 996-6444

TORSO — Neck round, muscular, rather outstretched, slightly arched and tapered from head to body. Skin well fitting with no loose folds. Topline horizontal, straight and firm from withers to hip joints. The loin section, viewed from above, is relatively short, broad and strong, but blending smoothly into the back. The croup is medium long, sloping gradually. Tail strong at the base, the last vertebra to reach the hock. At rest the dog holds it low, the tip bent back level with the hock. When in action he raises it and gives it a curl, which is strongest toward the tip, without forming a hook. Tail should not be carried too high nor turned to one side. Chest not broad but deep, the lowest point should reach the elbow, forming a smooth ascendant curve to the abdomen. Abdomen moderately developed, neither tucked-up nor paunchy.

FOREQUARTERS — Legs straight, parallel, perpendicular to the ground. Shoulders long and oblique, laid flat against the body, forming a sharp angle (approximately 90 degrees) with the upper arm. Top of the shoulder blades should be roughly a thumb's width apart. Arms should move in a direction exactly parallel to the axis of the body. Forearms long and well muscled. Bone flat rather than round. Pasterns short and strong, slightly sloped. Feet round (cat-footed), toes curved close together, well padded, strong nails. Nail color can vary from black to transparent.

HINDQUARTERS — Legs powerful without heaviness, moving in the same pattern as the limbs of the forequarters. Thighs broad and heavily muscled. Stifles clearly defined, with upper shank at right angles to the hip bones. Bone flat rather than round. Hocks moderately bent. Metatarsi short, perpendicular to the ground, parallel to each other when viewed from the rear. Dewclaws, if any, should be removed. Feet slightly elongated, toes curved close together, heavily padded, strong nails. Nail color may vary from black to transparent.

GAIT — The gait is lively and graceful, covering the maximum of ground. Always in motion, seemingly never tiring, he shows facility of movement rather than a hard driving action. He tends to single-track at a fast gait, the legs both front and rear converging toward the center line of gravity of the dog. The back line should remain firm and level, parallel to the line of motion with no crabbing. His natural tendency is to move in a circle rather than a straight line.

DISQUALIFICATIONS

Ears — hanging, as on a hound. Tail — cropped or stump. Color — white markings anywhere except as specified. Teeth — pronounced undershot. Size — males under 22½ or over 27½ inches in height; females under 20½ or over 25½ inches in height.

Approved May 12, 1959

BERNESE MOUNTAIN DOG STANDARD

GENERAL APPEARANCE — A well-balanced dog, active and alert; a combination of sagacity, fidelity and utility. *Height*—Dogs, 23 inches to 27½ inches; bitches, 21 inches to 26 inches at shoulder.

HEAD — Skull flat, defined stop and strong muzzle. Dewlaps very slightly developed, flews not too pendulous, jaw strong with good, strong teeth. Eyes dark, hazel-brown, full of fire. Ears V-shaped, set on high, not too pointed at tips and rather short. When in repose, hanging close to head; when alert, brought slightly forward and raised at base.

BODY — Rather short than too long in back, compact and well ribbed up. Chest broad with good depth of brisket. Loins strong and muscular. *Legs and Feet* — Forelegs perfectly straight and muscular, thighs well developed and stifles well bent. Feet round and compact. Dewclaws should be removed.

TAIL — Of fair thickness and well covered with long hair, but not to form a flag; moderate length. When in repose, should be carried low, upward swirl permissible; when alert, may be carried gaily, but may never curl or be carried over back.

COAT — Soft and silky with bright, natural sheen; long and slightly wavy but may never curl. *Color and Markings* — Jet-black with russet-brown or deep tan markings on all four legs, a spot just above forelegs, each side of white chest markings and spots over eyes, which may never be missing. The brown on the forelegs must always be between the black and white. *Preferable, but not a condition, are*—White feet, tip of tail, pure white blaze up foreface, a few white hairs on back of neck, and white star-shaped markings on chest. When the latter markings are missing, it is not a disqualification.

FAULTS — Too massive in head, light or staring eyes, too heavy or long ears, too narrow or snipy muzzle, undershot or overshot mouth, pendulous dewlaps, too long or Setterlike body, splay or hare feet, tail curled or carried over back, cowhocks and white legs.

SCALE OF POINTS

General appearance	15	Coat	10
Size and height	5	Color and markings	15
Head	15		
Body	15		
Legs and feet	15		
Tail	10	Total	100

Approved April 13, 1937

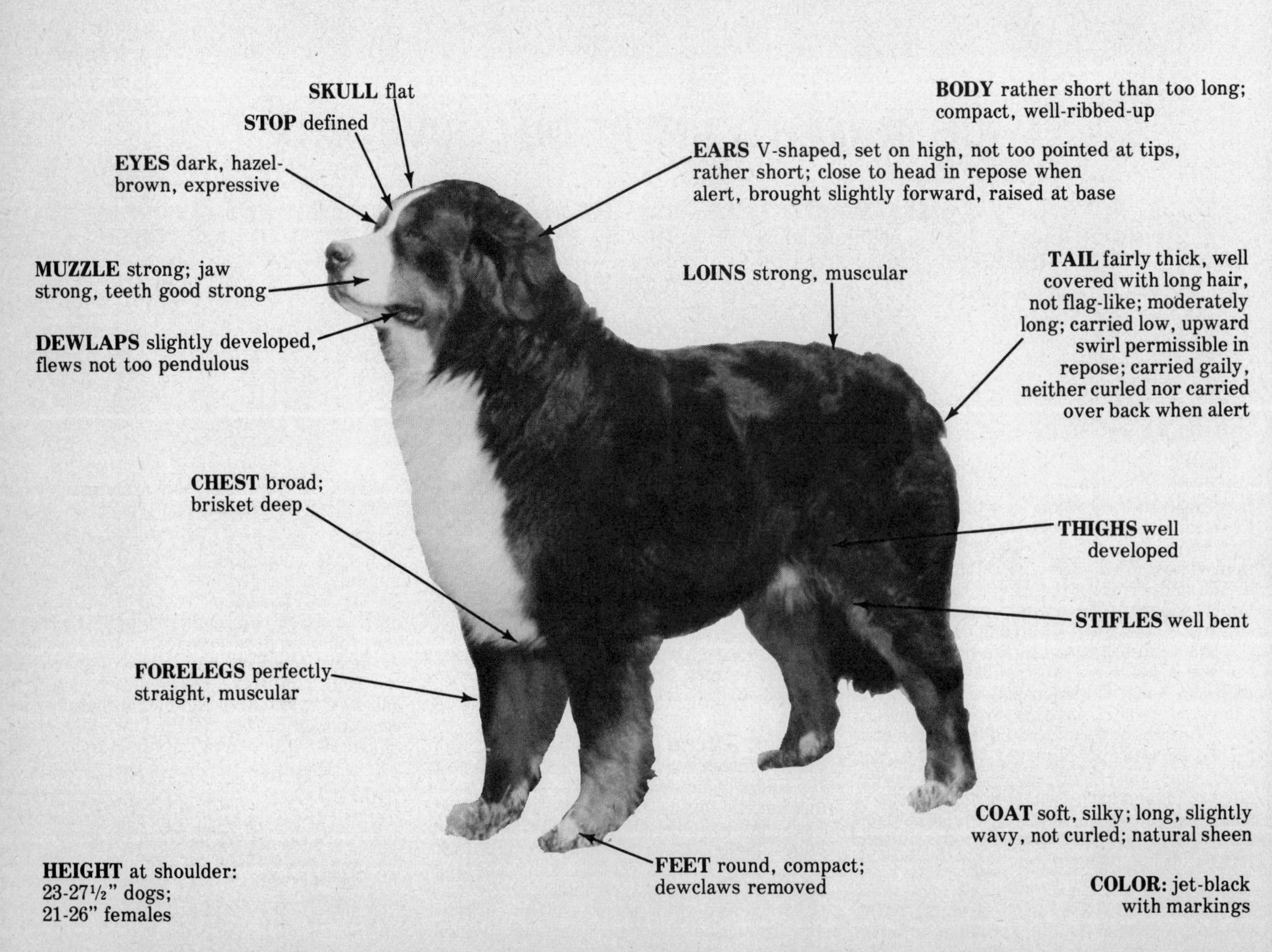

CH. SANCTUARY WOODS GORDO

WE WERE FORTUNATE IN ACQUIRING, DURING THE EMBRYONIC STAGE OF OUR BREEDING PROGRAM, SOUND AND TYPEY STOCK. THIS BOON HELPED TO ATTAIN THE REWARDING AND RESOUNDING SUCCESSES THE MON PLAISIR BERNESE HAVE EXPERIENCED AS SHOW DOGS PAR EXCELLANCE AND AS TREASURED COMPANIONS. ACUTELY AWARE OF THE STANDARD, AND THE TRADITIONAL ROLE FOR WHICH HE IS ACCLAIMED, HOLDING TO THE CONVICTION THAT NATURE AND THOSE DEPENDENT UPON HIS SERVICES WERE THE ULTIMATE ARCHITECTS IN HIS DESIGN AND DEMEANOR, WE HAVE DILIGENTLY ADHERED TO THE ESTABLISHED CHARACTERISTICS OF THE BERNESE MOUNTAIN DOG. IT IS NOT ONLY OUR OBJECTIVE, BUT OUR RESPONSIBILITY, TO BREED AND EXHIBIT THOSE INDIVIDUALS WHICH MOST NEARLY APPROACH THE PINNACLE OF PERFECTION CONTAINED WITHIN THE GUIDELINES OF THE A.K.C. THE PROOF OF THIS THEORY IS EVINCED IN THE CONSISTENT AND UNIFORM QUALITY OF OUR PUPPIES, THE HAPPINESS THEY HAVE BROUGHT TO THOSE WHOM THEY OWN, AND THE ACCOLADES AND APPLAUSE OUR MATURE DOGS HAVE RECEIVED IN THE ARENA. CH. SANCTUARY WOODS GORDO, WHO ILLUSTRATES THE BREED STANDARD IN THIS AND OTHER BOOKS, SETS THE STANDARD FOR MON PLAISIR; THAT IS A TRUE MARK OF DISTINCTION.

Several types of Swiss working dogs, thought to have descended from the Mastiff type, were identified by careful study and promoted in the last years of the 19th century. The most popular of these breeds has proved to be the Bernese Mountain Dog. These dogs descend from guard dogs and drovers but in recent years have been best known as draught dogs. Their job was to pull wagons to market. For this and previous jobs, of course, they had to be powerful, intelligent, and biddable. They are also lovable pets. Active and alert, the Bernese Mountain Dog combines sagacity, fidelity, utility, and beauty. The soft, silky, long, and slightly wavy coat must be jet black with deep tan marking on all four legs and tan spots just above each foreleg, on each side of the white chest marking, and over both eyes. White feet, tail tip, facial blaze, and star-shaped marking on chest are highly valued. This breed is essentially unknown in Britain or, indeed, anywhere but continental Europe and the U.S. About 200 are registered annually in the U.S., the breed ranking 96th.

GENERAL APPEARANCE — The Boxer is a medium-sized, sturdy dog, of square build, with short back, strong limbs, and short, tightfitting coat. His musculation, well developed, should be clean, hard and appear smooth (not bulging) under taut skin. His movements should denote energy. The gait is firm yet elastic (springy), the stride free and ground covering, the carriage proud and noble. Developed to serve the multiple purposes of guard, working, and escort-dog, he must combine elegance with substance and ample power, not alone for beauty but to insure the speed, dexterity, and jumping ability essential to arduous hike, riding expedition, police or military duty. Only a body whose individual parts are built to withstand the most strenuous efforts, assembled as a complete and harmonious whole, can respond to these combined demands. Therefore, to be at his highest efficiency he must never be plump nor heavy and, while equipped for great speed, he must never be racy.

The head imparts to the Boxer a unique individual stamp, peculiar to him alone. It must be in perfect proportion to the body, never small in comparison to the over-all picture. The muzzle is his most distinctive feature, and great value is to be placed on its being of correct form and in absolute proper proportion to the skull.

In judging the Boxer, first consideration should be given to general appearance; next, over-all balance, including the desired proportions of the individual parts of the body to each other, as well as the relation of substance to elegance—to which an attractive color or arresting style may contribute. Special attention is to be devoted to the head, after which the dog's individual components are to be examined for their correct construction and function, and efficiency of gait evaluated.

GENERAL FAULTS — Head not typical, plump, bulldoggy appearance, light bone, lack of balance, bad condition, lack of noble bearing.

HEAD — The beauty of the head depends upon the harmonious proportion of the muzzle to the skull. The muzzle should always appear powerful, never small in its relationship to the skull. The head should be clean, not showing deep wrinkles. Folds will normally appear upon the forehead when the ears are erect, and they are always indicated from the lower edge of the stop running downward on both sides of the muzzle. The dark mask is confined to the muzzle and is in distinct contrast to the color of the head. Any extension of the mask to the skull, other than dark shading around the eyes, creates a sombre, undesirable expression. When white replaces any of the black mask, the path of any upward extension should be between the eyes. The muzzle is powerfully developed in length, width and depth. It is not pointed, narrow, short or shallow. Its shape is influenced first through the formation of both jawbones, second through the placement of the teeth, and third through the texture of the lips.

The Boxer is normally undershot. Therefore, the lower jaw protrudes beyond the upper and curves slightly upward. The upper jaw is broad where attached to the skull and maintains this breadth except for a very slight tapering to the front. The incisor teeth of the lower jaw are in a straight line, the canines preferably up front in the same line to give the jaw the greatest possible width. The line of incisors in the upper jaw is slightly convex toward the front. The upper corner incisors should fit snugly back of the lower canine teeth on each side, reflecting the symmetry essential to the creation of a sound, non-slip bite.

The lips, which complete the formation of the muzzle, should meet evenly. The upper lip is thick and padded, filling out the frontal space created by the projection of the lower jaw. It rests on the edge of the lower lip and, laterally, is supported by the fangs (canines) of the lower jaw. Therefore, these fangs must stand far apart and be of good length so that the front surface of the muzzle is broad and squarish and, when viewed from the side, forms an obtuse angle with the topline of the muzzle. Over-protrusion of the overlip or underlip is undesirable. The chin should be perceptible when viewed from the side as well as from the front without being overrepandous (rising above the bite line) as in the Bulldog. The Boxer must not show teeth or tongue when the mouth is closed. Excessive flews are not desirable.

The top of the skull is slightly arched, not rotund, flat, nor noticeably broad, and the occiput not too pronounced. The forehead forms a distinct stop with the topline of the muzzle, which must not be forced back into the forehead like that of a bulldog. It should not slant down (down-faced) nor should it be dished, although the tip of the nose should lie somewhat higher than the root of the muzzle. The forehead shows just a slight furrow between the eyes. The cheeks, though covering powerful masseter muscles compatible with the strong set of teeth, should be relatively flat and not bulge, maintaining the clean lines of the skull. They taper into the muzzle in a slight, graceful curve. The

TEETH sound, powerful bite; lower incisors in straight line; canines preferably up front in the same line; upper incisors slightly rounded. Upper corner incisors fit snugly back of lowers

LIPS upper, thick, padded, lower edge rests on ledge of lower lip; lower must not rise above front of upper lip; lower must be perceptible viewed from front; teeth, tongue must not show when mouth is closed

SKULL top slightly arched; occiput not too pronounced

EARS high set, slipped to point, fairly long, shell not too broad; carried erect

NECK round, length ample; strong, muscular, clean; no dewlap; distinctly marked nape, elegant arch

BACK short, straight, broad, muscular; withers clearly defined; loins short, muscular. Croup slightly sloped, broad

TAIL: set-high rather than too deep; clipped; carried upward

SHOULDERS long, sloping, close-lying; not too muscular

PELVIS long; broad in females

THIGHS broad, curved; breech musculation strongly developed; long

HINDQUARTER JOINTS well-angulated; in balance with forequarters; thighs broad, curved

FEET: Strong pads; rear toes slightly longer than front, catlike

HIND LEGS straight, viewed from rear; hocks clean, not distended; hock joints perpendicular to ground

COLOR: Fawn, in various shades from light yellow to dark red or mahogany: brindle should have black stripes on fawn background; stripes clearly defined, covering top of body; white marking not rejected

UNDERLINE graceful curve

RIBS well-arched, extending far to rear

ELBOWS not too close, yet not off too far

PASTERNS clearly defined, slight slant but almost perpendicular to ground

DISQUALIFICATIONS—White or black ground color, or entirely white or black or any color other than fawn or brindle. (White markings allowed but must not exceed one-third of ground color)

HEAD: muzzle to be in correct relationship to skull, never too small; clean with neither deep wrinkles nor dewlap; typical, unique

EYES dark brown; not too small nor protruding nor deep-set; expression of energy and intelligence; dark rims

STOP distinct but neither forced into forehead nor sloping; furrow between eyes

NOSE broad, black, slightly turned up somewhat higher than muzzle; nostrils broad

JAWS wide; lower protrudes beyond upper; bends slightly upward; upper broad where attached to skull; undershot; bite powerful, sound

MUZZLE square, powerfully developed in length, breadth, depth; not pointed, narrow, short, shallow

CHEEKS no protrusion

MASK dark, confined to muzzle; in distinct contrast to head color, a REQUIRED trait

UPPER ARM long, forms right angle to shoulder blade

CHEST deep, reaching to elbows; depth, half of height at withers

FEET small, tightly arched toes (cat's paws); tough pads, turning neither in nor out

COAT short, shiny, smooth, tight to body

HEIGHT: adult males 22½" to 25", not under, females 21" to 23½", not over, at withers

FORELEGS straight, parallel; bones strong, firmly joined

BODY well-balanced; medium-sized; square in profile, sturdy, short; muscular, clean, powerfully developed; skin taut; equipped for speed, never racy

CH. SALGRAY'S AMBUSH

GRAND PRIZE FUTURITY WINNER, AMERICAN BOXER CLUB, 1967. BEST OF BREED, AMERICAN BOXER CLUB SPECIALTY, 1968 (FROM PUPPY CLASS). BEST OF BREED, AMERICAN BOXER CLUB SPECIALTY, 1968. MANY TIMES B.I.S AND GROUP WINNER. OUTSTANDING SIRE OF MORE THAN 20 CHAMPIONS.

SALGRAY BOXERS
(MR. & MRS. DANIEL M. HAMILBURG)
90 HOLLAND ROAD
BROOKLINE, MASSACHUSETTS 02146

ears are set at the highest points of the sides of the skull, cut rather long without too broad a shell, and are carried erect. The dark-brown eyes, not too small, protruding or deep-set, and encircled by dark hair, should impart an alert, intelligent expression. Their mood-mirroring quality combined with the mobile skin furrowing of the forehead gives the Boxer head its unique degree of expressiveness. The nose is broad and black, very slightly turned up; the nostrils broad with the naso-labial line running between them down through the upper lip which, however, must not be split.

Faults: Lack of nobility and expression, sombre face, unserviceable bite. Pinscher or Bulldog head, sloping top line of muzzle, muzzle too light for skull, too pointed a bite (snipy). Teeth or tongue showing with mouth closed, driveling, split upper lip. Poor ear carriage, light ("Bird of Prey") eyes.

NECK — Round, of ample length, not too short; strong, muscular and clean throughout without dewlap; distinctly marked nape with an elegant arch running down to the back.

Faults: Dewlap.

BODY — In profile, the build is of square proportions in that a horizontal line from the front of the forechest to the rear projection of the upper thigh should equal a vertical line dropped from the top of the withers to the ground.

CHEST AND FOREQUARTERS — The brisket is deep, reaching down to the elbows; the depth of the body at the lowest point of the brisket equals half the height of the dog at the withers. The ribs, extending far to the rear, are well arched but not barrel-shaped. Chest of fair width and forechest well defined, being easily visible from the side. The loins are short and muscular; the lower stomach line, lightly tucked up, blends into a graceful curve to the rear. The shoulders are long and sloping, close-lying, and not excessively covered with muscle. The upper arm is long, closely approaching a right angle to the shoulder blade. The forelegs, viewed from the front, are straight, stand parallel to each other, and have strong, firmly-joined bones. The elbows should not press too closely to the chest wall or stand off visibly from it. The forearm is straight, long, and firmly muscled. The pastern joint is clearly defined but not distended. The pastern is strong and distinct, slightly slanting, but standing almost perpendicular to the ground. The dewclaws may be removed as a safety precaution. Feet should be compact, turning neither in nor out, with tightly arched toes (cat feet) and tough pads.

Faults: Chest too broad, too shallow or too deep in front, loose or over-muscled shoulders, chest hanging between shoulders, tied-in or bowed-out elbows, turned feet, hare feet, hollow flanks, hanging stomach.

BACK — The withers should be clearly defined as the highest point of the back; the whole back short, straight and muscular with a firm topline.

Faults: Roach back, sway back, thin lean back, long narrow loins, weak union with croup.

HINDQUARTERS — Strongly muscled with angulation in balance with that of forequarters. The thighs broad and curved, the breech musculature hard and strongly developed. Croup slightly sloped, flat and broad. Tail attachment high rather than low. Tail clipped, carried upward. Pelvis long and, in females especially, broad. Upper and lower thigh long, leg well angulated with a clearly defined, well-let-down hock joint. In standing position, the leg below the hock joint (metatarsus) should be practically perpendicular to the ground with a slight rearward slope permissible. Viewed from behind, the hind legs should be straight with the hock joints leaning neither in nor out. The metatarsus should be short, clean and strong, supported by powerful rear pads. The rear toes just a little longer than the front toes, but similar in all other respects. Dewclaws, if any, may be removed.

Faults: Too rounded, too narrow, or falling off of croup, low-set tail, higher in back than in front; steep, stiff, or too-slightly-angulated hindquarters, light thighs, bowed or crooked legs, cowhocks, over-angulated hock joint (sickle hocks), long metatarsus (high hocks), hare feet, hindquarters too far under or too far behind.

GAIT — Viewed from the side, proper front and rear angulation is manifested in a smoothly-efficient, level-backed, ground-covering stride with powerful drive emanating from a freely operating rear. Although the front legs do not contribute impelling power, adequate "reach" should be evident to prevent interference, overlap or "sidewinding" (crabbing). Viewed from the front, the shoulders should remain trim and the elbows not flare out. The legs are parallel until gaiting narrows the track in proportion

[continued on page 159]

BULLMASTIFF STANDARD

GENERAL APPEARANCE — That of a symmetrical animal, showing great strength; powerfully built but active. The dog is fearless yet docile, has endurance and alertness. The foundation breeding was 60% Mastiff and 40% Bulldog.

HEAD — Skull large, with a fair amount of wrinkle when alert; broad, with cheeks well developed. Forehead flat. Muzzle broad and deep; its length, in comparison with that of the entire head, approximately as 1 is to 3. Lack of foreface with nostrils set on top of muzzle is a reversion to the Bulldog and is very undesirable. Nose black with nostrils large and broad. Flews not too pendulous, stop moderate, and the mouth (bite) preferably level or slightly undershot. Canine teeth large and set wide apart. A dark muzzle is preferable. *Eyes* — Dark and of medium size. *Ears* — V-shaped and carried close to the cheeks, set on wide and high, level with occiput and cheeks, giving a square appearance to the skull; darker in color than the body and medium in size.

NECK — Slightly arched, of moderate length, very muscular, and almost equal in circumference to the skull.

BODY — Compact. Chest wide and deep, with ribs well sprung and well set down between the forelegs. *Forequarters* — Shoulders muscular but not loaded, and slightly sloping. Forelegs straight, well boned and set well apart; elbows square. Pasterns straight, feet of medium size, with round toes well arched. Pads thick and tough, nails black. *Back* — Short, giving the impression of a well balanced dog. *Loins* — Wide, muscular and slightly arched, with fair depth of flank. *Hindquarters* — Broad and muscular with well developed second thigh denoting power, but not cumbersome. Moderate angulation at hocks. Cowhocks and splay feet are bad faults. *Tail* — Set on high, strong at the root and tapering to the hocks. It may be straight or curved, but never carried hound fashion.

COAT — Short and dense, giving good weather protection. *Color* — Red, fawn or brindle. Except for a very small white spot on the chest, white marking is considered a fault.

SIZE — Dogs, 25 to 27 inches at the shoulder, and 110 to 130 pounds weight. Bitches, 24 to 26 inches at the shoulder, and 100 to 120 pounds weight. Other things being equal, the heavier dog is favored.

Approved February 6, 1960

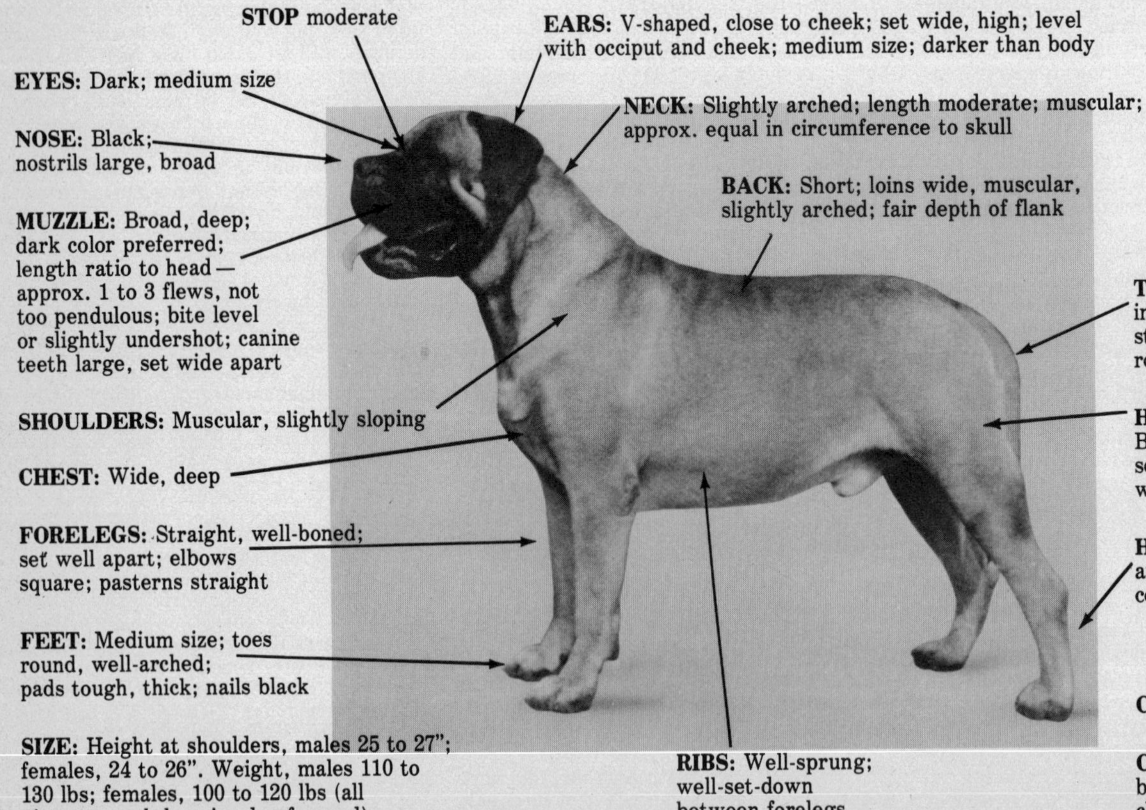

HEAD: Skull large, broad; fair wrinkle; cheeks well-developed; forehead flat
APPEARANCE: Powerfully built but active endurance with alertness; compact; symmetrical
STOP moderate
EARS: V-shaped, close to cheek; set wide, high; level with occiput and cheek; medium size; darker than body
EYES: Dark; medium size
NECK: Slightly arched; length moderate; muscular; approx. equal in circumference to skull
NOSE: Black; nostrils large, broad
BACK: Short; loins wide, muscular, slightly arched; fair depth of flank
MUZZLE: Broad, deep; dark color preferred; length ratio to head — approx. 1 to 3 flews, not too pendulous; bite level or slightly undershot; canine teeth large, set wide apart
TAIL: Set high, reaching to hocks; carriage straight or curved; root strong, tapering
SHOULDERS: Muscular, slightly sloping
HINDQUARTERS: Broad, muscular; second thigh well-developed
CHEST: Wide, deep
FORELEGS: Straight, well-boned; set well apart; elbows square; pasterns straight
HOCKS of moderate angulation; not cow-hocked
FEET: Medium size; toes round, well-arched; pads tough, thick; nails black
COAT: Short, dense
SIZE: Height at shoulders, males 25 to 27"; females, 24 to 26". Weight, males 110 to 130 lbs; females, 100 to 120 lbs (all virtues equal, heavier dog favored)
RIBS: Well-sprung; well-set-down between forelegs
COLOR: Red, fawn or brindle; white spot on chest not faulted

AM. CAN. CH. RAMAPO TORNE'S RED STEVE

STEVE WAS ACTIVELY CAMPAIGNED TO A TOTAL OF 186 BREED WINS AND COMPILED A THEN RECORD NUMBER OF GROUP PLACINGS AND GROUP WINS: NUMBER 1 BULLMASTIFF 1969 AND 1970. STEVE HOLDS THESE "ALL-TIME" BREED RECORDS: TOTAL CONSECUTIVE BOB WINS — 112. TOTAL SPECIALTY WINS — 7. TOTAL CONSECUTIVE NATIONAL SPECIALTY WINS — 4. AFTER 2 YEARS IN RETIREMENT STEVE ATTENDED HIS 5TH SPECIALTY AND AGAIN WENT BOB BECOMING THE FIRST WINNER FROM THE VETERAN CLASS.

VIRGIL MILLETT
"BAY EDGE"
250 BAY AVENUE
HUNTINGTON, N.Y. 11743
(516) 427-6585

Dogs of the Bullmastiff type were bred in Britain in the latter part of the 19th century to serve as nocturnal guards against poachers. The Mastiff, massive and powerful but slow and benign, and the Bulldog, aggressive but small, were chosen to be the parents. The descendant type, the Bullmastiff, was swift, powerful, and apparently sufficiently aggressive to achieve its purpose. The present day breed descends from such crosses. The Bullmastiff is powerful, symmetrical, active, and fearless but docile. The skull is large; the scalp with fair wrinkle, when the dog is alert. The muzzle is broad and deep. The body is compact; the back short. The coat is short and dense. Color is red, fawn, or brindle with dark muzzle. Dogs stand 25 to 27 inches at the shoulder and weigh 110 to 130 pounds. The Bullmastiff of today is very adaptable as a companion and pet. Some 600 are registered annually with the AKC; the breed taking 73rd.

COLLIE [ROUGH] STANDARD   COLLIE [SMOOTH] STANDARD

GENERAL CHARACTER — The collie is a lithe, strong, responsive, active dog, carrying no useless timber, standing naturally straight and firm. The deep, moderately wide chest shows strength, the sloping shoulders and well-bent hocks indicate speed and grace, and the face shows high intelligence. The Collie presents an impressive, proud picture of true balance, each part being in harmonious proportion to every other part and to the whole. Except for the technical description that is essential to this Standard and without which no Standard for the guidance of breeders and judges is adequate, it could be stated simply that no part of the Collie ever seems to be out of proportion to any other part. Timidity, frailness, sullenness, viciousness, lack of animation, cumbersome appearance and lack of over-all balance impair the general character.

HEAD — The head properties are of great importance. When considered in proportion to the size of the dog the head is inclined to lightness and never appears massive. A heavy-headed dog lacks the necessary bright, alert, full-of-sense look that contributes so greatly to expression. Both in front and profile view the head bears a general resemblance to a well-blunted lean wedge, being smooth and clean in outline and nicely balanced in proportion. On the sides it tapers gradually and smoothly from the ears to the end of the black nose, without being flared out in backskull ("cheeky") or pinched in muzzle ("snipy"). In profile view the top of the backskull and the top of the muzzle lie in two approximately parallel, straight planes of equal length, divided by a very slight but perceptible stop or break. A mid-point between the inside corners of the eyes (which is the center of a correctly placed stop) is the center of balance in length of head.

The end of the smooth, well-rounded muzzle is blunt but not square. The underjaw is strong, clean-cut and the depth of skull from the brow to the under part of the jaw is not excessive. The teeth are of good size, meeting in a scissors bite. *Overshot or undershot jaws are undesirable, the latter being more severely penalized.* There is a very slight prominence of the eyebrows. The backskull is flat, without receding either laterally or backward and the occipital bone is not highly peaked. The proper width of backskull necessarily depends upon the combined length of skull and muzzle and the width of the backskull is less than its length. Thus the correct width varies with the individual and is dependent upon the extent to which it is supported by length of muzzle. Because of the importance of the head characteristics, *prominent head faults are very severely penalized.*

EYES — Because of the combination of the flat skull, the arched eyebrows, the slight stop and the rounded muzzle, the foreface must be chiseled to form a receptacle for the eyes and they are necessarily placed obliquely to give them the required forward outlook. Except for the blue merles, they are required to be matched in color. They are almond-shaped, of medium size and never properly appear to be large or prominent. The color is dark and the eye does not show a yellow ring or a sufficiently prominent haw to affect the dog's expression. The eyes have a clear, bright appearance, expressing intelligent inquisitiveness, particularly when the ears are drawn up and the dog is on the alert. In blue merles, dark brown eyes are preferable, but either or both eyes may be merle or china in color without specific penalty. A large, round, full eye seriously detracts from the desired "sweet" expression. *Eye faults are heavily penalized.*

EARS — The ears are in proportion to the size of the head and, if they are carried properly and unquestionably "break" naturally, are seldom too small. Large ears usually cannot be lifted correctly off the head, and even if lifted, they will be out of proportion to the size of the head. When in repose the ears are folded lengthwise and thrown back into the frill. On the alert they are drawn well up on the backskull and are carried about three-quarters erect, with about one-fourth of the ear tipping or "breaking" forward. *A dog with prick ears or low ears cannot show true expression and is penalized accordingly.*

NECK — The neck is firm, clean, muscular, sinewy and heavily frilled. It is fairly long, carried upright with a slight arch at the nape and imparts a proud, upstanding appearance showing off the frill.

BODY — The body is firm, hard and muscular, a trifle long in proportion to the height. The ribs are well-rounded behind the well-sloped shoulders and the chest is deep, extending to the elbows. The back is strong and level, supported by powerful hips and thighs and the croup is sloped to give a well-rounded finish. The loin is powerful and slightly arched. *Noticeably fat dogs, or dogs in poor flesh, or with skin disease, or with no undercoat are out of condition and are moderately penalized accordingly.*

[continued on page 159]

Example of a Rough Coated Collie

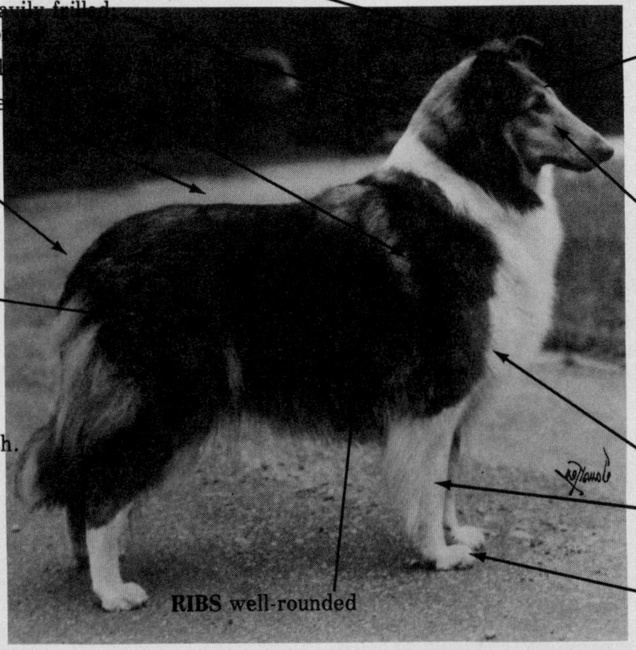

APPEARANCE: Lithe, strong, active; each part harmoniously in proportion, truly balanced. Body firm, hard, muscular; standing firm, straight. Length trifle longer than height

EARS in proportion to head; when alert ¾ erect with ¼ breaking

NECK firm, hard, muscular; he... long, slightly arched, carried up...

SHOULDERS well...

BACK strong, level; croup slope... loins powerful, slightly arched

TAIL moderately long; reaching to hocks or below; carried gaily when moving or alert (not over back); "swirl" end; profuse hair

HINDQUARTERS muscular, sinewy; powerful hips and thighs; hocks well-bent, turning neither in nor out; coat smooth below hocks; stifles well-bent

VARIETIES: Rough and Smooth. Same standard except coat

SIZE: Height, males, 24-26"; females, 22-24". Weight, males 60-75 lbs; females, 50-65 lbs

COLORS: Sable and white, tri-color, blue merle, white — no preference. S/W — from gold to mahogany, white markings; blaze permissible. Tri — predominantly black, white markings, tan shadings. Blue merle — mottled blue-gray and black, white markings, usually tan shadings. White — sable or tri markings preferred

RIBS well-rounded

HEAD inclined to lightness; never massive; front and profile view is well-blunted, lean wedge; clean, smooth, nicely balanced; tapering from ears to end of nose; neither snipy nor cheeky. Backskull and muzzle approx. parallel planes (equal length); backskull flat, not receding, width less than length. Occiput not highly peaked; foreface chiseled

EXPRESSION very important

EYES dark; almond-shaped; set obliquely; medium size (neither large nor prominent; no yellow rings or prominent haw; match in color (except for blue merles with dark brown preferred, but either or both eyes may be merle or china)

STOP slight but perceptible; midpoint of balance in head length

MUZZLE smooth, well-rounded; end blunt (not square); underjaw strong, clean-cut. Teeth good size; scissors bite. Nose black

CHEST deep; extending to elbows

FORELEGS straight, muscular. Pasterns flexible without weakness; well-feathered to back of pasterns

FEET: comparatively small; oval shaped; soles tough, well-padded; toes close together, well-arched

COAT (Rough) well-fitting, profuse, especially on mane and frill; properly textured; abundant except on head and legs; smooth face or mask. Outer coat straight, harsh; inner coat soft, dense. (Smooth) coat dense, hard

CH. JAGWYN'S SHADOW OF THE HAWK

SIRE: CH. BLACK HAWK OF KASAN (TOP PRODUCING WORKING DOG). DAM: CH. CUL MOR'S BIRKEN SHAW (TOP PRODUCING WORKING BITCH).

HANDLER: MARY O'CONNOR

PATRICIA B. MORROW (PATMOR COLLIES)
2637 HOLLISTON COURT
ATLANTA, GEORGIA 30340

LEGS — The forelegs are straight and muscular, with a fair amount of bone considering the size of the dog. A cumbersome appearance is undesirable. *Both narrow and wide placement are penalized.* The forearm is moderately fleshy and the pasterns are flexible but without weakness. The hind legs are less fleshy, muscular at the thighs, very sinewy and the hocks and stifles are well bent. *A cowhocked dog or a dog with straight stifles is penalized.* The comparatively small feet are approximately oval in shape. The soles are well padded and tough, and the toes are well arched and close together. When the collie is not in motion the legs and feet are judged by allowing the dog to come to a natural stop in a standing position so that both the forelegs and the hind legs are placed well apart, with the feet extending straight forward. Excessive "posing" is undesirable.

GAIT — The gait or movement is distinctly characteristic of the breed. A sound Collie is not out at the elbows but it does, nevertheless, move toward an observer with its front feet tracking comparatively close together at the ground. The front legs do not "cross over," nor does the Collie move with a pacing or rolling gait. Viewed from the front, one gains the impression that the dog is capable of changing its direction of travel almost instantaneously, as indeed it is. When viewed from the rear, the hind legs, from the hock joint to the ground, move in comparatively close-together, parallel, vertical planes. The hind legs are powerful and propelling. Viewed from the side, the gait is smooth not choppy. The reasonably long, "reaching" stride is even, easy, light and seemingly effortless.

TAIL — The tail is moderately long, the bone reaching to the hock joint or below. It is carried low when the dog is quiet, the end having an upward twist or "swirl." When gaited or when the dog is excited it is carried gaily but not over the back.

COAT — The well-fitting, proper-textured coat is the crowning glory of the rough variety of Collie. It is abundant except on the head and legs. The outer coat is straight and harsh to the touch. *A soft, open outer coat or a curly outer coat, regardless of quantity, is penalized.* The undercoat, however, is soft, furry and so close together that it is difficult to see the skin when the hair is parted. The coat is very abundant on the mane and frill. The face or mask is smooth. The forelegs are smooth and well feathered to the back of the pasterns. The hind legs are smooth below the hock joints. Any feathering below the hocks is removed for the show ring. The hair on the tail is very profuse and on the hips it is long and bushy. The texture, quantity and the extent to which the coat "fits the dog" are important points.

COLOR — The four recognized colors are sable and white, tri-color, blue merle and white. There is no preference among them. The sable and white is predominantly sable (a fawn sable color of varying shades from light gold to dark mahogany) with white

DOBERMAN PINSCHER STANDARD

GENERAL CONFORMATION AND APPEARANCE — The appearance is that of a dog of medium size, with a body that is square; the height, measured vertically from the ground to the highest point of the withers, equalling the length measured horizontally from the forechest to the rear projection of the upper thigh. *Height* at the withers — *Dogs* 26 to 28 inches, ideal about 27½ inches; *Bitches* 24 to 26 inches, ideal about 25½ inches. Length of head, neck and legs in proportion to length and depth of body. Compactly built, muscular and powerful, for great endurance and speed. Elegant in appearance, of proud carriage, reflecting great nobility and temperament. Energetic, watchful, determined, alert, fearless, loyal and obedient.

The judge shall dismiss from the ring any shy or vicious Doberman.

SHYNESS — A dog shall be judged fundamentally shy if refusing to stand for examination, it shrinks away from the judge; if it fears an approach from the rear; if it shies at sudden and unusual noises to a marked degree.

VICIOUSNESS — A dog that attacks or attempts to attack either the judge or its handler, is definitely vicious. An aggressive or belligerent attitude towards other dogs shall not be deemed viciousness.

HEAD — Long and dry, resembling a blunt wedge in both frontal and profile views. When seen from the front, the head widens gradually toward the base of the ears in a practically unbroken line. Top of skull flat, turning with slight stop to bridge of muzzle, with muzzle line extending parallel to top line of skull. Cheeks flat and muscular. Lips lying close to jaws. Jaws full and powerful, well filled under the eyes.

EYES — Almond shaped, moderately deep set, with vigorous, energetic expression. Iris, of uniform color, ranging from medium to darkest brown in black dogs; in reds, blues, and fawns the color of the iris blends with that of the markings, the darkest shade being preferable in every case.

TEETH — Strongly developed and white. Lower incisors upright and touching inside of upper incisors — a true scissors bite. *42 correctly placed teeth,* 22 in the lower, 20 in the upper jaw. Distemper teeth shall not be penalized.

DISQUALIFYING FAULTS — Overshot more than 3/16 of an inch. Undershot more than 1/8 of an inch. Four or more missing teeth.

EARS — Normally cropped and carried erect. The upper attachment of the ear, when held erect, is on a level with the top of the skull.

NECK — Proudly carried, well muscled and dry. Well arched, with nape of neck widening gradually toward body. Length of neck proportioned to body and head.

BODY — Back short, firm, of sufficient width, and muscular at the loins, extending in a straight line from withers to the *slightly* rounded croup. *Withers* pronounced and forming the highest point of the body. *Brisket* reaching deep to the elbow. *Chest* broad with forechest well defined. *Ribs* well sprung from the spine, but flattened in lower end to permit elbow clearance. *Belly* well tucked up, extending in a curved line from the brisket. *Loins* wide and muscled. *Hips* broad and in proportion to body, breadth of hips being approximately equal to breadth of body at rib cage and shoulders. *Tail* docked at approximately second joint, appears to be a continuation of the spine, and is carried only slightly above the horizontal when the dog is alert.

FOREQUARTERS — *Shoulder Blade* sloping forward and downward at a 45 degree angle to the ground meets the upper arm at an angle of 90 degrees. Length of shoulder blade and upper arm are equal. Height from elbow to withers approximately equals height from ground to elbow. *Legs,* seen from front and side, perfectly straight and parallel to each other from elbow to pastern; muscled and sinewy, with heavy bone. In normal pose and when gaiting, the elbows lie close to the brisket. *Pasterns* firm and almost perpendicular to the ground. *Feet* well arched, compact, and catlike, turning neither in nor out. Dewclaws may be removed.

HINDQUARTERS — The angulation of the hindquarters balances that of the forequarters. *Hip Bone* falls aways from spinal column at an angle of about 30 degrees, producing a slightly rounded, well-filled-out croup. *Upper Shanks,* at right angles to the hip bones, are long, wide, and well muscled on both sides of thigh, with clearly defined stifles. Upper and lower shanks are of equal length. While the dog is at rest, hock to heel is perpendicular to the ground. Viewed from the rear, the legs are straight, parallel to each other, and wide enough apart to fit in with a properly built body. *Cat Feet,* as on front legs, turning neither in nor out. Dewclaws, if any, are generally removed.

BODY square, medium size; compactly built; muscular, powerful; height at withers equals length

HEAD long, dry, as blunt wedge; widening toward base of ears; skull top flat; muzzle line parallel to skull top

TEETH strongly developed; scissors bite

EARS normally cropped, carried erect; upper attachment on level with skull top when erect

EYES almond-shaped, moderately deep-set; dark color desirable

NECK upright, well-muscled, dry; arched, nape widening gradually toward body; length proportioned to body and head

STOP slight

WITHERS pronounced; forming highest point of body

NOSE solid black, dark brown, dark gray, dark tan according to coat color

BACK short, firm, sufficient width; muscular at loin; straight line from withers to slightly rounded croup; loins wide, muscular

LIPS close to jaws

HIPS broad in proportion to body; hip bone falling away from spinal column at 30° angle

JAWS full, powerful, well-filled under eyes; cheeks flat, muscular

TAIL docked at approx. second joint, set on line with spine

SHOULDERS: Blades slope forward and downward 45 degrees meet upper arm at angle of 90 degrees

HINDQUARTERS: shanks long, wide, well-muscled; stifle clearly defined, parallel; upper and lower shanks of equal length

CHEST broad; forechest well-defined; brisket reaching deep to elbow

HOCKS turning neither in nor out; hock to heel perpendicular to ground

LEGS straight; parallel, muscled, sinewy; bone heavy; elbow close to brisket

FEET well-arched, compact, catlike; turning neither in nor out

BELLY well-tucked-up

COLORS: Black, red, blue and fawn with markings; white on chest, 1/2" square or less, permissible

RIBS: Well-sprung from spine

COAT smooth, short, hard; thick, close-lying

DISQUALIFICATIONS: Shyness, viciousness. Overshot more than 3/16" or undershot more than 1/8". Four or more missing teeth

SIZE: Height 26-28" males; 24-26 females

PASTERNS firm; almost perpendicular to ground

CH. DEVIL TREES BLACK SHAFT

SHAFT FINISHED HIS CHAMPIONSHIP AT ONE YEAR OF AGE AND STARTED HIS SPECIALS CAREER IN JANUARY 1974. IN 12 MONTHS OF SHOWING HE HAS ACCUMULATED 70 BOB, 13 GROUP I'S, 3 SPECIALTY BIS, 3 ALL BREED BIS.

OWNER
SHEILA & GEORGE WEST
RT. 124
POUND RIDGE, NEW YORK

HANDLER
JEFFREY LYNN BRUCKER
5071 PEACHTREE
DUNWOODY ROAD
ATLANTA, GEORGIA 30342

GAIT — Free, balanced, and vigorous, with good reach in the forequarters and good driving power in the hindquarters. When trotting, there is strong rear-action drive. Each rear leg moves in line with the foreleg on the same side. Rear and front legs are thrown neither in nor out. Back remains strong and firm. When moving at a fast trot, a properly built dog will singletrack.

COAT, COLOR, MARKINGS — *Coat*, smooth-haired, short, hard, thick and close lying. Invisible gray undercoat on neck permissible. *Allowed Colors* — Black, red, blue, and fawn (Isabella). *Markings* — Rust, sharply defined, appearing above each eye and on muzzle, throat and forechest, on all legs and feet, and below tail. *Nose* solid black on black dogs, dark brown on red ones, dark gray on blue ones, dark tan on fawns. White patch on chest, not exceeding 1/2 square inch, permissible.

FAULTS — *The foregoing description is that of the ideal Doberman Pinscher. Any deviation from the above described dog must be penalized to the extent of the deviation.*

DISQUALIFICATIONS

Overshot more than 3/16 of an inch; undershot more than 1/8 of an inch. Four or more missing teeth.

Approved October 14, 1969

GERMAN SHEPHERD DOG STANDARD

GENERAL APPEARANCE — The first impression of a good German Shepherd Dog is that of a strong, agile, well-muscled animal, alert and full of life. It is well balanced, with harmonious development of the forequarter and hindquarter. The dog is longer than tall, deep-bodied, and presents an outline of smooth curves rather than angles. It looks substantial and not spindly, giving the impression, both at rest and in motion, of muscular fitness and nimbleness without any look of clumsiness or soft living. The ideal dog is stamped with a look of quality and nobility—difficult to define, but unmistakable when present. Second sex characteristics are strongly marked, and every animal gives a definite impression of masculinity or femininity, according to its sex.

CHARACTER — The breed has a distinct personality marked by direct and fearless, but not hostile, expression, self-confidence, and a certain aloofness that does not lend itself to immediate and indiscriminate friendships. The dog must be approachable, quietly standing its ground and showing confidence and willingness to meet overtures without itself making them. It is poised, but when the occasion demands, eager and alert; both fit and willing to serve in its capacity as companion, watchdog, blind leader, herding dog, or guardian, whichever the circumstances may demand. The dog must not be timid, shrinking behind its master or handler; it should not be nervous, looking about or upward with anxious expression or showing nervous reactions, such as tucking of tail, to strange sounds or sights. Lack of confidence under any surroundings is not typical of good character. Any of the above deficiencies in character which indicate shyness must be penalized as very serious faults. It must be possible for the judge to observe the teeth and to determine that both testicles are descended. Any dog that attempts to bite the judge must be disqualified. The ideal dog is a working animal with an incorruptible character combined with body and gait suitable for the arduous work which constitutes its primary purpose.

HEAD — The head is noble, cleanly chiseled, strong without coarseness, but above all not fine, and in proportion to the body. The head of the male is distinctly masculine, and that of the bitch distinctly feminine. The muzzle is long and strong with the lips firmly fitted, and its top line is parallel to the top line of the skull. Seen from the front, the forehead is only moderately arched, and the skull slopes into the long, wedge-shaped muzzle without abrupt stop. Jaws are strongly developed. *Ears*—Ears are moderately pointed, in proportion to the skull, open toward the front, and carried erect when at attention, the ideal carriage being one in which the center lines of the ears, viewed from the front, are parallel to each other and perpendicular to the ground. A dog with cropped or hanging ears must be disqualified. *Eyes*—Of medium size, almond-shaped, set a little obliquely and not protruding. The color as dark as possible. The expression keen, intelligent and composed. *Teeth*—42 in number—20 upper and 22 lower—are strongly developed and meet in a scissors bite in which part of the inner surface of the upper incisors meet and engage part of the outer surface of the lower incisors. An overshot jaw or a level bite is undesirable. An undershot jaw is a disqualifying fault. Complete dentition is to be preferred. Any missing teeth other than first premolars is a serious fault.

NECK — The neck is strong and muscular, clean-cut and relatively long, proportionate in size to the head and without loose folds of skin. When the dog is at attention or excited, the head is raised and the neck carried high; otherwise typical carriage of the head is forward rather than up and but little higher than the top of the shoulders, particularly in motion.

FOREQUARTERS — The shoulder blades are long and obliquely angled, laid on flat and not placed forward. The upper arm joins the shoulder blade at about a right angle. Both the upper arm and the shoulder blade are well muscled. The forelegs, viewed from all sides, are straight and the bone oval rather than round. The pasterns are strong and springy and angulated at approximately a 25° angle from the vertical.

FEET — The feet are short, compact, with toes well arched, pads thick and firm, nails short and dark. The dewclaws, if any, should be removed from the hind legs. Dewclaws on the forelegs may be removed, but are normally left on.

PROPORTION — The German Shepherd Dog is longer than tall, with the most desirable proportion as 10 to 8½. The desired height for males at the top of the highest point of the shoulder blade is 24 to 26 inches; and for bitches, 22 to 24 inches. The length is measured from the point of the prosternum or breastbone to the rear edge of the pelvis, the ischial tuberosity.

BODY — The whole structure of the body gives an impression of depth and solidity without bulkiness. *Chest*—Commencing at the prosternum, is well filled and carried well down between the legs. It is deep and capacious, never shallow, with ample room

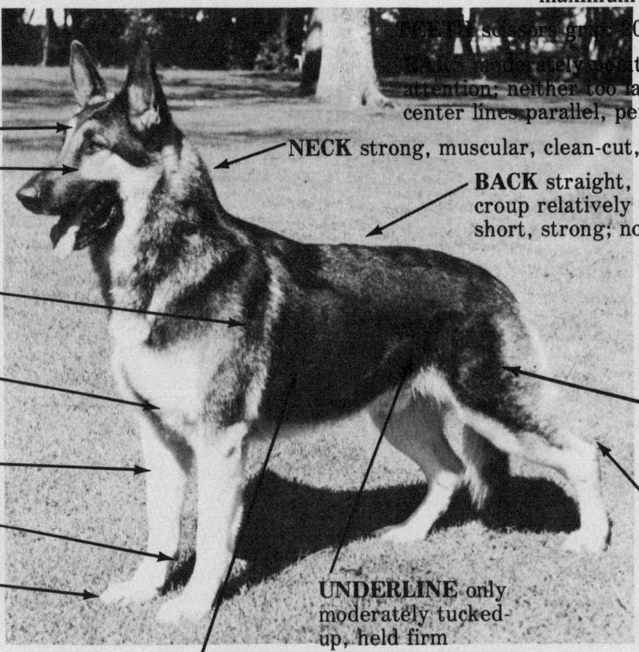

HEAD noble, cleanly chiseled, neither coarse nor refined; head of the male distinctly masculine, of the female distinctly feminine

SKULL: forehead moderately arched

EYES medium size, almond-shaped, slightly oblique, dark, not protruding; very expressive

STOP not abrupt

MUZZLE long, strong; lips firmly fitted; top line parallels top line of skull; jaws strongly developed

SHOULDERS: blades long, flat; meet upper arm at right angles

FORECHEST well-filled, well down between legs, carried forward; deep, capacious

LEGS straight; bone oval

PASTERNS strong, springy; angulated at 25 degrees

FEET strong, compact; toes well-arched; pads thick, firm; nails short, dark

DISQUALIFICATIONS: White in color; nose not predominantly black; cropped ears; hanging ears; docked tail; undershot jaw; attempting to bit judge

APPEARANCE: Body well-developed, sturdy, agile, deep, longer than tall; proportion 10:8½; temperament, expression, gait important

GAIT important; long, effortless trot, covering maximum ground with minimum steps

TEETH scissors grip; 20 upper, 22 lower, strongly developed

EARS moderately pointed, open toward front; erect at attention; neither too large nor too small; Front view—center lines parallel, perpendicular to ground; never cropped

NECK strong, muscular, clean-cut, relatively long; no loose folds of skin

BACK straight, strongly developed; from withers to croup relatively short; firm; withers high; loin broad, short, strong; not too long from last rib to thigh

CROUP long, gradually sloping

TAIL bushy, last vertebra extending to hock; low-set; wet smoothly into croup; in repose tail curves sabre-like; never lifted beyond line at right angles with topline

HINDQUARTERS broad, well muscled, upper thigh bone parallels shoulder blade—lower parallels upper arm; metatarsus (between hock joint and foot) short, strong

HOCK short, clean, sharply defined; strong, turning neither in nor out

UNDERLINE only moderately tucked-up, held firm

RIBS well-sprung, long, neither flat nor barrel-shaped; carried down to breastbone; carried well back

HEIGHT at shoulder: males 24"-26", females 22"-24"

COLOR: Strong rich colors preferred. Nose black.

COAT double; outer coat dense, coarse, straight, harsh, lying close to body

for lungs and heart, carried well forward, with the prosternum showing ahead of the shoulder in profile. *Ribs*—Well sprung and long, neither barrel-shaped nor too flat, and carried down to a sternum which reaches to the elbows. Correct ribbing allows the elbows to move back freely when the dog is at a trot. Too round causes interference and throws the elbows out; too flat or short causes pinched elbows. Ribbing is carried well back so that the loin is relatively short. *Abdomen*—Firmly held and not paunchy. The bottom line is only moderately tucked up in the loin.

TOPLINE — *Withers* — The withers are higher than and sloping into the level back. *Back*—The back is straight, very strongly developed without sag or roach, and relatively short. The desirable long proportion is not derived from a long back, but from overall length with relation to height, which is achieved by length of forequarter and length of withers and hindquarter, viewed from the side. *Loin*—Viewed from the top, broad and strong. Undue length between the last rib and the thigh, when viewed from the side, is undesirable. *Croup*—Long and gradually sloping. *Tail*—Bushy, with the last vertebra extended at least to the hock joint. It is set smoothly into the croup and low rather than high. At rest, the tail hangs in a slight curve like a sabre. A slight hook, sometimes carried to one side, is faulty only to the extent that it mars general appearance. When the dog is excited or in motion, the curve is accentuated and the tail raised, but it should never be curled forward beyond a vertical line. Tails too short, or with clumpy ends due to ankylosis, are serious faults. A dog with a docked tail must be disqualified.

HINDQUARTERS — The whole assembly of the thigh, viewed from the side, is broad, with both upper and lower thigh well muscled, forming as nearly as possible a right angle. The upper thigh bone parallels the shoulder blade while the lower thigh bone parallels the upper arm. The metatarsus (the unit between the hock joint and the foot) is short, strong and tightly articulated.

GAIT — A German Shepherd Dog is a trotting dog, and its structure has been developed to meet the requirements of its work. *General Impression* — The gait is outreaching, elastic, seemingly without effort, smooth and rhythmic, covering the maximum amount of ground with the minimum number of steps. At a walk it covers a great deal of ground, with long stride of both hind legs and forelegs. At a trot the dog covers still more ground with even longer stride, and moves powerfully but easily, with co-ordination and balance so that the gait appears to be the steady motion of a well-lubricated machine. The feet travel close to the ground on both forward reach and backward push. In order to achieve ideal movement of this kind, there must be good muscular development and ligamentation. The hindquarters deliver, through the back a powerful forward thrust which slightly lifts the whole animal and drives the body

[continued on page 159]

GIANT SCHNAUZER STANDARD

GENERAL DESCRIPTION—The Giant Schnauzer should resemble, as nearly as possible, in general appearance, a larger and more powerful version of the Standard Schnauzer, on the whole a bold and valiant figure of a dog. Robust, strongly built, nearly square in proportion of body length to height at withers, active, sturdy and well-muscled. Temperament which combines spirit and alertness with intelligence and reliability. Composed, watchful, courageous, easily trained deeply loyal to family, playful, amiable in repose, and a commanding figure when aroused. The sound, reliable temperament, rugged build, and dense weather-resistant wiry coat make for one of the most useful, powerful, and enduring working breeds.

HEAD—Strong, rectangular in appearance, and elongated; narrowing slightly from the ears to the eyes, and again from the eyes to the tip of the nose. The total length of the head is about one-half the length of the back (withers to set-on of tail). The head matches the sex and substance of the dog. The top line of the muzzle is parallel to the top line of the skull; there is a slight stop which is accentuated by the eyebrows.

SKULL — (Occiput to Stop). Moderately broad between the ears; occiput not too prominent. Top of skull flat; skin unwrinkled.

CHEEKS -Flat, but with well-developed chewing muscles; there is no "cheekiness" to disturb the rectangular head appearance (with beard).

MUZZLE –Strong and well-filled under the eyes; both parallel and equal in length to the topskull; ending in a moderately blunt wedge. The nose is large, black, and full. The lips are tight, and not overlapping, black in color.

BITE –A full complement of sound white teeth (6/6 incisors, 2/2 canines, 8/8 premolars, 4/6 molars) with a scissors bite. The upper and lower jaws are powerful and well-formed. *Disqualifying Faults*—Overshot or undershot.

EARS –When cropped, identical in shape and length with pointed tips. They are in balance with the head and are not exaggerated in length. They are set high in the skull and carried perpendicularly at the inner edges with as little bell as possible along the other edges. When uncropped, the ears are V-shaped button ears of medium length and thickness, set high and carried rather high and close to the head.

EYES—Medium size, dark brown, and deep-set. They are oval in appearance and keen in expression with lids fitting tightly. Vision is not impaired nor eyes hidden by too long eyebrows.

NECK –Strong and well-arched, of moderate length, blending cleanly into the shoulders, and with the skin fitting tightly at the throat; in harmony with the dog's weight and build.

BODY — Compact, substantial, short-coupled, and strong, with great power and agility. The height at the highest point of the withers equals the body length from breastbone to point of rump. The loin section is well-developed as short as possible for compact build.

FOREQUARTERS–The forequarters have flat, somewhat sloping shoulders and high withers. Forelegs are straight and vertical when viewed from all sides with strong pasterns and good bone. They are separated by a fairly deep brisket which precludes a pinched front. The elbows are set close to the body and point directly backwards.

CHEST—Medium in width, ribs well-sprung but with no tendency toward a barrel chest; oval in cross section; deep through the brisket. The breastbone is plainly discernible, with strong forechest; the brisket descends at least to the elbows, and ascends gradually toward the rear with the belly moderately drawn up. The ribs spread gradually from the first rib so as to allow space for the elbows to move close to the body.

SHOULDERS—The sloping shoulder blades (scapulae) are strongly-muscled yet flat. They are well laid back so that from the side the rounded upper ends are in a nearly vertical line above the elbows. They slope well forward to the point where they join the upper arm (humerus), forming as nearly as possible a right angle. Such an angulation permits the maximum forward extension of the forelegs without binding or effort. Both shoulder blades and upper arm are long, permitting depth of chest at the brisket.

BACK — Short, straight, strong, and firm.

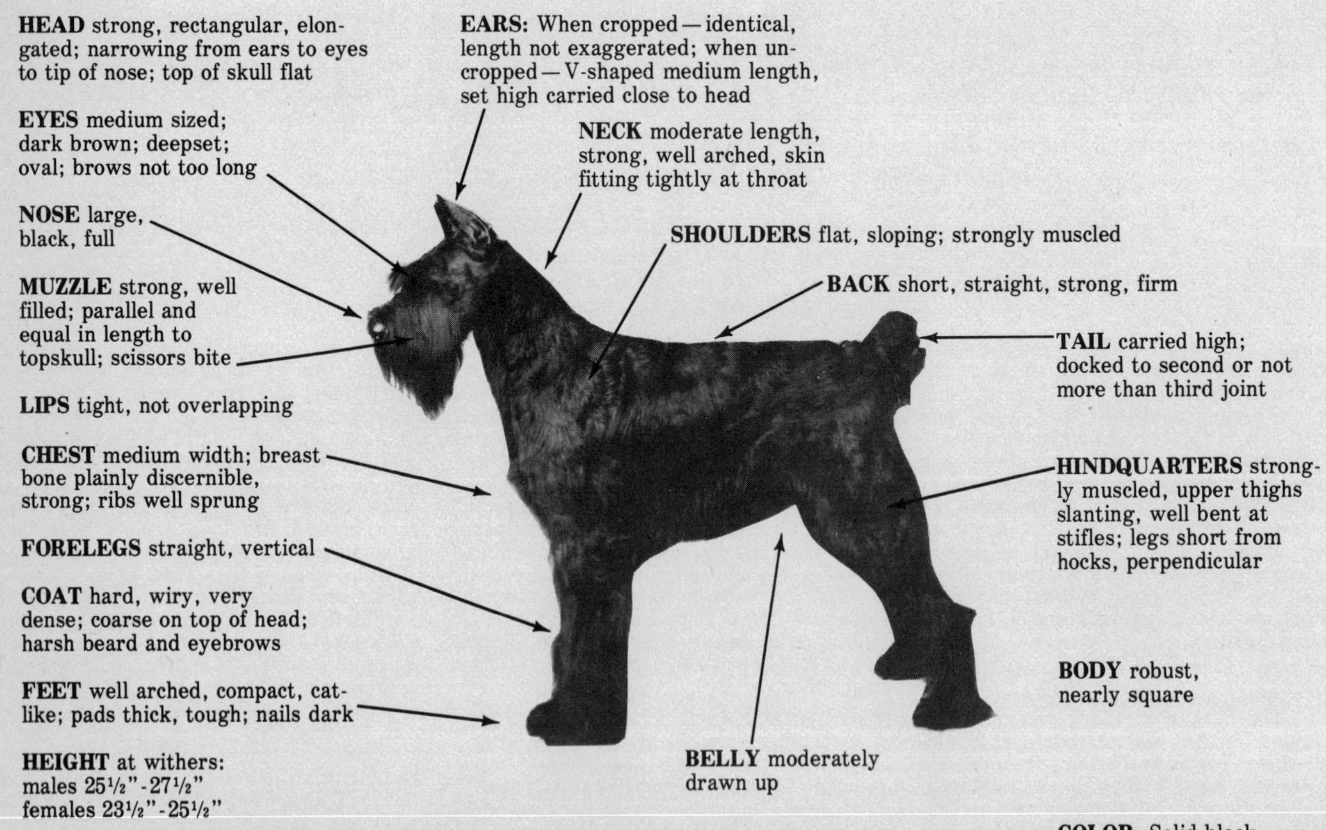

HEAD strong, rectangular, elongated; narrowing from ears to eyes to tip of nose; top of skull flat
EYES medium sized; dark brown; deepset; oval; brows not too long
NOSE large, black, full
MUZZLE strong, well filled; parallel and equal in length to topskull; scissors bite
LIPS tight, not overlapping
CHEST medium width; breast bone plainly discernible, strong; ribs well sprung
FORELEGS straight, vertical
COAT hard, wiry, very dense; coarse on top of head; harsh beard and eyebrows
FEET well arched, compact, catlike; pads thick, tough; nails dark
HEIGHT at withers: males 25½"-27½" females 23½"-25½"
DISQUALIFICATIONS: Overshot or undershot
EARS: When cropped — identical, length not exaggerated; when uncropped — V-shaped medium length, set high carried close to head
NECK moderate length, strong, well arched, skin fitting tightly at throat
SHOULDERS flat, sloping; strongly muscled
BACK short, straight, strong, firm
TAIL carried high; docked to second or not more than third joint
HINDQUARTERS strongly muscled, upper thighs slanting, well bent at stifles; legs short from hocks, perpendicular
BODY robust, nearly square
BELLY moderately drawn up
COLOR: Solid black or pepper & salt

TAIL — The tail is set moderately high and carried high in excitement. It should be docked to the second or not more than the third joint (approximately one and one-half to about three inches long at maturity).

HINDQUARTERS –The hindquarters are strongly-muscled, in balance with the forequarters; upper thighs are slanting and well bent at the stifles with the second thighs (tibiae) approximately parallel to an extension of the upper neckline. The legs from the hock joint to the feet are short, perpendicular to the ground while the dog is standing naturally, and from the rear parallel to each other. The hindquarters do not appear over-built or higher than the shoulders. Croup full and slightly rounded.

FEET –Well-arched, compact and catlike, turning neither in nor out, with thick tough pads and dark nails.

DEWCLAWS –Dewclaws, if any, on hind legs should be removed; on the forelegs, may be removed.

GAIT–The trot is the gait at which movement is judged. Free, balanced and vigorous, with good reach in the forequarters and good driving power in the hindquarters. Rear and front legs are thrown neither in nor out. When moving at a fast trot, a properly built dog will single-track. Back remains strong, firm, and flat.

COAT –Hard, wiry, very dense; composed of a soft undercoat and a harsh outer coat which, when seen against the grain, stands slightly up off the back, lying neither smooth nor flat. Coarse hair on top of head; harsh beard and eyebrows, the Schnauzer hallmark.

[*continued on p. 232*]

STANDARD OF POINTS

1. General Conformation		
[a] General appearance	10	
[b] Color and markings	8	
[c] Size	5	
[d] Condition of coat	4	
[e] Substance	3	30
2. Movement		
[a] Gait	10	
[b] Rear end [croup, legs, paws]	10	
[c] Front end [Shoulders, legs, paws]	8	28
3. Head		
[a] Head conformation	12	
[b] Teeth	4	
[c] Eyes [nose and ears]	4	20
4. Torso		
[a] Neck	6	
[b] Loin and back	6	
[c] Chest	4	
[d] Ribs and brisket	4	20
5. Tail		2
Total		100

1. GENERAL CONFORMATION .... 30 points

(a) General Appearance (10 points) — The Great Dane combines in its distinguished appearance dignity, strength and elegance with great size and powerful, well-formed, smoothly muscled body. He is one of the giant breeds, but is unique in that his general conformation must be so well-balanced that he never appears clumsy and is always a unit — the Apollo of dogs. He must be spirited and courageous — never timid. He is friendly and dependable. This physical and mental combination is the characteristic which gives the Great Dane the majesty possessed by no other breed. It is particularly true of this breed that there is an impression of great masculinity in dogs as compared to an impression of femininity in bitches. The male should appear more massive throughout than the bitch, with larger frame and heavier bone. In the ratio between length and height, the Great Dane should appear as square as possible. In bitches, a somewhat longer body is permissible. *Faults:* Lack of unity; timidity; bitchy dogs; poor musculature; poor bone development; out of condition; rickets; doggy bitches.

(b) Color and Markings (8 points) — (i) *Color:* Brindle Danes. Base color ranging from light golden yellow to deep golden yellow always brindled with strong black cross stripes. The more intensive the base color and the more intensive the brindling, the more attractive will be the color. Small white marks at the chest and toes are not desirable. *Faults:* Brindle with too dark a base color; silver-blue and grayish-blue base color; dull (faded) brindling; white tail tip.

(ii) Fawn Danes. Golden yellow up to deep golden yellow color with a deep black mask. The golden deep-yellow color must always be given the preference. Small white spots at the chest and toes are not desirable. *Faults:* Yellowish-gray, bluish-yellow, grayish-blue, dirty yellow color (drab color), lack of black mask.

(iii) Blue Danes. The color must be a pure steel blue as far as possible without any tinge of yellow, black or mouse gray. *Faults:* Any deviation from a pure steel-blue coloration.

(iv) Black Danes. Glossy black. *Faults:* Yellow-black, brown-black or blue-black. White markings, such as stripes on the chest, speckled chest and markings on the paws are permitted but not desirable.

(v) Harlequin Danes. Base color: pure white with black torn patches irregularly and well-distributed over the entire body; pure white neck preferred. The black patches should never be large enough to give the appearance of a blanket nor so small as to give a stippled or dappled effect. (Eligible, but less desirable are a few gray spots, also pointings where instead of a pure white base with black spots there is a white base with single black hairs showing through which tend to give a salt and pepper or dirty effect.) *Faults:* White base color with a few large spots; bluish-gray pointed background.

(c) Size (5 points) — The male should not be less than 30 inches at the shoulders, but it is preferable that he be 32 inches or more, providing he is well proportioned to his height. The female should not be less than 28 inches at the shoulders, but it is preferable that she be 30 inches or more, providing she is well proportioned to her height.

(d) Condition of Coat (4 points) — The coat should be very short and thick, smooth and glossy. *Faults:* Excessively long hair (stand-off coat); dull hair (indicating malnutrition, worms and negligent care).

(e) Substance (3 points) — Substance is that sufficiency of bone and muscle which rounds out a balance with the frame. *Faults:* Lightweight whippety Danes; coarse, ungainly proportioned Danes; always there should be balance.

2. MOVEMENT .... 28 points

(a) Gait (10 points) — Long, easy, springy stride with no tossing or rolling of body. The back line should move smoothly, parallel to the ground. The gait of the Great Dane

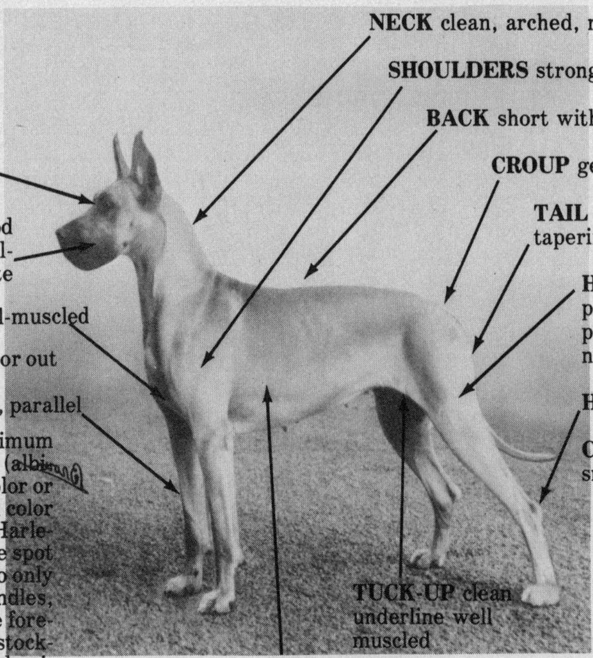

HEAD massive, long, narrow, large, angular, finely chiseled; forehead to nose bridge parallel, nose to stop equal to stop to slightly developed occiput

EYES almond shaped, dark; size medium; well-developed eyebrows

STOP well-defined

NOSE large, black; bridge broad

MUZZLE square, good depth; flews full; teeth well-developed; scissors bite

CHEST broad, deep, well-muscled

ELBOWS turning neither in nor out

FORELEGS straight, strong, parallel

DISQUALIFICATIONS: Under minimum height. Whites without black marks (albinos). Merles: Solid mouse-gray color or base with black or white or both color spots white base with mouse-spots. Harlequins and solid colors; where a large spot extends coatlike over entire body, so only neck, legs, tail tip are white. Brindles, fawn blues, and blacks; with white forehead line, white collars, high white stockings, white bellies. Danes with predominantly blue, gray, yellow or brindled spots. Docked tail. Split nose

FEET round, not turned; firm, highly arched; nails short, dark

PASTERNS strong, slight slope forward

RIBS well-sprung, not slab-sided nor barrel-like

TUCK-UP clean underline well muscled

APPEARANCE: Of great size; powerful, well-balanced; elegant, dignified, courageous, friendly

EARS set high, not too far apart, held erect

NECK clean, arched, muscular, long, free from throatiness

SHOULDERS strong, sloping, laid well-back for long strides

BACK short with gentle, even slope; loins arched strong

CROUP generous, slight slope to tail root

TAIL set high, thick at root, tapering in length to hocks

HINDQUARTERS muscular, powerful; thighs broad, legs parallel; hocks turning neither in nor out

HOCKS angulation moderate

COAT: Short, thick, smooth, glossy

HEIGHT: Males, 32" or more preferred (not less than 30"); females, 30" or more preferred (not less than 28")

COLORS: Brindle (base color, light to deep golden yellow); fawn, golden to deep yellow, deep, black mask; steel blue, black; Harlequin (base color white)

should denote strength and power. The rear legs should have drive. The forelegs should track smoothly and straight. The Dane should track in two parallel straight lines. *Faults:* Short steps. The rear quarters should not pitch. The forelegs should not have a hackney gait (forced or choppy stride). When moving rapidly the Great Dane should not pace for the reason that it causes excessive side-to-side rolling of the body and thus reduces endurance.

(b) Rear End (Croup, Legs, Paws) (10 points) — The croup must be full, slightly drooping and must continue imperceptibly to the tail root. Hind legs, the first thighs (from hip joint to knee) are broad and muscular. The second thighs (from knee to hock joint) are strong and long. Seen from the side, the angulation of the first thigh with the body, of the second thigh with the first thigh, and the pastern root with the second thigh should be very moderate, neither too straight nor too exaggerated. Seen from the rear, the hock joints appear to be perfectly straight, turned neither towards the inside nor towards the outside. *Faults:* A croup which is too straight; a croup which slopes downward too steeply; and too narrow a croup. Hind legs: Soft, flabby, poorly muscled thighs; cowhocks which are the result of the hock joint turning inward and the hock and rear paws turning outward; barrel legs, the result of the hock joints being too far apart; steep rear. As seen from the side, a steep rear is the result of the angles of the rear legs forming almost a straight line; overangulation is the result of exaggerated angles between the first and second thighs and the hocks and is very conducive to weakness. The rear legs should never be too long in proportion to the front legs.

Paws, round and turned neither towards the inside nor towards the outside. Toes short, highly arched and well closed. Nails short, strong and as dark as possible. *Faults:* Spreading toes (splay foot); bent, long toes (rabbit paws); toes turned towards the outside or towards the inside. Furthermore, the fifth toe on the hind legs appearing at a higher position and with wolf's claw or spur; excessively long nails; light-colored nails.

(c) Front End (Shoulders, Legs, Paws) (8 points) — *Shoulders* — The shoulder blades must be strong and sloping and seen from the side, must form as nearly as possible a right angle in its articulation with the humerus (upper arm) to give a long stride. A line from the upper tip of the shoulder to the back of the elbow joint should be as nearly perpendicular as possible. Since all dogs lack a clavicle (collar bone) the ligaments and muscles holding the shoulder blade to the rib cage must be well developed, firm and secure to prevent loose shoulders. *Faults:* Steep shoulders, which occur if the shoulder blade does not slope sufficiently; overangulation; loose shoulder which occur if the Dane is flabbily muscled, or if the elbow is turned toward the outside: loaded shoulders.

Forelegs — The upper arm should be strong and muscular. Seen from the side or front the strong lower arms run absolutely

[continued on page 159]

GENERAL APPEARANCE —The Komondor is characterized by imposing strength, courageous demeanor and pleasing conformation. In general he is a big muscular dog with plenty of bone and substance.

NATURE AND CHARACTERISTICS — As a houseguard as well as a guardian of herds he is, when grown up, an earnest, courageous, and very faithful dog. The young dog, however, is just as playful as any other puppy. He is much devoted to his master and will defend him against attack by any stranger. On account of this trait he is not used for driving the herds, but only for guarding them. His special task is to protect the animals, and he lives during the greater part of the year in the open air without protection against strange dogs and all kinds of beasts of prey.

HEAD—The head of the Komondor is covered all over with long hair, and thus the head looks somewhat short, in comparison to the seemingly wide forehead. When the hair is smoothed, it will be seen that the skull is somewhat arched if viewed from the side; the forehead is not wide, but appears, however, wider through the rich growth of hair. The stop is moderate, it is the starting point of the muzzle which is somewhat shorter than the length of the skull. The top line of the muzzle is straight and about parallel with the line of the top of the skull. The muzzle should be fairly square. The lips cover the teeth closely and are black. The muzzle is mostly covered by long hair. The edges of the muzzle are black or steel blue-gray. The jaws are powerful, and the teeth are level and close together evenly.

Distinctly undershot or overshot bite is a serious fault. *Ears*—The ears are rather low set and hang along the side of the head. They are medium-sized, and their surface is covered with long hair. *Eyes*—The eyes express fidelity. They are medium-sized and almond-shaped, not too deeply set and surrounded by rough, unkempt hair. The iris of the eyes is of coffee or darker brown color, light color is not desirable. Blue-white eyes are disqualifying. The edges of the eyelids are slate-gray. *Muzzle*—In comparison to the length given in the head description, the muzzle is wide, coarse and not pointed. The nostrils are wide. The color of the nose is black. Komondorok with flesh-colored noses must absolutely be excluded from breeding. A slate-colored or dark brown nose is undesirable but may, however, be accepted for breeding purposes.

NECK — The neck is covered with long hair, is muscular, of medium length, moderately arched. The head erect. No dewlap is allowed.

BODY—The body is characterized chiefly by the powerful, deep chest which is muscular and proportionately wide. The height at the top of the shoulders is 23½ inches to 31½ inches, the higher, the better. The shoulders slope into the neck without apparent protrusion. The body is moderately long and level. Back and loins are wide. The rump is wide, muscular, moderately sloping towards the root of the tail. The body should be somewhat drawn up at the rear, but not Greyhoundlike. *Tail*—The tail is a straight continuation of the rump-line, and reaches down to the hocks slightly curved upwards

at its end. It is covered in its full length with long hair, which when the dog is at ease almost touches the ground. When the dog is excited the tail is raised up to the level of the back. The tail should not be docked. Komondorok born with short tails must be excluded even for breeding purposes.

FORELEGS—The forelegs should be straight, well boned and muscular. Viewed from any side, the legs are like vertical columns. The upper arm joins the body closely, without loose elbows. The legs are covered all around by long, evenly hanging hair. *Hindquarters and Legs*—The steely, strong bone structure is covered with highly developed muscles, and the legs are evenly covered with long hair, hanging down in matted clods. The legs should be straight as viewed from the rear. Stifles well bent. Dewclaws must be removed. The body and the legs should about form a rectangle. *Feet*—The feet should be strong, rather large and with close, well-arched toes. The hind feet are stronger, and all are covered with long hair. The nails are black or slate-gray. The pads are hard, elastic and black.

COAT—Characteristic of the breed is the dense weather-resisting double coat. The puppy coat is relatively soft, but it shows a tendency to fall into cords. In the mature dog the coat consists of a dense, soft, woolly undercoat, much like the puppy coat, and a coarser outer coat that is wavy or curly. The coarser hairs of the outer coat trap the softer undercoat forming permanent strong cords that are felty to the touch. A grown dog is covered with a heavy coat of these tassel-like

HEAD erect; covered with long hair; forehead not wide. Skull somewhat arched (sideview); stop moderate. Distinctly undershot or overshot is a serious fault.

EYES medium-size; almond-shaped; not set too deep; iris coffee or dark brown; eyelid edges slate-gray; surrounded by rough, unkempt hair

MUZZLE somewhat shorter than skull length; wide, coarse; not pointed, fairly square; mostly covered by long hair; edges black or steel-gray; topline straight, parallel with skull top

NOSE black (slate or dark brown permitted for breeding); nostrils wide

JAWS powerful; teeth level, close evenly; lips black, closely cover teeth

CHEST powerful, deep; muscular proportionately wide

FORELEGS straight; well-boned muscular; upper arms join body closely; no loose elbows; long, even hair all around

FEET rather large; strong (hind feet stronger); covered with long hair; close, well-arched toes; black or slate-gray nails; hard, elastic, black pads

COAT long, dense, soft wooly, ragged; inclined to form permanent strong cords that are felty to the touch; length varies on various body parts; longest on things, tail, rump; not too curly; shortest around mouth and lower parts of the leg up to the hocks.

APPEARANCE: Big, strong, muscular; good bone, substance; imposing. Nature faithful, courageous

EARS medium; rather low-set; hang along side of head; long hair

NECK medium length; muscular; moderately arched; no dewlap; long haired. Shoulders smooth; sloping into neck

BACK wide, moderately long; level. Loins wide. Rump wide, muscular; moderate slope to tail root

TAIL: Extension of rump-line; reaches to hocks; end slightly curved; never docked; long hair its full length almost touching ground as ease; tail is raised to back level at excitement

HINDQUARTERS: Steely, strong bones; highly-developed muscles

HIND LEGS straight (rear view); dewclaws removed; even, long hair hanging— in matted clods. Stifles well-bent.

COLOR: White

SIZE: The bigger the better — min. height, males 25½"; females, 23½"

DISQUALIFICATIONS Blue-white eyes. Color other than white. Bobtails. Flesh-colored nose. Short, smooth hair on head and legs. Failure of the coat to cord by two years of age.

UNDERLINE somewhat drawn-up

CH. SZENTIVANI INGO ("DUNA")

"DUNA" IS A HUNGARIAN IMPORT, BRED BY EVERS VILMOSNE, SIRED BY THE FAMOUS C.A.C.I.B. OHEGYI ALADAR. HE WAS HANDLED THROUGHOUT HIS SHOW CAREER BY ROBERT J. STEBBINS FOR OWNER MARION J. LEVY JR. SHOWN 168 TIMES, WITH 165 BOB, HIS SHOW RECORD INCLUDES FOUR ALL-BREED BIS AND 86 GROUP PLACEMENTS. HE WAS #8 DOG ALL-BREEDS IN THE U.S. (PHILLIPS SYSTEM) IN 1972, AN ASTONISHING RECORD FOR SUCH A RARE BREED, AND ONE WHICH ATTRACTED THE ATTENTION OF THE U.S. DOG FANCY TO THE KOMONDOR AND THE CORDED COAT. BRED SPARINGLY, HE HAS SIRED 7 CHAMPIONS AND 1 C.D.

HANDLER: ROBERT J. STEBBINS

HERCEGVAROS KOMONDOROK
MARION J. LEVY JR.
102 RUSSELL ROAD
PRINCETON, N.J. 08540
(609) 924-0199

cords, which form themselves naturally, and once formed, require no care other than washing. Too curly a coat is not desired. Straight or silky coat is a serious fault. Short, smooth hair on the head and legs is a disqualification. Failure of the coat to cord by two years of age is a disqualification.

The coat is longest at the rump, loins and tail. It is of medium length on the back, shoulders and chest. Shorter on the cheeks, around the eyes, ears, neck, and on the extremities. It is shortest around the mouth and lower part of the legs up to the hocks.

SIZE—The bigger the Komondor, the better, a minimum height of $25\frac{1}{2}$ inches at top of shoulders for males and $23\frac{1}{2}$ inches for females is required.

FAULTS—Light or flesh-colored nose, albino or blue eyes, highly set and small ears. Short, smooth hair, on the head and legs, strongly curled tail, color other than white.

DISQUALIFICATIONS

Blue-white eyes. Color other than white. Bobtails. Flesh-colored nose. Short, smooth hair on head and legs. Failure of the coat to cord by two years of age.

KUVASZ
STANDARD

GENERAL CHARACTERISTICS — A spirited dog of keen intelligence, determination, courage and curiosity. Very sensitive to praise and blame. Primarily a one-family dog. Devoted, gentle and patient without being overly demonstrative. Always ready to protect loved ones even to the point of self-sacrifice. Extremely strong instinct to protect children. Polite to accepted strangers, but rather suspicious and very discriminating in making new friends. Unexcelled guard, possessing ability to act on his own initiative at just the right moment without instruction. Bold, courageous and fearless. Untiring ability to work and cover rough terrain for long periods of time. Has good scent and has been used to hunt game.

GENERAL APPEARANCE — A working dog of larger size, sturdily built, well balanced, neither lanky nor cobby. White in color with *no markings*. Medium boned, well muscled, without the slightest hint of bulkiness or lethargy. Impresses the eye with strength and activity combined with lightfootedness, moves freely on strong legs. Trunk and limbs form a horizontal rectangle slightly deviated from the square. Slightly inclined croup. Hindquarters are particularly well developed. Any tendency to weakness or lack of substance is a decided fault.

MOVEMENT — Easy, free and elastic. Feet travel close to the ground. Hind legs reach far under, meeting or even passing the imprints of the front legs. Moving toward an observer, the front legs do not travel parallel to each other but rather close together at the ground. When viewed from the rear, the hind legs (from the hip joint down) also move close at the ground. As speed increases, the legs gradually angle more inward until the pads are almost single-tracking. Unless excited, the head is carried rather low at the level of the shoulders. Desired movement cannot be maintained without sufficient angulation and firm slimness of body.

HEIGHT — Measured at the withers; dogs, 28 to 30 inches; bitches, 26 to 28 inches.

WEIGHT — Dogs, approximately 100 to 115 pounds; bitches, approximately 70 to 90 pounds.

COLOR — White.

HEAD — Proportions are of great importance as the head is considered to be the most beautiful part of the Kuvasz. Length of head measured from tip of nose to occiput is slightly less than half the height of the dog at the withers. Width is half the length of the head. The skull is elongated but not pointed. The stop is defined, never abrupt, raising the forehead gently above the plane of the muzzle. The longitudinal midline of the forehead is pronounced, widening as it slopes to the muzzle. Cheeks flat, bony arches above the eyes. The skin dry, no excess flews.

MUZZLE — Length in proportion to the length of the head, top straight, not pointed, underjaw well developed. Inside of the mouth preferably black.

NOSE — Large, black, nostrils well opened.

LIPS — Black, closely covering the teeth. The upper lip covers tightly the upper jaw only. Lower lip tight and not pendulous.

BITE — Dentition full, scissor bite preferred. Level bite acceptable.

EYES — Almond-shaped, set well apart, somewhat slanted. In profile, the eyes are set slightly below the plain of the muzzle. Lids tight, haws should not show. Dark brown, the darker the better.

EARS — V-shaped, tip is slightly rounded. Rather thick, they are well set back between the level of the eye and the top of the head. When pulled forward the tip of the ear should cover the eye. Looking at the dog face to face, the widest part of the ear is about level to the eye. The inner edge of the ear lies close to the cheek, the outer edge slightly away from the head forming a V. In the relaxed position, the ears should hold their set and are not cast backward. The ears should not protrude above the head.

NECK — Muscular, without dewlap, medium length, arched at the crest.

FOREQUARTERS — Shoulders muscular. The scapula and humerus form a right angle, are long and of equal length. Legs are medium boned, straight and well muscled. Elbows neither in nor out. When viewed from the side, the forechest protrudes slightly in front of the shoulders. The joints are dry, hard. Dewclaws on the forelegs should not be removed.

BODY — Forechest is well developed, chest deep with long well-sprung ribs reaching almost to the elbows. Shoulders long with withers higher than back. Back is of medium length, straight, firm and quits broad. The loin is short, muscular and tight. The croup well muscled, slightly sloping. The brisket is deep, well developed and runs parallel to the ground. The stomach is well tucked up.

BONE — In proportion to size of body. Medium, hard. Never heavy or coarse.

HEAD: Proportionate to body

SIZE: Height at shoulder, 26" males; females somewhat less

APPEARANCE: Sturdy build; free moving; strong, active

well-ribbed-up; sturdy

SKULL broad, flat

EARS rather small,
kull level; lying
close to
ringe

STOP not too decided

NECK
ing shoulders

BACK fairly
loins

EYES dark; size medium; set wide apart, slightly oblique

NOSE black; nostrils well developed

MUZZLE clean cut, square covered with short, fine hair; flews black

HINDQUARTERS strong, hindlegs parallel; slight feathering on back legs

TAIL moderate length, reaching below hocks; hair thick, fairly long

CHEST deep, fairly broad

FORELEGS straight, well muscled; bone strong; hair short on front

HOCKS turning neither in nor out

FEET strong, well-shaped; turning neither in nor out; not splayed

ELBOWS in, well let down

COLOR: Pure white

COAT long on neck and croup; shorter, slightly wavy on sides

HAMRALVI COPERNICUS CHEFLER

THIS 9-MONTH-OLD MALE IS PICTURED HERE TO ILLUSTRATE THE CORRECTNESS OF HIS BREED TYPE. SON OF OUTSTANDING PARENTS, HE WAS CHOSEN AS THE FOUNDATION FOR CHEFLER KENNELS. THE RARE ACCUMULATION OF MANY SOUGHT AFTER QUALITIES ENHANCE HIS VALUE AS A STUD DOG.

OWNERS:
PETE AND JUDY OEFLER
705 UTICA AVE.
VENTURA, CA. 93003
(805) 647-7428 or (213) 547-9039

HINDQUARTERS — The portion behind the hip joint is moderately long producing wide, long and strong muscles of the upper thigh. The femur is long, creating well-bent stifles. Lower thigh is long, dry, well muscled. Metatarsus is short, broad and of great strength. Dewclaws if any are removed.

TAIL — Carried low, natural length reaching at least to the hocks. In repose it hangs down resting on the body, the end but slightly lifted. In state of excitement, the tail may be elevated to the level of the loin the tip slightly curved up. Ideally there should not be much difference in the carriage of the tail in state of excitement or in repose.

FEET — Well padded. Pads resilient, black. Feet are closed tight forming round "cat feet." The rear paws somewhat longer, some hair between the toes the less the better. Dark nails are preferred.

SKIN — The skin is heavily pigmented. The more slate gray or black pigmentation the better.

COAT — The Kuvasz has a double coat formed by a guard hair and fine undercoat. The texture of the coat is medium coarse. The coat ranges from quite wavy to straight. Distribution follows a definite pattern over the body regardless of coat type. The head, muzzle, ears and paws are covered with short, smooth hair. The neck has a mane that extends to and covers the chest. Coat on the front of the forelegs up to the elbows and the hind legs below the thighs is short and smooth. The backs of the forelegs are feathered to the pastern with hair 2 to 3 inches long. The body and sides of the thighs are covered with a medium length coat. The back of the thighs and the entire tail is covered with hair 4 to 6 inches long. It is natural for the Kuvasz to lose most of the long coat during hot weather. Full luxuriant coat comes in seasonably depending on climate. Summer coat should not be penalized.

FAULTS — The foregoing description is that of the ideal Kuvasz. Any deviation from the above-described dog must be penalized to the extent of the deviation.

DISQUALIFICATIONS

Overshot bite. Undershot bite. Dogs smaller than 26 inches. Bitches smaller than 24 inches. Any color other than white.

Approved October 1, 1974

GENERAL CHARACTER AND SYMMETRY—Large, massive, symmetrical and well-knit frame. A combination of grandeur and good nature, courage and docility.

GENERAL DESCRIPTION OF HEAD—In general outline giving a massive appearance when viewed from any angle. Breadth greatly to be desired. *Skull*—Broad and somewhat rounded between the ears, forehead slightly curved, showing marked wrinkles which are particularly distinctive when at attention. Brows (superciliary ridges) moderately raised. Muscles of the temples well developed, those of the cheeks extremely powerful. Arch across the skull a flattened curve with a furrow up the center of the forehead. This extends from between the eyes to halfway up the skull. *Ears*—Small, V-shaped, rounded at the tips. Leather moderately thin, set widely apart at the highest points on the sides of the skull continuing the outline acros the summit. They should lie close to the cheeks when in repose. Ears dark in color, the blacker the better, conforming to the color of the muzzle. *Eyes*—Set wide apart, medium in size, never too prominent. Expression alert but kindly. The stop between the eyes well marked but not too abrupt. Color of eyes brown, the darker the better and showing no haw.

FACE AND MUZZLE—Short, broad under the eyes and running nearly equal in width to the end of the nose. Truncated, *i.e.*, blunt and cut off square, thus forming a right angle with the upper line of the face. Of great depth from the point of the nose to underjaw. Underjaw broad to the end and slightly rounded. Canine teeth healthy, powerful and wide apart. Scissors bite preferred but a moderately undershot jaw permissible providing the teeth are not visible when the mouth is closed. Lips diverging at obtuse angles with the septum and sufficiently pendulous so as to show a modified square profile. Nose broad and always dark in color, the blacker the better, with spread flat nostrils (not pointed or turned up) in profile. Muzzle dark in color, the blacker the better. Muzzle should be half the length of the skull, thus dividing the head into three parts—one for the foreface and two for the skull. In other words, the distance from tip of nose to stop is equal to one-half the distance between the stop and the occiput. Circumference of muzzle (measured midway between the eyes and nose) to that of the head (measured before the ears) as 3 is to 5.

NECK — Powerful and very muscular, slightly arched, and of medium length. The neck gradually increases in circumference as it approaches the shoulder. Neck moderately "dry" (not showing an excess of loose skin).

CHEST AND FLANKS — Wide, deep, rounded and well let down between the forelegs, extending at least to the elbow. Forechest should be deep and well defined. Ribs extremely well rounded. False ribs deep and well set back. There should be a reasonable, but not exaggerated, cut-up. *Shoulder and Arm*—Slightly sloping, heavy and muscular. No tendency to looseness of shoulders.

FORELEGS AND FEET — Legs straight, strong and set wide apart, heavy-boned. Elbows parallel to body. Feet heavy, round and compact with well-arched toes. Pasterns strong and bent only slightly. Black nails preferred.

HIND LEGS: Hindquarters broad, wide and muscular. Second thighs well developed, hocks set back, wide apart and parallel when viewed from the rear. *Back and Loins*—Back muscular, powerful and straight. Loins wide and muscular, slightly rounded over the rump.

TAIL—Set on moderately high and reaching to the hocks or a little below. Wide at the root, tapering to the end, hanging straight in repose, forming a slight curve but never over the back when dog is in action.

COAT—Outer coat moderately coarse. Undercoat dense, short and close lying.

COLOR—Apricot, silver fawn or dark fawn-brindle. Fawn-brindle should have fawn as a background color which should be completely covered with very dark stripes. In any case muzzle, ears and nose must be dark in color, the blacker the better, with similar color tone around the orbits, extending upwards between them.

SIZE — Dogs, minimum, 30 inches at the shoulder; bitches, minimum, 27½ inches at the shoulder.

SCALE OF POINTS

General character and symmetry	10
Height and substance	10
Skull	10
Face and muzzle	12
Ears	5
Eyes	5
Chest and ribs	10
Forelegs and feet	10
Back, loins and flanks	10
Hind legs and feet	10
Tail	3
Coat and color	5
Total	100

Approved July 8, 1941

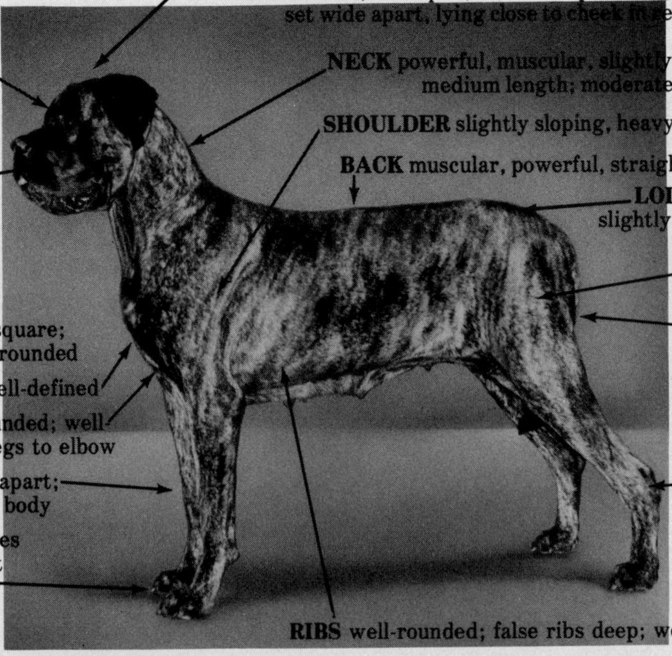

HEAD massive; good breadth desired; furrow up center of forehead; circumference of muzzle to head, 3 to 5

TEETH powerful; canine set wide apart; scissors bite preferred

BROWS moderately raised; temple muscles well-developed

STOP well-marked, not abrupt

NOSE broad, dark; nostrils spread flat

MUZZLE dark in color, half length of skull; cheeks powerfully muscled

EYES set wide apart, medium sized, not too prominent; expression alert, kindly; brown in color; darker preferred; no haw

FACE short, broad under eyes; square; under jaw broad to end, slightly rounded

FORECHEST deep, well-defined

CHEST wide, deep, rounded; well-let-down between forelegs to elbow

LEGS straight, strong, set wide apart; heavily boned; elbows parallel to body

FEET heavy, round, compact; toes well-arched; pastern strong, bent slightly; black nails preferred

BODY large, massive, symmetrical, well-knit

SKULL broad, rounded between ears; forehead slightly curved; marked wrinkles

EARS small, V-shaped; round at tips; leather moderately thin, set wide apart, lying close to cheek in repose; dark in color

NECK powerful, muscular, slightly arched, medium length; moderately "dry"

SHOULDER slightly sloping, heavy, muscular

BACK muscular, powerful, straight

LOINS wide, muscular, slightly rounded over rump

HINDQUARTERS broad, wide, muscular; second thighs well-developed

TAIL set moderately high, reaching to hocks; tapering to tip; hanging straight at repose; slight curve in action but not over back

HOCKS set back, wide apart, turning neither in nor out

RIBS well-rounded; false ribs deep; well-set-back; a reasonable cut-up

COLOR: Apricot; silver fawn; dark fawn-brindle (background fawn with dark stripes); muzzle, ears, nose, around eye sockets, dark

SIZE: Males, 30" minimum at shoulders; females, 27½" minimum

COAT double; outer, moderately coarse; under, dense, short, close lying

CH. THUNDERHILL'S ABBESS

TOP MASTIFF IN THE U.S. 1973. PLACED GROUP 4 1973. PLACED GROUP 3 1974. 14 TIMES BEST OF BREED.
HANDLER: ALAN LEVINE

EDWARD A. GERACE
GREENBRANCH FARM
BOX 100, RD 5
FLEMINGTON, N.J. 08822
(303) 495-4209

The Mastiff has been associated with Britain since the days of the Roman Empire. The dogs were bred and kept for war or guard duty, and for the sports of bull-, lion- or bear-baiting. Their long if not always glorious history was almost truncated at the time of the second World War when few Mastiffs could be kept in Britain and fewer bred. A small population, however, has been reestablished. The Mastiff is large, massive, symmetrical, and well-built. It is courageous but docile. Breadth is the key to the head and muzzle; substance, to the body. The coat is short and coarse. Colors are apricot, silver fawn, or dark fawn-brindle. The muzzle, ears, and nose must be dark in all cases. Dogs stand a minimum of 30 inches at the shoulder. The body must also be massive in girth. The Mastiff is a loyal and intelligent guard dog. Its size, of course, limits its role as a house dog. Some 500 are registered annually in the U.S.; the breed ranking 79th. Rather few are shown.

GENERAL APPEARANCE — The Newfoundland is large, strong, and active, at home in water and on land, and has natural life-saving instincts. He is a multipurpose dog capable of heavy work as well as of being a devoted companion for child and man. To fulfill its purposes the Newfoundland is deep bodied, well muscled, and well coordinated. A good specimen of the breed has dignity and proud head carriage. The length of the dog's body, from withers to base of tail, is approximately equal to the height of the dog at the withers. However, a bitch is not to be faulted if the length of her body is slightly greater than her height. The dog's appearance is more massive throughout than the bitch's, with larger frame and heavier bone. The Newfoundland is free moving with a loosely slung body. When he moves, a slight roll is perceptible. Complete webbing between the toes is always present. Large size is desirable but never at the expense of gait, symmetry, balance or conformation to the Standard herein described.

HEAD — The head is massive with a broad skull, slightly arched crown, and strongly developed occipital bone. The slope from the top of the skull to the tip of the muzzle has a definite but not steep stop. The forehead and face is smooth and free of wrinkles; the muzzle is clean-cut and covered with short, fine hair. The muzzle is square, deep, and fairly short; its length from stop to tip of nose is less than from stop to occiput. The nostrils are well developed. The bitch's head follows the same general conformation as the dog's but is feminine and less massive. A narrow head and a snipey or long muzzle are to be faulted.

The *eyes* are dark brown, relatively small, and deep-set; they are spaced wide apart and have no haw showing. Round, protruding, or yellow eyes are objectionable.

The *ears* are relatively small and triangular with rounded tips. They are set well back on the skull and lie close to the head. When the ear is brought forward it reaches to the inner corner of the eye on the same side.

The *teeth* meet in a scissors or level bite.

The Newfoundland's expression is soft and reflects the character of the breed; benevolent, intelligent, dignified, and of sweet disposition. The dog never looks or acts either dull or ill-tempered.

NECK — The neck is strong and well set on the shoulders. It is long enough for proud head carriage.

BODY — The Newfoundland's chest is full and deep with the brisket reaching at least down to the elbows. The back is broad, and the topline is level from the withers to the croup, never roached, slack, or swayed. He is broad at the croup, is well muscled, and has very strong loins. The croup slopes at an angle of about 30 degrees. Bone structure is massive throughout but does not give a heavy, sluggish appearance.

FOREQUARTERS — When the dog is not in motion, the forelegs are perfectly straight and parallel with the elbows close to the chest. The layback of the shoulders is about 45 degrees, and the upper arm meets the shoulder blade at an angle of about 90 degrees. The shoulders are well muscled. The pasterns are slightly sloping.

HINDQUARTERS — Because driving power for swimming, pulling loads, or covering ground efficiently is dependent on the hindquarters, the rear assembly of the Newfoundland is of prime importance. It is well muscled, the thighs are fairly long, the stifles well bent, and the hocks wide and straight. Cowhocks, barrel legs, or pigeon toes are to be seriously faulted.

FEET — The feet are proportionate to the body in size, cat-foot in type, well-rounded and tight with firm, arched toes, and with webbing present. Dewclaws on the rear legs are to be removed.

TAIL — The tail of the Newfoundland acts as a rudder when he is swimming. Therefore, it is broad and strong at the base. The tail reaches down a little below the hocks. When the dog is standing the tail hangs straight down, possibly a little bent at the tip, when the dog is in motion or excited, the tail is carried straight out or slightly curved, but it never curls over the back. A tail with a kink is a serious fault.

GAIT — The Newfoundland in motion gives the impression of effortless power, has good reach, and strong drive. A dog may appear symmetrical and well balanced when standing, but, if he is not structurally sound, he will lose that symmetry and balance when he moves. In motion, the legs move straight forward; they do not swing in an arc nor do the hocks move in or out in relation to the line of travel. A slight roll is present. As the dog's speed increases from a walk to a trot, the feet move in under the center line of the body to maintain balance. Mincing, shuffling, crabbing, too close moving, weaving, hackney action, and pacing are all faults.

SIZE — The average height for dogs is 28 inches, for bitches 26 inches. The average weight for dogs is 150 pounds, for bitches, 120 pounds. Large size is desirable but is not to be favored over correct gait, symmetry, and structure.

HEAD broad, massive; strongly developed occipital bone; stop definite but not steep
APPEARANCE: Deep bodied, well muscled, massive; dignity, intelligence, benevolence important
EARS small triangular, well set back, close to head; hair short, fine
EYES small; rather deeply set; wide apart; dark brown; no haw
NECK strong; well set on shoulders
BACK broad, straight topline
MUZZLE short; clean-cut; rather square; covered with short, fine hair
TAIL broad, strong at base; reaches a little below hocks; covered with long dense hair
CHEST full, deep; brisket reaches to elbows; shoulders well muscled
HINDQUARTERS well muscled; thighs long; stifles well bent; hocks wide, straight
FORELEGS straight, parallel; elbows in
FEET proportionate to body, cat type; toes firm, arched, webbed
COAT water resistant, double coat; straight, flat

SIZE: Average height — males 28"; females 26"

COLOR: Black; slight bronze tinge, or white splash on chest, toes not objectionable. Other than black, same standard except color which may be almost any; most encouraged — white and black (Landseers) or bronze; beauty of markings important. Blacks with white toes, breast and tail tip considered "blacks"

DISQUALIFICATIONS: Markings other than white on a solid-colored dog

Average weight — males 150 lbs; females 120 lbs

LITTLE BEAR'S LOVE SONG

18 LITTLE BEARS ARE GROUP 1 WINNERS. 6 LITTLE BEARS HAVE 1 OR MORE BIS. AM. CAN. CH. LITTLE BEAR'S JAMES THURBER HAD 7 BIS; HE WAS THE BIS RECORD HOLDER UNTIL CH. NEWTON. AS OF NOW 105 CHAMPION. A BREED RECORD.

HANDLER: ROSIL A. NESBERG

LITTLE BEAR KENNELS, REG.
ESTABLISHED IN 1949
VADIM ALEXIUS CHERN
BEAR HILL ROAD, R.D. 1
NEW MILFORD, CONN. 06776
(203) 354-3344

The Newfoundland seemingly originated in Newfoundland several hundred years ago. Some authorities believe that the breed's ancestry includes the Great Pyrenees while others credit native breeds, the Tibetan Mastiff, and even Viking dogs. In all likelihood, the native Newfoundland was greatly refined after being imported into Britain during the early part of the 19th century. The breed was presumably built for working in all weather and in the water. The coat is unusually heavy and the undercoat oily and highly waterproof. In the late 19th century, the Newfoundland was used frequently as a sledge-hauling dog. The Newfoundland is large and strong, at home on land and in the water. Its bearing is dignified; its proportions square, bone heavy, and muscle abundant. Movement is free with a slight roll. The theme is largeness but never at the expense of balance and movement. Average height, for dogs, is 28 inches and weight 150 lbs. Approved colors are black (the tail tip, toes, and a chest splash may be white), bronze, black and white (called Landseer), or almost any other. In the Landseer, beauty of markings is very important. The Newfoundland has proved to be an excellent companion and house dog. About 2,000 are registered annually with the AKC, the breed ranking 50th.

COAT — The Newfoundland has a water-resistant double coat. The outer coat is moderately long and full but not shaggy. It is straight and flat with no curl, although it may have a slight wave. The coat, when rubbed the wrong way, tends to fall back into place. The undercoat, which is soft and dense, is often less dense during summer months or in tropical climates but is always found to some extent on the rump and chest. An open coat is to be seriously faulted. The hair on the head, muzzle, and ears is short and fine, and the legs are feathered all the way down. The tail is covered with long dense hair, but it does not form a flag.

COLOR — Black. A slight tinge of bronze or a splash of white on chest and toes is not objectionable. Black dogs that have only white toes and white chest and white tip to tail should be exhibited in the classes provided for "black."

OTHER THAN BLACK — Should in all respects follow the black except in color, which may be almost any, so long as it disqualifies for the black class, but the colors most to be encouraged are bronze or white and black (Landseer) with black head marked with narrow blaze, even marked saddle and black rump extending on to tail. Beauty in markings to be taken greatly into consideration.

DISQUALIFICATIONS

Markings other than white on a solid-colored dog.

Approved June 9, 1971

OLD ENGLISH SHEEPDOG STANDARD

SKULL — Capacious and rather squarely formed, giving plenty of room for brain power. The parts over the eyes should be well arched and the whole well covered with hair. *Jaw* — Fairly long, strong, square and truncated. The top should be well defined to avoid a Deerhound face. (The attention of judges is particularly called to the above properties, as a long, narrow head is a deformity.) *Eyes* — Vary according to the color of the dog. Very dark preferred, but in the glaucous or blue dogs a pearl, walleye or china eye is considered typical. (A light eye is most objectionable.) *Nose* — Always black, large and capacious. *Teeth* — Strong and large, evenly placed and level in opposition. *Ears* — Medium-sized, and carried flat to side of head, coated moderately.

LEGS — The forelegs should be dead straight, with plenty of bone, removing the body a medium height from the ground, without approaching legginess, and well coated all around. *Feet* — Small, round; toes well arched, and pads thick and hard. *Tail* — It is preferable that there should be none. Should never, however, exceed 1½ or 2 inches in grown dogs. When not natural-born bobtails, however, puppies should be docked at the first joint from the body and the operation performed when they are from three to four days old.

NECK AND SHOULDERS — The neck should be fairly long, arched gracefully and well coated with hair. The shoulders sloping and narrow at the points, the dog standing lower at the shoulder than at the loin.

BODY — Rather short and very compact, ribs well sprung and brisket deep and capacious. *Slabsidedness highly undesirable*. The loin should be very stout and gently arched, while the hindquarters should be round and muscular and with well-let-down hocks, and the hams densely coated with a thick, long jacket in excess of any other part.

COAT — Profuse, but not so excessive as to give the impression of the dog being overfat, and of a good hard texture; not straight, but shaggy and free from curl. *Quality and texture of coat to be considered above mere profuseness*. Softness or flatness of coat to be considered a fault. The undercoat should be a waterproof pile, when not removed by grooming or season.

COLOR — Any shade of gray, grizzle, blue or blue-merled with or without white markings or in reverse. *Any shade of brown or fawn to be considered distinctly objectionable and not to be encouraged.*

SIZE — Twenty-two inches and upwards for dogs and slightly less for bitches. Type, character and symmetry are of the greatest importance and are on no account to be sacrificed to size alone.

GENERAL APPEARANCE AND CHARACTERISTICS — A strong, compact-looking dog of great symmetry, practically the same in measurement from shoulder to stern as in height, absolutely free from legginess or weaselness, very elastic in his gallop, but in walking or trotting he has a characteristic ambling or pacing movement, and his bark should be loud, with a peculiar "pot-casse" ring in it. Taking him all round, he is a profusely, but not *excessively* coated, thick-set, muscular, able-bodied dog with a most intelligent expression, free from all Poodle or Deerhound character. *Soundness should be considered of greatest importance.*

SCALE OF POINTS

Skull	5
Eyes	5
Ears	5
Teeth	5
Nose	5
Jaw	5
Foreface	5
Neck and shoulders	5
Body and loins	10
Hindquarters	10
Legs	10
Coat [texture, quality and condition]	15
General appearance and movement	15
Total	100

Approved October 13, 1953

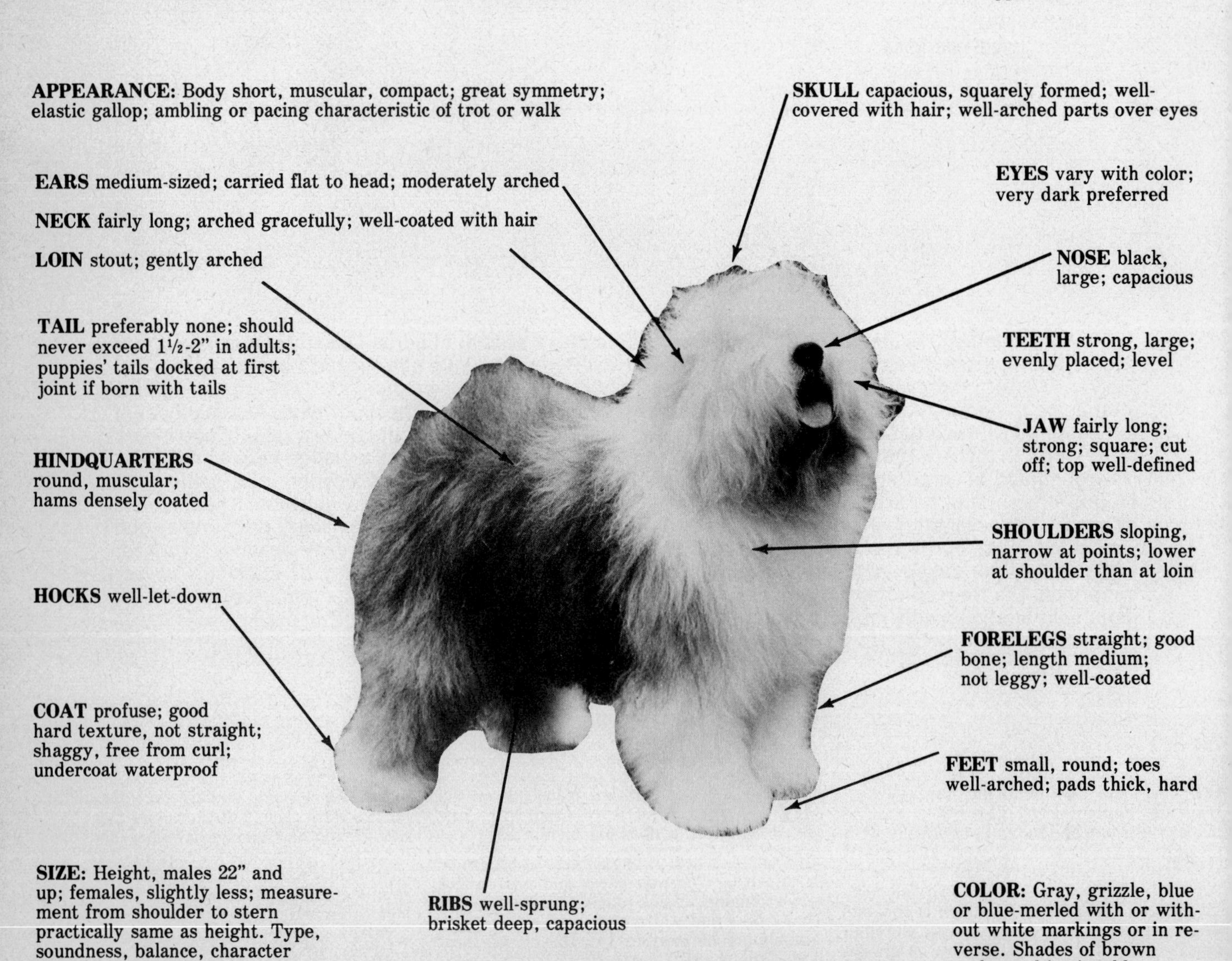
APPEARANCE: Body short, muscular, compact; great symmetry; elastic gallop; ambling or pacing characteristic of trot or walk
SKULL capacious, squarely formed; well-covered with hair; well-arched parts over eyes
EARS medium-sized; carried flat to head; moderately arched
EYES vary with color; very dark preferred
NECK fairly long; arched gracefully; well-coated with hair
LOIN stout; gently arched
NOSE black, large; capacious
TAIL preferably none; should never exceed 1½-2" in adults; puppies' tails docked at first joint if born with tails
TEETH strong, large; evenly placed; level
JAW fairly long; strong; square; cut off; top well-defined
HINDQUARTERS round, muscular; hams densely coated
SHOULDERS sloping, narrow at points; lower at shoulder than at loin
HOCKS well-let-down
FORELEGS straight; good bone; length medium; not leggy; well-coated
COAT profuse; good hard texture, not straight; shaggy, free from curl; undercoat waterproof
FEET small, round; toes well-arched; pads thick, hard
SIZE: Height, males 22" and up; females, slightly less; measurement from shoulder to stern practically same as height. Type, soundness, balance, character more important than size
RIBS well-sprung; brisket deep, capacious
COLOR: Gray, grizzle, blue or blue-merled with or without white markings or in reverse. Shades of brown or fawn objectionable

CH. FEZZIWIG VICE VERSA

AM. CAN. BDA. CH. FEZZIWIG VICE VERSA HAS ATTAINED THE GOAL SET FOR HIS FAMILY AND ADDED SOME FINE PRECEDENTS OF HIS OWN.

HE HAS PROVEN HIMSELF TO BE A GREAT SHOW DOG OF ENDURING QUALITY WITH OVER FIVE YEARS OF CONSISTENT RECOGNITION AS A SPECIALTY, SUPPORTED SHOW, GROUP AND BEST-IN-SHOW WINNER. HE SWEPT TO HIS U.S. CHAMPIONSHIP OVER SPECIALS WITH A FIRST WIN FROM PUPPY CLASS. HE EARNED REPEATEDLY THE RARE COMMENT, ONCE KNOWN TO "CEILING ZERO" AND "RAGGEDY ANDY," WHICH WAS, "ALMOST IMPOSSIBLE TO FAULT BY THE STANDARD."

HIS GREATEST PRECEDENTS ARE SET BY STUD WORK. THERE HAVE BEEN MANY MANY OCCASIONS WHERE HIS BOB WAS IN THE COMPANY OF ONE OF THE MANY HE SIRED, OR OF A KENNEL MATE. IN 1974 HE MOVED INTO A TRULY UNIQUE STUD POSITION. AT THE LARGE SUPPORTED TRENTON SHOW HE HAD A SON BOW AND A DAUGHTER BOS, AND AGAIN AT BUCKS COUNTY, ANOTHER SON BOW AND ANOTHER DAUGHTER BOS. ALL DOGS MENTIONED HAVE BEEN BY DIFFERENT DAMS. HIS LATEST '74 COMBINATION WAS STILL ANOTHER DAUGHTER BOS AT UNION COUNTY. THIS IS WHAT IT'S ALL ABOUT!!

FEZZIWIG KENNELS
MR. & MRS. HENDRIK VAN RENSSELAER
R.D. YOUNGS ROAD
BASKING RIDGE, NEW JERSEY 07920

The Old English Sheepdog was the staple sheepdog of parts of England, perhaps 200 years ago, and has more recently, been used as a drover's dog, as well. Bred to be weather and bramble resistant as well as a powerful deterrent to marauders, the Old English Sheepdog is also a good worker with flocks. Breed ancestry is quite separate from that of the Collie. Related breeds appear to include the Bearded Collie, the Briard, and the Russian Owtcharka. The Old English Sheepdog is a strong, compact dog of great symmetry and square proportions, moving with an elastic gait at the gallop but with an ambling walk. It is one of the few breeds with a specified bark, described as "pot-casse"—low pitched, full, and ringing.

STANDARD

GENERAL APPEARANCE — A dog of medium size, vigorous, alert, and extremely active. By nature affectionate, he is a devoted and home-loving companion, sensibly suspicious of strangers and therefore an excellent guard. Striking and highly characteristic is the shaggy coat which centuries ago fitted him for the strenuous work of herding the flocks on the plains of Hungary.

HEAD — Of medium size, in proportion to the body. The skull is slightly domed and not too broad. Stop clearly defined but not abrupt, neither dished nor downfaced, with a strong muzzle of medium length ending in a nose of good size. Teeth are strong and comparatively large, and the bite may be either level or scissors. Flews tight. *Ears* — Hanging and set fairly high, medium size, and V-shaped. *Eyes* — Deep-set and rather large, should be dark brown, but lighter color is not a serious fault.

NECK AND SHOULDERS — Neck strong and muscular, of medium length, and free of throatiness. Shoulders clean-cut and sloping, with elbows close.

BODY — The chest is deep and fairly broad with ribs well sprung. Back of medium length, straight and level, the rump sloping moderately. Fairly broad across the loins and well tucked up. *Tail* — Occasionally born bobtail, which is acceptable, never cut. The tail is carried curled over the back when alert, carried low with the end curled up when at rest. *Legs and Feet* — Forelegs straight, strong, and well boned. Feet round and compact with thick-cushioned pads and strong nails. Hindquarters well developed, moderately broad through the stifle which is well bent and muscular. Dewclaws, if any, may be removed from both forelegs and hind legs.

COAT — Characteristic of the breed is the dense, weather-resisting double coat. The outer coat, long and of medium texture, is never silky. It may be straight, wavy, or slightly curly, the more curly coat appearing to be somewhat shorter. the undercoat is soft, woolly, and dense. The coat mats easily, the hair tending to cling together in bunches, giving a somewhat corded appearance even when groomed. The hair is profuse on the head, ears, face, stifles, and tail, and the feet are well haired between the toes. Usually shown combed, but may also be shown uncombed with the coat hanging in tight, even cords.

COLOR — Solid colors, black, rusty-black, various shades of gray, and white. The black usually appears weathered and rusty or slightly gray. The inter-mixture of hair of different colors is acceptable and is usually present in the grays, but must be uniform throughout the coat so that the over-all appearance of a solid color is maintained. Nose, flews, and eyelids are black.

HEIGHT — Males about 17 inches, and should not exceed 19 inches. Females about 16 inches, and should not exceed 18 inches.

SERIOUS FAULTS — Overshot or undershot. Lack of undercoat, short or sparse coat. White markings such as white paws or spot on chest. Flesh color on nose, flews, or eyelids. Coat with areas of two or more colors at the skin.

Approved April 12, 1960

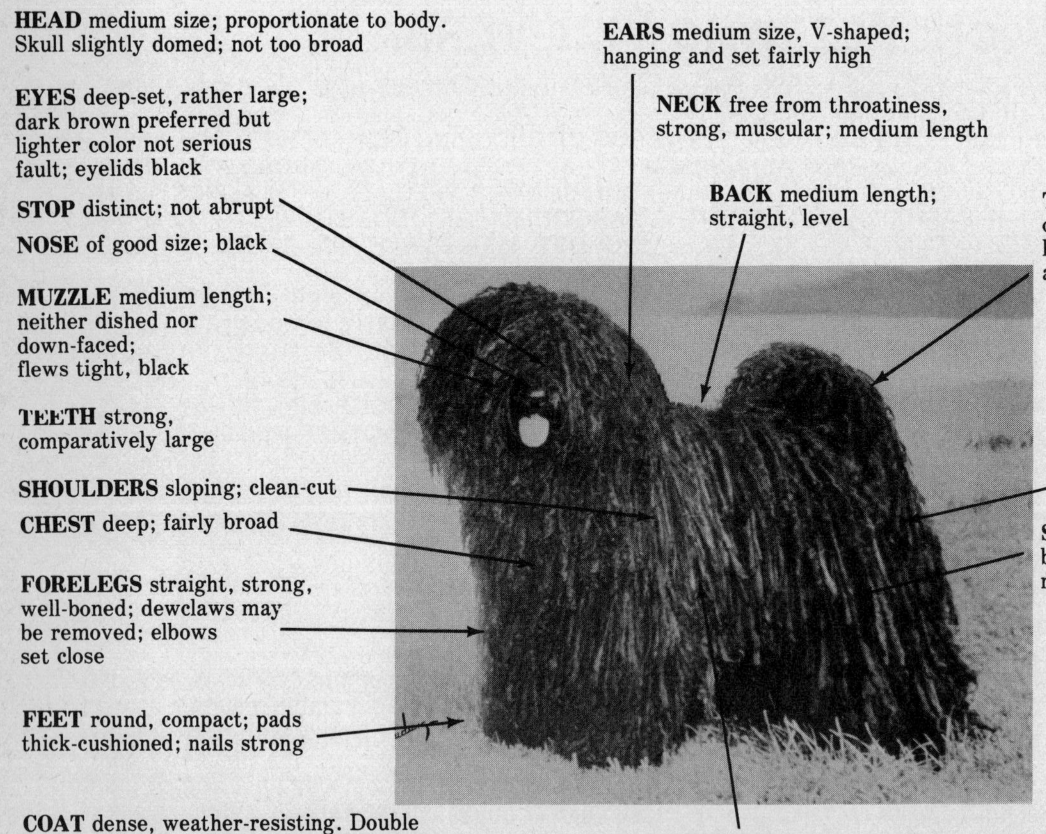

CH. SKYSYL HARVEY J. WALLBANGER

"HARVEY," SKYSYL'S THIRD BEST IN SHOW HOMEBRED, COMPLETED HIS CHAMPIONSHIP IN 3 SHOWS AS A PUPPY AND WAS #10 PULI. IN 1973 HE WAS #1 PULI AND IS LEADING IN 1974. HARVEY HAS DEFEATED ALL THE TOP PULI SPECIALS ACROSS THE U.S. HIS RECORD IS 1 B.I.S., 18 GROUP 1's. 15 GROUP 2's, 17 GROUP 3's, 19 GROUP 4's. HE IS THE SIRE OF SEVERAL QUALITY CHAMPIONS, MAKING HIM AN IDEAL BREEDERS PULI. SKYSYL SHOWS PULIK BOTH BRUSHED AND CORDED, QUALITY IS SUPREME.

HANDLER: MISS ANN J. BOWLEY
CO-OWNED
MRS. SCHUYLER OWEN
THE SKYSYL PULI KENNELS
SOUTH ROAD, CANAAN, N.H. 03741

The Puli is one of the traditional shepherd dogs of Hungary. The breed may well have been brought to Europe from the Asiatic steppes by the Magyars. In Hungarian, the plural is formed by adding *k* or *ik* to a noun. Thus, Pulik is the plural of Puli. The Puli is a medium-sized dog of great vigor, alertness, and spark. The coat is the striking characteristic of this breed. The outer coat is long and of medium texture. The undercoat is soft, woolly, and dense. If allowed to do so, the coat mats easily. The outer coat hairs form a cord around a core of undercoat hairs. The Puli may be shown thus corded or brushed out. The corded coat gives the dog a great deal of protection against weather and enemies in the field. Only solid colors are allowed. These include black, greys, and white. The black is often rusty or dull grey. The color varies in depth with the seasons and exposure to weather. This feature may derive from Asiatic or Tibetan ancestry. Males stand about 17 inches at the shoulder. The Puli is very intelligent and an enthusiastic worker. He may also be independent and bored if not kept busy. He is a one-family dog, suspicious of strangers. Pulik are not known in Britain. Some 750 are now registered annually in the U.S., the breed ranking 69th.

GENERAL APPEARANCE AND CHARACTER — The Rottweiler is a good-sized, strongly built, active dog. He is affectionate, intelligent, easily trained to work, naturally obedient and extremely faithful. While not quarrelsome, he possesses great courage and makes a splendid guard. His demeanor is dignified and he is not excitable.

HEAD — Is of medium length, the skull broad between the ears. Stop well pronounced as is also the occiput. Muzzle is not very long. It should not be longer than the distance from the stop to the occiput. Nose is well developed, with relatively large nostrils and is always black. Flews which should not be too pronounced are also black. Jaws should be strong and muscular; teeth strong — incisors of lower jaw must touch the inner surface of the upper incisors. Eyes are of medium size, dark brown in color and should express faithfulness, good humor and confidence. The ears are comparatively small, set high and wide and hang over about on a level with top of head. The skin on head should not be loose. The neck should be of fair length, strong, round and very muscular, slightly arched and free from throatiness.

FOREQUARTERS — Shoulders should be well placed, long and sloping, elbows well let down, but not loose. Legs muscular and with plenty of bone and substance, pasterns straight and strong. Feet strong, round and close, with toes well arched. Soles very hard, toe nails dark, short and strong. *Body* — The chest is roomy, broad and deep. Ribs well sprung. Back straight, strong and rather short. Loins strong and deep, and flanks should not be tucked up. Croup short, broad, but not sloping. *Hindquarters* — Upper thigh is short, broad and very muscular. Lower thigh very muscular at top and strong and sinewy at the bottom. Stifles fairly well bent, hocks strong. The hind feet are somewhat longer than the front ones, but should be close and strong with toes well arched. There should be no dewclaws. Tail should be short, placed high (on level with back) and carried horizontally. Dogs are frequently born with a short stump tail and when tail is too long it must be docked close to body.

COAT — Hair should be short, coarse and flat. The undercoat which is absolutely required on neck and thighs should not show through outer coat. The hair should be a little longer on the back of front and hind legs and on tail. *Color* — Black, with clearly defined markings on cheeks, muzzle, chest and legs, as well as over both eyes. Color of markings: tan to mahogany brown. A small spot of white on chest and belly is permissible but not desirable.

HEIGHT — Shoulder height for males is 23¾ to 27 inches, for females, 21¾ to 25¾ inches, but height should always be considered in relation to the general appearance and conformation of the dog.

FAULTS — Too lightly built or too heavily built, sway-back, roach back, too long body, lack of spring of ribs. Head too long and narrow or too short and plump. Lack of occiput, snipy muzzle, cheekiness, top line of muzzle not straight, light or flesh colored nose, hanging flews, overshot or undershot, loose skin on head, ears set too low, or ears too heavy, long or narrow or rose ear, or ears uneven in size. Light, small or slanting eyes, or lack of expression, neck too long, thin or weak, or very noticeable throatiness. Lack of bone and muscle, short or straight shoulders, front legs too close together or not straight, weak pasterns, splay feet, light nails, weak toes. Flat ribs, sloping croup. Too heavy or plump body. Flanks drawn up. Flat thighs, cowhocks or weak hocks, dewclaws. Tail set too high or too low or that is too long or too thin. Soft, too short, too long or too open coat, wavy coat or lack of undercoat. White markings on toes, legs, or other parts of body, markings not well defined or smudgy. The one-color tan Rottweiler with either black or light mask or with black streak on back as well as other colors such as brown or blue are not recognized and are believed to be cross bred, as is also a long-haired Rottweiler. Timid or stupid-appearing animals are to be positively rejected.

Approved April 9, 1935

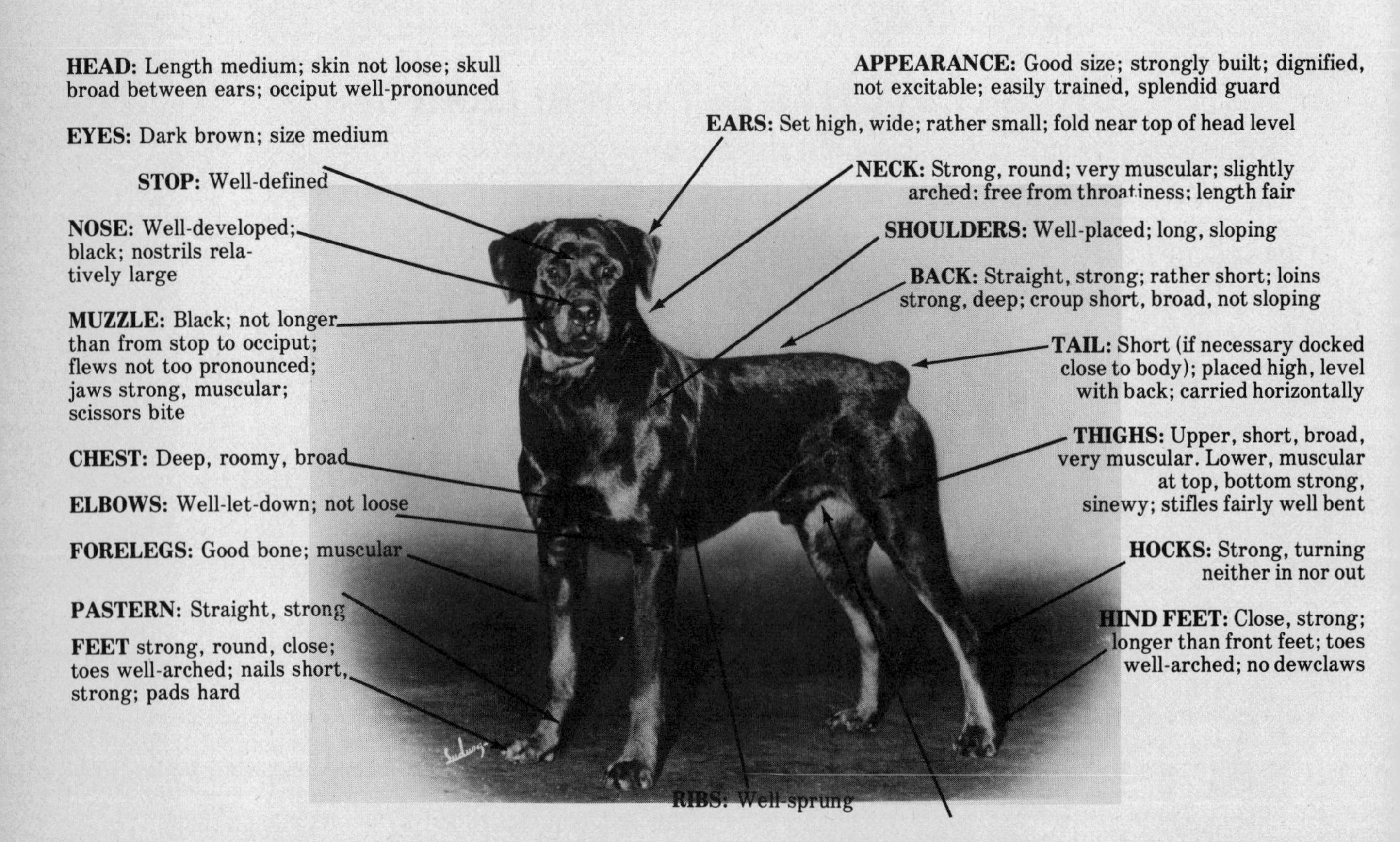

HEAD: Length medium; skin not loose; skull broad between ears; occiput well-pronounced
EYES: Dark brown; size medium
STOP: Well-defined
NOSE: Well-developed; black; nostrils relatively large
MUZZLE: Black; not longer than from stop to occiput; flews not too pronounced; jaws strong, muscular; scissors bite
CHEST: Deep, roomy, broad
ELBOWS: Well-let-down; not loose
FORELEGS: Good bone; muscular
PASTERN: Straight, strong
FEET strong, round, close; toes well-arched; nails short, strong; pads hard
APPEARANCE: Good size; strongly built; dignified, not excitable; easily trained, splendid guard
EARS: Set high, wide; rather small; fold near top of head level
NECK: Strong, round; very muscular; slightly arched; free from throatiness; length fair
SHOULDERS: Well-placed; long, sloping
BACK: Straight, strong; rather short; loins strong, deep; croup short, broad, not sloping
TAIL: Short (if necessary docked close to body); placed high, level with back; carried horizontally
THIGHS: Upper, short, broad, very muscular. Lower, muscular at top, bottom strong, sinewy; stifles fairly well bent
HOCKS: Strong, turning neither in nor out
HIND FEET: Close, strong; longer than front feet; toes well-arched; no dewclaws
RIBS: Well-sprung
COLOR: Black with distinct markings of tan to mahogany; white chest spot permissible
SIZE: Height males, 23¾ to 27"; females 21¾ to 25¾; considered in relation to conformation
UNDERLINE: No tuck-up; almost straight
COAT: Short, coarse, flat; undercoat required on neck, thighs (must not show); hair longer on tail, back of legs

CH. EGON VAN LUCAS C.D.X.

28 BEST OF BREEDS. 1 GROUP 3 PLACING.

NUMBER 1

ROTTWEILER 1ST. QUARTER PHILLIPS SYSTEM.

SIRE OF 2 LITTERS.

NOW BEING TRAINED FOR TRACKING DEGREE.

HANDLER: DOUGLAS BUNDOCK

MILDRED GARZINI
9501 EAST ROAD
REDWOOD VALLEY, CALIFORNIA 95470

The Rottweiler has an old and courageous history. This dog worked with the Roman armies when they climbed the Alps. They were able to be used on guard and tirelessly negotiate over the rough terrain. Today's Rottweiler has developed from the Roman cattle dogs. These dogs were adapted from the dogs that guarded the livestock in the town of Rottweil, which was in the center of the livestock country. The dogs excelled in pulling carts and in being a guardian and companion to their masters. After serving in this capacity for many years the Rottweiler was adopted for army and police work in which capacity they still faithfully serve.

GENERAL — Powerful, proportionately tall figure, strong and muscular in every part, with powerful head and most intelligent expression. In dogs with a dark mask the expression appears more stern, but never ill-natured.

HEAD — Like the whole body, very powerful and imposing. The massive skull is wide, slightly arched and the sides slope in a gentle curve into the very strongly developed, high cheek bones. Occiput only moderately developed. The supra-orbital ridge is very strongly developed and forms nearly a right angle with the horizontal axis of the head. Deeply imbedded between the eyes and starting at the root of the muzzle, a furrow runs over the whole skull. It is strongly marked in the first half, gradually disappearing toward the base of the occiput. The lines at the side of the head diverge considerably from the outer corner of the eyes toward the back of the head. The skin of the forehead, above the eyes, forms rather noticeable wrinkles, more or less pronounced, which converge toward the furrow. Especially when the dog is in action, the wrinkles are more visible without in the least giving the impression of morosity. Too strongly developed wrinkles are not desired. The slope from the skull to the muzzle is sudden and rather steep.

The muzzle is short, does not taper, and the vertical depth at the root of the muzzle must be greater than the length of the muzzle. The bridge of the muzzle is not arched, but straight; in some dogs, occasionally, slightly broken. A rather wide, well-marked, shallow furrow runs from the root of the muzzle over the entire bridge of the muzzle to the nose. The flews of the upper jaw are strongly developed, not sharply cut, but turning in a beautiful curve into the lower edge, and slightly overhanging. The flews of the lower jaw must not be deeply pendant. The teeth should be sound and strong and should meet in either a scissors or an even bite; the scissors bite being preferable. The undershot bite, although sometimes found with good specimens, is not desirable. The overshot bite is a fault. A black roof to the mouth is desirable. *Nose* (Schwamm) — Very substantial, broad, with wide open nostrils, and, like the lips, always black.

EARS — Of medium size, rather high set, with very strongly developed burr (Muschel) at the base. They stand slightly away from the head at the base, then drop with a sharp bend to the side and cling to the head without a turn. The flap is tender and forms a rounded triangle, slightly elongated toward the point, the front edge lying firmly to the head, whereas the back edge may stand somewhat away from the head, especially when the dog is at attention. Lightly set ears, which at the base immediately cling to the head, give it an oval and too little marked exterior, whereas a strongly developed base gives the skull a squarer, broader and much more expressive appearance.

EYES — Set more to the front than the sides, are of medium size, dark brown, with intelligent, friendly expression, set moderately deep. The lower eyelids, as a rule, do not close completely and, if that is the case, form an angular wrinkle toward the inner corner of the eye. Eyelids which are too deeply pendant and show conspicuously the lachrymal glands, or a very red, thick haw, and eyes that are too light, are objectionable.

NECK — Set high, very strong and in action is carried erect. Otherwise horizontally or slightly downward. The junction of head and neck is distinctly marked by an indentation. The nape of the neck is very muscular and rounded at the sides which makes the neck appear rather short. The dewlap of throat and neck is well-pronounced: too strong development, however, is not desirable.

SHOULDERS — Sloping and broad, very muscular and powerful. The withers are strongly pronounced. *Chest* — Very well arched, moderately deep, not reaching below the elbows. *Back* — Very broad, perfectly straight as far as the haunches, from there gently sloping to the rump, and merging imperceptibly into the root of the tail. *Hindquarters* — Well-developed. Legs very muscular. *Belly* — Distinctly set off from the very powerful loin section, only little drawn up.

TAIL — Starting broad and powerful directly from the rump is long, very heavy, ending in a powerful tip. In repose it hangs straight down, turning gently upward in the lower third only, which is not considered a fault. In a great many specimens the tail is carried with the end slightly bent and therefore hangs down in the shape of an *f*. In action all dogs carry the tail more or less turned upward. However, it may not be carried too erect or by any means rolled over the back. A slight curling of the tip is sooner admissible.

FOREARMS — Very powerful and extraordinarily muscular. *Forelegs* — Straight, strong. *Hind Legs* — Hocks of moderate angulation. Dewclaws are not desired; if present, they must not obstruct gait. *Feet* — Broad, with strong toes, moderately closed,

HEAD powerful, imposing; furrow over forehead deeply imbedded between eyes, runs back toward occiput

SKULL massive, wide, slightly arched, sloping at sides; cheek bones well-developed, occiput slightly developed; forehead skin wrinkled

EYES: Size moderate; dark brown; lower eyelids form angular wrinkly toward inner corner; not too pendant

STOP deep, sudden

NOSE substantial, broad; nostrils, well-dilated; black

MUZZLE short, depth good; does not taper; bridge straight; flews on upper jaw strongly developed; gracefully curved, overhanging; furrow from stop runs length of muzzle bridge; lower flews not pendant; dewlaps clearly noticeable; lips black

CHEST well-arched; moderately deep; not below elbows

FOREARMS very powerful; extremely muscular

FORELEGS straight, strong

FEET broad; toes strong, moderately well-closed; knuckles rather high

HEIGHT (minimum): males 27½"; females 25½"

COLOR: White with red, red with white; red, various shades; brindle patches, white markings. Never one color or without white

TEETH sound, strong; even bite or scissors (more desirable); undershot not desirable but overshot a fault; black mouth roof desirable

EARS: Size medium; rather high-set; strongly developed burr; flap tender; stand away from head at base, drop with sharp bend, front edge clinging to head; square, broad appearance

NECK very strong; set on high; carried erect in action, or horizontal; muscular; round at sides; distinct indentation marks junction of head and neck; dewlap well-pronounced

SHOULDERS sloping, broad; very muscular, powerful

BACK very broad; straight; gentle slope to rump

TAIL long, heavy, bushy; root broad; tapering to blunt end; straight down in repose, lower third gently curving; more or less turned-up in action but never too erect or rolled over back

HINDQUARTERS well-developed; loins powerful; thighs very muscular

HIND LEGS slightly bent at hocks; dewclaws not desired; if present, must not obstruct gait

WITHERS strongly defined

BELLY distinct, slight tuck-up

BODY powerful; strong, muscular

COAT dense, shorthaired, tough, lying smooth; not rough to touch. Two varieties: longhaired and shorthaired

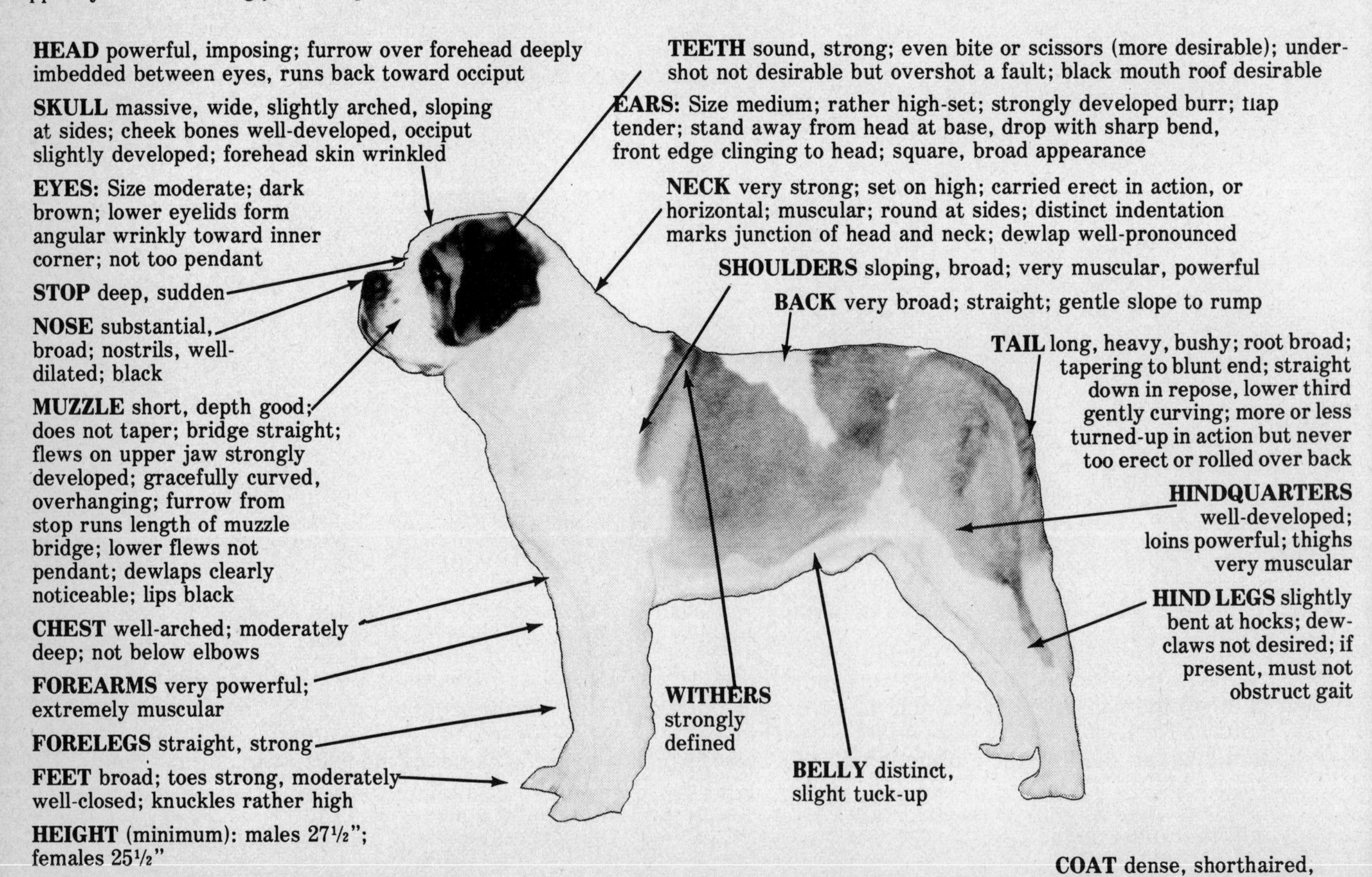

"HIGH CHATEAU'S GERO"

"GERO"; AN OUTSTANDING 2-YEAR-OLD SMOOTH-COATED SAINT BERNARD BRED BY HIGH CHATEAU KENNELS, CO-OWNED BY DIANE PEARLSTEIN & WINNIE VOGEL. HE WILL BE CAMPAIGNED THROUGHOUT THE NATION BY HIS HANDLER BRUCE C. CRABB. HIS EXCEPTIONAL TYPE AND TRUE SAINTLY TEMPERAMENT ARE A PERSONIFICATION OF THE STANDARD AND THESE COUPLED WITH HIS OVERALL SOUNDNESS, BALANCE AND TRUE MOVEMENT; MAKE HIM THE SAINT TO APPEAL TO ALL JUDGES . . . .

and with rather high knuckles. The so-called dewclaws which sometimes occur on the inside of the hind legs are imperfectly developed toes. They are of no use to the dog and are not taken into consideration in judging. They may be removed by surgery.

COAT—Very dense, short-haired (stockhaarig), lying smooth, tough, without however feeling rough to the touch. The thighs are slightly bushy. The tail at the root has longer and denser hair which gradually becomes shorter toward the tip. The tail appears bushy, not forming a flag. *Color*—White with red or red with white, the red in its various shades; brindle patches with white markings. The colors red and brown-yellow are of entirely equal value. Necessary markings are: white chest, feet and tip of tail, nose band, collar or spot on the nape; the latter and blaze are very desirable. Never of one color or without white. Faulty are all other colors, except the favorite dark shadings on the head (mask) and ears. One distinguishes between mantle dogs and splash-coated dogs.

HEIGHT AT SHOULDER — Of the dog should be 27½ inches minimum, of the bitch 25½ inches. Female animals are of finer and more delicate build.

Considered as faults are all deviations from the standard, as for instance a sway-back and a disproportionately long back, hocks too much bent, straight hindquarters, upward growing hair in spaces between the toes, out at elbows, cowhocks and weak pasterns.

LONGHAIRED

The longhaired type completely resembles the shorthaired type except for the coat which is not shorthaired (stockhaarig) but of medium length plain to slightly wavy, never rolled nor curly and not shaggy either. Usually, on the back, especially from the region of the haunches to the rump, the hair is more wavy, a condition, by the way, that is slightly indicated in the shorthaired dogs. The tail is bushy with dense hair of moderate length. Rolled or curly hair on the tail is not desirable. A tail with parted hair, or a flag tail, is faulty. Face and ears are covered with short and soft hair; longer hair at the base of the ear is permissible. Forelegs only slightly feathered; thighs very bushy.

Approved May 12, 1959

GENERAL CONFORMATION — (a) *General Appearance* — The Samoyed, being essentially a working dog, should present a picture of beauty, alertness and strength, with agility, dignity and grace. As his work lies in cold climates, his coat should be heavy and weather resistant, well groomed, and of good quality rather than quantity. The male carries more of a "ruff" than the female. He should not be long in the back as a weak back would make him practically useless for his legitimate work, but at the same time, a close-coupled body would also place him at a great disadvantage as a draft dog. Breeders should aim for the happy medium a body not long but muscular, allowing liberty, with a deep chest and well-sprung ribs, strong neck, straight front and especially strong loins. Males should be masculine in appearance and deportment without unwarranted aggressiveness; bitches feminine without weakness of structure or apparent softness of temperament. Bitches may be slightly longer in back than males. They should both give the appearance of being capable of great endurance but be free from coarseness. Because of the depth of chest required, the legs should be moderately long. A very short-legged dog is to be deprecated. Hindquarters should be particularly well developed, stifles well bent and any suggestion of unsound stifles or cowhocks severely penalized. General appearance should include movement and general conformation, indicating balance and good substance.

(b) *Substance* — Substance is that sufficiency of bone and muscle which rounds out a balance with the frame. The bone is heavier than would be expected in a dog of this size but not so massive as to prevent the speed and agility most desirable in a Samoyed. In all builds, bone should be in proportion to body size. The Samoyed should never be so heavy as to appear clumsy nor so light as to appear racy. The weight should be in proportion to the height.

(c) *Height* — Males — 21 to 23½ inches; females — 19 to 21 inches at the withers. An oversized or undersized Samoyed is to be penalized according to the extent of the deviation.

(d) *Coat* (Texture & Condition) — The Samoyed is a double-coated dog. The body should be well-covered with an undercoat of soft, short, thick, close wool with longer and harsh hair growing through it to form the outer coat, which stands straight out from the body and should be free from curl. The coat should form a ruff around the neck and shoulders, framing the head (more on males than on females). Quality of coat should be weather resistant and considered more than quantity. A droopy coat is undesirable. The coat should glisten with a silver sheen. The female does not usually carry as long a coat as most males and it is softer in texture.

(e) *Color* — Samoyeds should be pure white, white and biscuit, cream, or all biscuit. Any other colors disqualify.

MOVEMENT — (a) *Gait* — The Samoyed should trot, not pace. He should move with a quick agile stride that is well timed. The gait should be free, balanced and vigorous, with good reach in the forequarters and good driving power in the hindquarters. When trotting, there should be a strong rear action drive. Moving at a slow walk or trot, they will not single track, but as speed increases the legs gradually angle inward until the pads are finally falling on a line directly under the longitudinal center of the body. As the pad marks converge the forelegs and hind legs are carried straight forward in traveling, the stifles not turned in nor out. The back should remain strong, firm and level. A choppy or stilted gait should be penalized.

(b) *Rear End* — Upper thighs should be well developed. Stifles well bent — approximately 45 degrees to the ground. Hocks should be well developed, sharply defined and set at approximately 30 per cent of hip height. The hind legs should be parallel when viewed from the rear in a natural stance, strong, well developed, turning neither in nor out. Straight stifles are objectionable. Double jointedness or cowhocks are a fault. Cowhocks should only be determined if the dog has had an opportunity to move properly.

(c) *Front End* — Legs should be parallel and straight to the pasterns. The pasterns should be strong, sturdy and straight, but flexible with some spring for proper let-down of feet. Because of depth of chest, legs should be moderately long. Length of leg from the ground to the elbow should be approximately 55 per cent of the total height at the withers — a very short-legged dog is to be deprecated. Shoulders should be long and sloping, with a lay-back of 45 degrees and be firmly set. Out at the shoulders or out at the elbow should be penalized. The withers separation should be approximately 1 - 1½ inches.

(d) *Feet* — Large, long, flattish — a harefoot, slightly spread but not splayed; toes arched; pads thick and tough, with protective growth of hair between the toes. Feet should turn neither in nor out in a natural stance but may turn in slightly in the act of pulling. Turning out, pigeon-toes, round or

SKULL wedge-shaped, broad, slightly crowned; should form equilateral triangle from inner base of ears to center of stop
EYES dark preferred; set well apart; deep-set; almond shaped with lower lid slanting toward base of ear; dark rims preferred
STOP well-defined, not too abrupt
NOSE black preferred; brown, liver or Dudley not penalized
LIPS black preferred; slight turn-up at corners
JAWS and TEETH strong; well-set teeth: snug scissors bite
MUZZLE medium length, width; neither coarse nor snipy; of good depth; should taper toward nose; in proportion to skull
SHOULDERS long, sloping, firmly set: lay-back of 45 degrees
CHEST deep; ribs well-sprung; perfect depth approximates point of elbows; deepest part near ninth rib
FORELEGS parallel and straight to pasterns; moderately long; from ground to elbow approx. 55 per cent of total height at withers
FEET large, long, flattish; slightly spread but not splayed (harefoot); toes arched; pads thick, tough; hair between toes; should turn neither in nor out
COAT double-coated; body well-covered; undercoat soft, short thick, close; outercoat stands straight out; weather resistant; high sheen
PASTERNS strong, sturdy; straight; flexible
EARS strong, thick, erect, triangular, slightly rounded at tips; set well apart but within outer edge of head; length same as distance from inner base of ear to outer corner of eye; well-covered inside with hair; hair full and stand-off before ears
NECK strong, well-muscled; carried proudly erect; blending into shoulders with graceful arch; ruff around neck and shoulders
BACK withers form highest part; straight to loin; medium length, muscular; bitches may be slightly longer; croup full, slightly sloping to tail root; loins strong, slightly arched
WITHERS separation approx. 1 - 1½"
TAIL moderately long; profusely covered; carried forward over back or side when alert; neither high nor low set
HINDQUARTERS muscular, well-developed
STIFLES well-bent, approximately 45 degrees to ground
HIND LEGS parallel when viewed from rear; strong; well-developed
HOCKS well-developed, sharply defined, set at approx. 30 per cent of hip height
BODY muscular; bone heavy in proportion to body size
EXPRESSION of "Samoyed smile" important
COLOR pure white, white and biscuit, cream or all biscuit
UNDERLINE swings up in pleasing curve; tightly muscled
SIZE: Weight in proportion to height; height, males, 21" to 23½" at withers; females, 19" to 21"; over- or undersize penalized
DISQUALIFICATIONS: Any color other than listed. Blue eyes

CH. WINTERWAY'S BEOWULF

ONE OF THE LEADING SAMOYEDS IN THE COUNTRY AND AN OUTSTANDING REPRESENTATIVE OF THE BREED.

T. J. QUIGLEY
TAYMYR SAMOYEDS
11604 SOURWOOD LANE
RESTON, VA. 22091
(703) 860-1310

cat-footed or splayed are faults. Feathers on feet are not too essential but are more profuse on females than on males.

HEAD — (a) *Conformation* — Skull is wedge-shaped, broad, slightly crowned, not round or apple-headed, and should form an equilateral triangle on lines between the inner base of the ears and the center point of the stop. *Muzzle* — Muzzle of medium length and medium width, neither coarse nor snipy; should taper toward the nose and be in proportion to the size of the dog and the width of skull. The muzzle must have depth. *Stop* — Not too abrupt, nevertheless well defined. *Lips* — Should be black for preference and slightly curved up at the corners of the mouth, giving the "Samoyed smile." Lip lines should not have the appearance of being coarse nor should the flews drop predominately at corners of the mouth.

EARS — Strong and thick, erect, triangular and slightly rounded at the tips; should not be large or pointed, nor should they be small and "bear-eared." Ears should conform to head size and the size of the dog; they should be set well apart but be within the border of the outer edge of the head; they should be mobile and well covered inside with hair; hair full and stand-off before the ears. Length of ear should be the same measurement as the distance from inner base of ear to outer corner of eye.

EYES — Should be dark for preference; should be placed well apart and deep-set; almond-shaped with lower lid slanting toward an imaginary point approximating the base of ears. Dark eye rims for preference. Round or protruding eyes penalized. Blue eyes disqualifying.

NOSE — Black for preference but brown, liver, or Dudley nose not penalized. Color of nose sometimes changes with age and weather.

JAWS AND TEETH — Strong, well set teeth, snugly overlapping with scissors bite. Undershot or overshot should be penalized.

(b) *Expression* — The expression, referred to as "Samoyed expression," is very important and is indicated by sparkle of the eyes, animation and lighting up of the face when alert or intent on anything. Expression is made up of a combination of eyes, ears and mouth. The ears should be erect when alert; the mouth should be slightly curved up at the corners to form the "Samoyed smile."

TORSO — (a) *Neck* — Strong, well muscled, carried proudly erect, set on sloping shoulders to carry head with dignity when at attention. Neck should blend into shoulders with a graceful arch.

(b) *Chest* — Should be deep, with ribs well sprung out from the spine and flattened at the sides to allow proper movement of the shoulders and freedom for the front legs. Should not be barrel-chested. Perfect depth of chest approximates the point of elbows, and the deepest part of the chest should be back of the forelegs — near the ninth rib. Heart and lung room are secured more by body depth than width.

(c) *Loin and Back* — The withers forms the highest part of the back. Loins strong and slightly arched. The back should be straight to the loin, medium in length, very muscular and neither long nor short-coupled. The dog should be "just off square" — the length being approximately 5 per cent more than the height. Females allowed to be slightly longer than males. The belly should be well shaped and tightly muscled and, with the rear of the thorax, should swing up in a pleasing curve (tuck-up). Croup must be full, slightly sloping, and must continue imperceptibly to the tail root.

TAIL — The tail should be moderately long with the tail bone terminating approximately at the hock when down. It should be profusely covered with long hair and carried forward over the back or side when alert, but sometimes dropped when at rest. It should not be high or low set and should be mobile and loose — not tight over the back. A double hook is a fault. A judge should see the tail over the back once when judging.

DISPOSITION — Intelligent, gentle, loyal, adaptable, alert, full of action, eager to serve, friendly but conservative, not distrustful or shy, not overly aggressive. Unprovoked aggressiveness to be severely penalized.

DISQUALIFICATIONS

Any color other than pure white, cream, biscuit, or white and biscuit. Blue eyes.

Approved April 9, 1963

SHETLAND SHEEPDOG STANDARD

PREAMBLE—The Shetland Sheepdog, like the Collie, traces to the Border Collie of Scotland, which, transported to the Shetland Islands and crossed with small, intelligent, longhaired breeds, was reduced to miniature proportions. Subsequently crosses were made from time to time with Collies. This breed now bears the same relationship in size and general appearance to the Rough Collie as the Shetland Pony does to some of the larger breeds of horses. Although the resemblance between the Shetland Sheepdog and the Rough Collie is marked, there are differences which may be noted.

GENERAL DESCRIPTION — The Shetland Sheepdog is a small, alert, rough-coated, long-haired working dog. He must be sound, agile and sturdy. The outline should be so symmetrical that no part appears out of proportion to the whole. Dogs should appear masculine; bitches feminine.

SIZE—The Shetland Sheepdog should stand between 13 and 16 inches at the shoulder. *Note:* Height is determined by a line perpendicular to the ground from the top of the shoulder blades, the dog standing naturally, with forelegs parallel to line of measurement. *Disqualification:* Heights below or above the desired size range are to be disqualified from the show ring.

COAT—The coat should be double, the outer coat consisting of long, straight, harsh hair; the undercoat short, 'furry, and so dense as to give the entire coat its "stand-off" quality. The hair on face, tips of ears and feet should be smooth. Mane and frill should be abundant, and particularly impressive in males. The forelegs well feathered, the hind legs heavily so, but smooth below the hock joint. Hair on tail profuse. *Note:* Excess hair on ears, feet, and on hocks may be trimmed for the show ring. *Faults:* Coat short or flat, in whole or in part; wavy, curly, soft or silky. Lack of undercoat. Smooth-coated specimens. *Color*—Black, blue merle, and sable (ranging from golden through mahogany); marked with varying amounts of white and/or tan. *Faults:* Rustiness in a black or a blue coat. Washed out or degenerate colors, such as pale sable and faded blue. Self-color in the case of blue merle, that is, without any merling or mottling and generally appearing as a faded or dilute tricolor. Conspicuous white body spots. Specimens with more than 50 per cent white shall be so severely penalized as to effectively eliminate them from competition. *Disqualification:* Brindle.

TEMPERAMENT—The Shetland Sheepdog is intensely loyal, affectionate, and responsive to his owner. However, he may be reserved toward strangers but not to the point of showing fear or cringing in the ring. *Faults:* Shyness, timidity, or nervousness. Stubbornness, snappiness, or ill temper.

HEAD—The head should be refined and its shape, when viewed from top or side, be a long, blunt wedge tapering slightly from ears to nose, which must be black. *Skull and Muzzle*—Top of skull should be flat, showing no prominence at nuchal crest (the top of the occiput). Cheeks should be flat and should merge smoothly into a well-rounded muzzle. Skull and muzzle should be of equal length, balance point being inner corner of eye. In profile the top line of skull should parallel the top line of muzzle, but on a higher plane due to the presence of a slight but definite stop. Jaws clean and powerful. The deep, well-developed underjaw, rounded at chin, should extend to base of nostril. Lips tight. Upper and lower lips must meet and fit smoothly together all the way around. Teeth level and evenly spaced. Scissors bite. *Faults:* Too angled head. Too prominent stop, or no stop. Overfill below, between, or above eyes. Prominent nuchal crest. Domed skull. Prominent cheekbones. Snipy muzzle. Short, receding, or shallow under-jaw, lacking breadth and depth. Overshot or undershot, missing or crooked teeth. Teeth visible when mouth is closed. *Eyes*—Medium size with dark, almond-shaped rims, set somewhat obliquely in skull. Color must be dark, with blue or merle eyes permissible in blue merles only. *Faults:* Light, round, large or too small. Prominent haws. *Ears*—Small and flexible, placed high, carried three-fourths erect, with tips breaking forward. When in repose the ears fold lengthwise and are thrown back into the frill. *Faults:* Set too low. Hound, prick, bat, twisted ears. Leather too thick or too thin.

EXPRESSION — Contours and chiseling of the head, the shape, set and use of ears, the placement, shape and color of the eyes, combine to produce expression. Normally the expression should be alert, gentle, intelligent and questioning. Toward strangers the eyes should show watchfulness and reserve, but no fear.

NECK—Neck should be muscular, arched, and of sufficient length to carry the head proudly. *Faults:* Too short and thick.

BODY — In over-all appearance the body should appear moderately long as measured from shoulder joint to ischium (rearmost ex-

SKULL flat, no prominence at occiput; cheeks flat merging smoothly into well-rounded muzzle; skull and muzzle of equal length (balance point inner corner of eye); topline of skull parallels topline of muzzle
HEAD refined; viewed from top or side, long, blunt-wedged tapering from ears to nose; jaws clean, powerful; underjaw deep, well-developed, rounded at chin and extending to base of nostril; lips tight-fitting all around; teeth level, evenly spaced; scissors bite
EYES set somewhat obliquely; size medium, dark; almond-shaped rims; blue or merle eyes permissible in blue merles only
EARS small, flexible, placed high; carried ¾ths erect, tips breaking forward; in repose ears fold lengthwise, thrown back into frill
NECK muscular, arched, of sufficient length to carry head proudly
BACK short, level, strongly muscled
STOP slight but definite
FOREQUARTERS: shoulders slope 45-degree angle forward and downward to joint; at withers separated only by vertebra, sloping outward for rib spring; upper arm joins blade at approx. right angle; elbow joint equidistant from ground and from withers
TAIL: last vertebra should reach hock joint; carriage at rest straight down or, slight upward curve; when alert, lifted but not over back; hair profuse
HINDQUARTERS slight arch at loins; croup—gradual slope to rear; hipbone (pelvis) set at 30-degree angle to spine; thighs broad, muscular; thighbone set at angle corresponding to shoulder blade and upper arm; hind legs heavily feathered
CHEST deep; brisket reaches to point of elbow
FORELEGS straight from all angles, muscular, clean; bone strong; well-feathered
STIFLES distinctly angulated; length equals or exceeds thighbones
TUCK-UP moderate
BODY moderately long, sturdy, all parts in proportion to whole
HOCK clean-cut, angular, sinewy; bone good; strong ligamentation; no feather below joint
RIBS well-sprung, flattened at lower half for free play of foreleg, shoulder
FEET oval, compact; toes well-arched, fitting tightly together; pads deep, tough; nails hard, strong
METATARSUS short, straight viewed from all angles; dewclaws removed; hair smooth below joint
COLOR: Black, blue merle, sable (golden through mahogany); marked with varying amounts of white and/or tan
PASTERNS strong, sinewy, flexible; dewclaws may be removed
COAT: outer coat of long hair; straight, harsh; undercoat short, furry, so dense it gives "stand-off" quality; hair on face, ear tips and feet smooth; mane, frill abundant
DISQUALIFICATIONS: Heights below or above specified range—13" to 16". Brindle color
SIZE: at shoulder, 13" to 16"; neither under nor over

PIXIE DELL MILLER'S HIGH LIFE

A REFRESHING SOUND, STYLISH YOUNG HOPEFUL FROM PIXIE DELL — A KENNEL KNOWN FOR ITS MANY SHELTIE GREATS. BRED BY MR. & MRS. A. RAYMOND MILLER AND NOW UNDER THE JOINT OWNERSHIP OF MARIE K. MILLER AND MILDRED B. NICOLL. SO FAR HE HAS 3 BOB AND 3 BOW. HERE HE IS PICTURED WITH JUDGE MRS. CHARLOTTE CLEM MACGOWAN.

tremity of the pelvic bone), but much of this length is actually due to the proper angulation and breadth of the shoulder and hindquarter, as the back itself should be comparatively short. Back should be level and strongly muscled. Chest should be deep, the brisket reaching to point of elbow. The ribs should be well sprung, but flattened at their lower half to allow free play of the foreleg and shoulder. Abdomen moderately tucked up. *Faults:* Back too long, too short, swayed or roached. Barrel ribs. Slab side. Chest narrow and/or too shallow.

FOREQUARTERS — From the withers the shoulder blades should slope at a 45-degree angle forward and downward to the shoulder joints. At the withers they are separated only by the vertebra, but they must slope outward sufficiently to accommodate the desired spring of rib. The upper arm should join the shoulder blade at as nearly as possible a right angle. Elbow joint should be equidistant from the ground or from the withers. Forelegs straight viewed from all angles, muscular and clean, and of strong bone. Pasterns very strong, sinewy and flexible. Dewclaws may be removed. *Faults:* Insufficient angulation between shoulder and upper arm. Upper arm too short. Lack of outward slope of shoulders. Loose shoulders. Turning in or out of elbows. Crooked legs. Light bone. *Feet* (*front and hind*) — Feet should be oval and compact with the toes well arched and fitting tightly together. Pads deep and tough, nails hard and strong. *Faults:* Feet turning in or out. Splay-feet. Hare-feet. Cat-feet.

HINDQUARTERS — There should be a slight arch at the loins, and the croup should slope gradually to the rear. The hipbone (pelvis) should be set at a 30-degree angle to the spine. The thigh should be broad and muscular. The thighbone should be set into the pelvis at a right angle corresponding to the angle of the shoulder blade and upper arm. Stifle bones join the thighbone and should be distinctly angled at the stifle joint. The over-all length of the stifle should at least equal the length of the thighbone, and preferably should be clean-cut, angular, sinewy, with good bone and strong ligamentation. The hock (metatarsus) should be short and straight viewed from all angles. Dewclaws should be removed. Feet (*see* Forequarters). *Faults:* Croup higher than withers. Croup too straight or too steep. Narrow thighs. Cowhocks. Hocks turning out. Poorly defined hock joint. *Feet* (*see* Forequarters). *Tail* — The tail should be sufficiently long so that when it is laid along the back edge of the hind legs the last vertebra will reach the hock joint. Carriage of tail at rest is straight down or in a slight upward curve. When the dog is alert the tail is normally lifted, but it should not be curved forward over the back. *Faults:* Too short. Twisted at end.

GAIT — The trotting gait of the Shetland Sheepdog should denote effortless speed and smoothness. There should be no jerkiness, nor stiff, stilted, up-and-down movement. The drive should be from the rear, true and

[*continued on page 160*]

SIBERIAN HUSKY STANDARD

GENERAL APPEARANCE—The Siberian Husky is a medium-sized working dog of powerful but graceful build. His moderately compact and well-furred body, erect ears, and brush tail curved over the back suggest the Northern heritage of the capable sled dog. His characteristic gait is free and effortless but unbelievably strong when called upon to pull. And the keen and friendly expression in his slightly oblique eyes indicates the amenable disposition of the good companion.

HEAD—*Skull*—Of medium size, in proportion to the body; a trifle rounded on top and tapering gradually to the eyes, the width between the ears medium to narrow. Muzzle medium long, that is, the distance from nose to stop is about equal to the distance from stop to occiput. Skull and muzzle are finely chiseled. Lips dark and close-fitting, the jaws strong, and the teeth meeting in a scissors bite. *Faults:* Head too heavy; skull too wide; the muzzle either bulky, snipy, or coarse. *Ears*—Medium in size, set high, and carried erect. When at attention, they are practically parallel to each other. They are moderately rounded at the tips and well furred on the inner side. *Faults:* Too large, too low-set, and not strongly erect. *Eyes*—Set a trifle obliquely, their expression keen but friendly, interested, and even mischievous. Color may be either brown or blue, one brown eye and one blue eye being permissible but not desirable. *Faults:* Eyes set too obliquely.

NOSE—Preferably black, with brown allowed in specimens of reddish-colored coats; and flesh-colored nose and eye rims allowed in white dogs. The nose that is temporarily pink-streaked in winter is permissible but not desirable.

NECK — Strong, arched, and fairly short.

BODY—Moderately compact but never cobby. Chest deep and strong but not too broad, the ribs well sprung and deep. Shoulders powerful and well laid back. Back of medium length and strong, the back line level. Loins taut, lean, and very slightly arched. *Faults:* Weak or slack back; roach back.

LEGS AND FEET — *Legs* — The legs are straight and well muscled, with bone substantial but not heavy. Hindquarters powerful with good angulation. Well bent at stifles. Dewclaws on the rear legs, if any, are to be removed. *Feet*—Oval in shape, medium in size; compact and well furred between the toes. Pads tough and deeply cushioned. In short, a typical snowshoe foot, somewhat webbed between the toes. *Faults:* Bone too light or too heavy; insufficient bend at stifles; weak pasterns; feet soft and/or splayed.

TAIL—A well-furred brush carried over the back in a sickle curve when the dog runs or stands at attention, and trailing out behind when working or in repose. When carried up, the typical tail does not curl to either side of the body, nor does it snap flat to the back. The tail hair is usually of medium length, although length varies somewhat with over-all coat length.

COAT — Double. The undercoat is dense, soft and downy, and should be of sufficient length and density to support the outer coat. The outer coat is very thick, smooth-textured and soft, giving a smooth, full-furred appearance and a clean-cut outline. It is usually medium in length; a longer coat is allowed so long as the texture is soft and remains the same in any length. *Faults:* Harsh texture, or a rough look which obscures the clean-cut outline of the dog; absence of undercoat, except while actually shedding.

COLOR—All colors and white, and all markings are allowed. The various shades of wolf, and the silver grays, tan and black with white points are most usual. A variety of markings, especially on the head, are common to the breed, these including many striking and unusual patterns not found in other breeds. The cap-like mask and spectacles are typical.

SIZE—Both height and weight are very important. *Height*—Dogs, from 21 to 23½ inches at the shoulder; bitches, from 20 to 22 inches. *Weight*—Dogs, from 45 to 60 pounds; bitches, from 35 to 50 pounds. Dogs over 23½ inches and bitches over 22 inches are to be disqualified.

SUMMARY—Most important of the Siberian Husky's characteristics are medium size and moderate bone, soft coat, high-set ears, ease and freedom of action, and good disposition. A gait, or a general appearance in any way clumsy, heavy, or unwieldy is to be penalized. In addition to the faults already noted, obvious structural faults common to all breeds, such as cowhocks, for instance, are as undesirable in the Siberian Husky as in any other breed, even though they are not specifically mentioned therein.

DISQUALIFICATION

Height over 23½ inches in dogs; over 22 inches in bitches.

Approved March 12, 1963

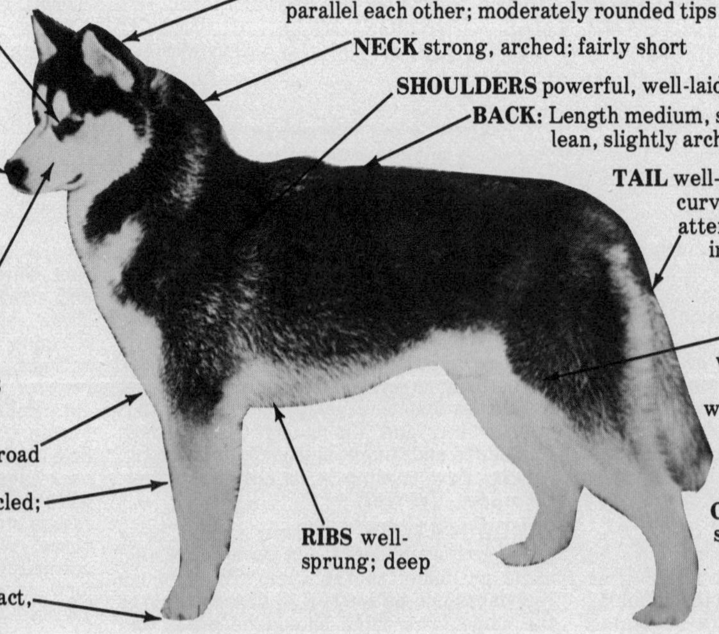

HEAD: Skull, medium size, in proportion to body; trifle rounded on top, tapering gradually to eyes; width between ears medium to narrow; finely chiseled

APPEARANCE: Of medium size; moderate bone; powerful, graceful; never cobby; moderately compact, well-furred body; gait, free, effortless, unbelievably strong; amenable disposition

EYES set trifle oblique, expression keen, friendly, interested, mischievous; color brown or blue—one brown, one blue permissible but not desirable; flesh-colored eye rims allowed in white dogs

EARS of medium size, high-set, carried erect; at attention, practically parallel each other; moderately rounded tips; inner side, well-furred

NECK strong, arched; fairly short

SHOULDERS powerful, well-laid-back

BACK: Length medium, strong; topline level; loins taut, lean, slightly arched, weak or roach back faulted

NOSE: black preferred; brown allowed with reddish coats; flesh-colored allowed in white dogs; pink-streaked allowed in winter but not desirable

TAIL well-furred brush; carriage, a sickle curve over back when running or at attention; trailing when working or in repose; does not curl to either side nor snap flat to back; hair of medium length

MUZZLE medium long; from nose to stop about equal from stop to occiput; finely chiseled; lips dark, close-fitting; jaws strong; scissors bite

HINDQUARTERS straight, well-muscled; bone substantial, not heavy; powerful; stifles well-bent; good angulation; dewclaws, if any, to be removed

CHEST deep, strong, not too broad

FORELEGS straight, well-muscled; bone substantial, not heavy; weak pasterns faulted

RIBS well-sprung; deep

COAT double; undercoat dense, soft, downy, of sufficient length and density to support outercoat. Outercoat very thick; texture smooth, soft, giving full-furred appearance; outline clean-cut; length medium, longer allowed if texture is soft

FEET oval, size medium; compact, well-furred between toes; pads tough, deeply cushioned; a "snowshoe foot," somewhat webbed

SIZE: Height at shoulder, dogs, 21-23½"; bitches, 20-22". Weight, dogs, 45-60 lbs; bitches, 35-50 lbs; both height, weight important

DISQUALIFICATIONS: Dogs over 23½"; bitches over 22"

COLORS: All colors and white; all markings allowed; cap-like mask and spectacles typical

CH. ARAHAZ' DYENGI

DYENGI WENT BEST OF WINNERS AT HIS LAST 5 SHOWS TO COMPLETE HIS CHAMPIONSHIP IN AUG. 1974. HIS SIRE, BOTH GRANDSIRES AND ALL 4 GREAT GRANDSIRES ARE AKC CHAMPIONS. DYENGI WILL BE SPECIALED ON A LIMITED BASIS IN 1975. HE IS THE 11th CHAMPION FOR HIS BREEDER/OWNERS. COOPER/WHITE-BLUE EYES. SIRE: CH. ARAHAZ' RED ROCKET. DAM: SUNTRANA FLAMING STAR.

The Siberian Husky was developed by certain peoples of Siberia as a sled dog, guard, and companion. The ancestral stock appears to have been of the Spitz type. Huskies were introduced to Alaska during the first decade of the 20th century in response to a fad for dog-sled racing. Some 16,000 are registered annually. The Siberian Husky is medium-sized, quick and light on his feet, free and graceful in action. His compact build, semi-erect coat, erect ears, and brush tail reveal his Spitz or Nordic affinities. Well-muscled Siberian Huskies carry no excess weight. All coat colors are allowed. Interesting and unique facial markings are common but not required. The Siberian Husky is friendly and gentle, alert and outgoing. He does not act like a guard dog. He is a tractable, agreeable companion.

STANDARD SCHNAUZER STANDARD

GENERAL APPEARANCE — The Standard Schnauzer is a robust, heavy-set dog, sturdily built with good muscle and plenty of bone; square-built in proportion of body-length to height. His nature combines high-spirited temperament with extreme reliability. His rugged build and dense harsh coat are accentuated by the hallmark of the breed, the arched eyebrows, bristly mustache, and luxuriant whiskers.

HEAD — Strong, rectangular, and elongated; narrowing slightly from the ears to the eyes and again to the tip of the nose. The total length of the head is about one-half the length of the back measured from the withers to the set-on of the tail. The head matches the sex and substance of the dog. The top line of the muzzle is parallel with the top line of the skull. There is a slight stop which is accentuated by the wiry brows.

SKULL (Occiput to Stop) — Moderately broad between the ears with the width of the skull not exceeding two-thirds the length of the skull. The skull must be flat; neither domed nor bumpy; skin unwrinkled.

CHEEKS — Well-developed chewing muscles, but not so much that "cheekiness" disturbs the rectangular head form.

MUZZLE — Strong, and both parallel and equal to length to the topskull; it ends in a moderately blunt wedge with wiry whiskers accenting the rectangular shape of the head. Nose is large, black and full. The lips should be black, tight and not overlapping.

EYES — Medium size; dark brown; oval in shape and turned forward; neither round nor protruding. The brow is arched and wiry, but vision is not impaired nor eyes hidden by too long an eyebrow.

BITE — A full complement of white teeth, with a strong, sound scissors bite. The canine teeth are strong and well developed with the upper incisors slightly overlapping and engaging the lower. The upper and lower jaws are powerful and either overshot or undershot. *Faults;* A level bite is considered undesirable but a lesser fault than an overshot or undershot mouth.

EARS — Evenly shaped, set high and carried erect when cropped. If uncropped, they are small, V-shaped button ears of moderate thickness and carried rather high and close to the head.

NECK — Strong, of moderate thickness and length, elegantly arched and blending cleanly into the shoulders. The skin is tight, fitting closely to the dry throat with no wrinkles or dewlaps.

SHOULDERS — The sloping shoulder blades are strongly muscled yet flat and well laid back so that the rounded upper ends are in a nearly vertical line above the elbows. They slope well forward to the point where they join the upper arm, forming as nearly as possible a right angle when seen from the side. Such an angulation permits the maximum forward extension of the forelegs without binding or effort.

CHEST — Of medium width with well-sprung ribs, and if it could be seen in cross-section would be oval. The breastbone is plainly discernible. The brisket must descend at least to the elbows and ascend gradually to the rear with the belly moderately drawn up.

BODY — Compact, strong, short-coupled and substantial so as to permit great flexibility and agility. The height at the highest point of the withers equals the length from breastbone to point of rump. *Faults:* Too slender or shelly; too bulky or coarse; excessive tuck-up.

BACK — Strong, stiff, straight and short, with a well-developed loin section; the distance from the last rib to the hips as short as possible. The top line of the back should not be absolutely horizontal, but should have a slightly descending slope from the first vertebra of the withers to the faintly curved croup and set-on of the tail.

FORELEGS — Straight, vertical and without any curvature when seen from all sides; set moderately far apart; with heavy bone; elbows set close to the body and pointing directly to the rear.

HINDQUARTERS — Strongly muscled, in balance with the forequarters, never appearing higher than the shoulders. Croup full and slightly rounded. Thighs broad with well-bent stifles. The second thigh, from knee to hock, is approximately parallel with an extension of the upper-neck line. The legs, from the clearly defined hock joint to the feet, are short and perpendicular to the ground and when viewed from the rear are parallel to each other.

FEET — Small and compact, round with thick pads and strong black nails. The toes are well closed and arched (cats paws) and pointing straight ahead.

HEAD strong, rectangular, elongated; narrowing from ears to eyes to tip of nose; top line of muzzle parallels top line of skull; luxuriant beard and eyebrows
APPEARANCE: Robust, heavy set, square-built; good muscle, plenty of bone
EARS even shape; set high, carried erect when cropped; uncropped, small, V-shape, close to head; carriage high; moderately thick
DISQUALIFICATIONS: Vicious dogs; males under 18" or over 20", females under 17" or over 19" in height
SKULL flat; moderately broad but not more than 2/3 of length
NECK strong, moderate thickness and length; skin tight, dry
SHOULDERS sloping, strongly
EYES medium size; dark brown, oval; turned forward; brow arched, wiry
NOSE large, black, full
MUZZLE strong, blunt; whiskers wire; jaw level, powerful, square; teeth strong, sound, white, scissors bite
TAIL set moderately high, carried erect; corpped to not less than 1" , not more than 2"
CHEEKS: Well developed; lips black, tight, not overlapping
CHEST moderately broad; breastbone reaching to elbows; extending slowly backward
HINDQUARTERS strongly muscled; croup full, slightly rounded; thighs broad; stifles well-bent
FORELEGS straight, vertical, good bone; elbows close to body, turning neither in nor out
FEET small, compact, round, thick pads; nails strong, black; toes well closed, arched, straight
COAT hard, wirly; outercoat dense, harsh; undercoat soft
SIZE: Ideal height for males, 18½" to 19½"; for females 17½" to 18½"

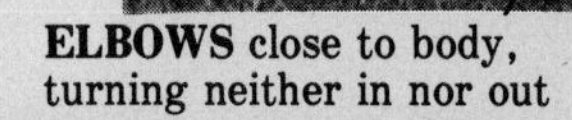

ELBOWS close to body, turning neither in nor out
BELLY moderately drawn-up
COLOR: Pepper and salt or pure black

CH. LAUSBUB GAUNER

CH. LAUSBUB WILHELM TELL EX. CH. LAUSBUBEN'S HEDWIG TELL. B.O.B. MINUTEMAN STANDARD SCHNAUZER SPEC. B.O.B. VINICKER BOCKER STANDARD SCHNAUZER SPEC. B.O.B. POTOMAC VALLEY STANDARD SCHNAUZER SPEC.

OWNER
ARNOLD M. MEIROWSKY M.D.
OLD HILLSBORO RD.
FRANKLIN, TENN.
(615) 269-4143

HANDLER
GUENTER BEHR
R.D. 1
MILFORD, N.J. 08848
(201) 996-2220

DEWCLAWS — Dewclaws, if any, on the hind legs are generally removed. Dewclaws on the forelegs may be removed.

TAIL — Set moderately high and carried erect. It is docked to not less than 1 inch nor more than 2 inches. *Faults:* Squirrel tail.

HEIGHT — Ideal height at the highest point of the shoulder blades, 18½ to 19½ inches for males and 17½ inches to 18½ inches for females. Dogs measuring over or under these limits must be faulted in proportion to the extent of the deviation. Dogs measuring more than one-half inch over or under these limits must be disqualified.

COAT — Tight, hard, wiry and as thick as possible, composed of a soft, close undercoat and a harsh outer coat which, when seen against the grain, stands up off the back, lying neither smooth nor flat. The outer coat (body coat) is trimmed (by plucking) only to accent the body outline. When in show condition, the outer coat's proper length is approximately 1½ inches, except on the ears, head, neck, chest, belly and under the tail where it may be closely trimmed to give the desired typical appearance of the breed.

On the muzzle and over the eyes the coat lengthens to form luxuriant beard and eyebrows; the hair on the legs is longer than that on the body. These "furnishings" should be of harsh texture and should not be so profuse so as to detract from the neat appearance or working capabilities of the dog. *Faults:* Soft, smooth, curly, wavy or shaggy; too long or too short; too sparse or lacking undercoat; excessive furnishings; lack of furnishings.

COLOR — Pepper and salt or pure black.

Pepper and Salt — The typical pepper and salt color of the topcoat results from the combination of black and white hairs, and white hairs banded with black. Acceptable are all shades of pepper and salt from dark iron-gray to silver gray. Ideally, pepper and salt Standard Schnauzers have a gray undercoat, but a tan or fawn undercoat is not to be penalized. It is desirable to have a darker facial mask that harmonizes with the particular shade of coat color. Also, in pepper and salt dogs, the pepper and salt mixture may fade out to light gray or silver white in the eyebrows, whiskers, cheeks, under throat, across chest, under tail, leg furnishings, under body, and inside legs.

Black — Ideally the black Standard Schnauzer should be a true rich color, free from any fading or discoloration or any admixture of gray or tan hairs. The undercoat should also be solid black. However, increased age or continued exposure to the sun may cause a certain amount of fading and burning. A small white smudge on the chest is not a fault. Loss of color as a result of scars from cuts and bites is not a fault.

Faults: Any color other than specified, and any shadings or mixtures thereof in the top-

[*continued on page 232*]

WELSH CORGI [CARDIGAN] STANDARD

GENERAL APPEARANCE — Low set, sturdily built, with heavy bone and deep chest. Overall silhouette long in proportion to height, culminating in low tail set and fox-like brush. Expression alert and foxy, watchful yet friendly. General impression: a handsome, powerful small dog, capable of both speed and endurance, intelligent, sturdy, but not coarse.

HEAD AND SKULL — Skull moderately wide and flat between the ears, with definite though moderate stop. Muzzle to measure about three inches in length, or in proportion to the skull as three to five. Muzzle medium, i.e., neither too pointed nor too blunt but somewhat less fine than the Pembroke. Nose black. Nostrils of moderate size. Underjaw clean cut and strong.

EYES — Medium to large, and rather widely set, with distinct corners. Color dark to dark amber but clear. Blue eyes, or one dark and one blue eye, permissible in blue merles.

MOUTH — Teeth strong and regular, neither overshot nor undershot. Pincer (level) bite permissible but scissors bite preferred, e.g., the inner side of the front teeth resting closely over the front of the lower front teeth.

EARS — Large and prominent in proportion to size of dog. Slightly rounded at the tips, moderately wide at the base, and carried erect, set well apart and well back, sloping slightly forward when erect. Flop ears a serious fault.

NECK — Muscular, well developed, especially in males, and in proportion to dog's build; fitting into strong, well shaped shoulders.

FOREQUARTERS — Chest broad, deep, and well let down between forelegs. Forelegs short, strong, and slightly bowed around chest, and with distinct but not exaggerated crook below the carpus. Elbows close to side. A straight terrier-like front is a fault.

BODY — Long and strong, with deep brisket, well sprung ribs with moderate tuck-up of loin. Top line level except for slight slope of spine above tail.

HINDQUARTERS — Strong, with muscular thighs. Legs short and well boned.

FEET — Round and well padded. Hind dewclaws, if any, should be removed. Front dewclaws may be removed.

TAIL — Long to moderately long resembling a fox brush. Should be set fairly low on body line, carried low when standing or moving slowly, streaming out when at a dead run, lifted when tracking or excited, but never curled over the back. A rat tail or a whip tail are faults.

COAT — Medium length but dense. Slightly harsh texture but neither wiry nor silky. Weather resistant. An overly short coat or a long and silky and/or curly coat are faults. Normal grooming and trimming of whiskers is permitted. Any trimming that alters the natural length of the coat is not permitted and is a serious fault. A distinctly long coat is a disqualification.

SIZE — Height approximately 12 inches at the highest point of the shoulder blades. Length usually between 36 and 44 inches from nose to tip of tail. In considering the height, weight, and length of a dog, overall balance is a prime factor.

COLORS — Red, sable, red-brindle, black-brindle, black, tri-color, blue merle. Usually with white flashings on chest, neck, feet, face or tip of tail. No preferences among these colors. A dog predominantly white in color should be seriously faulted. Pure white is a disqualification.

DISQUALIFICATIONS

A distinctly long coat and pure white.

Approved February 11, 1967

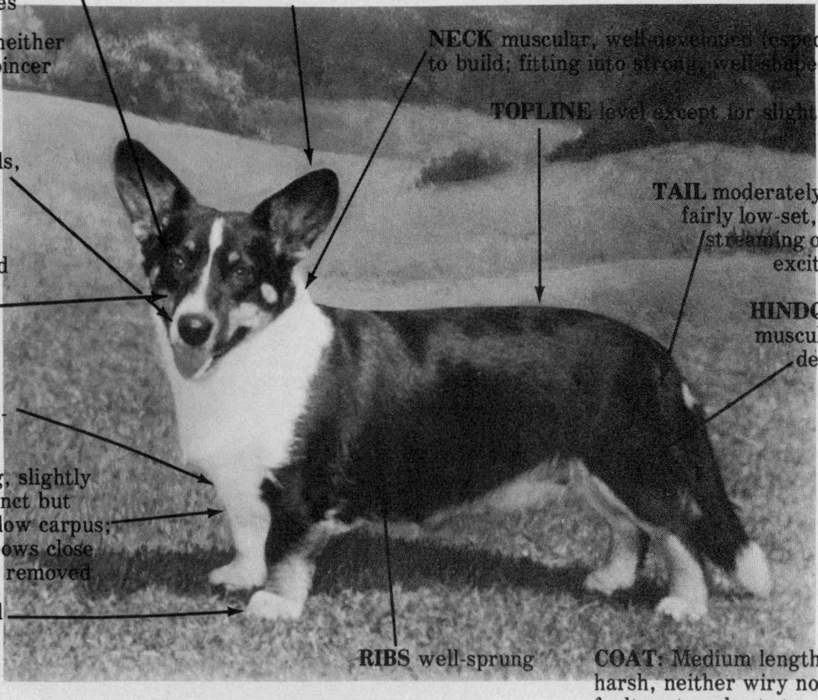

SKULL moderately wide, flat between ears; stop, definite though moderate

EYES medium to large, rather widely set; corners, distinct; dark to dark amber, clear; blue permissible, also one dark and one blue in blue merles

TEETH strong, regular; neither overshot nor undershot; pincer (level) bite permissible; scissors bite preferred

NOSE black; nostrils, moderate size

MUZZLE in proportion to skull 3';5, about 3" in length; neither too pointed nor too blunt; somewhat less fine than Pembroke; underjaw, clean, strong

CHEST broad, deep, well-let-down; brisket deep

FORELEGS short, strong, slightly bowed around chest; distinct but not exaggerated crook below carpus; straight front, a fault; elbows close to side; dewclaws may be removed

FEET round, well-padded (see legs for dewclaws)

APPEARANCE: Low-set, sturdy; bone heavy; chest deep; tail-set low; brush foxlike; expression, alert, foxy; overall silhouette, long in proportion to height; tuck-up, moderate; small, powerful, capable of speed, endurance

EARS large, prominent; slightly rounded at tips; moderately wide at base; carriage erect, sloping slightly forward; set well apart, well back; flop ears a serious fault

NECK muscular, well-developed (especially males), in proportion to build; fitting into strong, well-shaped shoulders

TOPLINE level except for slight slope to tail-set

TAIL moderately long, similar to fox brush; fairly low-set, on body line; carriage low, streaming out at dead run; lifted when excited; never curled over back

HINDQUARTERS strong; thighs muscular; legs short, well-boned; dewclaws should be removed

SIZE: Approx. 12" at high point of shoulder blades; LENGTH — 36" to 44" from nose to tip of tail; balance a prime factor

RIBS well-sprung

COAT: Medium length, dense; texture slightly harsh, neither wiry nor silky; weather-resistant; faults — too short, too long, silky, curly; trimming whiskers permitted; trimming to alter length of coat not permitted.
DISQUALIFICATION: Distinctly long coat

COLORS: Red, sable, red-brindle, black-brindle, black, tricolor, blue merle; Usually white flashings on chest, neck, feet, face, tip of tail; no preference among colors; fault, predominately white. **DISQUALIFICATION:** Pure white

CH. BRYMORE'S TALIESIN

GROUP WINNING CARDIGAN WELSH CORGI. # 1 IN THE NATION 1974.

TAMERLANE FARMS
MRS. J. BRUCE MOREY & CHAS. INGOLD
6N501 DENKER ROAD
ST. CHARLES, ILL. 60174

The Cardigan Welsh Corgi is one of the British Isles' oldest breeds of dogs. The breed is said to trace back to the migration of the Celts in 1200 B.C., where he was treated as an important member of the community. The great value of these dogs is their ability to work with cattle. Rather than herding the Corgi nips at their heels and drives them whatever distance he wishes. He possesses excellent speed, intelligence, agilitly and temperament.

WELSH CORGI [PEMBROKE] STANDARD

GENERAL APPEARANCE — Low-set, strong, sturdily built, alert and active, giving an impression of substance and stamina in a small space; outlook bold, expression intelligent and workmanlike. The movement should be free and active, elbows fitting closely to the sides, neither loose nor tied. Forelegs should move well forward, without too much lift, in unison with thrusting action of hind legs.

HEAD AND SKULL — Head to be foxy in shape and appearance, with alert and intelligent expression, skull to be fairly wide and flat between the ears; moderate amount of stop. Length of foreface to be in proportion to the skull as three is to five. Muzzle slightly tapering. Nose black. *Eyes* — Well set, medium size, hazel in color and blending with color of coat. *Ears* — Pricked, medium-sized, slightly pointed. A line drawn from the tip of the nose through the eye should, if extended, pass through, or close to, the tip of the ear.

MOUTH — Teeth level, or with the inner side of the upper front teeth resting closely on the front of the under ones.

NECK — Fairly long.

FOREQUARTERS — Legs short and as straight as possible: "Straight as possible" means straight as soundness and deep broad chest will permit. It does not mean terrier-straight. Ample bone carried right down to the feet. Elbows should fit closely to the sides, neither loose nor tied. Forearm should curve slightly round the chest. *Body* — Of medium length, with well-sprung ribs. Not short-coupled or terrierlike. Level top line. Chest broad and deep, well let down between the forelegs. *Hindquarters* — Strong and flexible, slightly tapering. Legs short. Ample bone carried right down to the feet. Hocks straight when viewed from behind. *Feet* — Oval, the two center toes slightly in advance of two outer toes, pads strong and well arched. Nails short. *Tail* — Short, preferably natural.

COAT — Of medium length and dense; not wiry. *Color* — Self colors in red, sable, fawn, black and tan, or with white markings on legs, chest and neck. Some white on head and foreface is permissible.

WEIGHT AND SIZE — Dogs, 20 to 24 pounds; bitches, 18 to 22 pounds. Height, from 10 to 12 inches at shoulder.

Approved February 10, 1952

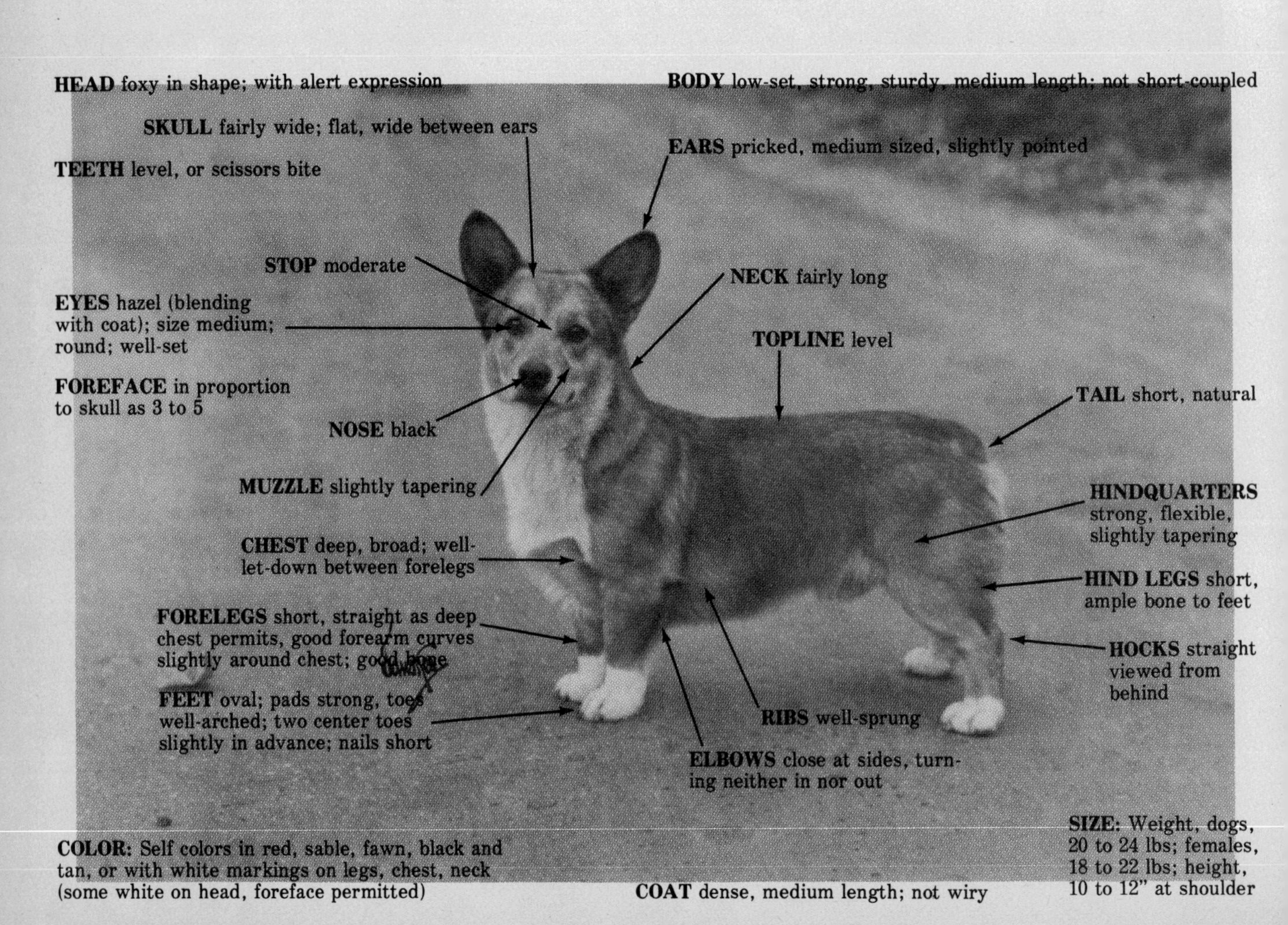

HEAD foxy in shape; with alert expression
SKULL fairly wide; flat, wide between ears
TEETH level, or scissors bite
STOP moderate
EYES hazel (blending with coat); size medium; round; well-set
FOREFACE in proportion to skull as 3 to 5
NOSE black
MUZZLE slightly tapering
CHEST deep, broad; well-let-down between forelegs
FORELEGS short, straight as deep chest permits, good forearm curves slightly around chest; good bone
FEET oval; pads strong, toes well-arched; two center toes slightly in advance; nails short
COLOR: Self colors in red, sable, fawn, black and tan, or with white markings on legs, chest, neck (some white on head, foreface permitted)
BODY low-set, strong, sturdy, medium length; not short-coupled
EARS pricked, medium sized, slightly pointed
NECK fairly long
TOPLINE level
TAIL short, natural
HINDQUARTERS strong, flexible, slightly tapering
HIND LEGS short, ample bone to feet
HOCKS straight viewed from behind
RIBS well-sprung
ELBOWS close at sides, turning neither in nor out
SIZE: Weight, dogs, 20 to 24 lbs; females, 18 to 22 lbs; height, 10 to 12" at shoulder
COAT dense, medium length; not wiry

CH. BEKONPENN COUNT DORONICUM C.D.

SHOWN TAKING BEST OF BREED AT ONLY 13 MO. OLD IN HIS SECOND U.S. SHOW. ALTHOUGH COUNT'S FIRST LITTER WAS WHELPED JUST 20 MONTHS AGO, HE ALREADY HAS NINE OFFSPRING WHO HAVE EITHER FINISHED CHAMPIONSHIP OR ARE WELL ON THEIR WAY TO THEIR TITLE. PUPPIES AVAILABLE. THE COUNT IS ONE OF THE SEVERAL TOP STUDS OWNED BY:

LARKLAIN KENNELS, REG.
(MRS. ELAINE P. ERGANBRIGHT)
3700 So. Garrison
Denver, CO 80235
(303) 985-2882

The Pembroke Welsh Corgi is a variation on the theme of the Cardigan variety. Both breeds strongly resemble a Swedish herding dog, the Vastgotaspets, but which, if either, give ancestry to the other is not known. These little dogs were bred principally to herd cattle by nipping at their heels. They are small, alert, and agile to avoid kicks. Earlier in the century, the Pembrooke and Cardigan Welsh Corgis were interbred, though they had not been to any extent in their home counties in Wales. The Pembroke Welsh Corgi is a low-set, sturdy, active, substantial dog with great endurance. It should appear neither coarse nor racy. It should stand 10-12 inches at the withers and weigh up to 30 lbs. The tail is absent or docked as short as possible. Movement is free and smooth. Acceptable colors include red, sable, fawn, and black and tan, with or without white markings. White is acceptable on legs, chest, neck, muzzle, underparts, and as a narrow blaze on the head. The Corgi is shown in natural condition. The Pembroke Welsh Corgi is a charming, intelligent, reliable family dog. It owes its popularity, perhaps in part, to its having been among the favored pets of King George VI and the present Queen Elizabeth of England. Some 2,500 are registered annually with the AKC, the breed ranking 47th.

AKITA
STANDARD

GENERAL APPEARANCE — Large, powerful, alert, with much substance and heavy bone. The broad head, forming a blunt triangle, with deep muzzle, small eyes and erect ears carried forward in line with back of neck, is characteristic of the breed. The large, curled tail, balancing the broad head, is also characteristic of the breed.

HEAD — Massive but in balance with body; free of wrinkle when at ease. Skull flat between ears and broad; jaws square and powerful with minimal dewlap. Head forms a blunt triangle when viewed from above. *Fault:* Narrow or snipy head.

Muzzle — Broad and full. Distance from nose to stop is to distance from stop to occiput as 2 is to 3. *Stop* — Well defined, but not too abrupt. A shallow furrow extends well up forehead.

Nose — Broad and black. Liver permitted on white Akitas, but black always preferred. *Disqualification:* Butterfly nose or total lack of pigmentation on nose.

Ears — The ears of the Akita are characteristic of the breed. They are strongly erect and small in relation to rest of head. If ear is folded forward for measuring length, tip will touch upper eye rim. Ears are triangular, slightly rounded at tip, wide at base, set wide on head but not too low, and carried slightly forward over eyes in line with back of neck. *Disqualification:* Drop or broken ears.

Eyes — Dark brown, small, deep-set and triangular in shape. Eye rims black and tight.

Lips and Tongue — Lips black and not pendulous; tongue pink.

Teeth — Strong with scissors bite preferred, but level bit acceptable. *Disqualification:* — Noticeably undershot or overshot.

NECK AND BODY — *Neck* — Thick and muscular; comparatively short, widening gradually toward shoulders. A pronounced crest blends in with base of skull.

Body — Longer than high, as 10 is to 9 in males; 11 to 9 in bitches. Chest wide and deep; depth of chest is one-half height of dog at shoulder. Ribs well sprung, brisket well developed. Level back with firmly-muscled loin and moderate tuck-up. Skin pliant but not loose. *Serious Faults:* Light bone, rangy body.

TAIL — Large and full, set high and carried over back or against flank in a three-quarter, full, or double curl, always dipping to or below level of back. On a three-quarter curl, tip drops well down flank. Root large and strong. Tail bone reaches hock when let down. Hair coarse, straight and full, with no appearance of a plume. *Disqualification:* Sickle or uncurled tail.

— *Forequarters* — Shoulders strong and powerful with moderate layback. Forelegs heavy-boned and straight as viewed from front. Angle of pastern 15 degrees forward from vertical. *Faults:* Elbows in or out, loose shoulders.

Hindquarters — Width, muscular development and comparable to forequarters. Upper thighs well developed. Stifle moderately bent and hocks well let down, turning neither in nor out.

Dewclaws On front legs generally not removed; dewclaws on hind legs generally removed.

Feet — Cat feet, well knuckled up with thick pads. Feet straight ahead.

COAT — Double-coated. Undercoat thick, soft, dense and shorter than outer coat. Outer coat straight, harsh and standing somewhat off body. Hair on head, legs and ears short. Length of hair at withers and rump approximately two inches, which is slightly longer than on rest of body, except tail, where coat is longest and most profuse. *Fault:* Any indication of ruff or feathering.

COLOR — Any color including white; brindle; or pinto. Colors are brilliant and clear and markings are well balanced, with or without mask or blaze. White Akitas have no mask. Pinto has a white background with large, evenly placed patches covering head and more than one-third of body. Undercoat may be a different color from outer coat.

GAIT — Brisk and powerful with strides of moderate length. Back remains strong, firm and level. Rear legs move in line with front legs.

SIZE — Males 26 to 28 inches at the withers; bitches 24 to 26 inches. *Disqualification:* Dogs under 25 inches; bitches under 23 inches.

TEMPERAMENT — Alert and responsive, dignified and courageous. Aggressive toward other dogs.

DISQUALIFICATIONS

Butterfly nose or total lack of pigmentation on nose. Drop or broken ears. Noticeably undershot or overshot. Sickle or uncurled tail. Dogs under 25 inches; bitches under 23 inches.

GENERAL APPEARANCE: Large, powerful, alert, with much substance and heavy bone. The large, curled tail balances the broad head

TEMPERAMENT: Alert, responsive, dignified, courageous. Aggressive towards other dogs

COAT: Double coat; undercoat thick and soft, dense and shorter than outer. Outer is straight, harsh and standing off body

HEAD: Massive, in balance with body. Forms a blunt triangle when viewd from above

BODY: Larger than high, chest wide, deep

TAIL: Large, full, set high, carried over back or against flank

NECK: Thick and muscular

EARS: Strongly erect, small, triangular; carried slightly forward over eyes in line with back of neck

MUZZLE: Broad and full. Distance from nose to stop is to distance from stop to occiput as 2 is to 3

NOSE: Broad and black

TEETH: Strong, scissors bite preferred

FOREQUARTERS: Shoulders strong, powerful, moderate layback. Forelegs heavy boned and straight viewed from front. Faults: elbows in or out, loose shoulders

HINDQUARTERS: Width well developed. Stifle moderately bent, hock well let down, turning neither in nor out

RIBS: Well sprung

DEWCLAWS: Front legs, generally not removed; hind legs, generally removed

FEET: Cat feet

WASSERMAN

DISQUALIFICATIONS: Butterfly nose or total lack of pigmentation on nose; drop or broken ears, noticeably under- or overshot; sickle or uncurled tail; dogs under 25", bitches under 23"

SIZE: Males, 26-28 inches; Females, 24-26 inches

COLOR: Any color. Brilliant and clear, markings balanced with or without mask or blaze. Undercoat may be different color

BELGIAN MALINOIS
STANDARD

GENERAL APPEARANCE — The Belgian Malinois is a well-balanced, square dog, elegant in appearance, with an exceedingly proud carriage of the head and neck. The dog is strong, agile, well-muscled, alert and full of life. It stands squarely on all fours and viewed from the side, the topline, forelegs, and hindlegs, closely approximate a square. The whole conformation gives the impression of depth and solidity without bulkiness. The expression indicates alertness, attention and readiness for activity, and the gaze is intelligent and questioning. The male is usually somewhat more impressive and grand than its female counterpart, which has a distinctly feminine look.

SIZE AND SUBSTANCE — Males 24-26 inches in height, females 22-24 inches measured at the withers. The length, measured from point of breast bone to point of rump, should equal the height, but bitches may be slightly longer. Bone structure is moderately heavy in proportion to height so that the dog is well balanced throughout and neither spindly nor leggy nor cumbersome and bulky.

COAT — Comparative short, straight, with dense undercoat. Very short hair on the head, ears, and lower legs. The hair is somewhat longer around the neck where it forms a collarette, and on the tail and the back of the thighs.

COLOR — Rich fawn to mahogany, with black overlay. Black mask and ears. The under parts of the body, tail, and breeches are lighter fawn, but washed out fawn color on the body is a fault. The tips of the toes may be white and a small white spot on the chest is permitted.

HEAD — Cleancut and strong, overall size in proportion to the body. *Skull* — Top flattened rather than rounded, the width approximately the same as the length but no wider. *Stop* — Moderate. *Muzzle, Jaws, Lips* — Muzzle moderately pointed, avoiding any tendency to snipiness, and approximately equal in length to that of the topskull. The jaws are strong and powerful. The lips tight and black, with no pink showing on the outside. *Ears* — Triangular in shape, stiff, erect, and in proportion to the head in size. Base of the ear should not come below the center of the eye. *Eyes* — Brown, preferably dark brown, medium size, slightly almond shaped, not protruding. *Nose* — Black, without spots or discolored areas. *Teeth* — A full complement of strong, white teeth, evenly set and meeting in an even bite or a scissors bite, neither overshot nor undershot.

TORSO — *Neck* — Round and rather outstretched, tapered from head to body, well muscled, with tight skin. *Topline* — The withers are slightly higher and slope into the back which must be level, straight, and firm from withers to hip joints. The loin section, viewed from above, is relatively short, broad and strong, but blending smoothly into the back. The croup is medium long, sloping gradually. *Tail* — Strong at the base, bone to reach hock. At rest it is held low, the tip bent back level with the hock. In action it is raised with a curl, which is strongest towards the tip, without forming a hook. *Chest* — Not broad, but deep. The lowest point reaches the elbow, forming a smooth ascendant curve to the abdomen, which is moderately developed, neither tucked-up nor paunchy.

FOREQUARTERS — SHOULDER — Long and oblique, laid flat against the body, forming a sharp angle (approximately 90 degrees) with the upper arm.

LEGS — Straight, strong, and parallel to each other. Bone oval rather than round. Length and substance well proportioned to the size of the dog. *Pastern* — Medium length, strong and very slightly sloped. Dewclaws may be removed. *Feet* — Round (cat-footed), toes curved close together, well padded. Nails strong and black except that they may be white to match white toe tips.

HINDQUARTERS — THIGHS — Broad and heavily muscled. The upper and lower thigh bones approximately parallel the shoulder blade and upper arm respectively, forming a relatively sharp angle at stifle joint. *Legs* — Length and substance well proportioned to the size of the dog. Bone oval rather than round. Legs are parallel to each other. The angle at the hock is relatively sharp, although the Belgian Malinois does not have extreme angulation. Metatarsus medium length, strong, and slightly sloped. Dewclaws, if any, should be removed. *Feet* — Slightly elongated, toes curved close together, well padded. Nails strong and black except that they may be white to match white toe tips.

GAIT — Smooth, free and easy, seemingly never tiring, exhibiting facility of movement rather than a hard driving action. The dog tends to single track at a fast gait, the legs, both front and rear, converging toward the center line of gravity of the dog, while the backline remains firm and level, parallel

[continued on page 159]

APPEARANCE: Well-balanced, squarely built, elegant; well-muscled, active, agile, alert; carriage of head and neck, proud; gait smooth, untiring. Substance: Bone structure moderately heavy, neither spindly, leggy nor bulky. Side view of topline, forelegs and hind legs approx. square

SIZE: Dogs 24 - 26"; females 22 - 24"

DISQUALIFICATIONS: Ears hanging; cropped or stump tail; dogs over 27½" or under 22½"; females over 25½" or under 20½"

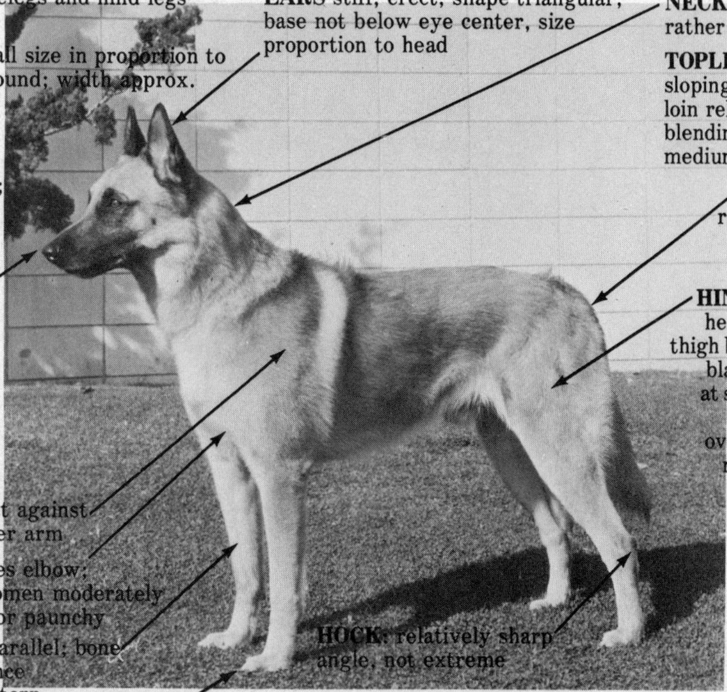

HEAD strong, clean-cut; over-all size in proportion to body; skull top flattened, not round; width approx. same as length, no wider

MUZZLE moderately pointed, not snipey; approx. length as topskull; jaws strong, powerful; lips tight, black, no pink showing outside; teeth strong, white; even or scissor bite; full complement; not over or undershot

NOSE black; no spots or discolored areas

STOP moderate

EYES brown, dark preferred; size medium; slightly almond-shaped, not protruding

SHOULDERS long, oblique, flat against body; approx. 90° angle to upper arm

CHEST deep, not broad; reaches elbow; smooth curve to abdomen; abdomen moderately developed, neither tucked-up nor paunchy

FORELEGS straight, strong, parallel; bone oval, not round; length, substance proportioned to size of dog; pastern strong, slightly sloped, length medium; dewclaws may be removed

FEET round, catlike; toes curve close together; well-padded; nails strong, black (or white to match toe tips)

EARS stiff, erect; shape triangular; base not below eye center, size proportion to head

HOCK: relatively sharp angle, not extreme

HIND FEET slightly elongated; toes curve close together; well padded; nails strong, black (or white to match toe tips); dewclaws, if any, should be removed

NECK well-muscled, tapered, round, rather outstretched; skin tight

TOPLINE: Withers slightly higher, sloping to level, straight, firm back; loin relatively short, broad, strong, blending smoothly into back; croup medium long, sloping gradually

TAIL: Strong at base; bone to reach hock; at rest, held low, tip bent level with hock; raised in action with curl but no hook

HINDQUARTERS: Thighs broad, heavily muscled; upper and lower thigh bones approx. parallel shoulder blade and upper arm; sharp angle at stifle joint; length, substance in proportion to size of dog; bone oval not round; mtatarsus length, medium strong, slightly sloped; legs parallel, dewclaws, if any, should be removed

COAT comparatively short, straight; undercoat dense; hair shorter on head, ears, lower legs, longer on thighs, neck, tail; forms collarete around neck

COLOR: Rich fawn to mahogany; black overlay; black mask, ears, underparts of body, tail, breeches, lighter; white spot on chest, white toe tips permitted

THE BOUVIER DES FLANDRES is a rough-coated dog of notably rugged appearance as befitting an erstwhile cattle driver and farmers' helper of Flandres, and later an ambulance dog and messenger in World War I. He is a compact-bodied, powerfully built dog of upstanding carriage and alert, intelligent expression.

HEAD—The head is medium long, with the skull slightly longer than the muzzle. *Skull*—Almost flat on top, moderately wide between the ears, and sloping slightly toward the muzzle. The brow is noticeably arched over the eyes. The stop is shallow, and the under-eye fill-in good. *Ears*—Rough-coated, set high on the head and cropped to a triangular contour. They stand erect and are carried straight up. *Eyes*—Neither protruding nor sunken, the eyes are set a trifle obliquely in the skull and not too far apart. They are of medium size and very nearly oval. Preferred color, a dark nut-brown. Black eyes, although not considered faulty, are less desirable as contributing to a somber expression. Light-colored eyes, and staring or wild expression are faulty. *Muzzle*—Wide, deep and well filled out, the width narrowing toward the tip of the nose. Cheeks are clean or flat-sided, the jaws powerful, and the lips dry and tight-fitting. A narrow muzzle, suggestive of weakness, is faulty. *Teeth* — Strong and white, with the canines set well apart, the teeth meet in a scissors bite. *Nose*—Black and well developed, the nostrils wide open. Across the top the contour is a trifle rounded as opposed to flat. Brown, pink and spotted noses are faulty.

NECK AND SHOULDERS — The neck is well rounded, slightly arched, and carried almost upright, its thickness gradually increasing as it fits gracefully into the shoulders. Clean and dry at the throat. The shoulders are long and sloping.

BODY—The brisket is deep, extending down at least to the point of the elbows, and of moderate width. *Back*—Short, strong and straight. *Loins*—Short, taut, and slightly arched in topline, while the rump is broad and square rather than sloping. Ribs are deep and well sprung. As advantageous for breeding purposes, slightly greater length of loin is permissible in bitches.

TAIL—Set high, carried up, and docked to about 4 inches.

LEGS AND FEET — The leg bones, although only moderate in girth, are made to appear heavy because of their covering with thick, rough hair. *Forelegs*—Straight as viewed from the front or side, with elbows turned neither in nor out. *Hind Legs*—Hindquarters are firm and well muscled, with large, powerful hams. Legs are strong and sturdy with hocks well let down and wide apart. They are slightly angulated at stifle and hock joints. Viewed from the back, they are absolutely parallel. *Feet*—Round, compact, with toes arched and close. The nails are black, the pads thick and tough.

COAT—Rough, touseled and unkempt in appearance, the coat is capable of withstanding the hardest work in the most inclement weather. *Topcoat*—Harsh, rough and wiry, and so thick that when separated by the hand the skin is hardly visible. *Undercoat*—Fine and soft in texture, and thicker in winter. On the skull the hair is shorter and almost smooth. On the brows it is longer, thus forming eyebrows. Longer growth on muzzle and underjaw from mustache and beard. On the legs it is thick and rough, on the feet rather short. Soft, silky or woolly topcoats are faulty. *Color*—From fawn to black; pepper and salt, gray and brindle. A white star on the chest is allowed. Chocolate brown with white spots is faulty.

HEIGHT — Dogs from 23½ to 27½ inches; bitches, a minimum of 22¾ inches.

SCALE OF POINTS

Coat	20
Head [eyes, ears, skull, foreface]	20
Shoulders and style	10
Hindquarters [hams and legs]	10
Back, loan, brisket, belly	15
Feet and legs	10
Symmetry, size and character	15
Total	100

Approved April 14, 1959

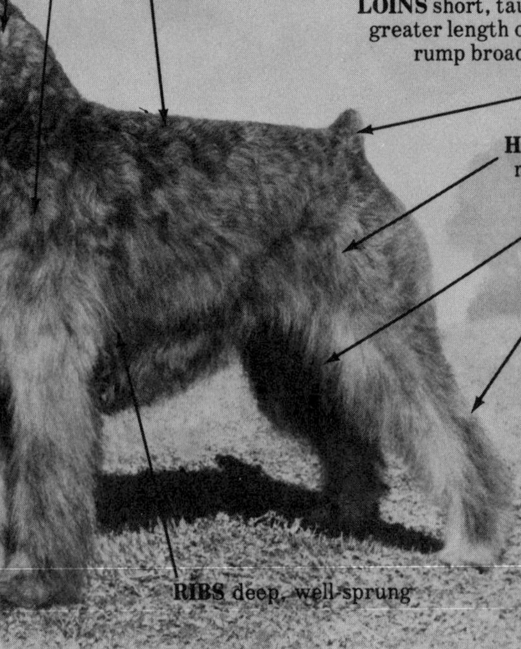
HEAD medium long; skull slightly longer than muzzle
SKULL almost flat on top; moderately wide between ears, sloping slightly toward muzzle; brow noticeably arched over eyes; under-eye fill-in good
TEETH strong, white; canines set well apart; scissors bite
EARS set high; cropped to triangular contour; carred erect; rough-coated
STOP shallow
NECK well-rounded, slightly arched, carried almost upright; thickness gradually increasing to fit gracefully into shoulders
EYES neither protruding nor sunken; set trifle obliquely, not too far apart; size medium; almost oval; dark, nut-brown color preferred; black less desirable; light eyes a fault
SHOULDERS long, sloping
BACK short, strong, straight
NOSE black, well-developed; nostrils wide open; top contour trifle rounded
LOINS short, taut, slightly arched in topline; greater length of loin permissible in bitches; rump broad, square rather than sloping
TAIL set high, carried up; docked to about 4"
MUZZLE wide, deep, well-filled-out; width narrows toward tip of nose; cheeks clean or flat-sided; jaws powerful; lips dry, tight-fitting
HINDQUARTERS firm, well-muscled with large, powerful hams; legs strong, sturdy
THROAT clean, dry
STIFLE slightly angulated
BRISKET deep, extending at least to point of elbows; of moderate width
HOCKS well-let-down; wide apart; slightly angulated; parallel viewed from rear
FORELEGS straight viewed from front or side; elbows turned neither in nor out; bones moderate in girth (appear heavier because of hair)
FEET round, compact; toes arched, close; nails black; pads thick, tough
COAT rough, touseled; outercoat harsh, rough, wiry, very thick; undercoat fine, soft texture, thicker in winter; skull hair short, almost smooth; hair longer on brows; longer hair forms mustache and beard; leg hair thick, rough; on feet, short
SIZE: Height, dogs 23½" to 27½"; bitches a minimum of 22¾"
COLOR: Fawn to black; pepper and salt; gray and brindle; white star on chest allowed
RIBS deep, well-sprung

GENERAL APPEARANCE — A strong and substantially built dog, fitted for field work, lithe, muscular, and well proportioned, alert and active. *Size*—Height at shoulders: Dogs, 23 to 27 inches; bitches, 22 to 25½ inches. Young dogs may be below the minimum.

HEAD—Large and rather long. Stop well marked and placed at equal distance from top of head and tip of nose. Forehead very slightly rounded. Line from stop to tip of nose straight. Teeth strong, white, and meeting exactly even. Muzzle neither narrow nor pointed. Nose rather square than rounded, always black. Hair heavy and long on top of head, the ears, and around the muzzle forming eyebrows standing out and not veiling the eyes too much. Eyes horizontal, well opened, dark in color and rather large; intelligent and gentle in expression. *Ears*—Placed high, alert, may be cropped or left natural. If cropped the ears are carried erect; if uncut they should not be too large or carried too flat. There shall be preference shown to either cropped or uncropped ears.

CONFORMATION — Neck muscular and distinct from the shoulders. Chest broad and deep. Back straight. Rump slightly sloped. Legs muscular with heavy bones. Hock not too near the ground, making a well-marked angle, the leg below the hock being not quite vertical. *Tail*—Uncut, well feathered, forming a crook at the end, carried low and twisted neither to right nor left. The length of the tail should equal the distance from the root of the tail to the point of the hock. *Feet*—Strong, round, with toes close together and hard pads; nails black.

COAT — Long, slightly wavy, stiff and strong. *Color*—All solid colors are allowed except white. Dark colors are preferable. Usual colors: black, and black with some white hairs, dark and light gray, tawny, and combinations of two of these colors, provided there are no marked spots and the transition from one to the other takes place gradually and symmetrically.

DEWCLAWS — Two dewclaws on each hind leg are required. A dog with only one cannot be given a prize.

FAULTS—Muzzle pointed. Eyes small, almond-shaped or light in color. Rump straight or too sloped. White spot on the breast (a large white spot is very bad). Tail too short or carried over the back. White nails.

DISQUALIFICATIONS

Size below the limit. Absence of dewclaws. Short hair on the head, face or feet. Tail lacking or cut. Nose light in color or spotted. Eyes spotted. Hair curled. White hair on feet. Spotted colors of the coat.

Approved March 12, 1963

HEAD large; rather long. Sop well-marked; equal distance from top of head to nose tip. Forehead slightly rounded
APPEARANCE: Strong, substantially built; lithe, muscular, well-proportioned; alert, active
EYES horizontal; dark, rather large; well-opened; intelligent, expressive
EARS placed high; alert; no preference between cropped or natural (carried erect if cropped, not too large or carried too flat if uncut)
NECK muscular; distinct from shoulders
RUMP slightly sloped
BACK straight
NOSE rather square, black; line from stop to tip of nose straight
TAIL uncut, well-feathered; carried low; twisted neither to right nor left; length should equal distance from tail root to point of hock
MUZZLE: Neither narrow nor pointed. Teeth strong, white; meeting exactly even
HOCK not too near ground; well-marked angle; leg not quite vertical below; two dewclaws required on each hind leg
CHEST broad; deep
LEGS muscular; bone heavy
COLOR: All solid colors except white; dark colors preferred. Usual: Black; black with some white hairs; dark and light gray; tawny; combinations of any two colors (without marked spots and transition ween gradual, symme cal)
FEET strong, round; toes close together; pads hard; nails black
DISQUALIFICATIONS: Size below limit; only one or absence of dewclaws; short hair on head, face, feet; tail lacking or cut; nose light in color or spotted; eyes spotted; hair curled; white hair on feet; spotted coat colors
COAT slightly wavy; long; stiff, strong. Hair heavy, long on top of head, ears; around muzzle forming stand-out eyebrows not veiling eyes too much
SIZE: Mature height at shoulders, males, 23 to 27", females, 22 to 25½

GREAT PYRENEES STANDARD

GENERAL APPEARANCE — A dog of immense size, great majesty, keen intelligence, and kindly expression; of unsurpassed beauty and a certain elegance, all white or principally white with markings of badger, gray, or varying shades of tan. In the rolling, ambling gait it shows unmistakably the purpose for which it has been bred, the strenuous work of guarding the flocks in all kinds of weather on the steep mountain slopes of the Pyrenees. Hence soundness is of the greatest importance and absolutely necessary for the proper fulfillment of his centuries' old task.

SIZE — The average height at the shoulder is 27 inches to 32 inches for dogs, and 25 inches to 29 inches for bitches. The average length from shoulder blades to root of tail should be the same as the height in any given specimen. The average girth is 36 inches to 42 inches for dogs and 32 inches to 36 inches for bitches. The weight for dogs runs 100 to 125 pounds and 90 to 115 pounds for bitches. A dog heavily boned; with close cupped feet; double dewclaws behind and single dewclaws in front.

HEAD — Large and wedge-shaped, measuring 10 inches to 11 inches from dome to point of nose, with rounding crown, furrow only slightly developed and with no apparent stop. *Cheeks* — Flat. *Ears* — V-shaped, but rounded at the tips, carried low and close to the head except when raised at attention. *Eyes* — Of medium size set slightly obliquely, dark rich brown in color with close eyelids, well pigmented. *Lips* — Close-fitting, edged with black. *Dewlaps* — Developed but little. The head is in brief that of a brown bear, but with the ears falling down. *Neck* — Short, stout and strongly muscular.

BODY — Well-placed shoulders set obliquely, close to the body. *Back and Loin* — Well coupled, straight and broad. *Haunches* — Fairly prominent. *Rump* — Sloping slightly. *Ribs* — Flat-sided. *Chest* — Deep. *Tail* — Of sufficient length to hang below the hocks, well plumed, carried low in repose, and curled high over the back, "making the wheel" when alert.

COAT — Created to withstand severe weather, with heavy fine white undercoat and long flat thick outer coat of coarser hair, straight or slightly undulating.

QUALITIES — In addition to his original age-old position in the scheme of pastoral life as protector of the shepherd and his flock, the Great Pyrenees has been used for centuries as a guard and watchdog on the large estates of his native France, and for this he has proven ideal. He is as serious in play as he is in work, adapting and molding himself to the moods, desires and even the very life of his human companions, through fair weather and foul, through leisure hours and hours fraught with danger, responsibility and extreme exertion; he is the exemplification of gentleness and docility with those he knows, of faithfulness and devotion for his master even to the point of self-sacrifice; and of courage in the protection of the flock placed in his care and of the ones he loves.

SCALE OF POINTS

Head		
Shape of Skull	5	
Ears	5	
Eyes	5	
Muzzle	5	
Teeth	5	25
General Conformation		
Neck	5	
Chest	5	
Back	5	
Loins	5	
Feet	5	25
Coat		10
Size and Soundness		25
Expression and General Appearance		15
Total		100

Approved February 13, 1935

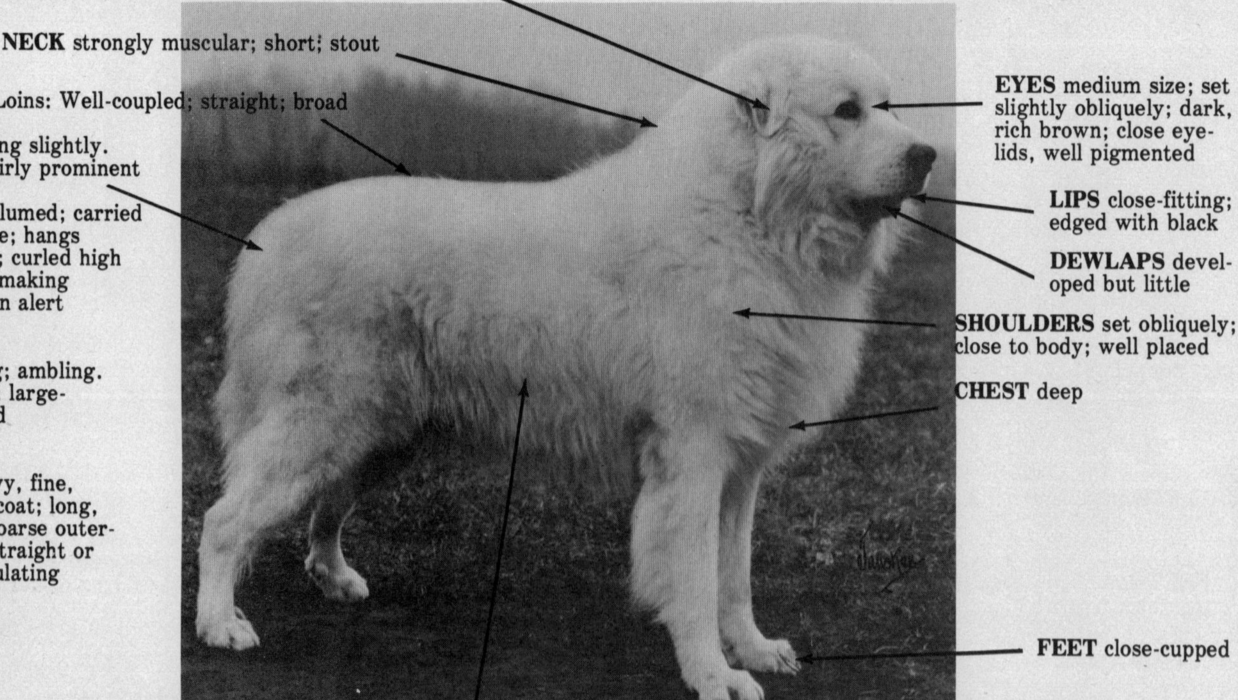
APPEARANCE: Immense size; majestic, elegant; keenly intelligent; kindly; sound; heavily-boned
EARS V-shaped; tips rounded; medium size; set parallel with eyes; carried low, close to head
NECK strongly muscular; short; stout
BACK and Loins: Well-coupled; straight; broad
RUMP sloping slightly. Haunches fairly prominent
TAIL well-plumed; carried low in repose; hangs below hocks; curled high over back ("making wheel") when alert
GAIT rolling; ambling. Legs strong; large-boned; sound
COAT: Heavy, fine, white undercoat; long, flat, thick, coarse outer-coat—hair straight or slightly undulating
COLORS: All white; principally white with badger, varying tan-shades or gray markings
RIBS flat-sided
HEAD large, wedge-shaped; resembling brown bear with ears hanging; measuring 10"-11" from dome to point of nose; rounding crown; no apparent stop. Cheeks flat
EYES medium size; set slightly obliquely; dark, rich brown; close eyelids, well pigmented
LIPS close-fitting; edged with black
DEWLAPS developed but little
SHOULDERS set obliquely; close to body; well placed
CHEST deep
FEET close-cupped
SIZE huge: Height, males, 27"-32"; females, 25" to 29". Average length from shoulder blades to tail root the same as height. Girth, males, 36"-42"; females, 32"-36" Weight, males, 100-125 lbs; females, 90-115 lbs

[Belgian Malinois cont'd. from p. 155]

to the line of motion with no crabbing. The Belgian Malinois shows a marked tendency to move in a circle rather than a straight line.

FAULTS — Any deviation from these specifications is a fault, the degree to which a dog is penalized depending on the extent to which the dog deviates from the standard and the extent to which the particular fault would actually affect the working ability of the dog.

DISQUALIFICATION

Ears hanging, as on a hound. Tail — cropped or stump. Males under 22½ or over 27½ inches in height. Females under 20½ or over 25½ inches in height.

Approved April 13, 1965

[Boxer cont'd. from p. 113]

to increasing speed, then the legs come in under the body but should never cross. The line from the shoulder down through the leg should remain straight, although not necessarily perpendicular to the ground. Viewed from the rear, a Boxer's breech should not roll. The hind feet should "dig in" and track relatively true with the front. Again, as speed increases, the normally broad rear track will become narrower.

Faults: Stilted or inefficient gait, pounding, paddling or flailing out of front legs, rolling or waddling gait, tottering hock joints, crossing over or interference—front or rear, lack of smoothness.

HEIGHT—Adult males—22½ to 25 inches; females—21 to 23½ inches at the withers. Males should not go under the minimum nor females over the maximum.

COAT — Short, shiny, lying smooth and tight to the body.

COLOR—The colors are fawn and brindle. Fawn in various shades from light tan to dark deer red or mahogany, the deeper colors preferred. The brindle variety should have clearly-defined black stripes on fawn background. White markings on fawn or brindle dogs are not to be rejected and are often very attractive, but must be limited to one-third of the ground color and are not desirable on the back of the torso proper. On the face, white may replace a part or all of the otherwise essential black mask. However, these white markings should be of such distribution as to enhance and not detract from the true Boxer expression.

CHARACTER AND TEMPERAMENT — These are of paramount importance in the Boxer. Instinctively a "hearing" guard dog, his bearing is alert, dignified and self-assured even at rest. In the show ring, his behavior should exhibit constrained animation. With family and friends, his temperament is fundamentally playful, yet patient and stoical with children. Deliberate and wary with strangers, he will exhibit curiosity but, most importantly, fearless courage and tenacity if threatened. However, he responds promptly to friendly overtures when honestly rendered. His intelligence, loyal affection and tractability to discipline make him a highly desirable companion.

Faults: Lack of dignity and alertness, shyness, cowardice, treachery and viciousness (belligerency toward other dogs should not be considred viciousness.)

DISQUALIFICATIONS

Boxers with white or black ground color, or entirely white or black, or any color other than fawn or brindle. [White markings, when present, must not exceed one-third of the ground color.]

Approved January, 1968

[Collies cont'd. from p. 117]

markings usually on the chest, neck, legs, feet and the tip of the tail. A blaze may appear on the foreface or backskull or both. The tri-color is predominantly black, carrying white markings as in a sable and white and has tan shadings on and about the head and legs. The blue merle is a mottled or "marbled" color, predominantly blue-gray and black with white markings as in the sable and white and usually has tan shadings as in the tri-color. The white is predominantly white, preferably with sable or tri-color markings. Blue merle coloring is undesirable in whites.

SIZE — Dogs are from 24 to 26 inches at the shoulder and weight from 60 to 75 pounds. Bitches are from 22 to 24 inches at the shoulder, weighing from 50 to 65 pounds. *An undersize or an oversize Collie is penalized according to the extent to which the dog appears to be undersize or oversize.*

EXPRESSION — Expression is one of the most important points in considering the relative value of Collies. *Expression,* like the term "character" is difficult to define in words. It is not a fixed point as in color, weight or height and it is something the uninitiated can properly understand only by optical illustration. In general, however, it may be said to be the combined product of the shape and balance of the skull and muzzle, the placement, size, shape and color of the eye and the position, size and carriage of the ears. An expression that shows sullenness or which is suggestive of any other breed is entirely foreign. The Collie cannot be judged properly until its expression has been carefully evaluated.

Smooth

The Smooth Variety of Collie is judged by the same Standard as the Rough Variety, except that the references to the quantity and the distribution of the coat are not applicable to the Smooth Variety, which has a hard, dense, smooth coat.

Approved March 10, 1959

[German Shepherd cont'd. from p. 121]

forward. Reaching far under, and passing the imprint left by the front foot, the hind foot takes hold of the ground; then hock, stifle and upper thigh come into play and sweep back, the stroke of the hind leg finishing with the foot still close to the ground in a smooth followthrough. The over-reach of the hindquarter usually necessitates one hind foot passing outside and the other hind foot passing inside the track of the forefeet, and such action is not faulty unless the locomotion is crab-wise with the dog's body sideways out of the normal straight line. *Transmission* — The typical smooth, flowing gait is maintained with great strength and firmness of back. The whole effort of the hindquarter is transmitted to the forequarter through the loin, back and withers. At full trot, the back must remain firm and level without sway, roll, whip or roach. Unlevel topline with withers lower than the hip is a fault. To compensate for the forward motion imparted by the hindquarters, the shoulder should open to its full extent. The forelegs should reach out close to the ground in a long stride in harmony with that of the hindquarters. The dog does not track on widely separated parallel lines, but brings the feet inward toward the middle line of the body when trotting in order to maintain balance. The feet track closely but do not strike nor cross over. Viewed from the front, the front legs function from the shoulder joint to the pad in a straight line. Viewed from the rear, the hind legs function from the hip joint to the pad in a straight line. Faults of gait, whether from front, rear or side, are to be considered very serious faults.

COLOR — The German Shepherd Dog varies in color, and most colors are permissible. Strong rich colors are preferred. Nose black. Pale, washed-out colors and blues and livers are serious faults. A white dog or a dog with a nose that is not predominantly black, must be disqualified.

COAT — The ideal dog has a double coat of medium length. The outer coat should be as dense as possible, hair straight, harsh and lying close to the body. A slightly wavy outer coat, often of wiry texture, is permissible. The head, including the inner ear and foreface, and the legs and paws are covered with short hair, and the neck with longer and thicker hair. The rear of the forelegs and hind legs has somewhat longer hair extending to the pastern and hock, respectively. Faults in coat include soft, silky, too long outer coat, woolly, curly, and open coat.

Approved April 9, 1968

[Great Dane cont'd. from p. 125]

straight to the pastern joints. Seen from the front, the forelegs and the pastern roots should form perpendicular lines to the ground. Seen from the side, the pastern root should slope only very slightly forward. *Faults:* Elbows turned toward the inside or toward the outside, the former position caused mostly by too narrow or too shallow a chest, bringing the front legs too closely together and at the same time turning the entire lower part of the leg outward; the latter position causes the front legs to spread too far apart, with the pastern roots and paws usually turned inwards. Seen from the side, a considerable bend in the pastern toward the front indicates weakness and is in most cases connected with stretched and spread toes (splay foot); seen from the side a forward bow in the forearm (chair leg); an excessively knotty bulge in the front of the pastern joint. *Paws* — Round and turned neither toward the inside nor toward the outside. Toes short, highly arched and well closed. Nails short, strong and as dark as possible. *Faults:* Spreading toes (splay foot), bent, long toes (rabbit paws); toes turned toward the outside or toward the inside; light-colored nails.

3. HEAD .... 20 points

(**a**) **Head Conformation** (12 points) — Long, narrow, distinguished, expressive, finely chiseled, especially the part below the eyes (which means that the skull plane under and to the inner point of the eye must slope without any bony protuberance in a pleasing line to the full square jaw), with strongly pronounced stop. The masculinity of the male is very pronounced in the expression and structure of head (this subtle difference should be evident in the dog's head through massive skull and depth of muzzle); the bitch's head may be more delicately formed. Seen from the side, the forehead must be sharply set off from the bridge of the nose. The forehead and the bridge of the nose must be straight and parallel to one another.

Seen from the front, the head should appear narrow, the bridge of the nose should be as broad as possible. The cheek muscles must show slightly but under no circumstances should they be too pronounced (cheeky). The muzzle part must have full flews and must be as blunt vertically as possible in front; the angles of the lip must be quite pronounced. The front part of the head, from the tip of the nose up to the center of the stop should be as long as the rear part of the head from the center of the stop to the only slightly developed occiput. The head should be angular from all sides and should have definite flat planes and its dimensions should be absolutely in proportion to the general appearance of the Dane. *Faults:* Any deviation from the parallel planes of skull and foreface; too small a stop; a poorly defined stop or none at all; too narrow a nose bridge; the rear of the head spreading laterally in a wedgelike manner (wedge head); an excessively round upper head (apple head); excessively pronounced cheek musculature; pointed muzzle; loose lips hanging over the lower jaw (fluttering lips) which create an illusion of a full deep muzzle. The head should be rather shorter and distinguished than long and expressionless.

(**b**) **Teeth** (4 points) — Strong, well developed and clean. The incisors of the lower jaw must touch very lightly the bottoms of the inner surface of the upper incisors (scissors bite). If the front teeth of both jaws bite on top of each other, they wear down too rapidly. *Faults:* Even bite; undershot and overshot; incisors out of line; black or brown teeth; missing teeth.

(**c**) **Eyes** (4 points) — Medium size, as dark as possible, with lively intelligent expression; almond-shaped eyelids, well-developed eyebrows. *Faults:* Light-colored, piercing, amber-colored, light blue to a watery blue, red or bleary eyes; eyes of different colors; eyes too far apart; Mongolian eyes; eyes with pronounced haws; eyes with excessively drooping lower eyelids. In blue and black Danes, lighter eyes are permitted but are not desirable. In harlequins, the eyes should be dark. Light colored eyes, two eyes of different color and walleyes are permitted but not desirable.

Nose (0 points) — The nose must be large and in the case of brindled and "single-colored" Danes, it must always be black. In harlequins, the nose should be black; a black spotted nose is permitted; a pink-colored nose is not desirable.

Ears (0 points) — Ears should be high, set not too far apart, medium in size of moderate thickness, drooping forward close to the cheek. Top line of folded ear should be about level with the skull. *Faults:* Hanging on the side, as on a Foxhound. Cropped ears; high set; not set too far apart, well pointed but always in proportion to the shape of the head and carried uniformly erect.

4. TORSO .... 20 points

(**a**) **Neck** (6 points) — The neck should be firm and clean, high-set, well arched, long, muscular and sinewy. From the chest to the head, it should be slightly tapering, beautifully formed, with well-developed nape. *Faults:* Short, heavy neck, pendulous throat folds (dewlaps).

(**b**) **Loin and Back** (6 points) — The withers forms the highest part of the back which slopes downward slightly toward the loins which are imperceptibly arched and strong. The back should be short and tensely set. The belly should be well shaped and tightly muscled, and, with the rear part of the thorax, should swing in a pleasing curve (tuck-up). *Faults:* Receding back; sway back; camel or roach back; a back line which is too high at the rear; an excessively long back; poor tuck-up.

(**c**) **Chest** (4 points) — Chest deals with that part of the thorax (rib cage) in front of the shoulders and front legs. The chest should be quite broad, deep and well muscled. *Faults:* A narrow and poorly muscled chest; strong protruding sternum (pigeon breast).

(**d**) **Ribs and Brisket** (4 points) — Deals with that part of the thorax back of the shoulders and front legs. Should be broad, with the ribs sprung well out from the spine and flattened at the side to allow proper movement of the shoulders extending down to the elbow joint. *Faults:* Narrow (slab-sided) rib cage; round (barrel) rib cage; shallow rib cage not reaching the elbow joint.

5. TAIL .... 2 points

Should start high and fairly broad, terminating slender and thin at the hock joint. At rest, the tail should fall straight. When excited or running, slightly curved (saberlike). *Faults:* A too high, or too low set tail (the tail set is governed by the slope of the croup); too long or too short a tail; tail bent too far over the back (ring tail); a tail which is curled; a twisted tail (sideways); a tail carried too high over the back (gay tail); a brush tail (hair too long on lower side). Cropping tails to desired length is forbidden.

FAULTS

Disqualification Faults: Deaf Danes. Danes under minimum height. White Danes without any black marks (albinos). Merles, a solid mouse-gray color or a mouse-gray base with black or white or both color spots or white base with mouse-gray spots. Harlequins and solid-colored Danes in which a large spot extends coatlike over the entire body so that only the legs, neck and the point of the tail are white. Brindle, fawn, blue and black Danes with white forehead line, white collars, high white stockings and white bellies. Danes with predominantly blue, gray, yellow, or also brindled spots. Docked tails. Split noses.

The faults below are important according to their grouping (very serious, serious, minor) and not according to their sequence as placed in each grouping:

Very serious: Lack of unity. Poor bone development. Poor musculature. Lightweight whippety Danes. Rickets. Timidity. Bitchy dog. Sway-back. Roach back. Cowhocks. Pitching gait. Short steps. Undershot teeth.

Serious: Out of condition. Coarseness. Any deviation from the standard on all coloration. Deviation from parallel planes of skull and foreface. Wedgehead. Poorly defined stop. Narrow nose bridge. Snipy muzzle. Any color but dark eyes in fawns and brindles. Mongolian eyes. Missing teeth. Overshot teeth. Heavy neck. Short neck. Dewlaps. Narrow chest. Narrow rib cage. Round rib cage. Shallow rib cage. Loose shoulders. Steep shoulders. Elbows turned inward. Chair legs (front). Knotty bulge in pastern joint (adult dog). Weak pastern roots. Receding back. Too long a back. Back high in rear. In harlequins, a pink nose. Poor tuck-up (except in bitches that have been bred). Too straight croup. Too sloping croup. Too narrow croup. Overangulation. Steep rear. Too long rear legs. Poorly muscled thighs. Barrel legs. Paws turned outward. Rabbit paws. Wolf's claw. Hackney gait.

Minor: Doggy bitches: Small white marks on chest and toes — blues, blacks, brindles and fawns. Few gray spots and pointings on Harlequins. In Harlequins, black-spotted nose. White-tipped tail except on Harlequins. Excessively long hair. Excessively dull hair. Apple head. Small stop. Fluttering lips. Eyes too far apart. Drooping lower eyelids. Haws. Any color but dark eyes in blacks, blues and harlequins. Discolored teeth. Even bite. Pigeon breast. Loaded shoulders. Elbows turned outward. Paws turned inward. Splay foot. Excessively long toenails. Light nails (except in harlequins). Low-set tail. Too long a tail. Too short a tail. Gay tail. Curled tail. Twisted tail. Brush tail.

DISQUALIFICATIONS

Danes under minimum height. White Danes without any black marks [*albinos*]. *Merles, a solid mouse-gray or a mouse-gray base with black or white or both color spots or white base with mouse-gray spots. Harlequins and solid-colored Danes in which a large spot extends coatlike over the entire body so that only the legs, neck and the point of the tail are white. Brindle, fawn, blue and black Danes with white forehead line, white collars, high white stockings and white bellies. Danes with predominantly blue, gray, yellow or also brindled spots. Docked tails. Split noses.*

Approved November 14, 1944

[*Shetland Sheepdog cont'd. from p. 145*]

straight, dependent upon correct angulation, musculation, and ligamentation of the entire hindquarter, thus allowing the dog to reach well under his body with his hind foot and propel himself forward. Reach of stride of the foreleg is dependent upon correct angulation, musculation and ligamentation of the forequarters, together with correct width of chest and construction of rib cage. The foot should be lifted only enough to clear the ground as the leg swings forward. Viewed from the front, both forelegs and hind legs should move forward almost perpendicular to ground at the walk, slanting a little inward at a slow trot, until at a swift trot the feet are brought so far inward toward center line of body that the tracks left show two parallel lines of footprints actually touching a center line at their inner edges. *There should be no crossing of the feet nor throwing of the weight from side to side. Faults:* Stiff, short steps, with a choppy, jerky movement. Mincing steps, with a hopping up and down, or a balancing of weight from side to side (often erroneously admired as a "dancing gait" but permissible in young puppies).

[*continued on page 232*]

GROUP 4

TERRIERS

AIREDALE TERRIER STANDARD

HEAD — Should be well balanced with little apparent difference between the length of skull and foreface. *Skull* should be long and flat, not too broad between the ears and narrowing very slightly to the eyes. Scalp should be free from wrinkles, stop hardly visible and cheeks level and free from fullness. *Ears* should be V-shaped with carriage rather to the side of the head, not pointing to the eyes, small but not out of proportion to the size of the dog. The topline of the folded ear should be above the level of the skull. *Foreface* should be deep, powerful, strong and muscular. Should be well filled up before the eyes. *Eyes* should be dark, small, not prominent, full of terrier expression, keenness and intelligence. *Lips* should be tight. *Nose* should be black and not too small. *Teeth* should be strong and white, free from discoloration or defect. Bite either level or vise-like. A slightly overlapping or scissors bite is permissible without preference.

NECK — Should be of moderate length and thickness gradually widening towards the shoulders. Skin tight, not loose. *Shoulders and Chest* — Shoulders long and sloping well into the back. Shoulder blades flat. From the front, chest deep but not broad. The depth of the chest should be approximately on a level with the elbows.

BODY — Back should be short, strong and level. Ribs well sprung. Loins muscular and of good width. There should be but little space between the last rib and the hip joint.

Hindquarters — Should be strong and muscular with no droop. *Tail* — The root of the tail should be set well up on the back. It should be carried gaily but not curled over the back. It should be of good strength and substance and of fair length.

LEGS — *Forelegs* should be perfectly straight, with plenty of muscle and bone. *Elbows* should be perpendicular to the body, working free of sides. *Thighs* should be long and powerful with muscular second thigh, stifles well bent, not turned either in or out, hocks well let down parallel with each other when viewed from behind. *Feet* should be small, round and compact with a good depth of pad, well cushioned; the toes moderately arched, not turned either in or out.

COAT — Should be hard, dense and wiry, lying straight and close, covering the dog well over the body and legs. Some of the hardest are crinkling or just slightly waved. At the base of the hard very stiff hair should be a shorter growth of softer hair termed the undercoat. *Color* — The head and ears should be tan, the ears being of a darker shade than the rest. Dark markings on either side of the skull are permissible. The legs up to the thighs and elbows and the under-part of the body and chest are also tan and the tan frequently runs into the shoulder. The sides and upper parts of the body should be black or dark grizzle. A red mixture is often found in the black and is not to be considered objectionable. A small white blaze on the chest is a characteristic of certain strains of the breed.

SIZE — Dogs should measure approximately 23 inches in height at the shoulder; bitches, slightly less. Both sexes should be sturdy, well muscled and boned.

MOVEMENT — Movement or action is the crucial test of conformation. Movement should be free. As seen from the front the forelegs should swing perpendicular from the body free from the sides, the feet the same distance apart as the elbows. As seen from the rear the hind legs should be parallel with each other, neither too close nor too far apart, but so placed as to give a strong well-balanced stance and movement. The toes should not be turned either in or out. Yellow eyes, hound ears, white feet, soft coat, being much over or under the size limit, being undershot or overshot, having poor movement, are faults which should be severely penalized.

SCALE OF POINTS

Head	10	Color	5
Neck, shoulders and chest	10	Size	10
Body	10	Movement	10
Hindquarters and tail	10	Gen. characteristics and expression	15
Legs and feet	10		
Coat	10	Total	100

Approved July 14, 1959

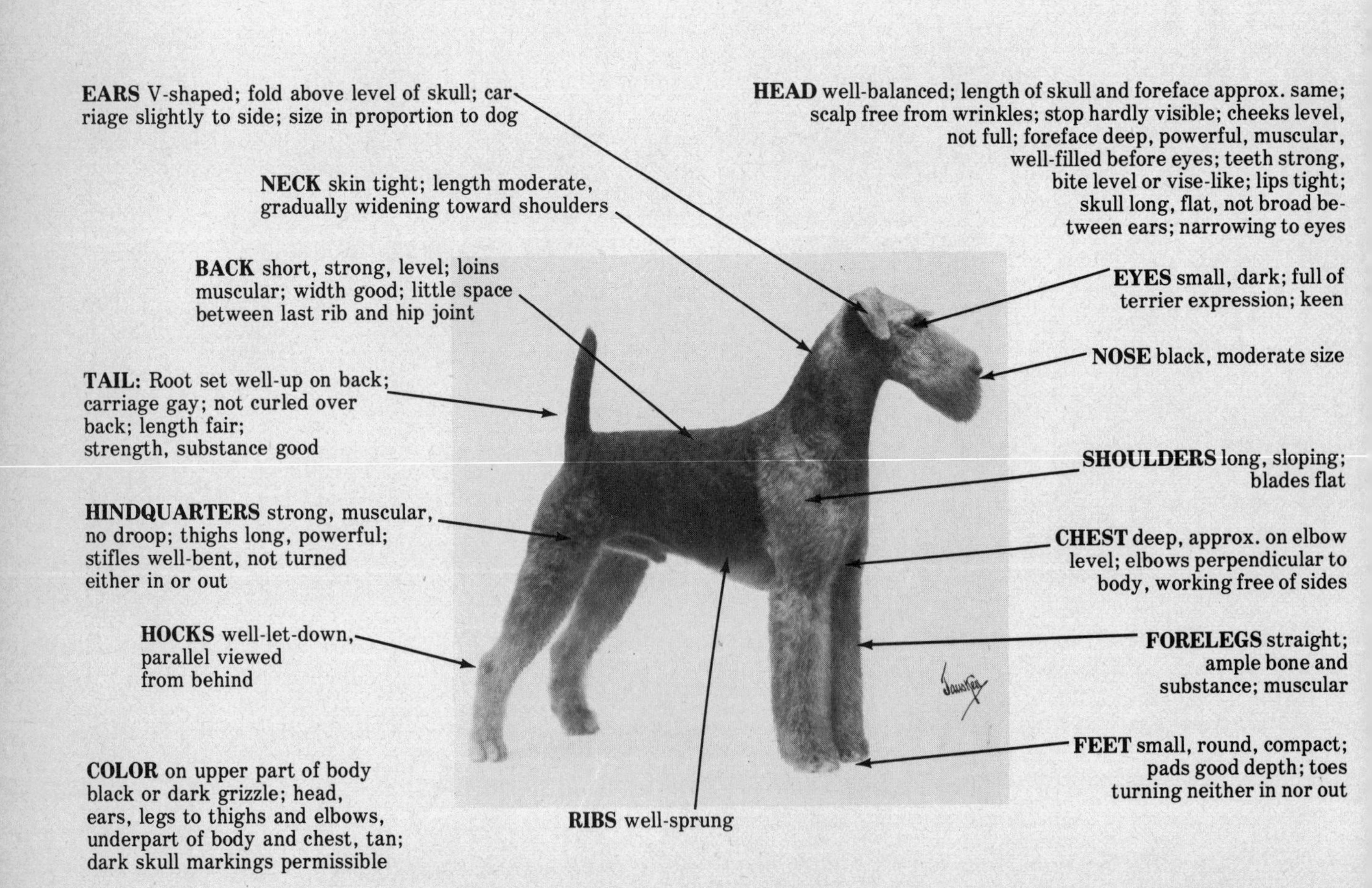
EARS V-shaped; fold above level of skull; carriage slightly to side; size in proportion to dog
HEAD well-balanced; length of skull and foreface approx. same; scalp free from wrinkles; stop hardly visible; cheeks level, not full; foreface deep, powerful, muscular, well-filled before eyes; teeth strong, bite level or vise-like; lips tight; skull long, flat, not broad between ears; narrowing to eyes
NECK skin tight; length moderate, gradually widening toward shoulders
BACK short, strong, level; loins muscular; width good; little space between last rib and hip joint
EYES small, dark; full of terrier expression; keen
NOSE black, moderate size
TAIL: Root set well-up on back; carriage gay; not curled over back; length fair; strength, substance good
SHOULDERS long, sloping; blades flat
HINDQUARTERS strong, muscular, no droop; thighs long, powerful; stifles well-bent, not turned either in or out
CHEST deep, approx. on elbow level; elbows perpendicular to body, working free of sides
HOCKS well-let-down, parallel viewed from behind
FORELEGS straight; ample bone and substance; muscular
FEET small, round, compact; pads good depth; toes turning neither in nor out
COLOR on upper part of body black or dark grizzle; head, ears, legs to thighs and elbows, underpart of body and chest, tan; dark skull markings permissible
RIBS well-sprung
COAT hard, dense, wiry; lying straight, close; slight wave permitted; undercoat short, soft
SIZE: Height, dogs approx. 23"; bitches slightly less

AM. CAN. CH. EDENS SPRING HEPATICA

PICTURED GOING B.O.W. AT THE MONTGOMERY COUNTY NATIONAL AIREDALE TERRIER SPEC. "SAL" FINISHED HIS CHAMPIONSHIP IN TWO WEEKENDS AND HAS SEVERAL GROUP PLACEMENTS TO HIS CREDIT.

ELIZABETH B. HOISINGTON
7524 RALEIGH LA GRANGE RD.
CORDORA, TENN. 38018

HANDLER
GUENTER BEHR
R.D. 1
MILFORD, N.J. 08848
(201) 996-2220

The Airedale Terrier originated as a working terrier of the Yorkshire district of England. The breed appears to have derived from several now-extinct country terriers crossed with Otter Hounds. Too large to go to ground (pursue prey into their underground burrows and there subdue them), Airedale Terriers are nevertheless highly valued for hunting otters and badgers as well as many smaller mammalian pests. The largest of the terriers, Airedales have a hard, dense, wiry coat which is black or dark grizzle on the back and sides and otherwise tan. Used for hunting in England, and as working dogs in Germany, Airedale Terriers have been continually popular as companions and show dogs in the United States. They rank among the most popular terriers, 39th among all breeds, accounting for about 7,000 registrations per year with the AKC. Relatively fewer appear in the show ring. Airedale Terriers rank only 5th among terriers in numbers in competition.

AUSTRALIAN TERRIER STANDARD

GENERAL APPEARANCE — A small sturdy, rough-coated terrier of spirited action and self-assured manner.

HEAD — Long, flat-skulled, and full between the eyes, with the stop moderate. The muzzle is no longer than the distance from the eyes to the occiput. Jaws long and powerful, teeth of good size meeting in a scissors bite, although a level bite is acceptable. Nose black. *Ears* set high on the skull and well apart. They are small and pricked, the leather either pointed or slightly rounded and free from long hairs. *Eyes* small, dark, and keen in expression; not prominent. Light-colored and protruding eyes are faulty.

NECK — Inclined to be long, and tapering into sloping shoulders; well furnished with hair which forms a protective ruff.

BODY — Low-set and slightly longer from the withers to the root of the tail than from the withers to the ground. *Chest* medium wide, and deep, with ribs well sprung but not round. Topline level. *Tail* set on high and carried erect but not too gay; docked leaving two-fifths. *Legs and Feet* — Forelegs straight and slightly feathered to the carpus or so-called knee; they are set well under the body with elbows close and pasterns strong. Hindquarters strong and well muscled but not heavy; legs moderately angulated at stifles and hocks, with hocks well let down. Bone medium in size. Feet are small, clean, and catlike, the toes arched and compact, nicely padded and free from long hair. Nails strong and black.

COAT — Outer coat harsh and straight, and about two and one half inches all over the body. Under coat short and soft. The topknot, which covers only the top of the skull, is of finer texture and lighter color than the body coat.

COLOR — "May be blue-black or silver-black, with rich tan markings on head and legs, sandy color or clear red. The blue-black is bluish at the roots and dark at the tips. In the silver-blacks each hair carries black and silver alternating with black at the tips. The tan is rich and deep, the richer the better. In the sandies, any suggestion of smuttiness is undersirable."

GAIT — Straight and true; sprightly, indicating spirit and assurance.

TEMPERAMENT — That of a hard-bitten terrier, with the aggressiveness of the natural ratter and hedge hunter, but as a companion friendly, affectionate, and biddable.

SIZE — Shoulder height, about 10 inches. Average weight 12 to 14 pounds.

Approved October 13, 1970

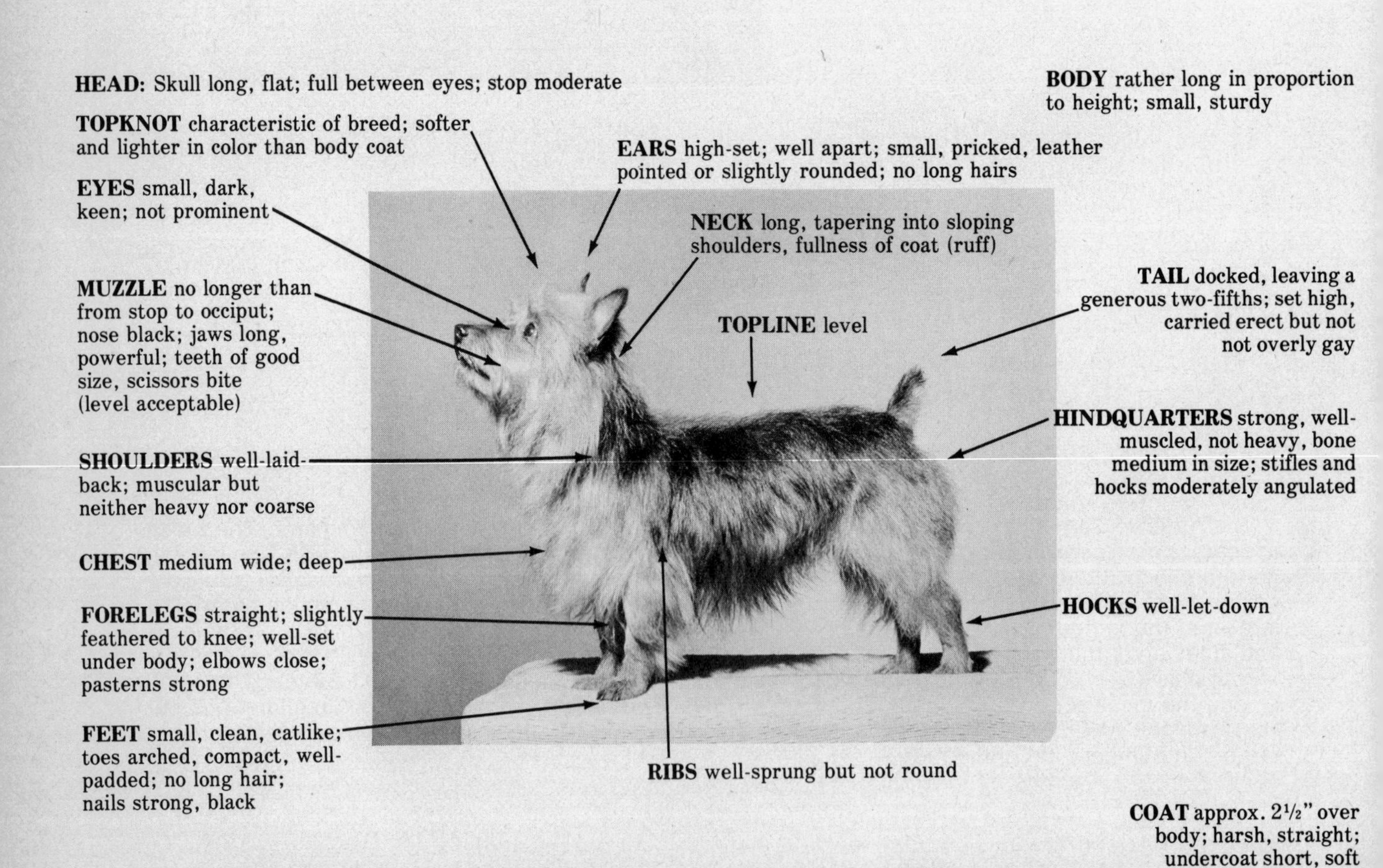

HEAD: Skull long, flat; full between eyes; stop moderate
BODY rather long in proportion to height; small, sturdy
TOPKNOT characteristic of breed; softer and lighter in color than body coat
EARS high-set; well apart; small, pricked, leather pointed or slightly rounded; no long hairs
EYES small, dark, keen; not prominent
NECK long, tapering into sloping shoulders, fullness of coat (ruff)
MUZZLE no longer than from stop to occiput; nose black; jaws long, powerful; teeth of good size, scissors bite (level acceptable)
TOPLINE level
TAIL docked, leaving a generous two-fifths; set high, carried erect but not not overly gay
SHOULDERS well-laid-back; muscular but neither heavy nor coarse
HINDQUARTERS strong, well-muscled, not heavy, bone medium in size; stifles and hocks moderately angulated
CHEST medium wide; deep
FORELEGS straight; slightly feathered to knee; well-set under body; elbows close; pasterns strong
HOCKS well-let-down
FEET small, clean, catlike; toes arched, compact, well-padded; no long hair; nails strong, black
RIBS well-sprung but not round
COAT approx. 2½" over body; harsh, straight; undercoat short, soft
COLOR blue-black, silver-black, with rich tan markings; red and sandy color
SIZE: Height approx. 10" at shoulder; weight approx. 12 to 14 lbs

AM. CAN. BDA. CH.
SEREN'S BRONWYN

AM. CAN. BDA. CH.
WILLELVA'S RAGAMUFFIN

SHOWN TAKING THEIR FOURTH BEST IN SHOW BRACE UNDER DISTINGUISHED TERRIER JUDGE MR. ROBERT GRAHAM. "WINNIE" AND "MUFFIN" ARE BOTH 3 COUNTRY CHAMPIONS. "MUFFIN" WAS THE "TOP AUSSIE" FEMALE IN THE COUNTRY IN 1972, OWNER HANDLED.

MRS. BARBARA A. ASHLEY
ASHBAR'S KENNELS
361 MOUNTAIN ROAD
WEST HARTFORD, CT.
(203) 521-8126

The Australian Terrier was developed over the last one hundred years in Australia from several small British breeds—Cairn, Yorkshire, Silky, Norwich, Irish, Scottish, and Dandy Dinmont Terriers. The result has been a distinctive, small, game, and hard-working breed. The coat is harsh, straight, and measures about 2½ inches on the body. The color may be sandy, red, or blue-black or silver-black with rich tan markings. The gait is straight, true, spirited, and assured. Average weight is 12 to 14 pounds. Admitted to AKC registry in 1960, the Australian Terrier has firmly established itself as a companion and a show dog in the U.S. About 12,000 are registered per year, the breed ranks 59th.

BORDER TERRIER STANDARD

SINCE THE Border Terrier is a working terrier of a size to go to ground and able, within reason, to follow a horse, his conformation should be such that he be ideally built to do his job. No deviations from this ideal conformation should be permitted, which would impair his usefulness in running his quarry to earth and in bolting it therefrom. For this work he must be alert, active and agile, and capable of squeezing through narrow apertures and rapidly traversing any kind of terrain. His head, "like that of an otter," is distinctive, and his temperament ideally exemplifies that of a Terrier. By hard as nails, "game as they come" and driv- obedient, and easily trained. In the field he is hard as nails, "Game as they come" and driving in attack. It should be the aim of Border Terrier breeders to avoid such over-emphasis of any point in the Standard as might lead to unbalanced exaggeration.

GENERAL APPEARANCE — He is an active terrier of medium bone, strongly put together, suggesting endurance and agility, but rather narrow in shoulder, body and quarter. The body is covered with a somewhat broken though close-fitting and intensely wiry jacket. The characteristic "otter" head with its keen eye, combined with a body poise which is "at the alert," gives a look of fearless and implacable determination characteristic of the breed. The proportions should be that the height at the withers is slightly greater than the distance from the withers to the tail, *i.e.*, by possibly 1-1½ inches in a 14-pound dog.

WEIGHT — Dogs, 13-15½ pounds, bitches, 11½-14 pounds, are appropriate weights for Border Terriers in hard-working condition.

HEAD — Similar to that of an otter. Moderately broad and flat in skull with plenty of width between the eyes and between the ears. A slight, moderately broad curve at the stop rather than a pronounced indentation. Cheeks slightly full. *Ears* — Small, V-shaped and of moderate thickness, dark preferred. Not set high on the head but somewhat on the side, and dropping forward close to the cheeks. They should not break above the level of the skull. *Eyes* — Dark hazel and full of fire and intelligence. Moderate in size, neither prominent nor small and beady. *Muzzle* — Short and "well filled." A dark muzzle is characteristic and desirable. A few short whiskers are natural to the breed. *Teeth* — Strong, with a scissors bite, large in proportion to size of dog. *Nose* — Black, and of a good size.

NECK — Clean, muscular and only long enough to give a well-balanced appearance. It should gradually widen into the shoulder.

SHOULDERS — Well laid back and of good length, the blades converging to the withers gradually from a brisket not excessively deep or narrow.

FORELEGS — Straight and not too heavy in bone and placed slightly wider than in a Fox Terrier. *Feet* — Small and compact. Toes should point forward and be moderately arched with thick pads.

BODY — Deep, fairly narrow and of sufficient length to avoid any suggestion of lack of range and agility. Deep ribs carried well back and not oversprung in view of the desired depth and narrowness of the body. The body should be capable of being spanned by a man's hands behind the shoulders. Back strong but laterally supple, with no suspicion of a dip behind the shoulder. Loin strong and the under line fairly straight. *Tail* — Moderately short, thick at the base, then tapering. Not set on too high. Carried gaily when at the alert, but not over the back. When at ease, a Border may drop his stern.

HINDQUARTERS — Muscular and racy, with thighs long and nicely molded. Stifles well bent and hocks well let down.

COAT — A short and dense undercoat covered with a very wiry and somewhat broken top coat which should lie closely, but it must not show any tendency to curl or wave. With such a coat a Border should be able to be exhibited almost in his natural state, nothing more in the way of trimming being needed than a tidying-up of the head, neck and feet. *Hide* — Very thick and loose fiiting.

MOVEMENT — Straight and rhythmical before and behind, with good length of stride and flexing of stifle and hock. The dog should respond to his handler with a gait which is free, agile and quick.

COLOR — Red, grizzle and tan, blue and tan, or wheaten. A small amount of white may be allowed on the chest but white on the feet should be penalized.

SCALE OF POINTS

Head, ears, neck and teeth	20
Legs and feet	15
Coat and skin	10
Shoulders and chest	10
Eyes and expression	10
Back and loin	10
Hindquarters	10
Tail	5
General appearance	10
Total	100

Approved March 14, 1950

BODY deep; sufficently long; fairly narrow; bone medium; of endurance, agility

TAIL moderately short, thick at base, tapering; set-on not too high; carriage gay but not over back

HIDE thick, loose fitting

HINDQUARTERS muscular, racy; thighs long, nicely moulded

HOCKS well-let-down; stifles well bent

FEET small, compact; toes pointing forward; moderately arched; pads thick

COAT short; dense undercoat; wiry close top coat; no tendency to curl or wave; no trimming, just "tidying-up"

SIZE: Height at withers greater than from withers to tail-set, (i. e. 1 to 1½" in 14-lb. dog); weight—males, 13 to 15½ lbs.; females, 11½ to 14 lbs.

EARS small, V-shaped, moderate thickness, dark; set somewhat on side, dropping forward close to cheeks; should not break above skull level

BACK strong, supple, no dip behind shoulder; loin strong

UNDERLINE fairly straight

RIBS well-back, deep; not over-sprung

HEAD otter-like, moderately broad; skull flat; width between ears and eyes

TEETH strong, scissors bite, large

STOP moderate, broad curve rather than marked indentation

EYES dark, moderate size; neither prominent nor small or beady; expressive

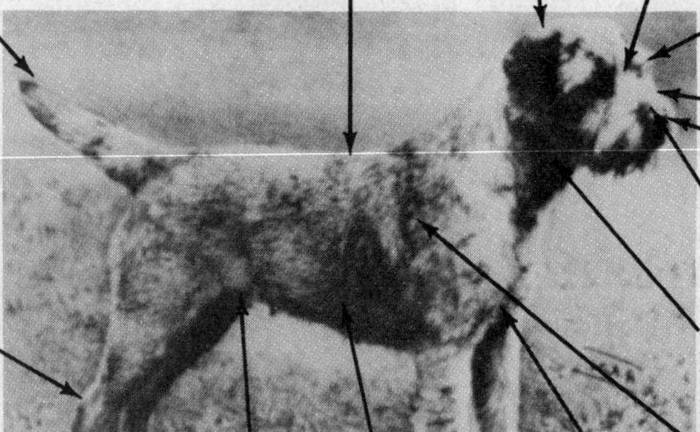

CHEEKS slightly full

MUZZLE short, well-filled, dark; slightly whiskered

NOSE good size, black

NECK clean, muscular, gradual widening to shoulders; not too long

SHOULDERS well-laid-back, good length, blades converging to withers

BRISKET not too deep or narrow

FORELEGS straight, not too heavy in bone; slightly wider than Fox Terrier

COLOR—Red; grizzle and tan; blue and tan; wheaten; small bit of white allowed on chest; white on feet penalized

CH. MONTY OF ESSENHIGH

BEST OF BREED AT THE BORDER TERRIER CLUB OF AMERICA SPECIALTY FROM THE CLASSES UNDER JUDGE MR. STANLEY DANGERFIELD. "MONTY" IS UNDEFEATED IN THE BREED.

OWNER
KATE J. SEEMANN
WILSON POINT
SOUTH NORWALK, CONN. 06854

AGENT/HANDLER
CLIFFORD HALLMARK
60 EAST MAIN STREET
MENDHAM, N.J. 07945
201—543-4842

The Border Terrier originated on the borders of the Cheviot Hills. This breed had the job of being the worker for sportsmen, farmers, and shepherds. Among the assets that this little dog possesses is his tireless hard-working attitude, weather-resisting coat, and climbing ability. He is a fearless hunter of the fox.

CAIRN TERRIER STANDARD

GENERAL APPEARANCE — That of an active, game, hardy, small working terrier of the short-legged class; very free in its movements, strongly but not heavily built, standing well forward on its forelegs, deep in the ribs, well coupled with strong hindquarters and presenting a well proportioned build with a medium length of back, having a hard, weather-resisting coat; head shorter and wider than any other terrier and well furnished with hair giving a general foxy expression.

SKULL — Broad in proportion to length with a decided stop and well furnished with hair on the top of the head, which may be somewhat softer than the body coat. *Muzzle* — Strong but not too long or heavy. Teeth large — mouth neither overshot nor undershot. Nose black. *Eyes* — Set wide apart, rather sunken, with shaggy eyebrows, medium in size, hazel or dark hazel in color, depending on body color, with a keen terrier expression. *Ears* — Small, pointed, well carried erectly, set wide apart on the side of the head. Free from long hairs.

TAIL — In proportion to head, well furnished with hair but not feathery. Carried gaily but must not curl over back. Set on at back level.

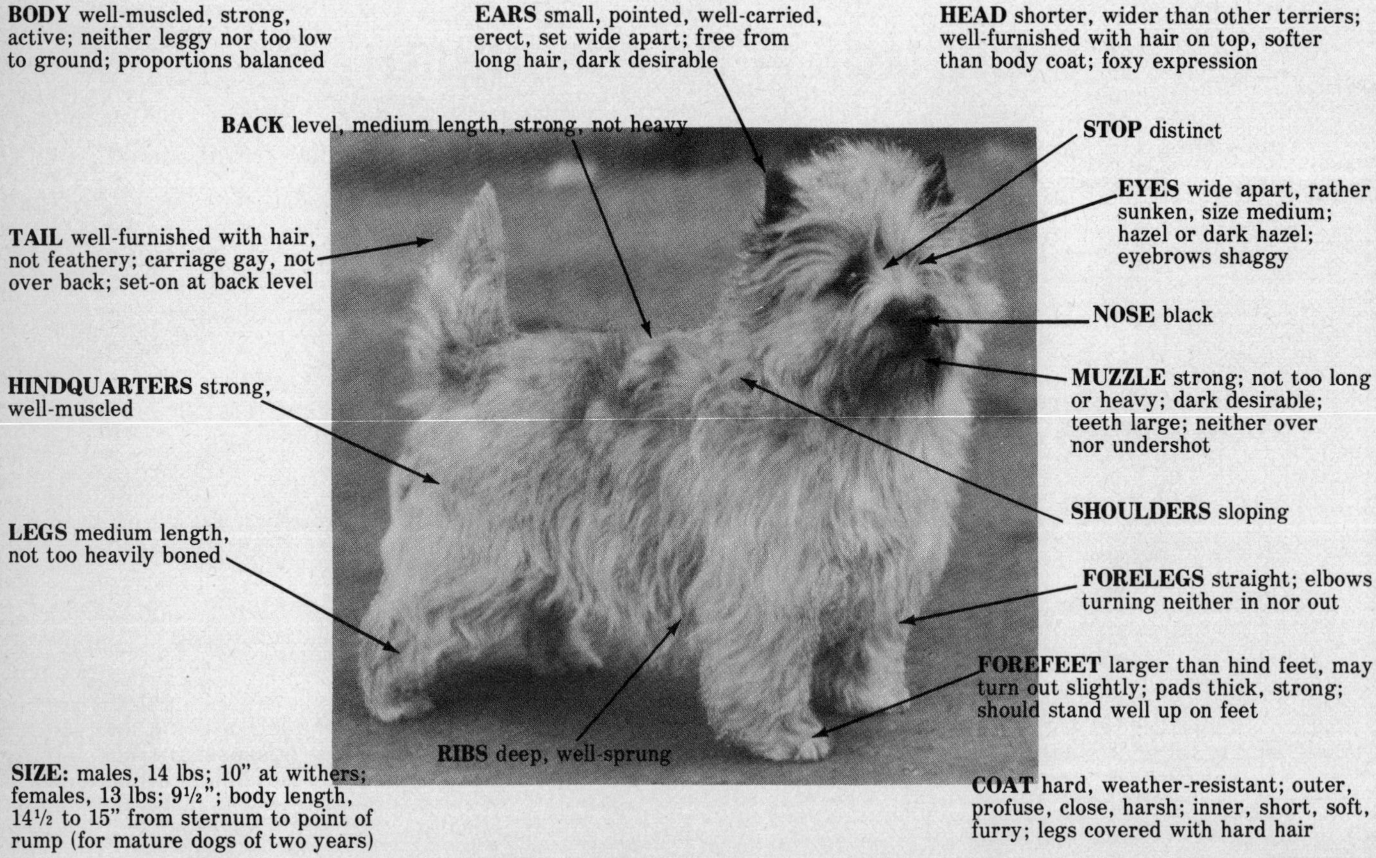

BODY — Well muscled, strong, active body with well-sprung, deep ribs, coupled to strong hindquarters, with a level back of medium length, giving an impression of strength and activity without heaviness. *Shoulders, Legs and Feet* — A sloping shoulder, medium length of leg, good but not too heavy bone; forelegs should not be out at elbows, and be perfectly straight, but forefeet may be slightly turned out. Forefeet larger than hind feet. Legs must be covered with hard hair. Pads should be thick and strong and dog should stand well up on its feet.

COAT — Hard and weather resistant. Must be double-coated with profuse harsh outer coat and short, soft, close furry undercoat. *Color* — May be of any color except white. Dark ears, muzzle and tail tip are desirable.

IDEAL SIZE — Involves the weight, the height at the withers and the length of body. Weight for bitches, 13 pounds, for dogs, 14 pounds. Height at the withers — bitches, 9½ inches, dogs, 10 inches. Length of body from 14¼ to 15 inches from the front of the chest to back of hindquarters. The dog must be of balanced proportions and appear neither leggy nor too low to ground; and neither too short nor too long in body. Weight and measurements are for matured dogs at two years of age. Older dogs may weigh slightly in excess and growing dogs may be under these weights and measurements.

CONDITION — Dogs should be shown in good hard flesh, well muscled and neither too fat or thin. Should be in full good coat with plenty of head furnishings, be clean, combed, brushed and tidied up on ears, tail, feet and general outline. Should move freely and easily on a loose lead, should not cringe on being handled, should stand up on their toes and show with marked terrier characteristics.

FAULTS

1. *Skull* — Too narrow in skull. 2. *Muzzle* — Too long and heavy a foreface; mouth overshot or undershot. 3. *Eyes* — Too large, prominent, yellow, and ringed are all objectionable. 4. *Ears* — Too large, round at points, set too close together, set too high on the head; heavily covered with hair. 5. *Legs and Feet* — Too light or too heavy bone. Crooked forelegs or out at elbow. Thin, ferrety feet; feet let down on the heel or too open and spread. Too high or too low on the leg. 6. *Body* — Too short back and compact a body, hampering quickness of movement and turning ability. Too long, weedy and snaky a body, giving an impression of weakness. Tail set on too low. Back not level. 7. *Coat* — Open coats, blousy coats, too short or dead coats, lack of sufficient undercoat, lack of hard hair on the legs. Silkiness or curliness. A slight wave permissible. 8. *Nose* — Flesh or light-colored nose. 9. *Color* — White on chest, feet or other parts of body.

Approved May 10, 1938

BODY well-muscled, strong, active; neither leggy nor too low to ground; proportions balanced
EARS small, pointed, well-carried, erect, set wide apart; free from long hair, dark desirable
HEAD shorter, wider than other terriers; well-furnished with hair on top, softer than body coat; foxy expression
BACK level, medium length, strong, not heavy
STOP distinct
EYES wide apart, rather sunken, size medium; hazel or dark hazel; eyebrows shaggy
TAIL well-furnished with hair, not feathery; carriage gay, not over back; set-on at back level
NOSE black
HINDQUARTERS strong, well-muscled
MUZZLE strong; not too long or heavy; dark desirable; teeth large; neither over nor undershot
SHOULDERS sloping
LEGS medium length, not too heavily boned
FORELEGS straight; elbows turning neither in nor out
FOREFEET larger than hind feet, may turn out slightly; pads thick, strong; should stand well up on feet
RIBS deep, well-sprung
SIZE: males, 14 lbs; 10" at withers; females, 13 lbs; 9½"; body length, 14½ to 15" from sternum to point of rump (for mature dogs of two years)
COAT hard, weather-resistant; outer, profuse, close, harsh; inner, short, soft, furry; legs covered with hard hair
COLOR: Any except white; dark ears, muzzle, tail tip desirable

CH. FOXGROVE SUSANELLA

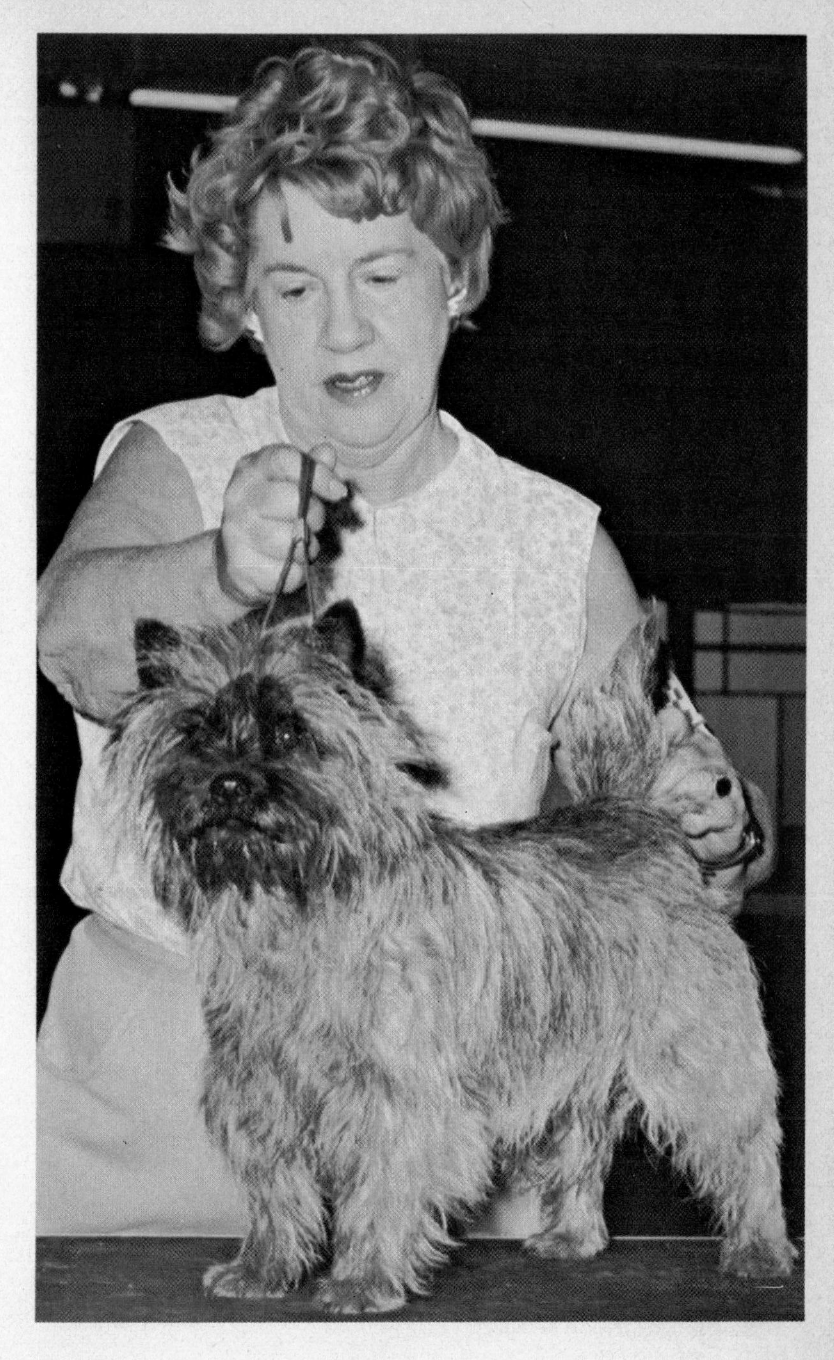

IMPORTED IN JUNE AFTER TOP WINS IN BRITAIN OF BEST CAIRN AT CRUFTS AND C.C. WINNER AT SOUTHERN CAIRN CLUB OPEN SHOW. NOW AN AMERICAN AND CANADIAN CHAMPION. SHE WAS BEST OF BREED AT THE CAIRN TERRIER SPECIALTY AT MONTGOMERY COUNTY. SUSANELLA WON GROUP FIRST AT UKC AND GROUP SECOND AT WORCESTER KENNEL CLUB.

MRS. BETTY HYSLOP
PRESCOTT ROAD
BROOKVILLE, ONTARIO, CANADA
HOUSE: (613) 345-5837
KENNEL: (613) 345-5836

The Cairn Terrier originated in the Western Highlands of Scotland. The breed was meant to work in rock terrain against otters, badgers, and foxes. Their name was only chosen in 1910, such was their "honest" life. Apparently not till the early 20th century were white dogs separated out from the colored ones, the white ones becoming part of the ancestry of West Highland White Terriers. Cairn Terriers today may be of any solid color except white. The Cairn Terrier must be active, game, hardy, free moving, "natural", and small, but of good substance. The face has a foxy expression. Very adaptable as companions and pets, Cairns have been very popular in England and are among the most popular of the Terriers in the U.S. Some 7,500 are registered annually, the breed ranking 35th. The breed is well represented in show competition but, as seems to be the case for many natural breeds, does not excel in Group wins.

FOX TERRIER [SMOOTH] STANDARD

FOX TERRIER [WIRE] STANDARD

The following shall be the standard of the Fox Terrier amplified in part in order that a more complete description of the Fox Terrier may be presented. The standard itself is set forth in ordinary type, the amplification in italics.

HEAD — The skull should be flat and moderately narrow, gradually decreasing in width to the eyes. Not much stop should be apparent, but there should be more dip in the profile between the forehead and the top jaw than is seen in the case of a Greyhound. The cheeks must not be full. The ears should be V-shaped and small, of moderate thickness, and drooping forward close to the cheek, not hanging by the side of the head like a Foxhound. *The topline of the folded ear should be well above the level of the skull.* The jaws, upper and lower, should be strong and muscular and of fair punishing strength, but not so as in any way to resemble the Greyhound or modern English Terrier. There should not be much falling away below the eyes. This part of the head should, however, be moderately chiseled out, so as not to go down in a straight slope like a wedge. The nose, toward which the muzzle must gradually taper, should be black. *It should be noticed that although the foreface should gradually taper from eye to muzzle and should tip slightly at its juncture with the forehead, it should not "dish" or fall away quickly below the eyes, where it should be full and well made up, but relieved from "wedginess" by a little delicate chiseling.* The eyes and the rims should be dark in color, *moderately* small and rather deep-set, full of fire, life and intelligence and as nearly as possible circular in shape. *Anything approaching a yellow eye is most objectionable.* The teeth shuld be as nearly as possible together, *i.e., the points* of the upper (*incisors*) teeth on the outside of or *slightly overlapping* the lower teeth. *There should be apparent little difference in length between the skull and foreface of a well-balanced head.*

NECK — Should be clean and muscular, without throatiness, of fair length, and gradually widening to the shoulders. *Shoulders* — Should be long and sloping, well laid back, fine at the points, and clearly cut at the withers. *Chest* — Deep and not broad. *Back* — Should be short, straight (*i.e., level*), and strong, with no appearance of slackness. *Brisket should be deep, yet not exaggerated. Loin* — Should be very powerful, *muscular* and very slightly arched. The foreribs should be moderately arched, the back ribs deep *and well sprung*, and the dog should be well ribbed up.

HINDQUARTERS — Should be strong and muscular, quite free from droop or crouch; the thighs long and powerful; *stifles well curved and turned neither in nor out;* hocks *well bent* and near the ground *should be perfectly upright and parallel each with the other when viewed from behind*, the dog standing well up on them like a Foxhound, and not straight in the stifle. *The worst possible form of hindquarters consists of a short second thigh and a straight stifle. Stern* — Should be set on rather high and carried gaily, but not over the back or curled. It should be of good strength, anything approaching a "pipe-stopper" tail being especially objectionable.

LEGS — The forelegs viewed from any direction must be straight with bone strong right down to the feet, showing little or no appearance of ankle in front, and being short and straight in pasterns. Both forelegs and hind legs should be carried straight forward in traveling, the stifles not turning outward. The elbows should hang perpendicularly to the body, working free of the sides. *Feet* — Should be round, compact and not large; the soles hard and tough; the toes moderately arched and turned neither in nor out.

COAT — Should be smooth, flat, but hard, dense and abundant. The belly and under side of the thighs should not be bare. *Color* — White should predominate; brindle, red, or liver markings are objectionable. Otherwise this point is of little or no importance.

SYMMETRY, SIZE AND CHARACTER — The dog must present a generally gay, lively and active appearance; bone and strength in a small compass are essentials, but this must not be taken to mean that a Fox Terrier should be cloddy, or in any way coarse — speed and endurance must be looked to as well as power, and the symmetry of the Foxhound taken as a model. The terrier, like the hound, must on no account be leggy, nor must he be too short in the leg. He should stand like a cleverly made hunter, covering a lot of ground, yet with a short back, as before stated. He will then attain the highest degree of propelling power, together with the greatest length of stride that is compatible with the length of his body. Weight is not a certain criterion of a terrier's fitness for his work — general shape, size and contour are the main points; and if a dog can gallop and stay, and follow his fox up a drain, it matters little what his weight is to a pound or so. *According to present-day requirements, a full-sized, well-balanced dog should not exceed 15½ inches at the withers, the bitch being proportionately lower — nor should*

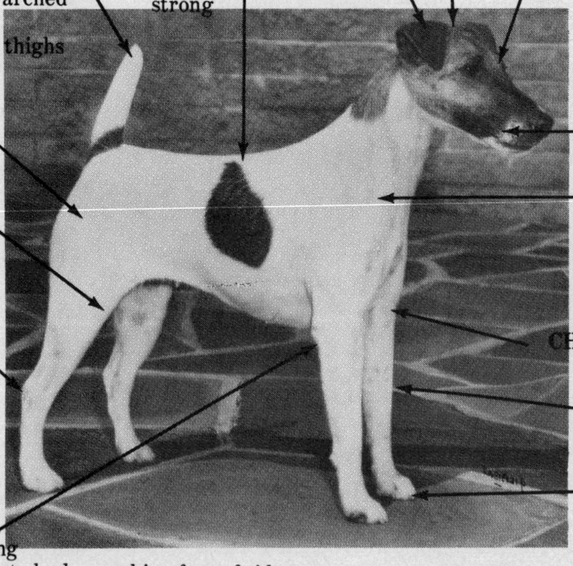

EARS V-shaped, small, moderately thick, foreward close to cheek; top line of folded ear well above skull level

NECK clean, muscular, length fair; widening to shoulders; not throaty

TAIL: Set high; carriage gay, not over back or curled

LOIN powerful, muscular, slightly arched

HINDQUARTERS strong, muscular, thighs long, powerful; free from crouch

STIFLES well-bent, turning neither in nor out

HOCKS well-bent, straight, parallel

DISQUALIFICATIONS: Nose—quite white, cherry or spotted. Ears—prick, tulip or rose. Mouth—much under - or overshot

ELBOWS hang perpendicular to body, working free of sides

BACK short, straight, strong

SKULL flat, moderately narrow; gradually decreasing in width to eyes

STOP slight, only a dip

EYES dark, moderately small, deep set, expressive, circular, rims dark

FOREFACE not "dished"; moderate chisleing; cheeks not full; same length as skull; nose black

JAWS strong, muscular, unwedge-like; teeth—close scissors bite

SHOULDERS long, sloping, well-laid-back, clearly cut at withers; fine at points

FORERIBS moderately arched; backribs deep, well-sprung

CHEST deep, not broad; brisket deep

FORELEGS straight, good bone; neither leggy nor too short, showing little of ankle

FEET round, compact, small; soles hard; toes moderately arched, turning neither in nor out; pasterns short, straight

COLOR white should predominate

COAT—TWO VARIETIES: Smooth—flat, smooth, hard, dense, abundant; belly and undersides of thighs not bare. Wire variety, same standard except coat—hard, wiry not woolly or silky, not too long

SIZE: Balance, proportion important; full-sized dog should not exceed 15½" at withers; 12" from withers to tail-set; head 7" to 7¼"; weight 18 lbs. Bitch proportionately less, weight 2 lbs less with margin of 1 lb. either way

CH. GRAMBRAE SERENE

AN IRISH IMPORT, "IRISH" WAS UNDEFEATED GAINING HIS CHAMPIONSHIP. LATER DURING HIS "FINEST HOURS" HE WAS WITH RIC CHASHOUDIAN ANNEXING BEST OF BREEDS, GROUP PLACINGS, AND WINNING SPECIALTIES. ALL OF THESE HAVE BEEN PUBLICIZED AND ARE WELL KNOWN. ONE OF THE MAIN STAYS IN A KENNEL HOUSING MANY CHAMPIONS, "IRISH" IS A HOUSE DOG, GUARDIAN, GOOD FRIEND TO ALL. HE IS NOW RETIRED FROM THE SHOW RING.

HANDLER—RIC CHASHOUDIAN

CRAG CREST KENNELS
MR. & MRS. FRED KUSKA
ROUTE 1, BOX 2255
COLFAX, CA. 95713
(916) 637-4144

the length of back from withers to root of tail exceed 12 inches, while, to maintain the relative proportions, the head should not exceed 7¼ inches or be less than 7 inches. A dog with these measurements should scale 18 pounds in show condition — a bitch weighing some 2 pounds less — with a margin of 1 pound either way.

BALANCE — *This may be defined as the correct proportions of a certain point, or points, when considered in relation to a certain other point or points. It is the keystone of the terrier's anatomy. The chief points for consideration are the relative proportions of skull and foreface; head and back; height at withers and length of body from shoulder-point to buttock — the ideal of proportion being reached when the last two measurements are the same. It should be added that, although the head measurements can be taken with absolute accuracy, the height at withers and length of back and coat are approximate, and are inserted for the information of breeders and exhibitors rather than as a hard and fast rule.*

MOVEMENT — *Movement, or action, is the crucial test of conformation. The terrier's legs should be carried straight forward while traveling, the forelegs hanging perpendicular and swinging parallel with the sides, like the pendulum of a clock. The principal propulsive power is furnished by the hind legs, perfection of action being found in the terrier possessing long thighs and muscular second thighs well bent at the stifles, which admit of a strong forward thrust or "snatch" of the hocks. When approaching, the forelegs should form a continuation of the straight line of the front, the feet being the same distance apart at the elbows. When stationary, it is often difficult to determine whether a dog is slightly out at shoulder, but, directly he moves, the defect — if it exists — becomes more apparent, the forefeet having a tendency to cross, "weave," or "dish." When, on the contrary, the dog is tied at the shoulder, the tendency of the feet is to move wider apart, with a sort of paddling action. When the hocks are turned in — cowhock — the stifles and feet are turned outward, resulting in a serious loss of propulsive power. When the hocks are turned outwards the tendency of the hind feet is to cross, resulting in an ungainly waddle.*

N.B. — Old scars or injuries, the result of work or accident, should not be allowed to prejudice a terrier's chance in the show ring, unless they interfere with its movement or with its utility for work or stud.

THE DOG PICTURED ABOVE IS A FINE EXAMPLE OF THE SMOOTH COAT VARIETY.

Ch. Foxden Bracer

Ch. Downsbragh Speak Easy

Ch. Ronnoco Resolute

Ch. Downsbragh Night Stick

Ch. Dynamite of Delwin

Ch. Flornell Prestonian Jewel

Preparing a Fox Terrier for Exhibition

by Percy Roberts

Ch. Foxden Sugar Plum

THE art of preparing a Wirehaired Fox Terrier for the true fancier of the breed should be a pleasure, providing one knows how to go about the job. Every amateur exhibitor knows how he would like his dog to look, but fails in the preparation of same, because he has not started off on the right foot.

In the first place, it is important that the would-be trimmer have a decent dog to work on. It is useless trying to trim a dog that does not measure up to the standard in a major degree. So, we will take it for granted that the dog is worthy of being exhibited.

I would suggest taking all the coat down with a non-cutting comb, in other words, plucking it. This applies to skull, ears, neck, shoulders, body and tail. Where longer hair is necessary, such as on the foreface, legs and quarters, it is as well not to strip out entirely but remove all old and ragged hairs. Tidy around the feet; by this I mean the outside of the toes towards the pad, not on the top side of the foot. This will give emphasis to the fact that the dog has a good round foot and a tight pad. The quarters should be gradually tapered down to a nice thick pad of hair that continues on down below the hock to the foot.

When this part of the preparation is completed, it is then advisable to give the dog a good rubbing and massage with some light, soothing oil, and the writer knows of nothing better for this purpose than pure olive oil and yellow sulphur—about one ounce of sulphur to sixteen ounces of oil. It is advisable to leave this on overnight and the next day. Then, before putting the dog away for the night, a good bath will remove all scurf, dandruff and other skin impurities from the surface of the skin, which will enable the new coat to come through at its best.

File the nails back to the quick once a week. From this time on, the dog should be systematically groomed daily, not so much with a brush as by hand. This serves a threefold purpose. It encourages the circulation under the skin which hastens the new coat coming through, it teaches the dog to stand for handling by a judge, and incidentally he learns to pose as he should in the ring.

After about a month of this treatment, it will be noticed that the dog has a new, even coat all over and now is the time when the would-be trimmer has to get in his best licks and prove how much he knows of the anatomy of his dog. It is well to clean skull, cheeks, ears, throat, and sides of neck down tight. Scale the shoulders down somewhat but not as tight as one does the throat. Take all the long hairs from underneath the loin and below root of tail. Tidy up any rough hairs on the body, taking them out, and continuing the grooming process as before described.

After two weeks of this, it is up to the prospective exhibitor to keep touching his dog up wherever he feels his make and shape could be improved, always keeping in mind that the happy medium is preferable to any exaggerations, such as too profuse whiskers and leg hair. Once the dog starts to come into shape, the writer knows no more pleasure than one gets trimming here and there about the dog, improving the picture until the finished article is achieved. The untold pleasure the general ensemble of his dog will give the intended exhibitor will well repay him for all efforts expended.

Since the passage of the new Kennel Club rule re artificial coloring, it is important that as few hairs are cut as possible, for where a hair is cut, it just dies, but where a hair is pulled out, a new one grows. Hence, the dog always appears in fresh bloom.

Twenty-four hours before the show, the dog should be bathed, thoroughly dried, combed out and have a light towel or blanket put on overnight before the show. This will help lay the coat as it was before washing.

With regard to chalk, the writer has never been able to see why a Wire or Smooth Fox Terrier should be smothered in chalk. It only needs a little on legs and feet, underneath the body, on whiskers, tail, and hocks, if the dog has been properly washed. One will find after removing all the chalk from the coat with a brush, the hair in these places will have a more substantial appearance. One can usually depend on the back and sides of the dog always being clean, so a flick of chalk there will complete the picture. This will be done just before the dog is taken into the ring.

The preparation of a Smooth Fox Terrier calls for a somewhat different technique although the principles are the same. One should have a pair of barber's thinning shears and a very sharp pocket knife. The frills down each side of the neck should be removed gradually. By this I mean that after each cut of the shears, the frill should be combed down. Then use the shears again and so on, until one has a neat and tidy neckline. The same applies to underneath tail and back of tail. See that all long hairs are removed from the under part of the loin. The thinning shears can be used again for this purpose, after which the dog will have a clean-cut outline. Use the sharp knife on the inside edges of the ears, whittling them down so that the ear will look nicely tapered off without being barbered. Use the shears again for around the toes and back of pad and the long hairs usually found on the back of the elbows, after which a good rubbing over all the trimmed parts with a strip of smooth emery cloth is advised.

It is well to make up one's mind that trimming a Smooth cannot be done in thirty minutes, so it is advised to work slowly, and the finished article will have much more pleasing results. Bathe and clean the night before the show as suggested for Wires. Application of chalk to a Smooth follows the same general principles as that for Wires. Another suggestion I would offer is to observe how the top professionals have their dogs turned out and endeavor by continued application to achieve similar results.

If these few hints are followed, the general appearance of the dog when taken into the ring will be a pleasure to his owner and a compliment to the judge.

ENG. & AM. CH. BRIARTEX TAVERN

IMPORTED FROM ENGLAND WITH 7 CC'S TO HIS CREDIT THIS IDEAL WIRE FOX TERRIER IS OF CORRECT SIZE AND WEIGHT. HE QUICKLY GAINED HIS AMERICAN TITLE WITH 1 GROUP FIRST, 1 GROUP SECOND, 2 GROUP THIRDS, AND 1 GROUP FOURTH FROM THE CLASSES. THIS ELEGANT YOUNG DOG SHOWS GREAT PROMISE FOR THE FUTURE.

OWNER
CONSTANCE JONES
BLACKBURN ROAD
SEWICKLEY, PA. 15143

AGENT/HANDLER
CLIFFORD HALLMARK
60 EAST MAIN STREET
MENDHAM, N.J. 07945
(201) 543-4842

Wire

This variety of the breed should resemble the smooth sort in every respect except the coat, which should be broken. The harder and more wiry the texture of the coat is, the better. On no account should the dog look or feel woolly; and there should be no silky hair about the poll or elsewhere. The coat should not be too long, so as to give the dog a shaggy appearance, but, at the same time, it should show a marked and distinct difference all over from the smooth species.

SCALE OF POINTS

Head and ears	15
Neck	5
Shoulders and chest	10
Back and loin	10
Hindquarters	15
Stern	5
Legs and feet	15
Coat	15
Symmetry, size and character	10
Total	100

DISQUALIFICATIONS

Nose — White, cherry or spotted to a considerable extent with either of these colors. Ears — Prick, tulip or rose. Mouth — Much undershot, or much overshot.

KERRY BLUE TERRIER STANDARD

HEAD — Long, but not exaggerated and in good proportion to the rest of the body. Well balanced, with little apparent difference between the length of the skull and foreface. (20 points) *Skull* — Flat, with very light stop, of but moderate breadth between the ears, and narrowing very slightly to the eyes. *Cheeks* — Clean and level, free from bumpiness. *Ears* — V-shaped, small but not out of proportion to the size of the dog, of moderate thickness, carried forward close to the cheeks with the top of the folded ear slightly above the level of the skull. A "dead" ear houndlike in appearance is very undesirable. *Foreface* — Jaws deep, strong and muscular. Foreface full and well made up, not falling away appreciably below the eyes but moderately chiseled out to relieve the foreface from wedginess. *Nose* — Black, nostrils large and wide. *Teeth* — Strong, white and either level or with the upper (incisors) teeth slightly overlapping the lower teeth. An undershot mouth should be strictly penalized. *Eyes* — Dark, small, not prominent, well placed and with a keen terrier expression. Anything approaching a yellow eye is very undesirable.

NECK — Clean and moderately long, gradually widening to the shoulders upon which it should be well set and carried proudly. (5 points) *Shoulders and Chest* — Shoulders fine, long and sloping, well laid back and well knit. Chest deep and of but moderate breadth. (10 points) *Legs and Feet* — Legs moderately long with plenty of bone and muscle. The forelegs should be straight from both front and side view, with the elbows hanging perpendicularly to the body and working clear of the sides in movement, the pasterns short, straight and hardly noticeable. Both forelegs and hind legs should move straight forward when traveling, the stifles turning neither in nor out. (10 points) Feet should be strong, compact, fairly round and moderately small, with good depth of pad free from cracks, the toes arched, turned neither in nor out, with black toenails.

BODY — Back short, strong and straight (*i.e.*, level), with no appearance of slackness. Loin short and powerful with a slight tuck-up, the ribs fairly well sprung, deep rather than round. (10 points) *Hindquarters and Stern* — Hindquarters strong and muscular with full freedom of action, free from droop or crouch, the thighs long and powerful, stifles well bent and turned neither in nor out, hocks near the ground and, when viewed from behind, upright and parallel with each other, the dog standing well up on them. Tail should be set on high, of moderate length and carried gaily erect, the straighter the tail the better. (10 points)

COLOR — The correct mature color is anly shade of blue gray or gray blue from deep slate to light blue gray, or a fairly uniform color throughout except that distinctly darker to black parts may appear on the muzzle, head, ears, tail and feet. (10 points) Kerry color, in its process of "clearing" from an apparent black at birth to the mature gray blue or blue gray, passes through one or more transitions — involving a very dark blue (darker than deep slate), shades or tinges of brown, and mixtures of these, together with a progressive infiltration of the correct mature color. Up to 18 months such deviations from the correct mature color are permissible without preference and without regard for uniformity. Thereafter, deviation from it to any significant extent must be severely penalized. Solid black is never permissible in the show ring. Up to 18 months any doubt as to whether a dog is black or a very dark blue should be resolved in favor of the dog, particularly in the case of a puppy. Black on the muzzle, head, ears, tail and feet is permissible at any age. *Coat* — Soft, dense and wavy. A harsh, wire or bristle coat should be severely penalized. In show trim the body should be well covered but tidy, with the head (except for the whiskers) and the ears and cheeks clear. (15 points)

GENERAL CONFORMATION AND CHARACTER — The typical Kerry Blue Terrier should be upstanding, well knit and in good balance, showing a well developed and muscular body with definite Terrier style and character throughout. A low-slung Kerry is not typical. (10 points)

HEIGHT — The ideal Kerry should be 18½ inches at the withers for a dog, slightly less for a bitch. In judging Kerries, a height of 18-19½ inches for a dog, and 17½-19 inches for a bitch should be given primary preference. Only where the comparative superiority of a specimen outside of the ranges noted clearly justifies it, should greater latitude be taken. In no case should it extend to a dog over 20 inches or under 17½ inches, or to a bitch over 19½ inches or under 17 inches. The minimum limits do not apply to puppies. *Weight* — The most desirable weight for a fully developed dog is from 33-40 pounds, bitches weighing proportionately less.

DISQUALIFICATIONS

Solid black. Dewclaws on hind legs.

Approved September 15, 1959

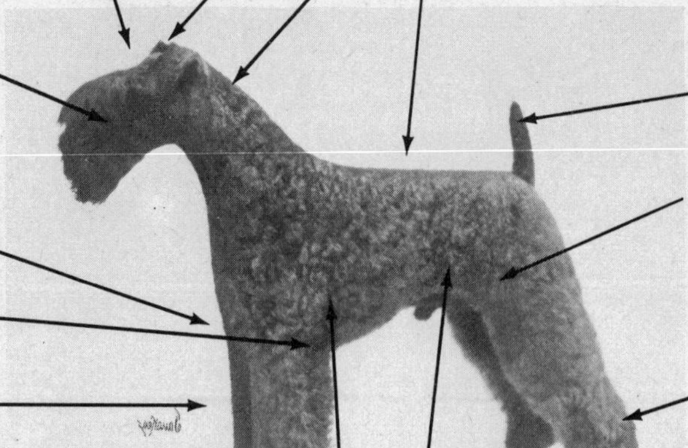

HEAD well-balanced; fairly long; good proportion to body; foreface and skull length approx. same

SKULL flat; stop slight; narrowing slightly to eyes; moderate breadth between ears

EYES dark, small; well-placed; expression keen

NOSE black; nostrils large, wide

CHEEKS clean, level; free from bumpiness

JAWS deep, strong; foreface full, well-made-up, moderately chiseled; teeth white, strong, level or upper slightly overlapping lower

CHEST deep; breadth moderate

ELBOWS: Turning neither in nor out; hanging perpendicular to body; working clear of sides

FORELEGS moderately long; good bone; muscular, straight

FEET strong, compact; fairly round; moderately small; pads of good depth, no cracks; toes arched; nails black

COLOR: When mature: any shade of blue-gray or gray-blue (deep slate to light blue-gray); color fairly uniform except darker on muzzle, head, ears, tail, feet. Color deviations ("clearing") permissible to 18 months

DISQUALIFICATION: Solid black; dewclaws on hind legs

APPEARANCE: Upstanding; well-knit in good balance; muscular, well-developed; terrier style and character

EARS: V-shaped; proportionately small; carried forward, close to cheeks; top folds slightly above skull level; thickness moderate

NECK clean; moderately long; proudly arched, blending into long, sloping shoulders; well-laid-back

BACK short, strong, straight; loin short, powerful

TAIL set high; length moderate; carried gaily, erect, straight

THIGH long, powerful

HINDQUARTERS muscular, strong; no droop or crouch; stifles turned neither in nor out

HOCKS firm, short; rear view, metatarsi parallel; stance well up

TUCK-UP slight

RIBS deep; fairly well-sprung

PASTERNS short, straight

COAT soft, dense, wavy

SIZE: Height, male 18 to 19½" at withers, ideal; female, 17½ to 19". Weight, male, 33 to 40 lbs; female, slightly less

CH. MORBLEU TONI OF TONTINE

BREEDER: MARGARET VILLERS. SIRE: CH. TONTINE'S SOMETHING ELSE. DAM: CH. LONDONERRY 'LIL. "TONI" STARTED HER SHOW CAREER SEPT. 1974, WINNING HER POINTS HANDILY AND 5 BOS AWARDS FROM THE CLASSES BOTH ON THE EAST COAST AND WEST COAST TO FINISH IN DECEMBER 1974. SHE WILL BE WIDELY SPECIALED ALL OF 1975.

HANDLER: RAYMOND PERRY

LUCILLE MYERS
9761 W. 11TH STREET
SANTA ANA, CALIFORNIA

The Kerry Blue Terrier originated in the southwest of Ireland but otherwise the ancestry of the breed is not known. There are many points of similarity among the Kerry Blue, Irish and Soft-Coated Wheaten Terriers. In Ireland, the Kerry is a utility dog used for working, sporting, and companionship. The Kerry Blue Terrier is large, ideally 18½ inches at the withers and between 33 and 40 pounds in weight. The soft, dense, wavy, and carefully trimmed coat, when mature, must be of blue gray shade. About 900 are now registered annually in the U.S., the breed ranking 64th.

MANCHESTER TERRIER [STANDARD] STANDARD

MANCHESTER TERRIER [TOY] STANDARD

HEAD — Long, narrow, tight-skinned, almost flat, with a slight indentation up the forehead; slightly wedge-shaped, tapering to the nose, with no visible cheek muscles, and well filled up under the eyes; tight-lipped jaws, level in mouth, and functionally level teeth, or the incisors of the upper jaw may make a close, slightly overlapping contact with the incisors of the lower jaw. *Eyes* — Small, bright, sparkling and as near black as possible; set moderately close together; oblong in shape, slanting upwards on the outside; they should neither protrude nor sink in the skull. *Nose* — Black.

EARS (*Toy Variety*) — Of moderate size; set well up on the skull and rather close together; thin, moderately narrow at base; with pointed tips; naturally erect carriage. Wide, flaring, blunt-tipped or "bell" ears are a serious fault; cropped or cut ears shall disqualify.

EARS (*Standard Variety*) — Erect, or button, small and thin; smaller at the root and set as close together as possible at the top of the head. If cropped, to a point, long and carried erect.

NECK AND SHOULDERS — The neck should be a moderate length, slim and graceful; gradually becoming larger as it approaches, and blend smoothly with the sloping shoulders; free from throatiness; slightly arched from the occiput.

CHEST — Narrow between the legs; deep in the brisket.

BODY — Moderately short, with robust loins; ribs well sprung out behind the shoulders; back slightly arched at the loin, and falling again to the tail to the same height as the shoulder. *Legs* — Forelegs, straight, of proportionate length, and well under body. Hind legs should not turn in or out as viewed from the rear; carried back; hocks well let down. *Feet* — Compact, well arched, with jet black nails; the two middle toes in the front feet rather longer than the others; the hind feet shaped like those of a cat. *Tail* — Moderately short, and set on where the arch of the back ends; thick where it joins the body, tapering to a point, not carried higher than the back.

COAT — Smooth, short, thick, dense, close and glossy; not soft.

COLOR — Jet black and rich mahogany tan, which should not run or blend into each other but abruptly forming clear, well-defined lines of color division. A small tan spot over each eye; a very small tan spot on each cheek, the lips of the upper and lower jaws should be tanned, extending under the throat, ending in the shape of the letter V; the inside of the ears partly tanned. Tan spots, called rosettes, on each side of the chest above the front legs, more pronounced in puppies than in adults. There should be a black "thumb mark" patch on the front of each foreleg between the pastern and the knee. There should be a distinct black "pencil mark" line running lengthwise on the top of each toe on all four feet. The remainder of the forelegs to be tan to the knee. Tan on the hind legs should continue from the penciling on the feet up the inside of the legs to a little below the stifle joint; the outside of the hind legs to be black. There should be tan under the tail, and on the vent, but only of such size as to be covered by the tail. White in any part of the coat is a serious fault, and shall disqualify whenever the white shall form a patch or stripe measuring as much as one-half inch in its longest dimension.

WEIGHT (*Toy Variety*) — Not exceeding 12 pounds. It is suggested that clubs consider dividing the American-bred and open classes by weight as follows: 7 pounds and under, over 7 pounds and not exceeding 12 pounds.

WEIGHT (*Standard Variety*) — Over 12 pounds and not exceeding 22 pounds. Dogs weighing over 22 pounds shall be disqualified. It is suggested that clubs consider dividing the American-bred and open classes by weight as follows: over 12 pounds and not exceeding 16 pounds, over 16 pounds and not exceeding 22 pounds.

DISQUALIFICATIONS

Color — White in any part of the coat, forming a patch or stripe measuring as much as ½-inch in its longest dimension.

Weight (*Standard Variety*) — Over 22 pounds.

Ears (*Toy Variety*) — *Cropped or cut ears.*

Approved June 12, 1962

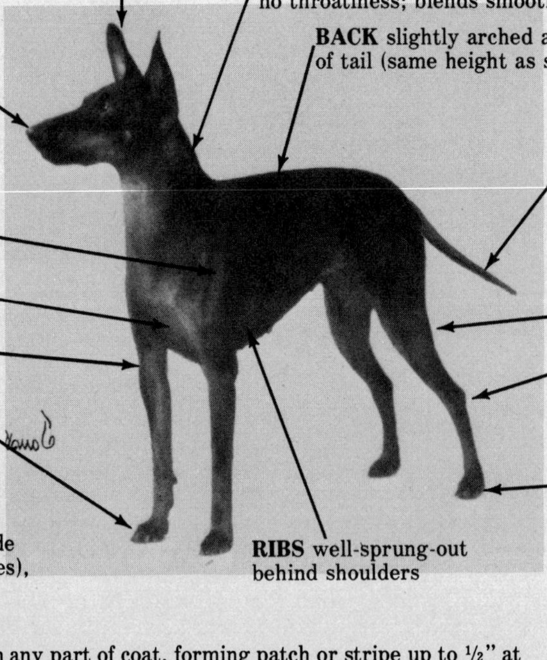

HEAD long, narrow, tight-skinned; almost flat; slight indentation up forehead; slightly wedge-shaped, tapering to nose; well-filled under eyes; no visible cheek muscles; tight-lipped jaws, mouth level; functional, level teeth — or incisors of upper jaw make close, slightly overlapping contact with lower incisors

EARS erect or button, small, thin; smaller at root; set high on skull, close together; if cropped to a point, long, carried erect; (*see* Toy variety)

BODY moderately short

NECK moderately long, slim, graceful; slightly arched; no throatiness; blends smoothly into shoulders

NOSE black

BACK slightly arched at loin, falling to set-on of tail (same height as shoulder); loins robust

EYES small; near black as possible; moderately close together; shape oblong; slanting upward on outside; neither protruding nor sunken; bright, sparkling

TAIL moderately short; set on where arch of back ends; thick at root tapering to point; not carried higher than back

SHOULDERS sloping

CHEST narrow between legs; brisket deep

HIND LEGS turning neither in nor out; carried back

FORELEGS straight, strong, well under body; length proportionate

HOCKS well-let-down

FOREFEET compact, well-arched; two middle toes longer; nails jet black

HINDFEET catlike

COLOR: Jet black, rich mahogany tan; clear, well-defined lines between colors; tan over each eye, on each check, lips extending under throat ending in V, inside of ears, above front legs on chest (rosettes), on forelegs, inside of hind legs, "pencil marks" on toes, under tail

RIBS well-sprung-out behind shoulders

COAT smooth, short, thick, dense, close, glossy; not soft

SIZE: Weight not exceeding 12 lbs. (Standard variety 12 to 22 lbs)

DISQUALIFICATIONS: Color — White in any part of coat, forming patch or stripe up to ½" at longest dimension. Weight, Standard variety — not under 12 or over 22 lbs. Toy variety — not over 12 lbs. Toy variety — cropped or cut ears

CH. BAM-SAW PETER

PICTURED WINNING BIS AT THE 1974 NATIONAL SPECIALTY OF THE A.M.T.C. UNDER JUDGE MRS. JAMES CARTER; PICTURED ALSO IS KAYLEEN HILLEBRAND, DISTRICT GOVERNOR OF M.T.C.A. SIRE: CH. RED ROOF RAILLERY. DAM: FRANCESCA OF RED ROOF.

BAM-SAW KENNELS — C. EVANS SAWYER, M.D.
MANCHESTER TERRIERS — STANDARDS & TOYS
BUTLER ROAD
MONSON, MASS. 01057

History tells us that the Manchester Terrier was developed in England from the mating of a Whippet to a well-known rat-killing dog. This explains the reason for the Manchester Terrier having a roach back. Due to the increasing popularity of this type of dog in the city of Manchester the breed took on this name. Before 1959 the Manchester Terrier was registered as two separate breeds, one a medium size and the other a toy. However, after this date they have been considered two varieties.

MINIATURE SCHNUAZER STANDARD

GENERAL APPEARANCE — The Miniature Schnauzer is a robust, active dog of terrier type, resembling his large cousin, the Standard Schnauzer, in general appearance, and of an alert, active disposition. He is sturdily built, nearly square in proportion of body length to height, with plenty of bone, and without any suggestion of toyishness.

HEAD — Strong and rectangular, its width diminishing slightly from ears to eyes, and again to the tip of the nose. The forehead is unwrinkled. The topskull is flat and fairly long. The foreface is parallel to the topskull, with a slight stop, and is at least as long as the topskull. The muzzle is strong in proportion to the skull; it ends in a moderately blunt manner, with thick whiskers which accentuate the rectangular shape of the head. *Teeth*—The teeth meet in a scissors bite. That is, the upper front teeth overlap the lower front teeth in such a manner that the inner surface of the upper incisors barely touches the outer surface of the lower incisors when the mouth is closed. *Eyes* — Small, dark brown and deep-set. They are oval in appearance and keen in expression. *Ears* — When cropped the ears are identical in shape and length, with pointed tips. They are in balance with the head and not exaggerated in length. They are set high on the skull and carried perpendicularly at the inner edges, with as little bell as possible along the outer edges. When uncropped, the ears are small and V-shaped, folding close to the skull.

NECK — Strong and well-arched, blending into the shoulders, and with the skin fitting tightly at the throat.

BODY—Short and deep, with the brisket extending at least to the elbows. Ribs are well sprung and deep, extending well back to a short loin. The underbody does not present a tucked-up appearance at the flank. The topline is straight; it declines slightly from the withers to the base of the tail. The over-all length from chest to stern bone equals the height at the withers.

FOREQUARTERS — The forequarters have flat, somewhat sloping shoulders and high withers. Forelegs are straight and parallel when viewed from all sides. They have strong pasterns and good bone. They are separated by a fairly deep brisket which precludes a pinched front. The elbows are close, and the ribs spread gradually from the first rib so as to allow space for the elbows to move close to the body. *Hindquarters*—The hindquarters have strong-muscled, slanting thighs: they are well bent at the stifles and straight from hock to so-called heel. There is sufficient angulation so that, in stance, the hocks extend beyond the tail. The hindquarters never appear overbuilt or higher than the shoulders. *Feet*—Short and round (cat-feet) with thick, black pads. The toes are arched and compact.

ACTION—The trot is the gait at which movement is judged. The dog must gait in a straight line. Coming on, the forelegs are parallel, with the elbows close to the body. The feet turn neither inward nor outward. Going away, the hind legs are parallel from the hocks down, and travel wide. Viewed from the side, the forelegs have a good reach, while the hind legs have a strong drive with good pick-up of hocks.

TAIL — Set high and carried erect. It is docked only long enough to be clearly visible over the topline of the body when the dog is in proper length of coat.

COAT — Double, with a hard, wiry outer coat and a close undercoat. The body coat should be plucked. When in show condition, the proper length is not less than three-quarters of an inch except on neck, ears and skull. Furnishings are fairly thick but not silky.

SIZE — From 12 to 14 inches. Ideal size 13½ inches. (*See disqualifications.*)

COLOR — The recognized colors are salt and pepper, black and silver, and solid black. The typical color is salt and pepper in shades of gray; tan shading is permissible. The salt and pepper mixture faes out to light gray or silver white in the eyebrows, whiskers, cheeks, under throat, across chest, under tail, leg furnishings under body, and inside legs. The light underbody hair is not to rise higher on the sides of the body than the front elbows.

The black and silvers follow the same pattern as the salt and peppers. The entire salt-and-pepper section must be black.

Black is the only solid color allowed. It must be a true black with no gray hairs and no brown tinge except where the whiskers may have become discolored. A small white spot on the chest is permitted.

FAULTS

Type — Toyishness, raciness, or coarseness. *Structure* — Head coarse and cheeky. Chest too broad or shallow in brisket. Tail set low. Sway or roach back. Bowed or cowhocked hindquarters. Loose elbows. *Action* — Sidegaiting. Paddling in front, or high hackney knee action. Weak hind action. *Coat* — Too soft or too smooth and slick in appearance. *Temperament* — Shyness or viciousness. *Bite* — Undershot or overshot jaw. Level bite. *Eyes* — Light and/or large and prominent in appearance.

DISQUALIFICATIONS

Dogs or bitches under 12 inches or over 14 inches. Color solid white or white patches on the body.

Approved May 13, 1958

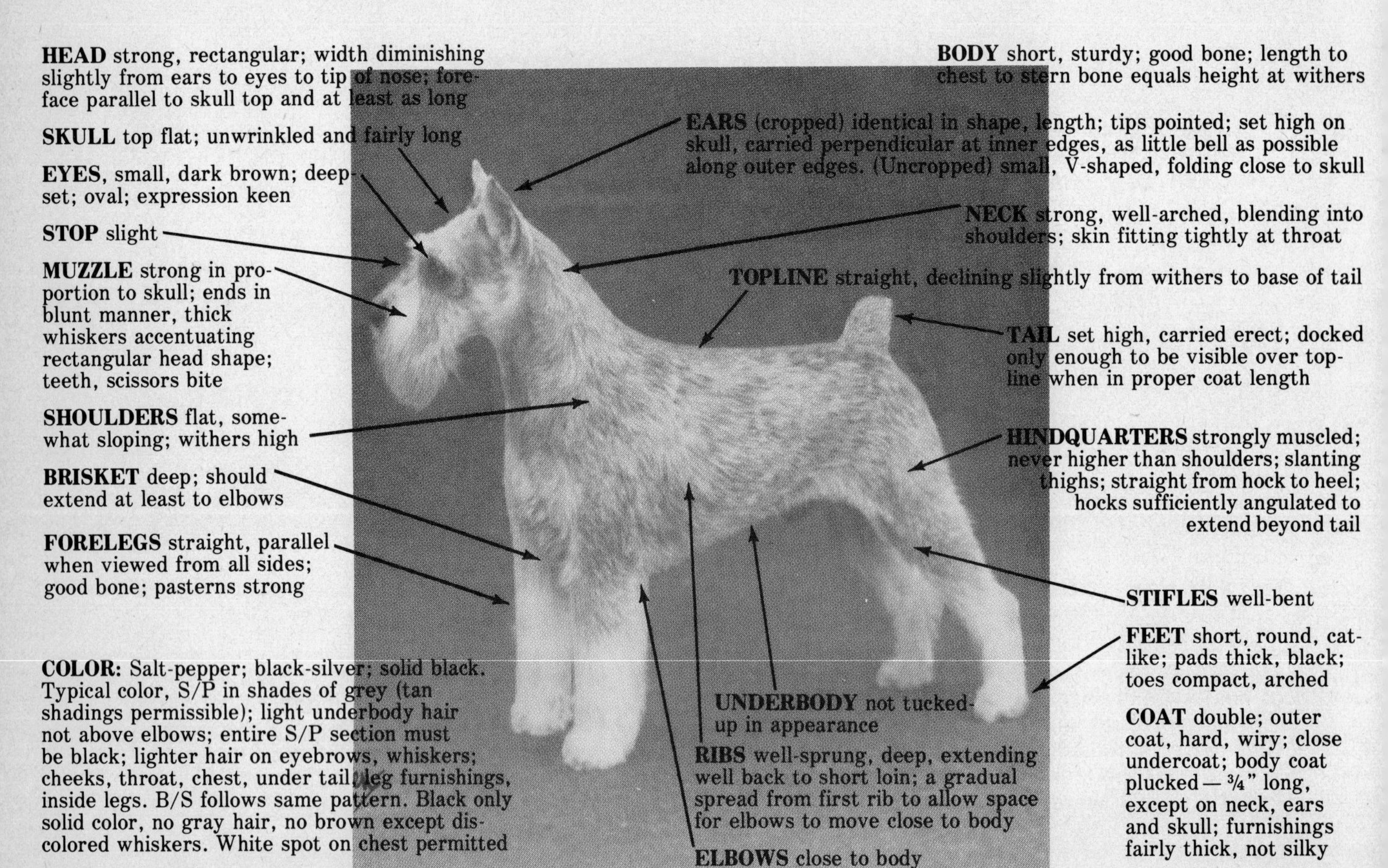
HEAD strong, rectangular; width diminishing slightly from ears to eyes to tip of nose; foreface parallel to skull top and at least as long
SKULL top flat; unwrinkled and fairly long
EYES, small, dark brown; deep-set; oval; expression keen
STOP slight
MUZZLE strong in proportion to skull; ends in blunt manner, thick whiskers accentuating rectangular head shape; teeth, scissors bite
SHOULDERS flat, somewhat sloping; withers high
BRISKET deep; should extend at least to elbows
FORELEGS straight, parallel when viewed from all sides; good bone; pasterns strong
COLOR: Salt-pepper; black-silver; solid black. Typical color, S/P in shades of grey (tan shadings permissible); light underbody hair not above elbows; entire S/P section must be black; lighter hair on eyebrows, whiskers; cheeks, throat, chest, under tail, leg furnishings, inside legs. B/S follows same pattern. Black only solid color, no gray hair, no brown except discolored whiskers. White spot on chest permitted
SIZE: From 12 to 14"; ideal height, 13½"
BODY short, sturdy; good bone; length to chest to stern bone equals height at withers
EARS (cropped) identical in shape, length; tips pointed; set high on skull, carried perpendicular at inner edges, as little bell as possible along outer edges. (Uncropped) small, V-shaped, folding close to skull
NECK strong, well-arched, blending into shoulders; skin fitting tightly at throat
TOPLINE straight, declining slightly from withers to base of tail
TAIL set high, carried erect; docked only enough to be visible over topline when in proper coat length
HINDQUARTERS strongly muscled; never higher than shoulders; slanting thighs; straight from hock to heel; hocks sufficiently angulated to extend beyond tail
STIFLES well-bent
FEET short, round, catlike; pads thick, black; toes compact, arched
COAT double; outer coat, hard, wiry; close undercoat; body coat plucked—¾" long, except on neck, ears and skull; furnishings fairly thick, not silky
UNDERBODY not tucked-up in appearance
RIBS well-sprung, deep, extending well back to short loin; a gradual spread from first rib to allow space for elbows to move close to body
ELBOWS close to body
DISQUALIFICATIONS: Dogs or bitches under 12" or over 14". Color—solid white or white patches on body

INT., MEX., AM., CH. KAZELS FAVORITE

JUDGE: MRS. TOM STEVENSON OWNER/HANDLER: MRS. K. L. CHURCH

THIS EXCEPTIONAL MINIATURE SCHNAUZER IS AMASSING AN OUTSTANDING RECORD WHICH INCLUDES 94 BESTS OF BREED; 4 ALL-BREED BEST IN SHOW; 2 AMSC SPECIALTY BEST OF BREED; AND MANY OTHER GROUP PLACEMENTS. HE HAS APPEARED IN THE TOP TEN BREED AND GROUP RANKINGS 3 CONSECUTIVE YEARS, TOPPING ALL SYSTEMS IN 1972, SETTING A NEW RECORD, AND WAS NUMBER 10 ALL TERRIERS.

MRS. K. L. CHURCH
#3 CHURCH ESTATES ROAD
ROUTE 3
HILLSBORO, MISSOURI 63050

The Miniature Schnauzer took its origin in Germany. Initially, the Schnauzer (now the Standard Schnauzer) was probably bred from Poodle, Wolf Spitz, and old Pinscher stock. The size was brought down by selection and by Affenpinscher crosses. Miniature Schnauzers of today have found prime favor as companions and pets. The Miniature Schnauzer is assigned to the Terrier Group because of its vermin destroying propensities and its general appearance, although it shares little or no common ancestry with the other terriers, all of which are of British background. The Miniature Schnauzer is active and robust, resembling both the Standard and the Giant Schnauzer, sturdily built, square in proportion, and of good substance. No suggestion of toyishness is allowed. The double coat, with hard, wiry outer hairs, must be pepper and salt, black and silver, or solid black. Tan shading is permissible in the former. Dogs and bitches must stand between 12 and 14 inches at the shoulder. Miniature Schnauzers are currently by far the most popular terriers in the U.S. Their popularity seems to be shading off slightly. Miniature Schnauzers rank 12th among all breeds in numbers in show competition, far ahead of the next ranking Scottish Terriers.

NORWICH TERRIER STANDARD

HEAD — Skull wide, slightly rounded with good width between the ears. Muzzle strong but not long or heavy, with slightly "foxy" appearance. Length about one-third less than the measurement from the occiput to the bottom of the stop, which should be well defined. *Faults:* A long narrow head; over square muzzle; highly rounded dome. *Ears* — Prick or drop. If pricked, small, pointed, erect and set well apart. If dropped, neat, small, with break just above the skull line, front edge close to cheek, and not falling lower than the outer corner of the eye. *Faults:* Oversize; poor carriage. *Eyes* — Very bright, dark and keen. Full of expression. *Faults:* Light or protruding eyes. *Jaw* — Clean, strong, tight lipped, with strong, large, closely-fitting teeth; scissors bite. *Faults:* A bite over or undershot. *Neck* — Short and strong, well set on clean shoulders.

BODY — Moderately short, compact and deep with level topline, ribs well sprung. *Faults:* Long weak back, loaded shoulders. *Legs* — Short and powerful and as straight as is consistent with the short legs for which we aim. Sound bone, round feet, thick pads. *Faults:* Out at elbow, badly bowed, knuckled over. Too light in bone. *Quarters* — Strong, rounded, with great powers of propulsion. *Faults:* Cowhocks. *Tail* — Medium docked, carriage not excessively gay.

COLOR — All shades of red, wheaten, black and tan and grizzle. White markings on the chest, though allowable, are not desirable. *Faults:* White markings elsewhere or to any great extent on the chest. *Coat* — As hard and wiry as possible, lying close to the body, with a definite undercoat. Top coat absolutely straight; in full coat longer and rougher forming almost a mane on shoulders and neck. Hair on head, ears and muzzle, except for slight eyebrows and slight whiskers, is absolutely short and smooth. These dogs should be shown with as nearly a natural coat as possible. A minimum amount of tidying is permissible but excessive trimming, shaping and clipping shall be heavily penalized by the judge. *Faults:* Silky or curly coat.

WEIGHT — Ideal, 11 to 12 pounds.

HEIGHT — Ideal, 10 inches at the withers.

GENERAL APPEARANCE — A small, low rugged terrier, tremendously active. A perfect demon yet not quarrelsome and of a lovable disposition, and a very hardy constitution. Honorable scars from fair wear and tear shall not count against.

DISQUALIFICATION

Cropped ears shall disqualify.

June 10, 1969

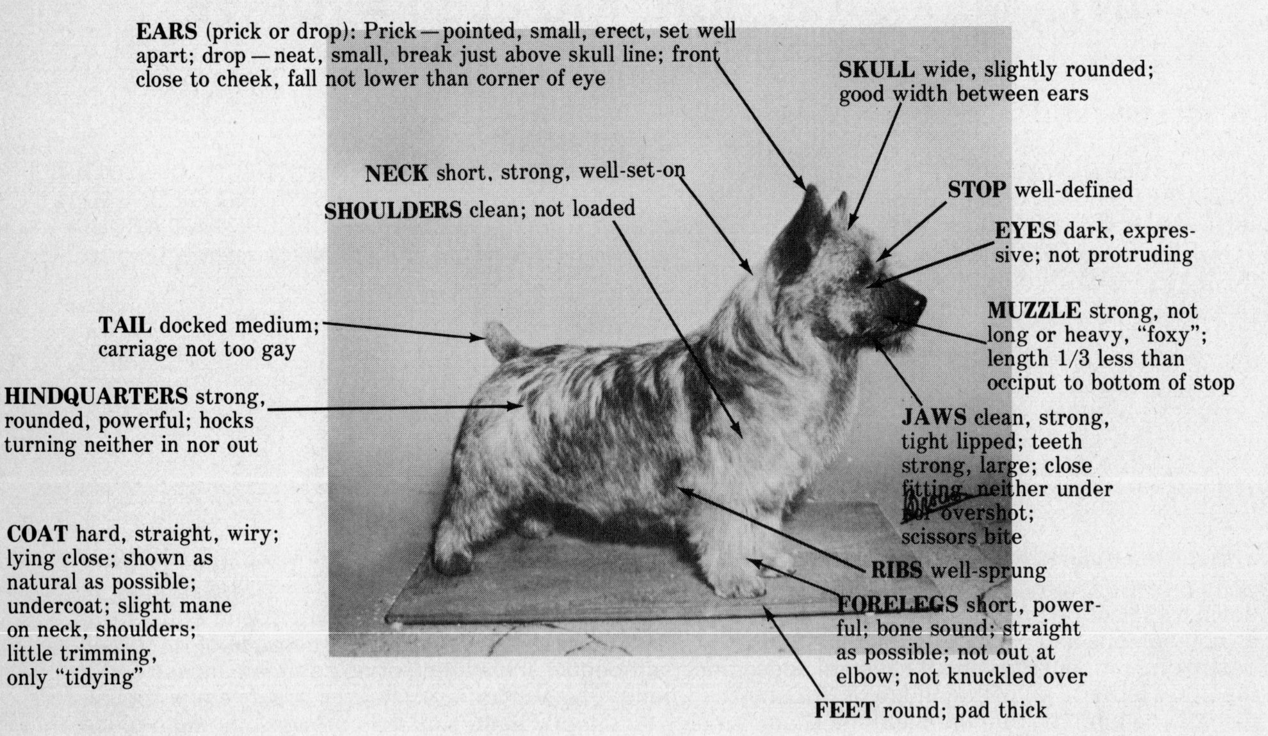

BODY moderately short, compact; topline level
EARS (prick or drop): Prick—pointed, small, erect, set well apart; drop—neat, small, break just above skull line; front close to cheek, fall not lower than corner of eye
SKULL wide, slightly rounded; good width between ears
NECK short, strong, well-set-on
SHOULDERS clean; not loaded
STOP well-defined
EYES dark, expressive; not protruding
MUZZLE strong, not long or heavy, "foxy"; length 1/3 less than occiput to bottom of stop
TAIL docked medium; carriage not too gay
HINDQUARTERS strong, rounded, powerful; hocks turning neither in nor out
JAWS clean, strong, tight lipped; teeth strong, large; close fitting, neither under nor overshot; scissors bite
COAT hard, straight, wiry; lying close; shown as natural as possible; undercoat; slight mane on neck, shoulders; little trimming, only "tidying"
RIBS well-sprung
FORELEGS short, powerful; bone sound; straight as possible; not out at elbow; not knuckled over
FEET round; pad thick

COLOR: Red, red-wheaten, black and tan, grizzle. White on chest allowed but not desirable

DISQUALIFICATION: Cropped ears

SIZE: Height—10" at withers ideal

WEIGHT: Ideal—11 to 12 lbs

AM. AND CAN. CH.
ICKWORTH NIMROD

BRED IN ENGLAND BY MISS A.L. HAZELDINE, NIMROD HAD TWO C.C.s BEFORE WE BROUGHT HIM TO THIS COUNTRY. HE IS BY HANLEY CASTLE BROCK EX NANFAN NYMPH. IN 1972 NIMROD WON THE NORWICH TERRIER SPECIALTY OVER SIXTY ENTRIES. IN 1974 HE WAS UNDEFEATED IN CANADA IN FIVE CONSECUTIVE SHOWS TO QUALIFY FOR HIS CHAMPIONSHIP. HE ALSO HAD SEVERAL GROUP PLACEMENTS THERE. NIMROD IS THE SIRE OF CH. BADGEWOOD MONTY COLLINS WHO WON TWENTY-FIVE BEST OF BREEDS IN 1974. CH. BADGEWOOD DUCHESS OF NORFOLK,NIMROD'S DAUGHTER, WAS THE WINNER OF THE SWEEPSTAKES AT THE 1974 NORWICH TERRIER SPECIALTY. CH. BADGEWOOD MISS ALICE IS ANOTHER OF HIS CHAMPION OFFSPRING.

MR. AND MRS. PHILIP S.P. FELL
BADGEWOOD KENNELS
COVE ROAD, OYSTER BAY
LONG ISLAND, N.Y. 11771
(516) 922-3952

The ancestory of the Norwich Terrier has not been established. The breed seems to have originated in East Anglia and one can guess that several earlier terrier strains contributed their genes. The breed was recognized by the English Kennel Club in 1923. In 1964, the drop-ear type, in England, was divided off as the Norfolk Terrier. In the U.S., both prick-ear and drop-ear types are shown as a single breed. This small, low, rugged, and active terrier is demonic but not quarrelsome. The hard, wiry, and absolutely straight coat is shown with a minimum of tidying. Acceptable colors are red, wheaten, black and tan, and grizzle. Eleven to 12 pounds is the ideal weight; 10 inches at the withers is the ideal height. Highly prized as pets and in the field, Norwich Terriers have nevertheless remained rather scarce. Some 300 are registered annually, the breed ranking 91st. As seems to be the case for the "natural" breeds, in general, Norwich Terriers are not shown in number and rarely score group wins.

HEAD — *Skull* (5 points) — Long, of medium width, slightly domed and covered with short, hard hair. It should not be quite flat, as there should be a slight stop or drop between the eyes. *Muzzle* (5 points) — In proportion to the length of skull, with not too much taper toward the nose. Nose should be black and of good size. The jaws should be level and square. The nose projects somewhat over the mouth, giving the impression that the upper jaw is longer than the lower. The teeth should be evenly placed, having a scissors or level bite, with the former being preferable. *Eyes* (5 points) — Set wide apart, small and of almond shape, not round. Color to be dark brown or nearly black. To be bright, piercing and set well under the brow. *Ears* (10 points) — Small, prick, set well up on the skull, rather pointed but not cut. The hair on them should be short and velvety.

NECK (5 points) — Moderately short, thick and muscular, strongly set on sloping shoulders, but not so short as to appear clumsy.

CHEST (5 points) — Broad and very deep, well let down between the forelegs.

BODY (15 points) — Moderately short and well ribbed up with strong loin, deep flanks and very muscular hindquarters. *Legs and Feet* (10 points) — Both forelegs and hind legs should be short and very heavy in bone in proportion to the size of the dog. Forelegs straight or slightly bent with elbows close to the body. Scottish Terriers should not be out at the elbows. Stifles should be well bent and legs straight from hock to heel. Thighs very muscular. Feet round and thick with strong nails, forefeet larger than the hind feet. *Note:* The gait of the Scottish Terrier is peculiarly its own and is very characteristic of the breed. It is not the square trot or walk that is desirable in the long-legged breeds. The forelegs do not move in exact parallel planes — rather in reaching out incline slightly inward. This is due to the shortness of leg and width of chest. The action of the rear legs should be square and true and at the trot both the hocks and stifles should be flexed with a vigorous motion. *Tail* (2½ points) — Never cut and about 7 inches long, carried with a slight curve but not over the back.

COAT (15 points) — Rather short, about 2 inches, dense undercoat with outer coat intensely hard and wiry.

SIZE AND WEIGHT (10 points) — Equal consideration must be given to height, length of back and weight. Height at shoulder for either sex should be about 10 inches. Generally, a well-balanced Scottish Terrier dog of correct size should weigh from 19 to 22 pounds and a bitch, from 18 to 21 pounds. The principal objective must be symmetry and balance.

COLOR (2½ points) — Steel or iron gray, brindled or grizzled, black, sandy or wheaten. White markings are objectionable and can be allowed only on the chest and that to a slight extent only.

GENERAL APPEARANCE (10 points) — The face should wear a keen, sharp and active expression. Both head and tail should be carried well up. The dog should look very compact, well muscled and powerful, giving the impression of immense power in a small size. *Penalties:* Soft coat, round or very light eye, overshot or undershot jaw, obviously oversize or undersize, shyness, timidity or failure to show with head and tail up are faults to be penalized. No judge should put to Winners or Best of Breed any Scottish Terrier not showing real terrier character in the ring.

SCALE OF POINTS

Skull	5	Tail	2½
Muzzle	5	Coat	15
Eyes	5	Size	10
Ears	10	Color	2½
Neck	5	General appearance	10
Chest	5		
Body	15	Total	100
Legs and feet	10		

Approved June 10, 1947

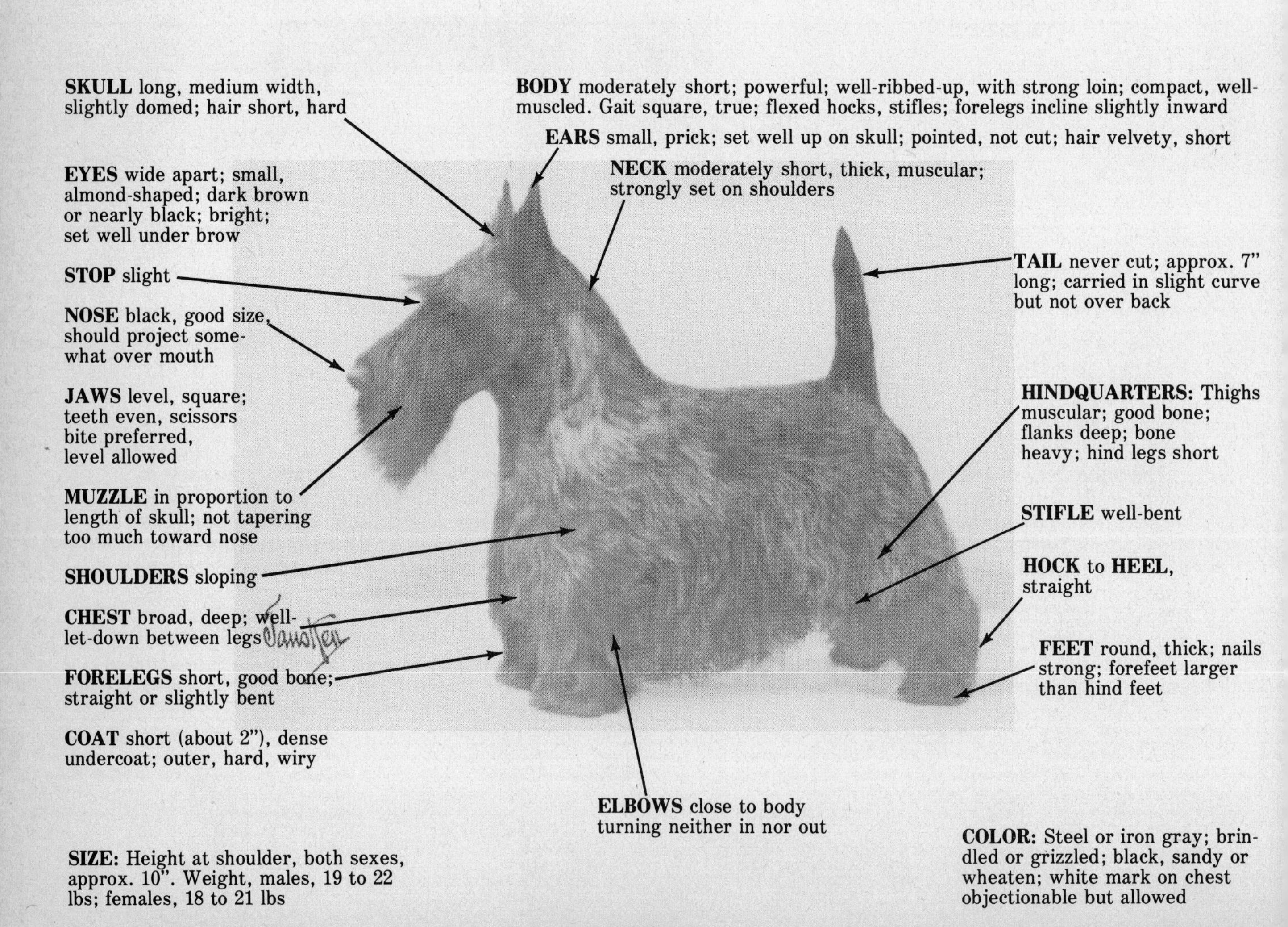
SKULL long, medium width, slightly domed; hair short, hard
BODY moderately short; powerful; well-ribbed-up, with strong loin; compact, well-muscled. Gait square, true; flexed hocks, stifles; forelegs incline slightly inward
EARS small, prick; set well up on skull; pointed, not cut; hair velvety, short
EYES wide apart; small, almond-shaped; dark brown or nearly black; bright; set well under brow
NECK moderately short, thick, muscular; strongly set on shoulders
STOP slight
TAIL never cut; approx. 7" long; carried in slight curve but not over back
NOSE black, good size, should project somewhat over mouth
JAWS level, square; teeth even, scissors bite preferred, level allowed
HINDQUARTERS: Thighs muscular; good bone; flanks deep; bone heavy; hind legs short
MUZZLE in proportion to length of skull; not tapering too much toward nose
STIFLE well-bent
SHOULDERS sloping
HOCK to HEEL, straight
CHEST broad, deep; well-let-down between legs
FEET round, thick; nails strong; forefeet larger than hind feet
FORELEGS short, good bone; straight or slightly bent
COAT short (about 2"), dense undercoat; outer, hard, wiry
ELBOWS close to body turning neither in nor out
COLOR: Steel or iron gray; brindled or grizzled; black, sandy or wheaten; white mark on chest objectionable but allowed
SIZE: Height at shoulder, both sexes, approx. 10". Weight, males, 19 to 22 lbs; females, 18 to 21 lbs

CH. BURBURY'S SIR LANCELOT

95 BOB, 32 GROUP PLACINGS, 3 GROUP FIRSTS, 4 GROUP FIRSTS IN BERMUDA, 5 SPECIALTY BEST IN SHOWS. SCOTTISH TERRIER CLUB OF SOUTHERN CALIFORNIA, GREATER MIAMI SCOTTISH TERRIER CLUB 1973 & 1974, SCOTTISH TERRIER CLUB OF AMERICA ROTATING SPECIALTY AT DETROIT, GREATER WASHINGTON, D.C. SPECIALTY, BEST OF BREEDS AT WESTMINSTER, TRENTON, BOARDWALK, PHILADELPHIA, SANTA BARBARA, MIAMI, BEVERLY HILLS, EASTERN. SIRE: DUNBAR'S SPECIAL AGENT. DAM: BURBURY EMBERS OF EDMINEL. BREEDER: LAURA LEE BURDICK.

HANDLER: PETER GREEN

LINDA CATLIN
CANTRAY KENNELS
BARRINGTON HILLS, ILL. 60010
(312) 381-0061

The origins of the Scottish Terrier are obscure. One deduces that they derived from the basic, rough coated, British, terrier stock which was bred differentially, locally, according to need and to taste. The Scottish Terrier was developed to be tough, weatherproof, courageous, and ready to dig after foxes and other pests of the day. The breed's identity was officially recognized in 1882. Originally preferred in brindle shades, black is now the most commonly seen coloring. Greys, reds, grizzles and wheatens are also seen. A Scottish Terrier must be keen, compact, and powerful. Symmetry and balance are equally important. Originally bred for a hard, outdoor life, the Scottish Terrier has proved very adaptable and popular as a companion and as a showman. They are excellent watch dogs. Some 10,000 are registered annually in the U.S., placing them second among terriers and 30th among all breeds. Scottish Terriers also rank second among terriers in numbers in show competition.

SKYE TERRIER STANDARD

GENERAL APPEARANCE — The Skye Terrier is a dog of style, elegance, and dignity; agile and strong with sturdy bone and hard muscle. Long, low, and lank — he is covered with a profuse coat that falls straight down either side of the body over oval-shaped ribs. The hair well feathered on the head veils forehead and eyes to serve as protection from brush and briar as well as amid serious encounters with other animals. He stands with head high and long tail hanging, and moves with a seemingly effortless gait. Of suitable size for his hunting work, strong in body, quarters, and jaw.

TEMPERAMENT — That of the typical working terrier capable of overtaking game and going to ground, displaying stamina, courage, strength, and agility. Fearless, good-tempered, loyal, and canny, he is friendly and gay with those he knows and reserved and cautious with strangers.

HEAD — Long and powerful, strength being deemed more important than extreme length. Moderate width at the back of the skull tapers gradually to a strong muzzle. The stop is slight. The dark muzzle is just moderately full as opposed to snipy, and the nose is always black. A Dudley, flesh-colored, or brown nose shall disqualify. Powerful and absolutely true jaws and mouth with the incisor teeth closing level, or with the upper teeth slightly overlapping the lower. *Eyes* — Brown, preferably dark brown, medium in size, close-set, and alight with life and intelligence. *Ears* — Symmetrical and gracefully feathered. They may be carried prick or drop. When prick, they are medium in size, placed high on the skull, erect at their outer edges, and slightly wider at the peak than at the skull. Drop ears, somewhat larger in size and set lower, hang flat against the skull.

NECK — Long and gracefully arched, carried high and proudly.

BODY — Pre-eminently long and low. The backline is level, the chest deep, with oval-shaped ribs. The sides appear flattish due to the straight falling and profuse coat.

LEGS AND FEET — *Forequarters* — Legs short, muscular, and straight as possible. "Straight as possible" means straight as soundness and chest will permit; it does not mean "terrier straight." Shoulders well laid back, with tight placement of shoulder blades at the withers, and elbows should fit closely to the sides and be neither loose nor tied. Forearm should curve slightly around the chest. *Hindquarters* — Strong, full, well developed, and well angulated. Legs short, muscular, and straight when viewed from behind. *Feet* — Large hare-feet preferably pointing forward, the pads thick and nails strong and preferably black.

MOVEMENT — The legs proceed straight forward when traveling. When approaching, the forelegs form a continuation of the straight line of the front, the feet being the same distance apart as the elbows. The principal propelling power is furnished by the hind legs, which travel straight forward. Forelegs should move well forward, without too much lift. The whole movement may be termed free, active, and effortless and give a more or less fluid picture.

TAIL — Long and well feathered. When hanging, its upper section is pendulous, following the line of the rump, its lower section thrown back in a moderate arc without twist or curl. When raised, its height makes it appear a prolongation of the backline. Though not to be preferred, the tail is sometimes carried high when the dog is excited or angry. When such carriage arises from emotion only, it is permissible. But the tail should not be constantly carried above the level of the back nor hang limp.

COAT — Double. Undercoat short, close, soft, and woolly. Outer coat hard, straight, and flat, 5½ inches long without extra credit granted for greater length. The body coat hangs straight down each side, parting from head to tail. The head hair, which may be shorter and softer, veils forehead and eyes and forms a moderate beard and apron. The long feathering on the ears falls straight down from the tips and outer edges, surrounding the ears like a fringe and outlining their shape. The ends of the hair should mingle with the coat at the sides of the neck.

COLOR — The coat must be one over-all color at the skin but may be of varying shades of the same color in the full coat, which may be black, blue, dark or light gray, silver, platinum, fawn, or cream. The dog must have no distinctive markings except for the desirable black points of ears, muzzle, and tip of tail, all of which points are preferably dark even to black. The shade of head and legs should approximate that of the body. There must be no trace of pattern, design, or clear-cut color variations, with the exception of the breed's only permissible white which occasionally exists on the chest not exceeding 2 inches in diameter.

The puppy coat may be very different in color from the adult coat. As it is growing and clearing, wide variations of color may occur; consequently this is permissible in dogs under 18 months of age. However, even in puppies there must be no trace of pattern, design, or clear-cut variations with the exception of the black band of varying width frequently seen encircling the body coat of

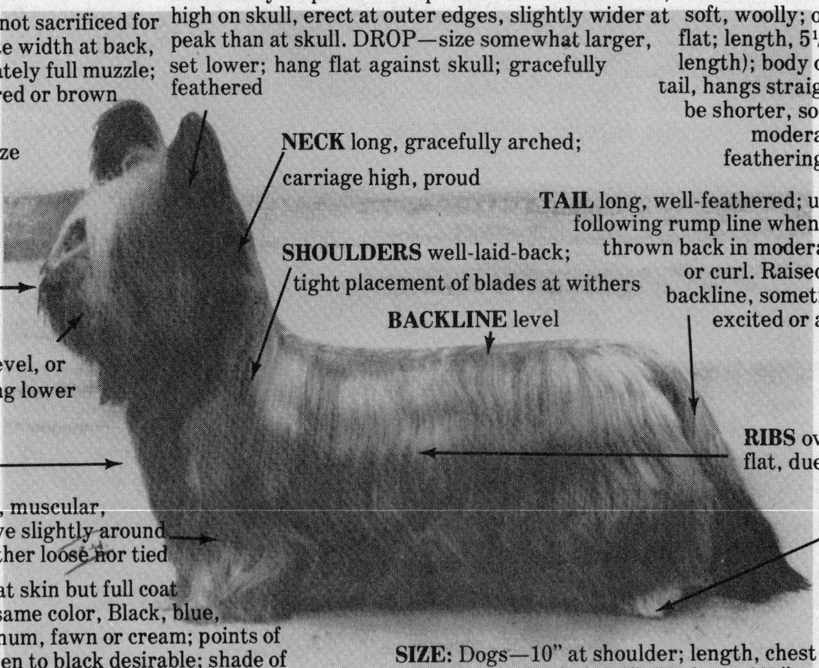

APPEARANCE: Elegant, dignified, agile, strong; bone sturdy; muscle hard; size suitable for hunting, long, lank, low. Temperament: Courageous, loyal, gay but reserved with strangers. Covered with profuse coat; stands with head high; gait effortless

HEAD long, powerful; strength not sacrificed for extreme length; skull of moderate width at back, tapering to strong, dark, moderately full muzzle; stop slight. A Dudley, flesh colored or brown nose shall disqualify.

EYES brown, dark preferred; size medium; close-set, expressive

NOSE always black

JAWS powerful; teeth closing level, or upper teeth slightly overlapping lower

CHEST deep

FOREQUARTERS: Legs short, muscular, straight as possible (should curve slightly around chest); elbows close to side, neither loose nor tied

COLOR: One solid, even color at skin but full coat of adult may vary in shades of same color, Black, blue, dark or light grey, silver, platinum, fawn or cream; points of ears, muzzle, tail tip, dark—even to black desirable; shade of head, legs, approximate body color; no trace of pattern, design or two clear-cut colors (white permitted on chest not to exceed 2" in diameter). A black band of varying width encircling body on cream dog under 18 months, not to be penalized

EARS may be prick or drop. PRICK—medium size, high on skull, erect at outer edges, slightly wider at peak than at skull. DROP—size somewhat larger, set lower; hang flat against skull; gracefully feathered

NECK long, gracefully arched; carriage high, proud

SHOULDERS well-laid-back; tight placement of blades at withers

BACKLINE level

COAT: Double; undercoat short, close, soft, woolly; outercoat hard, straight, flat; length, 5½" (no credit for greater length); body coat parted from head to tail, hangs straight down; head hair may be shorter, softer, veiling eyes, forms moderate beard and apron; ear feathering mingles with neck coat

TAIL long, well-feathered; upper section pendulous following rump line when hanging; lower section thrown back in moderate arc without twist or or curl. Raised, tail is prolongation of backline, sometimes carried high when excited or angry (no penalty when a matter of spirit)

RIBS oval-shaped; sides appear flat, due to coat

FEET large, hare-feet, preferably pointing forward; pads thick; nails strong, preferably black

SIZE: Dogs—10" at shoulder; length, chest bone over tail at rump, 20"; head 8½", tail 9". Bitches—9½" at shoulder; length, chest bone over tail at rump, 19"; head, 8"; tail 8½". Ideal length to height, 2:1 ratio. Slightly higher or lower, either sex, is acceptable if other dimensions are proportionate. Dogs 8" or less at withers and bitches 7½" or less at withers to be penalized

CH. TALISKER'S FANFRALOUCHE
CH. GLAMOOR GOOD GRACIOUS

CH. TALISKER'S FANFRALOUCHE, #4 SKYE TERRIER BITCH, KNIGHT SYSTEM, FOR 1973 AND FIRST HALF OF 1974, IS FROM THE LAST LITTER OF MRS. ADAM'S FAMOUS TALISKER KENNELS. "FANNY" HAS BEEN SHOWN SINCE OCTOBER 1972, ACHIEVING HER CHAMPIONSHIP NINE MONTHS LATER. SINCE THEN SHE HAS NUMEROUS BOB AND BOS AWARDS TO HER CREDIT.

CH. GLAMOOR GOOD GRACIOUS ("MITZI"), WHO WON WINNERS BITCH IN THE FEBRUARY 1974 SKYE TERRIER SPECIALTY SHOW IN NEW YORK, FINISHED HER CHAMPIONSHIP WITH A FIVE-POINT MAJOR AS WINNER BITCH AND BEST OF WINNERS AT THE WESTCHESTER KC SHOW.

COMING FROM SUCH ILLUSTRIOUS PARENTS AS WALTER AND ADELE GOODMAN'S CH. GLAMOOR GANG BUSTER AND CH. GLAMOOR GOOD NEWS, WESTMINSTER BEST IN SHOW WINNER, SHE IS WELL ON HER WAY TO BECOMING FAMOUS IN HER OWN RIGHT.

HANDLER: JANE PAUL & OWNER

DR. NICHOLAS M. JUHASZ & IRMA JUHASZ
701 FERNMERE AVENUE
INTERLAKEN, ASBURY PARK, N.J. 07712

the cream-colored dog, and the only permissible white which, as in the adult dog, occasionally exists on the chest not exceeding 2 inches in diameter.

SIZE — *Dogs:* Shoulder height, 10 inches. Length, chest bone over tail at rump, 20 inches. Head, 8½ inches. Tail, 9 inches. *Bitches:* Shoulder height, 9½ inches. Length, chest bone over tail at rump, 19 inches. Head, 8 inches. Tail, 8½ inches. A slightly higher or lower dog of either sex is acceptable, providing body, head, and tail dimensions are proportionately longer or shorter. The ideal ratio of body length to shoulder height is 2 to 1, which is considered the correct proportion.

Measurements are taken with the Skye standing in natural position with feet well under. A box caliper is used vertically and horizontally. For the height, the top bar should rest on the withers. The head is measured from the tip of the nose to the back of the occipital bone, and the tail from the root to tip. Dogs 8 inches or less at the withers and bitches 7½ inches or less at the withers are to be penalized.

Approved February 8, 1964

SOFT-COATED WHEATEN TERRIER STANDARD

GENERAL APPEARANCE — The Soft-Coated Wheaten Terrier is a medium-sized, hardy, well-balanced sporting terrier covered abundantly with a soft, naturally wavy coat of a good clear wheaten color. The breed requires moderation in all points and any exaggerated features are to be shunned. The head is only moderately long, is well balanced and should be free of any coarseness; the back is level with tail set on high and carried gaily; legs straight in front and muscular behind with well-laid-back shoulders and well-bent stifles to provide a long graceful stride. The dog should present an overall appearance of a hardy, active and happy animal, strong and well-coordinated.

HEAD — Well balanced and moderately long, profusely covered with coat which may fall forward to shade the eyes.

Skull — Flat and not too wide with no suggestion of coarseness. Skull and foreface about equal length.

Cheeks — Clean and stop well defined.

Muzzle — Square, powerful and strong, with no suggestion of snipiness. Lips are tight and black.

Nose — is black and large for size of the dog.

EYES — Dark hazel or brown, medium in size and well protected under a strong brow; eye rims black.

EARS — Break level with the skull and drop slightly forward close to the cheeks rather than pointing to the eyes; small to medium in size.

TEETH — Large, clean and white with either level or scissors bite.

NECK — Medium in length, strong and muscular, well covered with protective coat.

SHOULDERS — Well laid back, clean and smooth.

BODY — Body is compact; back strong and level. Ribs are well sprung but without roundness to provide a deep chest with relatively short coupling.

Length of back from point of withers to base of tail should measure about the same as from point of withers to ground.

Tail is docked and well set on, carried gaily but never over the back.

LEGS AND FEET — Forelegs, straight and well boned; hind legs well developed with well bent stifles; hocks well let down, turned neither in nor out.

Feet are round and compact with good depth of pad. Nails dark.

Dewclaws on forelegs may be removed; dewclaws on hind legs should be removed.

COAT — Abundant, soft and wavy, of a good clear wheaten color; may be shaded on the ears and muzzle.

The Soft-Coated Wheaten Terrier is a natural dog and should so appear. Dogs that appear to be overly trimmed should be penalized.

Coat on ears may be left natural or relieved of the fringe to accent smallness.

Coat color and texture do not stabilize until about 18-24 months and should be given some latitude in young dogs.

For show purposes the coat may be tidied up merely to present a neat outline but may not be clipped, plucked or styled.

SIZE — Dogs should measure 18-19 inches at the withers and should weigh between 35-45 pounds, bitches somewhat less.

MOVEMENT — Free; gait graceful and lively, having reach in front and good drive behind; straight action fore and aft.

TEMPERAMENT — Good tempered, spirited and game; exhibits less aggressiveness than is sometimes encouraged in terriers in the show ring; alert and intelligent.

MAJOR FAULTS — Overshot. Undershot. Coat texture deviation. Any color save wheaten.

GENERAL APPEARANCE: Medium-sized sporting terrier, requiring moderation in all points. Presents an overall appearance of a hardy, active, happy, strong, and well coordinated animal

COAT: Abundant, soft and wavy, of a good clear wheaten color. Overly trimmed dogs should be penalized. Coat color and texture do not stabilize till 18-24 months

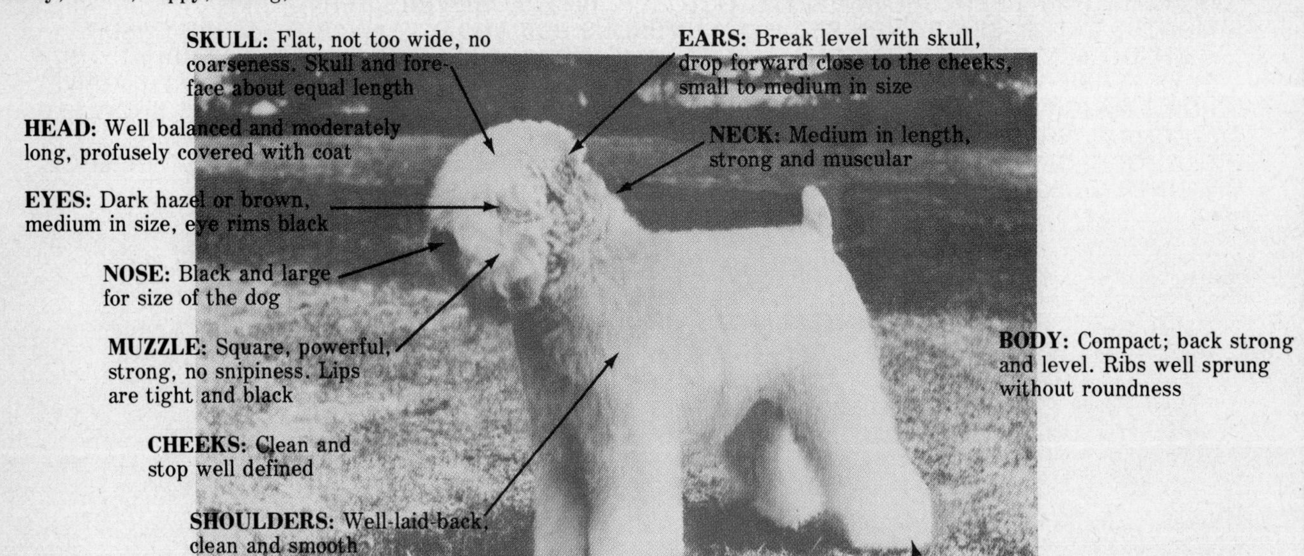

MAJOR FAULTS: Overshot. Undershot. Coat texture deviation. Any color save wheaten

TEMPERAMENT: Good tempered, spirited, game, less aggressiveness than is sometimes encouraged in terriers in the show ring; alert and intelligent

SIZE: Dogs 18-19 inches at withers; weight between 35-45 pounds, bitches somewhat less

HOLMENOCKS HAPHAZARD

NEARING CHAMPIONSHIP WITH MAJOR WINS UNDER MR. ROBERT MOORE AND MISS GENE SIMMONDS WHERE HAPHAZARD WENT ON TO BOB. ALSO BOS UNDER MRS. TOM STEVENSON AT OX RIDGE.

OWNER
KNOCKNAHILLA REG.
MARIE L. AVALLONE
161 PRITEHARD AVENUE
THORNWOOD, NEW YORK 10594

HANDLER/AGENT
BERTRAM TORMEY
PINES BRIDGE ROAD
KATONAH, NEW YORK

The Soft-Coated Wheaten Terrier is a native of Ireland where it was an all-round working dog used for driving cattle, standing guard, and killing vermin. Dogs stand 18-19 inches at the shoulder and weigh 35-45 pounds. The coat must be wheaten in color, abundant, long, and slightly wavy. The dog is presented naturally. The Soft-Coated Wheaten Terrier is believed to be one of the old, traditional breeds of Ireland and to have been ancestral to other breeds but in recent decades, it has not enjoyed popularity in either Ireland or England. The breed achieved full AKC recognition in 1973. Registrations will probably not exceed 200 in 1974.

STAFFORDSHIRE BULL TERRIER STANDARD

CHARACTERISTICS — From the past history of the Staffordshire Bull Terrier the modern dog draws his character of indomitable courage, high intelligence, and tenacity. This, coupled with his affection for his friends, and children in particular, his off-duty quietness, and trustworthy stability makes him the foremost all-purpose dog.

GENERAL APPEARANCE — The Staffordshire Bull Terrier is a smooth-coated dog. He should be of great strength for his size and, although muscular, should be active and agile.

HEAD AND SKULL — Short, deep through, broad skull, very pronounced cheek muscles, distinct stop, short foreface, black nose.

EYES — Dark preferable, but may bear some relation to coat colour. Round, of medium size, and set to look straight ahead.

EARS — Rose or half-pricked and not large. Full drop or prick to be penalized.

MOUTH — The mouth should be level, i.e., the incisors of the bottom jaw should fit closely inside the incisors of the top jaw, and the lips should be tight and clean. The badly undershot or overshot mouth to be heavily penalized.

NECK — Muscular, rather short, clean in outline and gradually widening towards the shoulders.

FOREQUARTERS — Legs straight and well boned, set rather wide apart, without looseness at the shoulders, and showing no weakness at the pasterns, from which point the feet turn out a little.

BODY — The body should be close-coupled, with a level topline, wide front, deep brisket, well-sprung ribs, and rather light in the loins.

HINDQUARTERS — The hindquarters should be well muscled, hocks let down with stifles well bent. Legs should be parallel when viewed from behind.

FEET — The feet should be well padded, strong, and of medium size.

TAIL — The tail should be of medium length, low set, tapering to a point and carried rather low. It should not curl much, and may be likened to an old-fashioned pump handle.

COAT — Smooth, short, and close to the skin.

COLOUR — Red, fawn, white, black or blue, or any of these colours with white. Brindle or any shade of brindle with white. Black-and-tan or liver colour are not permitted to be exhibited.

WEIGHT AND SIZE — Weight: Dogs, 28 to 38 lb. Bitches, 24 to 34 lbs. Height (at shoulder): 14 to 16 in., these heights being related to the weights.

FAULTS — To be penalized in accordance with the severity of the faults: Light eyes or pink eye-rims, except that where the coat surrounding the eye is white, the rim may be pink. Tail too long or badly curled. Non-conformation to the limits of weight or height. Full drop and prick ears. Undershot or overshot mouths. The following faults should debar a dog from winning any prize: Pink (Dudley) nose. Badly undershot or overshot mouth. Badly undershot — where the lower jaw protrudes to such an extent that the incisors of the lower jaw do not touch those of the upper jaw. Badly overshot — where the upper jaw protrudes to such an extent that the incisors of the upper jaw do not touch those of the lower jaw.

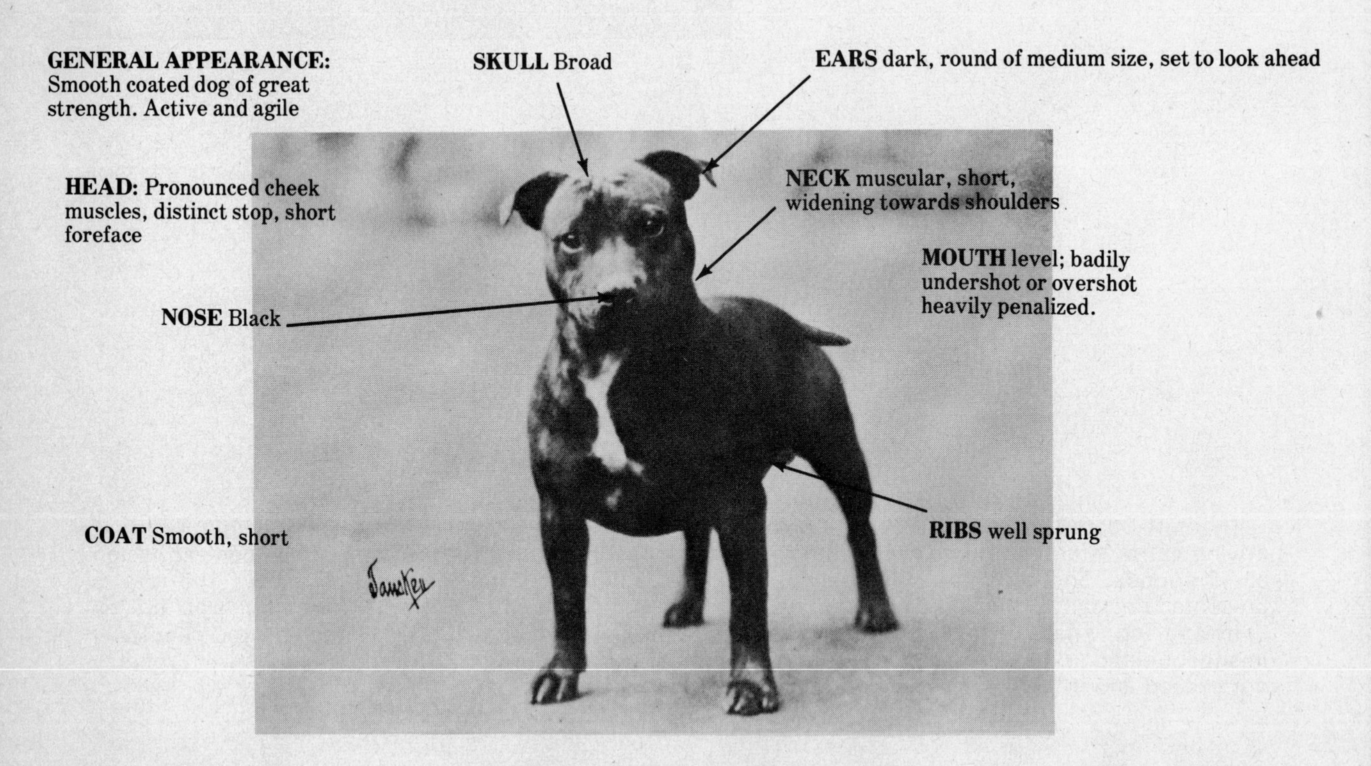

GAMECOCK ANOTHER BRINSLEY LAD

"LAD" WENT FROM THE PUPPY CLASS TO BEST OF OPPOSITE SEX AT THE STAFFORDSHIRE BULL TERRIER CLUB OF AMERICA SPECIALTY SHOW ON MARCH 10, 1973. AT THE NATIONAL CAPITAL KENNEL CLUB SHOW HE WAS BEST STAFFORDSHIRE BULL TERRIER DOG AND WON THE MISCELLANEOUS GROUP. ON OCTOBER 7, 1973 HE WAS BEST IN SHOW AT THE SPECIALTY OF THE STAFFORDSHIRE BULL TERRIER CLUB.

The Staffordshire Bull Terrier was the *original* Bull and Terrier cross around 1800 in England, both of its ancestors, the English Bulldog and the old English Terrier are extinct. In 1935, the breed was recognized by the Kennel Club in England. In 1966, no fewer than 1,228 Staffordshire Bull Terriers were registered by the Kennel Club, which made the Stafford the most popular smooth-coated Terrier, the fifth most popular Terrier and the 27th most popular breed on the all-breed list. The Stafford is recognized and represented in at least thirty-five countries, including the United States and Canada, around the world from Finland to New Zealand.

WEST HIGHLAND WHITE TERRIER STANDARD

GENERAL APPEARANCE — The West Highland White Terrier is a small, game, well-balanced, hardy-looking Terrier, exhibiting good showmanship, possessed with no small amount of self-esteem, strongly built, deep in chest and back ribs, straight back and powerful hindquarters on muscular legs, and exhibiting in marked degree a great combination of strength and activity. The coat should be about 2 inches long, white in color, hard, with plently of soft undercoat. The dog should be neatly presented. Considerable hair should be left around the head to act as a frame for the face to yield a typical Westie expression.

COLOR AND PIGMENTATION — Coat should be white, as defined by the breed's name. Nose should be black. Black pigmentation is most desirable on lips, eye-rims, pads of feet, nails and skin. *Faults:* Any coat color other than white and nose color other than black are serious faults.

COAT — Very important and seldom seen to perfection; must be double-coated. The outer coat consists of straight hard hair, about 2 inches long, with shorter coat on neck and shoulders, properly blended. *Faults:* Any silkiness or tendency to curl is a serious fault, as is an open or single coat.

SIZE — Dogs should measure about 11 inches at the withers, bitches about one inch less. *Faults:* Any specimens much over or under height limits are objectionable.

SKULL — Should be fairly broad, being in proportion to his powerful jaw, not too long, slightly domed, and gradually tapering to the eyes. There should be a defined stop, eyebrows heavy. *Faults:* A too long or too narrow skull.

MUZZLE — Should be slightly shorter than the skull, powerful and gradually tapering to the nose, which should be large. The jaws should be level and powerful, the teeth well set and large for the size of the dog. There shall be 6 incisor teeth between the canines of both lower and upper jaws. A tight scissors bite with upper incisors slightly overlapping the lower incisors or level mouth are equally acceptable. *Faults:* Muzzle longer than skull. Teeth much undershot or overshot are a serious fault, as are teeth defective or missing.

EARS — Small, carried tightly erect, set wide apart and terminating in a sharp point. They must never be cropped. The hair on the ears should be short, smooth and velvety, and trimmed free of fringe at the tips. *Faults:* Round-pointed, drop, broad and large ears are very objectionable, as are mule-ears, ears set too closely together or not held tightly erect.

EYES — Widely set apart, medium in size, dark in color, slightly sunk in the head, sharp and intelligent. Looking from under heavy eyebrows, they give a piercing look. *Faults:* Too small, too full or light-colored eyes are very objectionable.

NECK — Muscular and nicely set on sloping shoulders. *Faults:* Short neck or too long neck.

CHEST — Very deep and extending at least to the elbows with breadth in proportion to size of the dog. *Fault:* Shallow chest.

BODY — Compact and of good substance, level back, ribs deep and well arched in the upper half of rib, presenting a flattish side appearance, loins broad and strong, hindquarters strong, muscular, and wide across the top. *Faults:* Long or weak back; barrel ribs; high rump.

LEGS AND FEET — Both forelegs and hind legs should be muscular and relatively short, but with sufficient length to set the dog up so as not to be too close to the ground. The shoulder blades should be well laid back and well knit at the backbone. The chest should be relatively broad and the front legs spaced apart accordingly. The front legs should be set in under the shoulder blades with definite body overhang before them. The front legs should be reasonably straight and thickly covered with short hard hair. The hind legs should be short and sinewy; the thighs very muscular and not set wide apart, with hocks well bent. The forefeet are larger than the hind ones, are round, proportionate in size, strong, thickly padded, and covered with short hard hair; they may properly be turned out a slight amount. The hind feet are smaller and thickly padded. *Faults:* Steep shoulders, loaded shoulders, or out at the elbows. Too light bone. Cowhocks, weak hocks and lack of angulation. A "Fiddle-front" is a serious fault.

TAIL — Relatively short, when standing erect it should never extend above the top of the skull. It should be covered with hard hairs, no feather, as straight as possible, carried gaily but not curled over the back. The tail should be set on high enough so that the spine does not slope down to it. The tail must never be docked. *Faults:* Tail set too low; tail too long or carried at half mast or over back.

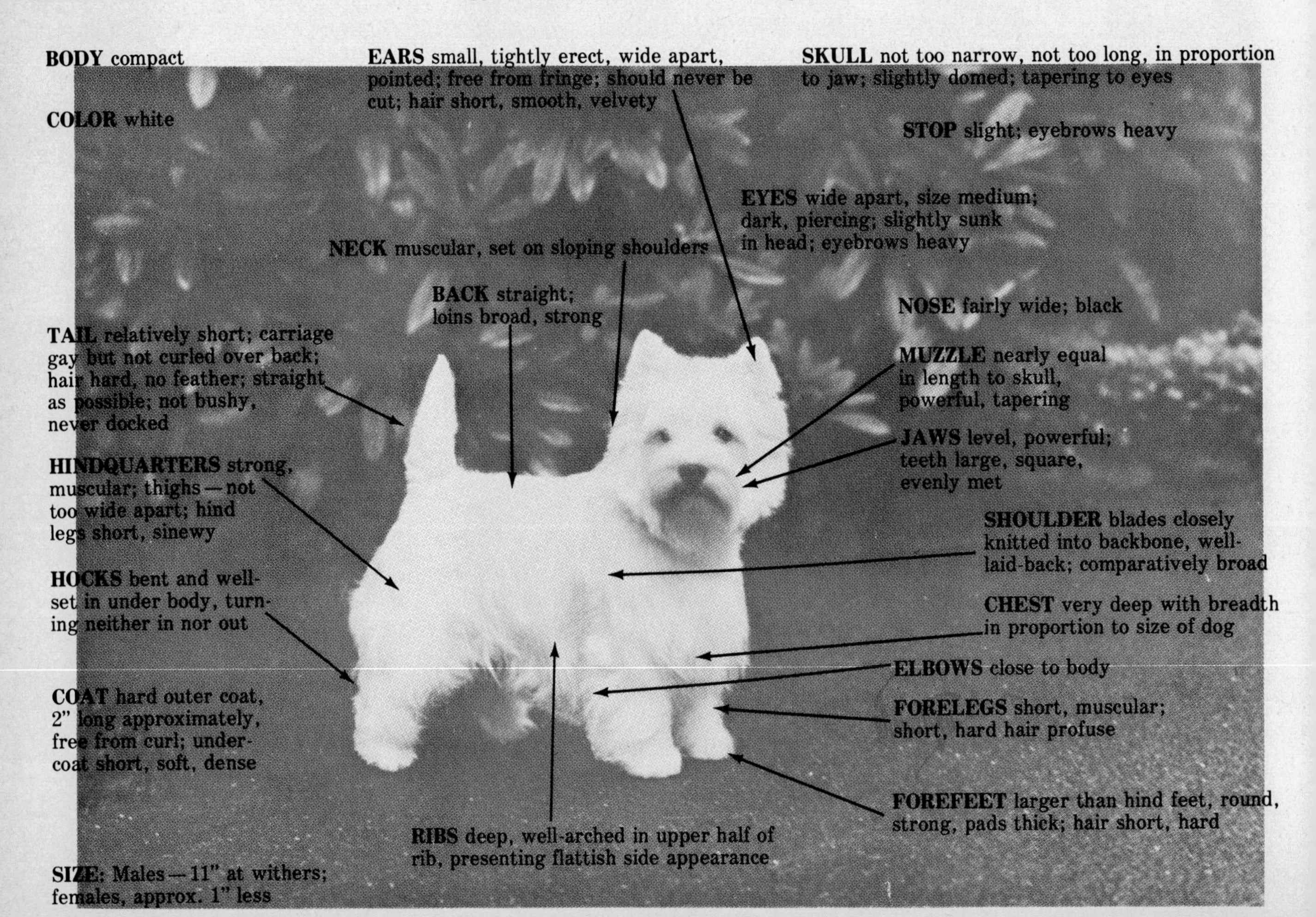
BODY compact
EARS small, tightly erect, wide apart, pointed; free from fringe; should never be cut; hair short, smooth, velvety
SKULL not too narrow, not too long, in proportion to jaw; slightly domed; tapering to eyes
COLOR white
STOP slight; eyebrows heavy
EYES wide apart, size medium; dark, piercing; slightly sunk in head; eyebrows heavy
NECK muscular, set on sloping shoulders
BACK straight; loins broad, strong
NOSE fairly wide; black
TAIL relatively short; carriage gay but not curled over back; hair hard, no feather; straight as possible; not bushy, never docked
MUZZLE nearly equal in length to skull, powerful, tapering
JAWS level, powerful; teeth large, square, evenly met
HINDQUARTERS strong, muscular; thighs—not too wide apart; hind legs short, sinewy
SHOULDER blades closely knitted into backbone, well-laid-back; comparatively broad
HOCKS bent and well-set in under body, turning neither in nor out
CHEST very deep with breadth in proportion to size of dog
ELBOWS close to body
COAT hard outer coat, 2" long approximately, free from curl; under-coat short, soft, dense
FORELEGS short, muscular; short, hard hair profuse
FOREFEET larger than hind feet, round, strong, pads thick; hair short, hard
RIBS deep, well-arched in upper half of rib, presenting flattish side appearance
SIZE: Males—11" at withers; females, approx. 1" less

CH. BRAIDHOLME WHITE TORNADO OF BINATE

BEFORE HIS IMPORTATION FROM ENGLAND, "NIKKI" WAS NAMED BEST IN SHOW AT THE BIRMINGHAM KC AT 13 MONTHS OF AGE. AT THE 1973 WEST HIGHLAND WHITE TERRIER CLUB OF AMERICA SPECIALTY HELD AT THE ALL TERRIER MONTGOMERY COUNTY KC, "NIKKI" WAS BOB FROM THE OPEN DOG CLASS AND WENT ON TO GROUP 4. IN 1974 HE REPEATED HIS BOB VICTORY AT THE W.H.W.T. SPECIALTY AND WENT ON TO THE COVERTED BEST IN SHOW AWARD. THIS FINE ENGLISH IMPORT IS A MULTIPLE BIS WINNER AND RANKS AMONG THE TOP TERRIERS IN THE COUNTRY.

OWNERS
MR. & MRS. GEORGE H. SEEMANN, JR
WILSON POINT
SOUTH NORWALK, CONN. 06854

AGENT/HANDLER
CLIFFORD HALLMARK
60 EAST MAIN STREET
MENDHAM, N.J. 07945
201—543-4842

MOVEMENT — Should be free, straight and easy all around. In front, the leg should be freely extended forward by the shoulder. The hind movement should be free, strong and fairly close. The hocks should be freely flexed and drawn close under the body; so that when moving off the foot the body is thrown or pushed forward with some force. *Faults:* Stiff, stilty or too wide movement behind. Lack of reach in front, and/or drive behind.

TEMPERAMENT — Must be alert, gay, courageous and self-reliant, but friendly. *Faults:* Excess timidity or excess pugnacity.

Approved December 10, 1968

AMERICAN STAFFORDSHIRE TERRIER STANDARD

GENERAL IMPRESSION — The American Staffordshire Terrier should give the impression of great strength for his size, a well put-together dog, muscular, but agile and graceful, keenly alive to his surroundings. He should be stocky, not long-legged or racy in outline. His courage is proverbial.

HEAD — Medium length, deep through, broad skull, very pronounced cheek muscles, distinct stop; and ears are set high. *Ears* — Cropped or uncropped, the latter preferred. Uncropped ears should be short and held half rose or prick. Full drop to be penalized. *Eyes* — Dark and round, low down in skull and set far apart. No pink eyelids. *Muzzle* — Medium length, rounded on upper side to fall away abruptly below eyes. Jaws well defined. Underjaw to be strong and have biting power. Lips close and even, no looseness. Upper teeth to meet tightly outside lower teeth in front. Nose definitely black.

NECK — Heavy, slightly arched, tapering from shoulders to back of skull. No looseness of skin. Medium length. *Shoulders* — Strong and muscular with blades wide and sloping. *Back* — Fairly short. Slight sloping from withers to rump with gentle short slope at rump to base of tail. Loins slightly tucked.

BODY — Well-sprung ribs, deep in rear. All ribs close together. Forelegs set rather wide apart to permit of chest development. Chest deep and broad.

TAIL — Short in comparison to size, low set, tapering to a fine point; not curled or held over back. Not docked. *Legs* — The front legs should be straight, large or round bones, pastern upright. No resemblance of bend in front. Hindquarters well-muscled, let down at hocks, turning neither in nor out. Feet of moderate size, well-arched and compact. Gait must be springy but without roll or pace.

COAT — Short, close, stiff to the touch, and glossy. *Color* — Any color, solid, parti, or patched is permissible, but all white, more than 80 per cent white, black and tan, and liver not to be encouraged.

SIZE — Height and weight should be in proportion. A height of about 18 to 19 inches at shoulders for the male and 17 to 18 inches for the female is to be considered preferable.

FAULTS — Faults to be penalized are Dudley nose, light or pink eyes, tail too long or badly carried, undershot or overshot mouths.

Approved June 10, 1936

HEAD medium length; broad skull; very pronounced cheek muscles

APPEARANCE: Impression of great strength for size; well-put-together, stocky; not long-legged or racy; muscular; agile

STOP distinct

EARS: Cropped or uncropped (latter preferred). Uncropped short, held half rose or prick

EYES dark, round; set low in skull; wide apart

NECK heavy; slightly arched; tapering from shoulders to back of skull; dry; length medium

NOSE definite black

BACK fairly short; slight slope from withers to rump; gentle slope from rump to tail-set. Loins slightly tucked

MUZZLE medium length; rounded upper side; falling away abruptly below eyes

TAIL short compared to size; low-set; tapering to fine point; not curled or held over back; not docked

JAWS well-defined; underjaw strong, with biting power. Teeth have tight scissors bite. Lips close, even; no looseness

HINDQUARTERS well-muscled

SHOULDERS strong, muscular; blades wide, sloping

HOCKS well-let-down; turning neither in nor out

CHEST deep, broad

SIZE: Height and weight in proportion. Preferred: Male, 18" to 19" at shoulder; female, 17" to 18"

FORELEGS straight, large; wide apart; bones round. Pasterns upright

FEET well-arched, compact; size moderate

RIBS well-sprung; close together; deep in rear

COAT short, close; stiff to touch; glossy

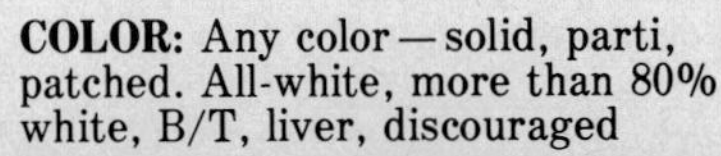

COLOR: Any color—solid, parti, patched. All-white, more than 80% white, B/T, liver, discouraged

BEDLINGTON TERRIER STANDARD

GENERAL APPEARANCE — A graceful, lithe, well balanced dog with no sign of coarseness, weakness or shelliness. In repose the expression is mild and gentle, not shy or nervous. Aroused, the dog is particularly alert and full of immense energy and courage. Noteworthy for endurance, Bedlingtons also gallop at great speed, as their body outline clearly shows.

HEAD — Narrow but deep and rounded. Shorter in skull and longer in jaw. Covered with a profuse topknot which is lighter than the color of the body, highest at the crown, and tapering gradually to just back of the nose. There must be no stop and the unbroken line from crown to nose end reveals a slender head without cheekiness or snipeyness. Lips are black in the blue and tans and brown in all other solid and bi-colors.

EYES — Almond shaped, small, bright, and well sunk with no tendency to tear or water. Set is oblique and fairly high on the head. Blues have dark eyes; blues and tans less dark with amber lights; sandies, sandies and tans — light hazel; liver, livers and tans slightly darker. Eye rims are black in the blue and blue and tans and brown in all other solid and bi-colors.

EARS — Triangular with rounded tips. Set on low and hanging flat to the cheek in front with a slight projection at the base. Point of greatest width approximately three inches. Ear tips reach the corners of the mouth. Thin and velvety in texture, covered with fine hair forming a small silky tassel at the tip.

NOSE — Nostrils large and well defined. Blues and blues and tans have black noses. Livers, livers and tans, sandies, sandies and tans have brown noses.

JAWS — Long and tapering. Strong muzzle well filled up with bone beneath the eye. Close fitting lips, no flews.

TEETH — Large, strong and white. Level or scissors bite. Lower canines clasp the outer surface of the upper gum just in front of the upper canines. Upper premolars and molars lie outside those of the lower jaw.

NECK AND SHOULDERS — Long tapering neck with no throatiness, deep at the base and rising well up from the shoulders which are flat and sloping with no excessive musculature. The head is carried high.

BODY — Muscular and markedly flexible. Chest deep. Flat ribbed and deep through the brisket, which reaches to the elbows. Back has a good natural arch over the loin creating a definite tuck-up of the underline. Body slightly greater in length than height. Well muscled quarters are also fine and graceful.

LEGS AND FEET — Lithe and muscular. The hind legs are longer than the forelegs, which are straight and wider apart at the chest than at the feet. Slight bend to pasterns which are long and sloping without weakness. Stifles well angulated. Hocks strong and well let down, turning neither in nor out. Long hare feet with thick, well closed up, smooth pads. Dewclaws should be removed.

COAT — A very distinctive mixture of hard and soft hair standing well out from the skin. Crisp to the touch but not wiry, having a tendency to curl, especially on the head and face. When in show trim must not exceed one inch on body; hair on legs is slightly longer.

TAIL — Set low, scimitar shaped, thick at the root and tapering to a point which reaches the hock. Not carried over the back nor tight to the underbody.

COLOR — Blue, sandy, liver, blue and tan, sandy and tan, liver and tan. In bi-colors the tan markings are found on the legs, chest, under the tail, inside the hindquarters and over each eye. The topknots of all adults should be lighter than the body color. Patches of darker hair from an injury are not objectionable as it is only temporary. Darker body pigmentation of all colors to be encouraged.

HEIGHT — The preferred Bedlington Terrier dog measures 16½ inches at the withers, the bitch 15½ inches. Under 16 inches or over 17½ inches for dogs and under 15 inches or over 16½ inches for bitches are serious faults. Only where comparative superiority of a specimen outside these ranges clearly justifies it, should greater latitude be taken.

WEIGHT — To be proportionate to height within the range of 17 to 23 pounds.

GAIT — Unique lightness of movement. Springy in the slower paces, not stilted or hackneyed. Must not cross, weave or paddle.

Approved September 12, 1967

GENERAL APPEARANCE: Graceful, lithe, well-balanced; no coarseness, shelliness or weakness. Expression mild, gentle. When aroused, dog is alert, full of immense energy, courage. Noteworthy for endurance, speed; unique lightness of movement

HEAD carried high; narrow, deep, rounded; skull shorter, jaw longer, tapering; no stop, line from crown to nose unbroken; No cheekiness or snipeyness; lips black in blue and tans, brown in all other solid and bi-colors; topknot profuse, highest at crown, tapering to just back of nose, color lighter than body; muzzle strong, well filled with bone beneath eye; lips close fitting, no flews

EARS triangular, tips rounded, low-set, hanging flat to cheek in front with slight projection at base; greatest width, approx. 3"; ear tips reach corners of mouth; texture velvety, thin; covered with fine hair, small tassel at tip

TAIL set low; scimitar-shaped; root thick, tapering to point that reaches hock, not carried over back nor tight to underbody

BACK has good, natural arch over loin, creating definite tuck-up of underline

NOSE: Nostrils large, well-defined; blues and blue/tans, black in color; livers, liver/tans, sandies, sandie/tans, brown in color

EYES almond-shaped, small, bright, well-sunk, no tendency to tear; set obliquely, fairly high. Blues have dark eyes; blues and tans, less dark with amber lights; sandies, sandies/tans, light hazel; liver, liver/tans, slightly darker. Rims black in blue and blue/tans; brown in all solid and bi-colors

COAT: Very distinctive mixture of hard and soft hair standing well out from skin; crisp to touch but not wiry; a tendency to curl, especially on head, face. Show trim must not exceed one inch of body, leg hair, slightly longer

TEETH large, strong, white. Level or scissors bite

HIND LEGS longer than forelegs; stifles well-angulated; hocks strong, well-let-down, turning neither in nor out; dewclaws should be removed

NECK long, tapering, no throatiness; deep at base, rising well up from shoulders; head carried high

CHEST deep; flat ribbed, brisket deep, reaching to elbows

FEET: Hare feet; pads thick, well-closed-up, smooth

SHOULDERS flat, sloping, no excessive musculature

FORELEGS straight, wider apart at chest than feet; pasterns slightly bent, long sloping without weakness

BODY muscular, markedly flexible; slightly greater in length than height; quarters well-muscled

SIZE: Dog, 16½" at withers, bitch, 15½. Over 17½ and under 16" for dogs and over 16½ and under 15" for bitches are serious faults. Only superior specimens' outside limits considered. WEIGHT: In proportion to height, within 17 to 23 lbs.

White

THE BULL TERRIER must be strongly built, muscular, symmetrical and active, with a keen determined and intelligent expression, full of fire but of sweet disposition and amenable to discipline.

THE HEAD should be long, strong and deep right to the end of the muzzle, but not coarse. Full face it should be oval in outline and be filled completely up giving the impression of fullness with a surface devoid of hollows or indentations, *i.e.*, egg shaped. In profile it should curve gently downwards from the top of the skull to the tip of the nose. The forehead should be flat across from ear to ear. The distance from the tip of the nose to the eyes should be perceptibly greater than that from the eyes to the top of the skull. The underjaw should be deep and well defined. *The Lips* should be clean and tight. *The Teeth* should meet in either a level or in a scissors bite. In the scissors bite the upper teeth should fit in front of and closely against the lower teeth, and they should be sound, strong and perfectly regular.

THE EARS should be small, thin and placed close together. They should be capable of being held stiffly erect, when they should point upwards. *The Eyes* should be well sunken and as dark as possible, with a piercing glint and they should be small, triangular and obliquely placed; set near together and high up on the dog's head. Blue eyes are a disqualification. *The Nose* should be black, with well developed nostrils bent downwards at the tip.

THE NECK should be very muscular, long, arched and clean, tapering from the shoulders to the head and it should be free from loose skin.

THE CHEST should be broad when viewed from in front, and there should be great depth from withers to brisket, so that the latter is nearer the ground than the belly.

THE BODY should be well rounded with marked spring of rib, the back should be short and strong. The back ribs deep. Slightly arched over the loin. The shoulders should be strong and muscular but without heaviness. The shoulder blades should be wide and flat and there should be a very pronounced backward slope from the bottom edge of the blade to the top edge. Behind the shoulders there should be no slackness or dip at the withers. The underline from the brisket to the belly should form a graceful upward curve.

THE LEGS should be big boned but not to the point of coarseness; the forelegs should be of moderate length, perfectly straight, and the dog must stand firmly upon them. The elbows must turn neither in nor out, and the pasterns should be strong and upright. The hind legs should be parallel viewed from behind. The thighs very muscular with hocks well let down. Hind pasterns short and upright. The stifle joint should be well bent with a well developed second thigh. *The Feet* round and compact with well arched toes like a cat.

THE TAIL should be short, set on low, fine, and ideally should be carried horizontally. It should be thick where it joins the body, and should taper to a fine point.

THE COAT should be short, flat, harsh to the touch and with a fine gloss. The dog's skin should fit tightly. *The Color* is white, though markings on the head are permissible. Any markings elsewhere on the coat are to be severely faulted. Skin pigmentation is not to be penalized.

MOVEMENT — The dog shall move smoothly, covering the ground with free, easy strides, fore and hind legs should move parallel each to each when viewed from in front or behind. The forelegs reaching out well and the hind legs moving smoothly at the hip and flexing well at the stifle and hock. The dog should move compactly and in one piece but with a typical jaunty air that suggests agility and power.

FAULTS — Any departure from the foregoing points shall be considered a fault, and the seriousness of the fault shall be in exact proportion to its degree, *i.e.*, a very crooked front is a very bad fault; a rather crooked front is a rather bad fault; and a slight crooked front is a slight fault.

DISQUALIFICATION

Blue eyes.

Colored

The Standard for the Colored Variety is the same as for the White except for the subhead "Color" which reads: *Color*. Any color other than white, or any color with white markings. Other things being equal, the preferred color is brindle. A dog which is predominantly white shall be disqualified.

DISQUALIFICATIONS

Blue eyes. Any dog which is predominantly white.

Approved September 10, 1968

VARIETIES: Two, white and colored. Standard for colored same as white. COLORED: Any color other than white, or any color with white markings. Other things being equal, the preferred color is brindle

HEAD long, strong, deep; full face, egg-shaped; profile gently curves from top of skull to nose tip; forehead flat; distance from tip of nose to eyes greater than eyes to occiput

EARS erect; small, thin; placed close together

NECK muscular, arched, long, clean, free from loose skin, tapering

SHOULDERS strong, muscular, without heaviness; blades wide, flat; slope pronounced; no dip at withers

BACK short, strong; loins slightly arched

TAIL set low; short, fine; carried horizontally; thick at base tapering to fine point

THIGHS well-developed, muscular

HIND LEGS parallel viewed from rear

STIFLE JOINT well-bent

HOCKS well-let-down; hock to heel short, upright

UNDERLINE graceful upward curve

RIBS well-rounded, back ribs deep

PASTERNS strong, upright

EYES obliquely placed, triangular, small, dark, well-sunken, set near together and high on head

TEETH level or scissor bite

NOSE black; well-developed nostrils bent downward at tip

MUZZLE strong, full

LIPS tight, clean

UNDERJAW deep, well-defined

CHEST deep, broad

ELBOWS turning neither in nor out

FORELEGS moderate in length, big boned, straight

FEET round, compact; toes well-arched, catlike

COAT short, flat, harsh, glossy; skin fits tightly

DISQUALIFICATIONS: For whites — any markings other than on head; for coloreds — predominantly white in color

HEAD — Strongly made and large, not out of proportion to the dog's size, the muscles showing extraordinary development, more especially the maxillary. *Skull* broad between the ears, getting gradually less towards the eyes, and measuring about the same from the inner corner of the eye to back of skull as it does from ear to ear. The forehead well domed. The head is *covered* with very soft silky hair, which should not be confined to a mere topknot, and the lighter in color and silkier it is the better. The *Cheeks*, starting from the ears proportionately with the skull have a gradual taper towards the muzzle, which is deep and strongly made, and measures about three inches in length, or in proportion to skull as 3 is to 5. The *Muzzle* is covered with hair of a little darker shade than the topknot, and of the same texture as the feather of the forelegs. The top of the muzzle is generally bare for about an inch from the back part of the nose, the bareness coming to a point towards the eye, and being about 1 inch broad at the nose. The nose and inside of *Mouth* black or dark-colored. The *Teeth* very strong, especially the canines, which are of extraordinary size for a small dog. The canines mesh well with each other, so as to give the greatest available holding and punishing power. The incisors in each jaw are evenly spaced and six in number, with the upper incisors overlapping the lower incisors in a tight, scissors bite.

EYES — Set wide apart, large, full, round, bright, expressive of great determination, intelligence and dignity; set low and prominent in front of the head; color, a rich dark hazel.

EARS — Pendulous, set well back, wide apart, and low on the skull, hanging close to the cheek, with a very slight projection at the base, broad at the junction of the head and tapering almost to a point, the forepart of the ear tapering very little — like the tapering being mostly on the back part, the forepart of the ear coming almost straight down from its junction with the head to the tip. They should harmonize in color with the body color. In the case of a Pepper dog they are covered with a soft straight brownish hair (in some cases almost black). In the case of a Mustard dog the hair should be mustard in color, a shade darker than the body, but not black. All should have a thin feather of light hair starting about 2 inches from the tip, and of nearly the same color and texture as the topknot, which gives the ear the appearance of a *distinct point*. The animal is often 1 or 2 years old before the feather is shown. The cartilage and skin of the ear should not be thick, but rather thin. Length of ear from 3 to 4 inches.

NECK — Very muscular, well-developed and strong, showing great power of resistance, being well set into the shoulders.

BODY — Long, strong and flexible; ribs well sprung and round, chest well developed and let well down between the forelegs; the back rather low at the shoulder, having a slight downward curve and a corresponding arch over the loins, with a very slight gradual drop from top of loins to root of tail; both sides of backbone well supplied with muscle. *Tail* — Rather short, say from 8 inches to 10 inches, and covered on the upper side with wiry hair of darker color than that of the body, the hair on the under side being lighter in color and not so wiry, with nice feather about 2 inches long, getting shorter as it nears the tip; rather thick at the root, getting thicker for about four inches, then tapering off to a point. It should not be twisted or curled in any way, but should come up with a curve like a scimitar, the tip, when excited, being in a perpendicular line with the root of the tail. It should neither be set on too high nor too low. When not excited it is carried gaily, and a little about the level of the body.

LEGS — The forelegs short, with immense muscular development and bone, set wide apart, the chest coming well down between them. The feet well formed *and not flat*, with very strong brown or dark-colored claws. Bandy legs and flat feet are objectionable. The hair on the forelegs and feet of a Pepper dog should be tan, varying according to the body color from a rich tan to a pale fawn; of a Mustard dog they are of a darker shade than its head, which is a creamy white. In both colors there is a nice feather, about two inches long, rather lighter in color than the hair on the forepart of the leg. The hind legs are a little longer than the forelegs, and are set rather wide apart but not spread out in an unnatural manner, while the feet are much smaller; the thighs are well developed, and the hair of the same color and texture as the forelegs, but having no feather or dewclaws; the whole claws should be dark; but the claws of all vary in shade according to the color of the dog's body.

COAT — This is a very important point; the hair should be about 2 inches long; that from

SKULL broad between ears, less toward eyes; approx.
covering of hair on top of head
HEAD large, strongly made; not out of proportion to dog's size
TEETH strong, canines very large; upper slightly overlapping lower; neither under nor overshot
EYES wide apart, large, full, round; expressive of great determination, intelligence and dignity; dark hazel
NOSE and inside of mouth black or dark colored
MUZZLE measures in proportion to skull as 3" is to 5". Top generally bare 1" wide at nose to point at stop
CHEEKS gradually taper toward muzzle
CHEST well-developed, well let-down between forelegs
FORELEGS short, wide apart; muscular
FEET well-formed, not flat; claws strong, brown; nice feathering
EARS pendulous; leather thin; set well-back,
low on skull, hanging close to
part straight, back part tapering
(color and texture of top-
starting 2" from tip gives appearance of
distinct point
BODY long, strong, flexible
NECK muscular, well-developed, strong, well set into shoulders
BACK rather low at shoulder; having slight downward curve and corresponding arch over loins; with very slight gradual drop to root of tail
RIBS well-sprung, round
TAIL short 8-10"; thick at root and for 4", then tapering; not twisted or curled, scimitar-like curve; set neither too high nor too low; hair upper wiry, darker; hair underside softer, lighter with 2" feathering
HINDLEGS longer than fore, wide apart; feet smaller; thighs well-developed; no feathering or dewclaws
WEIGHT: 18 to 24 pounds preferred
COAT 2" long; on body from skull to tail root a mixture of hard (crisp not wiry) hair with soft undercoat; penciled
COLOR: Pepper (dark bluish black to light silvery gray, intermediate shades preferred) or mustard (reddish brown to pale fawn)
SIZE: Height 8-11" at shoulder; length from shoulder to tail root not more than twice height, preferably 1-2" less

HEAD — Long, but in nice proportion to the rest of the body; the skull flat, rather narrow between the ears, and narrowing slightly toward the eyes; free from wrinkle, with the stop hardly noticeable except in profile. The jaws must be strong and muscular, but not too full in the cheek, and of good punishing length. The foreface must not fall away appreciably between or below the eyes; instead, the modeling should be delicate. An exaggerated foreface, or a noticeably short foreface, disturbs the proper balance of the head and is not desirable. The foreface and the skull from occiput to stop should be approximately equal in length. Excessive muscular development of the cheeks, or bony development of the temples, conditions which are described by the fancier as "cheeky," or "strong in head," or "thick in skull" are objectionable. The "bumpy" head, in which the skull presents two lumps of bony structure above the eyes, is to be faulted. The hair on the upper and lower jaws should be similar in quality and texture to that on the body, and of sufficient length to present an appearance of additional strength and finish to the foreface. Either the profuse, goat-like beard, or the absence of beard, is unsightly and undesirable.

TEETH — Should be strong and even, white and sound; and neither overshot nor undershot.

LIPS — Should be close and well-fitting, almost black in color.

NOSE — Must be black.

EYES — Dark brown in color; small, not prominent; full of life, fire and intelligence, showing an intense expression. The light or yellow eye is most objectionable, and is a bad fault.

EARS — Small and V-shaped; of moderate thickness; set well on the head, and dropping forward closely toward the outside corner of the eye. The top of the folded ear should be well above the level of the skull. A "dead" ear, hound-like in appearance, must be severely penalized. It is not characteristic of the Irish Terrier. The hair should be much shorter and somewhat darker in color than that on the body.

NECK — Should be of fair length and gradually widening toward the shoulders; well and proudly carried, and free from throatiness. Generally there is a slight frill in the hair at each side of the neck, extending almost to the corner of the ear.

SHOULDERS AND CHEST — Shoulders must be fine, long, and sloping well into the back. The chest should be deep and muscular, but neither full nor wide.

BODY — The body should be moderately long. The short back is not characteristic of the Irish Terrier, and is extremely objectionable. The back must be strong and straight, and free from an appearance of slackness or "dip" behind the shoulders. The loin should be strong and muscular, and slightly arched, the ribs fairly sprung, deep rather than round, reaching to the level of the elbow. The bitch may be slightly longer than the dog.

HINDQUARTERS — Should be strong and muscular; thighs powerful; hocks near the ground; stifles moderately bent.

STERN — Should be docked, taking off about one quarter. It should be set on rather high, but not curled. It should be of good strength and substance; of fair length and well covered with harsh, rough hair.

FEET AND LEGS — The feet should be strong, tolerably round, and moderately small; toes arched and turned neither out nor in, with dark toenails. The pads should be deep, and must be perfectly sound and free from corns. Cracks alone do not necessarily indicate unsound feet. In fact, all breeds have cracked pads occasionally, from various causes.

Legs moderately long, well set from the shoulders, perfectly straight, with plenty of bone and muscle; the elbows working clear of the sides; pasterns short, straight, and hardly noticeable. Both fore and hind legs should move straight forward when traveling; the stifles should not turn outwards. "Cowhocks" — that is, the hocks turned in and the feet turned out — are intolerable. The legs should be free from feather and covered with hair of similar texture to that on the body to give proper finish to the dog.

COAT — Should be dense and wiry in texture, rich in quality, having a broken appearance, but still lying fairly close to the body, the hairs growing so closely and strongly together that when parted with the fingers the skin is hardly visible; free of softness or silkiness, and not so longs as to alter the outline of the body, particularly in the hindquarters. On the sides of the body the coat is never as harsh as on the back and

[continued on page 200]

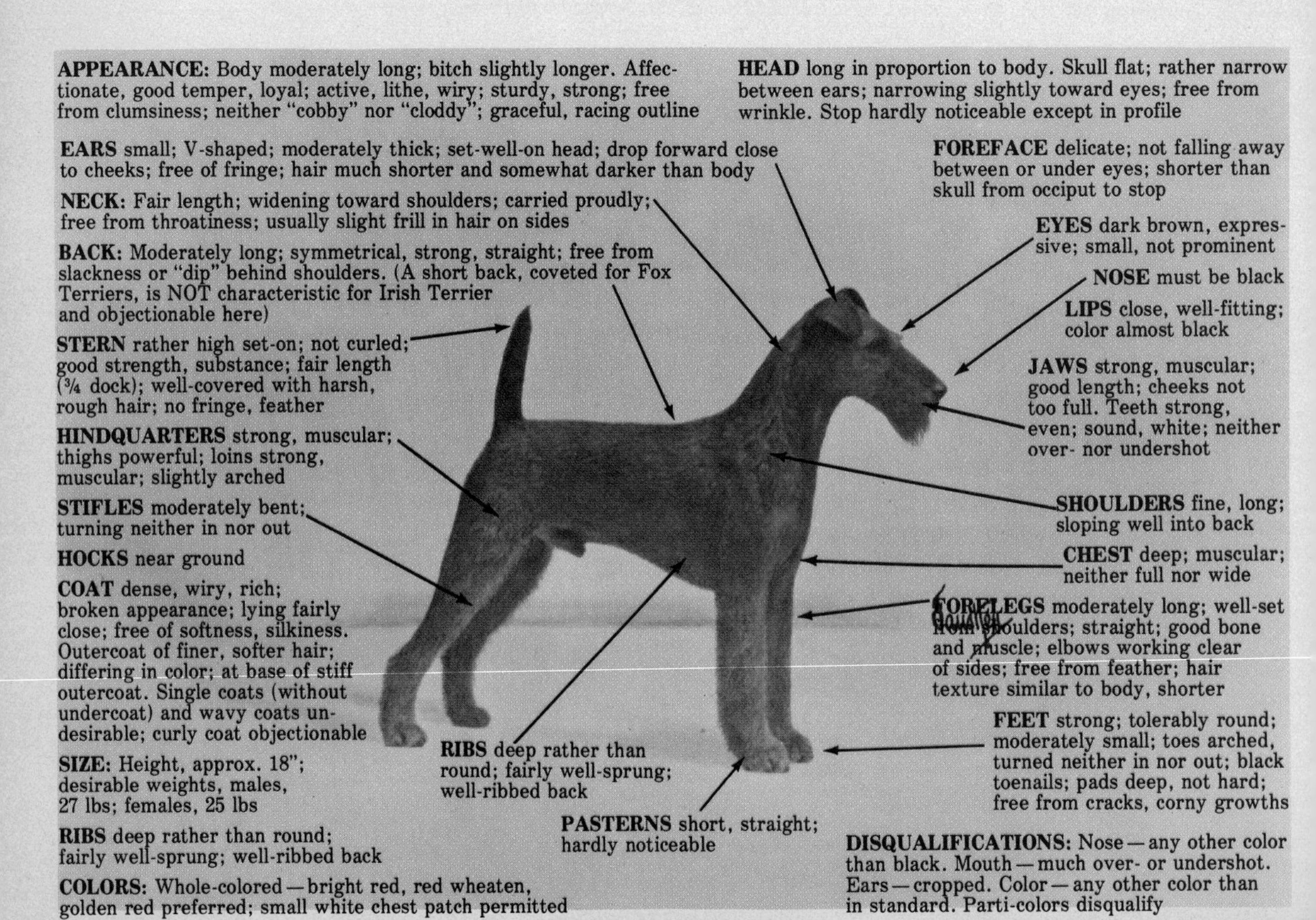

APPEARANCE: Body moderately long; bitch slightly longer. Affectionate, good temper, loyal; active, lithe, wiry; sturdy, strong; free from clumsiness; neither "cobby" nor "cloddy"; graceful, racing outline
HEAD long in proportion to body. Skull flat; rather narrow between ears; narrowing slightly toward eyes; free from wrinkle. Stop hardly noticeable except in profile
EARS small; V-shaped; moderately thick; set-well-on head; drop forward close to cheeks; free of fringe; hair much shorter and somewhat darker than body
FOREFACE delicate; not falling away between or under eyes; shorter than skull from occiput to stop
NECK: Fair length; widening toward shoulders; carried proudly; free from throatiness; usually slight frill in hair on sides
EYES dark brown, expressive; small, not prominent
BACK: Moderately long; symmetrical, strong, straight; free from slackness or "dip" behind shoulders. (A short back, coveted for Fox Terriers, is NOT characteristic for Irish Terrier and objectionable here)
NOSE must be black
LIPS close, well-fitting; color almost black
STERN rather high set-on; not curled; good strength, substance; fair length (3/4 dock); well-covered with harsh, rough hair; no fringe, feather
JAWS strong, muscular; good length; cheeks not too full. Teeth strong, even; sound, white; neither over- nor undershot
HINDQUARTERS strong, muscular; thighs powerful; loins strong, muscular; slightly arched
STIFLES moderately bent; turning neither in nor out
SHOULDERS fine, long; sloping well into back
HOCKS near ground
CHEST deep; muscular; neither full nor wide
COAT dense, wiry, rich; broken appearance; lying fairly close; free of softness, silkiness. Outercoat of finer, softer hair; differing in color; at base of stiff outercoat. Single coats (without undercoat) and wavy coats undesirable; curly coat objectionable
FORELEGS moderately long; well-set from shoulders; straight; good bone and muscle; elbows working clear of sides; free from feather; hair texture similar to body, shorter
FEET strong; tolerably round; moderately small; toes arched, turned neither in nor out; black toenails; pads deep, not hard; free from cracks, corny growths
SIZE: Height, approx. 18"; desirable weights, males, 27 lbs; females, 25 lbs
RIBS deep rather than round; fairly well-sprung; well-ribbed back
PASTERNS short, straight; hardly noticeable
RIBS deep rather than round; fairly well-sprung; well-ribbed back
DISQUALIFICATIONS: Nose — any other color than black. Mouth — much over- or undershot. Ears — cropped. Color — any other color than in standard. Parti-colors disqualify
COLORS: Whole-colored — bright red, red wheaten, golden red preferred; small white chest patch permitted

LAKELAND TERRIER STANDARD

GENERAL APPEARANCE — The Lakeland Terrier is a small, workman-like dog of square, sturdy build and gay, friendly, self-confident demeanor. He stands on his toes as if ready to go, and he moves, lithe and graceful, with a straight-ahead, free stride of good length. His head is rectangular in contour, ears V-shaped, and wiry coat finished off with fairly long furnishings on muzzle and legs.

HEAD — Well balanced, rectangular, the length of skull equaling the length of the muzzle when measured from occiput to stop, and from stop to nosetip. *The skull* is flat on top and moderately broad, the cheeks almost straightsided, and the stop barely perceptible. *The muzzle* is broad with straight nose bridge and good fill-in beneath the eyes. *The nose* is black, except that liver-colored noses shall be permissible on liver-coated dogs. *Jaws* are powerful. *The teeth*, which are comparatively large, may meet in either a level, edge-to-edge bite or a slightly overlapping scissors bite. Specimens with teeth overshot or undershot are to be disqualified. *The ears* are small, V-shaped, their fold just above the top of the skull, the inner edge close to the cheeks, and the flap pointed down. *The eyes*, moderately small and somewhat oval in outline, are set squarely in the skull, fairly wide apart. Their normally dark color may be a warm brown or black. *The expression* depends upon the dog's mood of the moment; although typically alert, it may be intense and determined, or gay and even impish.

NECK — Reachy and of good length; refined but strong; clean at the throat, slightly arched, and widening gradually into the shoulders. The withers, that point at the back of the neck where neck and body meet, are noticeably higher than the level of the back.

BODY — In over-all length-to-height proportion, the dog is approximately square. The moderately narrow *chest* is deep; it extends to elbows which are held close to the body. Shoulder blades are sloping, that is, well laid back, their musculature lean and almost flat in outline. *The ribs* are well sprung and moderately rounded. *The back* is short and level in topline. *Loins* are taut and short, although they may be a trifle longer in bitches than in dogs. *Quarters* are strong, broad, and muscular.

LEGS AND FEET — Forelegs are strongly boned, clean, and absolutely straight as viewed from the front or side, and devoid of appreciable bend at the pasterns. *Hind legs* too are strong and sturdy, the second thighs long and nicely angulated at the stifles and the hocks. *Hocks* are well let down, with the bone from hock to toes straight and parallel to each other. The small *feet* are round, the toes compact and well padded, the nails strong. Dewclaws, if any are to be removed.

TAIL — Set high on the body, the tail is customarily docked so that when the dog is set up in show position, the tip of the docked tail is on an approximate level with the skull. In carriage it is gay or upright, although a slight curve in the direction of the head is considered desirable. The tail curled over the back is faulty.

COAT AND COLOR — Two-ply or double, the outer coat is hard and wiry in texture, the undercoat soft. Furnishings on muzzle and legs are plentiful as opposed to profuse. *The color* may be blue, black, liver, black and tan, blue and tan, red, red grizzle, grizzle and tan, or wheaten. Tan, as desirable in the Lakeland Terrier, is a light wheaten or straw color, with rich red or mahogany tan to be penalized. Otherwise, colors, as specified, are equally acceptable. Dark-saddled specimens (whether black grizzle or blue) are nearly solid black at birth, with tan points on muzzle and feet. The black recedes and usually turns grayish or grizzle at maturity, while the tan also lightens.

SIZE — The ideal *height* of the mature dog is 14½ inches from the withers to the ground, with up to a ½-inch deviation either way permissible. Bitches may measure as much as one inch less than dogs. The *weight* of the well-balanced, mature specimen in hard, show condition, averages approximately 17 pounds, those of other heights proportionately more or less.

Size is to be considered of lesser importance than other qualities, that is, when judging dogs of equal merit, the one nearest the ideal size is to be preferred. Symmetry and proportion, however, are paramount in the appraisal, since all qualities together must be considered in visualizing the ideal.

MOVEMENT — Straight and free, with good length of stride. Paddling, moving close, and toeing-in are faulty.

TEMPERAMENT — The typical Lakeland Terrier is bold, gay, and friendly, with a

[continued on page 200]

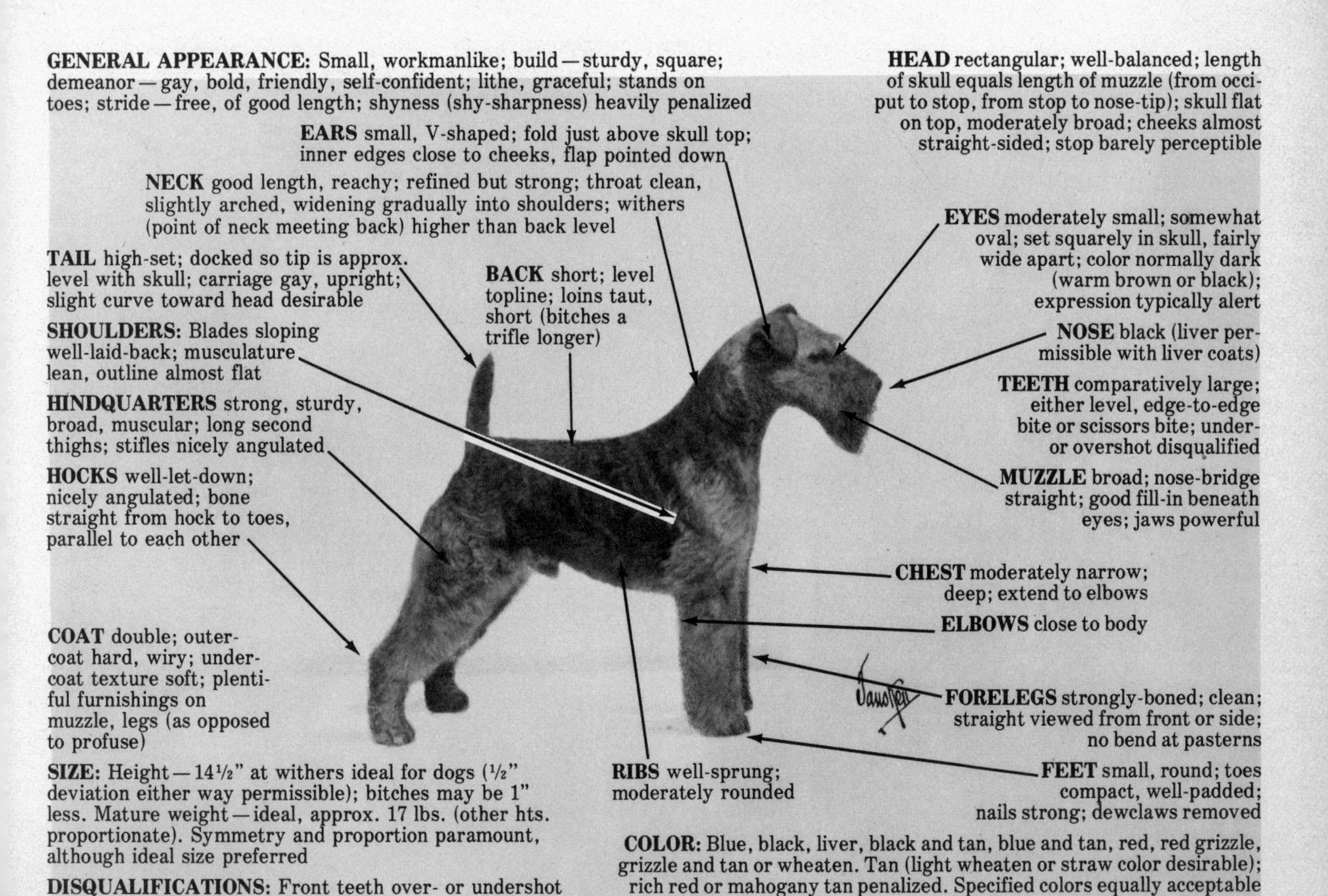

GENERAL APPEARANCE: Small, workmanlike; build—sturdy, square; demeanor—gay, bold, friendly, self-confident; lithe, graceful; stands on toes; stride—free, of good length; shyness (shy-sharpness) heavily penalized
EARS small, V-shaped; fold just above skull top; inner edges close to cheeks, flap pointed down
NECK good length, reachy; refined but strong; throat clean, slightly arched, widening gradually into shoulders; withers (point of neck meeting back) higher than back level
TAIL high-set; docked so tip is approx. level with skull; carriage gay, upright; slight curve toward head desirable
BACK short; level topline; loins taut, short (bitches a trifle longer)
SHOULDERS: Blades sloping well-laid-back; musculature lean, outline almost flat
HINDQUARTERS strong, sturdy, broad, muscular; long second thighs; stifles nicely angulated
HOCKS well-let-down; nicely angulated; bone straight from hock to toes, parallel to each other
COAT double; outer-coat hard, wiry; under-coat texture soft; plentiful furnishings on muzzle, legs (as opposed to profuse)
HEAD rectangular; well-balanced; length of skull equals length of muzzle (from occiput to stop, from stop to nose-tip); skull flat on top, moderately broad; cheeks almost straight-sided; stop barely perceptible
EYES moderately small; somewhat oval; set squarely in skull, fairly wide apart; color normally dark (warm brown or black); expression typically alert
NOSE black (liver permissible with liver coats)
TEETH comparatively large; either level, edge-to-edge bite or scissors bite; under- or overshot disqualified
MUZZLE broad; nose-bridge straight; good fill-in beneath eyes; jaws powerful
CHEST moderately narrow; deep; extend to elbows
ELBOWS close to body
FORELEGS strongly-boned; clean; straight viewed from front or side; no bend at pasterns
FEET small, round; toes compact, well-padded; nails strong; dewclaws removed
RIBS well-sprung; moderately rounded
SIZE: Height—14½" at withers ideal for dogs (½" deviation either way permissible); bitches may be 1" less. Mature weight—ideal, approx. 17 lbs. (other hts. proportionate). Symmetry and proportion paramount, although ideal size preferred
DISQUALIFICATIONS: Front teeth over- or undershot
COLOR: Blue, black, liver, black and tan, blue and tan, red, red grizzle, grizzle and tan or wheaten. Tan (light wheaten or straw color desirable); rich red or mahogany tan penalized. Specified colors equally acceptable

SEALYHAM TERRIER STANDARD

THE SEALYHAM should be the embodiment of power and determination, ever keen and alert, of extraordinary substance, yet free from clumsiness.

HEIGHT — At withers about 10½ inches. *Weight* — 23-24 pounds for dogs; bitches slightly less. It should be borne in mind that size is more important than weight.

HEAD — Long, broad and powerful, without coarseness. It should, however, be in perfect balance with the body, joining neck smoothly. Length of head roughly three-quarters height at withers, or about an inch longer than neck. Breadth between ears a little less than one-half length of head. *Skull* — Very slightly domed, with a shallow indentation running down between the brows, and joining the muzzle with a moderate stop. *Cheeks* — Smoothly formed and flat, without heavy jowls. *Jaws* — Powerful and square. Bite level or scissors. Overshot or undershot bad faults. *Teeth* — Sound, strong and white, with canines fitting closely together. *Nose* — Black, with large nostrils. White, cherry or butterfly bad faults. *Eyes* — Very dark, deeply set and fairly wide apart, of medium size, oval in shape with keen terrier expression. Light, large or protruding eye bad faults. Lack of eye rim pigmentation not a fault. *Ears* — Folded level with top of head, with forward edge close to cheek. Well rounded at tip, and of length to reach outer corner of eye. Thin, not leathery, and of sufficient thickness to avoid creases. Prick, tulip, rose or hound ears bad faults.

NECK — Length slightly less than two-thirds of height of dog at withers. Muscular without coarseness, with good reach, refinement at throat, and set firmly on shoulders. *Shoulders* — Well laid back and powerful, but not overmuscled. Sufficiently wide to permit freedom of action. Upright or straight shoulder placement highly undesirable.

LEGS — Forelegs strong, with good bones; and as straight as is consistent with chest being well let down between them. Down on pasterns, knuckled over, bowed, and out at elbow, bad faults. Hind legs longer than forelegs and not so heavily boned. *Feet* — Large but compact, round with thick pads, strong nails. Toes well arched and pointing straight ahead. Forefeet larger, though not quite so long as hind feet. Thin, spread or flat feet bad faults.

BODY — Strong, short-coupled and substantial, so as to permit great flexibility. Brisket deep and well let down between forelegs. Ribs well sprung.

BACK — Length from withers to set on of tail should approximate height at withers, or 10½ inches. Topline level, neither roached nor swayed. Any deviations from these measurements undesirable. *Hindquarters* — Very powerful, and protruding well behind the set on of tail. Strong second thighs, stifles well bent, and hocks well let down. Cowhocks bad fault.

TAIL — Docked and carried upright. Set on far enough forward so the spine does not slope down to it.

COAT — Weather-resisting, comprised of soft, dense undercoat and hard, wiry top coat. Silky or curly coat bad fault. *Color* — All white, or with lemon, tan or badger markings on head and ears. Heavy body markings and excessive ticking should be discouraged. *Action* — Sound, strong, quick, free, true and level.

SCALE OF POINTS

General character, balance and size		15
Head	5	
Eyes	5	
Mouth	5	
Ears	5	
Neck	5	25
Shoulders and brisket	10	
Body, ribs, & loin	10	
Hindquarters	10	
Legs and feet	10	
Coat	10	50
Tail	5	
Color [body marking & ticking]	5	10
Total		100

Approved March 12, 1935

BODY short, sturdy, strong; short-coupled; substantial

EARS folded level with top of head; forward edge close to cheek; length to reach outer corner of eye; tip rounded; thin, but of sufficient thickness to avoid creasing

NECK length slightly less than two-thirds of height; muscular; refined at throat; set firmly on shoulders

BACK equal to height from withers to set-on of tail; level

TAIL docked and carried upright; set high so spine does not slope down

HINDQUARTERS powerful, protruding well behind set-on of tail; strong second thighs; stifles well-bent

HIND LEGS longer, less bone than forelegs

HOCKS well-let-down

HIND FEET longer, not as large as forefeet

HEAD long, broad, powerful without coarseness; length approx. three-quarters height or one inch longer than neck; breadth between ears slightly less than one-half length of head

SKULL slightly domed, shallow indentation between brows

EYES dark, deeply set, fairly wide apart; oval, medium size; keen expression. Lack of pigmentation not a fault

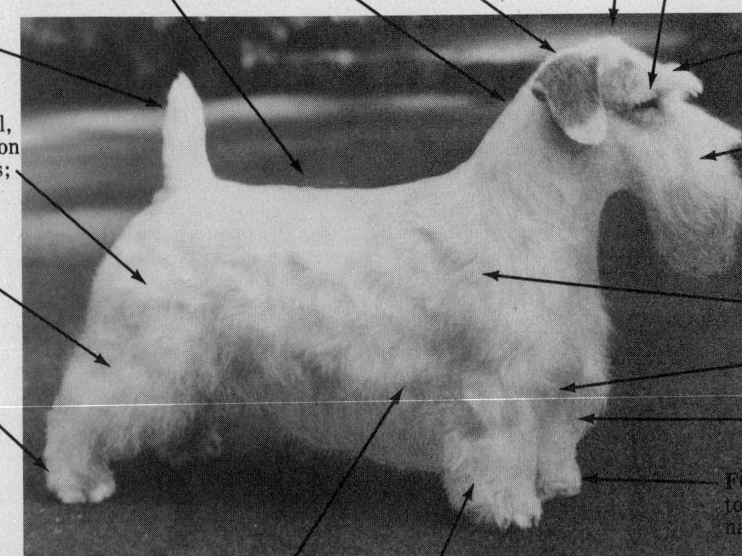

STOP moderate

NOSE black; nostrils large

JAWS: Powerful and square. Bite level or scissors. Overshot or undershot bad faults

CHEEKS smooth, flat; jowls not heavy

SHOULDERS well-laid-back, powerful; muscles smooth

BRISKET deep; well-let-down between legs

FORELEGS strong, good bone, straight as consistent with chest; elbows turning neither in nor out

FOREFEET large, compact, round; toes well-arched, straight; nails strong; pads thick

COAT weather-resisting; outer hard, wiry; undercoat soft, dense

COLOR: All white, or with lemon, tan or badger marking on head and ears

SIZE: Height at withers, approx. 10½". Weight, 23-24 pounds for dogs; bitches slightly less. Size more important than weight

RIBS well-sprung

PASTERNS firm, straight

HEAD — The skull should be flat, and rather wider between the ears than the Wire-haired Fox Terrier. The jaw should be powerful, clean-cut, rather deeper, and more punishing—giving the head a more masculine appearance than that usually seen on a Fox Terrier. Stop not too defined, fair length from stop to end of nose, the latter being of a black color. *Ears* — The ear should be V-shaped, small, not too thin, set on fairly high, carried forward and close to the cheek. *Eyes* — The eye should be small, not being too deeply set in or protruding out of skull, of a dark hazel color, expressive and indicating abundant pluck. *Neck* — The neck should be moderate length and thickness, slightly arched and sloping gracefully into the shoulders.

BODY — The back should be short, and well-ribbed up, the loin strong, good depth, and moderate width of chest. The shoulders should be long, sloping, and well set back. The hindquarters should be strong, thighs muscular and of good length, with the hocks moderately straight, well let down, and fair amount of bone. The stern should be set on moderately high, but too gaily carried. *Legs and Feet* — The legs should be straight and muscular, possessing fair amount of bone, with upright and powerful pasterns. The feet should be small, round and catlike.

COAT — The coat should be wiry, hard, very close and abundant. *Color* — The color should be black and tan, or black grizzle and tan, free from black penciling on toes.

SIZE — The height at shoulder should be 15 inches for dogs, bitches proportionately less. Twenty pounds shall be considered a fair average weight in working condition, but this may vary a pound or so either way.

SCALE OF POINTS

Head and jaws	10	Legs and feet	10
Ears	5	Coat	15
Eyes	5	Color	5
Neck and shoulders	10	Stern	5
Body	10	General appearance	15
Loins and hindquarters	10	Total	100

DISQUALIFICATIONS

(1) Nose — white, cherry or spotted to a considerable extent with either of these colors. (2) Ears — prick, tulip or rose. (3) Undershot jaw or pig-jawed mouth. (4) Black below hocks or white to an appreciable extent.

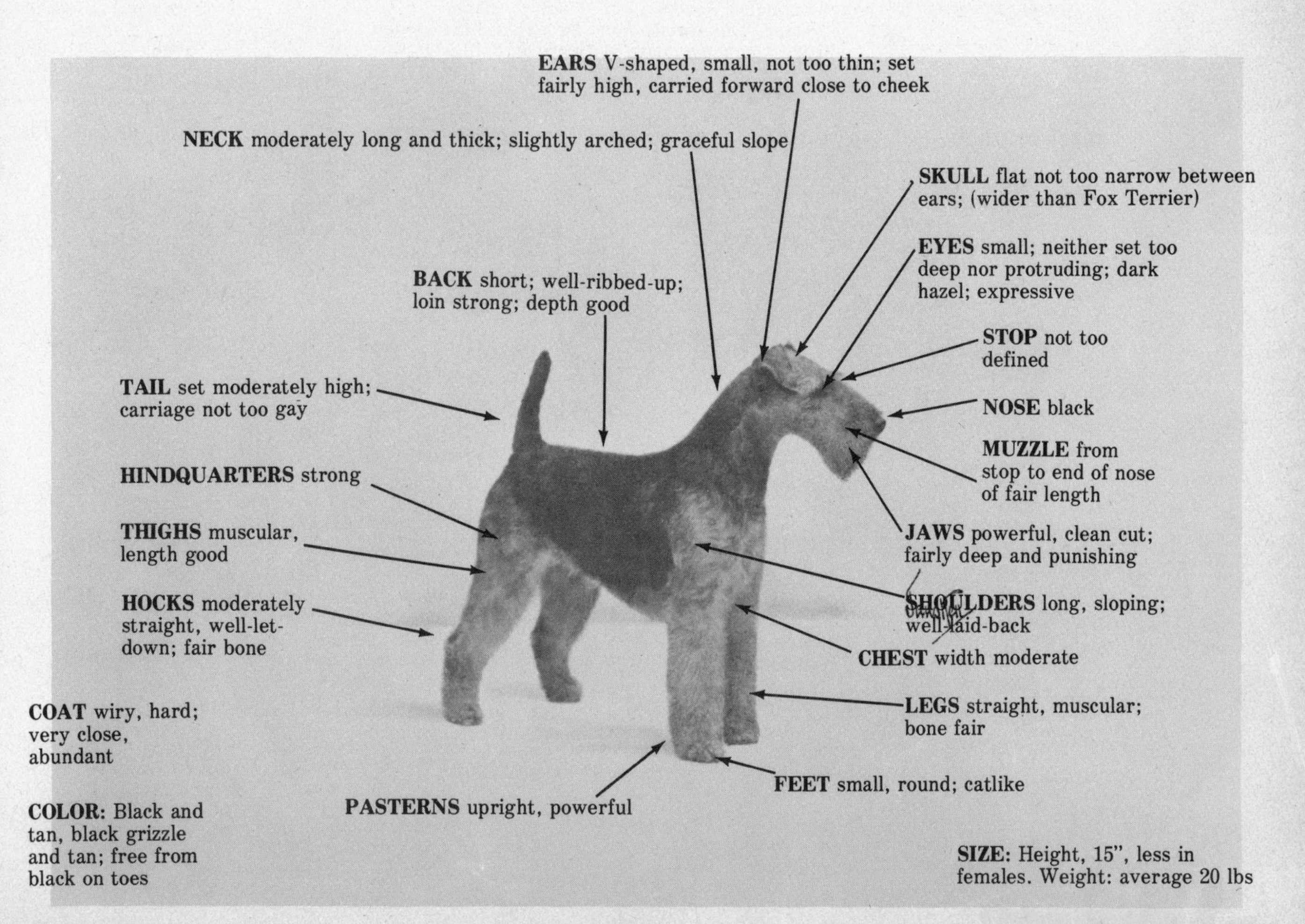
EARS V-shaped, small, not too thin; set fairly high, carried forward close to cheek
NECK moderately long and thick; slightly arched; graceful slope
SKULL flat not too narrow between ears; (wider than Fox Terrier)
EYES small; neither set too deep nor protruding; dark hazel; expressive
BACK short; well-ribbed-up; loin strong; depth good
STOP not too defined
TAIL set moderately high; carriage not too gay
NOSE black
MUZZLE from stop to end of nose of fair length
HINDQUARTERS strong
THIGHS muscular, length good
JAWS powerful, clean cut; fairly deep and punishing
HOCKS moderately straight, well-let-down; fair bone
SHOULDERS long, sloping; well-laid-back
CHEST width moderate
COAT wiry, hard; very close, abundant
LEGS straight, muscular; bone fair
FEET small, round; catlike
COLOR: Black and tan, black grizzle and tan; free from black on toes
PASTERNS upright, powerful
SIZE: Height, 15", less in females. Weight: average 20 lbs

[*Dandie Dinmont cont'd. from p. 195*]

skull to root of tail, a mixture of hardish and soft hair, which gives a sort of crisp feel to the hand. The hard should not be wiry; the coat is what is termed piley or penciled. The hair on the under part of the body is lighter in color and softer than on the top. The skin on the belly accords with the color of dog. *Color* — The color is pepper or mustard. The pepper ranges from a dark bluish black to a light silvery gray, the intermediate shades being preferred, the body color coming well down the shoulder and hips, gradually merging into the leg color. The mustards vary from a reddish brown to a pale fawn, the head being a creamy white, the legs and feet of a shade darker than the head. The claws are dark as in other colors. (Nearly all Dandie Dinmont Terriers have some white on the chest, and some have also white claws.)

SIZE — The height should be from 8 to 11 inches at the top of shoulder. Length from top of shoulder to root of tail should not be more than twice the dog's height, but preferably 1 or 2 inches less. *Weight* — The preferred weight from 18 to 24 pounds. These weights are for dogs in good working condition.

The relative value of the several points in the standard are apportioned as follows:

SCALE OF POINTS

Head	10	Coat	15
Eyes	10	Color	5
Ears	10	Size and weight	5
Neck	5	General appearance	5
Body	20		
Tail	5	Total	100
Legs and feet	10		

Approved June 10, 1969

[*Irish Terrier cont'd. from p. 196*]

quarters, but it should be plentiful and of good texture. At the base of the stiff outer coat there should be a growth of finer and softer hair, lighter in color, termed the undercoat. Single coats, which are without any undercoat, and wavy coats are undesirable; the curly and the kinky coats are most objectionable.

COLOR — Should be whole-colored: bright red, golden red, red wheaten, or wheaten. A small patch of white on the chest, frequently encountered in all whole-colored breeds, is permissible but not desirable. White on any other part of the body is most objectionable. Puppies sometimes have black hair at birth, which should disappear before they are full grown.

SIZE — The most desirable weight in show condition is 27 pounds for the dog and 25 pounds for the bitch. The height at the shoulder should be approximately 18 inches. These figures serve as a guide to both breeder and judge. In the show ring, however, the informed judge readily identifies the oversized or under-sized Irish Terrier by its conformation and general appearance. Weight is not the last word in judgment. It is of the greatest important to select, insofar as possible, terriers of moderate and generally accepted size, possessing the other various characteristics.

GENERAL APPEARANCE — The overall appearance of the Irish Terrier is important. In conformation he must be more than a sum of his parts. He must be all-of-a-piece, a balanced vital picture of symmetry, proportion and harmony. Furthermore, he must convey character. This terrier must be active, lithe and wiry in movement, with great animation; sturdy and strong in substance and bone structure, but at the same time free from clumsiness, for speed, power and endurance are most essential. The Irish Terrier must be neither "cobby" nor "cloddy," but should be built on lines of speed with a graceful, racing outline.

TEMPERAMENT — The temperament of the Irish Terrier reflects his early background: he was family pet, guard dog, and hunter. He is good tempered, spirited and game. It is of the utmost importance that the Irish Terrier show fire and animation. There is a heedless, reckless pluck about the Irish Terrier which is characteristic, and which, coupled with the headlong dash, blind to all consequences, with which he rushes at his adversary, has earned for the breed the proud epithet of "Daredevil." He is of good temper, most affectionate, and absolutely loyal to mankind. Tender and forebearing with those he loves, this rugged, stout-hearted terrier will guard his master, his mistress and children with utter contempt for danger or hurt. His life is one continuous and eager offering of loyal and faithful companionship and devotion. He is ever on guard, and stands between his home and all that threatens.

Approved December 10, 1968

[*Lakeland Terrier cont'd. from p. 197*]

selfconfident, cock-of-the-walk attitude. Shyness, especially shy-sharpness, in the mature specimen is to be heavily penalized.

SCALE OF POINTS

Head	15	Legs and feet	10
Eyes, ears, expression	15	Size and symmetry	10
Neck	5	Movement	10
Body	10	Temperament	10
Coat	15		
		Total	100

DISQUALIFICATION

The front teeth overshot or undershot.

Approved May 14, 1963

GROUP 5

TOYS

AFFENPINSCHER STANDARD

GENERAL APPEARANCE — Small, but rather sturdy in build and not delicate in any way. He carries himself with comical seriousness and he is generally quiet and a very devoted pal. He can get vehemently excited, however, when attacked and is fearless toward any aggressor.

COAT — A very important factor. It is short and dense in certain parts and shaggy and longer in others, but should be hard and wiry. It is longer and more loose and shaggy on the legs and around the eyes, nose and chin, giving the typical monkeylike appearance from whence comes his name. The best color is black, matching his eyes and fiery temperament. However, black with tan markings, red, gray and other mixtures are permissible. Very light colors and white markings are a fault.

HEAD — Should be round and not too heavy, with well-domed forehead.

EYES — Should be round, of good size, black and very brilliant.

EARS — Rather small, set high, pointed and erect, usually clipped to a point.

MUZZLE — Must be short and rather pointed with a black nose. The upper jaw is a trifle shorter than the lower jaw, while the teeth should close together; a slight undershot condition is not material. The teeth, however, should not show.

NECK — Short and straight.

BODY — The back should be straight with its length about equal to the height at the shoulder. Chest should be reasonably deep and the body should show only a slight tuck-up at the loin. *Legs* — Front legs should be straight as possible. Hind legs without much bend at the hocks and set well under the body. *Feet* — Should be round, small and compact. Turned neither in nor out, with preferably black pads and nails. *Tail* — Cut short, set and carried high.

SIZE — The smaller dog, if of characteristic type, is more valuable, and the shoulder height should not exceed 10¼ inches in any case.

Approved September 15, 1936

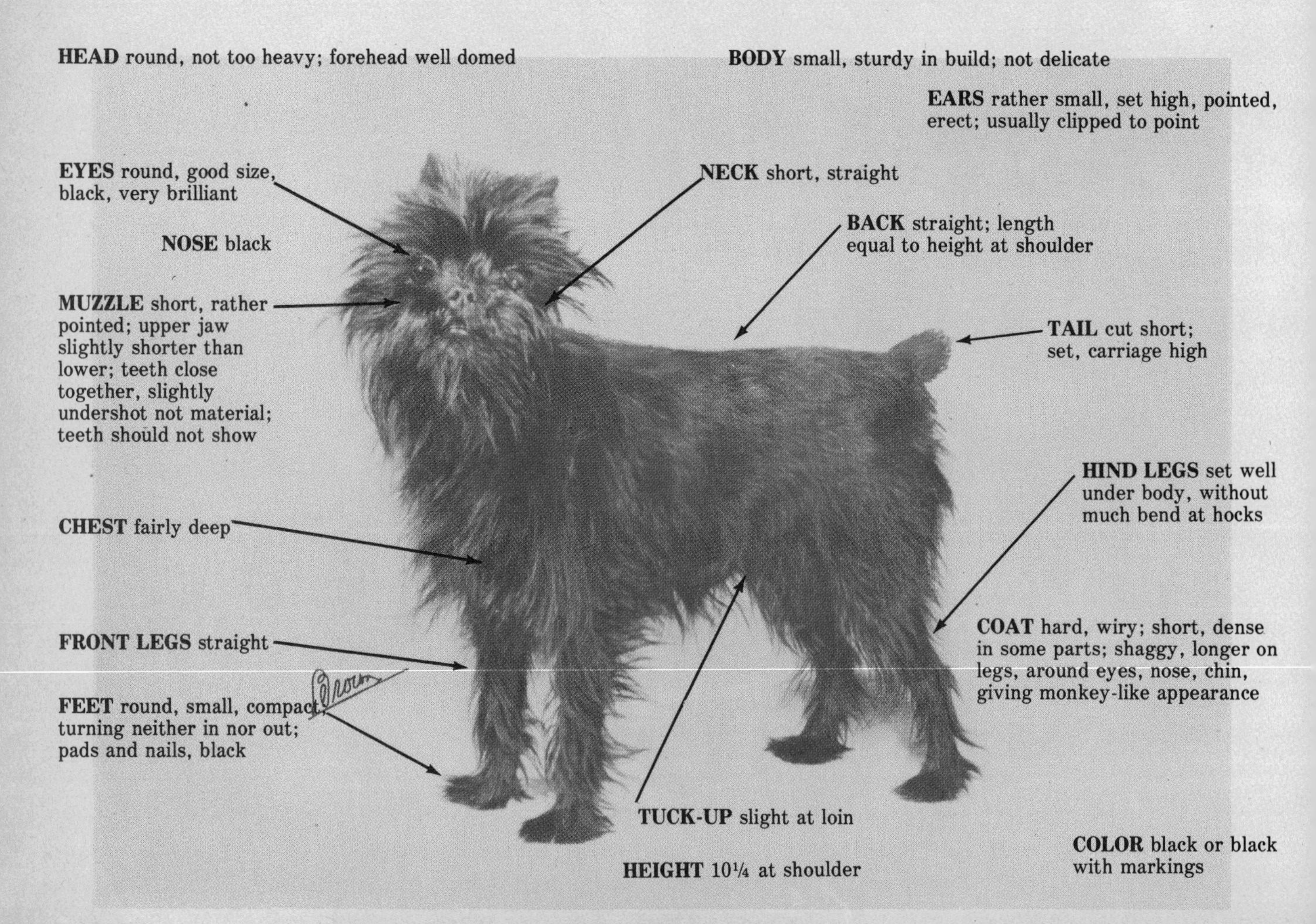
HEAD round, not too heavy; forehead well domed
BODY small, sturdy in build; not delicate
EARS rather small, set high, pointed, erect; usually clipped to point
EYES round, good size, black, very brilliant
NECK short, straight
NOSE black
BACK straight; length equal to height at shoulder
MUZZLE short, rather pointed; upper jaw slightly shorter than lower; teeth close together, slightly undershot not material; teeth should not show
TAIL cut short; set, carriage high
HIND LEGS set well under body, without much bend at hocks
CHEST fairly deep
COAT hard, wiry; short, dense in some parts; shaggy, longer on legs, around eyes, nose, chin, giving monkey-like appearance
FRONT LEGS straight
FEET round, small, compact; turning neither in nor out; pads and nails, black
TUCK-UP slight at loin
HEIGHT 10¼ at shoulder
COLOR black or black with markings

CH. AFF-AIRN WEE WINNIE WINKIE

CH. AFF-KINS KUTE-KINS KITTY KAT

WINNIE WAS #1 AFFENPINSCHER IN 1966 (PHILLIPS SYSTEM). SHE HAD A GROUP FIRST AT DELAWARE COUNTY UNDER MR. WILLIAM KENDRICK, AS WELL AS 1 GROUP SECOND, 2 GROUP THIRDS, AND 2 GROUP FOURTHS. WINKIE IS NOW 11 YEARS OLD, BORN ON DECEMBER 27, 1963. KITTY IS HER DAUGHTER WHO FINISHED WITH FOUR MAJORS.

EMILY KINSLEY STREMSKI
R.D. 4, BOX 179
NAZARETH, PA. 18064
(215) 759-0910

The Affenpinscher is one of the smaller breeds of dogs seen in America. He is an ancestor of another Toy dog the Brussels Griffon. He is a very intelligent, alert, terrier-like Toy dog. His coat texture is very stiff and wire-like. The Affenpinscher was first admitted to American Kennel Club registration in 1936.

BRUSSELS GRIFFON STANDARD

GENERAL APPEARANCE — A toy dog, intelligent, alert, sturdy, with a thick-set short body, a smart carriage and set-up, attracting attention by an almost human expression.

HEAD — *Skull* — Large and round, with a domed forehead. *Ears* — Small and set rather high on the head. May be shown cropped or natural. If natural they are carried semi-erect. *Eyes* — Should be set well apart, very large, black, prominent, and well open. The eyelashes long and black. Eyelids edged with black. *Nose* — Very black, extremely short, its tip being set back deeply between the eyes so as to form a lay-back. The nostrils large, the stop deep. *Lips* — Edged with black, not pendulous but well brought together, giving a clean finish to the mouth. *Jaws* — Chin must be undershot, prominent, and large with an upward sweep. The incisors of the lower jaw should protrude over the upper incisors, and the lower jaw should be rather broad. Neither teeth nor tongue should show when the mouth is closed. A wry mouth is a serious fault.

BODY AND LEGS — Brisket should be broad and deep, ribs well sprung, back level and short. *Neck* — Medium length, gracefully arched. *Tail* — Set and held high, docked to about one third. *Forelegs* — Of medium length, straight in bone, well muscled, set moderately wide apart and straight from the point of the shoulders as viewed from the front. Pasterns short and strong. *Hind legs* — Set true, thighs strong and well muscled, stifles bent, hocks well let down, turning neither in nor out. *Feet* — Round, small, and compact, turned neither in nor out. Toes well arched. Black pads and toenails preferred.

COAT — There are two distinct types of coat — rough and smooth. The rough coat should be wiry and dense, the harder and more wiry the better. On no account should the dog look or feel woolly, and there should be no silky hair anywhere. The coat should not be so long as to give a shaggy appearance, but should still be distinctly different all over from the smooth coat. The head should be covered with wiry hair slightly longer around the eyes, nose, cheeks, and chin, thus forming a fringe. The smooth coat is similar to that of the Boston Terrier or English Bulldog, with no trace of wire hair.

COLOR — In the rough-coated type, coat is either 1. reddish brown, with a little black at the whiskers and chin allowable, or 2. black and reddish brown mixed, usually, with black mask and whiskers, or 3. black with uniform reddish brown markings, usually appearing under the chin, on the legs, over the eyebrows, around the edges of the ears and around the vent, or 4. solid black. The colors of the smooth-coated type are the same as those of the rough-coated type except that solid black is not allowable. Any white hairs in either the rough or smooth coat are a serious fault, except for "frost" on the black muzzle of a mature dog, which is natural.

WEIGHT — Usually 8 to 10 pounds, and should not exceed 12 pounds. Type and quality are of greater importance than weight, and a smaller dog that is sturdy and well proportioned should not be penalized.

SCALE OF POINTS

Head		
Skull	5	
Nose and stop	10	
Eyes	5	
Chin and jaws	10	
Ears	5	35
Coat		
Color	12	
Texture	13	25
Body and General Conformation		
Body [brisket and rib]	15	
Legs	10	
Feet	5	
General Appearance [neck, topline, and tail carriage]	10	40
Total		100

DISQUALIFICATIONS

Dudley or butterfly nose, white spot or blaze anywhere on coat, hanging tongue, jaw overshot, solid black coat in the smooth type.

Approved February 6, 1960

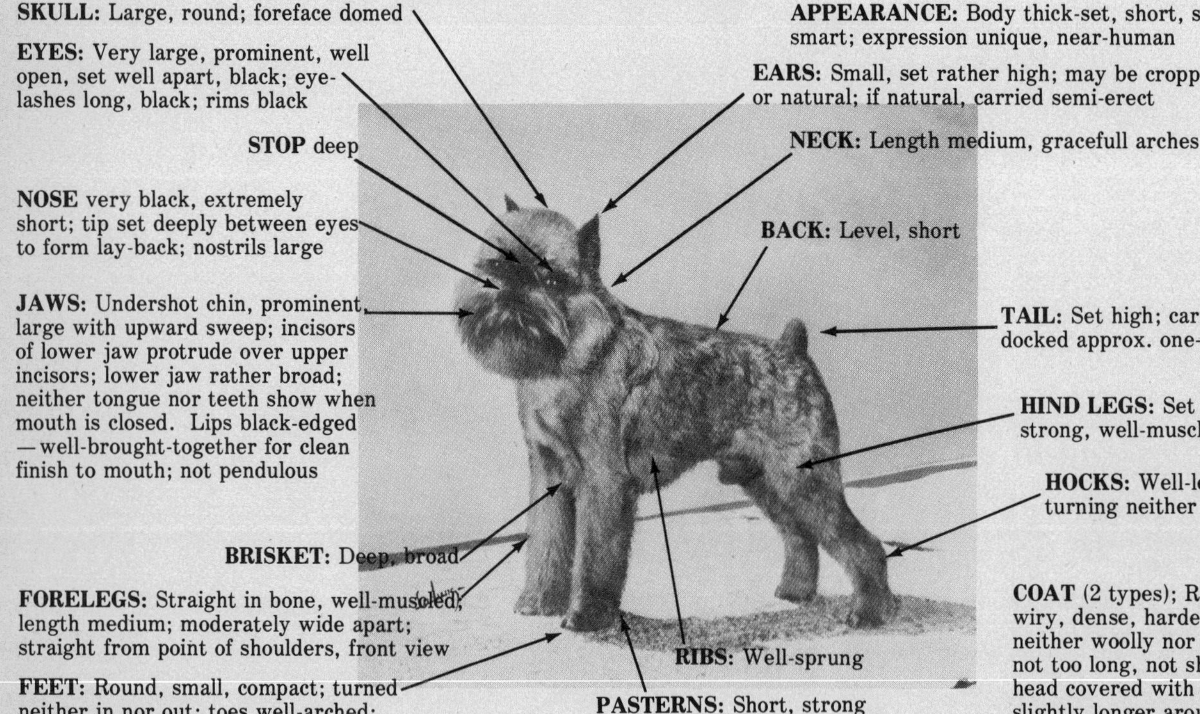

SKULL: Large, round; foreface domed
EYES: Very large, prominent, well open, set well apart, black; eyelashes long, black; rims black
STOP deep
NOSE very black, extremely short; tip set deeply between eyes to form lay-back; nostrils large
JAWS: Undershot chin, prominent, large with upward sweep; incisors of lower jaw protrude over upper incisors; lower jaw rather broad; neither tongue nor teeth show when mouth is closed. Lips black-edged —well-brought-together for clean finish to mouth; not pendulous
BRISKET: Deep, broad
FORELEGS: Straight in bone, well-muscled, length medium; moderately wide apart; straight from point of shoulders, front view
FEET: Round, small, compact; turned neither in nor out; toes well-arched; black preferred for pads, toenails
COLOR: Reddish brown (some black at whiskers, chin permitted); black and reddish brown mixed usually with black mask, whiskers; black with uniform reddish brown markings under chin, on legs, over eyebrows, edges of ears, around vent; black for rough-coated variety only; white hairs serious fault except for frost on black muzzle
APPEARANCE: Body thick-set, short, sturdy; carriage smart; expression unique, near-human
EARS: Small, set rather high; may be cropped or natural; if natural, carried semi-erect
NECK: Length medium, gracefull arches
BACK: Level, short
TAIL: Set high; carriage high; docked approx. one-third
HIND LEGS: Set true; thighs strong, well-muscled; stifles bent
HOCKS: Well-let-down; turning neither in nor out
COAT (2 types); Rough — very wiry, dense, harder the better; neither woolly nor silky; hair not too long, not shaggy; head covered with wiry hair slightly longer around eyes, nose, cheeks, chin forming fringe. Smooth — no trace of wiry hair
RIBS: Well-sprung
PASTERNS: Short, strong
SIZE: Weight, 8 to 10 lbs; should not exceed 12 lbs; type, quality more important than weight
DISQUALIFICATION: Dudley or butterfly nose; white spot or blaze anywhere on coat, hanging tongue; jaw overshot; solid black coat in smooth type

CH. SKIBBEREEN OLLIVERSON

BEST OF BREED, PROGRESSIVE DOG CLUB (TOY DOGS ONLY), 1974; BEST OF BREED, AMERICAN BRUSSELS GRIFFON ASSOCIATION SPECIALTY SHOW, WESTCHESTER K.C., 1973; WINNERS DOG, AMERICAN BRUSSELS GRIFFON ASSOCIATON SPECIALTY SHOW, WESTCHESTER K.C., 1972, ATTAINING CHAMPIONSHIP; TWELVE OTHER BESTS OF BREED AT MAJOR SHOWS.

COBURG KENNELS
223 OLD HIGHWAY, BRIDGEWATER TOWNSHIP
SOMERVILLE, NEW JERSEY 08876

The Brussels Griffon originated in Belgium. Documentation is lacking but ancestry allegedly includes the Affenpinscher, native Belgian mongrels, and the Pug. Two varieties are recognized, the Rough coated and the Smooth. The latter is also called Petit Brabancon. The Brussels Griffon is a toy dog, intelligent and alert, with a thick-set, square body. The Rough coated variety resembles an Affenpinscher in some ways while the Smooth vaguely suggests a Pug. The head is large, round, and domed. The eyes are very large and set well apart. The nose is very short. The chin is prominent and the bite undershot. The back is level and short; the legs of good substance. The Rough-coated variety may be reddish brown, black and reddish brown mixed, black with reddish brown markings, or solid black. The Smooth variety may be any of these except solid black. Weight is usually 8 to 10 lbs. The Brussels Griffon is independent and may be hard to train. They are said to have many breeding difficulties, hence a low reproductive rate. About 200 are registered with the AKC annually. The breed ranks 95th. The Smooth coat is relatively the more rarely seen in the show ring.

CHIHUAHUA [SMOOTH COAT] STANDARD

HEAD — A well-rounded "apple dome" skull, with or without molera. Cheeks and jaws lean. Nose moderately short, slightly pointed (self-colored, in blond types, or black). In moles, blues, and chocolates, they are self-colored. In blond types, pink nose permissible.

EARS — Large, held erect when alert, but flaring at the sides at about an angle of 45 degrees when in repose. This gives breadth between the ears. In Long Coats, ears fringed. (Heavily fringed ears may be tipped slightly, never down.)

EYES — Full, but not protruding, balanced, set well apart — dark ruby, or luminous. (Light eyes in blond types permissible.)

TEETH — Level or scissors bite. Overshot or undershot bite or any distortion of the bite should be penalized as a serious fault.

NECK AND SHOULDERS — Slightly arched, gracefully sloping into lean shoulders, may be smooth in the very short types, or with ruff about neck preferred. In Long Coats, large ruff on neck desired and preferred. Shoulders lean, sloping into a slightly broadening support above straight forelegs that are set well under, giving a free play at the elbows. Shoulders should be well up, giving balance and soundness, sloping into a level back. (Never down or low.) This gives a chestiness, and strength of forequarters, yet not of the "Bulldog" chest; plenty of brisket.

BACK AND BODY — Level back, slightly longer than height. Shorter backs desired in males. Ribs rounded (but not too much "barrel-shaped"). *Hindquarters* — Muscular, with hocks well apart, neither out nor in, well let down, with firm sturdy action. *Tail* — Moderately long, carried sickle either up or out, or in a loop over the back, with tip just touching the back. (Never tucked under.) Hair on tail in harmony with the coat of the body, preferred furry in Smooth Coats. In Long Coats, tail full and long (as a plume). *Feet* — Small, with toes well split up but not spread, pads cushioned, with fine pasterns. (Neither the hare nor the cat-foot.) A dainty, small foot with nails moderately long.

COAT — In the Smooth, the coat should be soft texture, close and glossy. (Heavier coats with undercoats permissible.) Coat placed well over body with ruff on neck, and more scanty on head and ears. In Long Coats the coat should be of a soft texture, either flat or slightly curly, with undercoat preferred. Ears fringed (heavily fringed ears may be tipped slightly, never down), feathering on feet and legs, and pants on hind legs. Large ruff on neck desired and preferred. Tail full and long (as a plume). *Color* — Any color — solid, marked or splashed.

WEIGHT — A well-balanced little dog not to exceed 6 pounds.

GENERAL APPEARANCE — A graceful, alert, swift-moving little dog with saucy expression. Compact, and with terrierlike qualities.

SCALE OF POINTS

Head, including ears	20
Body, including tail	20
Coat	20
Legs	20
General Appearance and Action	20
Total	100

DISQUALIFICATIONS

Cropped tail, bobtail. Broken down or cropped ears. Any dog over 6 pounds in weight. In Long Coats, too thin coat that resembles bareness.

EARS large; held erect when alert; flaring 45 degrees in repose

NECK slightly arched; gracefully sloping into shoulders

BACK level, slightly longer than height; shorter back for males

TAIL moderately long; carried cycle either up or out, or in loop with tip touching back; Longcoats with full plume; bobtail or tailless permitted if so born

HINDQUARTERS muscular; hocks well apart; neither in nor out; well-let-down; firm, sturdy

COLOR: Any color; solid, marked, splashed

SIZE: Weight, 1 to 6 lbs; 2 to 4 preferred

DISQUALIFICATIONS: Cropped tail, broken down or cropped ears. Longhairs—too thin coat that resembles bareness

HEAD well-rounded; skull "apple-domed"

EYES full, balanced; set well apart, dark; not protruding; light eyes in blonds allowed

JAWS lean; teeth level; cheeks lean

SHOULDERS lean, well up, sloping to back

CHEST reasonably deep, plenty of brisket

FORELEGS straight, set well under shoulders; fine pasterns

FEET small, dainty; neither hare nor catlike; toes well-split-up but not spread; pads cushioned; nails moderately long

RIBS somewhat rounded

PASTERNS fine

COAT—Smooths, texture soft, close, glossy, ruff at neck, scanty coat on head and ears; Longcoats, either flat or slightly curly; ears fringed; texture soft, feathering on feet; legs, with pants; large ruff on neck

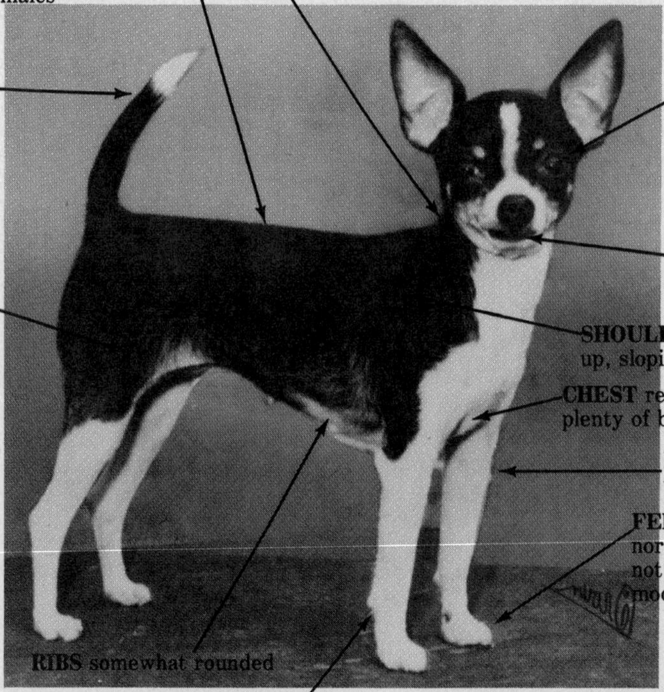

CH. BUCKMAN'S ANGUS OF CEDAR RIDGE

3½ POUNDS OF DYNAMITE, HIS CAREER BEGAN AT 7 MONTHS OF AGE. AT 7½ MONTHS HE WENT BOB UNDER MR. TOM STEVENSON ENROUTE TO GROUP 4 UNDER DR. W. FIELD JR. AT MISSISSIPPI STATE KC. ANGUS COMPLETED HIS CHAMPIONSHIP WITH EASE, FINISHING AT NINE MONTHS WITH THREE 4 POINT MAJORS. SPECIALED IN ONLY 10 SHOWS ANGUS HAS 8 BOB. AT BATON ROUGE ANGUS WENT BOB AND GROUP 3 UNDER MRS. YOUNG. AT BIRMINGHAM HE WAS BOB OVER A LARGE ENTRY UNDER MISS IRIS DE LA TORRE BUENO (PICTURED(. THIS LITTLE DOG EXCELS IN BRED TYPE, SOUNDNESS AND SHOWMANSHIP. OWNER/HANDLED.

SALLIE BUCKMAN
4145 COLEMAN ROAD
MEMPHIS, TENN. 38128

A HISTORY OF THE CHIHUAHUA
APPEARS AT THE BOTTOM OF
PAGE 209

Excerpts from:

The Dog That Came In From The Cold

By Tom Stevenson

In the beginning it was the little dog that opened the door to man's hearth and heart, the little dog that turned up occasionally among the dogs outside that man depended on for survival in a primitive world. Too small to run with the pack, too weak to survive without help, his size made him a reject in nature's scheme for survival. Unless . . . .

Though life was a grim proposition, there were men capable of pity. With help, the little misfit would survive. He did. He moved in with the family. He took over. He became a thing to be esteemed, an item of value, a rare thing. A tiny replica of the fierce hunter-killers outside, he was something to laugh at, a toy to enjoy. He kept the women company, played with the children and reproduced himself within his size limitations. The smaller he was, the more he was sought after. Bred selectively to fill a demand, toy dogs found a place in the offerings of merchants who came to barter for the necessities and the luxuries that men exchanged.

When trade routes were developed he was carried as a curiosity to far-off places. While other dogs moved slowly with migrating peoples and armies, the toys were being offered as a commodity in the markets of the world. He went from the Mediterranean basin in a caravan to be sold as a small wonder in a Chinese court. He sailed to Britain with a cargo of wine and oil, to become a lady's plaything in a country house. He carried with him the genes of his ancestors, stamping his get with the mark of his origins.

The toy dog was developed by selective breeding for size alone. The breeds as we know them came later, refinements in shape and form to satisfy a concept that was meaningful in the land: the little lion of Buddha for the temple court; the tiny replica of the Egyptian god; the feathered and brightly colored creature as decorative as a bird and the pocket-sized caricature of the mighty hunters and dogs of war. As individual breeds emerged they became more than ever curiosities to be acquired from the strange peoples that had created them. Now there were new empires, served by merchant fleets. Returning officers and dignitaries brought home exotic little dogs of the Orient to a country of animal lovers. English breeders had their own green thumb to cultivate and improve on what already seemed perfection.

In this melting pot of toy blood, there now appeared strange new looks, oriental faces on familiar spaniel bodies, sleek greyhound lines giving grace to little working terriers, Foo Dog heads on rough little ratters. Again, new breeds were made.

So it becomes a challenge now to identify the ingredients. If there was meaning in their creation, then there is a need to understand the way they were used and the concept of the breeder—the picture he had in mind—in bringing them to being. To lose the past is to lose one's way into the future. The evidence is still at hand, the qualities of mind that govern the way they think and move; residuals of instinct that furnish the compulsion to hunt, to herd, to guard; coat, balance, structure, Some analyses are easy and direct: the Pomeranian, for instance, of wolf stock, a tiny replica of the dogs that were and still are used for freighting and hunting in the Arctic. At other times the game gets more complicated, particularly when many families and much travel is involved and the end product is made in the image of gods we had never imagined.

The pattern of emergence from large ancestors, of being shaped through selective breeding in a form meaningful in a particular culture applies to the Chihuahua in his isolated land. In Mayan art, he appears centuries ago with his toyish head and natural body, making one feel that he was made little centuries ago when he became a temple dog. Descriptions of his foot in breed standards and references to digging or burrowing may indicate terrier ancestors. As the tiniest of dogs, he too may be valuable as a size reducer abroad.

So we may speculate, on where they came from and the workings of the minds that shaped them. These are mysteries for each to resolve as best he can. But one thing, a certainty beyond any speculation, is that the toy dog has moved into our hearts permanently. He satisfies a need, he keeps us amused and, perhaps best of all, he demands no return. He keeps us aware that no man lives on bread alone and the best things in life are free.

CH MOM-SON S PRESLEEN OPAL

"OPAL" A PROUD AND SHOWY BITCH HANDLED TO HER CHAMPIONSHIP JUNE 6, 1973 BY ARLIENE KONST. SINCE THEN HAS BEEN SPECIALTIED BY JERRY RIGDEN, AND NOW HAS 20 BEST OF BREEDS, AND 10 BEST OF OPP SEX TO BEST OF VARIETY TO HER CREDIT. PICTURE ABOVE SHOWS "OPAL" WITH HER PROUD NEW OWNER, HANDLER ARLIENE WINNING BEST OF OPP SEX TO BEST OF VARIETY AND THEN GOING ON TO WIN BEST OF OPP SEX TO BEST OF BREED AT THE CHIHUAHUA CLUB OF MICHIGAN, NOV. 25, 1974. THERE WERE 51 DOGS ENTERED UNDER JUDGE DELORES WOODS.

HANDLER: ARLIENE KONST & JERRY RIGDEN

ARLIENE KONST & FRANCYL KONST
549 SOLON RD
CHAGRIN FALLS, OHIO 44022

One must conclude after reading as many authorities as possible that the origin of the Chihuahua is not known beyond the fact that the modern breed was found in Mexico. Attempts to trace these dogs to pre-Columbian Mexico or to various European or Asiatic roots are not convincing. The origin of the long-coated variety seems, if anything, more obscure. Nevertheless, the breed is distinctive and, above all, popular. The Chihuahua is the smallest of the recognized dog breeds, two to four pounds being the preferred weight range, but good smaller examples are also seen. It is a graceful, alert, tiny dog with a saucy expression. The head is domed and may have a gap in the bony skully called the molera. The ears are large and held erect when alert. The eyes are full. The neck and shoulders are graceful, the back level. The coat in the Smooth variety is soft, close, and glossy, with a ruff on the neck. In the long-coated variety, the coat is soft, either flat or slightly curled, the ears fringed, the feet and legs feathered, the hind legs panted. A large neck ruff is valued. Chihuahuas have been continually popular since their introduction into the U.S. and Europe. Some 22,000 are registered annually with the AKC, the breed ranking 13th. Neither variety is shown in proportion to the numbers registered and neither variety garners its share of Group wins or placements.

GENERAL APPEARANCE — That of a lively, high-bred little dog with dainty appearance, smart, compact carriage and profuse coat. These dogs should be essentially stylish in movement, lifting the feet high when in action, carrying the tail (which is heavily feathered, proudly curved or plumed) over the back. In size they vary considerably, but the smaller they are the better, provided type and quality are not sacrificed. When divided by weight, classes should be under and over 7 pounds.

HEAD — Should be large for the size of the dog, with broad skull, rounded in front. *Eyes* — Large, dark, lustrous, rather prominent and set wide apart. *Ears* — Small and V-shaped, nicely feathered, set wide apart and high on the head and carried slightly forward. *Nose* — Very short in the muzzle part. The end or nose proper should be wide, with open nostrils, and must be the color of the dog's markings, *i.e.*, black in black-marked dogs, and red or deep flesh color in red or lemon-marked dogs. It shall be a disqualification for a black and white Japanese Spaniel to have a nose any other color than black.

NECK — Should be short and moderately thick.

BODY — Should be squarely and compactly built, wide in chest, "cobby" in shape. The length of the dog's body should be about its height. *Tail* — Must be well twisted to either right or left from root and carried up over back and flow on opposite side; it should be profusely covered with long hair (ring tails not desirable). *Legs* — The bones of the legs should be small, giving them a slender appearance, and they should be well feathered. *Feet* — Small and shaped somewhat long; the dog stands up on its toes somewhat. If feathered, the tufts should never increase in width of the foot, but only its length a trifle.

COAT — Profuse, long, straight, rather silky. It should be absolutely free from wave or curl, and not lie too flat, but have a tendency to stand out, especially at the neck, so as to give a thick mane or ruff, which with profuse feathering on thighs and tail gives a very showy appearance. *Color* — The dogs should be either black and white or red and white, *i.e.*, parti-colored. The term red includes all shades of sable, brindle, lemon and orange, but the brighter and clearer the red the better. The white should be clear white, and the color, whether black or red, should be evenly distributed, patches over the body, cheek and ears.

SCALE OF POINTS

Head and neck	10	Feet and legs	5
Eyes	10	Coat and markings	15
Ears	5	Action	5
Muzzle	10	Size	10
Nose	5		
Body	15	Total	100
Tail	10		

DISQUALIFICATIONS

In black and whites, a nose any other color than black.

HEAD large for size of dog; broad skull, rounded in front

APPEARANCE: Lively, smart; high-stepping action; dainty; compact carriage. Body square, cobby

EYES large, dark; rather prominent; set wide apart; lustrous

EARS small, V-shaped; wide apart; carried slightly forward, high on head; nicely feathered

NECK moderately thick; short

NOSE: Very short muzzle part; and wide, open nostrils. Color: Black in black-marked dogs; red or deep flesh for red or lemon-marked

TAIL very heavily feathered; proudly curved or plumed over back; well-twisted either right or left from root, flowing over opposite side

CHEST wide

COAT long, straight, rather silky; profuse; absolutely free from curl or wave; not too flat, tendency to stand out; thick neck mane (or ruff); profuse feathering on thighs and tail

LEGS small-boned; slender; well-feathered

FEET small; shaped long to some degree; stands somewhat on toes, any feathering should add to length not width of foot

SIZE: Considerable variation, the smaller the better without sacrifice of type or quality. When divided by weight, should be over or under 7 lbs

COLOR: Black and white, red and white. Red includes all shades of sable, brindle, lemon, orange (but the brighter and clearer red the better). White should be clear; colors evenly-distributed patches over body, cheeks, ears

DISQUALIFICATIONS: Nose color other than black in black and whites

CH. SOMETHIN SPECIAL'S SHASHI-KO

SASHI'S CAREER HAS BEEN SOMEWHAT UNUSUAL. SHE STARTED WITH AN UNEXPECTED BOB AT RAMAPO KC ON 11-18-73; THEN WENT ON TO A FIVE POINT MAJOR AT NATIONAL CAPITAL KC ON 3-10-74. AT THIS SHOW SHE WAS HANDLED BY A JUNIOR HANDLER, DONNA GALE BOCCIA. AFTER THIS, AT THE SUGGESTION OF DONNA'S MOTHER, SHE WAS HANDLED BY JOHN J. MARSH WHO FINISHED HER AT LANCASTER KC 5-12-74 JUST BEFORE A TORNADO SWEPT AWAY THE TENTS!

HANDLER: JOHN J. MARSH

SOMETHIN SPECIAL CHINS
G. W. ARTHUR, M.D.
149 EAST 29TH STREET
NEW YORK, N.Y. 10016
(212) MU 6-1517

The Japanese Spaniel, which is also called the Chin and the Japanese, has apparently been among the pampered pets of the Japanese nobility for several centuries. The resemblance of the Japanese Spaniel to the Pug, Pekingese, and the Tibetan Spaniel is striking and not surprising as these three breeds are themselves related. Undoubtedly ancestors of these three breeds contributed to the ancestry of the Japanese Spaniel which only reached Britain and the U.S. permanently and in numbers in the latter part of the 19th century. The Japanese Spaniel is a happy, lively lap-dog of dainty appearance and compact build, carrying a profuse coat and a profusely plumed tail, its action is stylish. Size is variable but the smaller dogs are preferred provided type and quality are not sacrificed. Weight classes may be provided, over and under 7 lbs. These dogs must be either black and white or red and white, red encompassing a wide range of sables, brindles, oranges, and lemons. Clear colors are preferred and the color should be distributed in even patches over the body, cheeks, and ears. The nose color should be like that of the coat. These elegant little dogs, which are still immensely popular in Japan, have experienced some ups and downs in the West. They are now registered to the tune of about 300 annually in the U.S., the breed ranking 89th. They are among the more rarely seen of the Toy Group, ranking 16th in the group in numbers in competition.

MINIATURE PINSCHER STANDARD

GENERAL APPEARANCE — The Miniature Pinscher was originated in Germany and named the "Reh Pinscher" due to his resemblance in structure and animation to a very small specie of deer found in the forests. This breed is structurally a well-balanced, sturdy, compact, short-coupled, smooth-coated toy dog. He is naturally well groomed, proud, vigorous and alert. The natural characteristic traits which identify him from other toy dogs are his precise Hackney gait, his fearless animation, complete self-possession, and his spirited presence. *Faults:* Structurally lacking in balance, too long- or short-coupled, too coarse or too refined (lacking in bone development causing poor feet and legs), too large or too small, lethargic, timid or dull, shy or vicious, low in tail placement and poor in action (action not typical of the breed requirements). Knotty overdeveloped muscles.

HEAD — In correct proportion with the body. *From Top* — Tapering, narrow with well-fitted but not too prominent foreface which should balance with the skull. No indication of coarseness. *From Front* — Skull appears flat, tapering forward toward the muzzle. Muzzle itself strong rather than fine and delicate, and in proportion to the head as a whole; cheeks and lips small, taut and closely adherent to each other. Teeth in perfect alignment and apposition. *From Side* — Well-balanced with only a slight drop to the muzzle, which should be parallel to the top of the skull. *Eyes* — Full, slightly oval, almost round, clear, bright and dark even to a true black; set wide apart and fitted well into the sockets. *Ears* — Well-set and firmly placed, upstanding (when cropped, pointed and carried erect in balance with the head). *Nose* — Black only (with the exception of chocolates, which may have a self-colored nose).

Faults: Too large or too small for the body, too coarse or too refined, pinched and weak in foreface, domed in skull, too flat and lacking in chiseling, giving a vapid expression. *Jaws and teeth* overshot or undershot. *Eyes* too round and full, too large, bulging, too deep-set or set too far apart; or too small, set too close (pig eyes). Light-colored eyes not desirable. *Ears* poorly placed, low-set hanging ears (lacking in cartilage) which detract from head conformation. (Poorly cropped ears if set on the head properly and having sufficient cartilage should not detract from head points, as this would be a man-made fault and automatically would detract from general appearance.) *Nose* any color other than black (with the exception of chocolates which may have a self-colored nose).

NECK — Proportioned to head and body. Slightly arched, gracefully curved, clean and firm, blending into shoulders, length well-balanced, muscular and free from a suggestion of dewlap or throatiness. *Faults:* Too straight or too curved; too thick or too thin; too long or short; knotty muscles; loose, flabby or wrinkled skin.

BODY — *From Top* — Compact, slightly wedge-shaped, muscular with well-sprung ribs. *From Side* — Depth of brisket, the base line of which is level with the points of the elbows; short and strong in loin with belly moderately tucked up to denote grace in structural form. Back level or slightly sloping toward the rear. Length of males equals height at withers. Females may be slightly longer. *From Rear* — High tail-set; strong, sturdy upper shanks, with croup slope at about 30 degrees; vent opening not barreled. *Forequarters* — Forechest well-developed and full, moderately broad, shoulders clean, sloping with moderate angulation, coordinated to permit the true action of the Hackney pony. *Hindquarters* — Well-knit muscular quarters set wide enough apart to fit into a properly balanced body.

Faults: From Top — Too long, too short, too barreled, lacking in body development. *From Side* — Too long, too short, too thin or too fat, hips higher or considerably lower than the withers, lacking depth of chest, too full in loin, sway back, roach back or wry back. *From Rear* — Quarters too wide or too close to each other, overdeveloped, barreled vent, underdeveloped vent, too sloping croup, tail set low. *Forequarters* — Forechest and spring of rib too narrow (or too shallow and underdeveloped), shoulders too straight, too loose, or too short and overloaded with muscles. *Hindquarters* — too narrow, undermuscled or overmuscled, too steep in croup.

LEGS AND FEET — Strong bone development and small clean joints; feet catlike, toes strong, well-arched and closely knit with deep pads and thick, blunt nails. *Forelegs and Feet* — As viewed from the front straight and upstanding, elbows close to body, well-knit, flexible yet strong with perpendicular pasterns. *Hind Legs* — All adjacent bones should appear well-angulated with well-muscled thighs or upper shanks, with clearly well-defined stifles, hocks short, set well apart turning neither in nor out; while at rest should stand perpendicular to the ground and upper shanks, lower shanks and hocks parallel to each other.

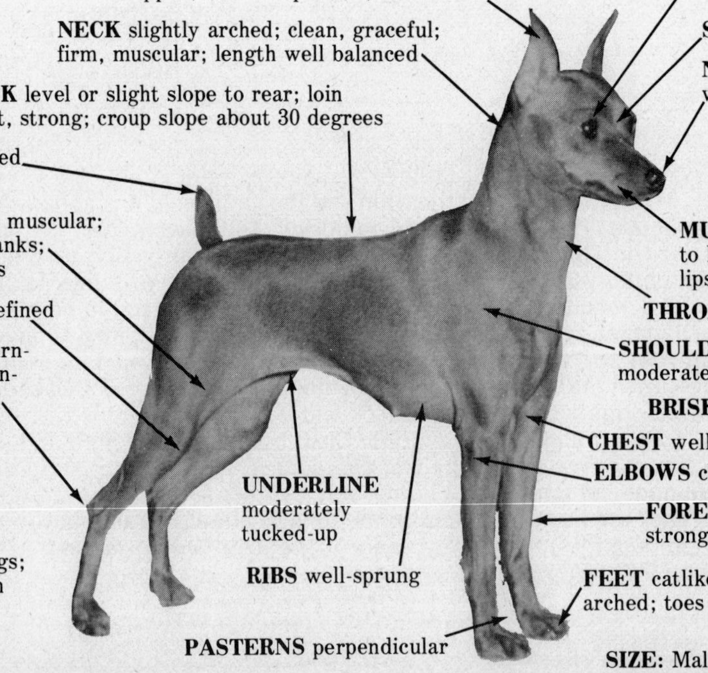

APPEARANCE: Structurally well balanced; sturdy, compact; vigorous, alert; hackney gait; spirited

BODY squarely-built, compact; slightly wedge-shaped, muscular

EARS placed firmly, upstanding; when cropped, ears are pointed, carried erect

NECK slightly arched; clean, graceful; firm, muscular; length well balanced

BACK level or slight slope to rear; loin short, strong; croup slope about 30 degrees

TAIL-set high; docked ½-1"; held erect

HINDQUARTERS well-knit, muscular; fairly wide; sturdy upper shanks; good bone; small, clean joints

STIFLES well-defined

HOCKS short, well-apart, turning neither in nor out; perpendicular to ground; parallel to each other from hock to heel

COLOR: Solid red or stag; lustrous black with sharply defined tan, rust-red markings; solid brown or chocolate with rust or yellow markings

UNDERLINE moderately tucked-up

RIBS well-sprung

PASTERNS perpendicular

HEAD tapering, narrow, not coarse; foreface in balance with skull; skull flat, tapering toward muzzle

TEETH alignment perfect; neither over nor undershot

EYES full, only slightly oval, dark; wide apart, well into sockets

STOP slight

NOSE black (except chocolates which may have self-colored noses)

MUZZLE strong, in proportion to head; parallel to top of skull; lips, cheeks small and taut

THROAT clean

SHOULDERS clean, sloping, moderate angulation

BRISKET deep; level with elbows

CHEST well developed, full; moderately broad

ELBOWS close to body

FORELEGS straight, well-knit; flexible, strong; bone good; joints small, clean

FEET catlike, turning neither in nor out; well-arched; toes strong; pads thick; nails blunt

SIZE: Male, length equals height at withers; females, slightly longer; ideal, 11 to 11½" at withers; oversize or too fat a fault

COAT smooth, hard, short; straight and lustrous

DISQUALIFICATIONS: Color — Thumb marks or any area of white on feet or forechest exceeding ½" in its longest dimension. Size — Either sex measuring under 10" or over 12½"

CH. JAY MAC'S IMPOSSIBLE DREAM

BRED BY THE JOHN McNAMARA'S, HER TYPE IS A LOVELY REPRESENTATION OF THE MINIATURE PINSCHER. FONDLY KNOWN BY MANY AS "IMPY" SHE WAS #1 MIN PIN FOR 1973 AND 1974 AND PLACED AMONGST THE STRONGEST CONTENDERS FOR TOP TOY BOTH YEARS. "IMPY" HAS HAD A GREAT SHOW CAREER ON BOTH COASTS, STARTING IN THE EAST OWNED BY MRS. DOROTHY TURCO SHE AMASSED A RECORD OF 35 TOY GROUPS, 3 SPECIALTIES, 9 BIS HANDLED BY DICK VAUGHAN. IN MARCH 1974 SHE WAS SOLD TO MRS. DOROTHY DE MARIA. ALTHOUGH SHE WAS HELD OUT OF THE RING FOR 6 WEEKS TO GET ACQUAINTED WITH HER NEW HANDLER JOE WATERMAN, SHE CONTINUED ON TO WIN 36 MORE GROUPS, 1 SPECIALTY, AND 6 BIS IN 1974.

HANDLER: JOE WATERMAN

DOROTHY DE MARIA
11848 SUSAN AVENUE
DOWNEY, CALIFORNIA 90241

Faults: Too thick or thin bone development, large joints, spreading flat feet. *Forelegs and Feet* — bowed or crooked, weak pasterns, feet turning in or out, loose elbows. *Hind Legs* — Thin undeveloped stifles, large or crooked hocks, loose stifle joints.

TAIL — Set high, held erect, docked to ½ to 1 inch. *Faults:* Set too low, too thin, drooping, hanging or poorly docked.

COAT — Smooth, hard and short, straight and lustrous, closely adhering to and uniformly covering the body. *Faults:* Thin, too long, dull; upstanding; curly; dry; area of various thickness or bald spots.

COLOR — 1. Solid red or stag red. 2. Lustrous black with sharply defined tan, rust-red markings on cheeks, lips, lower jaw, throat, twin spots above eyes and chest, lower half of forelegs, inside of hind legs and vent region, lower portion of hocks and feet. Black pencil stripes on toes. 3. Solid brown or chocolate with rust or yellow markings. *Faults:* Any color other than listed; very dark or sooty spots. *Disqualifications* — Thumb marks or any area of white on feet or forechest exceeding one-half (½) inch in its longest dimension.

SIZE — Desired height 11 inches to 11½ inches at the withers. A dog of either sex measuring under 10 inches or over 12½ inches shall be disqualified. *Faults:* Oversize; undersize; too fat; too lean.

SCALE OF POINTS

General appearance and movement— [*very important*]	30	**Body**	15
Skull	5	**Feet**	5
Muzzle	5	**Legs**	5
Mouth	5	**Color**	5
Eyes	5	**Coat**	5
Ears	5	**Tail**	5
Neck	5	**Total**	100

DISQUALIFICATIONS

Color — Thumb marks or any area of white on feet or forechest exceeding one-half (½) inch in its longest dimension. Size — A dog of either sex measuring under 10 or over 12½ inches.

Approved May 13, 1958

PAPILLON STANDARD

GENERAL APPEARANCE — The Papillon is a small, friendly, elegant Toy Dog of fine boned structure, light, dainty and of lively action; distinguished from other breeds by its beautiful butterfly-like ears.

HEAD — Small. The skull of medium width, and slightly rounded between the ears. A well defined stop is formed where the muzzle joins the skull. The muzzle is fine, abruptly thinner than the head, tapering to the nose. The length of the muzzle from the tip of nose to stop is approximately one-third the length of the head from tip of nose to occiput.

NOSE — Black, small, rounded, and slightly flat on top. *Disqualification:* Pink, spotted or liver-colored.

EYES — Dark, round, not bulging, of medium size and alert in expression. The inner corner of the eyes is on a line with the stop. Eye rims black.

MOUTH — Lips are tight, thin, and black. Teeth meet in a scissors bite. Tongue must not be visible when jaws are closed. *Fault:* Overshot or undershot.

EARS — The ears of either the erect or drop type should be large with rounded tips and set on the sides and towards the back of the head. (1) Ears of the erect type are carried obliquely and move like the spread wings of a butterfly. When alert, each ear forms an angle of approximately 45 degrees to the head. The leather should be of sufficient strength to maintain the erect position. (2) Ears of the drop type, known as Phalene, are similar to the erect type, but are carried drooping and must be completely down. *Fault:* Ears small, pointed, set too high, one ear up or ears partly down.

NECK — Of medium length.

BODY — Must be slightly longer than the height at withers. It is not a cobby dog. Topline straight and level. The chest is of medium depth with well sprung ribs. The belly is tucked up.

FOREQUARTERS — Shoulders well developed and laid back to allow freedom of movement. Forelegs slender, fine boned and must be straight. Removal of dewclaws on forelegs optional.

HINDQUARTERS — Well developed and well angulated. Hocks inclined neither in nor out. The hindlegs are slender, fine boned, and parallel when viewed from behind. Dewclaws, if any, must be removed from hindlegs.

FEET — Thin and elongated (harelike), pointing neither in nor out.

TAIL — Long, set high and carried well arched over the body. The plume may hang to either side of the body. *Fault:* Low-set tail, one not arched over back nor too short.

COAT — Abundant, long, fine, silky, flowing, straight with resilient quality, flat on back and sides of body. A profuse frill on chest. There is no undercoat. Hair short and close on skull, muzzle, front of forelegs and from hind feet to hocks. Ears well fringed with the inside covered with silken hair of medium length. Backs of the forelegs are covered with feathers diminishing to the pasterns. Hindlegs are covered to the hocks with abundant breeches (culottes). Tail is covered with a long flowing plume. Hair on feet is short but fine tufts may appear over toes and grow beyond them forming a point.

SIZE — Height at highest point of shoulder blades, 8 inches to 11 inches. Weight is in proportion to height. *Fault:* — Over 11 inches. Over 12 inches disqualifies.

GAIT — Free, quick, easy, graceful, not paddle footed, or stiff in hip movements.

COLOR — White predominates with patches which may be any color except liver. Also tricolor (black and white with tan spots over the eyes, on the cheeks, in the ears and under the tail). Color must cover both ears and extend over both eyes. A clearly defined white blaze and nose band, together with symmetrical head markings, are preferable but not essential. The size, shape and placement of the patches on the body are without importance. A saddle is permissible. Among the allowable colors there is no preference. *Disqualification:* Liver color, coat of solid color, all white, or one with no white, white patches on ears or around eyes.

DISQUALIFICATIONS

Nose — Pink, spotted or liver-colored. Height — Over 12". Color — Liver-color, coat of solid color, all white, or one with no white. White patches on ears or around eyes.

Approved June 8, 1965

APPEARANCE: Small, light, dainty; action, lively, friendly; butterfly-like ears a distinguishing mark; not a cobby dog—slightly longer than height at withers

HEAD small; skull, medium width; slightly rounded between ears

STOP well-defined

NECK: length medium

NOSE black, small, rounded slightly flat on top

EYES dark, round, not bulging; size medium; inner corner of eye on line with stop; eye rims black

MOUTH: Lips tight, thin, black; tongue not visible when jaws are closed; scissors bite

MUZZLE fine, abruptly thinner than head, tapering to nose; length from tip of nose to stop approx. one-third length from tip of nose to occiput

SHOULDERS well-developed, laid back

CHEST: depth medium; belly tucked up

FORELEGS slender, fine-boned, straight; removal of dewclaws optional

SIZE: At withers, 8" to 11"; weight in proportion to height; fault over 11" disqualify over 12"

EARS: Either erect or drop, large; tips rounded; set on sides toward back of head. ERECT: Carried obliquely, move like spread wings of butterfly; alert, ear forms 45-degree angle to head; leather strong enough to maintain erect position. DROP: Known as "Phalene" type; carriage, drooping

COAT abundant, long, fine, silky, flowing, straight with resilient quality, flat on back and sides of body; no undercoat. Hair short, close on skull, muzzle, front of forelegs, from hocks to feet, feet (tufts over toes); ears fringed (inside, silken, medium length hair); feathering on backs of forelegs; abundant breeches; long, flowing plume; profuse frill on chest

TOPLINE straight, level

TAIL long, set high; carriage, well-arched over body; plume may hang to either side of body

FEET thin, elongated (harelike), turned neither in nor out

HINDQUARTERS well-developed, well-angulated; hocks inclined neither in nor out; legs slender, fine-boned, parallel (hind view); declaws, if any, must be removed

COLOR: White predominates with patches of any color except liver; also tricolor with correct tan spots; clearly defind white blaze and nose band with symmetrical head markings preferable but not essential; saddle permissible; no preference among allowable colors

DISQUALIFICATIONS: Over 12"; liver color; coat of solid color, all white or one with no white; white patches on ears or around eyes. Pink, spotted or liver-colored nose.

CH. CADAGA'S BRAVO

BRAVO'S KENNELMATE CH. CADAGA'S DE'JA HAD 20 GROUP 1; 37 GROUP 2; 17 GROUP 3; 17 GROUP 4; 156 BOB.

HANDLER: HOWARD NYGOOD

MRS. D. CHRISTIAN GAUSS
50 OENOKE LANE
NEW CANAAN, CONN. 06840
203-966-0312

Dogs believed to be direct ancestors of today's Papillons are depicted in continental European art from the late 13th century. The earlier examples appear to be dwarfed spaniels while the later type have the large, erect, obliquely carried ears that suggest a butterfly and gave rise to the current breed name. Indeed these dogs are still called spaniels in international competition. The favored dogs of royalty and nobility for centuries, Papillons only became established as a breed of wide, public interest in Britain and the U.S. after the 1st World War. The Papillon is a small, friendly, fine-boned, dainty, lively, but essentially normal, dogs without exaggerated features except for the beautiful butterfly ears. The ears can also be of the drop type. Such dogs are known as Phalene but both types are shown as one breed in the U.S. The coat is abundant, long, fine, silky, flowing, and straight. It is flat on the back and sides of the body with a profuse frill on the chest. There is no undercoat. The ears are fringed; the fore-legs are feathered; the hind-legs are covered to the hocks with breeches. The tail has a long flowing plume. White must predominate, with patches of any color but liver. Color must cover both ears and extend over both eyes with a clear white blaze and noseband. Papillons make delightful family companions. Some 400 are registered annually in the United States, the breed ranking 84th.

PEKINGESE STANDARD

EXPRESSION — Must suggest the Chinese origin of the Pekingese in its quaintness and individuality, resemblance to the lion in directions and independence and should imply courage, boldness, self-esteem and combativeness rather than prettiness, daintiness or delicacy.

SKULL — Massive, broad, wide and flat between the ears (not dome-shaped), wide between the eyes. *Nose* — Black, broad, very short and flat. *Eyes* — Large, dark, prominent, round, lustrous. *Stop* — Deep. *Ears* — Heart-shaped, not set too high, leather never long enough to come below the muzzle, nor carried erect, but rather drooping, long feather. *Muzzle* — Wrinkled, very short and broad, not overshot nor pointed. Strong, broad underjaw, teeth not to show.

SHAPE OF BODY — Heavy in front, well-sprung ribs, broad chest, falling away lighter behind, lionlike. Back level. Not too long in body; allowance made for longer body in bitch. *Legs* — Short forelegs, bones of forearm bowed, firm at shoulder; hind legs lighter but firm and well shaped. *Feet* — Flat, toes turned out, not round, should stand well up on feet, not on ankles.

ACTION — Fearless, free and strong, with slight roll.

COAT, FEATHER AND CONDITION — Long, with thick undercoat, straight and flat, not curly nor wavy, rather coarse, but soft; feather on thighs, legs, tail and toes long and profuse. *Mane* — Profuse, extending beyond the shoulder blades, forming ruff or frill round the neck.

COLOR — All colors are allowable. Red, fawn, black, black and tan, sable, brindle, white and parti-color well defined: black masks and spectacles around the eyes, with lines to ears are desirable. *Definition of a Parti-Color Pekingese* — The coloring of a parti-color dog must be broken on the body. No large portion of any one color should exist. White should be shown on the saddle. A dog of any solid color with white feet and chest is *not* a parti-color.

TAIL — Set high; lying well over back to either side; long, profuse, straight feather.

SIZE — Being a toy dog, medium size preferred, providing type and points are not sacrificed; extreme limit 14 pounds.

SCALE OF POINTS

Expression	5	Shape of Body	15
Skull	10	Legs and feet	15
Nose	5	Coat, feather and condition	15
Eyes	5	Tail	5
Stop	5	Action	10
Ears	5		
Muzzle	5		
		Total	100

FAULTS — Protruding tongue, badly blemished eye, overshot, wry mouth.

DISQUALIFICATIONS

Weight — over 14 pounds; Dudley nose.

Approved April 10, 1956

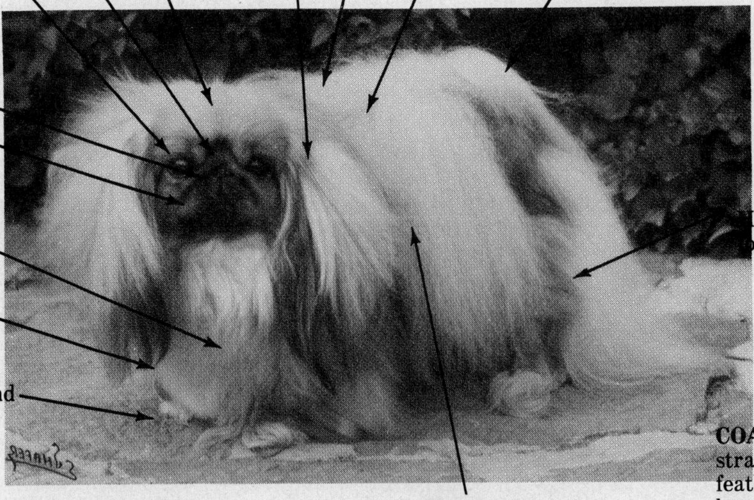

SKULL massive, broad, wide; flat between ears; not domed-shaped

BODY heavy in front; not too long; females, longer bodies

STOP deep

EARS heart-shaped, not set too high; not carried erect (rather drooping); long feathering; leather length not below muzzle

EYES large, dark, prominent, round lustrous; wide between eyes

MANE profuse, forming ruff or frill; extending beyond shoulder blades

TAIL—set high, lying over back to either side; long, profuse, straight feather

BACK level

MUZZLE wrinkled, very short, broad; not overshot or pointed

NOSE black, broad; very short, flat

JAW strong, broad underjaw; teeth must not show

CHEST broad, falling away behind

IND LEGS lighter than relegs; firm, well-shaped

FORELEGS short; forearm bones bowed; firm at shoulder; feather profuse

SIZE: Extreme weight limit 14 lbs; medium size preferred

FEET flat; toes turned out, not round

COAT long; undercoat thick, straight, flat; coarse but soft; feathering profuse on thighs, legs, tail, toes

DISQUALIFICATIONS: Weight—over 14 lbs. Dudley nose

RIBS well-sprung

COLOR: All allowed including partis; parti-colors must be broken on body with some white on saddle; black mask; spectacles around eyes; lines to ears desirable

APPEARANCE: Quaint, individual; expression implies courage, boldness, self-esteem and combativeness rather than daintiness or delicacy; lionlike; slightly rolling gait

CH. MASTERPIECE ZODIAC OF DUD-LEE'S

NUMBER ONE PEKINGESE IN AMERICA FOR 1974. HE IS UNDEFEATED IN THE BREED SINCE HIS PRESENT OWNERSHIP BEGAN; SHOWN 42 TIMES WITH 42 BOB. "ZODI" IS A MULTIPLE SPECIALTY AND ALL BREED BIS WINNER. HE IS A GREAT SHOW DOG AS WELL AS A GREAT SIRE. "ZODI" IS AT STUD ALONG WITH—

CH. DAN LEE DRAGONSEED
(ALL-TIME TOP AM. BRED PEKE)
CH. DAGBURY OF CALARTHA
(BIS WINNER, TOP PEKE '72 & '73)
CH. HI-SWINGER OF BROWN'S DEN
(BIS WINNER)
CH. YANKEE BERNARD
(GROUP WINNER)
CH. RICKSHAW'S RENNAISSANCE
(GROUP WINNER)
CH. DRAGON HAI FANFARE
(GROUP WINNER)

SEVERAL OTHER AMERICAN AND IMPORTED DOGS AT STUD, YOUNG STOCK IS AVAILABLE.

OWNER/HANDLED BY:
MRS. WALTER M. JEFFORDS, JR.
AND
MR. MICHAEL WOLF
ROLLING HILLS FARM
ANDREWS BRIDGE, PA 17509
(717) 529-2752

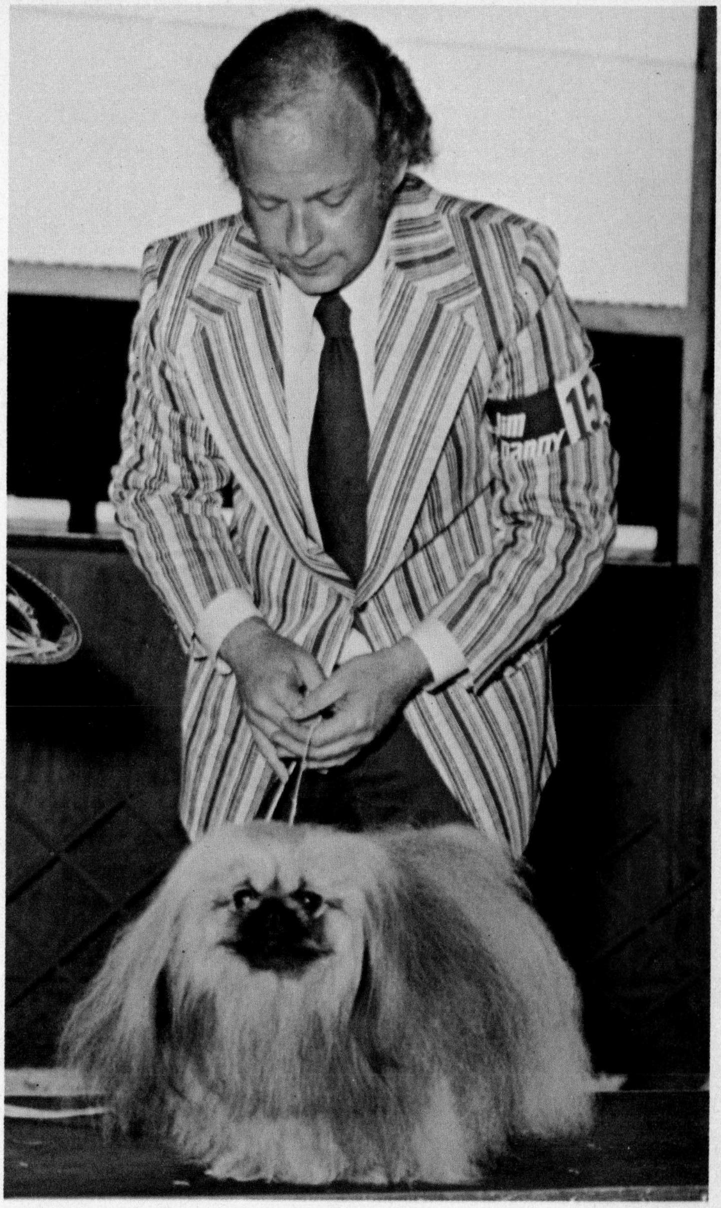

Dogs very like today's Pekingese are featured in Chinese paintings as far back as the early 18th century. Earlier paintings, sculptures, and descriptions certainly deal with dogs of similar type. During these years, the Pekingese were among the principal lap dogs of the Imperial Court. The breed became known and established in Europe in the mid-1800's. Their ancestry almost certainly included dogs of the Pug, Lhasa Apso, and Tibetan Spaniel type, each in unknown degree. The Pekingese expression is both quaint and individualistic, suggesting a lion in its implication of courage, self-esteem, and combativeness. The lion metaphor is enhanced as well by the mane-like ruff of the coat and commonly by the gold or fawn color. The skull is massive, broad, wide, and flat. The eyes large, dark, and prominent. The muzzle is very short, broad, and wrinkled; the nose very blunt and black. The body is heavy in front and lighter in back; the back level, the forelegs bowed. Action is free, strong, and slightly rolling. The coat is long, straight, and flat with feathering on the thighs, legs, tail, and toes. All colors are allowable including parti-color. Medium size is preferred, provided type and points are not sacrificed. The extreme upper limit is 14 pounds. In personality, the Pekingese is independent, courageous, loving, but not servile. Among the most popular breeds in both Britain and the United States for many years, the Pekingese is the most popular Toy breed today, other than the Toy Poodle, in the United States. Some 25,000 are registered annually; the breed ranking 12th. Considering the number registered, the number competing in shows is small. In this respect, they rank only 5th in the Toy Group.

STANDARD

GENERAL APPEARANCE, CARRIAGE AND CONDITION — That of a very active, intelligent and elegant-appearing dog, squarely built, well proportioned, moving soundly and carrying himself proudly. Properly clipped in the traditional fashion and carefully groomed, the Poodle has about him an air of distinction and dignity peculiar to himself.

HEAD AND EXPRESSION — (a) *Skull:* moderately rounded with a slight but definite stop. Cheek-bones and muscles flat. (b) *Muzzle:* long, straight and fine, with slight chiseling under the eyes. Strong without lippiness. The chin definite enough to preclude snipiness. Teeth white, strong and with a scissors bite. (c) *Eyes:* set far apart, very dark, oval in appearance and showing alert intelligence. (d) *Ears:* hanging close to the head, set at or slightly below eye level. The ear leather is long, wide, and thickly feathered, but the ear fringe should not be of excessive length.

NECK AND SHOULDERS — Neck well proportioned, strong and long enough to permit the head to be carried high and with dignity. Skin snug at throat. The neck rises from strong, smoothly muscled shoulders. The shoulder blade is well laid back and approximately the same length as the upper foreleg.

BODY — The chest deep and moderately wide with well sprung ribs. The back short, strong and slightly hollowed; the loins short, broad and muscular. Length of body and height at shoulder are in such proportion as to insure the desirable squarely built appearance.

TAIL — Straight, set on high and carried up, docked, but sufficient in length to insure a balanced outline.

LEGS — The forelegs are straight and parallel when viewed from the front. When viewed from the side with the leg vertical, the elbow is directly below the highest point of the shoulder blade. The hindlegs are muscular with width in the region of the stifles. The pasterns are strong and the stifles well bent. The length of the leg from the stifle joint to the hock joint is considerably greater than the length from the hock joint to the foot.

FEET — The feet are rather small, oval in shape with toes well arched and cushioned on thick firm pads. Nails short but not excessively shortened. The feet turn neither in nor out. Dewclaws may be removed.

COAT — QUALITY — Of naturally harsh texture, profuse and dense throughout.

CLIP — A Poodle may be shown in the "Puppy" clip or the "English Saddle" clip or the traditional "Continental" clip. A Poodle shown in any other type of clip shall be disqualified.

A Poodle under a year old may be shown in the "Puppy" clip with the coat long. The face, throat, feet and base of the tail are shaved. The entire shaven foot is visible. There is a pompon on the end of the tail. In order to give a neat appearance, a slight shaping of the coat is permissible; however, a Poodle in "Puppy" clip that is excessively scissored shall be dismissed.

Dogs one year old or older must be shown in either the "English Saddle" clip or the "Continental" clip.

In the "English Saddle" clip the face, throat, feet, forelegs and base of the tail are shaved, leaving puffs on the forelegs and a pompon on the end of the tail. The hindquarters are covered with a short blanket of hair except for a curved shaved area on each flank and two shaved bands on each hindleg. The entire shaven foot and a portion of the shaven leg above the puff are visible. The rest of the body is left in full coat but may be shaped in order to insure overall balance.

In the "Continental" clip the face, throat, feet and base of the tail are shaved. The hindquarters are shaved with pompons (optional) on the hips. The legs are shaved, leaving bracelets on the hindlegs and puffs on the forelegs. There is a pompon on the end of the tail. The entire shaven foot and portion of the shaven foreleg above the puff are visible. The rest of the body is left in full coat but may be shaped in order to insure overall balance.

In all clips the hair of the topknot may be held in place by an elastic band or barette. The hair is only of sufficient length to present a smooth outline.

COLOR — The coat is an even and solid color at the skin. In blues, grays, silvers, browns, cafe-au-laits, apricots, and creams the coat may show varying shades of the same color. This is frequently present in the somewhat darker feathering of the ears and in the tipping of the ruff. While clear colors are definitely preferred, such natural variations in the shading of the coat is not to be considered a fault. Brown and cafe-au-lait Poodles have liver-colored noses, eye-rims and lips, dark toenails and dark amber eyes. Black, blue, gray, silver, cream and white Poodles

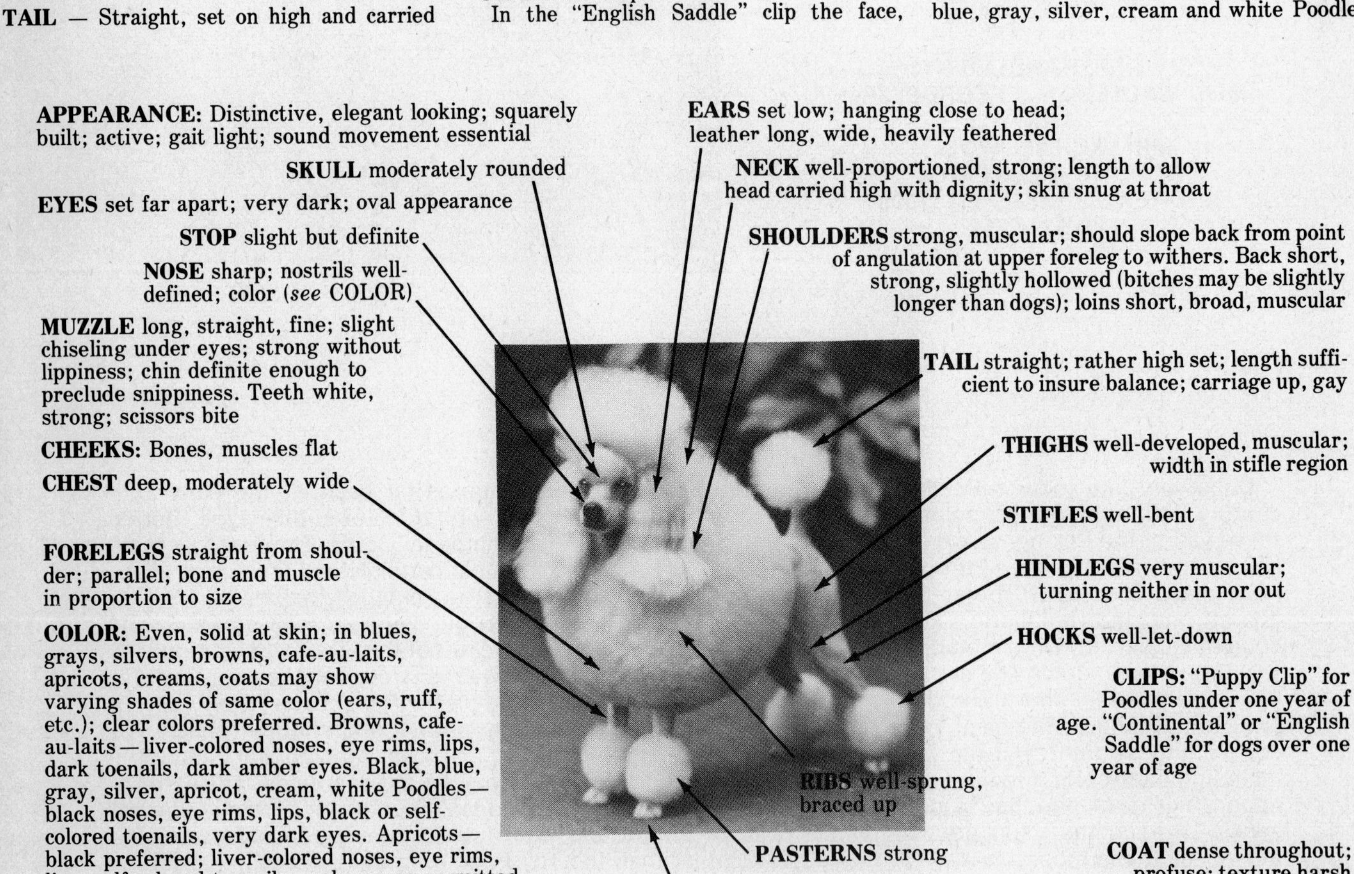
APPEARANCE: Distinctive, elegant looking; squarely built; active; gait light; sound movement essential
SKULL moderately rounded
EYES set far apart; very dark; oval appearance
STOP slight but definite
NOSE sharp; nostrils well-defined; color (*see* COLOR)
MUZZLE long, straight, fine; slight chiseling under eyes; strong without lippiness; chin definite enough to preclude snippiness. Teeth white, strong; scissors bite
CHEEKS: Bones, muscles flat
CHEST deep, moderately wide
FORELEGS straight from shoulder; parallel; bone and muscle in proportion to size
COLOR: Even, solid at skin; in blues, grays, silvers, browns, cafe-au-laits, apricots, creams, coats may show varying shades of same color (ears, ruff, etc.); clear colors preferred. Browns, cafe-au-laits — liver-colored noses, eye rims, lips, dark toenails, dark amber eyes. Black, blue, gray, silver, apricot, cream, white Poodles — black noses, eye rims, lips, black or self-colored toenails, very dark eyes. Apricots — black preferred; liver-colored noses, eye rims, lips, self-colored toenails, amber eyes permitted
DISQUALIFICATIONS: Parti-colors where coat is not even solid color at skin but variegated in patches of two or more colors. Only specified clips allowed in show ring; only specified sizes for each variety permitted
EARS set low; hanging close to head; leather long, wide, heavily feathered
NECK well-proportioned, strong; length to allow head carried high with dignity; skin snug at throat
SHOULDERS strong, muscular; should slope back from point of angulation at upper foreleg to withers. Back short, strong, slightly hollowed (bitches may be slightly longer than dogs); loins short, broad, muscular
TAIL straight; rather high set; length sufficient to insure balance; carriage up, gay
THIGHS well-developed, muscular; width in stifle region
STIFLES well-bent
HINDLEGS very muscular; turning neither in nor out
HOCKS well-let-down
CLIPS: "Puppy Clip" for Poodles under one year of age. "Continental" or "English Saddle" for dogs over one year of age
RIBS well-sprung, braced up
PASTERNS strong
COAT dense throughout; profuse; texture harsh
FEET rather small; oval; turning neither in nor out; toes arched, close; pads hard, thick, well-cushioned
SIZE determines 3 varieties: STANDARD, over 15" at withers; MINIATURE, over 10" (to 15") at withers; TOY, 10" or under at withers

CH. PEEPLE'S SAHARA

MULTIPLE GROUP & BEST IN SHOW WINNER
INCLUDING IN 1974
TOY GROUP WESTMINSTER KENNEL CLUB
BEST OF BREED POODLE CLUB OF AMERICA

OWNER
ROBERT A. KOEPPEL
NEW YORK CITY

HANDLER
RICHARD L. BAUER
MAHOPAC, NEW YORK

have black noses, eye-rims and lips, black or self-colored toenails and very dark eyes. In the apricots, while the foregoing coloring is preferred, liver-colored noses, eye-rims and lips, and amber eyes are permitted but are not desirable.

Parti-colored dogs shall be disqualified. The coat of a parti-colored dog is not an even solid color at the skin but is of two or more colors.

GAIT — A straightforward trot with light springy action and strong hindquarter drive. Head and tail carried high. Forelegs and hindlegs move parallel turning neither in nor out. Sound movement is essential.

SIZE

STANDARD — The Standard Poodle is over 15 inches at the highest point of the shoulders. Any Poodle which is 15 inches or less in height shall be disqualified from competition as a Standard Poodle.

MINIATURE — The Miniature Poodle is 15 inches or under at the highest point of the shoulders, with a minimum height in excess of 10 inches. Any Poodle which is over 15 inches or 10 inches or less at the highest point of the shoulders shall be disqualified from competition as a Miniature Poodle.

TOY — The Toy Poodle is 10 inches or under at the highest point of the shoulders. Any Poodle which is more than 10 inches at the highest point of the shoulders shall be disqualified from competition as a Toy Poodle.

VALUE OF POINTS

General appearance, temperament, carriage and condition	30
Head, expression, ears, eyes and teeth	20
Body, neck, legs, feet and tail	20
Gait	20
Coat, color and texture	10

MAJOR FAULTS

Eyes: round in appearance, protruding, large or very light.
Jaws: undershot, overshot or wry mouth.
Feet: flat or spread.
Tail: set low, curled or carried over the back.
Hindquarters: cow hocks.
Temperament: shyness or sharpness.

DISQUALIFICATIONS

Clip: A dog in any type of clip other than those listed under "Coat" shall be disqualified.

Parti-colors: The coat of a parti-colored dog is not an even solid color at the skin but is of two or more colors. Parti-colored dogs shall be disqualified.

Size: A dog over or under the height limits specified under "Size" shall be disqualified.

Approved November 10, 1970

SHIH TZU
STANDARD

GENERAL APPEARANCE — Very active, lively and alert, with a distinctly arrogant carriage. The Shih Tzu is proud of bearing as befits his noble ancestry, and walks with head well up and tail carried gaily over the back.

HEAD — Broad and round, wide between the eyes. Muzzle square and short, but not wrinkled, about one inch from tip of nose to stop. *Definite Stop. Eyes* — Large, dark and round but not prominent, placed well apart. Eyes should show warm expression. *Ears* — Large, with long leathers, and carried drooping; set slightly below the crown of the skull; so heavily coated that they appear to blend with the hair of the neck. *Teeth* — level or slightly undershot bite.

FOREQUARTERS — Legs short, straight, well boned, muscular, and heavily coated. Legs and feet look massive on account of the wealth of hair.

BODY — Body between the withers and the root of the tail is somewhat longer than the height at the withers; well coupled and sturdy. Chest broad and deep, shoulders firm, back level.

HINDQUARTERS — Legs short, well boned and muscular, are straight when viewed from the rear. Thighs well rounded and muscular. Legs look massive on account of wealth of hair.

FEET — Of good size, firm, well padded, with hair between the pads. Dewclaws, if any, on the hind legs are generally removed. Dewclaws on the forelegs may be removed.

TAIL — Heavily plumed and curved well over the back; carried gaily, set on high.

COAT — A luxurious, long, dense coat. May be slightly wavy but *not* curly. Good woolly undercoat. The hair on top of the head may be tied up.

COLOR — All colors permissible. Nose and eye rims black, except that dogs with liver markings may have liver noses and slightly lighter eyes.

GAIT — Slightly rolling, smooth and flowing, with strong rear action.

SIZE — Height at withers — 9 to 10½ inches — should be no more than 11 inches nor less than 8 inches. Weight of mature dogs — 12 to 15 pounds — should be no more than 18 pounds nor less than 9 pounds. However, type and breed characteristics are of the greatest importance.

FAULTS — Narrow head, overshot bite, sniping, pink on nose or eye rims, small or light eyes, legginess, sparse coat, lack of definite stop.

Approved May 13, 1969

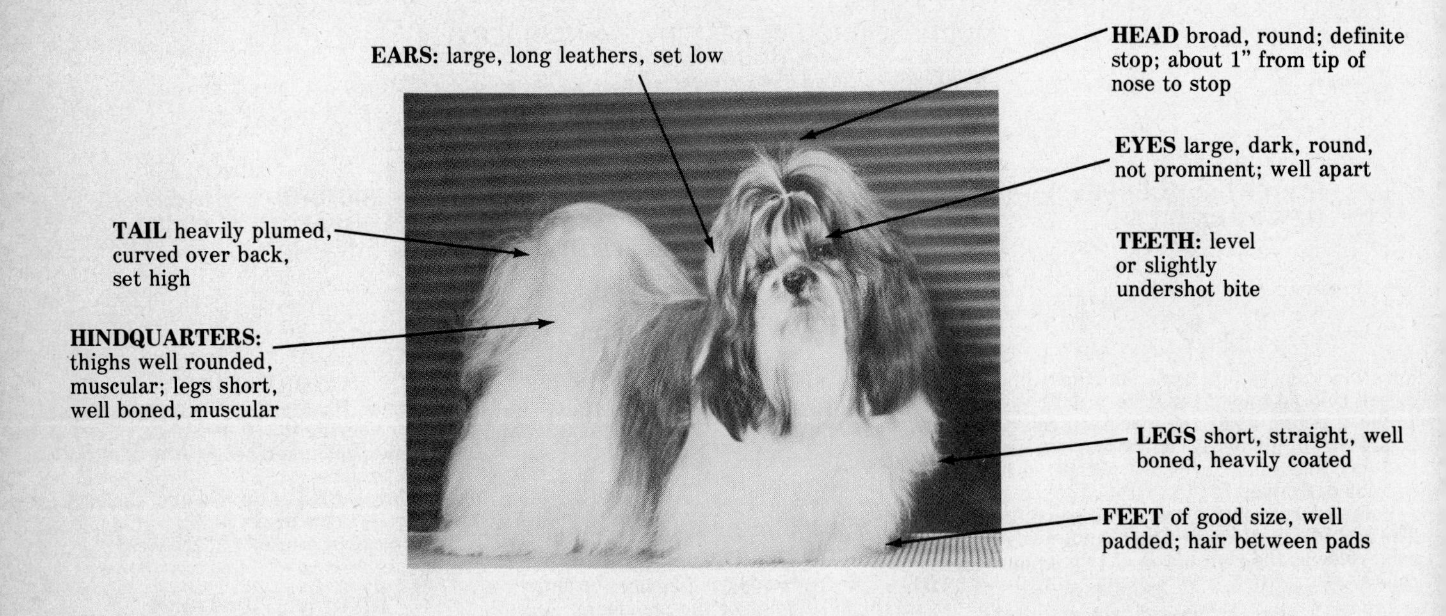

APPEARANCE: Active, lively, alert; arrogant carriage; walks with head well up, tail over back
EARS: large, long leathers, set low
HEAD broad, round; definite stop; about 1" from tip of nose to stop
EYES large, dark, round, not prominent; well apart
TAIL heavily plumed, curved over back, set high
TEETH: level or slightly undershot bite
HINDQUARTERS: thighs well rounded, muscular; legs short, well boned, muscular
LEGS short, straight, well boned, heavily coated
FEET of good size, well padded; hair between pads
COLOR: All colors permissible; nose and eye rims black; dogs with liver markings may have liver noses, lighter eyes
COAT: Luxurious, long, dense; not curly
SIZE: Height, 9" to 10½" but not less than 8" or over 11". Weight: mature dogs 12-15 lbs. but not less than 9 lbs. nor over 18 lbs.

CH. WITCH'S WOOD YUM YUM

TOP WINNING SHIH TZU OF ALL TIME. HER RECORD IS 40 BIS, 136 TOY GROUP I'S, 236 TOTAL GROUP PLACEMENTS, 257 BEST OF BREED. TOP TOY ALL SYSTEMS 1973. SHE IS A FOUR-YEAR-OLD BITCH NOW RETIRED AND AT HOME WITH HER OWNERS, READY TO START HER NEW CAREER, "MOTHERHOOD."

HANDLER: JOHN M. MURDOCK

DR. & MRS. J. WESLEY EDEL
FT. LAMAR ROAD, JAMES ISLAND
CHARLESTON, S.C.

The Shih Tzu is of Chinese origin proximally but ultimately derived from Tibet. The most likely hypothesis is that dogs very like the modern Lhasa Apsos were bred by variety in Tibet, often as the pampered pets of the upper classes. They were on occasion sent to the Chinese Imperial Court as gifts and tribute. Crosses there with Pekingese or dogs ancestral to the Pekingese would have introduced the shorter muzzle, domed head, shorter legs, and other features that today differentiate the Shih Tzu from the Lhasa Apso. Indeed, the Shih Tzu, or its predecessors, may well have given the Pekingese, in turn, its heavy coat. Pugs and Tibetan Spaniels may also have entered the mix. Shih Tzu means little lion in Chinese and it is the Shih Tzu and its ancestors which are believed to have been the models of the Tibetan lion dogs which have been so popular in Chinese art. The Shih Tzu is loving, intelligent, and robust. These dogs must have very good substance. Weights of 12-15 lbs. and heights at the shoulder of 9-12½ inches are the preferred size ranges. The coat is luxurious, dense, and long with a good woolly undercoat. The hair on the head may be tied up. All colors are permissible. Given full recognition by the AKC early in 1969, the Shih Tzu has found ready acceptance as a pet and show dog of exceptional charm and beauty almost totally lacking in irritability. Just four years after recognition, over 7,000 are now registered annually in the United States and the breed ranks 36th. The Shih Tzu ranks 2nd in numbers in competition in the Toy Group and first in the number of Toy Group wins.

SILKY TERRIER STANDARD

THE SILKY TERRIER is a lightly built, moderately low-set toy dog of pronounced terrier character and spirited action.

HEAD — The head is strong, wedge-shaped, and moderately long. The skull is a trifle longer than the muzzle, in proportion about three-fifths for the skull, two-fifths for the muzzle. *Skull* — Flat, and not too wide between the ears. *Stop* — Shallow. *Ears* — Small, V-shaped and pricked. They are set high and carried erect without any tendency to flare obliquely off the skull.

EYES — Small, dark in color, and piercingly keen in expression. Light eyes are a fault. *Teeth* — Strong and well aligned; scissors bite. A bite markedly undershot or overshot is a serious fault. *Nose* — The nose is black.

NECK AND SHOULDERS — The neck fits gracefully into sloping shoulders. It is medium long, fine and to some degree crested along its top line.

BODY — Low-set, about one-fifth longer than the dog's height at the withers. A too short body is a fault. The back line is straight, with a just perceptible rounding over the loins. Brisket medium wide, and deep enough to extend down to the elbows.

Tail — The tail is set high and carried erect or semierect but not over-gay. It is docked and well coated but devoid of plume.

FOREQUARTERS — Well laid back shoulders, together with good angulation at the upper arm, set the forelegs nicely under the body. Forelegs are strong, straight and rather fine-boned. **Hindquarters** — Thighs well muscled and strong, but not so developed as to appear heavy. Legs moderately angulated at stifles and hocks, with the hocks low and equidistant from the hock joints to the ground. *Feet* — Small, cat-like, round, compact. Pads are thick and springy while the nails are strong and dark colored. White or flesh colored nails are a fault. The feet point straight ahead, with no turning in or out. Dewclaws, if any, are removed.

COAT — Flat, in texture fine, glossy, silky; on matured specimens the desired length of coat from behind the ears to the set-on of the tail is from five to six inches. On the top of the head the hair is so profuse as to form a topknot, but long hair on face and ears is objectionable. Legs from knee and hock joints to feet should be free from long hair. The hair is parted on the head and down over the back to the root of the tail. *Color* — Blue and tan. The blue may be silver blue, pigeon blue or slate blue, the tan deep and rich. The blue extends from the base of the skull to the tip of the tail, down the forelegs to the pasterns, and down the thighs to the hocks. On the tail the blue should be very dark. Tan appears on muzzle and cheeks, around the base of the ears, below the pasterns and hocks, and around the vent. There is a tan spot over each eye. The topknot should be silver or fawn.

TEMPERAMENT — The keenly alert air of the terrier is characteristic, with shyness or excessive nervousness to be faulted. The manner is quick, friendly, responsive.

MOVEMENT — Should be free, light footed, lively, and straightforward. Hindquarters should have strong propelling power. Toeing in or out is to be faulted.

SIZE — Weight ranges from eight to ten pounds. Shoulder height from nine to ten inches. Pronounced diminutiveness (such as a height of less than 8 inches) is not desired; it accentuates the quality of toyishness as opposed to the breed's definite terrier character.

Approved April 14, 1959

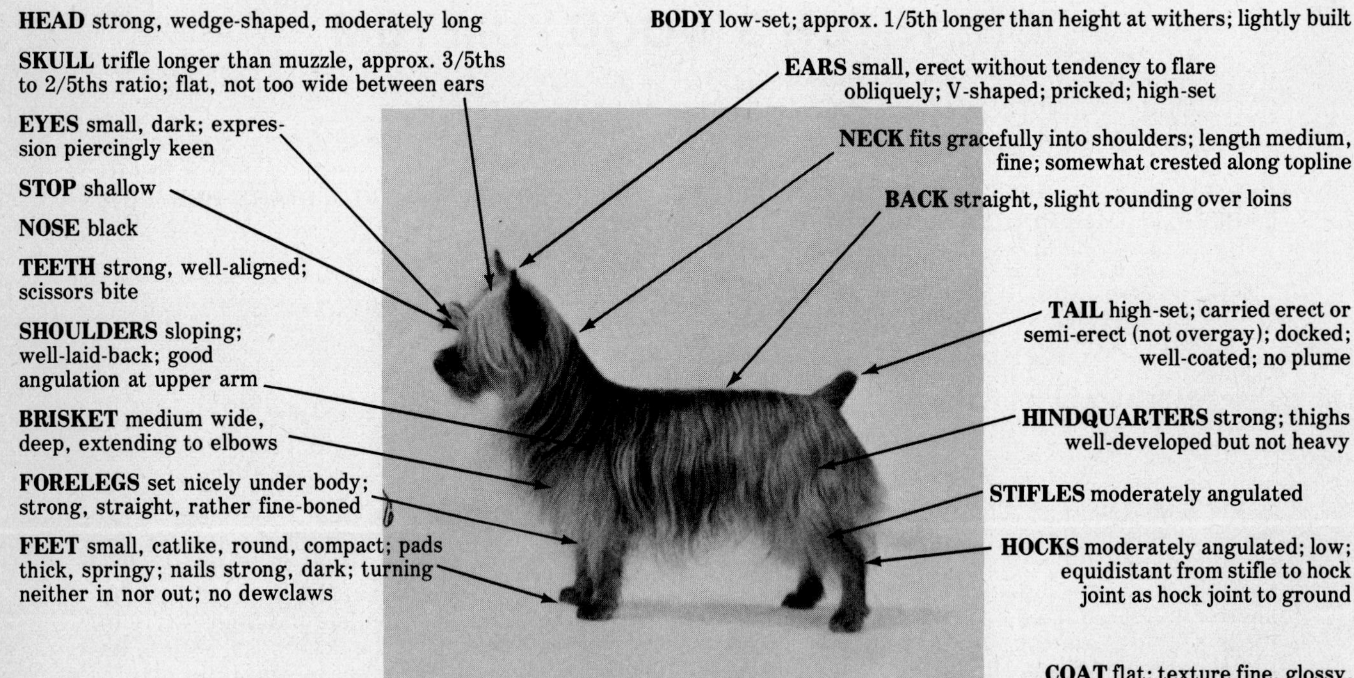

HEAD strong, wedge-shaped, moderately long
SKULL trifle longer than muzzle, approx. 3/5ths to 2/5ths ratio; flat, not too wide between ears
EYES small, dark; expression piercingly keen
STOP shallow
NOSE black
TEETH strong, well-aligned; scissors bite
SHOULDERS sloping; well-laid-back; good angulation at upper arm
BRISKET medium wide, deep, extending to elbows
FORELEGS set nicely under body; strong, straight, rather fine-boned
FEET small, catlike, round, compact; pads thick, springy; nails strong, dark; turning neither in nor out; no dewclaws
BODY low-set; approx. 1/5th longer than height at withers; lightly built
EARS small, erect without tendency to flare obliquely; V-shaped; pricked; high-set
NECK fits gracefully into shoulders; length medium, fine; somewhat crested along topline
BACK straight, slight rounding over loins
TAIL high-set; carried erect or semi-erect (not overgay); docked; well-coated; no plume
HINDQUARTERS strong; thighs well-developed but not heavy
STIFLES moderately angulated
HOCKS moderately angulated; low; equidistant from stifle to hock joint as hock joint to ground
COAT flat; texture fine, glossy, silky; hair length 5" to 6" from behind ears to tail-set; profuse hair on head forms topknot; long hair on face, ears objectionable; no long hair from knee and hock joints to feet; hair is parted from head down over back to root of tail
COLOR: Blue and tan; blue may be silver-blue, pigeon-blue or slate-blue; tan deep, rich; blue extends from skull to tail tip (tail very dark) and down legs to pasterns and hocks; tan on muzzle, cheeks, base of ear, below pasterns, hocks, around vent; tan spot over each eye; topknot silver or fawn
WEIGHT from 8 to 10 lbs.
HEIGHT at withers from 9" to 10" (pronounced diminutiveness such as less than 8" not desirable)
TEMPERAMENT of pronounced terrier character; action spirited; keenly alert; friendly, responsive

CH. ROYALINE DON JUAN OF CASANOVA, "D.J."

AT FOUR YEARS OF AGE, "D.J." HAS ALREADY WON SEVEN ALL BREED BEST IN SHOWS THEREBY BREAKING ALL PREVIOUS SILKY TERRIER RECORDS. SIX OF THESE BIS WINS WERE ACHIEVED IN 1974 AGAINST TOP COMPETITION IN CALIFORNIA. 1973 AND 1974 WESTMINSTER BEST OF BREED WINNER. 1974 PHILLIPS SYSTEM NO. 1 SILKY TERRIER AND NO. 3 TOY DOG. BEST IN SHOW WINNER OF THE PRESTIGIOUS BEVERLY HILLS KC WINTER SHOW IN 1974 AGAINST THE TOP DOGS IN THE NATION. SHOW RECORD TO DATE: 7 ALL BREED BEST IN SHOWS, 1 SPECIALTY BEST IN SHOW, 76 TOY GROUP PLACEMENTS, 29 GROUP FIRSTS, 104 BEST OF BREEDS.

HANDLER: DICK & MADELINE WEBB

ROBERT AND GLORIA FARRON
1230 LEONARD AVE.
PASADENA, CALIF. 91107
(213) 351-0553

The Silky Terrier is of Australian origin. It derives from crosses of the Australian and the Yorkshire Terrier. The Australian Terrier, in turn, was developed from half a dozen small British Terriers. The Silky Terrier was granted official recognition by the AKC in 1959 but has not yet found acceptance in Britain. The Silky is an alert, appealing dog of 8 to 19 pounds with a lustrous, silky, long (but not too long) coat of blue and tan. The Silky is lightly built, spirited, and clearly a terrier. The body is low-set and slightly longer than the height at the withers. The back line is straight, rounding just perceptibly over the loins. The tail is set high and carried erect or semi-erect. The tail is docked and well coated but not plumed. The Silky Terrier has proved to be an intelligent and vivacious pet and is said to be a good helper on the farm. Over 3,000 are now registered annually in the United States, the breed ranking 44th.

YORKSHIRE TERRIER
STANDARD

GENERAL APPEARANCE — That of a long-haired Toy Terrier whose blue and tan coat is parted on the face and from the base of the skull to the end of the tail and hangs evenly and quite straight down each side of body. The body is neat, compact and well proportioned. The dog's high head carriage and confident manner should give the appearance of vigor and self-importance.

HEAD — Small and rather flat on top, the skull not too prominent or round, the muzzle not too long, with the bite neither undershot nor overshot and teeth sound. Either scissor or level bite is acceptable. The nose is black. Eyes are medium in size and not too prominent: dark in color and sparkling with a sharp intelligent expression. Eye rims are dark. Ears are small V-shaped, carried erect and set not too far apart.

BODY — Well proportioned and very compact. The back is rather short, the back line level, with height at shoulder the same as at the rump.

LEGS AND FEET — Forelegs should be straight, elbows neither in nor out. *Hind legs* straight when viewed from behind, but stifles are moderately bent when viewed from the sides. *Feet* are round with black toe-nails. *Dew claws*, if any, are generally removed from the hind legs. Dew claws on the forelegs may be removed.

TAIL — Docked to a medium length and carried slightly higher than the level of the back.

COAT — Quality, texture and quantity of coat are of prime importance. Hair is glossy, fine and silky in texture. Coat on the body is moderately long and perfectly straight (not wavy). It may be trimmed to floor length to give ease of movement and a neater appearance, if desired. The fall on the head is long, tied with one bow in center of head or parted in the middle and tied with two bows. Hair on muzzle is very long. Hair should be trimmed short on tips of ears and may be trimmed on feet to give them a neat appearance.

COLORS — Puppies are born black and tan and are normally darker in body color, showing an intermingling of black hair in the tan until they are matured. Color of hair on body and richness of tan on head and legs are of prime importance in ADULT DOGS to which the following color requirements apply:

Blue — Is a dark steel blue, not a silver blue and not mingled with fawn, bronzy or black hairs.

Tan — All tan hair is darker at the roots than in the middle, shading to still lighter tan at the tips. There should be no sooty or black hair intermingled with any of the tan.

COLOR ON BODY — The blue extends over the body from back of neck, to root of tail. Hair on tail is a darker blue, especially at end of tail.

Headfall — A rich golden tan, deeper in color at sides of head, at ear roots and on the muzzle, with ears a deep rich tan. Tan color should not extend down on back of neck.

Chest and Legs — A bright rich tan, not extending above the elbow on the forelegs nor above the stifle on the hind legs.

WEIGHT — Must not exceed seven pounds.

Approved April, 1966

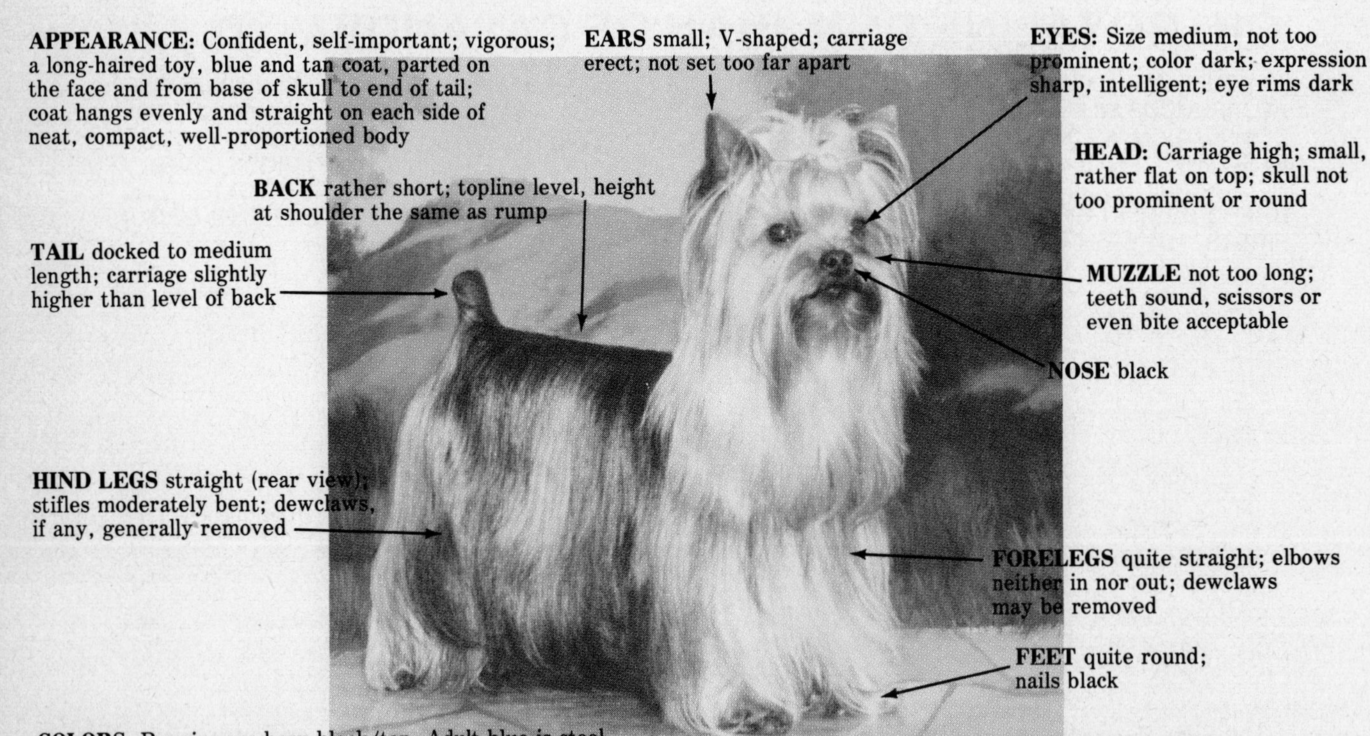

APPEARANCE: Confident, self-important; vigorous; a long-haired toy, blue and tan coat, parted on the face and from base of skull to end of tail; coat hangs evenly and straight on each side of neat, compact, well-proportioned body
EARS small; V-shaped; carriage erect; not set too far apart
EYES: Size medium, not too prominent; color dark; expression sharp, intelligent; eye rims dark
HEAD: Carriage high; small, rather flat on top; skull not too prominent or round
BACK rather short; topline level, height at shoulder the same as rump
TAIL docked to medium length; carriage slightly higher than level of back
MUZZLE not too long; teeth sound, scissors or even bite acceptable
NOSE black
HIND LEGS straight (rear view); stifles moderately bent; dewclaws, if any, generally removed
FORELEGS quite straight; elbows neither in nor out; dewclaws may be removed
FEET quite round; nails black
COLORS: Puppies are born black/tan. Adult blue is steel blue (not silver nor mingled with fawn, bronze or black hairs). Tan hair is darker at roots, shading lighter to tips (no sooty or black hair with tan). Blue extends over body from back of neck to tail root. Hair on tail darker blue, especially at end. Headfall rich, golden tan, deeper at sides, ear roots and on muzzle. Ears a deep, rich tan (tan should not extend down back of neck). Chest, legs, a bright, rich tan, not extending above elbows or above stifles
COAT quality, texture and quantity of prime importance: Texture glossy, fine glossy, silky; body coat long, straight (not wavy); may be trimmed to floor length; the headfall can be tied with one or two bows; muzzle hair long; hair on ear tips trimmed; hair on feet may be trimmed
WEIGHT: Must not exceed 7 pounds

CH. TRIVAR'S GOLD DIGGER

PICTURED WINNING BEST IN SHOW AT UPPER MARLBORO UNDER MR. VANCE EVANS. "GOLDY" IS SIRED BY CH. TRIVAR'S TYCOON, ONE OF THE TOP WINNING YORKIES OF THE BREED. WHILE BEING SHOWN, TYCOON AMASSED 30 GROUP 1's, MORE THAN ANY OTHER YORKIE BRED IN AMERICA. BRED, OWNED AND HANDLED BY JOHNNY ROBINSON AND MORRIS HOWARD.

TRIVAR
10030 GLENOLDEN DRIVE
POTOMAC, MARYLAND 20854

The Yorkshire Terrier was developed about 150 years ago in Yorkshire, England from a variety of British terriers and possibly the Maltese. The breed was developed at first as a working terrier but was subsequently bred down to toy size. The Yorkshire Terrier has a long blue and tan coat, parted down the back and face; the hair hangs straight. The body is neat and compact. The dog's carriage and bearing radiate vigor and self-confidence. The coat quality, texture, length, and color are very important. Weight must not exceed 7 pounds. The Yorkshire Terrier is hardy, game, protective, and easily trained. They make courageous and vivacious pets with the ways of a true terrier. In Britain they have recently ranked third among all breeds in popularity. Some 180,000 are registered annually in the United States; the breed ranking 17th. Yorkshire Terriers rank 3rd in numbers in show competition in the Toy group in 1972.

ENGLISH TOY SPANIEL [BLENHEIM & PRINCE CHARLES] [KING CHARLES & RUBY]

HEAD — Should be well domed, and in good specimens is absolutely semi-globular, sometimes even extending beyond the half-circle, and absolutely projecting over the eyes, so as nearly to meet the upturned nose. *Eyes* — The eyes are set wide apart, with the eyelids square to the line of the face — not oblique or foxlike. The eyes themselves are large and dark as possible, so as to be generally considered black, their enormous pupils, which are absolutely of that color, increasing the description. *Stop* — The stop, or hollow between the eyes, is well marked, as in the Bulldog, or even more so; some good specimens exhibit a hollow deep enough to bury a small marble in it. *Nose* — The nose must be short and well turned up between the eyes, and without any indication of artificial displacement afforded by a deviation to either side. The color of the end should be black, and it should be both deep and wide with open nostrils. A light-colored nose is objectionable, but shall not disqualify. *Jaw* — The muzzle must be square and deep, and the lower jaw wide between the branches, leaving plenty of space for the tongue, and for the attachment of the lower lips, which should completely conceal the teeth. It should also be turned up or "finished," so as to allow of its meeting the end of the upper jaw, turned up in a similar way as above described. A protruding tongue is objectionable, but does not disqualify. *Ears* — The ears must be long, so as to approach the ground. In an average-sized dog they measure 20 inches from tip to tip, and some reach 22 inches or even a trifle more. They should be set low down on the head and hang flat to the sides of the cheeks, and be heavy-feathered.

SIZE — The most desirable size is from 9 pounds to 12 pounds. *Shape* — In compactness of shape the Spaniels almost rival the Pug, but the length of coat adds greatly to the apparent bulk, as the body, when the coat is wetted, looks small in comparison with that dog. Still, it ought to be decidedly "cobby," with strong, stout legs, short broad back and wide chest.

COAT — The coat should be long, silky, soft and wavy, but not curly. There should be a profuse mane, extending well down in the front of the chest. The feather should be well displayed on the ears and feet, and in the latter case so thickly as to give the appearance of being webbed. It is also carried well up the back of the legs. In the Black and Tan the feather on the ears is very long and profuse, exceeding that of the Blenheim by an inch or more. The feather on the tail (which is cut to the length of about 1½ inches) should be silky, and from 3 to 4 inches in length, constituting a marked "flag" of a square shape, and not carried above the level of the back.

Colors of Two Varieties

KING CHARLES AND RUBY — The King Charles and Ruby types which comprise one show variety are solid-colored dogs. The King Charles are black and tan (considered a solid color), the black rich and glossy with deep mahogany tan markings over the eyes and on the muzzle, chest and legs. The presence of a few white hairs intermixed with the black on the chest is to be faulted, but a white patch on the chest or white appearing elsewhere disqualifies. The Ruby is a rich chestnut red and is whole-colored. The presence of a few white hairs intermixed with the red on the chest is to be faulted, but a white patch on the chest or white appearing elsewhere disqualifies.

BLENHEIM AND PRICE CHARLES — The Blenheim and Price Charles types which comprise the other show variety are broken-colored dogs. The Blenheim is red and white. The ground color is a pearly white which has bright red chestnut or ruby red markings evenly distributed in large patches. The ears and cheeks should be red, with a blaze of white extending from the nose up the forehead and ending between the ears in a crescentic curve. In the center of the blaze at the top of the forehead, there should be a clear "spot" of red, the size of a dime. The Prince Charles, a tri-colored dog, is white, black and tan. The ground color is a pearly white. The black consists of markings which should be evenly distributed in large patches. The tan appears as spots over the eyes, on the muzzle, chest and legs; the ears and vent should also be lined with tan. The Prince Charles has no "spot," that being a particular feature of the Blenheim.

King Charles, or Black and Tan. Prince Charles, White, with Black and Tan Markings. Ruby, or Red.

SCALE OF POINTS

Symmetry, condition, size and soundness of limb	20
Head	15
Stop	5
Muzzle	10
Eyes	10
Ears	15
Coat and feathering	15
Color	10
Total	100

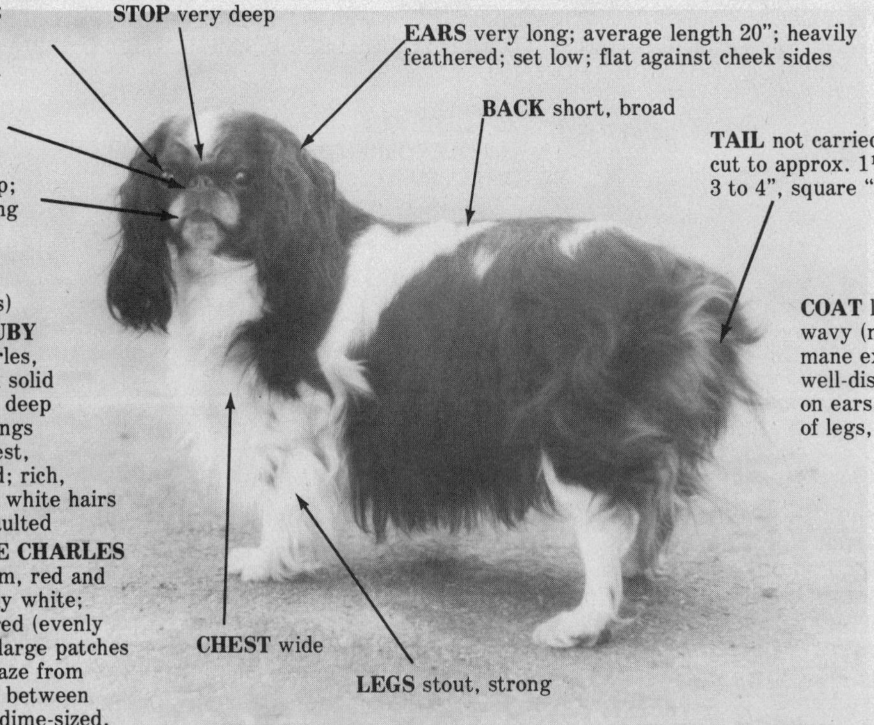

HEAD: Well-domed; semi-globular ideal; sometimes projecting over eyes, meeting upturned nose

BODY compact, cobby; thick-set; carriage smart

EYES wide apart; large, dark; lids square with face line; not oblique nor foxlike

STOP very deep

EARS very long; average length 20"; heavily feathered; set low; flat against cheek sides

NOSE short; well-turned-up between eyes; black, deep, wide; nostrils open

BACK short, broad

TAIL not carried over back level; cut to approx. 1½"; silky feathering 3 to 4", square "flag" shape

MUZZLE square, deep; lower jaw wide, turned up; teeth concealed; protruding tongue objectionable

TWO VARIETIES (divided by color patterns)

KING CHARLES and **RUBY** (solid-colored): King Charles, black and tan (considered solid color); rich, glossy black; deep mahogany tan; tan markings over eyes, on muzzle, chest, legs. Ruby, whole-colored; rich, chestnut red. Intermixed white hairs on chest permitted but faulted

BLENHEIM and **PRINCE CHARLES** (broken-colored): Blenheim, red and white; ground color pearly white; bright chestnut or ruby red (evenly distributed) markings in large patches on ears, cheeks; white blaze from nose up forehead, ending between ears in crescentic curve; dime-sized, red "spot" in blaze center, top of forehead. Prince Charles, tri-colored, white, black, tan ground color pearly white; black (evenly distributed) markings in large patches; tan spots over eyes, on muzzle, chest, legs, ears, vent (no forehead "spot")

COAT long, silky, soft, wavy (not curly); profuse mane extending over chest; well-displayed feathering on ears, feet, back of legs, tail

CHEST wide

LEGS stout, strong

SIZE: 9 to 12 lbs. desirable

DISQUALIFICATIONS: A white patch on chest or any other part of King Charles and Ruby

ITALIAN GREYHOUND STANDARD

DESCRIPTION — The Italian Greyhound is very similar to the Greyhound, but much smaller and more slender in all proportions and of ideal elegance and grace.

HEAD — Narrow and long, tapering to nose, with a slight suggestion of stop.

SKULL — Rather long, almost flat.

MUZZLE — Long and fine.

NOSE — Dark. It may be black or brown or in keeping with the color of the dog. A light or partly pigmented nose is a fault.

TEETH — Scissors bite. A badly undershot or overshot mouth is a fault.

EYES — Dark, bright, intelligent, medium in size. Very light eyes are a fault.

EARS — Small, fine in texture; thrown back and folded except when alerted, then carried folded at right angles to the head. Erect or button ears severely penalized.

NECK — Long, slender and gracefully arched.

BODY — Of medium length, short coupled; high at withers, back curved and drooping at hindquarters, the highest point of curve at start of loin, creating a definite tuck-up at flanks.

SHOULDERS — Long and sloping.

CHEST — Deep and narrow.

FORELEGS — Long, straight, set well under shoulder; strong pasterns, fine bone.

HINDQUARTERS — Long, well muscled thigh; hindlegs parallel when viewed from behind, hocks well let down, well bent stifle.

FEET — Hare foot with well arched toes. Removal of dew claws optional.

TAIL — Slender and tapering to a curved end, long enough to reach the hock; set low, carried low. Ring tail a serious fault, gay tail a fault.

COAT — Skin fine and supple, hair short, glossy like satin and soft to the touch.

COLOR — Any color and markings are acceptable except that a dog with the tan markings normally found on black and tan dogs of other breeds must be disqualified.

ACTION — High stepping and free, front and hind legs to move forward in a straight line.

SIZE — Height at withers, ideally 13" to 15".

Approved April 13, 1971

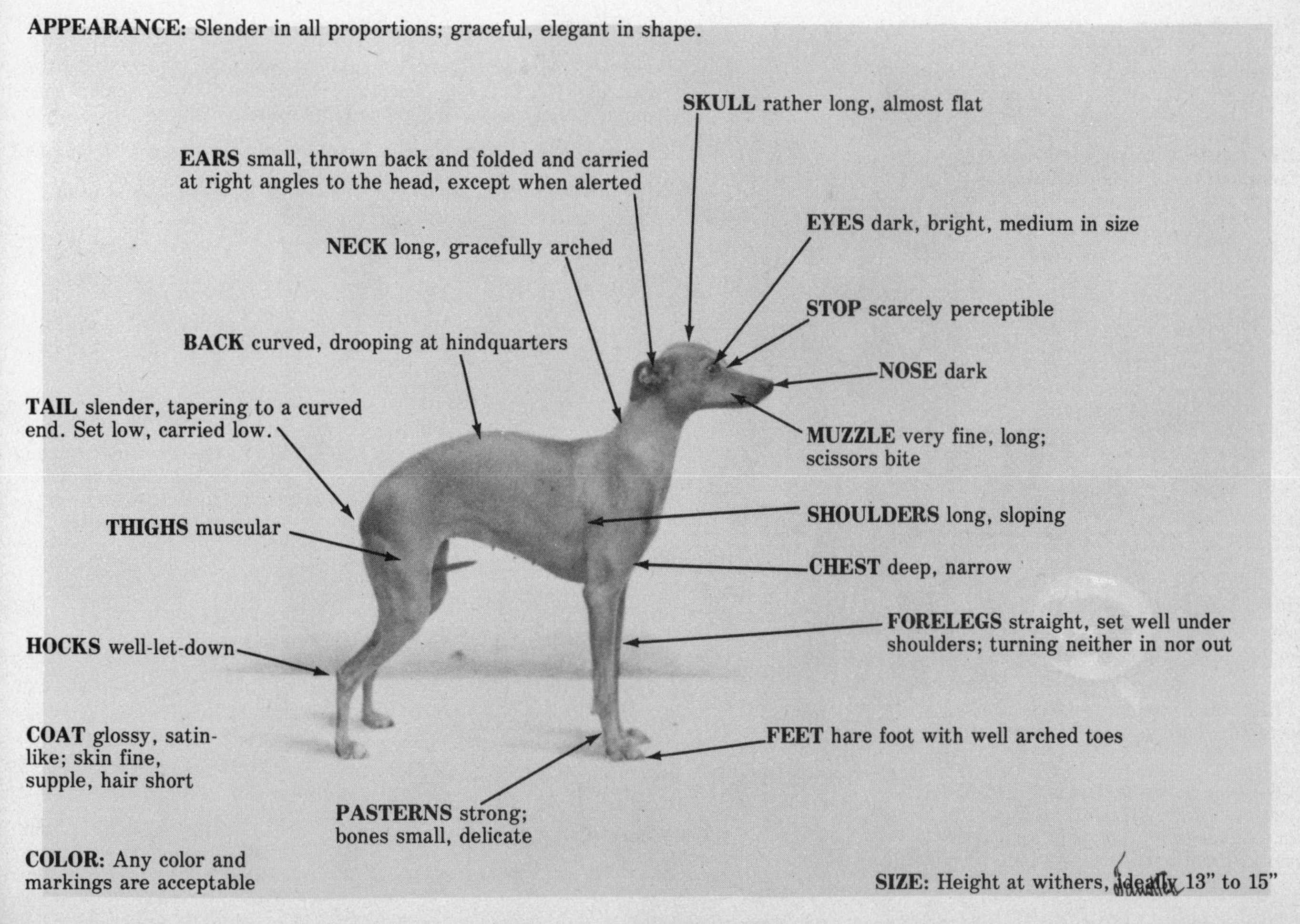

APPEARANCE: Slender in all proportions; graceful, elegant in shape.
SKULL rather long, almost flat
EARS small, thrown back and folded and carried at right angles to the head, except when alerted
EYES dark, bright, medium in size
NECK long, gracefully arched
STOP scarcely perceptible
BACK curved, drooping at hindquarters
NOSE dark
TAIL slender, tapering to a curved end. Set low, carried low.
MUZZLE very fine, long; scissors bite
THIGHS muscular
SHOULDERS long, sloping
CHEST deep, narrow
FORELEGS straight, set well under shoulders; turning neither in nor out
HOCKS well-let-down
COAT glossy, satin-like; skin fine, supple, hair short
FEET hare foot with well arched toes
PASTERNS strong; bones small, delicate
COLOR: Any color and markings are acceptable
SIZE: Height at withers, ideally 13" to 15"

MALTESE STANDARD

GENERAL APPEARANCE — The Maltese is a toy dog covered from head to foot with a mantle of long, silky, white hair. He is gentle-mannered and affectionate, eager and sprightly in action, and, despite his size, possessed of the vigor needed for the satisfactory companion.

HEAD — Of medium length and in proportion to the size of the dog. *The skull* is slightly rounded on top, the stop moderate. *The drop ears* are rather low set and heavily feathered with long hair that hangs close to the head. *Eyes* are set not too far apart; they are very dark and round, their black rims enhancing the gentle yet alert expression. *The muzzle* is of medium length, fine and tapered but not snipy. *The nose* is black. *The teeth* meet in an even, edge-to-edge bite, or in a scissors bite.

NECK — Sufficient length of neck is desirable as promoting a high carriage of the head.

BODY — Compact, the height from the withers to the ground equaling the length from the withers to the root of the tail. Shoulder blades are sloping, the elbows well knit and held close to the body. The back is level in topline, the ribs well sprung. The chest is fairly deep, the loins taut, strong, and just slightly tucked up underneath.

TAIL — A long-haired plume carried gracefully over the back, its tip lying to the side over the quarter.

LEGS AND FEET — Legs are fine-boned and nicely feathered. Forelegs are straight, their pastern joints well knit and devoid of appreciable bend. Hind legs are strong and moderately angulated at stifles and hocks. The feet are small and round, with toe pads black. Scraggly hairs on the feet may be trimmed to give a neater appearance.

COAT AND COLOR — The coat is single, that is, without undercoat. It hangs long, flat, and silky over the sides of the body almost, if not quite, to the ground. The long headhair may be tied up in a topknot or it may be left hanging. Any suggestion of kinkiness, curliness, or woolly texture is objectionable. Color, pure white. Light tan or lemon on the ear is permissible, but not desirable.

SIZE — Weight under 7 pounds, with from 4 to 6 pounds preferred. Over-all quality is to be favored over size.

GAIT — The Maltese moves with a jaunty, smooth, flowing gait. Viewed from the side, he gives an impression of rapid movement, size considered. In the stride, the forelegs reach straight and free from the shoulders, with elbows close. Hind legs to move in a straight line. Cowhocks or any suggestion of hind leg toeing in or out are faults.

TEMPERAMENT — For all his diminutive size, the Maltese seems to be without fear. His trust and affectionate responsiveness are very appealing. He is among the gentlest mannered of all little dogs, yet he is lively and playful as well as vigorous.

Approved November 12, 1963

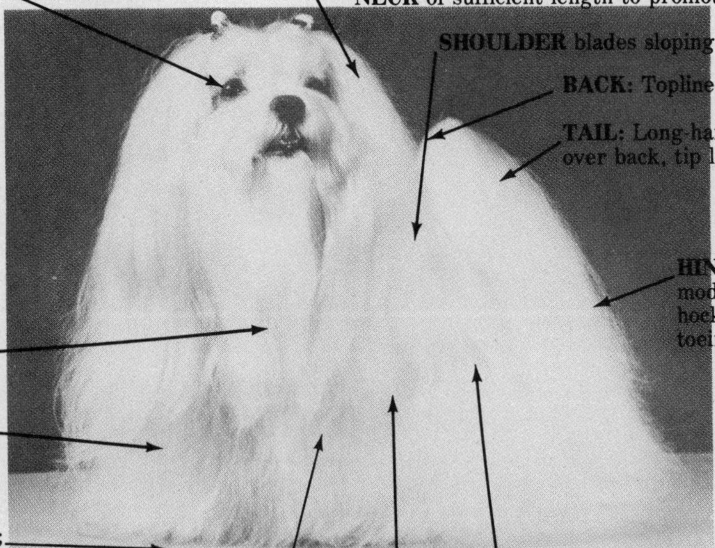

HEAD of medium length; skull top slightly rounded; stop moderate; muzzle of medium length, fine, tapered but not snipy; nose black; teeth, an even, edge-to-edge or scissors bite

BODY compact; height from withers to ground equal to length from withers to root of tail; covered with mantle of long, silky, white hair. TEMPERAMENT, gentle, affectionate, responsive, playful, fearless, vigorous. GAIT, jaunty, smooth, flowing; side view, movement seems rapid; forelegs reach straight and free from shoulders

EYES very dark, round; not too far apart; black rims enhance gentle but alert expression

EARS set rather low, drop; close to head; heavily feathered with long hair

NECK of sufficient length to promote high carriage of head

SHOULDER blades sloping

BACK: Topline level; loins taut, strong

TAIL: Long-haired plume carried gracefully over back, tip lying to side over quarter

HIND LEGS fine-boned, strong; moderately angulated at stifles, hocks; straight (cowhocks or toeing in or out are faults)

CHEST fairly deep

FORELEGS fine-boned, straight; pastern joints well-knit, devoid of appreciable bend; nicely feathered

FEET small, round; toe pads black; scraggly hairs may be trimmed

SIZE: Weight under 7 lbs; 4 to 6 lbs preferred; over-all quality favored over size

COAT single (no undercoat), flat, silky, long (almost to ground); headhair tied in topknot or left hanging; kinkiness, curliness or woolly texture objectionable

ELBOWS held close to body; well-knit

RIBS well-sprung

TUCK-UP just slight

COLOR: Pure white; light tan or lemon on ears permissible but not desirable

MANCHESTER TERRIER (TOY) STANDARD AND THE MANCHESTER TERRIER (STANDARD) STANDARD ARE THE SAME, THE ONLY VARIATION BEING IN THE EARS AND THE WEIGHT LIMIT. SEE PAGE 176 FOR THE ENTIRE STANDARD FOR BOTH VARIETIES. THE HISTORY OF THE TOY VARIETY APPEARS BELOW.

Manchester Terriers were developed in England as ratters. Indeed, many were pitted against rats for sport and excelled at their job. A great size range has been accepted both in England and the U.S. In England the smallest dogs are classified separately as English Toy Terriers (Black and Tan). In the U.S., two varieties, the standard and the toy are shown separately but registered together. The open class in each variety may be further divided by size. The Manchester Terrier must be black and tan. The two colors must not only be sharply delineated but many fine details of tan distribution must be fulfilled. Taken together, about 600 of the two varieties are registered annually in the U.S., the breed ranking 76th. The toy variety appears infrequently in show competition, ranking 15th in the Toy Group.

POMERANIAN STANDARD

APPEARANCE — The Pomeranian in build and appearance is a cobby, balanced, short-coupled dog. He exhibits great intelligence in his expression, and is alert in character and deportment.

HEAD — Well-proportioned to the body, wedge-shaped but not domed in outline, with a fox-like expression. There is a pronounced stop with a rather fine but not snipey muzzle, with no lippiness. The pigmentation around the eyes, lips, and on the nose must be black, except self-colored in brown and blue.

TEETH — The teeth meet in a scissors bite, in which part of the inner surface of the upper teeth meets and engages part of the outer surface of the lower teeth. One tooth out of line does not mean an undershot or overshot mouth.

EYES — Bright, dark in color, and medium in size, almond-shaped and not set too wide apart nor too close together.

EARS — Small, carried erect and mounted high on the head, and placed not too far apart.

NECK & SHOULDERS — The neck is rather short, its base set well back on the shoulders. The Pom is not straight-in-shoulder, but has sufficient lay-back of shoulders to carry the neck proudly and high.

BODY — The back must be short and the topline level. The body is cobby, being well ribbed and rounded. The brisket is fairly deep and not too wide.

LEGS — The forelegs are straight and parallel, of medium length in proportion to a well balanced frame. The hocks are perpendicular to the ground, parallel to each other from hock to heel, and turning neither in nor out. The Pomeranian stands well-up on toes.

TAIL — The tail is characteristic of the breed. It turns over the back and is carried flat, set high. It is profusely covered with hair.

COAT — Double-coated; a short, soft, thick undercoat, with longer, coarse, glistening outercoat consisting of guard hairs which must be harsh to the touch in order to give the proper texture for the coat to form a frill of profuse, standing-off straight hair. The front legs are well feathered and the hindquarters are clad with long hair or feathering from the top of the rump to the hocks.

COLOR — Acceptable colors to be judged on an equal basis; any solid color, any solid color with lighter or darker shadings of the same color, any solid color with sable or black shadings, parti-color, sable and black & tan. Black & tan is black with tan or rust, sharply defined, appearing above each eye and on muzzle, throat, and forechest, on all legs and feet and below the tail. Parti-color is white with any other color distributed in even patches on the body and a white blaze on head.

MOVEMENT — The Pomeranian moves with a smooth, free, but not loose action. He does not elbow out in front nor move excessively wide nor cow-hocked behind. He is sound in action.

SIZE — The weight of a Pomeranian for exhibition is 3 to 7 pounds. The ideal size for show specimens is from 4 to 5 pounds.

TRIMMING & DEWCLAWS — Trimming for neatness is permissible around the feet and up the back of the legs to the first joint; trimming of unruly hairs on the edges of the ears and around the anus is also permitted. Dewclaws, if any, on the hind legs are generally removed. Dewclaws on the forelegs may be removed.

CLASSIFICATIONS — The Open Classes at Specialty shows may be divided by color as follows: Open Red, Orange, Cream & Sable; Open Black, Brown & Blue: Open Any Other Allowed Color.

Approved March 9, 1971

APPEARANCE: Compact, short-coupled, well-balanced, well-knit; buoyant, active but docile

HEAD somewhat foxy, wedge-shaped; skull slightly flat, large in proportion to muzzle; hair smooth, short-coated; no lippiness; muzzle rather fine. Teeth, scissors grip

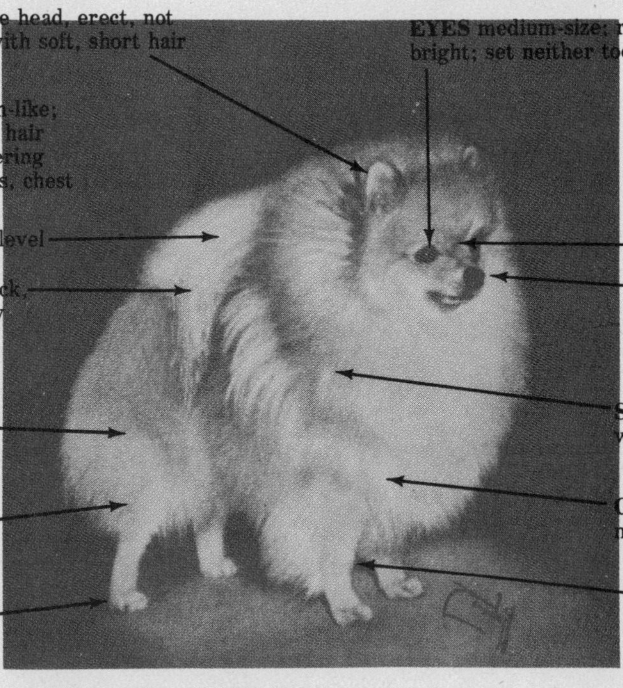

EARS small, high on the head, erect, not too far apart; covered with soft, short hair

EYES medium-size; rather oblique; dark, bright; set neither too wide nor too close

NECK rather short, well-set-in; lion-like; mane profuse; frill of long, straight hair sweeping from under jaw, also covering whole of front, top part of shoulders, chest

BACK short, level

STOP slight

TAIL turned over back, carried flat; profusely covered with long spreading hair

NOSE: Blues and browns self-colored; all others black

TEETH: Must be scissors bite

HIND LEGS well-feathered to hocks; fine in bone; free in action

SHOULDERS clean; well-laid-back

CHEST fairly deep; not too wide

HOCKS turning neither in nor out

FORELEGS perfectly straight; well-feathered; proportionately medium length

FEET small, compact; well up on toes

RIBS: Body well-ribbed-up

COAT double; undercoat soft, fluffy; outercoat long, perfectly straight, glistening; texture of guard hairs harsh to touch

SIZE: Weight, 3 to 7 lbs; ideal 4 to 5 lbs

STANDARD

SYMMETRY — Symmetry and general appearance, decidedly square and cobby. A lean, leggy Pug and a dog with short legs and a long body are equally objectionable. *Size and Condition* — The Pug should be *multum in parvo*, but this condensation (if the word may be used) should be shown by compactness of form, well-knit proportions, and hardness of developed muscle. Weight from 14 to 18 pounds (dog or bitch) desirable.

BODY — Short and cobby, wide in chest and well ribbed up. *Legs* — Very strong, straight, of moderate length and well under. *Feet* — Neither so long as the foot of the hare, nor so round as that of the cat; well-split-up toes, and the nails black.

MUZZLE — Short, blunt, square, but not up-faced. *Head* — Large, massive, round — not applehead, with no indentation of the skull. *Eyes* — Dark in color, very large, bold and prominent, globular in shape, soft and solicitous in expression, very lustrous, and, when excited, full of fire. *Ears* — Thin, small, soft, like black velvet. There are two kinds — the "rose" and "button." Preference is given to the latter.

MARKINGS — Clearly defined. The muzzle or mask, ears, moles on cheeks, thumb mark or diamond on forehead, back-trace should be as black as possible. *Mask* — The mask should be black. The more intense and well defined it is the better. *Wrinkles* — Large and deep. *Trace* — A black line extending from the occiput to the tail.

TAIL — Curled tightly as possible over the hip. The double curl is perfection.

COAT — Fine, smooth, soft, short and glossy, neither hard nor woolly.

COLOR — Silver or apricot-fawn. Each should be decided, to make the contrast complete between the color and the trace and the mask. Black.

SCALE OF POINTS

	Fawn	Black
Symmetry	10	10
Size	5	10
Condition	5	5
Body	10	10
Legs and feet	5	5
Head	5	5
Muzzle	10	10
Ears	5	5
Eyes	10	10
Mask	5	—
Wrinkles	5	5
Tail	10	10
Trace	5	—
Coat	5	5
Color	5	10
Total	100	100

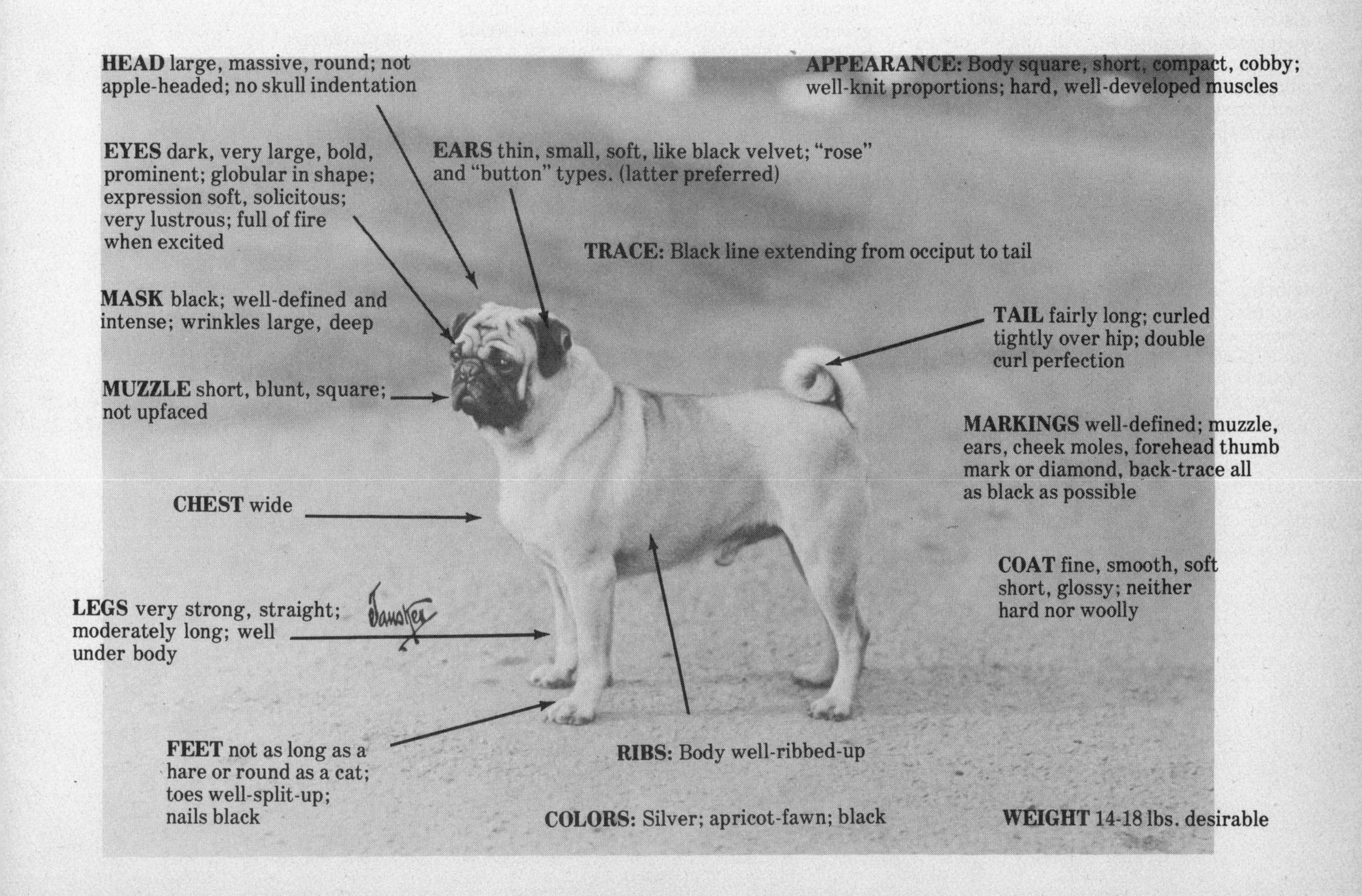

HEAD large, massive, round; not apple-headed; no skull indentation
APPEARANCE: Body square, short, compact, cobby; well-knit proportions; hard, well-developed muscles
EYES dark, very large, bold, prominent; globular in shape; expression soft, solicitous; very lustrous; full of fire when excited
EARS thin, small, soft, like black velvet; "rose" and "button" types. (latter preferred)
TRACE: Black line extending from occiput to tail
MASK black; well-defined and intense; wrinkles large, deep
TAIL fairly long; curled tightly over hip; double curl perfection
MUZZLE short, blunt, square; not upfaced
MARKINGS well-defined; muzzle, ears, cheek moles, forehead thumb mark or diamond, back-trace all as black as possible
CHEST wide
COAT fine, smooth, soft short, glossy; neither hard nor woolly
LEGS very strong, straight; moderately long; well under body
FEET not as long as a hare or round as a cat; toes well-split-up; nails black
RIBS: Body well-ribbed-up
COLORS: Silver; apricot-fawn; black
WEIGHT 14-18 lbs. desirable

[English Toy cont'd. from p. 226]

Blenheim, or White with Red Markings

Symmetry, condition, size and soundness of limb	15
Head	15
Stop	5
Muzzle	10
Eyes	10
Ears	10
Coat and feathering	15
Color and markings	15
Spot	5
Total	100

DISQUALIFICATIONS

King Charles and Ruby: A white patch on the chest, or white on any other part.

Approved July 14, 1959

[Giant Schanuzer cont'd. from p. 123]

COLOR — Solid black or pepper and salt.

BLACK—A truly pure black. A small white spot on the breast is permitted.

PEPPER AND SALT—Outer coat of a combination of banded hairs (white with black and black with white) and some black and white hairs, appearing grey from a short distance. *Ideally*—an intensely pigmented medium grey shade with "peppering" evenly distributed throughout the coat, and a grey undercoat. *Acceptable*—All shades of pepper and salt from dark iron-grey to silver-grey. Every shade of coat has a dark facial mask to emphasize the expression; the color of the mask harmonizes with the shade of the body coat. Eyebrows, whiskers, cheeks, throat, chest, legs, and under tail are lighter in color but include "peppering."

HEIGHT — The height at the withers of the male is 25½ to 27½ inches, and of the female, 23½ to 25½ inches, with the mediums being desired. Size alone should never take precedence over type, balance, soundness, and temperament. It should be noted that too small dogs generally lack the power and too large dogs, the agility and maneuverability, desired in a working dog.

FAULTS — The foregoing description is that of the ideal Giant Schnauzer. Any deviation from the above described dog must be penalized to the extent of the deviation.

The judge shall dismiss from the ring any shy or vicious Giant Schnauzer.

SHYNESS—A dog shall be judged fundamentally shy if, refusing to stand for examination, it repeatedly shrinks away from the judge; if it fears unduly any approach from the rear; if it shies to a marked degree at sudden and unusual noises.

VICIOUSNESS—A dog that attacks or attempts to attack either the judge or its handler, is definitely vicious. An aggressive or belligerent attitude towards other dogs shall not be deemed viciousness.

DISQUALIFICATIONS

Overshot or undershot.

Approved February 13, 1971

[Standard Schnauzer cont'd. from p. 149]

coat such as rust, brown, red, yellow or tan; absence of peppering; spotting or striping; a black streak down the back; or a black saddle without typical salt and pepper coloring — and gray hairs in the coat of a black; in blacks, any undercoat color other than black.

GAIT — Sound, strong, quick, free, true and level gait with powerful, well-angulated hindquarters that reach out and cover ground. The forelegs reach out in a stride balancing that of the hindquarters. At a trot, the back remains firm and level, without swaying, rolling or roaching. When viewed from the rear, the feet, though they may appear to travel close when trotting must not cross or strike. Increased speed causes feet to converge toward the center line of gravity. *Faults:* Crabbing or weaving; paddling, rolling, swaying; short, choppy, stiff, stilted rear action; front legs that throw out or in (East and West movers); hackney gait, crossing over, or striking in front or rear.

FAULTS — Any deviation from the specifications in the standard is to be considered a fault and should be penalized in proportion to the extent of the deviation. In weighing the seriousness of a fault, greatest consideration should be given to deviation from the desired alert, highly intelligent, spirited, reliable character of the Standard Schnauzer, and secondly to any deviation that detracts from the Standard Schnauzer's desired general appearance of a robust, active, square-built, wire-coated dog. Dogs that are shy or appear to be highly nervous should be seriously faulted and dismissed from the ring. Vicious dogs shall be disqualified.

DISQUALIFICATIONS

Vicious dogs. Males under 18 inches or over 20 inches in height. Females under 17 inches or over 19 inches in height.

Approved May 14, 1968

[Shetland Sheepdog cont'd. from p. 160]

Lifting of tront feet in hackneylike action, resulting in loss of speed and energy. Pacing gait.

SCALE OF POINTS

GENERAL APPEARANCE		
Symmetry	10	
Temperament	10	
Coat	5	25
HEAD		
Skull and stop	5	
Muzzle	5	
Eyes, ears and expression	10	20
BODY		
Neck and back	5	
Chest, ribs and brisket	10	
Loin, croup, and tail	5	20
FOREQUARTERS		
Shoulder	10	
Forelegs and feet	5	15
HINDQUARTERS		
Hip, thigh and stifle	10	
Hocks and feet	5	15
GAIT		
Gait—smoothness and lack of waste motion when trotting		5
Total		100

DISQUALIFICATIONS

Heights below or above the desired range, i.e., 13-16 inches. Brindle color.

Approved May 12, 1959

GROUP 6
NON-SPORTING DOGS

BICHON FRISE STANDARD

GENERAL APPEARANCE — A sturdy, lively dog of stable temperament, with a stylish gait and an air of dignity and intelligence.

COLOR — Solid white, or white with cream, apricot, or gray on the ears and/or body.

HEAD — Proportionate to the size of the dog. Skull broad and somewhat round, but not coarse; covered with a topknot of hair.

MUZZLE — Of medium length, not heavy or snipy. Slightly accentuated stop.

EARS — Dropped, covered with long flowing hair. The leather should reach approximately halfway the length of the muzzle.

EYES — Black or dark brown, with black rims. Large, round, expressive, and alert.

LIPS — Black, fine, never drooping.

NOSE — Black, round, pronounced.

BITE — Scissors.

NECK — Rather long, and gracefully and proudly carried behind an erect head.

SHOULDERS — Well laid back. Elbows held close to the body.

BODY — Slightly longer than tall. Well developed with good spring of ribs. The back inclines gradually from the withers to a slight rise over the loin. The loin is large and muscular. The brisket, well let down.

TAIL — Covered with long flowing hair, carried gaily and curved to lie on the back.

SIZE — The height at the withers should not exceed 12 inches nor be under 8 inches.

LEGS AND FEET — Strong bones; forelegs appearing straight, with well-knit pasterns. Hindquarters well angulated. Feet, resembling cat's paws, are tight and round.

COAT — Profuse, silky and loosely curled. There is an undercoat.

GROOMING — Scissored to show the eyes and give a full rounded appearance to the head and body. Feet should have hair trimmed to give a rounded appearance. When properly brushed, there is an overall "powder puff" appearance. Puppies may be shown in short coat, but the minimum show coat for an adult is two inches.

FAULTS — Cowhocks, snipy muzzle, poor pigmentation, protruding eyes, yellow eyes, undershot or overshot bite.

SERIOUS FAULTS — Corkscrew tail, black hair in the coat.

Approved April 4, 1973

GENERAL APPEARANCE: A sturdy, lively dog of stable temperament, with a stylish gait and an air of dignity and intelligence

COLOR: Solid white, white with cream, apricot, or gray on the ears and/or body

HEAD: Proportionate to dog, skull broad, somewhat round, not coarse, covered with topknot
EARS: Dropped, covered with long flowing hair. Leather reaches approximately halfway the length of muzzle
NOSE: Black, round, pronounced
TAIL: Covered with long flowing hair, carried gaily, curved to lie on back
MUZZLE: Medium length, not heavy or snipy. Slightly accentuated stop
SHOULDERS: Well-laid-back. Elbows close to the body
LEGS AND FEET: Strong boned, forelegs straight, well-knit pasterns. Hindquarters well angulated. Feet resemble cat's paws (tight and round)
SIZE: Not over 12" at withers, nor under 8"
BODY: Slightly longer than tall. Well developed. Back inclines gradually from withers to slight arch over loin. Loin large and muscular, brisket well let down

COAT: Profuse, silky and loosely curled, with an undercoat

SERIOUS FAULTS: Corkscrew tail, black hair in the coat

CH. CHAMINADE SYNCOPATION

"SNIDLEY" IS THE NUMBER ONE BICHON FRISE AND NUMBER THREE NON-SPORTING DOG IN THE NATION. HE ALREADY HAS 5 BEST IN SHOWS, 18 GROUP FIRSTS AND 21 GROUP PLACEMENTS. HE IS ALREADY THE SIRE OF 3 CHAMPIONS.

OWNER
MRS. WILLIAM TABLER
44 WOLVER HOLLOW ROAD
GLEN HEAD, LONG ISLAND, N.Y.

HANDLER
TED YOUNG, JR.
TEDWIN-FRANCE STREET
ROCKY HILL, CONN. 06067
(203) 529-8641

ASSISTED & GROOMED BY
JOHNNY PALUGA

The Bichon Frise is a small pure white dog with loosely curled coat. Though small in stature the Bichon is a hardy fun loving dog, he makes a fine companion and house pet. Since its recent acceptance by the American Kennel Club the Bichon has gained great popularity as a show dog.

BOSTER TERRIER STANDARD

GENERAL APPEARANCE — The general appearance of the Boston Terrier should be that of a lively, highly intelligent, smooth-coated, short-headed, compactly built, short-tailed, well-balanced dog of medium station, of brindle color and evenly marked with white. The head should indicate a high degree of intelligence, and should be in proportion to the size of the dog; the body rather short and well knit, the limbs strong and neatly turned; tail short; and no feature be so prominent that the dog appears badly proportioned. The dog should convey an impression of determination, strength and activity, with style of a high order; carriage easy and graceful. A proportionate combination of "color" and "ideal markings" is a particularly distinctive feature of a representative specimen, and a dog with a preponderance of white on body, or without the proper proportion of brindle and white on head, should possess sufficient merit otherwise to counteract its deficiencies in these respects. The ideal "Boston Terrier expression" as indicating "a high degree of intelligence," is also an important characteristic of the breed. "Color and markings" and "expression" should be given particular consideration in determining the relative value of "general appearance" to other points.

SKULL — Square, flat on top, free from wrinkles; cheeks flat; brow abrupt, stop well defined. *Eyes* — Wide apart, large and round, dark in color, expression alert, but kind and intelligent. The eyes should set square in the skull, and the outside corners should be on a line with the cheeks as viewed from the front. *Muzzle* — Short, square, wide and deep, and in proportion to skull; free from wrinkles; shorter in length than in width and depth, not exceeding in length approximately one-third of length of skull; width and depth carried out well to end; the muzzle from stop to end of nose on a line parallel to the top of the skull; nose black and wide, with well defined line between nostrils. The jaws broad and square, with short regular teeth. Bite even or sufficiently undershot to square muzzle. The chops of good depth but not pendulous, completely covering the teeth when mouth is closed. *Ears* — Carried erect, either cropped to conform to the shape of head, or natural bat, situated as near the corners of skull as possible.

Head Faults: — Skull "domed" or inclined; furrowed by a medial line; skull too long for breadth, or *vice versa*; stop too shallow; brow and skull too slanting. Eyes small or sunken; too prominent; light color or wall-eye; showing too much white or haw. Muzzle wedge-shaped or lacking depth; downfaced; too much cut out below the eyes; pinched or wide nostrils; butterfly nose; protruding teeth; weak lower jaw; showing turn-up, layback, or wrinkled. Ears poorly carried or in size out of proportion to head.

NECK — Of fair length, slightly arched and carrying the head gracefully; setting neatly into shoulders. *Neck Faults:* Ewe-necked; throatiness; short and thick.

BODY — Deep with good width of chest; shoulders sloping; back short; ribs deep and well sprung, carried well back to loins; loins short and muscular; rump curving slightly to set-on of tail; flank very slightly cut up. The body should appear short but not chunky. *Body Faults:* Flat sides; narrow chest; long or slack loins; roach back; sway-back; too much cut up in flank. *Elbows* — Standing neither in nor out. *Forelegs* — Set moderately wide apart and on a line with the point of the shoulders; straight in bone and well muscled; pasterns short and strong. *Hind Legs* — Set true; bent at stifles; short from hocks to feet; hocks turning neither in nor out; thighs strong and well muscled. *Feet* — Round, small and compact and turned neither in nor out; toes well arched. *Leg and Feet Faults:* Loose shoulders or elbows; hind legs too straight at stifles; hocks too prominent; long or weak pastern; splay feet.

GAIT — The gait of the Boston Terrier is that of a sure-footed, straight-gaited dog, forelegs and hind legs moving straight ahead in line with perfect rhythm, each step indicating grace with power. *Gait Faults:* There shall be no rolling, paddling or weaving when gaited and any crossing movement, either front or rear, is a serious fault.

TAIL — Set-on low; short, fine and tapering; straight; or screw; devoid of fringe or coarse hair, and not carried above horizontal. *Tail Faults:* A long or gaily carried tail; extremely gnarled or curled against body. (*Note:* The preferred tail should not exceed in length approximately half the distance from set-on to hock.)

IDEAL COLOR — Brindle with white markings. The brindle to be evenly distributed and distinct. Black with white markings permissible but brindle with white markings preferred. *Ideal Markings* — White muzzle, even white blaze over head, collar, breast, part or whole of forelegs, and hind legs below hocks. *Color and Markings Faults:* All white; absence of white marking; preponderance of white on body; without the proper proportion of brindle and white on head; or any variations detracting from the general appearance.

COAT — Short, smooth, bright and fine in texture. *Coat Faults:* Long or coarse; lacking luster.

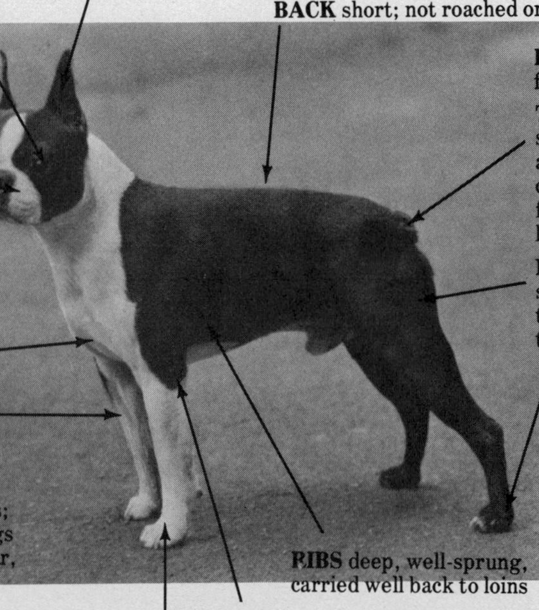

SKULL square, flat on top, no wrinkles; cheeks flat; brow abrupt
EYES wide apart, large, round, dark; set square in skull; outside corners on line with cheeks (front view)
STOP well-defined
NOSE black, wide; well-defined line between nostrils
MUZZLE short, square, wide, deep, proportion to skull, no wrinkles, shorter than width and depth; length not exceeding 1/3 of skull; width and depth same to end; topline of muzzle parallel to topline of skull
JAWS broad, square; bite even or slightly undershot to square muzzle; chops deep but not pendulous, covering teeth
CHEST deep: good width
FORELEGS straight, well-muscled; moderately wide apart and on line with point of shoulders
COLOR ideal brindle with white markkings; black with white permissible; ideal markings —white muzzle, even blaze over head, collar, breast forelegs, hind legs below hocks
DISQUALIFICATIONS: Solid black; black and tan; liver or mouse colors. Dudley nose. Docked tail or any artificial means to deceive judge
APPEARANCE: Body compact, well-balanced, medium size; short, not chunky; well-knit; carriage easy, graceful; high degree of intelligence; sure-footed, straight-gaited
EARS carried erect; either cropped to conform to head shape or natural bat shape; set as near skull corners as possible
NECK length fair; slightly arched; setting neatly into shoulders; not throaty
SHOULDERS sloping
BACK short; not roached or swayed; loins short, muscular
RUMP curving slightly to tail-set; flank slightly tucked up
TAIL set low; short, fine, tapering; straight or screw; carriage not above horizontal; no fringe or coarse hair; not docked; preferred tail not to exceed 1/2 length from set-on to hock
HIND LEGS set true; stifles bent; short from hocks to feet; hocks turning neither in nor out; thighs strong, well-muscled
FEET round, small, compact, turning neither in nor out; toes well-arched
SIZE: Lightweight, under 15 lbs; middleweight, 15-20 lbs; heavyweight, 20-25 lbs
COLOR ideal brindle with white markings; black with white permissible; ideal markings—white muzzle, even blaze over head, collar, breast, forelegs, hind legs below hocks
RIBS deep, well-sprung, carried well back to loins
ELBOWS turning neither in nor out
PASTERNS short, strong

CH. BEAU KAY'S GAY CHAPPIE

"CHAPPIE" IS A CONSISTENT BREED WINNER AND GROUP PLACING DOG. AMONG HIS WINS ARE BOB AT THE TRIANGLE BOSTON TERRIER SPECIALTY TWO YEARS IN A ROW, AND BEST IN SHOW AT THE BOSTON TERRIER CLUB OF AMERICA 1973 SPECIALTY SHOW. HE IS AT STUD ALONG WITH—

ENG. AND AM. CH. COURT BARTON EMERALD ISLE
ENG. AND AM. CH. COURT BARTON NIGHT PATROL
CH. MRS. JEFFORDS TEDDY

OWNER/HANDLED BY:
MRS. WALTER M. JEFFORDS, JR.
AND
MR. MICHAEL WOLF
ROLLING HILLS FARM
ANDREWS BRIDGE, PA 17509
(717) 529-2752

SCALE OF POINTS

General appearance	10	Hind legs	5
Skull	10	Gait	10
Eyes	5	Feet	5
Muzzle	10	Tail	5
Ears	2	Color	4
Neck	3	Ideal markings	5
Body	15	Coat	2
Elbows	4		
Forelegs	5	Total	100

WEIGHT — Not exceeding 25 pounds, divided by classes as follows: lightweight, under 15 pounds; middleweight, 15 and under 20 pounds; heavyweight, 20 and not exceeding 25 pounds.

DISQUALIFICATIONS

Solid black; black and tan; liver or mouse colors. Dudley nose. Docked tail or any artificial means used to deceive the judge.

Approved April 9, 1957

GENERAL APPEARANCE, ATTITUDE, EXPRESSION, Etc. — The perfect Bulldog must be of medium size and smooth coat; with heavy, thick-set, low-swung body, massive, short-faced head, wide shoulders and sturdy limbs. The general appearance and attitude should suggest great stability, vigor and strength. The disposition should be equable and kind, resolute and courageous (not vicious or aggressive), and demeanor should be pacific and dignified. These attributes should be countenanced by the expression and behavior.

GAIT — The style and carriage are peculiar, his gait being a loose-jointed, shuffling, sidewise motion, giving the characteristic "roll." The action must, however, be unrestrained, free and vigorous.

PROPORTION AND SYMMETRY — The "points" should be well distributed and bear good relation one to the other, no feature being in such prominence from either excess or lack of quality that the animal appears deformed or ill-proportioned. *Influence of Sex* — In comparison of specimens of different sex, due allowance should be made in favor of the bitches, which do not bear the characteristics of the breed to the same degree of perfection and grandeur as do the dogs.

SIZE — The size for mature dogs is about 50 pounds; for mature bitches, about 40 pounds.

COAT — The coat should be straight, short, flat, close, of fine texture, smooth and glossy. (No fringe, feather or curl.) *Color of Coat* — The color of coat should be uniform, pure of its kind and brilliant. The various colors found in the breed are to be preferred in the following order: (1) Red Brindle, (2) all other brindles, (3) solid white, (4) solid red, fawn or fallow, (5) piebald, (6) inferior qualities of all the foregoing. *Note:* A perfect piebald is preferable to a muddy brindle or defective solid color. Solid black is very undesirable, but not so objectionable if occurring to a moderate degree in piebald patches. The brindles to be perfect should have a fine, even and equal distribution of the composite colors. In brindles and solid colors a small white patch on the chest is not considered detrimental. In piebalds the color patches should be well defined, of pure color and symmetrically distributed.

SKIN — The skin should be soft and loose, especially at the head, neck and shoulders. *Wrinkles and Dewlap* — The head and face should be covered with heavy wrinkles, and at the throat, from jaw to chest, there should be two loose pendulous folds, forming the dewlap.

SKULL — The skull should be very large, and in circumference, in front of the ears, should measure at least the height of the dog at the shoulders. Viewed from the front, it should appear very high from the corner of the lower jaw to the apex of the skull, and also very broad and square. Viewed at the side, the head should appear very high, and very short from the point of the nose to occiput. The forehead should be flat (not rounded or domed), neither too prominent nor overhanging the face. *Cheeks* — The cheeks should be well rounded, protruding sideways and outward beyond the eyes. *Stop* — The temples or frontal bones should be very well defined, broad, square and high, causing a hollow or groove between the eyes. This indentation, or stop, should be both broad and deep and extend up the middle of the forehead, dividing the head vertically, being traceable to the top of the skull. *Eyes and Eyelids* — The eyes, seen from the front, should be situated low down in the skull, as far from the ears as possible, and their corners should be in a straight line at right angles with the stop. They should be quite in front of the head, as wide apart as possible, provided their outer corners are within the outline of the cheeks when viewed from the front. They should be quite round in form, of moderate size, neither sunken nor bulging, and in color should be very dark. The lids should cover the white of the eyeball, when the dog is looking directly forward, and the lid should show no "haw." *Ears* — The ears should be set high in the head, the front inner edge of each ear joining the outline of the skull at the top back corner of skull, so as to place them as wide apart, and as high, and as far from the eyes as possible. In size they should be small and thin. The shape termed "rose ear" is the most desirable. The rose ear folds inward at its back lower edge, the upper front edge curving over, outwards and backwards, showing part of the inside of the burr. (The ears should not be carried erect or prick-eared or buttoned and should never be cropped.)

FACE — The face, measured from the front of the cheekbone to the tip of the nose, should be extremely short, the muzzle being very short, broad, turned upwards and very deep from the corner of the mouth. *Nose* — The nose should be large, broad and black, its tip being set back deeply between the eyes. The distance from bottom of stop, between the eyes to the tip of nose should be as short as possible and not exceed the

HEAD massive, short-faced; very high; very short, nose to occiput

SKULL large, forehead flat, neither too prominent nor overhanging face; circumference measures height at shoulder

FACE short; muzzle short, broad, turned upward, very deep from corner of eye to corner of mouth; wrinkled

STOP well-defined; broad, deep; groove between eyes, up forehead; temples broad; square, high

EYES set low, far from ears; corners right angle with stop; round, moderate size, dark; no haw; wide apart

NOSE large, broad, black; tip set deeply between eyes; nostrils wide, large, black; divided by line

CHEEKS rounded, protruding sideways, outward beyond eyes

JAWS massive, broad, square, undershot; chops thick, broad, pendant, deep, overhanging lower jaws; 6 small even teeth between wide-apart canines

CHEST broad, deep, full; brisket capacious; sides full

FORELEGS short, stout; straight, muscular; set wide apart; calves well-developed with bowed outline; bones straight

FEET moderate size, compact, firmly set; toes compact, well-split-up; knuckles high; nails short, stubby; fore slightly out-turned or straight

SKIN soft, loose, especially on head, neck, shoulders; head, face covered with heavy wrinkles; at throat two loose pendulous folds form dewlap

SIZE: Weight 50 lbs males; 40 lbs females

DISQUALIFICATION: Dudley or flesh-colored nose

APPEARANCE: Body medium size, thick-set, low-swung; strong, massive, sturdy; of great stability; disposition kind, courageous, pacific, dignified; gait, characteristic free roll

EARS wide apart, set high; small, thin; neither erect nor cropped; "rose ear" desirable

NECK short, thick; deep, strong; arched at back

SHOULDERS muscular, heavy, widespread, slanting outward

BACK short, strong; broad at shoulders, narrow at loins; (slight dip, roach-backed or wheel-backed); loins higher than whithers

TAIL straight or screwed; short, hung low, tapering; carriage downwards; root thick; tip fine; never curved or curly

HIND LEGS strong, muscular, longer than forelegs; hocks slightly bent, well-let-down, lower leg short, straight, strong; stifles turned slightly outward; hocks in feet well outward

BELLY tucked-up; not rotund

RIBS well-rounded; deep from shoulder; well-let-down

ELBOWS low; stand well out, loose from body

COAT straight, short; flat, close; texture fine; smooth, glossy; no fringe or feather

COLOR: uniform; pure of its kind; brilliant; preference in order — 1. red brindle; 2. all other brindles; 3. solid white; 4. solid red, fawn or fallow; 5. piebald. Perfect piebald preferable to muddy brindle or defective solid

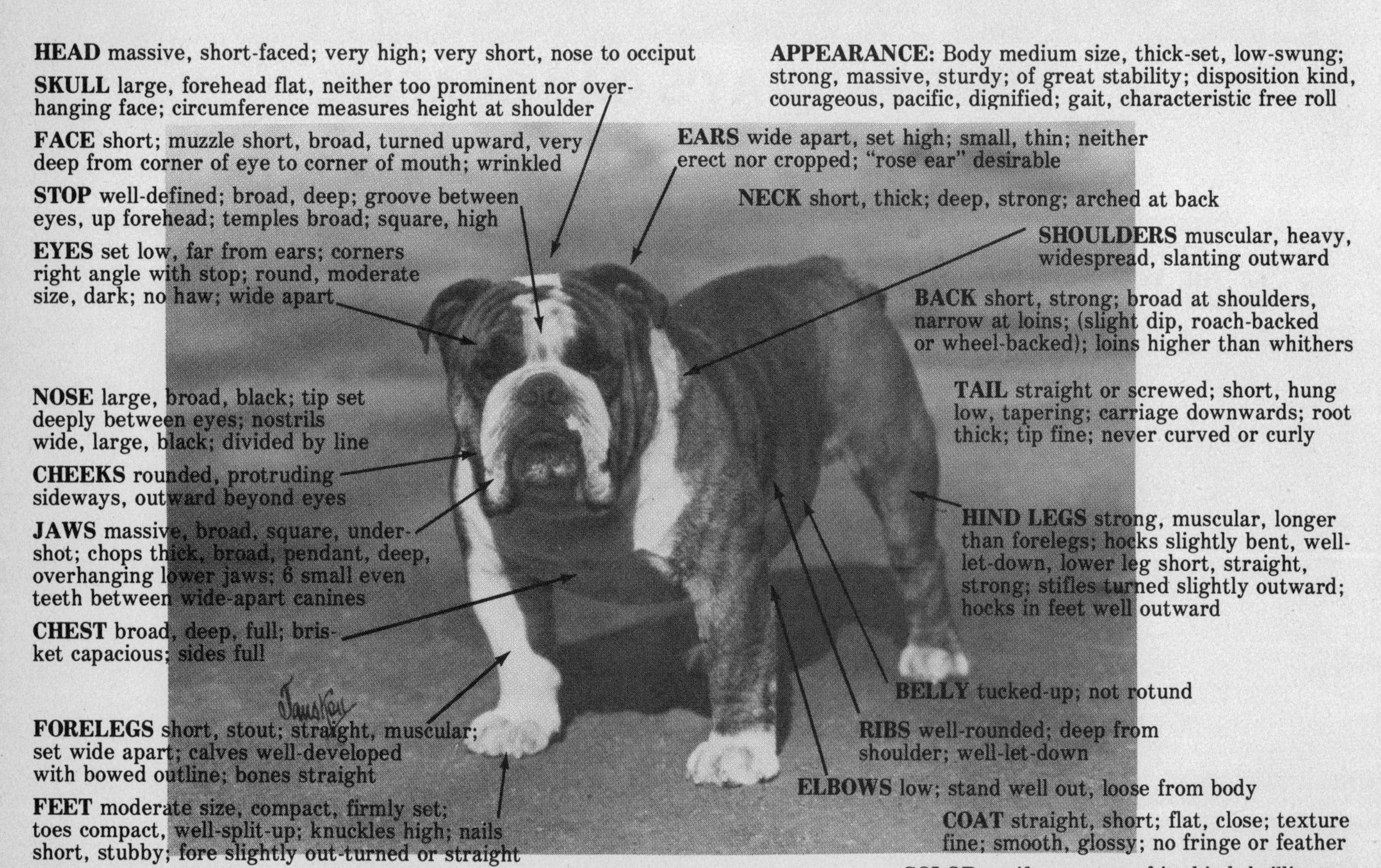

CH. HETHERBULL ARROGANT DYNAMO

DYNA, A GRANDDAUGHTER OF THE TOP WINNER AND PRODUCER, CH. HETHERBULL'S ARROGANCE, HAD A TOP CAREER IN THE CLASSES HIGHLIGHTED BY HER BOW AT THE B.C.A.I. SPECIALTY. IN THE WHELPING BOX, WHERE ANY GOOD BITCH MUST EARN THE RIGHT TO BE CALLED GREAT, DYNA HAS DONE EVEN BETTER. JUST THREE YEARS OLD, SHE HAS QUALIFIED FOR THE B.C.A. HALL OF FAME, BASED ON THE NUMBER OF CHAMPION GET PRODUCED, JOINING ARROGANCE, A TOP SIRE, WHOSE OFFSPRING ARE MAKING HIM A FOUNDATION OF THE BREED. DYNA PRESENTLY HAS 5 CHAMPION GET OUT OF A TOTAL OF NINE PUPPIES WHELPED, OTHERS POINTED AND THE PROSPECT OF FUTURE LITTERS. SHE HAS WON THE BROOD BITCH CLASS AT THE LAST TWO NATIONAL SPECIALTIES IN DENVER AND ATLANTA.

JEAN AND ROBERT A. HETHERINGTON
1 PULIS AVENUE
MAHWAH, NEW JERSEY 07430
(201) 891-5723

length from the tip of nose to the edge of under lip. The nostrils should be wide, large and black, with a well-defined line between them. Any nose other than black is objectionable and "Dudley" or flesh-colored nose absolutely disqualified from competition. *Chops* — The chops or "flews" should be thick, broad, pendant and very deep, completely overhanging the lower jaw at each side. They join the under lip in front and almost or quite cover the teeth, which should be scarcely noticeable when the mouth is closed. *Jaws* — The jaws should be massive, very broad, square and "undershot," the lower jaw projecting considerably in front of the upper jaw and turning up. *Teeth* — The teeth should be large and strong, with the canine teeth or tusks wide apart, and the 6 small teeth in front, between the canines, in an even, level row.

NECK — The neck should be short, very thick, deep and strong and well arched at the back. *Shoulders* — The shoulders should be muscular, very heavy, wide-spread and slanting outward, giving stability and great power.

CHEST — The chest should be very broad, deep and full.

BRISKET AND BODY — The brisket and body should be very capacious, with full sides, well-rounded ribs and very deep from the shoulders down to its lowest part, where it joins the chest. It should well let down between the shoulders and forelegs, giving the dog a broad, low, short-legged appearance. The body should be well ribbed up behind with the belly tucked up and not rotund. *Back* — The back should be short and strong, very broad at the shoulders and comparatively narrow at the loins. There should be a slight fall in the back, close behind the shoulders (its lowest part), whence the spine should rise to the loins (the top of which should be higher than the top of the shoulders), thence curving again more suddenly to the tail, forming an arch (a very distinctive feature of the breed), termed "roach back" or, more correctly, "wheel-back."

FORELEGS — The forelegs should be short, very stout, straight and muscular, set wide apart, with well developed calves, presenting a bowed outline, but the bones of the legs should not be curved or bandy, nor the feet brought too close together. *Elbows* — The elbows should be low and stand well out and loose from the body.

HIND LEGS — The hind legs should be strong and muscular and longer than the forelegs, so as to elevate the loins above the shoulders. Hocks should be slightly bent and well let down, so as to give length and strength from loins to hock. The lower leg should be short, straight and strong, with the stifles turned slightly outward and away from the body. The hocks are thereby made to approach each other, and the hind feet to turn outward. *Feet* — The feet should be moderate in size, compact and firmly set. Toes compact, well split up, with high knuckles and with short stubby nails. The

[continued on page 256]

CHOW CHOW STANDARD

GENERAL APPEARANCE — A massive, cobby, powerful dog, active and alert, with strong, musclar development, and perfect balance. Body squares with height of leg at shoulder; head, broad and flat, with short, broad, and deep muzzle, accentuated by a ruff; the whole supported by straight, strong legs. Clothed in a shining, offstanding coat, the Chow is a masterpiece of beauty, dignity, and untouched naturalness.

HEAD — Large and massive in proportion to size of dog, with broad, flat skull; well filled under the eyes; moderate stop; and proudly carried. *Expression* — Essentially dignified, lordly, scowling, discerning, sober, and snobbish — one of independence. *Muzzle* — Short in comparison to length of skull; broad from eyes to end of nose, and of equal depth. The lips somewhat full and overhanging. *Teeth* — Strong and level, with a scissors bite; should neither be overshot, nor undershot. *Nose* — Large, broad, and black in color. *Disqualification:* nose spotted or distinctly other color than black, except in blue Chows, which may have solid blue or slate noses. *Tongue* — A blue-black. The tissues of the mouth should approximate black. *Disqualification:* tongue red, pink, or obviously spotted with red or pink. *Eyes* — Dark, deep-set, of moderate size, and almond-shaped. *Ears* — Small, slightly rounded at tip, stiffly carried. They should be placed wide apart, on top of the skull, and set with a slight, forward tilt. *Disqualification:* drop ear or ears. A drop ear is one which is not stiffly carried or stiffly erect, but which breaks over at any point from its base to its tip.

BODY — Short, compact, with well-sprung ribs, and let down in the flank.

NECK — Strong, full, set well on the shoulders. *Shoulders* — Muscular, slightly sloping. *Chest* — Broad, deep, and muscular. A narrow chest is a serious fault.

BACK — Short, straight, and strong. *Loins* — Broad, deep, and powerful. *Tail* — Set well up and carried closely to the back, following line of spine at start.

FORELEGS — Perfectly straight, with heavy bone and upright pasterns. *Hind Legs* — Straight-hocked, muscular, and heavy boned. *Feet* — Compact, round, cat-like, with thick pads.

GAIT — Completely individual. Short and stilted because of straight hocks.

COAT — Abundant, dense, straight, and offstanding; rather coarse in texture with a soft, woolly undercoat. It may be any clear color, solid throughout, with lighter shadings on ruff, tail, and breechings.

DISQUALIFICATIONS

Nose spotted or distinctly other color than black, except in blue Chows, which may have solid blue or slate noses. Tongue red, pink or obviously spotted with red or pink. Drop ear or ears.

Approved March 11, 1941

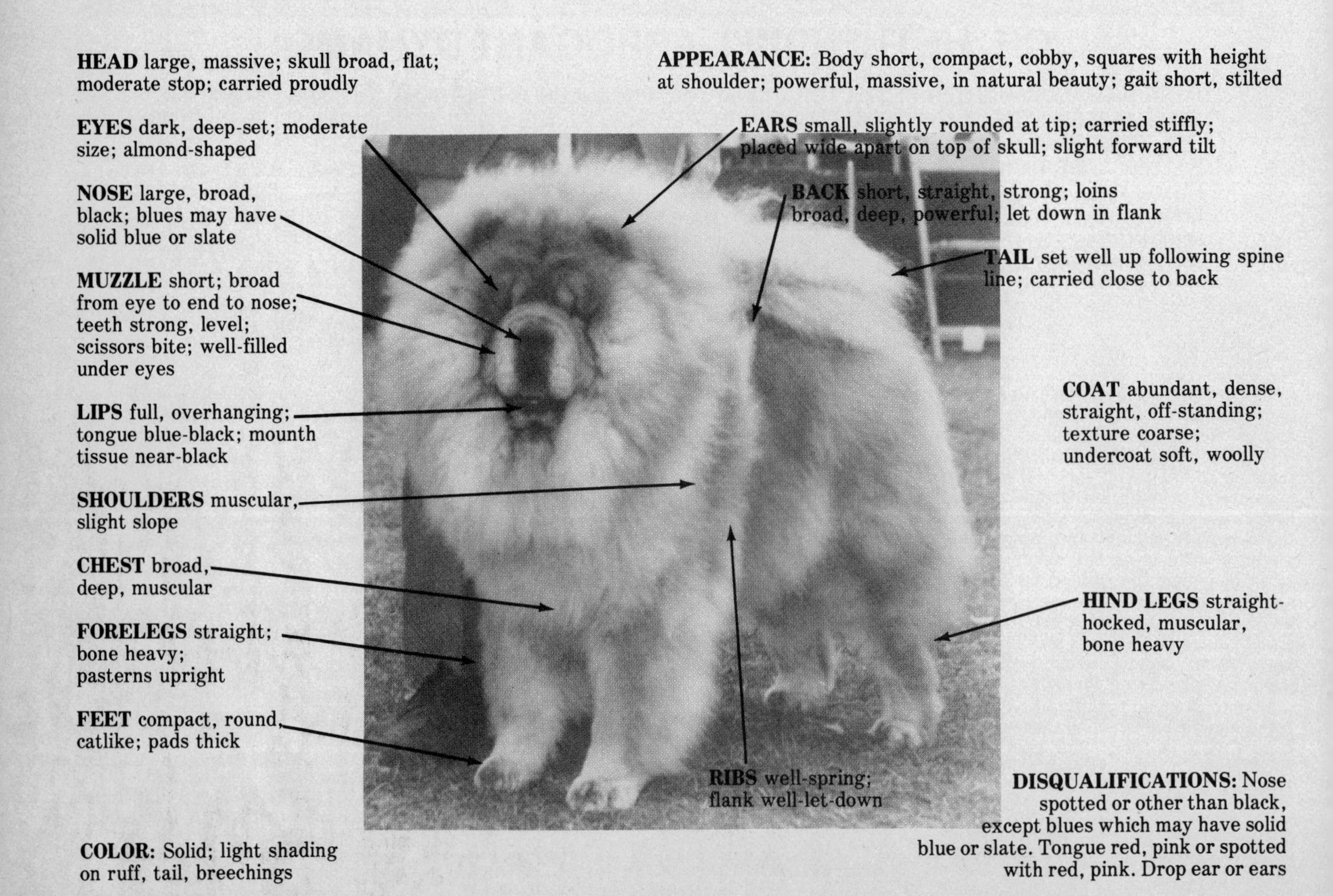
HEAD large, massive; skull broad, flat; moderate stop; carried proudly
APPEARANCE: Body short, compact, cobby, squares with height at shoulder; powerful, massive, in natural beauty; gait short, stilted
EYES dark, deep-set; moderate size; almond-shaped
EARS small, slightly rounded at tip; carried stiffly; placed wide apart on top of skull; slight forward tilt
NOSE large, broad, black; blues may have solid blue or slate
BACK short, straight, strong; loins broad, deep, powerful; let down in flank
TAIL set well up following spine line; carried close to back
MUZZLE short; broad from eye to end to nose; teeth strong, level; scissors bite; well-filled under eyes
COAT abundant, dense, straight, off-standing; texture coarse; undercoat soft, woolly
LIPS full, overhanging; tongue blue-black; mounth tissue near-black
SHOULDERS muscular, slight slope
CHEST broad, deep, muscular
HIND LEGS straight-hocked, muscular, bone heavy
FORELEGS straight; bone heavy; pasterns upright
FEET compact, round, catlike; pads thick
RIBS well-spring; flank well-let-down
DISQUALIFICATIONS: Nose spotted or other than black, except blues which may have solid blue or slate. Tongue red, pink or spotted with red, pink. Drop ear or ears
COLOR: Solid; light shading on ruff, tail, breechings

CH. LIONTAMER MARDI GRAS

SIRE: CH. EASTWOOD LIONTAMER OF ELSTER. DAM: GOTSCHALL'S VELVET NITE. BORN JAN. 8, 1968. REG. #99847. RECORD: BOB 145, GROUP PLACING 101 GROUP 1's 13, BIS 1. CHOW TOP TEN 6 YEARS. 1969 #5, 1970 #3, 1971 #3, 1972 #3, 1973 #7, (FIRST HALF) 1974 #9. MARDI, LIKE HIS SIRE, PROVED TO ALL DOGDOM, SPECTATORS, HANDLERS, JUDGES, AND CHILDREN THAT CHOWS ARE NOT "MEAN." HE IS A "LOVER BOY" TO ALL. MARDI HAS ALWAYS MET TOP COMPETITION IN THE GROUPS; HE HAS BEEN SHOWN IN 14 STATES.

MISS MARY ALICE ELLIOTT
45 CHERRY STREET
DENVER, COLORADO 80220

There is belief that the Chow developed through the breedings of the Samoyed and the Mastiff of Tibet. Hard to explain, however, is the fact that the Chow possesses a black tongue, since both of his putative ancestors do not have this, nor does any other breed. Today the Chow is a pet and show animal enjoyed by many. His entry into the American dog show scene was in 1890. At the Westminster Dog Show in New York, the dog named Takya placed third. Since that time his popularity has grown and his dog show success has prospered.

DALMATIAN STANDARD

THE DALMATIAN should represent a strong, muscular, and active dog; poised and alert; free of shyness; intelligent in expression; symmetrical in outline; and free from coarseness and lumber. He should be capable of great endurance, combined with a fair amount of speed.

HEAD—Should be of a fair length, the skull flat, proportionately broad between the ears, and moderately well defined at the temples, and not in one straight line from the nose to the occiput bone as required in a Bull Terrier. It should be entirely free from wrinkle. *Muzzle*—Should be long and powerful—the lips clean. The mouth should have a scissors bite. Never undershot or overshot. It is permissible to trim whiskers. *Eyes*—Should be set moderately well apart, and of medium size, round, bright, and sparkling, with an intelligent expression; their color greatly depending on the markings of the dog. In the black-spotted variety the eyes should be dark (black or brown or blue). In the liver-spotted variety they should be lighter than in the black-spotted variety (golden or light brown or blue). The rim around the eyes in the black-spotted variety should be black; in the liver-spotted variety, brown. Never flesh-colored in either. Lack of pigment a major fault. *Ears*—Should be set rather high, of moderate size, rather wide at the base, and gradually tapering to a rounded point. They should be carried close to the head, be thin and fine in texture, and preferably spotted. *Nose*—In the black-spotted variety should always be black; in the liver-spotted variety, always brown. A butterfly or flesh-colored nose is a major fault.

NECK AND SHOULDERS — The neck should be fairly long, nicely arched, light and tapering, and entirely free from throatiness. The shoulders should be oblique, clean, and muscular, denoting speed.

BODY, BACK, CHEST, AND LOINS — The chest should not be too wide, but very deep and capacious, ribs well sprung but never rounded like barrel hoops (which would indicate want of speed). Back powerful; loin strong, muscular and slightly arched. *Legs and Feet*—Of great importance. The forelegs should be straight, strong, and heavy in bone; elbows close to the body; feet compact, well-arched toes, and tough, elastic pads. In the hind legs the muscles should be clean, though well defined; the hocks well let down. Dewclaws may be removed from legs. *Nails*—In the black-spotted variety, black or white; or a nail may be both black and white. In the liver-spotted variety, brown or white; or a nail may be both brown and white.

GAIT—Length of stride should be in proportion to the size of the dog, steady in rhythm of 1, 2, 3, 4 as in the cadence count in military drill. Front legs should not paddle, nor should there be a straddling appearance. Hind legs should neither cross nor weave; judges should be able to see each leg move with no interference of another leg. Drive and reach are most desirable. Cowhocks are a major fault.

TAIL—Should ideally reach the hock joint, strong at the insertion, and tapering toward the end, free from coarseness. It should not be inserted too low down, but carried with a slight curve upwards, and never curled.

COAT — Should be short, hard, dense, and fine, sleek and glossy in appearance, but neither woolly nor silky. *Color and Markings* — Are most important points. The ground color in both varieties should be pure white, very decided, and not intermixed. The color of the spots in the black-spotted variety should be dense black; in the liver-spotted variety they should be liver brown. The spots should not intermingle, but be as round and well defined as possible, the more distinct the better. In size they should be from that of a dime to a half-dollar. The spots on the face, head, ears, legs, and tail to be smaller than those on the body. Patches, tri-colors, and any color markings other than black or liver constitute a disqualification. A true patch is a solid, sharply defined mass of black or liver that is appreciably larger than any of the markings on the dog. Several spots that are so adjacent that they actually touch one another at their edges do not constitute a patch.

SIZE — The desirable height of dogs and bitches is between 19 and 23 inches at the withers, and any dog or bitch over 24 inches at the withers is to be disqualified.

MAJOR FAULTS — Butterfly or flesh-colored nose. Cowhocks. Flat feet. Lack of pigment in eye rims. Shyness. Trichiasis (abnormal position or direction of the eyelashes).

FAULTS — Ring or low-set tail. Undersize or oversize.

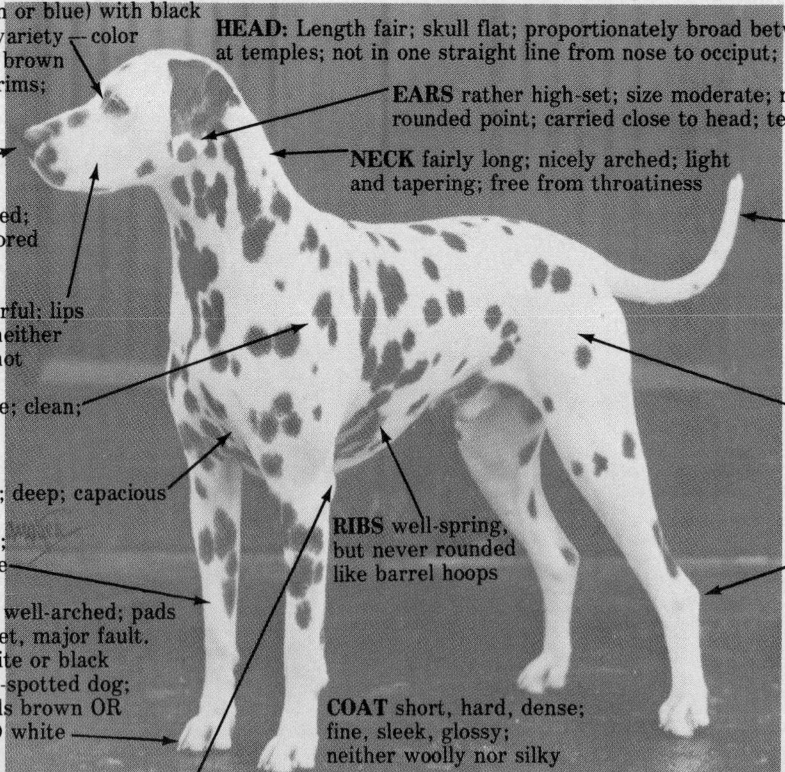

EYES: Moderately well apart; size medium; round bright; expression intelligent. Color depends greatly on markings—in black-spotted variety, eyes should be dark (black, brown or blue) with black rims. Liver-spotted variety—color lighter (golden, light brown or blue) with brown rims; lack of pigment, major fault

NOSE black for black-spotted dogs; brown for liver-spotted; butterfly or flesh-colored nose, major fault

MUZZLE long, powerful; lips clean; scissors bite; neither undershot nor overshot

SHOULDERS oblique; clean; muscular

CHEST not too wide; deep; capacious

FORELEGS straight; strong; heavy in bone

FEET compact; toes well-arched; pads tough, elastic; flat feet, major fault. NAILS black OR white or black AND white for black-spotted dog; for liver-spotted, nails brown OR white or brown AND white

DISQUALIFICATIONS: Any color other than black or liver; any size over 24" at withers; patches; tri-colors; undershot or overshot bite

APPEARANCE: Strong, muscular, active, poised, alert; not shy; symmetrical in outline; free from coarseness and lumbar; built for great endurance and fair speed; legs and feet of great importance

HEAD: Length fair; skull flat; proportionately broad between ears; moderately well-defined at temples; not in one straight line from nose to occiput; entirely free from wrinkle

EARS rather high-set; size moderate; rather wide at base, tapering to rounded point; carried close to head; texture fine, thin; preferably spotted

NECK fairly long; nicely arched; light and tapering; free from throatiness

RIBS well-spring, but never rounded like barrel hoops

COAT short, hard, dense; fine, sleek, glossy; neither woolly nor silky

ELBOWS close to body

BACK powerful; loin strong, muscular, slightly arched

TAIL should reach hock joint; strong at insertion, tapering toward end; free from coarseness; tail-set not too low; carried with slight upward curve; never curled

HINDQUARTERS: Muscles clean, though well-defined; dewclaws may be removed; cowhocks a major fault

HOCKS well-let-down, turning neigher in nor out

SIZE: Height at withers—dogs and bitches, between 19" to 23" desirable

GAIT: Stride length in proportion to size of dog; steady cadence; drive and reach desirable

COLOR, MARKINGS important; ground color, pure white for both varieties; black spots, dense black; liver spots, liver brown; spots must not intermingle—must be round, well-defined, distinct as possible; size of spots—from dime to half-dollar; spots on face, head, ears, legs, tail—smaller than spots on body

CH. COACHKEEPERS BLIZZARD OF QA

TOP WINNING DALMATIAN PICTURED ABOVE WINNING THE NON-SPORTING GROUP. HE IS A MULTIPLE GROUP AND BEST IN SHOW WINNER.

OWNER
MRS. ALAN R. ROBSON
R.D. BOX 210
GLEN MOORE, PA. 19343

HANDLER
BOBBY B. BARLOW
P.O. BOX 117
BEALLSVILLE, MARYLAND 12074

SCALE OF POINTS

Body, back, chest and loins	10
Coat	5
Color and markings	25
Ears	5
Gait	10
Head and eyes	10
Legs and feet	10
Neck and shoulders	10
Size, symmetry, etc.	10
Tail	5
Total	100

DISQUALIFICATIONS

Any color markings other than black or liver. Any size over 24 inches at the withers. Patches. Tri-colors. Undershot or overshot bite.

Approved December 11, 1962

GENERAL APPEARANCE — The French Bulldog should have the appearance of an active, intelligent, muscular dog, of heavy bone, smooth coat, compactly built, and of medium or small structure. *Proportion and Symmetry* — The points should be well distributed and bear good relation one to the other, no feature being in such prominence from either excess or lack of quality that the animal appears deformed or poorly proportioned. *Influence of Sex* — In comparison of specimens of different sex, due allowance should be made in favor of the bitches, which do not bear the characteristics of the breed to the same marked degree as do the dogs.

WEIGHT — A lightweight class under 22 pounds; heavyweight class, 22 pounds, and not over 28 pounds.

HEAD — The head should be large and square. The top of the skull should be flat between the ears; the forehead should not be flat but slightly rounded. The stop should be well defined, causing a hollow or groove between the eyes. The muzzle should be broad, deep and well laid back; the muscles of the cheeks well developed. The nose should be extremely short; nostrils broad with well defined line between them. The nose and flews should be black, except in the case of the lighter-colored dogs, where a lighter color nose is acceptable. The flews should be thick and broad,hanging over the lower jaw at the sides, meeting the underlip in front and covering the teeth which should not be seen when the mouth is closed. The underjaw should be deep, square, broad, undershot and well turned up. *Eyes* — The eyes should be wide apart, set low down in the skull, as far from the ears as possible, round in form, of moderate size, neither sunken nor bulging, and in color dark. No haw and no white of the eye showing when looking forward.

NECK — The neck should be thick and well arched, with loose skin at throat.

EARS — The ears shall hereafter be known as the bat ear, broad at the base, elongated, with round top, set high on the head, but not too close together, and carried erect with the orifice to the front. The leather of the ear, fine and soft.

BODY — The body should be short and well rounded. The chest, broad, deep and full, well ribbed with the belly tucked up. The back should be a roach back, with a slight fall close behind the shoulders. It should be strong and short, broad at the shoulders and narrowing at the loins. *Legs* — The forelegs should be short, stout, straight and muscular, set wide apart. The hind leg should be strong and muscular, longer than the forelegs, so as to elevate the loins above the shoulders. Hocks well let down. *Feet* — The feet should be moderate in size, compact and firmly set. Toes compact, well split up, with high knuckles and short, stubby nails; hind feet slightly longer than forefeet. *Tail* — The tail should be either straight or screwed (but not curly), short, hung low, thick root and fine tip; carried low in repose.

COLOR, SKIN AND COAT — Acceptable colors are: All brindle, fawn, white, brindle and white, and any color except those which constitute disqualification. The skin should be soft and loose, especially at head and shoulders, forming wrinkles. Coat moderately fine, brilliant, short and smooth.

SCALE OF POINTS

General Properties					
Proportion and symmetry	5				
Expression	5		**Body, Legs, etc.**		
Gait	4		**Shoulders**	5	
Color	4		**Back**	5	
Coat	2	20	**Neck**	4	
Head			**Chest**	3	
Skull	6		**Ribs**	4	
Cheeks and chops	2		**Brisket**	3	
Stop	5		**Belly**	2	
Ears	8		**Forelegs**	4	
Eyes	4		**Hind legs**	3	
Wrinkles	4		**Feet**	3	
Nose	3		**Tail**	4	40
Jaws	6				—
Teeth	2	40	**TOTAL**		100

DISQUALIFICATIONS

Other than bat ears; black and white, black and tan, liver, mouse or solid black [black means black without any trace of brindle]; eyes of different color; nose other than black except in the case of the lighter-colored dogs, where a lighter color nose is acceptable; hare lip; any mutilation; over 28 pounds in weight.

Approved February 11, 1947

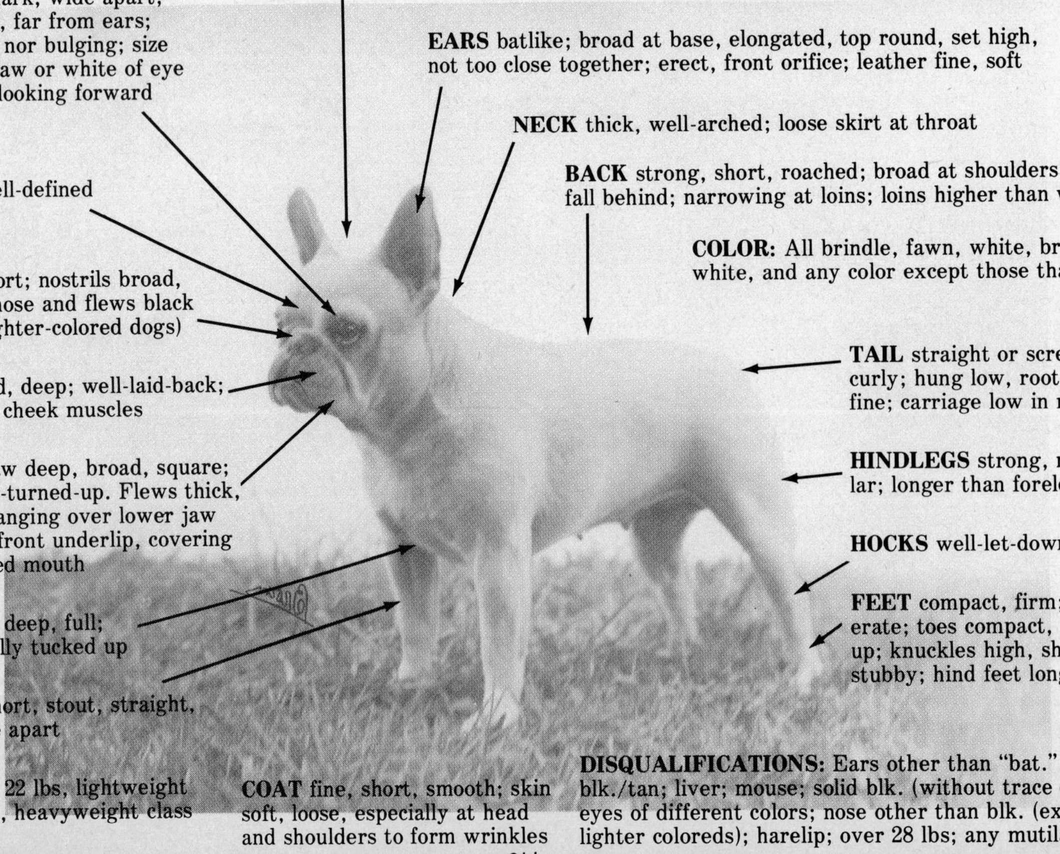

HEAD large, square

SKULL top flat between ears; forehead slightly rounded

APPEARANCE: Body short, compact, well-rounded; muscular; heavy bone; structure medium; well-balanced (no exaggeration); due allowance to females with traits lesser marked than males

EYES round, dark, wide apart; set low in skull, far from ears; neither sunken nor bulging; size moderate; no haw or white of eye showing when looking forward

EARS batlike; broad at base, elongated, top round, set high, not too close together; erect, front orifice; leather fine, soft

NECK thick, well-arched; loose skirt at throat

STOP well-defined

BACK strong, short, roached; broad at shoulders, slight fall behind; narrowing at loins; loins higher than withers

COLOR: All brindle, fawn, white, brindle and white, and any color except those that disqualify

NOSE very short; nostrils broad, line between; nose and flews black (variation in lighter-colored dogs)

MUZZLE broad, deep; well-laid-back; well-developed cheek muscles

TAIL straight or screwed; not curly; hung low, root thick, tip fine; carriage low in repose

JAWS, underjaw deep, broad, square; undershot; well-turned-up. Flews thick, black; broad; hanging over lower jaw sides; meeting front underlip, covering teeth with closed mouth

HINDLEGS strong, muscular; longer than forelegs

HOCKS well-let-down

CHEST broad, deep, full; well-ribbed; belly tucked up

FEET compact, firm; size moderate; toes compact, well-split-up; knuckles high, short; nails stubby; hind feet longer

FORELEGS short, stout, straight, muscular, wide apart

SIZE: Weight, 22 lbs, lightweight class; 22-28 lbs, heavyweight class

COAT fine, short, smooth; skin soft, loose, especially at head and shoulders to form wrinkles

DISQUALIFICATIONS: Ears other than "bat." Black/white; blk./tan; liver; mouse; solid blk. (without trace of brindle); eyes of different colors; nose other than blk. (except in lighter coloreds); harelip; over 28 lbs; any mutilation

CH. LAVENDERS FLEUR

BEST OF OPPOSITE SEX, WESTMINSTER KENNEL CLUB 1974. BEST OF BREED, EASTERN AND WORCESTER KENNEL CLUBS AND MULTIPLE BEST OF BREED WINNER.

HANDLER: DOROTHY HARDY

OWNERS
MR. & MRS. JOHN BUTLER PRIZER & ELIZABETH C. PEARSON
RAUHALA
8763 STENTON AVE.
CHESTNUT HILL
PHILADELPHIA, PA. 19118

The French Bulldog possesses very distinct features, one being the bat ear and the other the shape of the skull. The skull is level between the ears and slightly curved, forming a dome over the eyes. What a true representative of the breed should possess is a compact build, soundness and good balance, weight between 19 and 22 pounds, a smooth coat, and medium or small structure.

GENERAL APPEARANCE AND CONFORMATION — The Keeshond is a handsome dog, of well-balanced, short-coupled body, attracting attention not only by his alert carriage and intelligent expression, but also by his luxurious coat, his richly plumed tail, well curled over his back, and by his foxlike face and head with small pointed ears. His coat is very thick round the neck, fore part of the shoulders and chest, forming a lionlike mane. His rump and hind legs, down to the hocks, are also thickly coated forming the characteristic "trousers." His head, ears and lower legs are covered with thick short hair. The ideal height of fully matured dogs (over 2 years old), measured from top of withers to the ground, is: for males, 18 inches; bitches, 17 inches. However, size consideration should not outweigh that of type. When dogs are judged equal in type, the dog nearest the ideal height is to be preferred. Length of back from withers to rump should equal height as measured above.

HEAD — *Expression* — Expression is largely dependent on the distinctive characteristic called "spectacles" — a delicately penciled line slanting slightly upward from the outer corner of each eye to the lower corner of the ear, coupled with distinct markings and shadings forming short but expressive eyebrows. Markings (or shadings) on face and head must present a pleasing appearance, imparting to the dog an alert and intelligent expression. *Fault:* Absence of "spectacles." *Skull* — The head should be well proportioned to the body, wedge-shaped when viewed from above. Not only in muzzle, but the whole head should give this impression when the ears are drawn back by covering the nape of the neck and the ears with one hand. Head in profile should exhibit a definite stop. *Fault:* Apple head, or absence of stop. *Muzzle* — The muzzle should be dark in color and of medium length, neither coarse nor snipy, and well proportioned to the skull. *Mouth* — The mouth should be neither overshot nor undershot. Lips should be black and closely meeting, not thick, coarse or sagging; and with no wrinkle at the corner of the mouth. *Fault:* Overshot or undershot. *Teeth* — The teeth should be white, sound and strong (but discoloration from distemper not to penalize severely); upper teeth should just overlap the lower teeth. *Eyes* — Eyes should be dark brown in color, of medium size, rather oblique in shape and not set too wide apart. **Fault:** Protruding round eyes or eyes light of color.

EARS — Ears should be small, triangular in shape, mounted high on head and carried erect; dark in color and covered with thick, velvety, short hair. Size should be proportionate to the head — length approximating the distance from outer corner of the eye to the nearest edge of the ear. *Fault:* Ears not carried erect when at attention.

BODY — *Neck and Shoulders* — The neck should be moderately long, well shaped and well set on shoulders; covered with a profuse mane, sweeping from under the jaw and covering the whole of the front part of the shoulders and chest, as well as the top part of the shoulders. *Chest, Back and Loin* — The body should be compact with a short straight back sloping slightly downward toward the hindquarters; well ribbed, barrel well rounded, belly moderately tucked up, deep and strong of chest. *Legs* — Forelegs should be straight seen from any angle, and well feathered. Hind legs should be profusely feathered down to the hocks — not below, with hocks only slightly bent. Legs must be of good bone and cream in color. *Fault:* Black markings below the knee, penciling excepted. *Feet* — The feet should be compact, well rounded, catlike, and cream in color. Toes are nicely arched, with black nails. *Fault:* White foot or feet.

TAIL — The tail should be set on high, moderately long, and well feathered, tightly curled over back. It should lie flat and close to the body with a very light gray plume on top where curled, but the tip of the tail should be black. The tail should form a part of the "silhouette" of the dog's body, rather than give the appearance of an appendage. *Fault:* Tail not lying close to the back. *Action* — Dogs should show boldly and keep tails curled over the back. They should move cleanly and briskly; and the movement should be straight and sharp (not lope like a German Shepherd). *Fault:* Tail not carried over back when moving.

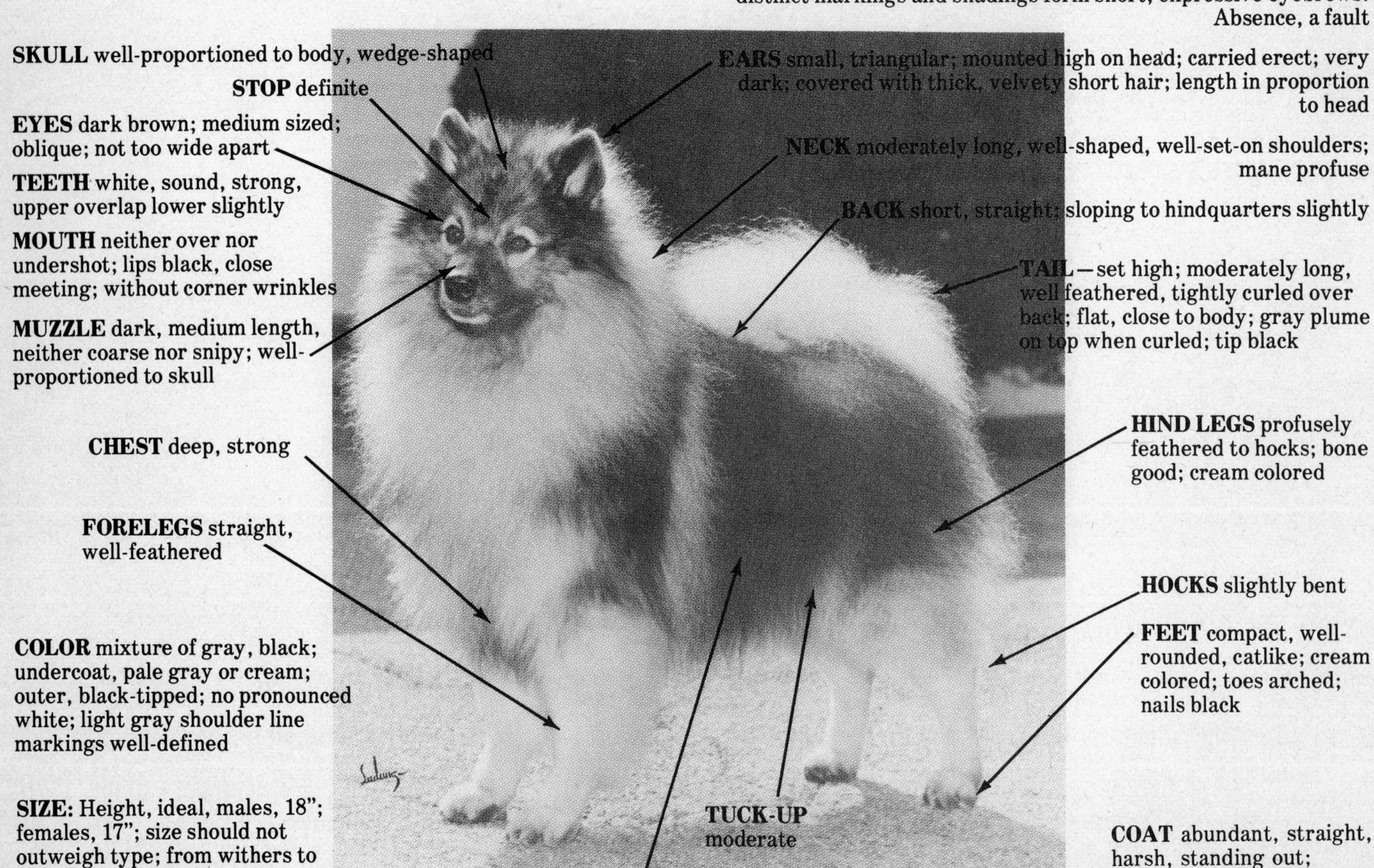

APPEARANCE: Well-balanced, short-coupled, compact; luxurious coat, plume, mane, "trousers"; gait sharp, brisk
HEAD: Face foxlike; hair smooth, soft, short; texture velvety; expression dependent on "spectacles" (delicately penciled lines slanting slightly upward from outer corners of eyes to lower corner of ears); distinct markings and shadings form short, expressive eyebrows. Absence, a fault
SKULL well-proportioned to body, wedge-shaped
STOP definite
EYES dark brown; medium sized; oblique; not too wide apart
TEETH white, sound, strong, upper overlap lower slightly
MOUTH neither over nor undershot; lips black, close meeting; without corner wrinkles
MUZZLE dark, medium length, neither coarse nor snipy; well-proportioned to skull
EARS small, triangular; mounted high on head; carried erect; very dark; covered with thick, velvety short hair; length in proportion to head
NECK moderately long, well-shaped, well-set-on shoulders; mane profuse
BACK short, straight; sloping to hindquarters slightly
TAIL—set high; moderately long, well feathered, tightly curled over back; flat, close to body; gray plume on top when curled; tip black
CHEST deep, strong
FORELEGS straight, well-feathered
HIND LEGS profusely feathered to hocks; bone good; cream colored
HOCKS slightly bent
FEET compact, well-rounded, catlike; cream colored; toes arched; nails black
COLOR mixture of gray, black; undercoat, pale gray or cream; outer, black-tipped; no pronounced white; light gray shoulder line markings well-defined
SIZE: Height, ideal, males, 18"; females, 17"; size should not outweigh type; from withers to rump equal to height
TUCK-UP moderate
RIBS well-ribbed, barrel well-rounded
COAT abundant, straight, harsh, standing out; undercoat thick, downy; no parting down back

CH. FLAKKEE INSTANT REPLAY

SPEEDY IS RAPIDLY APPROACHING THE POSITION OF TOP WINNING KEES IN THE HISTORY OF THE BREED. TO DATE HE HAS WON A TOTAL OF 183 BOB AWARDS, 124 GROUP FIRSTS AND 40 BEST IN SHOWS. HIS KENNEL MATE CH. FLAKKEE SWEEPSTAKES STILL HOLDS THE ALL TIME BEST IN SHOW RECORD WITH 46. SPEEDY HAS ALSO TOPPED THE NON-SPORTING GROUP (PHILLIPS SYSTEM) IN 1972 & '73 AND IS A LEADING CONTENDER FOR THE AWARD FOR 1974. WAS WINNER OF THE KEN-L-RATION AWARD FOR 1973.

HANDLER PORTER WASHINGTON

FLAKKEE KENNELS, REG.
4310 COMPTON BLVD.
LAWNDALE, CA. 90260

COAT — The body should be abundantly covered with long, straight, harsh hair; standing well out from a thick, downy undercoat. The hair on the legs should be smooth and short, except for a feathering on the front legs and "trousers," as previously described on the hind legs. The hair on the tail should be profuse, forming a rich plume. Head, including muzzle, skull and ears, should be covered with smooth, soft, short hair — velvety in texture on the ears. Coat must not part down the back. *Fault:* Silky, wavy or curly coats. Part in coat down the back.

COLOR AND MARKINGS — A mixture of gray and black. The undercoat should be very pale gray or cream (not tawny). The hair of the outer coat is black tipped, the length of the black tips producing the characteristic shading of color. The color may vary from light to dark, but any pronounced deviation from the gray color is not permissible. The plume of the tail should be very light gray when curled on back, and the tip of the tail should be black. Legs and feet should be cream. Ears should be very dark—almost black. Shoulder line markings (light gray) should be well defined. The color of the ruff and "trousers" is generally lighter than that of the body. "Spectacles" and shadings, as previously described, are characteristic of the breed and must be present to some degree. There should be no pronounced white markings.

VERY SERIOUS FAULT — Entirely black or white or any other solid color; any pronounced deviation from the gray color.

SCALE OF POINTS

General conformation and appearance		20
Head		
Shape	6	
Eyes	5	
Ears	5	
Teeth	4	20
Body		
Chest, back and loin	10	
Tail	10	
Neck and shoulders	8	
Legs	4	
Feet	3	35
Coat		15
Color and markings		10
		100

Approved July 12, 1949

LHASA APSO STANDARD

CHARACTER — Gay and assertive, but chary of strangers. *Size* — Variable, but about 10 inches or 11 inches at shoulder for dogs, bitches slightly smaller.

COLOR — Golden, sandy, honey, dark grizzle, slate, smoke, parti-color, black, white or brown. This being the true Tibetan Lion-dog, golden or lionlike colors are preferred. Other colors in order as above. Dark tips to ears and beard are an asset.

BODY SHAPE — The length from point of shoulders to point of buttocks longer than height at withers, well ribbed up, strong loin, well-developed quarters and thighs.

Coat — Heavy, straight, hard, not woolly nor silky, of good length, and very dense.

MOUTH AND MUZZLE — Mouth level, otherwise slightly undershot preferable. Muzzle of medium length; a square muzzle is objectionable.

HEAD — Heavy head furnishings with good fall over eyes, good whiskers and beard; skull narrow, falling away behind the eyes in a marked degree, not quite flat, but not domed or apple-shaped; straight foreface of fair length. Nose black about $1\frac{1}{2}$ inches long, or the length from tip of nose to eye to be roughly about one-third of the total length from nose to back of skull.

EYES — Dark brown, neither very large and full, nor very small and sunk.

EARS — Pendant, heavily feathered.

LEGS — Forelegs straight; both forelegs and hind legs heavily furnished with hair. *Feet* — Well feathered, should be round and catlike, with good pads.

TAIL AND CARRIAGE — Well feathered, should be carried well over back in a screw; there may be a kink at the end. A low carriage of stern is a serious fault.

Approved April 9, 1935

CHARACTER: Gay, assertive, chary of strangers

SKULL narrow, note quite flat but not domed; falling away behind eyes; foreface straight; length fair

HEAD: Heavy furnishings, good fall over eyes; whiskers, beard

EARS pendant, heavily feathered, dark tips desirable

TAIL well-feathered; carried well over back in screw; kink at end permitted

EYES dark brown; neither very large and full nor very small and sunken

NOSE black, approx. $1\frac{1}{2}$" long; tip to eye approx. $\frac{1}{3}$ of tip to occiput

MUZZLE medium length, not square; mouth level or slightly undershot

LEGS straight, heavily feathered

FEET round, catlike, well-feathered; pads good

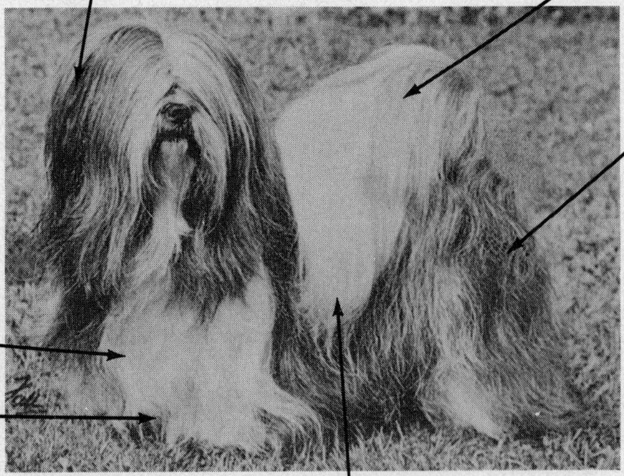

HINDQUARTERS well-developed; thighs muscular; loins strong

COAT heavy, straight, hard, of good length, very dense; neither woolly nor silky

SIZE: height, males 10 to 11"; females slightly smaller; length from withers to point of buttocks longer than height at withers

RIBS body well-ribbed-up

COLORS in order of preference: Golden, sandy, honey, dark grizzle, slate, smoke, parti-color, black, white, brown. Dark tips to ears; beard an asset

CH. KARNES KEE-O OF KORKY

2 YEARS OLD — OUT AS A SPECIAL FOR 2½ MONTHS OF LIMITED CAMPAIGNING. 19 BREEDS — 2 GROUP I'S AND 15 GROUP PLACEMENTS.
HANDLER: ROBERT D. SHARP

SUSAN C. HUTCHINS
201 EAST 62ND ST.
NEW YORK, N.Y. 10021

Tibet is the home of the Lhasa Apso where he is known as the *"Bark Lion Sentinel Dog."* They have a heavy coat which serves as protection from the climate. They are excellent guard dogs as well as faithful companions. Lhasas coats come in many different colors, however the lion-like golden color is the most preferred. As a result when one color is bred to another it is difficult to predict what color the puppies will be.

GENERAL APPEARANCE, CARRIAGE AND CONDITION — That of a very active, intelligent and elegant-appearing dog, squarely built, well proportioned, moving soundly and carrying himself proudly. Properly clipped in the traditional fashion and carefully groomed, the Poodle has about him an air of distinction and dignity peculiar to himself.

HEAD AND EXPRESSION — (a) *Skull:* moderately rounded, with a slight but definite stop. Cheek-bones and muscles flat. (b) *Muzzle:* long, straight and fine, with slight chiseling under the eyes. Strong without lippiness. The chin definite enough to preclude snipiness. Teeth white, strong and with a scissors bite. (c) *Eyes;* set far apart, very dark, oval in appearance and showing alert intelligence. (d) *Ears:* hanging close to the head, set at or slightly below eye level. The ear leather is long, wide, and thickly feathered, but the ear fringe should not be of excessive length.

NECK AND SHOULDERS — Neck well proportioned, strong and long enough to permit the head to be carried high and with dignity. Skin snug at throat. The neck rises from strong, smoothly muscled shoulders. The shoulder blade is well laid back and approximately the same length as the upper foreleg.

BODY—The chest deep and moderately wide with well sprung ribs. The back short, strong and slightly hollowed; the loins short, broad and muscular. Length of body and height at shoulder are in such proportion as to insure the desirable squarely built appearance.

TAIL—Straight, set on high and carried up, docked, but sufficient in length to insure a balanced outline.

LEGS — The forelegs are straight and parallel when viewed from the front. When viewed from the side with the leg vertical, the elbow is directly below the highest point of the shoulder blade. The hindlegs are muscular with width in the region of the stifles. The pasterns are strong and the stifles well bent. The length of the leg from the stifle joint to the hock joint is considerably greater than the length from the hock joint to the foot.

FEET—The feet are rather small, oval in shape with toes well arched and cushioned on thick firm pads. Nails short but not excessively shortened. The feet turn neither in nor out. Dewclaws may be removed.

COAT—*QUALITY:* of naturally harsh texture, profuse and dense throughout.

CLIP—A Poodle may be shown in the "Puppy" clip or the "English Saddle" clip or the traditional "Continental" clip. A Poodle shown in any other type of clip shall be disqualified.

A Poodle under a year old may be shown in the "Puppy" clip with the coat long. The face, throat, feet and base of the tail are shaved. The entire shaven foot is visible. There is a pompon on the end of the tail. In order to give a neat appearance, a slight shaping of the coat is permissible; however, a Poodle in "Puppy" clip that is excessively scissored shall be dismissed.

Dogs one year old or older must be shown in either the "English Saddle" clip or the "Continental" clip.

In the "English Saddle" clip the face, throat, feet, forelegs and base of the tail are shaved, leaving puffs on the forelegs and a pompon on the end of the tail. The hindquarters are covered with a short blanket of hair except for a curved shaved area on each flank and two shaved bands on each hindleg. The entire shaven foot and a portion of the shaven leg above the puff are visible. The rest of the body is left in full coat but may be shaped in order to insure overall balance.

In the "Continental" clip the face, throat, feet and base of the tail are shaved. The hindquarters are shaved with pompons (optional) on the hips. The legs are shaved, leaving bracelets on the hindlegs and puffs on the forelegs. There is a pompon on the end of the tail. The entire shaven foot and portion of the shaven forelegs above the puff are visible. The rest of the body is left in full coat but may be shaped in order to insure overall balance.

In all clips the hair of the topknot may be held in place by an elastic band or barrette. The hair is only of sufficient length to present a smooth outline.

COLOR—The coat is an even and solid color at the skin. In blues, grays, silvers, browns, cafe-au-laits, apricots, and creams the coat may show varying shades of the same color. This is frequently present in the somewhat darker feathering of the ears and in the tipping of the ruff. While clear colors are definitely preferred, such natural variation in the shading of the coat is not to be

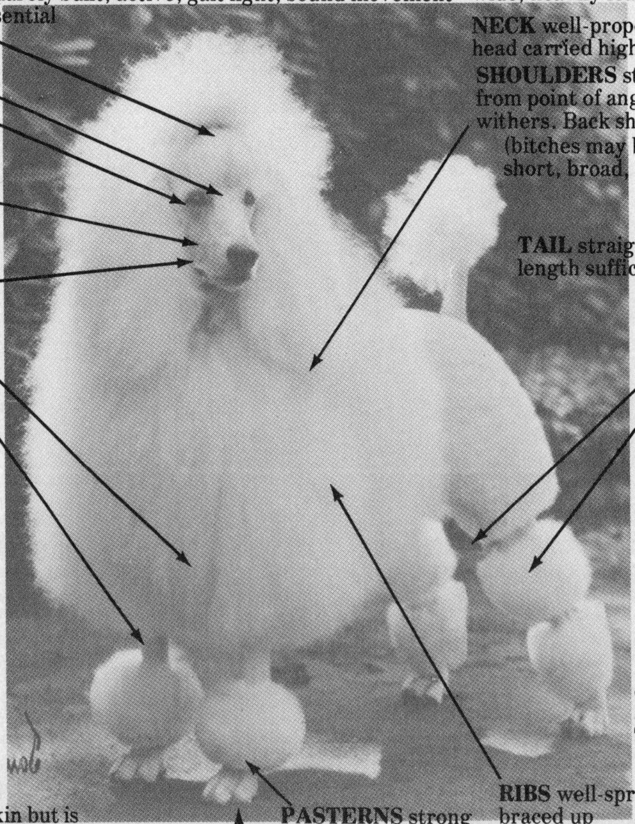

APPEARANCE: Distinctive, elegant looking; squarely built; active; gait light; sound movement essential

SKULL moderately rounded

STOP slight but definite

EYES set far apart; very dark; oval appearance

MUZZLE long, straight, fine; slight chiseling under eyes; strong without lippiness; chin definite enough to preclude snippiness. Teeth white, strong; scissors bite

CHEEKS: Bones, muscles flat

CHEST deep, moderately wide

FORELEGS straight parallel

COLOR even, solid at skin; in blues, grays, silvers, browns, cafe-au-laits, apricots, creams, coats may show varying shades of same color (ears, ruff, etc.); clear colors preferred but shadings not considered fault. Browns, cafe-au laits—liver-colored noses, eye rims, lips, dark toenails, dark amber eyes. Black, blue, gray, silver, cream, white Poodes—black noses, eye rims, lips, black or self-colored toenails, very dark eyes. Apricots—foregoing coloring preferred; liver-colored noses, eye rims, lips, amber eyes permitted

DISQUALIFICATIONS: Parti-colors where coat is not even solid color at skin but is of two or more colors. Only specified clips allowed in show ring; only specified sizes for each variety permitted

EARS set low; hanging close to head; leather long, wide, heavily feathered

NECK well-proportioned, strong; length to allow head carried high with dignity; skin snug at throat

SHOULDERS strong, muscular, should slope back from point of angulation at upper foreleg to withers. Back short, strong, slightly hollowed (bitches may be slightly longer than dogs); loins short, broad, muscular

TAIL straight; rather high set; docked length sufficient to insure balance; carriage up

STIFLES well-bent

HINDLEGS very muscular;

CLIPS: "Puppy Clip" for Poodles under one year of age. "Continental" or "English Saddle" for dogs over one year of age

COAT dense throughout; profuse; texture harsh

SIZE determines 3 varieties; STANDARD, over 15" at withers; MINIATURE, 15" or under at withers with min over 10"; TOY, 10" or under at withers

RIBS well-sprung; braced up

PASTERNS strong

FEET rather small; oval; turning neither in nor out; toes arched, close; pads hard, thick, well cushioned

AN OUTSTANDING REPRESENTATIVE OF THE BREED, "CHRIS" IS A POODLE GREAT IN THE MAKING. IN ADDITION TO HIS IMPRESSIVE SHOW RECORD WHICH INCLUDES THE NON-SPORTING GROUP AT INTERNATIONAL "CHRIS" PEDIGREE SPEAKS FOR ITSELF. SIRED BY OUR WESTMINSTER BEST IN SHOW WINNER CH. ACADIA COMMAND PERFORMANCE EX. HAUS BRAU ZULINNA, THIS FINE YOUNG DOG IS SIRING QUALITY GET.

HANDLER—LUC BOILEAU

OWNER
EDWARD B. JENNER
KNOLLAND FARMS
RICHMOND, ILLINOIS 60071
815—678-4217

CH. VISCARA VAGABOND KING

considered a fault. Brown and cafe-au-lait Poodles have liver-colored noses, eye-rims and lips, dark toenails and dark amber eyes. Black, blue, gray, silver, cream and white Poodles have black noses, eye-rims and lips, black or self-colored toenails and very dark eyes. In the apricots while the foregoing coloring is preferred, liver-colored noses, eyerims and lips, and amber eyes are permitted but are not desirable.

Parti-colored dogs shall be disqualified. The coat of a parti-colored dog is not an even solid color at the skin but is of two or more colors.

GAIT—A straightforward trot with light springy action and strong hindquarter drive. Head and tail carried high. Forelegs and hindlegs move parallel turning neither in nor out. Sound movement is essential.

SIZE

STANDARD—The Standard Poodle is over 15 inches at the highest point of the shoulders. Any Poodle which is 15 inches or less in height shall be disqualified from competition as a Standard Poodle.

MINIATURE—The Miniature Poodle is 15 inches or under at the highest point of the shoulders, with a minimum height in excess of 10 inches. Any Poodle which is over 15 inches or 10 inches or less at the highest point of the shoulders shall be disqualified from competition as a Miniature Poodle.

TOY—The Toy Poodle is 10 inches or under at the highest point of the shoulders. Any Poodle which is more than 10 inches at the highest point of the shoulders shall be disqualified from competition as a Toy Poodle.

VALUE OF POINTS

General appearance, temperament, carriage and condition	30
Head, expression, ears, eyes and teeth	20
Body, neck, legs. feet and tail	20
Gait	20
Coat, color and texture	10

MAJOR FAULTS

Eyes: round in appearance, protruding, large or very light.
Jaws: undershot, overshot or wry mouth.
Feet: flat or spread.
Tail: set low, curled or carried over the back.
Hindquarters: cow hocks.
Temperament: shyness or sharpness.

DISQUALIFICATIONS

Clip: A dog in any type of clip other than those listed under "Coat" shall be disqualified.

Parti-colors: The coat of a parti-colored dog is not an even solid color at the skin but is of two or more colors. Parti-colored dogs shall be disqualified.

Size: A dog over or under the height limits specified under "Size" shall be disqualified.

SCHIPPERKE STANDARD

APPEARANCE AND GENERAL CHARACTERISTICS — Excellent and faithful little watchdog, suspicious of strangers. Active, agile, indefatigable, continually occupied with what is going on around him, careful of things that are given him to guard, very kind with children, knows the ways of the household; always curious to know what is going on behind closed doors or about any object that has been moved, betraying his impressions by his sharp bark and upstanding ruff, seeking the company of horses, a hunter of moles and other vermin; can be used to hunt, a good rabbit dog. *Color* — Solid black.

HEAD — Foxlike, fairly wide, narrowing at the eyes, seen in profile slightly rounded, tapering muzzle not too elongated nor too blunt, not too much stop.

Nose — Small and black. *Eyes* — Dark brown, small, oval rather than round, neither sunken nor prominent. *Expression* — Should have a questioning expression: sharp and lively, not mean or wild. *Ears* — Very erect, small, triangular, placed high, strong enough not to be capable of being lowered except in line with the body. *Teeth* — Meeting evenly. A tight scissors bite is acceptable.

NECK — Strong and full, slightly arched, rather short. *Shoulders* — Muscular and sloping. *Chest* — Broad and deep in brisket.

BODY — Short, thick-set and cobby. Broad behind the shoulders, seeming higher in front because of ruff. Back strong, short, straight and level or slightly sloping down toward rump. Ribs well sprung. *Loins* — Muscular and well drawn up from the brisket but not to such an extent as to cause a weak and leggy appearance of the hindquarters. *Forelegs* — Straight under body, with bone in proportion, but not coarse. *Hindquarters* — Somewhat lighter than the foreparts, but muscular, powerful, with rump well rounded, tail docked to no more than 1 inch in length. *Feet* — Small, round and tight (not splayed), nails straight, strong and short.

COAT — Abundant and slightly harsh to the touch, short on the ears and on the front of legs and on the hocks, fairly short on the body, but longer around neck beginning back of the ears, and forming a ruff and a cape; a jabot extending down between the front legs, also longer on rear where it forms a culotte, the points turning inward. Undercoat dense and short on body, very dense around neck making ruff stand out. Culotte should be as long as the ruff.

WEIGHT — Up to 18 pounds.

FAULTS — Light eyes, large round prominent eyes, ears too long or too rounded, narrow head and elongated muzzle, too blunt muzzle, domed skull, smooth short coat with short ruff and culotte, lack of undercoat, curly or silky coat, body coat more than three (3) inches long, slightly overshot or undershot, sway-back, Bull Terrier shaped head, straight hocks. Straight stifles and shoulders, cowhocks, feet turning in or out, legs not straight when viewed from front. Lack of distinction between length of coat, ruff and culotte.

DISQUALIFICATIONS

Any color other than solid black. Drop or semi-erect ears. Badly overshot or undershot.

Approved May 12, 1959

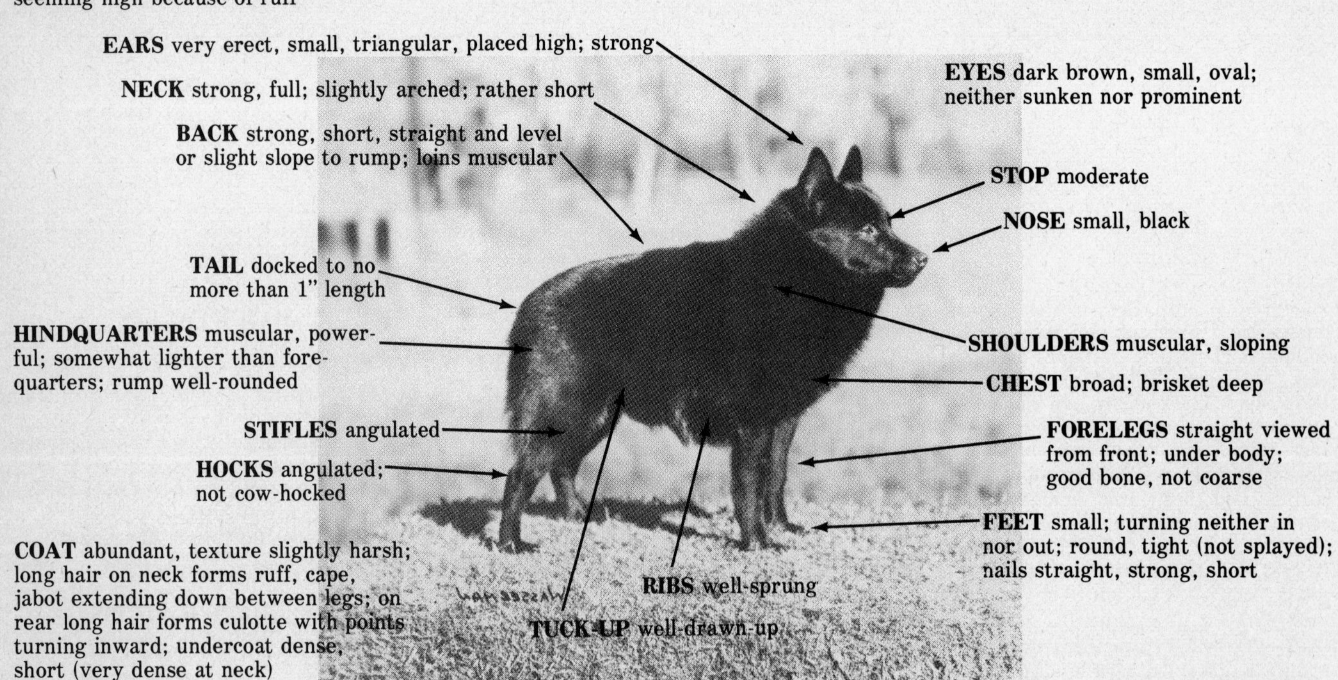

CH. ELFE-MIRS BILLIE-BILLY BI-HO

"BILLY" IS THE SCHIPPERKE TO WATCH.

HIS SHOW RECORD TO DATE INCLUDES: 4 ALL BREED BEST IN SHOWS, 1 NATIONAL SPECIALTY, 40 GROUP FIRSTS AND HE'S STILL GOING STRONG.

WITH MORE THAN 12 CHAMPION GET TO HIS CREDIT, "BILLY" IS WELL ON HIS WAY TO BECOMING ONE OF THE BREED'S TOP PRODUCERS.

HANDLER: FRAN WASSERMAN

FRAKARI KENNELS, REG.
R.D. 1, BOX 116A, RT. 79
MARLBORO, NEW JERSEY 07746

The Schipperke is of Belgian origin. Some authorities identify it as a Spitz breed while others think it to be a miniature version of the Belgian Sheepdog. The Schipperke seems, in any event, to have been a popular, plebian dog of Belgian homes and barges for well over 100 years. The Schipperke is individualistic, inquisitive, and alert. He is loyal and affectionate with his family but unsure of strangers. He makes an excellent companion, in a stable, attentive home. The Schipperke is distinctive in appearance. Basically of Spitz type, with foxlike face, outstanding coat, erect ears, and rather straight hocks, the Schipperke's tail is docked to no more than 1 inch. The abundant coat with ruff, jabot, and culotte, must be solid black. Weight is up to 18 pounds. Never yet widely popular in the United States, some 1,400 are registered annually, the breed ranking 56th.

TIBETAN TERRIER STANDARD

SKULL AND HEAD — Skull of medium length, not broad or coarse, narrowing slightly from ear to eye, not domed but not absolutely flat between the ears. The malar bones are curved, but should not be over-developed so as to bulge. There should be a marked stop in front of the eyes, but this must not be exaggerated. The head should be well furnished with long hair, falling forward over the eyes. The lower jaw should carry a small but not over-exaggerated amount of beard. Jaws between the canines should form a distinct curve. The length from the eye to tip of nose should be equal to that from eye to base of skull, not broad or massive.

NOSE — Black. Any color other than black shall disqualify.

EYES — Large, dark, neither prominent nor sunken; should be set fairly wide apart. Eyelids dark.

EARS — Pendant, not too close to the head, "V"-shaped, not too large; heavily feathered.

MOUTH — Level by preference but a slight undershot should not be penalized.

FOREQUARTERS — Legs straight, heavily furnished.

BODY — Compact and powerful. Length from point of shoulder to root ot tail equal to height at withers. Well ribbed up. Loin slightly arched.

HINDQUARTERS — Heavily furnished, hocks well let down.

FEET — The feet should be large, round, and heavily furnished with hair between the toes and pads. The dog should stand well down on its pads.

TAIL — Medium length, set on fairly high and carried in a gay curl over the back. Very well feathered. There is often a kink near the tip.

COAT — Double-coated. The undercoat fine wool, the top coat profuse, fine, but not silky or woolly; long; either straight or waved.

COLORED — Any color or colors including white.

WEIGHT AND SIZE — Average weight 22 to 23 pounds . . . but may be 18 to 30 pounds. Height from 14 to 16 inches.

FAULTS — Poor coat; mouth very undershot or overshot; a weak snipy foreface.

DISQUALIFICATION

Nose any color other than black.

SKULL AND HEAD: Of medium length, not broad or coarse; narrowing slightly from ear to eye. Marked stop in front of eyes. Head well furnished with hair falling over eyes. Lower jaw has small beard. Jaws between canines form a distinct curve. Length of eye to tip of nose is equal to that from eye to skull base

BODY: Compact and powerful. Length from point of shoulder to root of tail equal to height at withers. Well ribbed up, loin slightly arched

EYES: Large, dark, set fairly well apart

NOSE: Black

MOUTH: Level is preferred

EARS: Pendant, not too close to head, "V"-shaped

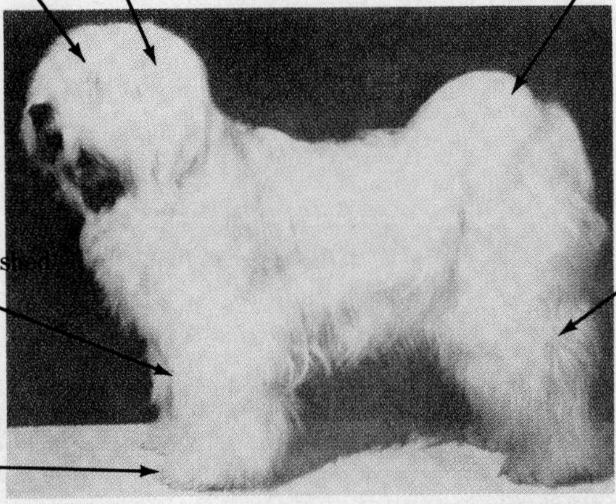

TAIL: Medium length, carried in a gay curl over back. Very well feathered

FOREQUARTERS: Legs straight, heavily furnished

HINDQUARTERS: Heavily furnished, hocks well let down

FEET: Large, round, heavily furnished. Dog stands well down on its pads

COLOR: Any color or colors, including white

COAT: Double coated. Undercoat fine wool, top coat profuse, fine, but not silky or wooly; long, either straight or waved

FAULTS: Poor coat; mouth very undershot or overshot; a weak snipy face

WEIGHT AND SIZE: Average 22 to 23 pounds—may be 18 to 30 pounds. Height from 14 to 16 inches

DISQUALIFICATION: Nose any color other than black

CH. ZIM SHA'S TASHA TI SONG

AMERICA'S FIRST CHAMPION. IN THE FIRST YEAR AFTER RECOGNITION, SEVEN GROUP PLACINGS. SIRE OF FOUR CHAMPIONS. FOUNDATION SIRE OF FOUR GENERATIONS OF CHAMPIONS AND MORE TO COME.
HANDLER: JOHN DAVIDSON

TI SONG TIBETAN TERRIERS
ANNE KELEMAN
755 ATHERTON AVE.
NOVATO, CALIFORNIA 94947

The Tibetan Terrier was apparently bred in Tibet to be a utility working dog and companion. It is a hardy, natural breed with an appealing "country" look. The body is square and compact. The coat is double, long, and shaggy. The height at the shoulder for a dog or bitch is 14 to 16 inches. All colors, including white, are acceptable. The Tibetan Terrier was recognized in Britain decades ago; it achieved AKC status in 1973. The breed is rare; probably about 200 will be registered in 1974.

[Bulldog cont'd. from p. 239]

front feet may be straight or slightly outturned, but the hind feet should be pointed well outward.

TAIL — The tail may be either straight or "screwed" (but never curved or curly), and in any case must be short, hung low, with decided downward carriage, thick root and fine tip. If straight, the tail should be cylindrical and of uniform taper. If "screwed" the bends or kinks should be well defined, and they may be abrupt and even knotty, but no portion of the member should be elevated above the base or root.

DISQUALIFICATION
Dudley or flesh-colored nose.

SCALE OF POINTS

General Properties		
Proportion and symmetry	5	
Attitude	3	
Expression	2	
Gait	3	
Size	3	
Coat	2	
Color of Coat	4	22
Head		
Skull	5	
Cheeks	2	
Stop	4	
Eyes and eyelids	3	
Ears	5	
Wrinkle	5	
Nose	6	
Chops	2	
Jaws	5	
Teeth	2	39
Body, Legs, etc.		
Neck	3	
Dewlap	2	
Shoulders	5	
Chest	3	
Ribs	3	
Brisket	2	
Belly	2	
Back	5	
Forelegs and Elbows	4	
Hind legs	3	
Feet	3	
Tail	4	39
Total		100

REPETITIOUS SHOW TERMS ABBREVIATED

BIS	best in show	KC	kennel club	CDX	companion dog excellent
BOS	best of opposite sex	Ch.	champion of record	UD	utility dog degree
GR1, GR2, etc.	placings in group	R/W	red and white	TD	tracking dog
BOB	best of breed	Bl/W	black and white	UDT	utility-tracking dog
BOW	best of winners	Bl/T	black and tan	O1, O2, etc.	placings in open class
WD or WB	winners dog or bitch	CC	challenge certificate	N1, N2, etc.	placings in novice class
RD or RB	reserve winners dog or bitch	JR.	junior	GN1, GN2, etc.	graduate novice
Am-bred	bred in America	P1, P2, etc.	placings in puppy class	TT	tracking test
BBE	bred by exhibitor				
BIM	best in match	OTC	obedience trial club	F. T. Ch.	field trial champion
AKC	American Kennel Club	CD	companion dog degree	Dual Ch.	bench-field champion

DOG ANATOMY

Superficial Structures

a External Jugular Vein
b Sternohyoideus Muscle
c Sternomastoideus Muscle
d Trapezius Muscle
e Omotransversarius Muscle
f Clavicular Head of Trapezius
g Cleido-mastoideus Muscle
h Rudimentary Clavicle
i Branch of Cephalic Vein
j Deltoideus Muscle
k Pectoralis Major Muscle
l Clavicular Head of Deltoideus
m Triceps Brachii Muscle
n Biceps Brachii Muscle
o Median Cubital Vein
p Common Digital Extensor Muscle
q Cephalic Vein
r Extensor Carpi Radialis Muscle
s Lateral Digital Extensor Muscle
t Abductor Pollicis Longus Muscle
u Extensor Carpi Ulnaris Muscle
v Flexor Carpi Ulnaris Muscle
w Back Portion of Pectoralis Major
x Latissimus Dorsi Muscle
y Rectus Abdominis Muscle
z External Oblique Abdominal Muscle
1 Temporal Muscle
2 Masseter Muscle
3 Parotid Salivary Gland
4 Mandibular Salivary Gland
5 External Intercostal Muscles
6 Dorsal Sacrococcygeus Muscle
7 Gluteus Medius Muscle
8 Coccygeus Muscle
9 Gluteus Maximus Muscle
10 Semitendinosus Muscle
11 Biceps Femoris Muscle
12 Small Saphenous Vein
13 Calcanean Tendon
14 Flexor Hallucis Longus Muscle
15 Peroneus Digiti Quinti Muscle
16 Peroneus Brevis Muscle
17 Peroneus Longus Muscle
18 Long Digital Extensor Muscle
19 Anterior Tibial Muscle

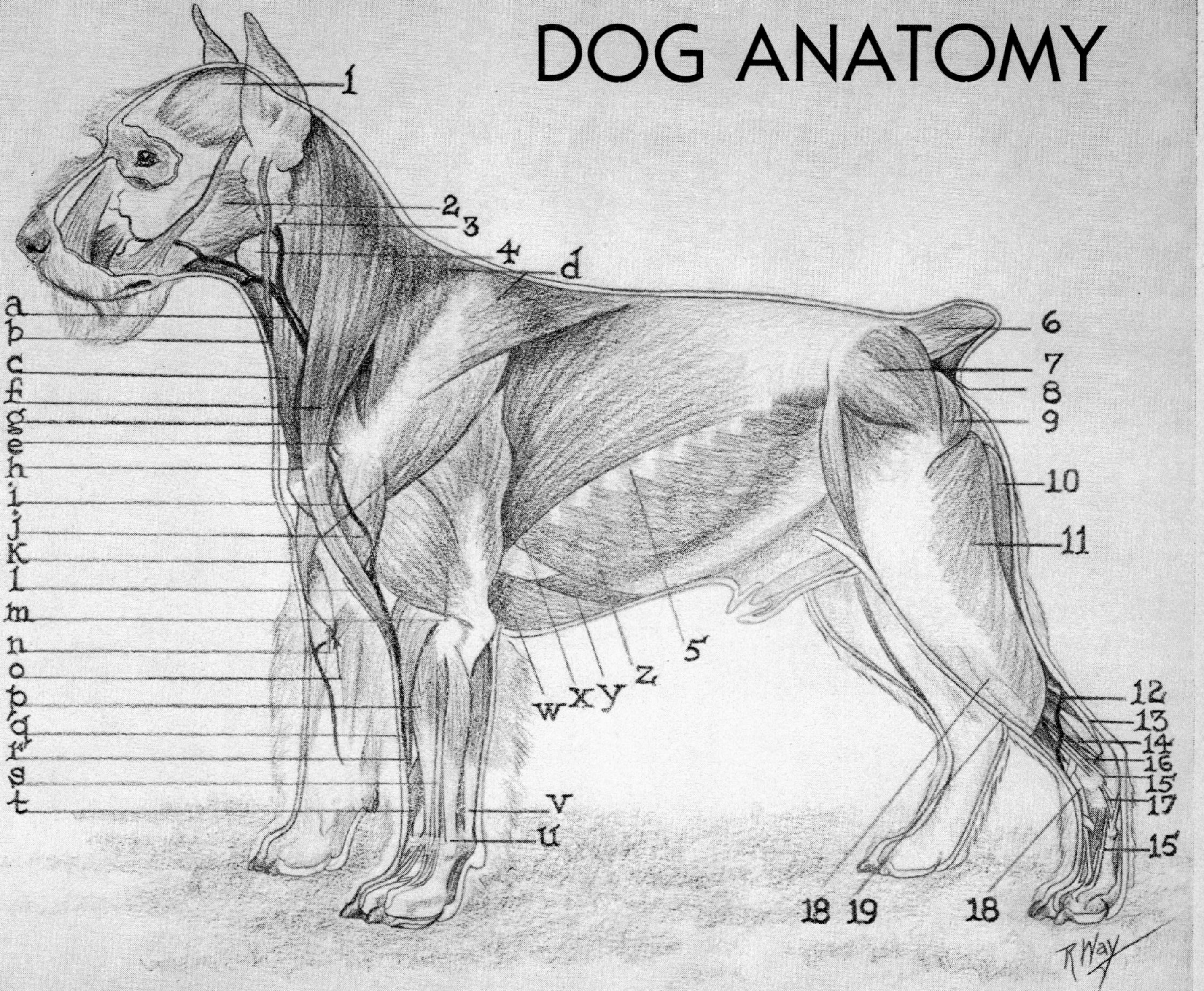

R Way

The Skeleton

1 Skull
2 Seven Cervical Vertebrae
3 Scapula
4 Ribs - Thirteen Pairs
5 Sternum
6 Humerus
7 Radius ; 7a Ulna
8 Carpal Bones
9 Metacarpal Bones
10 Phalangeal Bones
11 Thoracic Vertebrae - Thirteen
12 Lumbar Vertebrae - Seven
13 Sacrum
14 Coccygeal Vertebrae
15 Os Coxae
16 Femur
17 Os Penis
18 Patella
19 Fibula
20 Tibia
21 Tarsal Bones
22 Metatarsal Bones
23 Phalangeal Bones

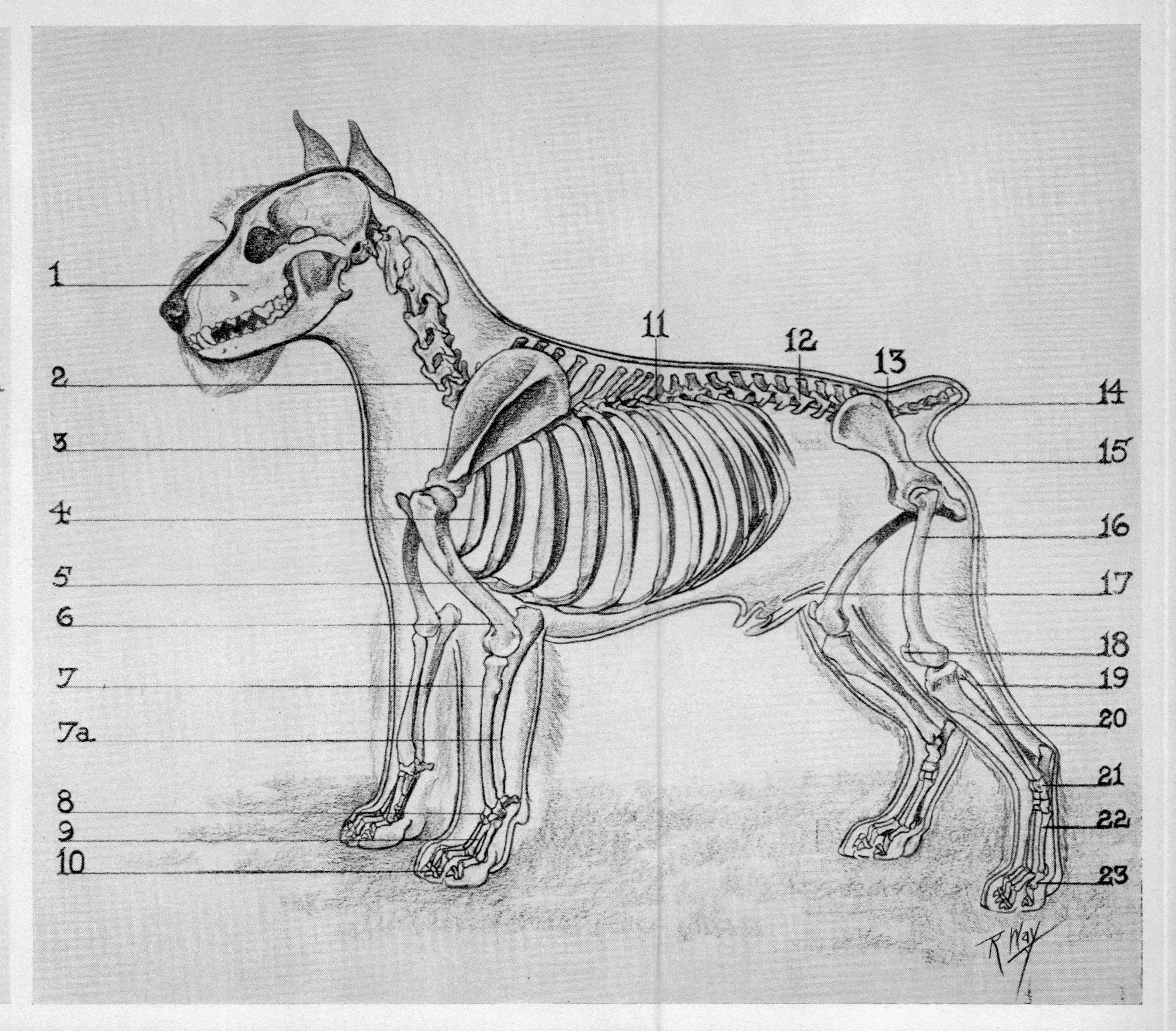

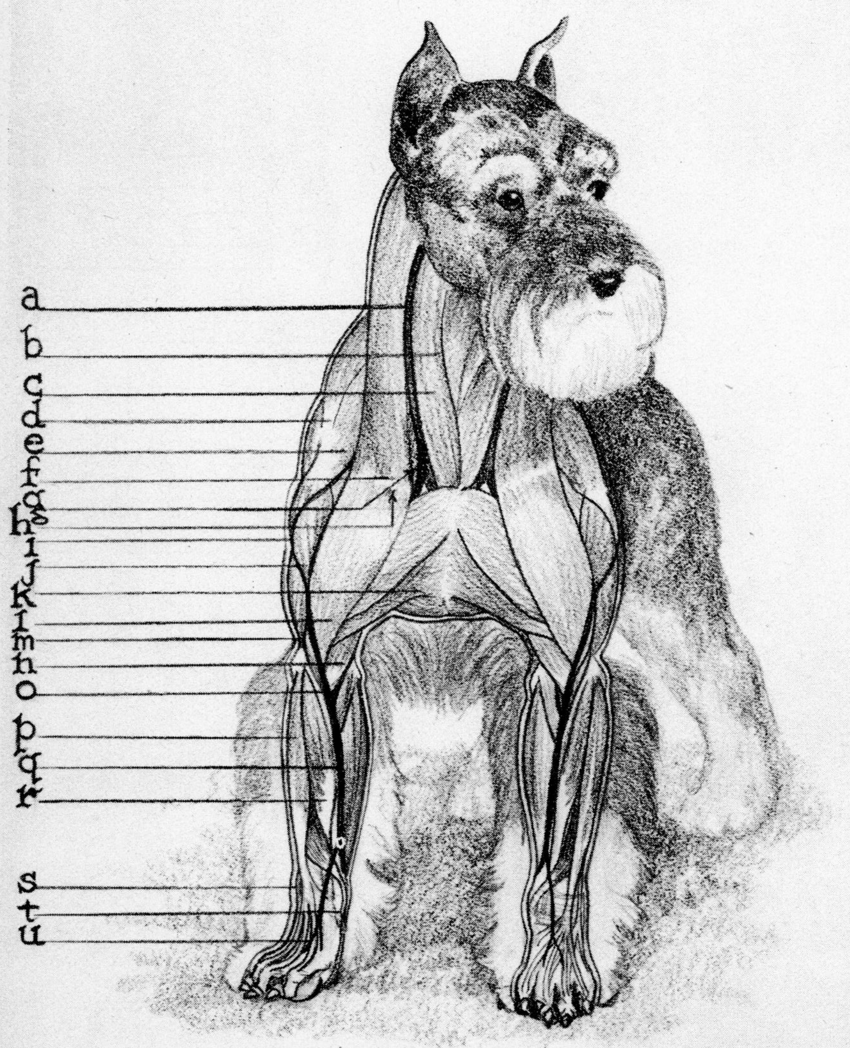

Superficial Structures

a External Jugular Vein
b Sternohyoideus Muscle
c Sternomastoideus Muscle
d Trapezius Muscle
e Omotransversarius Muscle
f Clavicular Head of Trapezius
g Cleido-mastoideus Muscle
h Rudimentary Clavicle
i Branch of Cephalic Vein
j Deltoideus Muscle
k Pectoralis Major Muscle
l Clavicular Head of Deltoideus
m Triceps Brachii Muscle
n Biceps Brachii Muscle
o Median Cubital Vein
p Common Digital Extensor Muscle
q Cephalic Vein
r Extensor Carpi Radialis Muscle
s Lateral Digital Extensor Muscle
t Abductor Pollicis Longus Muscle
u Accessory Cephalic Vein

The Bones

1 Skull
2 Cervical Vertebrae
3 Scapula
4 Ribs
5 Sternum
6 Humerus
7 Radius and Ulna
8 Carpal Bones
9 Metacarpal Bones
10 Phalangeal Bones

Superficial Structures

7 Gluteus Medius Muscle
9 Gluteus Maximus Muscle
6 Dorsal Sacrococcygeus Muscle
25 Obturator Internus Muscle
11 Biceps Femoris Muscle
10 Semitendinosus Muscle
21 Semimembranosus Muscle
22 Gracilis Muscle
23 Popliteal Lymph Gland
24 Gastrocnemius Muscle
12 Small Saphenous Vein
13 Calcanean Tendon
20 Superficial Digital Flexor Tendon

The Bones

14' Coccygeal Vertebrae
15' Os Coxae
16 Femur
19 Fibula
20' Tibia
21' Tarsal Bones
22' Metatarsal Bones
23' Phalangeal Bones

popular dogs

THE AMERICAN
BLUE BOOK OF DOG BREEDERS
DIRECTORY OF KENNELS

BLUE BOOK PATRONS

Cynthia A. Burns
Mrs. Peggy M. Borcherding
Prof. Donald C. Bunting
Leo P. & Lieselotte Cameron
Jean Q. Clark
Michael Coletta
Katherine R. Davison
Mrs. Anne E. Donohue
Mary W. Eckstein
Mrs. Charles W. Englehard
Mary V. Friedlander
Linda Goldstein
Judith Heckelman
Mrs. Frank S. Hess
Cheryl E. Hoerner
Mr. & Mrs. Michael R. Guinn
Mrs. S. V. Imslee
Cornelia A. Ingertsoll
Betty Gene Jones
Frances J. Johnston
Mrs. Norma Kantelis
Mrs. Georgia E. Kufeld
Meg Kulzcyk
Oliver M. Lombard
Susanne M. Leeds
Mary E. Leggett
Mrs. Lois Liska
Mr. & Mrs. Wm. R. Maloney
Mrs. Prescott J. Mollison
Mrs. Frances W. Nahrgang
David Napierkowski
Mrs. A. Cameron Pearson
Linda Puckett
Mrs. Cheever Porter
Robert T. Provan
J. E. Ralston
H. R. Ramsburg
Mrs. Kathy Rawlins
Violet O. Ringwald
Carolyn F. Ross
Katie Schaller
Mrs. Thomas Schettig
Pamela M. Slater
Mrs. George O. Smith
Mrs. Horatio J. Snyder
Dan & Terry Sredzinski
Mr. Pierre P. Stolkowski
Mrs. Blanche M. Tenerowicz
C. A. Thuesen
Mary Ann Wanatick
Barbara A. Weinig
Lorraine S. White

Breeds appear in alphabetical order. Kennels are listed within their breeds in accordance with geographical location —first alphabetical order by state, and then alphabetical order by city.

Abbreviations in listings: p.-puppies; d.-adult dogs; s.-studs.

For information or order forms write:

POPULAR DOGS DIRECTORY

Suite 1500, One Park Ave., New York, N.Y. 10016

AFFENPINSCHER

PA AFF-KIN'S K'S. Est. 1960. Emily Kinsley Strempski, RD#4 Box 179, Nazareth 18064. 215—759-0910. p.d.s.

TX BALU. Reg. Lucille Meystedt, Box 230, Rusk 75785. 214—743-2533. p.d.s.

BALU'S KENNELS
Reg. Established 1951
Only Selective Breeding
Home of 30 Champions
Known the World over for Quality Affenpinschers
Quality Not Quantity
L. E. MEYSTEDT
P.O. Box 230
Rusk, TX 75785
(214) 743-2533

AFGHAN HOUND

CT Mr. & Mrs. David D. Walden, Rd. 1, Box 365, No. Stonington 06359. 203—535-0370. p.

FL LARCH TREE, Mr. & Mrs. Wm. A. Clot, 6840 S.W. 119 St. Miami 33156. 305—661-1898. p.d.s.

FL Bonnie Newman, 2320 N. Hastings, Orlando 32808. 305—298-0738. p.

IL SHAHZADI. Reg. Kris Buchanan, Hickory Trace, Dunlap 61525. 309—243-5820.

IL ANDRAMI AFGHANS. J. & A Vikta, 108 Wolpers Road, Park Forest 60466. 312—481-3174. p.d.

IN JEJOLA AFGHANS. Richard & Ruth Granich, 2525 Rock Creek Drive, Bloomington 47401. 812—334-1638. p.

MA ZARNO. Dorothy S. Eaton, 65 Outlook Drive, Lexington 02173. 617—861-8608. p.d.

MA Mr. & Mrs. Stephen M. Edgell III, 8 Sheffield West, Winchester 01890. 617—729-2153. d.

MA Mrs. Roberta M. Kelly, 26 Whiting St., Lynn 01902. 617—593-2812. p.d.

MD KINGSWAY. Barbara J. Divers, Baltimore Zoo, Druid Hill Park, Baltimore 21217. 301—889-5149 or 444-2656. p.d.

NJ AFGHAN HOUNDS OF ZERVLISTAN, Jan & Bill Zervoulis, R.D. 1, Box 345, Mountain Rd., Basking Ridge 07920—647-1077. p.d.s.

NJ AFGHAN HOUNDS OF ALRICKHAN, Reg. F. A. von Ahrens, 6 Phillip Drive, Edison Township 08817. Champion Stud Service 201—575-9237. p.d.

NJ ARISTON AFGHAN HOUNDS. Elise Abraham, 786 Mabie St., New Milford 07646. 201—262-5541. p.d.s.

NY KANDAHARA. Lee & Jim Canalizo, 30 East Woodbine Dr. Freeport 11520. 516—FR 8-1153. p.d.s.

NY ZARDIN, Reg. Dr. Denton Sayer Cox, 530 East 72nd St. New York 10021. 212—879-4003. p.d.s.

NY Mrs. Loraine Patterson Munter, Preston Rd. Rye 10580. 914—967-3602. p.s.

NY SANDINA, Reg. Glorvina R. Schwartz, Tuxedo Park, Tuxedo 10987. 914—EL 1-2494. p.d.s.

PA WELL-DUN K'S. Evelyn E. Duncan, R.D. #1, Box 480, Boyertown 19512. 215—367-8027. p.d.s.

PA WINDSTILL. Est. 1962. Mary & James Dick, Box 383, Lake Harmony 18624. 717—722-0416. p.d.s.

PA HOUND HOLLOW K'S. Est. 1963. Romayne & Michael W. Switch, Meeting House Rd., R.D. 1, New Hope 18938. 215—862-2992. p.d.s.

PA STEP'S AFGHAN HOUNDS. Reg. Joan L. Stepanauckas, 1804 N. Main Ave., Scranton 18508. 717—342-2741. p.d.s.

PA BALLYWALSH K'S. Mr. & Mrs. Joseph H. Walsh, 1825 Diamond St., Sellersville 18960. 215—257-7375. p.d.s.

VA Mrs. Susan E. Tucker, 4210 Hillcrest Rd., Richmond 23225. 804—232-0407. p.d.

WV CROWN HILL K'S Est. July 1970. Patrick & Patricia Blizzard, 242 Midway Drive, Dunbar 25064.

AIREDALE TERRIER

BUCCANEER AIREDALES

CH. BUCCANEER'S BABETTE
Puppies, show prospects, and Stud Service
Ch. Buccaneer's Swashbuckler
Ch. Buccaneer's War Dance
Mrs. Jane B. Young
525 Dogwood Drive
Kingsport, Tenn. 37663
(615) 239-8602

CA AIREDALE TERRIER CLUB OF AMERICA, INC. Wilma Carter, Asst. Secy., 10344 Mann Drive, Monta Vista 95014. Booklets: Trimming—.50, Facts—.25, 1970 Decennial Year Book $6.00. Membership List on Request.

IL COUNSELOR K'S. Diane H. & Charles Orange, 5336 Westview Lane, Lisle 60532. 312—964-8898. p.d.s.

NJ Guenter Behr, R.D. 1, Milford 08848. 201—996-2220. p.d.s.

NJ QUERENCIA K'S, Reg. Countess Ercilia Le Ny, Miller Park Rd. Milford 08848. 201—996-2220. p.d.s.

PA BIRCHRUN K'S. Barbara Strebeigh, Birchrunville 19421.

AKITA

CA TOSHIRO AKITAS. Est. 1970. Ted & Susan dePolo & Al & Barbara Cox. 1325 Morningside Dr., Burbank 91506. 213—846-9710 or 395-5753. At Stud: Triple K Tomo-Go & son Toshi. p.s.

CA Gus D. Bell, 2110 Evergreen Springs Drive, Diamond Bar 91765.

CA KIN HOZAN. Harold & Bea Hunt, 11053 66th St., Mira Loma 91752. p.d.s.

MD SAKURA. B. L. Miller, 3646 Largo Rd., Upper Marlboro 20870 301—627-3905. p.d.s.

ALASKAN MALAMUTE

CA Tony Ducks, 1262 Clayton, San Francisco 94117. 415—864-7486. p.s.

DE NORTHWOOD K'S, Reg. Wayne & Ruth Zimmerman, 1516 Stony Run Dr., Wilmington 19803 302—478-6752. p.d.s.

MA SNOHEET. Wendell J. Knox, 27 Curve St., Lexington 02173. 1—617—862-9351. p.s.

MD Lorea T. Wright, P.O. Box 833, Severna Park 21146. 301—677-4209. p.d.s.

NJ BURBON K'S. Frank & Claire Bongarzone, Wayside Rd., R.D. 1, New Shrewsbury 07724. 201—542-0718. p.d.s.

NY Elaine Wishnow, 2351 E. 17 St. Brooklyn 11229. 212—781-3451. p.

ZARDAL KENNELS, Reg.

CH. ZARDAL BARANOF

Champion Stud Service, and puppies available for those who demand the highest quality.

AUDREY I. THOMAS
1160 Whalen Road
Penfield, New York 14526
(716) 377-2849

NY ASTORM K'S. Walter & Zaneta Pronsky, R.D. 1, Dearsboro Rd., Clinton 13323. 315—853-6368. p.d.s.

NY ZARDAL K'S, Reg. Audrey I. Thomas, 1160 Whalen Rd., Penfield 14526. 716—377-2849. p.d.s.

PA Mick & Kathie McCormick, R.D. 1, Butler 16001. 412—285-1466. p.d.s.

PA Richard & Doris Sassaman, #1 Driftwood 15832. 814—546-2542. p.

PA TAWECHI, Reg. Jon Cowen, 1172 Telegraph Rd., West Chester 19380. 215—696-0496. p.d.s.

VT Wilma Boar, P.O. Box 171, Ascutney 05030. 802—674-6419. p.d.

AMERICAN WATER SPANIELS

OH BARBARA SPISAK, 10292. Top Show Quality Puppies from Champion Stock. 513-885-3242. p.s.

AUSTRALIAN SHEPHERDS

CA BONNIE-BLU K'S. Phillip C. Wildhagen, 23911 Homezell Dr., Canoga Park 91304. 213—887-1841. p.d.s.

AUSTRALIAN TERRIER

GA Barbara E. Campbell, 2206 East Doublegate Dr., Albany 31701. p.s.

NJ COILTRAG K'S. Gertrude & Paul Arata, Jr., R.D. No. 1, Box 250, Egg Harbor 08215. 609—1142. p.d.s.

NJ PLEASANT PASTURES K'S. Reg. Est. 1944. Mrs. Milton Fox, 1411 Dorsett Dock Rd., Point Pleasant 08742. 201—889-0557.

PA Thomas W. Cripps, Box 546, R.D. 2, Northumberland 17857. 717—473-8801. p.d.s.

PA Mrs. Earl J. & Joel E. Hertz, 223 Kuhn Drive, East Berlin 17316. 717—259-0769. p.d.s.

WA TAMMIKIN K'S. Reg. Est. 1959. Gust S. and Shirley J.

AUST. CAN. AM. CH. TINEE TOWN TALEWAGGER, R.O.M. AND DAUGHTER, "WINNIE"

TAMMIKIN KENNELS, REG.

Puppies and Adults from Champions and Imports
Blue/Tans and Sandy/Reds
Excellent Temperaments
Guaranteed to please you be it for Show, Breeding or a Companionable Pet.
We love our Dogs and they show it.

Champions at stud with register of Merit Awards

FROM BEST IN SHOW BLOOD-LINES

GUST AND SHIRLEY LUND
2201-30th St.
Bellingham, Wash. 98225
(206) 733-8827

Lund, 2201 - 30th St., Bellingham 98225. 206—733-8827. p.d.s.

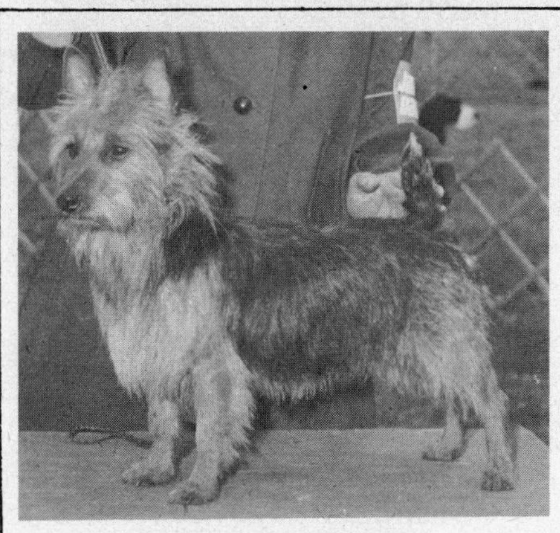

REGENCY KENNELS

Puppies occasionally   Ch. Stud Service

Home of 4 generations of champions
AUSTRALIAN TERRIERS

Ida Ellen and **Alice Ann Weinstock**
R.D. 3, Box 101
Quakertown, Pa. 18951

BASENJI

CA Roberta Frederick, P.O. Box 731, Eagle Mountain 92241. 714—392-4236. p.d.s.

CA TANDA. Andrew & Anne Logan, 14171 Flower St., Garden Grove 92643. 714—638-2690. p.d.s.

CA James & Ruth Shannon, 605 Tina Way, Livermore 94550. 415—443-9096. p.d.s.

KY K. A. Kent, 204 Lyndon Lane, Louisville 40222. 502—426-4146. p.d.s.

PA Diane M. Messmer, R.D. 2, Box 228, Lewisberry 17339. 717—938-2540. p.d.

RI Mr. & Mrs. Robert N. Forcier, 41 Thurman St., Warwick 02888. 401—781-6552. p.s.

BASSET HOUND

IL Mrs. Donald (Ruth) Bateman, P.O. Box 215, Warrenville 60555. 312—393-1297. p.d.

MD Barbara S. Borschow, 12515 Travilah Rd., Potomac 20854. 301—926-8632. p.d.s.

MD Carole M. Bowns, 19705 Meredith Dr., Derwood 20855. 948-8768. p.d.

MD Dr. Leonard Skolnick, Slippery Hill, Harwood 20776. 301—867-3182. p.d.s.

MD TIARA BASSETS. Ralph & Arvilla Webb, 6112 Muncaster Mill Rd., Derwood 20855. 301—301—948-8768. p.d.

MI JAGERSVEN, Reg. Mr. & Mrs. Finn Bergishagen, 2345 Lochaven, Union Lake 48085. 313—363-8212. p.d.s.

BEAGLE

PA HOLLYHOX BEAGLES. Mary Sease, 318 W. 4th St., Waynesboro 17268. 717—762-1952. p.d.

PA PLEASANT VIEW K'S. Reg. Est. 1900 William F. Steele, 1150 Wilmington Pike, West Chester 19380. 215—339-0217. p.d. Ch.s.

BEDLINGTON TERRIER

IL R. Robert & Roberta M Held, 22 S. Rammer Ave., Arlington Heights 60004. 312—259-2227.

IL Durbin C. & Janice S. Scheibe, 319 E. Blackstone Ave., Willow Springs 60480. 312—839-5099. p.s.

NJ ORMONT K'S. Est. 1969, Mr. & Mrs. Bertram Moser, 14 Baneberry Drive. Whitehouse Station 08889. 201—534-2589. p.d.s.

NY Cerelia K. Kiefer, Centerville Rd., R.D. 3, Pulaski 13142.

OH TARTANIA. Dolores Wendel, Route 3, Ashland 44805. 419—962-4564. p.d.s.

PA LEANING TREES K'S. Est. 1948. Oscar Crouthamel, 1506 Old Bethlehem Pike, Sellersville 18960. 215—257-4720. p.d.s.

BELGIAN SHEEPDOG

CA GREENFIELDS. Ellen K. Haro, P.O. Box 133, Davis 95616. 916—756-5550. p.d.s.

CA FASHION WALK K'S. Don and Carol Goodman, 53 Breaker Dr., Pittsburg 94565. Male For Sale, 10 pts, 1 maj. Ch. sire and dam. Ebon Will and A-Yacht lines. 415—458-2872.

IL Mrs. Mary Ann Weber, 9105 W. Belmont, Franklin Park 60131. 312—678-7275. p.d.

WA TAIANNE BELGIANS. Miss Bertine Pigott, 23129 Wachusetts Dr., Edmonds 98020. Inquiries invited & answered promptly. No Litter Lot Sales.

BELGIAN TERVUREN

CA WINDFAIR K'S. Gladys Y. Clark, 5011 La Canada Blvd. La Canada 91011. 213—790-0196. p.s.

GA Marguerite Horstman, Rt. 1, Box 203, Social Circle 30279. 404—464-3549. p.d.

IN SANG ROYAL K'S. Sallyann Comstock, Rt. 2, Box 133A, Hebron 46341. 219—996-6444.

IN Marteen Nolan, RR 1, Box 17, Hebron 46341. 219—996-3434. s.

BERNESE MOUNTAIN

NJ MON PLAISIR. Est. 1960, Joseph & Susanne Gagnon, Box 86, Route 579, Pattenburg 08860. 201—479-4536. p.d.s.

NJ Mrs. Esther Mueller, 673 Green Pond Rd., Rockaway 07866. 201—625-0756. p.d.s.

MON PLAISIR

BERNESE MOUNTAIN DOGS PAR EXCELLENCE

- **Puppies**
  Pet, Obedience & Show
  Fully Guaranteed
- **Stud Service**
  To Select Mates

Joseph and Susanne Gagnon
MON PLAISIR
Box 86, Route 579—Pattenburg, N.J. 08860
(201) 479-4536
Home of the Most Famous—
That's a True Mark of Distinction

BICHON FRISE

CA WARMAN'S BICHONS, Reg. Mr. & Mrs. R. M. Warman, 1416 De Anza Street, Barstow 92311. 714—252-3818. p.d.

CA VINTAGE YEAR K'S. Est. 1964. Harriet M. Kaiserman, Vintage Year Ranch, State, Rt. Box 21, Santa Margarita 93453. 805—438-5632. p.

CT Marion Chambers, P.O. Box 45, Woodstock 06281. 203—928-9737. p.d.s.

MA OVERLOOK PONDS K'S. Evelyn Farrar, 13 Huguenot Rd., Oxford 01540. 617—987-5575. d.

MD MARLE K'S. M. Thalheimer, Rt. 6 Box 137, Westminster 21157, 301—795-9621. p.d.s.

NY DURAH K'S. Edythe & Joel

S. Fishbach, 1047 Hendrix St., Brooklyn 11207. 212—257-0764 or 649-0599. p.s.

NY Amy Costello, 255-14 86th Ave., Floral Park 11001. 212—343-6497. p.s.

NY Mrs. Joan Rosenthal, 160 Brookville Lane, Glen Head 11545. 516—676-8555. s.

NY RIVAGE d'AMI K'S. Helen D. Temmel, 205 West Shore Dr., Massapequa 11758. 516—541-0061. d.s.

NY IDLE-HOURS BICHON FRISE. Mr. & Mrs. Robert Lawson, 110 Hollywood Dr., Oakdale 11769. 516—567-0388. p.d.s.

NY Doris La Rotonda, Verbank Club Road, Verbank 12585. p.d.s.

PA Mrs. Celeste G. Fleishman, Brushtown Rd., Gwynedd Valley 19437. 215—MI 6-2929. p.d.s.

PA Jean Rank, 1421 Charlton Hgts. Rd., Coracpolis 15108. 412—262-1764. p.d.s.

PA BEAU CHEVAL FARMS. Est. 1958. Mrs. Marlene J. Anderson, Box 69., Park Ave., Wycombe 18980 (outside Phila.). 215—598-7229. p.d.s.

VA Mrs. Roberta A. Jones, 14433 St. Germain Dr., Centreville 22020. 703—830-1028. p.d.

VA Mrs. Arthur W. Stowell, 5501 Virginia Beach Blvd., Virginia Beach 23462. 804—497-8030. p.d.s.

BLOODHOUND

NY CRAGSMOOR K'S. Matthew H. Stander, Henry Rd., Cragsmoor 12420. 914—647-8330. p.d.s.

ND Mrs. Vincent Brey, RR 1, Grand Forks 58201. 701—772-0617. p.d.s.

BORDER COLLIES

OH BRADFORDS' BORDER COLLIES are professionals, for herding, obedience work or companion dogs. Puppies, the latest in the best of bloodlines. R.D. 4 Wooster 44691. 216—264-4168 or 419—368-4124.

BORDER TERRIER

CT DALQUEST K'S. Reg., Margery B. Harvey & Marjory L. Van der Veer, R.R. 1, Box 276, North Windham 06256. 203—455-9150. p.d.s.

VA LITTLE FIR. Mr. & Mrs. David Van Gordon Kline, 8428 Old Mt. Vernon Rd., Alexandria 22309. 703—360-5457. p.d.s.

BORZOIS

CA WANT A WINNER; RANCHO GABRIEL'S 54 Champions are proof of the pudding. Gillette, 9020 Robbins Road, Sacramento 95823. 916—383-7671.

FL KALINKA BORZOI. Paul & Francoise Einstein, 7451 S. W. 47th Court, Miami 33143. 305—661-8103. p.d.s.

IN ZENCOR FARMS. Asa Mays, Jr., D.V.M., Route 11, Box 280-C, Bloomington 47401.

KS Donna S. Jewell, 3025 Lawn Silver Lake Rd., Topeka 66618. 913—235-1233. p.d.s.

MA JARI KENNELS. Jane E. Goulsten, 401 Village St., Medway 02053. 617—533-2590. p.d.

MI VALA RAMA K'S. Mrs. Grace D. Conally, 1310 Joliet Place, Detroit 48207. 313—963-6139. p.d.s.

NH GWEJON FARM. Mr. & Mrs. John M. Pinette, Winter St. Extension, R.F.D. #1, Claremont 03743. 603—542-6258. p.s.

NJ PHAEDRIAN. Frances Kubiak, New Road, Monmouth Junction 08852. 201—329-6879. d.s.

NY Dr. Roxann Schaubhut, 678 Union Blvd., West Islip 11795. 516—661-6560. p.d.s.

TX Emile & Carolynn Gilutin, 504 Myers Drive, Lake Dallas 75230. 214—363-2421.

TX JOBI K'S. Est. 1960. 18 Champions. Mrs. J. Bartholomay Jelke, 6625 Deihl Rd., Houston 77018. 713—462-6418. p.d.s.

VA Nancy O. Werlich, 301 N. Quaker Lane, Alexandria 22034. 703—370-1713. p.d.

BOSTON TERRIER

MD MAR-SAM KENNELS, Reg. Mrs. Samuel (Marie C.) Hawkins, Box 409, Ritchie Highway, Pasadena 21122. 301—766-8187. p.d.s.

MD DEN DOR EL, Reg. Dorothea L. & Erle W. Howard, 5878 Montgomery Rd. Elkridge 21227. 301—796-3321. p.d.s.

MA KORTNI K'S. Marsha L. Palmer & Joan E. Brennan, 406 Treble Cove Rd., N. Billerica 01862. 617—6743. p.s.

NY Harry M. Grifka, 84 Dart St., East Rockaway 11518. 516—LY 3-6147. p.

NY STAR Q BOSTON TERRIERS. INC. Dr. K. Eillen Hite, 215 E. 80th St., New York 10021. 212—BU 8-2283. p.d.s.

NY Elsie Peters, 10 Table Lane, Hicksville 11801. 516—796-3290. p.s.

PA STORMCREST, Reg. Dolores M. Surochak, Box 272 B, R.D. 2, Weatherly 18255. 717—427-8343. p.d.s.

RI Elaine L. Wheeler, 716 Post Rd. Warwick 02888. 401—467-4194. p.d.

BOUVIER DES FLANDRES

NY VLAANDEREN BOUVIERS, Reg. Sandi & Ralph Goldman, Boutonville Rd., Box 158, South Salem 10590. 914—763-3631. p.

PA DU CLOS DES CERBERES. Est. 1932. Belgium, 1942 U.S.A. Miss E. F. Bowles, Belco Farm, R.D. 2, Collegeville 19426. 215—489-2841. p.d.s.

PA Gladys & Carl May, R.D. 2 Box 52, Glenmoore 19343. 215—269-5490. p.s.

PA HANOVER FARM KENNEL. Dr. & Mrs. C. J. Bodarky, Hanover Farm, R.D. 1, Perkiomenville 18074. 215—754-7330. p.d.s.

PA Liliana B. Mees, 1200 Estate Drive, West Chester 19380. 215—692-6246. p.s.

SC BIBARCY. Reg. Est. 1950. Arthur M. & M. E. Pedersen, RR

#2, Box #542, Gaffney 29340. 803 489-1254. p.d.s.

CAN FLANDERS FIELD K'S. LTD. Dr. and Mrs. E. Houttuin, 570 Hazelhurst Road, Mississauga (Clarkson) Ontario. 416—822-5134. p.d.s.

BOXER

CT Richard & Jean McNickle, RFD 2, Box 519-A, Ledyard 06339. 203—536-0333. p.d.s.

CT AMRI BOXERS. Est. 1960. Mrs. Anne Marie H. Rowe, 165 Pilgrim Lane, Stratford 06497. 203—378-3873. p.d.s.

IL MY-R BOXERS. Lorraine C. Meyer, 807 Fairview Blvd., Rockford 61107.

ME THE EASTWOOD'S. 112 York St., York 03909. 207—363-3705. p.

MD MERRYWEY K'S. Miss Thelma V. Francis, 1601 S. Rolling Rd., (Relay) Baltimore 21227. 301—242-8161. p.d.s.

MN JADO K'S Mr. & Mrs. Christopher Healy, Route 2, New Ulm 56073. 507—354-5587. p.d.

NB WILLOW-RIDGE BOXER K'S. Dorothy Anderson, P.O. Box 27, Wahoo 68066. 402—443-3280.

NJ ELDIC K'S. Reg. Est. 1934. Mr. & Mrs. Richard Haeberle, Jr., Lees Hill Rd., R.D. 1, Basking Ridge 07920. 201—539-5555 or 539-2230. Jane Forsyth, Hdlr. p.d.s.

NJ TAWNY OAKS BOXERS, Reg. Ted & Joan Popadaniec, 19 Whitman St., Bloomfield 07003. 201—338-6143. p.d.

NJ HEN-RE'S BOXERS. Henry & Reta Emenecker, Sr. 79 E. Main St., Marlton 08053. 609—983-0303. p.d.s.

NJ RONEL BOXERS. B. R. & Eleanor Erickson, 155 Locust Drive, Union 07083. 201—688-0549. p.d.s.

BRIARD

CA Mrs. R. H. Englehart, 5868 Deerhead Road, Malibu 90265. 213—457-9697. p.

CA Mrs. Herman Ludwig, 9466 Riverview Ave., Lakeside 92040 714—448-1379. p.

FL BREEZY KNOLL FARM. L. Rae Thompson, 2919 John Moore Rd. Brandon 33511. 813—689-1768. p.

MI Barbara L. Ruby, 3132 Woodland Ridge, Orchard Lake 48033. 313—851-2386. p.s.

OH Mr. & Mrs. S. L. Davidson, 1 Sylvan Lane, Cincinnati 45215. 513—761-9029. p.

OH Mr. & Mrs. Charles Vetrone, 810 Harriet Ave., N.W., Canton 44703. 216—455-4277. p.

PA Mr. & Mrs. William F. Genari, 1150 Princeton Drive, Monroeville 15146. 412—373-3538. s.

BRITTANY SPANIEL

NM SPORTSMAN K'S. Puppies, excellent show and field championship pedigree. Liver & Orange, also trained dogs, Rt. 1, Box 212-S Las Cruces, 88001. 505—524-7908. p.d.s.

NY ROYALWIRTH K'S. Richard E. Wirth, 6203 Royalton Center Rd., Akron 14001. 716—542-9123. p.d.s.

PA Alicia A. Graham, 5235 Elmwood, Pittsburgh 15223. 412—882-8487. p.d.

PA Herbert W. Krumrine, 12 Reid Rd., R.D. 2, Coatesville 19320. 215—384-4619. p.d.

BRUSSELS GRIFFON

CA Richard A. Ball, 1637 W. El Segundo Blvd., Gardena 90249.

KY FABEL K'S. A. J. Carter, Jr., 1810 Pershing Ave. Louisville 40222. 502—426-5617. p.d.s.

MD MERRYWEY. Est. 1934. Miss Thelma V. Francis, 1601 S. Rolling Rd., (Relay) Baltimore 21227. 301—242-8161. p.d.s.

MD Howard S. Smith, Rt. 6, Box 133, Westminister 21157. 301—795-4495. d.

NY Miss Iris de la Torre Bueno, 400 Pelham Rd. New Rochelle 10805. 914—NE 2-2814. p.s.

NY GOLIGHTLY. Richard & Barbara Thomas, 1 West 67th St., New York 10023. 212—362-6700. p.d.s.

ENGLAND GAYSTOCK GRIFFONS. Mrs. Deborah Gaines, 27, Blandys Hill, Kintbury, Newbury, Berks. Phone: Kintbury 329

BULLDOG

IL IL LAKEVIEW K'S. Est. 1969. Bud Havens, Rt. 1, Elkville 62932. 618—568-5251. p.d.s.

KY Lewis & Emma Hatfield, Tates Creek Pike, Route 5, Box 25, Nicholasville 40356. 606—272-4049. p.d.

MA PILGRIM K'S. Est. 1948. (English Bulldogs). Earle D. Iveson, #45 Whiting Street, Hingham 02043. 617—749-1850. p.d.s.

NJ Mr. & Mrs. Robert A. Hetherington, Jr., 1 Pulis Ave., Mahwah 07430. 201—891-5723. p.d.s.

NJ ROMED BULLDOG K'S. Reg. Edgar G. E. Moss, R.D. 2, Box 535, Flemington 08822. 201—782-7619. p.d.s.

NY WAUGH'S. Reg. Mrs. Randall Waugh, 2 Hillcrest Drive, Box 143, Briarcliff Manor 10510. p.d.s.

NY Charles A. Westfield, Jr., 123 West Rogues Path, Huntington 11743. 516—692-7460.

NY Mr. & Mrs. David Wetherell, 1194 Seneca Creek Rd. West Seneca 14224. 716—674-8277. p.s.

TX Keith & Nancy Criss, Rt. 3, Box 225, Gatesville 76528. 817—865-7630. p.d.s.

VA Mr. & Mrs. R. G. Stockton, 1106 S. Albermarle Rd., Sterling 22170. 703—471-1727. p.d.

WA Bob & Carol Thoreson, 20718 N. E. 83rd St., Vancouver 98662. 206—892-0947. p.d.s.

WI Mr. & Mrs. Larry Nelson, Box 66, 620 Schofield St., Chetek 54728. 715—924-3267. p.d.s.

BULLMASTIFF

CA ROYALGUARD K'S. Sharon L. Sunberg, 18310 Cajalco Road, Perris 92370. All breeding stock OFA certified. Puppies Guaranteed. 714—689-0670. p.d.s.

MA Lucy Rowland, 154 Brattle St. Cambridge 02138. 617—354-5077. p.

NH BLACKBIRCH FARM.

Robert & Janet Treat, W. Nottingham 03291. 603—942-8160. p.d.s.

NJ Mr. Jeffry Glaser, 4 Rock Ledge Rd., R.D. 3, Randolph 07801. 201—361-1540. p.s.

PA Joseph E. Wisotzkey, Crow's Nest Lane, York 17403. p.d.s.

BULL TERRIER

IL Mrs. Anita Bartell, 9 Overlook Drive, Golf 60029.

PA BANBURY. Mrs. M. P. Mackay-Smith, R.D. 4, Box 548, Coatesville 19320. 215—486-0667. p.d.s.

PA Mrs. Brenda D. Weintraub, General Delivery, Fort Loudon 17224. 717—369-4453. p.

CAIRN TERRIER

THE CAIRN TERRIER CLUB OF AMERICA. For information and names of breeders, write Ross A. Obenauer, Secy. 15 Lakeview Circle, Skaneateles, NY 13152.

CA Doris & Baker Harris, 9786 Hawley Rd., El Cajon 92021. 714—445-5347. p.d.s.

CT Mrs. Luanne Klepps Craco, 30 Linden Lane, Madison 06443. 203—245-4845. p.d.

IL CRAIGDHU K'S. Mary S. Allen, 538 River Lane, Loves Park 61111.

KY CLACHMACUDDIN CAIRNS. Reg. Catherine J. Walls, P.O. Box 1117, Henderson 42420. p.

MS Mrs. Joe Marcum, Rt. 1, Box 44A, Clinton 39056. 601—924-0204.

NH SHEA-D-WILLOW K'S. Reg. Mr. & Mrs. Peter L. Shea, RFD 1, Weare Rd. Goffstown 03045. p.d.

NJ COILTRAG K'S. Gertrude & Paul Arata, Jr., R.D. 1, Box 250, Egg Harbor 08215. 609—965-1142. p.d.s.

NY ALBANOCH CAIRN TERRIERS. John J. Reynolds & Miss Alice T. Reynolds, 7312 Fifth Ave., Brooklyn 11209. 212—833-2098. p.d.s.

NY HAPPICAIRN. Susan Wofsey, 1116 Third Ave., New York 10021. 212—RE 4-5013. p.

NY Janet E. Sternberg, 3 Simmons Rd., Perry 14530. 716—237-2322. p.d.s.

OR Julia E. Hague, Rt. 1, Box 49A Beavercreek 97004. 503—632-3522. p.d.s.

PA John & Barbara Butchkoski, RD 3, Box 371, Stroudsburg 18360. 717—629-0838. p.d.s.

CANAAN DOG

(Not Recognized by the AKC)

MI BETH MA EMUNAH CANAANS. Mrs. Judith K. Ardine, 12568 Lakefield Rd., St. Charles 48655. 517—642-8776. p.s.

PA SPATTERDASH K'S. IKC Reg. Est. 1957. Jay C. Scheaffer, 2017 Chestnut St., Emmaus 18049. 215—965-4315. p.d.s.

CAVALIER KING CHARLES SPANIEL

KY SUTHERLAND K'S. EKC Reg. Est. 1957. Mrs. George Garvin Brown, Sutherland, Prospect 40059. 502—228-1171. p.

MA TARRYON CAVALIERS. Mrs. David H. Burnham, Hull House, Hull 02045. 617—925-9472.

ME KILSPINDIE CAVALIERS. Reg. EKC, Elizabeth I. Spalding, 190 Mountain Rd., Falmouth 04105. 207—797-3650.

NJ DIJERS CAVALIERS. Dr. & Mrs. Jerry Roseff, 1200 W. Cross St., Lakewood 08701. 201—364-1121.

NY MONT D' OR, Ann & Richard Golden, 53 Glenndale Drive, Oyster Bay Cove, L.I., 11771. 516—922-9344 or 45.

CHESAPEAKE BAY RETRIEVER

DE NEMOURS K'S. Reg. William D. Mathewson, Montchanin 19710 302—478-2673 or 655-2256. p.s.

MD Janet P. Horn, 18400 New Hampshire Ave., Ashton 20702.

NY FOREST VIEW. Dolores Lumsden, Marathon 13803. 607—849-3991 or 3915. p.d.s.

CHIHUAHUA

CA Candice & Bettie Lauber, 4038 47th St., San Diego 92105. 714—281-4875. p.

CT TERRYMONT. Reg. Herbert & E. Ruth Terry, 20 Blue Ridge Lane, Wilton 06897. 203—227-3177. p.d.s.

NY FOREST VIEW K'S. Ella M. Atkinson, Marathon 13803. 607—849-3915 or 3991. p.d.s.

CHOW CHOW

KS CISSY BOO K'S. Dr. Merle A. Hodges, 850 So. Santa Fe, Salina 67401. 913—827-5829.

MD PANDEE. Dr. I. P. Earle, Greencastle Rd. Laurel 20810. 301—776-7763. p.d.s.

TX CLAR-ELL-MO K'S. Clarence H. Moss, 214 Thorain Blvd., San Antonio 78212. 512—826-8115. P.d.s.

WI Harold & Adie Toudt, 5519 Highway 67, Dousman 53118. 414—965-2242. p.d.s.

CLUMBER SPANIEL

CT Mrs. Patricia L. Petrone, 20 Greenwood Ave., Darien 06820. 203—329-9282. p.s.

COCKER SPANIEL—ASCOB, BLACK, PARTI

AZ Dr. & Mrs. Benjamin Herman, 3451 Camino Suerte, Tucson 85715. 602—296-2129. p.d.s.

FL Hugh & Pat Campbell, Rt. 3, Box 668, Dade City 33525. 904—588-3614. p.s.

IN SANSTAR. Reg. Irene L. Peacock, 353 Grace Drive, Richmond 47374. 317—973-1162. p.d.s.

MD Donald Crawford, Jr., 3700 Milford Ave., Baltimore 21207. 301—664-8750. p.

MI LANCER K'S. Ron & Gloria Lancaster, 30 Wright, Kincheloe AFB 49788. 906—495-5836. p.d.s.

MI WEE WOLFE COCKERS. Reg. Mr. & Mrs. Spencer W. Wolfe, 510 Hillson Dr., Pontiac 48054. 313—681-3067. p.d.

MO SILVER MAPLE K'S. Reg. Ruth & Lee Kraeuchi, 2022 N. Ballas Rd., St. Louis 63131. 314—965-1630. p.d.s.

NJ GING'S. Lloyd W. Alton & Bill Gorodner, 957 East Glen Ave., Ridgewood 07450. 201—444-7216. p.d.s.

NJ Shirley D. & Felix Page, 3 Locust Court, Old Bridge 08857. 201—257-6565. p.d.s.

NY STONEHEDGE. Mary Elizabeth Gorr (Mrs. Richard H.) R.D. 4, Box 345, Katonah 10536. 914—CE 2-4269. p.d.s.

NY F. Leslie & Elaine C. Pinkowski, 2456 Fix Rd., Grand Island 14072. 716—773-4700. p.s.

NY DEBUT. Patricia Ann Swanson, 2390 Clair Ct., Yorktown Hgts.10598. 914—245-4789.

OH Louise Melneczyn, RR 6, Box 129, Lake Choctaw, London 43140 614—852-9753. p.d.s.

RI THURLYN ACRE K'S. Reg. Mrs. Thurston Steele, 595 Division St., East Greenwich 02818. 401—884-9530. p.d.

CAN. Mrs. Livia M. Whittall, 6226 Summit Ave., West Vancouver, British Columbia 604—921-9251. p.d.s.

COLLIE

AZ ASIL COLLIES. Lynn F. Davis, 5540 W. Windsor Ave., Phoenix 85035. 602—247-4036. p.d.s.

CT VERN HILL K'S. Reg. Ted & Ethel Mike, Cedar Swamp Rd., Coventry 06238. 203—643-9633 or 742-9478. p.d.

IN RUFLANE, Reg. Mr. & Mrs. Hans Boehringer, 242 Horn Rd., RR #6, Valparaiso 46383. 219—462-5275. p.d.s.

MA Carol E. Stuart, 440 Newman Ave. Seekonk 02771. 617—336-8228. p.

MD SILCREST K'S. Reg. Warren & Louise Johnson, Rt. 1, Box 163, Brandywine 20613. 301—888-1186. p.d.

MD COSMOS WORLD OF COLLIES. Reg. Mrs. Miriam Zilist, 15105 Cosmos Ct., Rockville 20853. 301—929-1412. p.d.

MS Ann W. Holbrook, 17 Sherman Ave., Pass Christian 39571. 601—452-9984. p.

NH GOLDMONT COLLIES. Evelyn L. Coburn, Winchester 03470. 603—239-6637. p.d.s.

NJ BRACH ERIN COLLIES. Patricia R. Ickes, R.D. #2, Stoney Corner, Stockton 08559. 201—996-2873. p.d.

NY HIGHBURN. Reg. William & Barbara Burns, 52 Phillips Ave., Highland 12528. 914—691-7994. p.d.

OR Ralph & Frances Burns, Dunroamin Ranch, Vida 97488. 503—896-3216. p.d.

CH. CO-SETT'S ZEPHYR LYNN

CO-SETT KENNELS, REG.

"Cockers with Personality"

Red-Buff-Black-Parti-Color

Puppies & Grown Dogs
for Pet, Show, or Breeding

EDWARD S. & LEDA E. FRY
P.O. Box 241 Lake Orion, MI 48035
(313) 693-8687

TWYNEFF KENNELS

BREEDERS OF CHAMPIONS IN ALL 3 COCKER SPANIEL VARIETIES

OFFERED AT STUD

CH. TWYNEFF PETER GUNN (pictured)

CH. TWYNEFF STARSHOOTER R/W
Sired by our top producing **CH. STONEWALK SHARPSHOOTER**

CH. MARPET BEACHCOMBER BUFF
Sire of 12 Champions, Buff and Black

Pedigrees and fees available on request

Puppies available occasionally - Reservations are recommended to secure the sex and variety desired

Rt2, Box 185 Antioch, IL 60002 (312) 395-0554

PA HICKORYBROOK FARM. Est. 1968. Howard & Pat Buerger, P.O. Box 304. Chalfont 18914. 215—249-3301. p.d.s.

PA Myrna Bizzarro, RD #4, Brooks Rd., Meadville 16335. 814—337-8134. p.d.

PA MYSTIC HILL COLLIES. Reg. Patricia A. Leonard, RD 1, Box 264, Edgemont Twp., Glen Mill 19342. 215-459-5002. p.d.s.

DACHSHUND

NATIONAL MINIATURE DACHSHUND CLUB INC., 2031 Lake Shore Blvd., Jacksonville, Fla. 32210. Smooth, Longhaired, Wirehaired AKC Reg.

CA DISTLEFINK. Barbara L. Powers, 4900 Glenalbyn Dr., Los Angeles 90065. 213—223-7040. p.d.s.

CA TRI-IVORY K'S. Sheila Farrington, 170 Nardi Lane, Martinez 94553. 415—228-3069. p.d.s.

CT MOOREHOPE K'S. Mr. & Mrs. W. H. Blair, 27 Pecksland Road, Greenwich 06830. 203—661-1967. p.d.s.

CT WILDEE'S. Diane Mae Coon, R.F.D. #5, Spicer Rd., Norwich 06360. 203—887-0910. p.s.

CT PATCHWORK. Miniature Longhairs, Pat Beresford, RFD #3, Winsted 06098. 203—379-7209. p.d.s.

IA Mrs. William L. Sebring, R.D. 1, Cambridge 50046. 515—383-4416. p.d.s.

MA SAMANTHA'S K'S. Arnold & Joan Greene, P.O. Box 587, Lenox 01240. 413—433-3111. p.

NH HARMO K'S. Est. 1955. (Smooth & Wirehaired). Mrs. Anna H. Boardman, Milford Rd., Amherst 03031. 603—673-2200. p.d.s.

NJ Ethel Carr, 190 Elberon Ave., Paterson 07502. 201—278-8173. p.s.

NJ Ms. Joyce Derks, 518 N. Main St., Box 84, Elmer 08318. 609—358-3218. p.d.s.

NY VILLANOL. Reg. Mr. & Mrs. Gordon H. Carvill, Miller Rd., RD 1, East Greenbush 12061. 518—477-5266 or 477-9555. p.d.s.

NY Frank & Mary Castoral, 29-32 172 St., Flushing 11358. 212—461-7969. p.s.

NY TORI-JARICE MINIATURE DACHSHUNDS. Reg. Hilda, Tom & Jeanne Rice, 764 Wyngate Drive East, Valley Stream 11580. 516—825-8122. p.d.s.

OH WAGATOMO K'S. Reg. Dr. Miles K. McElrath, 2691 North Cassady Ave., Columbus 43219. 614—471-6138. p.d.s.

PA MARDACHS K'S. Reg. Marjorie J. Creasy, 65 N. Pioneer Ave., Shavertown 18708. 717—696-2948. p.d.s.

PA K. Ann Evans & Marge Wilson, RD 4, Box 186, Hummelstown 17036. 717—566-3295. p.d

VT ROSE FARM K'S. Reg. Mrs. Pierce Onthank, Rose Farm, Shoreham 05770. 802—897-7611. p.d.s.

DALMATIAN

AL Sandra Huisinga, Rt. 12, Box 482, Biram 35215. 205—681-3644. d.s.

GA GRANVILLE. Dr. M. E. & E. E. Grotefend, Green Acre Farms, P.O. Box 1022, Douglas 31533. 912—384-8192.

GA ATLANTIS DALMATIANS. Emily Hoover, 295 West Crossville Road, Roswell 30075. 404—993-7812. p.d.s.

IN Mr. & Mrs. Robert Ingalls, Box 21, Bedford 47421. 812—275-6129. p.d.

MA Wendy Ann Bellavance, 18 Walnut St., Rehoboth 02769. 617—222-2626. p.d.s.

PA Mr. & Mrs. Richard M. Keith, Kettle Lane Farm, Box 67, Furlong, Bucks Co. 18925. 215—794-7173. p.d.s.

PA Lucille P. Shive (Groomer), 2238 Locust Lane, York 17404. 717—764-2753. p.

RI DELTALYN DALMATIANS. Reg. Robert A. & Judith M. Rivard, 25 Reardon Ave., Riverside 02915. 401—433-1877.

VA GREEN STAR K'S. Mrs. Marjorie Doane, 8101 Ox Road, Fairfax Sta. 22039.

DANDIE DINMONT TERRIER

CT Bruce Greenwood, Winwood, Old Green Rd., Sandy Hook 06482. 203—426-4915. p.d.s.

IN DANCAWAY K'S. Mr. and Mrs. John R. Brant, Jr., RR #3, Box 134, Zionsville 46077. 317-873-2025. p.d.s.

LA CARNGORME. Mrs. Dora L. Evans, 105 Judy Street, Denham Springs 70726. 504—664-7162.

MA CHARLIESHOPE FARM. Robert G. Neuhardt, M.D. 10 Mulberry Lane, Northboro 01532.

NY CLIFFIELD K'S. Miss Sarah H. Swift, Indian Hill Rd., Bedford Village 10506. 914—BE 4-3536. p.d.s.

NY Elaine Diamond, 8 Payne Circle, Hewlett 11557. 516—374-6278. p.

DOBERMAN PINSCHER

CT David Bratter, 42 Mountain Farms Rd., West Hartford 06117. 203—233-1381. p.

LA JAYMARES. Mr. & Mrs. Manuel J. Miyares, 1309 Poinsetta Dr., Metairie 70005. 504—834-5177. p.d.s.

MA Arnold & Joan Greene, P.O. Box 587, Lenox 01240. 413—433-3111.

MA GOLDMEDAL. Reg. Barbara Zagrodnick, 20 State St., Chelmsford 01824. 617—256-0646. p.d.s.

MI Madeline M. Kahl, 33557 W. Jefferson, Rockwood 48173. 616—379-9684. p.d.

NC DUNELM K'S. Mr. & Mrs. Arthur B. Ferguson, 22 Lebanon Circle, Burham 27705. 919—477-2247. p.d.s.

NY DE BELLA K'S. Est. 1963. Mrs. Robert Slonim, 91 Gates Ave., Central Islip 11722. 516—234-1286. p.d.s.

NY BRANDENDORF. A. J. Meshirer, 2 Peony Drive, Massapequa 11758.

NY H.B. LANG'S K'S. Est. 1969. Henry & Elizabeth Langert, 29 Petty Lane, Medford 11763. 516—289-8481. p.d.s.

NY DAMASYN, THE HOUSE OF DICTATOR. Peggy & Bob Adamson, Damasyn, 157 Parkway Drive, Roslyn heights, Long Island 11577. 516—621-9358.

NY TZAR KAHN. Reg. Joe Correia, 632 Edgemere Ave., Uniondale 11553. 516—IV 1-8092. p.d.s.

OH Carol Wilson, 22905 Ruple Rd. Brookpark 44142. 216—234-8304. p.s.

PA EDELHALL. Reg. A. G. Martin, 811 Weil St., Bethlehem 18015. 215—865-4076. p.d.s.

PA RICHLO D'S. Est. 1968. L.A. Walter, Robinson Place-River Rd., Yardley 19067. 215—493-3247. p.d.s.

ENGLISH COCKER SPANIEL

AL Miss Nell Berry, 105 Roberts Ave. Gadsden 35901. 205—547-8188. p.d.s.

CA SEVARG K'S. Virginia Graves, 4340 Occidental Rd. Santa Rosa, 95401. 707—546-4364. p.d.

CA Georgia Elizabeth Hauser, 1645 Stanford St., Santa Monica 90404. 213—828-7257. p.s.

MA Katherine R. Davison, Green Rd., Bolton 01740. 617—779-2700.

MA June Sheldon, 38 Charlton Rd. Dudley 01570. 617—943-7206. p.

MA GRAECROFT. Mrs. Augustus F. Doty, Jr., 41 White Pond Road, Stow 01775. 617—443-9825. p.d.s.

MI MAPLE LAWN. Reg. Mr. & Mrs. H. W. Glassen, 4300 Stall Rd., Lansing 48906. 517—482-7622. p.d.s.

MT CARACHELLE ENGLISH COCKERS. Linda Cunningham, 3326 Ravalli Place, Billings 59102. 406—656-6690. p.d.s.

NJ SPRUCERUN. Reg. Patricia J. Detmold, P.O. Box 317, Glen Gardner 08826. 201—832-7398. p.d.s.

NJ ON TIME FARM, Reg. Mr. & Mrs. Seymour F. Prager, RD 2, Califon 07830. 201—832-2312. p.d.s.

NY WOODLEA DICROFT K'S. J. Dike & The C. Hintons, 352 Lanning Road, Honeoye Falls 14472. 716—624-3475. p.d.s.

NY Betty Batchelder, Closter Rd. Palisades 10964. 914—El 9-2134. p.d.

NY KENOBO K'S. Helga Tustin, R.D., Box 1986, Knollwood Rd., Syosset 11791. 516—921-2358. p.d.s.

PA Jessie M. Dike & Lucille T. Hinton, Rt. 2, Butler 16001. 412—287-8566. p.d.s.

PA KELLIGREW K'S. Mr. & Mrs. George Kattermann, 437 Upper Gulph Road, Radnor 19087. 215—688-8094. All stock X-rayed. p.d.s.

CAN. RANZFEL K'S, Reg. Miss Virginia L. Lyne, 5310 Fairhome Rd., R.R. 7, Victoria, B.C. 604—479-2115. p.d.s.

ENGLISH SETTER

AZ SOLHEIM RANCH. Est. 1964. Mr. & Mrs. A. D. Solheim, Star Rt. 2, Box 344, Cave Creek 85331. 602—992-6885. OFA Parents. p.s.

FL Norman I. Segal, 20500 N. E. 22 Jct., N. Miami Beach 33160. 305—931-3947. p.s.

IL MARGAND K'S. Mrs. Andrew E. Hawn, P.O. Box 362, Mt., Carmel 62863.

MA GRAECROFT. Mrs. Augustus F. Doty, Jr., 41 White Pond Road, Stow 01775. 617—443-9825. p.d.s.

MI Donald O. & Helga Bienz, 1005 E. North St., Albion 49224. 517—629-6180. p.s.

NY Mrs. Linda Goldstein, 275 Central Park West, New York 10024. 212—873-0879.

ENGLISH SPRINGER SPANIEL

IL BELMAREL K'S, INC. C. P. Zeno & Thais O. Ladas, 19701 Governor's Highway, Homewood 60430. 312—798-3494. p.d.s.

IA Merle H. & Sally J. Ihne, Grandview 52752. 319—729-2261. p.d.

MA Reed F. Hankwitz, 419 Elm St., So. Dartmouth 02748.

MA WICK'S. Reg. Clifford L. Wedlock, 68 Concord Rd., Wayland 01778. 617—358-4843. p.

NJ Mrs. Harold E. (Patricia) Hanull, 9 Cresthill Rd., Trenton 08638. 609—882-9157. p.

PA WINGOVER. Benning & Edwards, Wingover Farm, Bethlehem Pike, RD 1, Ambler 19002. 215—643-1555 or 4358. p.d.s.

PA WAKEFIELD K'S. Mrs. W. J. Borie, Brushtown Rd., Gwynedd Valley 19437. 215—MI 6-3367. p.d.s.

PA HOLLY HILL K'S. Mrs. Kurt Semke, Pike-land Rd., R.D. 1, Malvern 19355. 215—935-9262. p.d.s.

PA JAYNE'S ENGLISH SPRINGER SPANIELS. Reg. Jayne E. & Paul M. Lowy, Cindy's Bark King Ranch, RD 2, Box 481, Washington 15301. 412—746-1611. p.d.s.

ENGLISH TOY SPANIEL

GA GODRIC K'S. Miss Miriam O. Goodridge, 6134 Rockbridge Rd., Stone Mountain 30083. 404—469-9012.

NY FOTHERINGAY. Reg. Bronwyn Thomas, 1 West 67 St., New York 10023. 212—362-6700. p.d.s.

FLAT COATED RETRIEVERS

CO CH-SIRED FLAT-COATS for family, show & field. Send for brochure. Sally J. Terroux, 14601 W. 72nd Ave., Golden 80401. 303—424-7703. p.d.s.

ATHERCROFT FLAT COATED RETRIEVERS

Home of history making - Bitch First **Best in Show** Flatcoat

"CH. ATHERCROFT BLAC IS BEAUTIFUL"

Puppies occasionally - Ch. Stud Service available

GLENN S. & BARBARA M. CONNER
1248 Gordon Rd.
Lyndhurst, OH 44124
(216) 461-5179

FIELD SPANIEL

VA GUNHILL. P. Carl Tuttle, Gunhill Farm, Rectortown 22140. 703—364-2509. p.d.s.

FOX TERRIER, SMOOTH

FL James R. & Carmen Gipson, 5411 Roosevelt Blvd., Jacksonville 32210. 904—384-6210. p.d.s.

NY SHOON. Martha Dildilian (Mrs. Ara T.), Old Trail, Fonda 12068. 518—853-3063. p.d.s.

FOX TERRIER, WIRE

CT George F. Skelly, 24 Woodford Dr, Bloomfield 06002. 203—242-6626. p.d.

FL TERRIKANE. Reg. Mr. & Mrs. John F. Kane, 22445 SW 127 Ave., Miami 33170. 305—248-5310. p.d.s.

GA Dorothea Carvelas, 103 Shields Rd., P.O. Box 611, Stockbridge 30281. 912—474-2641. p.d.s.

LA LILI JAY'S. Reg. Mrs. A. J. Jones, 2219 Virginia Ave., Shreveport 71103. 318—423-5445. p.d.s.

MD Mrs. Eve M. Ballich, Valley Rd., Stevenson 21153. 301—486-7812. p.d.s.

MS Mr. & Mrs. J. R. Burger, 151 Belvedere Circle, Biloxi 39531. 601—388-3108. p.d.

OH DENRICK. Eileen L. (Mrs. Norman F.) Lamson, 19385 Bowman Dr., Strongsville 44136. 216—238-6075. p.d.s.

PA Charles E. & Jane B. Slep, 2105 Hayden Dr., Johnstown 15905. 814—255-3394. p.d.

VA RAYLU. Reg. Robert O. & Gene S. Bigelow, Box 195, Rt. 2, Grafton Br., Yorktown 23692. 804—877-2475. p.d.s.

VA WYNDSYR. Suzanne & Nicholas Vracas, 13133 Vineyard Way, Woodbridge 22191. 703—491-3945. p.d.s.

WV Elizabeth R. King, Rt. 5, Box 175, Martinsburg 25401. 304—267-2305. p.

FRENCH BULLDOG

CA LAURELWOOD K'S. Reg. Est. 1932. Betty G. Nordfelt, P.O. Box 577, Ripon 95366. 209—599-4423. p.s.

GERMAN SHEPHERD DOG

CA Bill & Cindy Aston, 9253 Henley Way, Sacramento 95826. 916—363-7119. p.

CT LLENROC FARM. Reg. Noel A. Benson, Sunset Hill, Bethel 06801. 203—744-4629. p.d.s.

CT TYRONE. Reg. Mrs. L. J. Knowles, Tyrone Farm, Pomfret 06258. 203—928-3647. d.

FL Mrs. Zoa L. Sommer, P.O. Box 171, Gainesville 32601. 904—475-1346. p.d.

IL AVANTE GERMAN SHEPHERDS. Nicholas & Marilyn Baffa, 3934 W. 75th Place, Chicago 60652. 312—582-6227. p.d.

IL Agnes B. Kreydich, 10420 S. Shristiana Ave., Chicago 60655. 312—233-5113. p.

MA Ruth & Bernard Jensen, 14 Kay St., No. Grafton 01536. 617—839-2772. p.

MA George L. & Carol A. Morse, 12 Helen Circle, P.O. Box 146, East Longmeadow 01028. 413—525-6088. p.s.

MT RAIN BOE SHEPHERDS. Ray & Lee Boe, 121 Brickyard Ln., Billings 59101. 406—259-6728. p.

NC Barbara J. Friesel, Rt. 4, Box 336, Goldsboro 27530. 919—778-1377. p.d.

NH Joan A. Quimby, Rt. 1, Box 270, Gossville 03239. 603—736-4705. p.d.

NJ BRILAN. Reg. Paul & Joan Bridenbaugh, 14 Rye St., Piscataway 08854. 201—463-0169. p.

NY WONDER DOG K'S, Inc., 95 Jersey St., W. Babylon 11704. AKC registered puppies and adult dogs for sale. 516—643-2330.

NY TOP OF THE SKY K'S. Irene & Barbara Lukacs, 4161 Covert Rd., Burdett 14898. 914—679-9438. p.

NY Hiland & Carolyn Newkirk, 12 Yerry Hill Rd., Woodstock 12498. 914—679-9438. p.

NY Robert A. Wright, 2608 Phillips Rd., Castleton 12033. 518—477-8469. p.d.

NY MAUR-MAY K'S. Reg. Maureen Yentzen, Box 843, Cortland 13045. 607—756-9165. p.d.

OH Elizabeth J. & Irvin D. Kelley, Milcor Acres, 4932 Kirby Ave., Cincinnati 45223. 513—541-3523.

OH WALD FENSTER. Dave & Nan Owitz, 25665 Cook Rd., Olmsted Falls 44138. 216—235-1880.

PA BEE JAY K'S. Est. 1951. Miss Betty J. Irwin, 32 E. Holland Rd., Holland 18966. 215—357-3563. p.d.s.

PA Margaret M. Megahan, 780 Belmont Ave., Williamsport 17701.

PA BARONBERG. Reg. Carolyn M. & Jerry W. Berkstresser, 584 Summit Terrace, York 17403. 717—845-1047. p.d.s.

TX MURPHAUS K'S. Mrs. R. E. Murphy, 1869 Chris Craft Dr., Grapevine 76051. 817—481-1753. p.d.s.

VA KINGLAND. Reg. Mrs. Edwin H. King, 3100 (West) Old Gun Rd., Midlothian 23113. 804—272-1321. p.s.

VA HEXENGASSE GERMAN SHEPHERDS. Mary F. & Deborah R. Wingate, Rt. 1, Box 165A, Browntown Rd., Front Royal 22630. 703—635-8747. p.d.

GERMAN SHORTHAIRED POINTER

CA MACHTOLFF K'S. Est. 1965 Dennis Machtolff, 30470 San Francisquito Cyn. Saugus 91350. 805—259-4560. p.d.s.

MA Mr. & Mrs. William J. Foley, 400 Lincoln St., Stoughton 02072. 617—344-6120. p.d.s.

VA GUNHILL FARM. P. Carl Tuttle, Rectortown 22140.

GERMAN WIREHAIRED POINTER

MI JAGERSBO. Reg. Est. 1928. Erik Bergshangen Jr., P.O. Box 67, Birmingham 48012. 313—MI 4 -7717. p.d.s.

GIANT SCHNAUZER

MI BRANDENBURG K'S. John Ashe, 29614 Greenland, Livonia 48154. 313—425-9088. p.d.s.

NY Mr. & Mrs. Heinrich Groth-Honigtal, 1583 Burns Rd., Angola 14006. 716—947-4200. p.d.s.

NY CAMOLI K'S. Louis T. Padavan, Box 127, Remsenburg 11960.

GOLDEN RETRIEVER

CA KAZAK. Mrs. Bernadette Ballanger, Rancho de Oro, 13865 Elizabeth Lake Rd., Leona Valley 93550. 805—724-5216. p.d.s.

CA Robert J. Collins, 17970 Hatton St., Reseda 91335. 213—939-8077. p.

CA Robert H. Dunn, 26850 Eastvale, Palos Verdes Peninsula 90274. 714—541-1242. p.s.

CA Bill & Joan Young, 3315 Concord Blvd., Concord 94519. 415—689-2505. p.d.s.

IA GLORYBEE. Ralph & Jean Madsen, Rt. 1, Dumont 50625. 515—857-3346. p.d.

NJ Dr. & Mrs. L. C. Johnson, 12 Sergeant St., Princeton 08540. 609—921-7722. p.d.s.

NJ Dan & Laura Snelling, 510 Steel Gap Rd., Somerville 08876.

NY JOLLY K'S. Dr. John B. Lounsbury, P. O. Box 593. Billings 12510. 914—677-5602. p.d.

NY Jeffrey G. Pepper, 21 Christopher Dr., New City 10956. p.d.s.

VT FINDERNE K'S, Reg. Est. 1954. Mr. & Mrs. R. N. Hargrave, South Londonderry 05155. 802—824-5450. p.d.s.

GORDON SETTER

CA AULD SOD K'S. Charles R. & Karen Gard, 551 Union St., Encinitas 92024. 714—753-4494. p.d.s.

CT GORDON HILL. Mrs. Roland (Muriel) C. Clement, 71 Weed Ave., RR 2, Norwalk 06850. 203—838-8619. p.d.s.

CT Judith A. Cohan, 328 West Shepard Ave., Hamden 06514. 203—288-7258. p.s.

MA CHERIDAN. Mr. & Mrs. Daniel W. Dunham, 1 Oneida Ave., East Falmouth 02536. 617 477-1320. p.d.

MD KADON. Reg. Kay Monaghan, Box 85, Dogwood Rd., Woodlawn 21207. 301—944-6630. p.d.s.

NY SANGERFIELD K'S. Jean S. Look, Margaret Sanger & Fred Itzenplitz, Church St., E. Randolph 14730. 716—358-4585. p.d.s.

NY Mrs. Stephen R. Austin, 94 Reist St., Williamsville 14221.

PA CAMERON K'S. Reg. H. L. & M. L. Metzger, P.O. Box 111, Sinnamphoning 15861, 814—546-7791. p.s.

PA HICKORY SMOKE K's. Reg. Mr. & Mrs. Allen Ruess, Jefferis Rd., RD 1, Downington 19335. 215—942-2211. p.d.s.

PA Harold J. Schuster, Glenwood Manor, Penn. Valley Terr., Morrisville 19067. 215—295-7329. p.d.

VA ROCKAPLENTY K'S. Mrs. W. W. Clark, Star Route, Box S-78, Maurertown 22644. 703—436-3362. p.d.s.

GREAT DANE

CA Richard & Sue Rudman, 4643 Third St., La Mesa 92041. 714—460-4643. p.

CT LAZYCROFT, Reg. Yvonne Crofts, Lazycroft Farms, Wyassup Rd., North Stonington 06359. 203—535-2813. p.d.

CT SHERIDANE K'S. Reg. Michael Sherman, Rt. 66, Hebron 06248. 203—228-9089. p.d.

FL PINE HOLLOW K'S. Reg. N. Leon Duffer & W. R. Ptomey, M.D., 5524 No. Palafox Hgwy., Pensacola 32503. 904—968-6595. p.d.

IL TAMERLANE K'S. Mrs. J. Bruce Morey, Rt. 3, Box 1379, St. Charles 60174. 312—584-5997. p.s.

LA Kitten Irene Cary, 501 Brockenbraugh Ct., Metairie 70005. p.d.

MD STRAWSER'S HARLEQUINS. A. B. (Mrs. Neil) Strawser, 19 Stanmore Court, Potomac 20854. 301—299-4165. p.d.s.

MI Shirley Lawler, 2012 S. Washington Ave., Saginaw 48601. 517—755-9004. p.d.

MT Cleve & JoAnn Runyan, Rt. 3, Troy 59935. 406—295-4099. p.d.

NJ Virginia Budis, 363 So. Maple Ave., Basking Ridge 07920. 201—766-2392. p.d.

NY BLUE SPRUCE Patie (Mrs. Sidney) Glanz, Gage Rd., R.R. #5, Brewster 10509. 914—279-3600.

PA BREEZY'S DANE VILLA. Mrs. Beverly Hammerly, R.D. 1, Box 157, Hamburg 19526. 215—562-4144. p.d.s.

PA KNAJAR. Marjorie J. Knapp, Box A143, RD 2, New Hope 18938. 215—794-7664. p.d.s.

GREAT PYRENEES

CT ZODIAC K'S. Home of Am. & Can. Ch. Quibbletown Leo-The Lion, Mr. & Mrs. Walter R. Moore, 568 Brewster St., Bridgeport 06605. 203—333-2010. p.s.

KS SOLEIL K'S. Reg. Est. 1943. Mr. & Mrs. Jack W. Magoffin, Rt. 1, Sterling 67579. 316—278-3386. p.d.s.

OH CHERIWOOD K'S. Est. 1967. Mr. & Mrs. James Reynolds, 5490 Hayden Run Rd., Amlin 43002. 614—876-5335. p.s.

WI Robert M. Brown, D.V.M., 3360 Jackson Drive, Jackson 53037. 414—677-2897. p.d.s.

GREYHOUNDS

MA Elsie S. Neustadt, M.D., P.O. Box 1185, Hanover 02339.

IBIZAN HOUNDS

(AKC Miscellaneous Classification)

IBIZAN HOUND FANCIERS & EXHIBITORS OF U.S. For information on the breed contact: Miss Kathy Anders, Corres Secty., Forge Village Rd., Grotto Mass. 01450. 617—448-2293.

AZ ISHTAR IBIZANS. Richard & Laura Edwards, 2430 East Mc-Dowell, Phoenix 85008. 602—273-0468. Eng. import at stud. p.

PA LOS PODENCO'S. Peg Hamilton Ozlek, 1713 Bustleton Pike, Churchville 18966.

IRISH SETTER

CA KAMRON IRISH SETTERS. Ron & Renee Taylor, 18119. Topham St., Reseda 91335. 213—342-1317. p.s.

GA WILEIRE IRISH SETTERS. Mr. & Mrs. Robert A. Bragg, P.O. Box 275, Gray 31032. 912—986-3818. p.d.s.

GA BAYBERRY. Reg. Mr. & Mrs. William C. Brooks, 1645 Meadow View Lane, N.E. Gainesville 30501. 404—534-7768. p.d.s.

GA HARMONEY LANE K'S. Mr. & Mrs. Richard E. Smith, Rt. 2, Batesville Rd., Woodstock 30188. 404—475-4380. p.d.s.

IL WARMHEARTH. Reg. Robert A. Lemke, 419 Marcy St., Ottawa 61350. 815—434-4865. p.

IL RED GLORY K'S. Andres A. & Patricia E. Veile, R.R. 5, Quincy 62301. 217—222-8786. p.s.

MA LEMAR'S SETTERS. Steven R. & Susan Martin, 272 Summer St., Duxbury 02332. 413—585-2404. p.

MI Miss Mary Therese Watters, 759 E. Savidge, Spring Lake 49456. 616—842-7996. p.d.

MS INTELLIGENT CHAMPION-BRED Irish Setter Puppies for show, field or pet. Todd Bobo, 1155 Oakhurst, Clarksdale 38614. 601—624-4380.

NJ WESTWIND. Reg. Luz Holvenstot, Westwind-Naughright Rd., Long Valley 07853. 201—876-3614.

NY HONEYROCK K'S. 1967. Janice E. White, Honeyrock Farm, R.D., Shilling Rd., Palmyra 14522. 315—597-5977. (evenings & weekends). p.d.s.

NY Paul & Joan Ferguson, RD 4, Cemetery Rd., Rome 13440. 315—865-4805. p.d.s.

OH BEARAGON'S. Henry & Christine Niedzwiecki, 36290 Kinzel Rd., Avon 44011. 216—934-6468. p.d.s.

RI EAST BAY K'S. Karl F. Correia, 33 Harbour View Ave., Bristol 02809. 401—253-4429. p.

VA SPIRETOP. Constance Lyons, 3720 Willard Rd., Chantilly 22021. 703—378-5439.

IRISH TERRIER

CA C. C. Honey, 16470 Wagon Wheel Dr., Riverside 92506. 714 687-4739.

MD Charles F. & Laureen Ritter, 550 W. Allegheny Ave., Baltimore 21204. 301—821-8869. p.

MD George Kidd, 15401 Seneca Rd., Germantown 20767.

RI COTTERYNNE. Reg. Margaret A. Conneely, 1 Mayfair Dr.,, Rumford 02916. 401—434-6000. p.

IRISH WATER SPANIEL

CA FRAN-OAKS K'S. Reg. Mrs. J. W. Francis, 659 Camino El Dorado, Encinitas 92024. 714—753-1707. p.d.s.

IRISH WOLFHOUND

CA FLEETWIND K'S. Louis J. Hall, 3293 Marina Drive, Marina 93933.

CO Paul W. Palmer, M.D., 13775 Vollmer Rd., Colorado Springs 80908. 303—495-2758. p.d.s.

MD GREYSARGE. Reg. Celeste Winans Hutton, Box 260, Falls Rd., Cockeysville 21030. 301—252-2239. p.d.s.

NJ Capt. & Mrs. Robert H. Lang, 1 Oriole Terrace, Sparta 07871. 201—729-7112. p.

VA TRALEE. Mary & John Donovan, 2117 Great Falls St., Falls Church 22043. 703—532-2770. p.

ENGLAND. SUNNINGDALE K'S. Eringdale Wolfhounds, Etchinghill, Kent, Lyinge 87501. p.

ITALIAN GREYHOUND

KS Father Robert E. Watson. P.O. Box 20, Walnut 66780.

MA RAYRIDGE ITALIAN GREYHOUNDS. Reg. Raymond V. Filburn, Jr., 8 B Street, Reading 01867. 617—944-1199. p.d.s.

PA Donna J. Kemper, RD 1, Box 139, Port Matilda 16870. 814—237-7407. p.d.s.

JACK RUSSELL TERRIERS
(Not recognized by the AKC)

NJ HAMILTON FARM K'S. Est. 1967. Jack Russell Terriers, puppies, stud service, also "Jack Russell Book". Mrs. H. L. Crawford, III. Gladstone 07934. 201—234-0126.

KEESHOND

CA STAR-KEES' KEESHONDEN. Mrs. Robin Stark, 15120 Montebello Rd., Cupertino 95014. 408—867-3659. p.s.

GA John S. Ragland, 3136 Clairmont Rd. N.E., Atlanta 30329. 404—636-3229. p.d.

CA WISTONIA K'S. Mrs. Nan Greenwood, 4302 Compton Blvd., Lawndale 90260. 213—676-6488.

IL KEESHOND CLUB OF AMERICA, Marilyn Miller, 1060 So. Plum Grove Rd., Palatine 60067. 312—359-3589. p.d.s.

PA FAIRVILLE KEESHOND K'S. Reg. Mrs. M. K. Goebel, RD 1, Chadds Ford 19317. 215—388-6422. p.d.s.

PA RUTTKAY KEESHOND K'S. 9 West Ridge Pike, Royersford 19468. 215—489-7358. p.d.s.

KERRY BLUE TERRIER

CA TONTINE-MORBLEU K'S. Lucille Myers & Raymond Perry. 9761 West 11th St., Santa Ana 92703. 714-531-7473. p.d.s.

CA FALCONMOOR K'S. Reg. Henry & Hella Herwig, 1049 E. Mission Rd., San Marcos 92069. 714—745-2759.

CA TOWNSHEND. Edith (Mrs. Herd) Izant, 8311 S. La Sierra Ave., Whittier 90605.

FL KERRYMEAR K'S. Mr. & Mrs. John A. Sisto, 8395 S. W., 186th St., Miami 33157. 305—235-6047. p.d.s.

NY TWINHILLS K'S. Jean B. & Edwin W. Underhill, Lakeview, Box 15, RFD #2, Katonah 10536. 914—666-8631. p.d.s.

NY Winifred Gordon, RD 2, P.O. Box 566, New Paltz 12561. 914—255-1105. p.d.s.

KOMONDOR

NJ Barbara Soldo, 16 Center Ave.,Matawan 07747. 201—583-9332. p.

KUVASZOK

AR VON ELFIN K'S. Kuvaszok for 30 years. Puppies/Show Potential, Future breeders. Pets (Companion, guardian, workers). Honestly represented. Priced and guaranteed accordingly. X-Ray program since 1954. Temperament a must. Intelligence the most. Beauty always. Phone: (Station) 501—623-7941. Correspondence c/o Margaret Hutchinson, Rt. 7, Box 224, Hot Springs 71901.

LABRADOR RETRIEVER

CA Ceylon & Marjorie Brainard, 9465 Santa Lucia, Atascadero 93422. 805—466-1458.

FL AMA'S LABRADORS. Don & Rhonda Zepetello, 4800 S.W. 36th Court, Hollywood 33023. p.d.s.

IL ROSEBROOK K'S. Barry D. Rose, Rose Lane, Marseilles 61341. 815—795-4930. p.d.s.

MD SPENROCK K'S. Reg. Mrs. Edwin A. Churchill, Chesapeake City 21915. 301—885-5900.

MA Allan & Jeanne M. Young, 81 Parliment Dr., Franklin 02038. 617—528-9749. p.s.

MI FRANKLIN LABRADORS. Reg. Mrs. B. W. Ziesson, Box 32, Franklin 48025. 313—626-2613. p.s.

MI WHISKEY CREEK K'S. Est. 1961. Charlotte B. Todd, Rt. 2, Hart 49420. 616—873-3034. p.d.s.

NM SPORTSMEN K'S. Puppies, excellent show & field, championship pedigrees, Black, yellow, chocolate also trained dogs. Rt. 1, Box 212-S Las Cruces 88001. 505—524-7908. p.d.s.

NY LINDENMERE. Reg. Rose Babrow, 616 Bread & Cheese Hollow Rd., Ft. Salonga 11768. 516—757-7780. p.d.

NY Donald R. Tilly, Rt. 22, Bedford Village 10506. 914—234-3324. p.d.s.

NY ABRACADABRA. Mrs. Arthur B. de Garis, Abracadabra, Millbrook 12545. 914—677-3836. p.d.s.

OH NICKOLAI. Bonnie & Nick Nichols, 1964 Buttermilk Hill Rd., Delaware 43015. 614—362-5189. p.d.s.

OH HOPEDALE LABRADORS. Marie S. Toth, 14419 Sperry Rd., Newbury 44065. 216—338-3388. p.

PA Mr. & Mrs. Clifford E. Clarke, 691 West Valley Rd., Straffard-Wayne 19087. 215—687-0559. p.d

PA WATERVILLE LABRADORS. M.A. Dempster, Chestnut Parkway at Bridge, Wallingford 19086. 215—TR 2-1058. p.

RI George F. & Louise H. White, P.O. Box 286, Charlestown 02813. 401—364-6277. p.d.

WI SHAMROCK ACRES K'S. Sally B. McCarthy, Rt. 1, Waunakee 53597.

LAKELAND TERRIER

OH Donald J. & Barbara Riter, 11110 Fowlers Mill Rd., Chardon 44024. 216—286-3670. p.d.s.

LHASA APSO

CA Ann Crawford, 297 Chorro St., San Luis Obispo 93401. 805—544-9735. p.

CA Ruth E. Suse, 306 Willow St., Pacific Grove 93950. 408—373-5863. p.

CA HUGHES KISMET K'S. Est. 1963. Robert W. & Letha Hughes. 11089 Oleander Ave., Fontana 92335. 714—882-3898. p.d.s.

CA SHALU LHASA APSOS Dick & Judy Newton, 14300 MacLay Court, Saratoga 95070. 408—876-1322.—proven p.d.s.

IL BLAMA LHASA APSOS. Reg. B. C. Turner, 36 West 245 St., Indian Mounds Rd., Rt. 3, Box 433, St. Charles 60174. 312—584-0739. p.d.s.

KY LANRIC'S K'S. Richard Whitney, 257 Delmont Ave., Louisville 40206. 502—895-3870. p.d.

MO JEREC K'S. Reg. Est. 1950. Mrs. Joan R. Ernst, 8200 East 67, Kansas City 64133. 816—356-3174. p.d.s.

NJ Marion E. Banga, 53 Glenroy Rd., Fairfield 07006. 201—227-1837. p.d.

NJ Mrs. Paul Morgan, 12 Village Rd., Florham Park 07932. 201—377-4789. p.d.

NJ Mr. & Mrs. Joe R. Reed, RD 6, Almond Rd., Bridgeton 08302, 609—692-7831. p.d.s.

NJ Barbara Soldo, 16 Center Ave., Matawan 07747. 201—583-9332. p.s.

NV KARMA LHASA APSO K'S. (Puppies Only.) Successor to entire HAMILTON FARM K'S. OF Apsos. 6976 La Cienaga, Las Vegas 89109. 702—736-3730.

NY DuRAH K'S. Joel S. & Miss Edythe Fishbach, 1047 Hendrix St., Brooklyn 11207. 212—649-0599 or 257-0764. p.s.

NY Mrs. Patricia B. DeWitt, 131 Lodge Ave., Huntington Station 11746. 516—549-3881. p.s.

NY BAIJAI K'S. Frank and Audrey Holder, Freedom Plains Road, Pleasant Valley 12569. Stud Service and Show puppies available. 914—635-3952.

NY Mrs. Carroll Matthews, 468 Pellett Rd., Webster 14580. 716—671-6465. p.d.s.

NY Mr. & Mrs. Lawrence Scheur, 52 Stoneledge Court, Williamsville 14221. 716—633-1673. p.s.

PA PEKAY. Reg. Mr. & Mrs. H. William Farrow, Jr., 4116 Goshen Rd., Newtown Square 19073. 215—EL 6-6737. p.d.s.

PA Mr. & Mrs. Norman L. Herbel, 1862 West Maple Ave., Langhorne 19047. 215—757-7627. p.d.s.

PA POTALA K'S. Pet & Show Stock. Ch. Stud Service. Keke Blumberg, 848 Winter Rd., Rydal 19046. 215—887-2936. p.d.s.

SC VINCENT, Frank M. Rt. 1 Box 460, Bonneau 29431. 803—899-6766. p.d.s.

VA Mr. & Mrs. Wilson J. Browning, Jr., 1337 West Princess Anne Rd., Norfolk 23507. 804—625-3527. p.d.

MALTESE

CT Mrs. Dodie Ready, 295 Old Sherman Hill Rd., Woodbury 06798. 203—263-4051. p.d.s.

CT NYSSAMEAD MALTESE. Susan Weber, Box 484. Tariffville 06081. 203—658-1891. p.s.

IN JOANNE-CHEN'S MALTESE Joanne Hesse, Box 9, R.R. 1, New Haven 46774. 219—749-5595. p. Ch.s. Breeder of Top-winning Maltese and 8 BIS Maltese.

MA ELYSIAN FIELDS MALTESE. Miss Sally R. Cushman, Smith's Point, Manchester 01944. 617—526-7695. p.d.

MA SUGAR TOWNE K'S. Reg. Claudette LeMay, 2570 Acushnet Ave., New Bedford 02745. 617—995-5324. p.d.s.

MI Shirley R. Pearson, 1530 Rotsel, Pontiac 48053. 313—334-8793. p.d.s.

NB Dr. & Mrs. Roger T. Brown, 1417 South 136 St., Omaha 68144.

NY Margarette (Peg) Vicedomini, 626 W. Buffalo St., Ithaca 14850. 607—272-2903. p.

PA FAIENCE K'S. Reg. Est. 1945 Russell I. Jackson, Grange Ave., Providence Square, R.D. 1, Collegeville 19426. 215—489-7029. Puppies for show & breeding. Ch. stud service.

PA SHELMAR K'S. Est. 1943. Ms. Claire B. Keyburn, California Rd., R.D. 4P, Quakertown 18951. 215—536-3966. p.d.s.

MANCHESTER TERRIER

NY Mrs. D.C. Eldridge, 719 Hoop St., Olean 14760. 716—372-0296. p.d.s.

OH Lucinda E. Gundecker, Toys, P.O. Box 181, Upper Sandusky, 43351. 419—294-1363 evenings.

SC Robert A. Treynor, Rt. 3, Box 560A, John's Island 29455.

VA LANGHOLM—"WILLOW-LEDGE", Reg. Est. 1956. Mrs. Eve C. Olsen, Owner, Haywood 22722. 703—923-4536. p.s.

MASTIFF

CA RAMSGATE MASTIFFS. Dr. & Mrs. Dwayne L. Nash, Ramsgate Ranch, 12686 N. Curry Rd., Lodi 95240. 209—368-2101. p.d.

MA GOLDSBURY HOUSE. George & Louise Foot, Athol Rd., Warwick 01378. 413—544-6483. p.

MN SPICE HILL FARM. Barbara Lambert, 8320 Hidden Bay Trail, St. Paul 55109. 612—777-4736. Puppies from Berngarth, English breeding.

PA BEAU CHEVAL FARMS. Est. 1958. Mrs. Marlene J. Anderson, Box 69, Park Ave., Wycombe 18980 (outside Phila.) 215—598-7229. p.d.s.

CAN. NORTHWOOD K'S. I. Ozols, 67 Newton Drive, Willowdale, Ontario. Masstiff puppies of the Highest Quality. 416—225-8227. p.

MINIATURE SCHNAUZER

CA Dolores Walters, 3058 N. Lima St., Burbank 91504. 213—843-4359. p.d.s.

CA SHREVE'S RANCH. De Canine Tree (formerly Der Ruff

House) Est. 1951. Ernest & Dorothy Shreve, 12417 Denholm Dr., El Monte 91732. 213—579-2791. p.d.s.

CT BISHOP'S FOLLY. Mrs. Mildred Bishop, Petticoat Lane, East Haddam 06423. 203—873-8460. p.

CO Kathleen (Mrs. Donald G.) Knight, 12601 W. 49th Ave., Wheat Ridge 80033. 303—422-2917. p.d.s.

IL Dr. Jeanette Schulz, 2 South 656 Bob-O-Link Rd., Lombard 60148. 312—627-5347. p.s.

MD Charles D. Heath, 130 Tulip Dr., Gaithersburg 20760. 301—926-4732. p.d.

MD Mrs. Robert Doud, 4101 Landgreen St., Rockville 20853.

NY Aileen & Richard Santo, Edge Rd., Muttontown 11791. 516—364-9366. p.d.s.

OH KALENHEIM SCHNAUZERS. Mr. & Mrs. Leonard J. Heim, 2481 Royalton Rd. West, Broad Hts., 44147. 216—237-6079. p.d.

PA Mrs. J. M. Deaver, Brook side Farm, 110 Shippack Pike, Ambler 19002. 215—646-3047. p.d.s.

PA Barbara Fields, 3205 Burn Brae Dr., Dresher 19025. 215—OL 9-3513. p.d.s.

PA SIM-CAL. Miss Theresa Klemencic, 350 Chess St., Bridgeville 15017. 412—221-5457. p.s.

PA ROBCORD MINIATURE SCHNAUZER. Donald R. Peacock, RD 2, Snake Hill Rd., Doylestown 18901. 215—794-8610. p.d.s.

PA "RYDALBROOK." Est. 1958. Mrs. Ann W. Kaeppler, Rydalbrook Farm, Box 286, Pineville (Near New Hope) 18946. 215—343-6787 or 598-3119. p.d.s.

VA Elizabeth G. Edwards, 1424 Rutledge Ave., Charlottesville 22901. 703—295-2038. p.d.

VA Betty F. McKenzie, 146 Hill Prince Rd., Virginia Beach 23462. 703—497-3330. p.d.

VT SPICEWOOD. Mrs. Raymond R. Hurley, Star Rt., Bennington 05201. 802—442-4769. p.d.

WI WALK-A-WAY. Carroll Schroeder, Rt. 7, Drier Rd., Eau Claire 54701. p.s.

NEWFOUNDLAND

CA PEPPERTREE. Penelope Buell, 1306 N. Fuller St., Los Angeles 90046. 213—874-5840. p.d.s.

CT LITTLE BEAR K'S. Reg. Est. 1948. Vadim Alexis Chern, Bear Hill Rd., R.D. 1, New Milford 06776. 203—354-3344. p.d.s.

MA NAUTILUS K'S. Est. 1963. Robert & Seba Gaines, Greencroft, Ayer Road, Harvard 01451. 617—722-0620. p.d.s. Breeding Stock X-Rayed Sound.

MABlack and Landsees Newf. Puppies available. Stud Service. Visitors welcome. Write ALLISON ACRES, Flat Hill Road, Lunenburg 01462 or call 617—582-6665.

MA WILDEWOOD K'S. Norman & Sandra Beberman, 136 Wilder Rd., Fitchburg 01420. 617—342-2333. p.s.

MA SHIPSHAPE K'S. Reg. Mrs. Wilma Lister, Shipshape, Bog Rd., Marstons Mills 02648. 617—428-8958. p.d.s.

PA SOJOWASE K'S. Reg. Mr. & Mrs. James G. Schmoyer, R.D. 1, Germansville 18053. 215—767-6934. p.d.s.

PA KELLIGREW K'S. Mr. & Mrs. George Katterman, 437 Upper Gulph Rd., Radnor 19087. 215—688-8094.

VT SEAWARD K'S. Reg. Est. 1932. Elinor C. Ayers, Johnnycake St., Manchester Center 05255. 802—362-2746. p.d.s.

VT RADCLIFFE K'S. Stamford 01247. 802—694-1420. Richard R. and Nancy MacMahon. Mailing address: Box 954, No. Adams, Mass. 01247. p.d.s.

NORWEGIAN ELKHOUND

MI Mrs. Edward S. Forsyth, G-9194. N. Genesee Rd., Rt. 1, Mt. Morris 48458. 313—686-7428. p.d.s.

MO HILLSIDE K'S. Patricia Kelso, Rt. 1, Box 65B, Dittmer 63023. 314—285-2241. p.d.s.

NH WATERFALL K'S. Reg. Est. 1941. Mr. & Mrs. H.S. Dunning, Valley Farms, Walpole 03608. 603—756-4777. p.d.s.

VA Sylvia J. Caricofe Sizemore, 10604 Vale Rd., Oakton 22202. 703—938-4157. p.d.s.

CAN KARIN K'S. Mr. & Mrs. Karl S Innes, R.R. 2, Taunton Rd. E., Oshawa, Ontario L1H 7K5. 416—725-8772. p.d.s.

NORWICH TERRIER

MD KING'S PREVENTION K'S. (Prick Ear). Est. 1950. Mrs. Sterling Larrabee, King's Prevention, Chestertown 21620. 301—778-3611.

PA RYLAND K'S. Reg. Mrs. Willard K. Griffiin 321 Conestoga Rd., Devon 19333. 301—647-5471. p.

OLD ENGLISH SHEEPDOG

AZ Gail H. Fletcher, 7674 East Sutton Drive, Scottsdale 85260—948-1225. p.s.

MA LONDON OLD ENGLISH SHEEPDOGS. Emily London, 19 Pine Hill Road, Framingham 01701.

MA WOOLNSPICE K'S. Dr. & Mrs. Alfred D. Weiss, Conant Rd., Lincoln 01773. 617—259-9394. p.d.s.

MI CRYSTAL'S K'S. Colleen Paro, 120 Crystal Ave., Crystal Falls 49920. Pedigree, etc. on request. 906—875-6685. p.d.s.

MI BANBURY K'S. Dr. G. L. Sparschu, 2379 Military, Port Huron 48060. 313—984-4166. p.s.

NJ John R. Castor, Box 488, Whitehouse Statio 08889. p.d.s.

NJ Steven & Maureen Silberman, 139 Rock Rd. W., Green Brook 08812. 201—753-7898. p.d.s.

NY Mrs. Jean Thorkildsen, R.D. 2, Lake Rd., Ballston Lake 12019. 518—399-5670. p.

NY Stan & Sue Mannlein, 959 Westwood Ave., Staten Island 10314. 212—761-6149. p.s.

OH Cassandra Moulton, 361 Eldridge Rd., Aurora 44202. 216—562-7188. p.s.

PA PAT CULLEN K'S. R.D. 1, Box 197, Northampton 18067. 215—262-2287. p.d.s.

VA WILDERNESS. Jim & Patricia Govenides, 224 Brakehead Drive, Fredericksburg 22401. 703—371-2608. p.d.

OTTER HOUND

NC BARDILL'S K'S. Est. 1952. Mrs. Barbara M. Dillard, Rt. 5, Box 287, Henderson 27536. 919—492-0396. p.s.

NY Jane W. Steinau, Cantitoe Rd., RFD #1, Katonah 10536.

PAPILLON

CT CADAGA K. Catharine Davis Gauss, 50 Oenoke Lane, New Canaan 06840. 203—966-0312.

IL REBOB K'S. R. M. Smith, 7945 Ogden Ave., Lyons 60534. 312—442-9511. p.d.

PEKINGESE

CA Mrs. Judith F. Anderson, P.O. Box 926, Los Altos 94022, 415—961-7746. p.d.

CT PALACEGUARD K'S. Mr. & Mrs. W. H. Blair, 27 Pecksland Road, Greenwich 06830. 203—661-1967. p.d.s.

NY Richard Del Grosso, 353 W. 56th St., New York 10022.

NY CARALEA. Reg. Mary E. Spicer, 1819 Jefferson Rd. West, Pittsford 14534. 716—586-0307. p.d.

OH CHANGDOM-PEKINGESE. William Jay Switzer, 320 Hanna Ave. - Apt. #4, Bldg. #1, Love land 45140. 513—683-6097. p.

PA SENEG.Betty L. Miller, R. R.D.4, Box 314, Greensberg, 15601. 412—668-2600. p.d.s.

PA FREELAND. Mrs. Matthew H. Imrie, Lahaska 18931. 215—794-8418.

PA CLAYMORE K'S. Mrs. Robert I. Ballinger, Jr., 454 S. Ithan Ave., Villanova 19085. p.d.s.

SD TIKUO. Patricia A. O'Shea, 1505 Suburban Drive, Sioux Falls 57101. 605—339-0913. p.d.s.

WA Anne L. & Melvin H. Samek, Rt. 7, Box 7378, Bainbridge Island 98110. 206—842-4156. p.d.s.

CAN. ST. AUBREY-ELSDON K'S. Nigel Aubrey-Jones, 4170 Decarie Blvd., Montreal, Quebec. 514—488-6279 or 435-9167. p.d.s.

PHARAOH HOUNDS
(Not recognized by the AKC)

NY BELTARA K'S. Mrs. Rita Laventhall Sacks, 3 Ivy Pl., Huntington 11743.

POINTER

NY RUSTIC WOODS. Imported English dogs at stud (U.S. & Can. Champions-Group Winners). S. & A. Novick, 10 Chelmsford Drive, Muttontown 11545. 516—626-1532. p.d.s.

POMERANIAN

CA Pauline B. Hughes, 1726 Crest Dr., Encinitas 92024.

FL SCOTIA. Reg. Edna E. Girardot, P.O. Box 646, Floral City 32636. 904—726-2001. p.d.s.

IA Mrs. Norris McKamey, R.R. 1, Box 185, Bettendorf 52722. 319—355-7775. p.d.

IL VARNEY'S K'S. Betty & Richard Varney, Cavalier line puppies: Show, Breeding, Pet, Champion Stud service, 2600 Duffy Lane, Deerfield 60015. 312—945-8311.

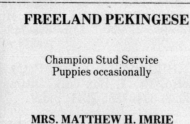

NC DORADO POMERANIANS. Carol A. Fama, 300 Pearch Orchard Dr., Greensboro 27405. 919—288-3215.

NJ GINGERBREAD K'S. Eugene L. Munson, 310 White Oak Ridge Rd., Short Hills 07078. 201—467-3439. p.

NY Peter A. & Maria C. Campbell, 37 Ave. D., Lake Ronkonkoma, L.I., 11779. 516—981-0527. p.d.

PA GLENARDEN K'S. Virginia K. Harris, R.D. 1, Mount Bethel 18343. 717—897-6808. p.d.s.

POODLE

AK PENALVER TOY POODLE'S Rebecca Penalver Weber, 5303 Eielson St., Anchorage 99502. 907—277-0093. p.s.

CA CHEZ-DORAL. Reg. Dorothy L. & Alfred E. Carlson, 29995 W. Mulholland Hwy., Agoura 91301. 213—889-6539. p.d.s.

CA Dr. Herbert I. & Merridy I. Cohen, 1525 Superior Ave., Newport Beach 92660. 714—642-0145. p.d.

CA Phillip W. & Barbara J. Glasscock, 17633 LeMay St., Van Nuys 91406. 213—345-9119. p.d.

CA Dorothy F. Hageman, 711 Furlong Rd., Sebastopol 95472. 707—823-2046. p.d.s.

CA Sarah G. Honig, 447 12th Ave., San Francisco 94118. 415—752-3568. s.

CA CHERAY. Reg. Miss Cherie Ellen Lempert, Montair Court, Danville 94526. p.

CA Alta E. Pierson, 2321 No. Santa Fe Ave., Compton 90222. 213—631-8798. p.d.s.

CA MAROSE K'S. Reg. Mrs. Harold Ringrose, 2450 Green St., San Francisco 94123. s.

CT AMOR POODLES. Judy Randi, 359 Third Ave., West Haven 06516. 203—933-8365. p.d.

DE ROUND TABLE K'S. (Miniature & Standard). Mrs. A.V. Keene, Box 44, RD 1, Middletown 19709. Quality Show puppies and Dogs usually available. 302—834-4662. p.d.s.

DE Wm D. McCorkle, 1409 River View Ave., Wilmington 19806. p.s.

FL NIKOLANE. Reg. Miss Saima S. Nikola, 1336-62nd Ave., So., St., Petersburg 33705. 813—867-4964. p.

MA Cynthia Becker, 60 Royal St., Allston 02134. 617—787-5140. p.

ME CIMEFLEURI. Reg. J. Melton Berube, Rt. 1, Box 74, Presque Isle 04769. 207—764-1259. p.d.s.

MD SUNSWEPT POODLES. Barbara P. Durst, Box 252B, Masemore Rd., Parkton 21120. 301—329-6464. p.d.s.

MD Marguerite & William Eaves I, 164 Sprint St. & Warns Lane, Frostburg 21532. 301—689-3003. p.d.

MD ANDECHEZ POODLES. Reg Blanche & Rebecca C. Tansil, Sunswept Lane, Rt. 1, Parkton 21120. 301—329-6318. p.d.s.

MD Dean & Joell Wright, Rt. 1, P.O. Box 83 G., Jarrettsville 21084. 301—557-7098. p.

NB PINAFORE K'S. Reg. Mrs. Philip J. Harney, 3315 N 80 St., Omaha 68134, 402—571-4868. p.d.s.

NH HARMO K'S. (Miniatures & Toys.) Mrs. Anna H. Boardman, Milford Rd., Amherst 03031. 603—673-2200. p.d.s.

NJ BLUE BELL K'S. Miniatures & Toys. Specializing in Apricots & Blacks. Mrs. Emily Wiech, 1558 Good Intent Rd., Deptford 08096. 609—227-2966. Puppies & young dogs available, also stud service.

NJ Mr. & Mrs. Robert E. Dunlap, 2327 Belvedere Drive, Scotch Plains 07076. 201—233-6865. p.d.s.

NJ SILVANDOR. Reg. Dorothy-Anne Griffin, 169 Summit Ave., Jersey City 07304. p.d.s.

NJ Mary O. Richardson, 418 South Columbia St., Woodbury 08096. 609—845-1296.

NY DEARBIT POODLES. Mrs. Edith A. Farrell, 6 Woolsey Ave., Bethpage L.I. 11714. 516—935-2083. p.d.s.

NY MAUXHURST. Reg. Miss Dereke (Derry) Jay Harvey, 200 Taxter Rd., Irvington 10533. 914-LY 1-8857. p.d.

NY JOURDAIN POODLES. Mrs. Henri Jourdain, 197 Roselle St., Mineola 11501. 516—747-6236. p.d.

NY HARIANN K'S. Reg. Ann & Harry Schneider, 7196 Lane Rd., Victor 14564, 716—924-3500. p.d.s.

PA Mr. & Mrs. Paul (Betty) Hollabaugh, 449 Woodlawn Ave., Sunbury 17801. 717—286-6672. p.d.

PA BLUET K'S. Marvin Mernick, 2765 Milford Lane, York 17402. p.d.

VA COPODO K'S (Standards). Wayne Quarles and Eugene Doebler, 11025 Oakton Rd., Oakton 22124. 703—385-8490. 8490.

WI SILVER SAND K'S. Reg. Betty L. Smith, R.R. 6, Box 105, Eau Claire 54701. 715—832-8216. p.d.s.

WI Dick & Carole Wallace, 808 LaFollette, Sponner 54801. 715—635-8191. p.

TX MEISTER PUDEL K'S. Reg. Dan & Marti Goodson, Sterling City Rt., Box 50, Big Spring 74720. 915—2634231. p.s.

FRANCE. DE LAMORLAYE K'S. Reg. in France. Est. 1935. Princess Amedee de Broglie, 41 Avenue Foch, Paris 75116. Tel:

727—8449. (Toys, Miniatures, Standards. Black, Brown, White, Silver.) p.d. Air Shipment to U.S.A. & all parts of the world.

PORTUGUESE WATER DOGS
(Not Recognized by the AKC)

PORTUGESE WATER DOG CLUB OF AMERICA (Portugese Kennel Club Registered and PWDCA registered) for information wirte: Mrs. Herbert Miller, Jr., Corres. Secy, "Farmion," 1 Greenley Road, New Canaan, Conn. 06840. 203—966-1997.

PUG

KS DONALDSON PUGS K'S. Wayne & Marie Donaldson, Garnett 66032. 913—448-3970. p.d.s.

MI Margaret Brown & Evelyn J. Brockway, Box 7, Douglas 49406. 616—857-2698. p.d.s.

MD MERRYWEY Est. 1934. Miss Thelma V. Francis, 1601 S. Rolling Rd., (Relay) Baltimore 21227. 301—242-8161. p.d.s.

MD FRECKLETON'S AERO. Ruth Freckleton, 6210 Auth Rd., Camp Springs 20023. 301—449-4495. p.d.s.

NY Elaine Diamond, 8 Payne Circle, P.O. Box 164. Hewlett 11557. 516—374-6278. p.

PA KOCH'S PUGS. Est. 1951. Miriam R. Koch, 7971 Grayson Rd., Harrisburg 17111. 717—564-1530. p.d.s.

PULI

CA HUNNIA K'S. Reg. Leslie & Klara Benis, 5845 Melvin Ave., Tarzana 91356. 213—345-2164. p.d.s.

CA Barbara Edwards, 105 Flying Mist Isle, Foster City 94404. 415—345-7959. p.d.

CT CEDWOOD. Ellanor H. Anderson 1155 Burlington Ave., Bristol 06010.

CT MARVIC K'S. Mr. and Mrs. Victor Stiff. Box 41, Canton Center 06020. 203—693-2377. p.

NH THE SKYSYL PULI K'S. Reg. Est. 1947. Mrs. Sylvia Curtis Owen, South Road, Canaan 02741. 603—523-4858. p.s.

OH Archie J. Bakay, 4645 Estes Drive, Kent 44240. 216—678-9467. p.s.

OH McMILLEN K'S. Ethel M. & Kyle F. McMillen, 7435 St. Peters Church Rd., N.E., Louisville 44641. 216—877-2794. p.d.s.

RHODESIAN RIDGEBACK

CA LION VISTA K'S. Chris & Janel Freed, 856 Barsby St., Vista 92083. p.d.

CA BATOKA K'S. Reg. Loraine H. Hulbert, 6304 Hickory Ave., Orangevale 95662. 916—988-1829. p.s.

CA DOUBLE E.E. RANCH. Mrs. Edith B. Kienast, P.O. Box 323, Woodland Hills 91364. 213—347-3897. p.s.

MA SHADYRIDGE K'S. Est. April 1961. Mrs. Ulla-Britt Ikengren, Groton Street, Dunstable 01827. 617—649-7020. p.d.s.

MA Ulla-Britt Ekengren, Groton St., Dunstable 01827. 617—649-7020. p.d.s.

MD ROLLING K'S. Reg. D. Jay Hyman, Rt. 109, Barnesville 20703. 301—948-5130. p.s.

NJ Suzanne C. & Frank J. Hills, Jr.,
Mine Mount Rd., Bernardsville 07924. 201—766-5490. p.s.

NJ Vonnabeth Thompson, 2 Bertrond St., Old Bridge 08857.

NY HOUNDS OF GRAYMOUR. Phyllis Lia, 46 Parker Ave., New City 10956. 914—634-2831. p.d.

NY KING HILL K'S. Susan P. & Thomas I. King, R.D. 1, Grace Moore Rd., Saratoga Springs 12866. 518—518-584-5615. Boarding. p.d.s.

OH KIMBIDA K'S. Reg. Est. 1967 Mrs. Ida Poore, Box 85, Gates Mills 44040. 216—423-3220. p.d.s.

SAINT BERNARD

CA Gloria F. & Lawrence S. Davy, Jr., 3148 Monterey St., Oxnard 93030. 805—483-3777. p.

IN Kenneth & Leona Rudisell, Rt. 6, Box 195, LaPorte 46350. 219—325-0413. p.

MA Mr. Edward A. Poor, Wheeler Lane, Acton 01720.

MA SERENITY HILLS K'S. John E. & Constance J. Brennan, Beaver Dam Rd., R.F.D. 1, Plymouth 02360. 413—224-8065. p.

MA KENBARK K'S. Reg. Kenneth & Patricia A. Greene, E. Grove St., Mtd. 6, Middleboro 02346. 617—947-9646 p.d.

MA Barbara & John Washburn, 168 Slater St., Attleboro 02703. 617—226-0554. p.d.s.

MD BILANE K'S. Bill & Anne Shockley, Box 365, R.D. 3, Elkton 21921. 301—398-6244. p.d.s.

NH CAVAJONE K'S. Reg. Bruce Crabb, Baboosic Lake Rd., Merrimack 03054. 603—424-5122. p.d.s.

NJ MON PLAISIR. Est. 1960, Joseph & Susanne Gagnon, Box 86, Route 579, Pattenburg 08860. 201—479-4536. p.d.s.

NY MONT D'OR. Ann & Richard Golden, 53 Drive, Oyster Bay Cove, L.I. 11771. 516—922-9344 or p.d.s.

NY VEDALYN. Daniel & Vera Lyons, 71 Eatondale Ave., Blue Point 11715. 516—363-6426. p.d.s.

NY DREHIL. Patricia Korn, 74 Croton Dam Rd., Ossining 10562.

OH GINJAC K'S. John & Virginia Howard, Box 287, Rt. 2, Centerburg 43011. 614—625-5464. p.d.s.

PA "SNOBELT SAINTS." Est. 1967. William & Kathleen Dunn, Box #88, Dallas 18612. 717—675-4221. p.

PA BEAU CHEVAL FARMS. Est. 1958. Mrs. Marlene J. Anderson, Box 69, Park Ave., Wycombe 18980 (outside Phila.). 215—598-7229. p.d.s.

WI RONDO ACRES. Otto and Amber Zills, R 1, Waupun 53963. 414—324-3262. Good temperament; top quality puppies. p.d.s.

SALUKI

CA SRINAGAR K'S. Reg. Dr. Winafred Lucas (Breeders over 125 Champs—Top Kennel All Breeds 1971.) P.O. Drawer 4, Crest Park 92326. 714—337-1179. p.d.s.

CT Mr. & Mrs. Lee S. Brodsky, 617 North St., Greenwich 06830. 203—661-4756. p.d.s.

IL Helen S. Borden, 1322-42nd Ave., Rock Island 61201. 309—786-0058. p.

MD DE FORET SALUKIS. David & Joanna Abraham, 16718 Cashell Rd., Rockville 20853. 301—924-3922. p.d.s.

NY Mr. & Mrs. Albert C. Landel, 8588 Abbott Hill Rd., Boston 14025. 716—941-5996. d.s.

OH Esther Bliss Knapp, Pine Paddocks, Valley City 44280. 216—225-5841.

SAMOYED

AL DIXIEFROST K'S. Dr. & Mrs. Harold W. Skalka, Rt. 1, Box 18, Sterrett 35147. p.d.s.

CA ASGARD SAMOYEDS. Ruth Mary Heckeroth, 822 S. Grade Rd., Alpine 92001. 714—445-3317.

MD Susanne B. Boyd, 4301 Damascus Rd., Gaithersburg 20760. 301—774-4846. p.d.

MO Mrs. Peggy M. Borcherding, 3969 Weber Rd., St. Louis 63123. 314—638-0453.

NY SNOW COUNTRY SAMOYEDS. Lyndon & Jean Schermerhorn. No. Gage Rd., Barneveld 13304. 315—896-4492. p.s.

OH STARFIRE SAMOYEDS. Reg. Addie & John Decker, 3404 38th St. S.W., Canton 44706. 216—484-4028. p.d.s.

VA SNO BEAR K'S. Jack & Maureen Armstrong, 910 South Buchanan, Arlington 22204. 703—979-1947. p.

VA Rita Bowling, 478 Dam Neck Rd., Virginia Beach 23454. 804—426-7170. s.

VA TAYMYR K'S. Thomas J. Quigley, 11604 Sourwood Lane, Reston 22091. 703—860-1310. p.s.

SCHIPPERKE

SCHIPPERKE CLUB OF AMERICA, INC. For breed information & breeder directory write Mr. Albert Haase, Secy., 1601 W. 55th Street, La Grange, Ill. 60525.

MD Vera M. McKeldin, 139 Greenmeadow Drive, Timonium 21093. 301—252-1973. p.

TN Russell F. Kent, Levi Road, Rt. 2, Hixson 37343.

SCOTTISH DEERHOUND

CT Mrs. Frederick Collins, 90 Ferris Hill Rd., New Canaan 06840. 203—966-2716. p.

NY GAYLEWARD K'S. Mrs. Gayle Gerber, Clinton Corners 12514. 914—868-1975. p.

SCOTTISH TERRIER

AK Thomas J. & Janus B. Beaman, 108 Davis St., Anchorage 99504. 907—333-6428. p.d.s.

AK Thomas B. & Marilyn E. Fischer, P.O. Box 167, Anchorage 99510. 907—333-1846. p.

CA Mildred Charves, 4767 Tully Rd., Modesto 95350.

FL HEATHERLANE. Mr. & Mrs. Nicholas Levandoski, 13000 SW 81st Ave., Miami 33156. 305—238-4147. p.d.s.

MI ANSTAMM K'S. Mrs. Anthony Stamm, 2097 South 4th St., Kalamazoo 49009. 616—375-0427. p.d.s.

NJ "SCOTTIEWOOD." Mrs. Marjorie Conover, R.D. 1, Box 49, Farmingdale 07727. 201—938-2545. p.d.s.

NJ KENJO. Kennan & Jeanne Glaser, Rd. 1, Church Rd., Mt. Laurel 08057. 609—234-5712. p.d.s.

OR BARRAGLEN. Mr. & Mrs. A.R. Bower, 150 Detrick Drive, Grants Pass 97526. 503—479-0509. p.d.

VA Betty F. McKenzie, 146 Hill Prince Rd., Virginia Beach 23462. 804—497-3330. p.

VA Mrs. John A. Munro, Rt. 1, Box 186, Barboursville 22923. 804—973-8731. p.

VA Mrs. John Gordon Myers, 112 Fifty Third St., Virginia Beach 23451. 804—428-9340. p.d.s.

SEALYHAM TERRIER

CA BARDON. Barbara & Don Davis, 13516 Egbert St., Sylmar 91342. 213—367-7090. p, p.d.s.

IN Mrs. Jeanne Pearson, 11835 Aboite Rd., R.R. 1, Roanoke 46783. 219—672-3277. p.s.

VA SUTLIFF FARMS. Mrs. Herny Sutliff, Jr., 3446 Kenmore Rd., Richmond 23225. 703—272-3360.

SHETLAND SHEEPDOG

CT DOXIEWYND. Reg. Mrs. Georgene M. Thomson, 147 Maple St., Somersville 06072. 203—749-2949. p.d.

GA COR-MIK K'S. Est. 1945. Mrs. Myron Gauger, Rt. No. 1, Box 2605, Perry 31069. 912—987-1808. Professiona handler.

MA ESLEE K'S. Reg. (Sables & Tri's) Esther B. Manning, 31 Shrewsbury St., No. Grafton 01536. 617—839-4685. Puppies occasionally in Blue, Tri, Sables.

MA Mrs. Marion Basile, 15 Powell Ave., Springfield 01118. 413—782-6619. p.

MD KIDWELLY K'S. Frank H. Hansen, 27 Timothy Rd., Brandywine 20613. 301—372-8249. p.d.s.

MD LINGARD. Reg. Jean Cunningham Jeu, 15815 Kruhm Rd., Burtonsville 20730. 301—384-5547.

MT Evelyn T. Meis, Rt. 1, Box 1074, Hamilton 59840. 406—363—1022. p.d.s.

NJ SANDMERE. Mrs. Louella M. Ericksen, 214 So. Hillside Ave., Succasunna 07876. 201—584-8644. p.d.s.

NJ Mrs. Cecilia & Jean Macmillan, 61 Riverside Dr., Denville 07834. 201—627-5798. p.d.

NJ Everett L. & Joyce van Blarcom, Jr., 117 Ridge Rd., Rahway 07065. p.d.

NY MALASHEL K'S. Elaine Wishnow, 2351 E. 17th St., Brooklyn 11229. 212—891-3451. p.d.

NY ALKAN SHELTIES. Al & Kandy Crocco, 11 Ben View Rd., Hyde Park 12538. 914—471-4320. p.d.s.

OH KILOREN K'S. Robert & Frances May, 9685 Washington St., Chagrin Falls 44022. 216—543-4411. p.d.s.

PA ASTOLAT. Reg. Constance B. Hubbard, R.D. 1, Box 505, Kunkletown 18058. 717—629-0365. p.d.s.

PA Judith Anne Volk, 3405 Plumstead Ave., Drexel Hill 19026. 215—CL 9-4075. p.d.

PA SHELMAR K'S. Est. 1943. Ms. Claire B. Keyburn, California Rd., R.D. 4P, Quakertown, 18951. 215—536-3966. p.d.s.

VA MALPSH. Reg. Mary A. Hayes, 485 Colony Rd., Newport News 23602. 804—877-1260. p.d.s.

SHIH TZU

CA WILLOWS SHIH TZU. Consuelo Bolsaks, 2905 Pioneer Drive, Redding 96001. 916—243-1391. p.d.s.

CA SEVARG K'S. Virginia Graves, 4340 Occidental Rd., Santa Rosa, 95401. 707—546-4364. p.d.

CT PAN DEN K'S. Mrs. B. Kaddo, Puppies, Stud service from top Scandinavian bloodlines. Pedigree on request. P.O. Box 816, Stratford 06075. 203—335-8931.

CT TUNXIS VALLEY. Marianne I. Fischer, 20 Elm Street, Unionville 06085. 203—673-2305. All Champion Sired. p.s.

CT Gail D. Gross, 22 Ridgecrest Rd., Wallingford 06492. 203—269-1291. p.

FL Robert A. & Betty J. Brooks, 635 Hanover Court, Spring Hill 33512. 904—683-2211. p.d.

MI Jane Seng, 34010 Edmonton, Farmington Hills 48024. 313—474-3901. p.d.s.

NY BLUE CHIP. Helen Senkow, 53 East Shore Drive, Babylon 11702.

NY HEAVENLY DYNASTY K'S. Jo Ann White, 650 Ocean Ave., Brooklyn 11226. p.d.s.

OH BON D'ART. Len & Bonnie Guggenheim, 3770 Carol, Rocky River 44116. 216—331-2759 or 331-8943. p.s.

PA Per-Axel and Jeanne Lindblom, 11 Cloverlee Lane, Newtown 18940.

TX UCHI OUI "HOUSE OF HAPPINESS", Reg. Frances M. Thornton, 101 Peaceful Drive, Converse 78109. 512—658-2151 or 828-3106.

SIBERIAN HUSKY

AK WHITE FOX K'S. Glenn & Phyllis Castleton, 1517 Turpin St., Anchorage 99504. 907—333-7594. p.d.

CO SUNBURST. Nancy I. Black, Box 727, Granby 80446. 303—725-3455.

CT Mrs. Jean Fournier, 17 Dominique Lane, Simsbury 06070. p.d.s.

CT IRLOCON. Reg. Mrs. Norman W. Harris, 60 Borglum Rd., Wilton 06897. 203—762-8280. p.d.s.

ID Terry G. & Elaine J. Martin, Rt. 3, Box 76A, Jerome 83338. 208—324-5110. p.d. (Racing Huskies)

IL KOYUKUK K'S. Dennis Hitchcock, Sherrard 61281. 309—593-9271. p.d.s.

MD Mrs. Carolyn McDonough Windsor, 8406 Maymeadow Court. Baltimore 21207. 301—655 6246. p.d.s.

MA Mr. & Mrs. William F. St. Lawrence, 202 Elmer Rd., So. Weymouth 02190. 617—335-8272. p.d

MI SHEBLIKO F. K'S. Reg. Marinette Miller, R.R. 1, Box 73-M35, Gwinn 49841. 906—346-9718. p.s.

NY SNOWMASS K'S. Dr. Barry & Gail Eton, 2196 Smith St., Merrick L.I. 11566. 516—378-0118. p.d.s.

NY Alfred & Elsa Marchesano, 99 Springtime Lane, Levittown 11756. 516—735-3653. p.d.s.

NY EU MOR K'S. Est. 1962. c/o Eunice Moreno & Lynne Witkin, 58 Neil Drive, Smithtown, L.I. 11787. Puppies of Quality from OFA clear Champion Studs and Bitches. 516—265-5567 or 516—234-5063.

NY Patricia A. McKee, 15 Lincoln Ave., Yonkers 10704. 914—237-9078. p.s.

NY Bert Welsford, Jr., 4934 Arthur Kill Rd., Staten Island 10307. 212—984-5604. p.d.

OH TONKA CHU. Reg. Michael & Charlotte de Sandis, Tonka Chu, RR 1, Highway 7, Newport 45768. 614—473-2036. p.s.

PA MINE CREEK K'S. Reg. J. Louise Nixon, R#1, Elkland 16920. 607—359-2157. p.d.

VT STOWBROOK. Reg. Mr. & Mrs. R. Robert Rivera, P.O. Box A1, Stowe 05672. 802—253-7687. p.d.

SILKY TERRIER

For information about the breed, write to SILKY TERRIER CLUB

OF AMERICA, INC., Dept. PD, P.O. Box 3521, San Francisco, California 94119.

AR AVONWYCK. Janean A. Wylie, 1915 Spring St., Little Rock 72206. 501—375-8817. p.

AR LARRAKIN SILKY TERRIERS. Reg. Betty & Jim Young, 1917 Spring St., Little Rock 72206. 501—372-2364. p.s.

CA D'UNDER. Howard A. Jensen & Paul G. Hefner, 776 Hayes St., San Francisco 94102. 415—861—1847. p.d.s.

CA ARTARMON-SANTA ROSA K'S. Reg. Mr. & Mrs. James T. Moss, 6065 Old Redwood Highway, Santa Rosa 95401. 707—542-6299. p.d.s

CA BONDI. Reg. Colonel & Mrs. Pavlas, 3315 Rubin Drive, Oakland 94602. 415—531-5873. p.d.s.

CT KATINA. Reg. Richard H. & Diane Nachman, Shoddy Mill Rd., Andover 06232. 203—742-7170. p.d.s.

CT SUNDOWNER K'S. Est. 1966. Champion bloodlines show and pet. Joan Caspersen, 22 Flaum Dr., West Haven 06516. 203—933-6342. p.d.s.

HI Mildred & William Carlstrom, 2088 Aaniu Loop, Pearl City 96782. 808—455-2171. p.d.

MD Mrs. Freda R. Kraus, Rt. 1, Box 366, Union Bridge 21791. 301—635-2437. p.d.

NJ Dr. & Mrs. Emigdio Lola, 737 Bowyer Ave., West End 07740. 201—229-4318. p.d.

NY "ELMIKES" K'S. Reg. Elsa Venisko, R.D. 2, Stony Ford Rd., Middletown 10940. 914—294-7267. p.d.s.

TN HARGILLS. Reg. Miss Harriett Gill, 1300 Morrell Rd., Knoxville 37919. 615—588-1962.

TX Mr. & Mrs. Michael Dyer, 7310-B Fondren Rd., Houston 77036. 713—771-1608. p.s.

TX Noble M. Moss, 9828 Vistadale Drive, Dallas 75238. 214—348-4110. p.d.s.

WA KIKU. Reg. Jon & Kay Magnussen, 4630 East Lake Sammamish Rd. No., Redmond 98052. 206—885-0194. p.d.s.

WI DAKLYN. Mary G. Drake, 4741 W. Rawson Ave., Franklin 53132. 414—421-5165. p.d.s.

SKYE TERRIER

CT William & Jane Bouton, Hampton Lane, New Canaan 06840. 203—966-8935. p.s.

MD ROYALIST SKYE TERRIER K'S. Reg. Mrs. Joseph Hexter, 14400 Brookmead Dr., Germantown 20767. 301—948-1196. p.d.s.

MN ROBLYN ACRES. Mr. & Mrs. Robert J. Boucher, 14890 Ostrum Trail North, Marine on St. Crois 55047. 612—433-2024. p.d.s.

MO WINDFLOWER. Reg. Ralph &Sandra Allen, 5290 Westminster Place, St. Louis 63108. 314—367-4444. p.d.s.

NY SKY SCOT K's. Leslie M. Becker, R.D. 2, Middleburgh 12122.

OK OLIVIA. Reg. Mrs. Olga Smid, 126 Windsor Drive, Chickasha 73018. 405—224-6168. p.d.s.

CAN CEILIDH. Reg. Donald E. Drury, University Post Office, Antigonish, Nova Scotia. 902—863-2022. p.s.

SOFT COATED WHEATEN TERRIER

CO Jacqueline Gottlieb, 370 Pinebrook Hills, Boulder 80302.

MA Gary H. Sherman, Cold Spring Rd., Williamstown 01267. 413—458-8667. p.d.

NY LEPRECAUN K'S. IKC Reg. Est. 1965. Harry & Juanita Wurzburger, 419 E. State St., Long Beach 11561. 516—431-4235. p.d.s.

SMOOTH FOX TERRIERS

CA BRONWYN. Eleanor B. Gilbert, 133 Via Alameda, Redondo Beach 90277.

STANDARD MANCHESTER TERRIER

CA Dr. & Mrs. William Crawford, 116 Carmel Valley Rd., Carmel Valley 93924. 408—659-3578. p.d.s.

STANDARD SCHNAUZER

CT NEMOSTAN K'S. Reg. Dr. & Mrs. Bernard O. Memoitin, 1318 Long Ridge Rd., Stamford 06903. 203—323-6767. p.d.s.

CT Robert & Florence Oehl, 5 Columbia St., Wallingford 06492. 203—269-7928. p.

NM WESTEFUCHS. Reg. Dr. & Mrs. High S. Murray, 1291 Vallecita Dr., Santa Fe 87501. p.d.s.

TN LAUSBUBEN K'S. Reg. Est. 1962. Arnold M. Meirowsky, M.D., Etzelhof, Old Hillsboro Rd., Franklin 37064. 615—269-4143. p.d.s.

WI VON LINK. Norbert & Cecelia Link, 7616-26 Ave., Kenosha 53140. 414—657-5275.

TIBETAN SPANIELS

CT AMROTH TIBETAN SPANIELS. Jay Child (Mrs. Patrick), 153 Cannon Street, Hamden 06518.

VIZSLA

AZ Marjorie J. Mehagian, 7043 N. Central, Phoenix 85020. 602—943-3205. p.s.

CA Elaine Saldivar, 4343 1/2 Burns Ave., Los Angeles 90029. 213—663-5868. p.d.s.

IL Mrs. Diane Stoeke, Rt. 1, Box 15, Sugar Grove 60554. 312—466-4679. p.d.s.

NY Dr. John B. Lounsbury, P.O. Box 593. Billings 12510. 914—677-5602. p.d.

NY GLEN COTTAGE K'S. John X. Strauz & Joseph F. Cunningham, R.D. 2, Middletown 10940.

NY BOWCOT. Reg. Dr. & Mrs. Bernard E. McGivern, Jr., 95 West Entry Rd., Country Club Grounds, Staten Island 10304. 212—987-7984 or 447-1251. p.d.s.

NV SAGEACRE. Reg. Mrs. Connie Johnson, 1066 Evans Ave., Reno 89502. 702—323-3882. p.s.

WEIMARANER

CT CEDAR HILL WEIMARANERS. Mr. & Mrs. R. N. Duncan, P.O. Box 96, Windsor 06095. 203—653-2959. p.d.s.

CT "MONOMOY". Reg. Mrs. John A. Mason, 564 W. Avon Rd., Avon 06001, 203—673-4914. p.d.s.

MD TOMAR. Mary Jean Knott, 4869 Avoca Ave., Ellicott City 21043.

NY WINTERWIND. Reg. Joseph G. & Dorothy Winter, 403 Beach 46 St., Far Rockaway 11691. 212—327-3433. p.d.s.

NY HOLBROOK ACRES. Est. 1964. Irene Marie Brown, 3 Knickerbocker Ave., Holbrook 11741. 516—585-4372. p.d.s.

OH C. Shirley Benedict, 1113 Waugh Dr., Hubbard 44425, 216—534-5119. p.s.

PA FLOTTHEIM'S K'S. Reg. Est. 1951. Mr. & Mrs. Adolf Haussermann, 505 Willow Ave., Ambler 19002. 215—MI 6-3138. p.d.s.

PA Malcolm L. Decker, Jr., 2 Goodrock Rd., Levittown 19057. 215—946-8332. p.d.s.

PA Marthena Scollon, 4909 Pulaski Ave., Philadelphia 19144. 215—VI 9-0285. p.d.s.

WELSH CORGI [Pembroke]

GA William P. & Beverly S. Hill, Ramblebriar Farm, 2329 Sewell Mill Rd., Marietta 30062. 404—971-0301. p.d.s.

IL HOHEIT. Kenneth Clayton, Rt., 2 Box 235, DeKalb 60115. 815—756-9720. p.d.s.

MA Caroline H. (Mrs. F. H.) Kierstead, RFD, Williamsburg 01096, 413—268-7084. p.s.

ME Mrs. Jonson Platt, P.O. Box 269, Kennebunkport 04046. 207—967-5553. p.d.

PA HICKORYBROOK FARM K'S. Est. 1968. Howard & Pat Buerger, P.O. Box 304, Chalfont 18914. 215—249-3301. p.d.s.

PA EHRSTAG. Reg. Ronald H. and Jane L. Shakely, RD 1, Renfrew 16053. 412—586-7106. p.d.s.

WELSH SPRINGER SPANIELS

PA SYLABRU ACRES. Est.

1969. Bruce & Sylvia Foreacre, 11 Locust St., West Chester 19380. 215—696-2998 or LO 6-4016. p.d.s.

WELSH TERRIER

CT PALACEGUARD K'S. Mr. & Mrs. W. H. Blair, 27 Pecksland Road, Greenwich 06830. 203—661-1967. p.d.s.

CT BARDWYN. Reg. Mrs. Bardi McLennan, 66 Lords Highway, Weston 06880. 203—227-3926. p.d.s.

IL JANTERRS WELSH TERRIERS. P.O. Box 70, Barington 60010. 312—658-5929. p.d.s.

IL ABADALE K'S. Reg. Mrs. M. King, 6431 No. Big Hollow Rd., Peoria 61614. 309—691-5859. p.d.s.

MD KITWYN. Reg. Mrs. Kathryn C. Creech, 14035 Forsythe Rd., Skyesville 21784. 301—442-2018. p.d.s.

MD QUEST END K'S. Maj. & Mrs. Richard M. Stacy, Box 327, Owings 20836. 301—257-6204 or 627-3308. p.d.

PA Mrs. Sheila Lyster Marshall, Hollow Rd., Birchrunville 19421. 215—827-7242. p.

VA Norma L. Aprahamian, 3615 Chellowe Rd., Richmond 23225. 804—272-4598. p.s.

PA LICKEN RUN K'S. A distinctive winning strain, all American-bred. For Show, Pet, Breeding. Champions at stud. W. Etter, 324 Forest Ave., Quakertown 18951. 215—536-4109. p.d.s.

WEST HIGHLAND WHITE TERRIER

CA Mrs. Harold Eisenberg, Jr., 17 Knoll Way, San Rafael 94903.

CT Howard & Louise Beringer, 1211 Raymond Hill Rd., Uncasville 06382. 203—848-3728. p.

CT HELLISTER K'S. Joan O. Capon, Guilford 06437. 203—457-0628. p.d.

FL BYLINE. Hugh S. & Colleen B. Pettis, 10230 Pan American Drive, Miami 33157. 305—232-1849. p.d.s.

MA Mrs. John C. Storey, 224 Hinckley Rd., Milton 02187. 617—696-5489.

MN WOODLAWN K'S. Reg. Mr. & Mrs. James F. Finley, 1333 12th Ave. N.W. New Brighton 55112. 612—633-2987. p.d.s.

MN SIRIUS ACRES. Reg. Mrs. Margery G. Jones, 4416 Highland Rd., Minnetonka 55343. 218—935-2244. p.d.s.

PA WHYTEHAVEN. Reg. Mr. & Mrs. Samuel A. Faust, Long Run Rd., R.D. 2, Schuylkill Haven 17972. 717—385-3967. p.d.s.

RI WYNDERGAEL K'S. Reg. Diane M. Fronczak, Pine Swamp Rd., Cumberland 02864. 401—762-5447. p.d.s.

RI HUNTINGHOUSE K'S. Est. 1934. Katherine Hayward, Hartford Pike, No. Scituate 02857. 401—647-3703. p.d.s.

CAN K'S. OF THE ROUGE. Reg. Mrs. J. H. Daniell-Jenkins, 1 Evelyn Ave., Rouge Hills, Pickering, Ontario L1V 1N3. 416—282-7934. p.s.

WHIPPET

FL KIPPEN K'S. Ingrid Wells, 330 Leah Miller Drive. Ft. Walton Beach 32548. 904—243-3208. p.d.

MA REDTOP. Reg. Rosemary E. & David L. Wortman, 37 Norcross Hill, Baldwinville 01436. 617—939-5451. p.d.s.

NY Mrs. Alexander J. McRae, 34 Westcliff Drive, Dix Hills, 11746. 516—HA 1-3484. p.d.

NY GORTICO K'S. Mrs. Gordon J. Pinkosz, R.D. 4, Box 560, Rockwell Rd., Kingston 12401.

OH COLONIAL ACRES K'S. Reg. Walter W. Schenck, 5373 Cincinnati, Dayton Rd., Middletown 45042. 513—777-2266. p.d.s.

YORKSHIRE TERRIER

MD CAROUSEL K'S. Mrs. Paul Jackson, 36 Washington St., Frostburg 21532. 301—689-9424. p.d.

MD Johnny A. Robinson, Jr., 10030 Glenolden Drive, Potomac 20854. 301—299-6428. p.d.s.

NJ YORKSMITH. Betty Smith, R.D. 2, Box 147, Blairstown 07825. 201—383-6077. p.d.s.

NY BLUE-CHIP. Helen Senkow, 53 East Shore Drive, Babylon 11702. p.d.s.

NY HESKETHANE. Reg. Beryl Hesketh, Box 203, Albany Post Rd., Gardiner 12525. 914—255-7597. p.d.s.

NY Fay Gold, P.O. Box 256, Times Square Station, New York 10036.

PA WINDSHAVEN. Mrs. Nancy Lee Webb, 394 Marple Rd., Broomall 19008. 215—353-0842. p.d.s.

PA WHEATLAND K'S. Est. 1959. Wildweir Lines, 2723 Columbia Ave., Lancaster 17603. 717—733-1224. p.d.s.

PA SHELMAR K'S. Est. 1943. Ms. Claire B. Keyburn, California Rd., R.D. 4P, Quakertown, 18951. 215—536-3966. p.d.s.

INDEX

INDEX